C000145033

Street by Street

NEWCASTLE UPON TYNE SUNDERLAND

DURHAM, GATESHEAD, SOUTH SHIELDS, TYNEMOUTH

Blyth, Chester-le-Street, Cramlington, North Shields, Peterlee, Ponteland, Seaham, Stanley, Washington, Whitley Bay

Ist edition May 2001

Published by AA Publishing (a trading name of Automobile Association Developments Limited, whose registered office is Norfolk House, Priestley Road, Basingstoke, Hampshire, RG24 9NY. Registered number 1878835).

Mapping produced by the Cartographic Department of The Automobile Association.

A CIP Catalogue record for this book is available from the British Library.

Printed by G. Canale & C. S.P.A., Torino, Italy

Ref: MX052

Key to map pages ii-iii

Key to map symbols iv-1

Enlarged scale pages 2-17

Street by Street 18-137

Index – towns & villages 138

Index – streets 139-166

Index – featured places 166-170

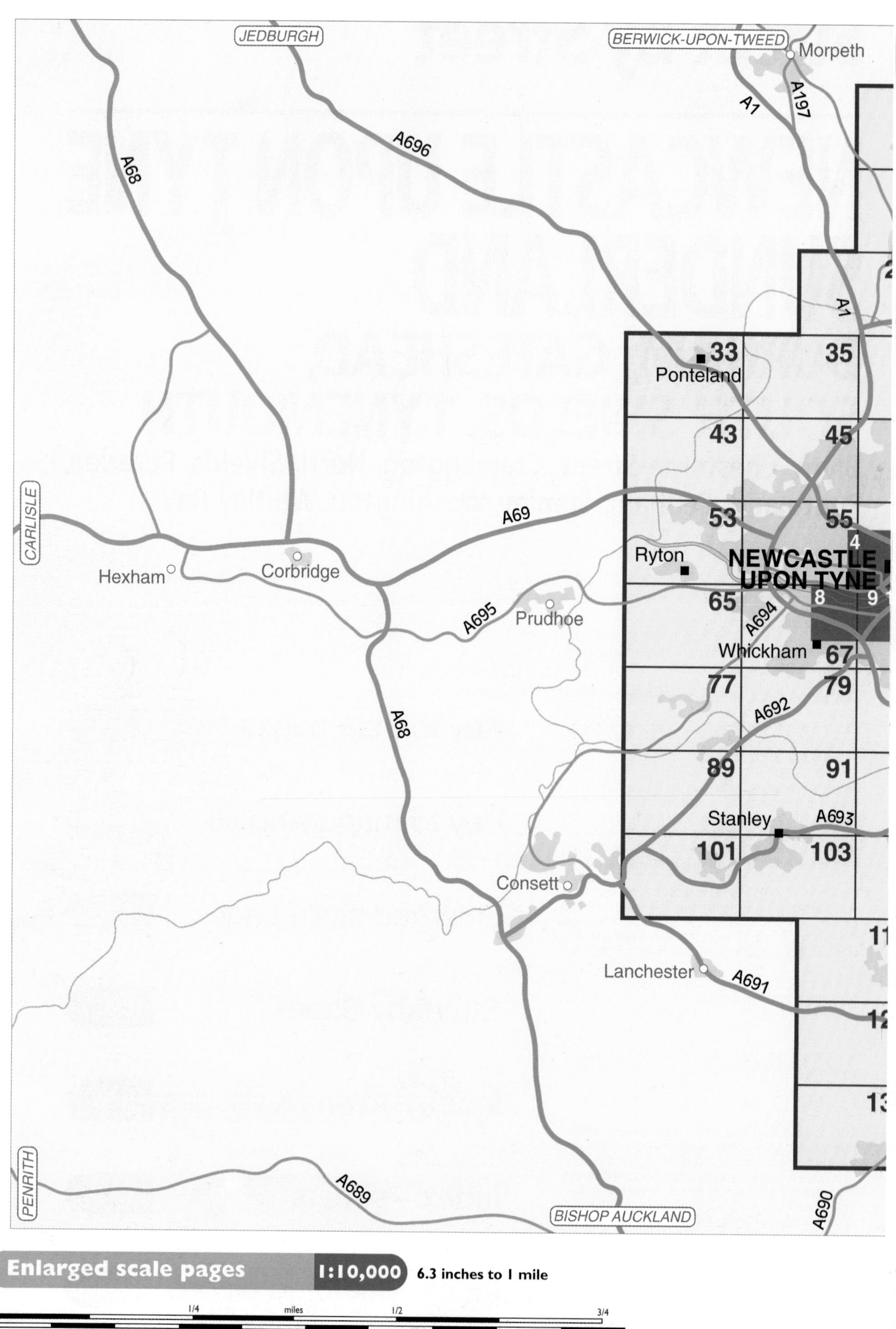

Enlarged scale pages 1:10,000

6.3 inches to 1 mile

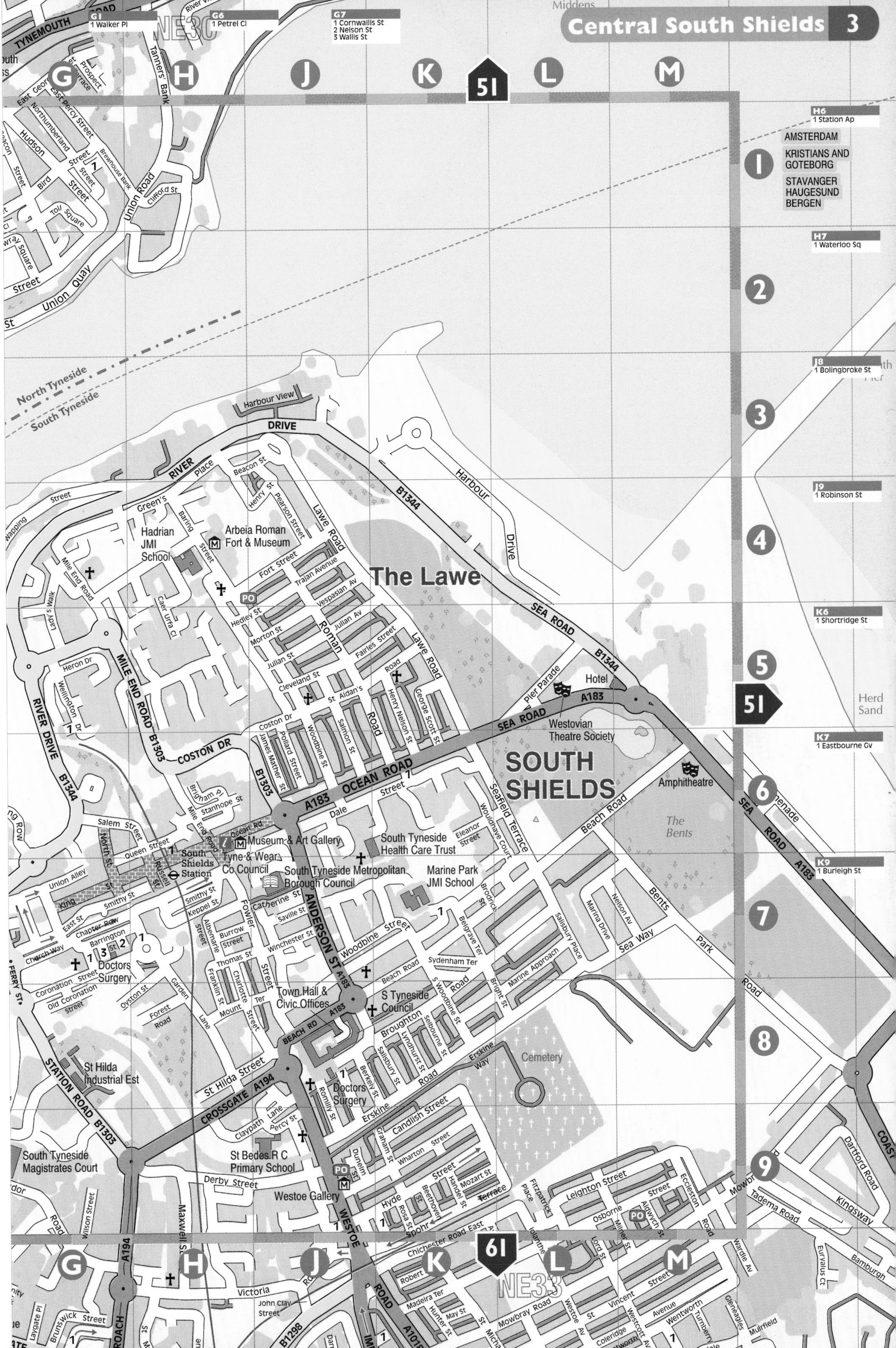

Central South Shields
3
G1 1 Walker Pl
G6 1 Petrel Cl
G7 1 Cornwallis St 2 Nelson St 3 Wallis St
H6 1 Station Ap
H7 1 Waterloo Sq
J8 1 Bolingbroke St
J9 1 Robinson St
K6 1 Shortridge St
K7 1 Eastbourne Gv
K9 1 Burleigh St
AMSTERDAM
KRISTIANS AND GOTEBORG
STAVANGER HAUGESUND BERGEN
TYNEMOUTH ROAD
NE30
NE33
51
61
Tanners' Bank
Union Road
Union Quay
Clifford St
Brewhouse Bank
East Percy Street
Northumberland Street
Hudson Street
Bird Street
Toll Square
Prospect Terrace
North Tyneside
South Tyneside
Harbour View
RIVER DRIVE
B1344
Harbour Drive
SEA ROAD
Lawe Road
Pearson Street
Beacon St
Henry St
Baring Street
Green's Place
Wapping Street
Hadrian JMI School
Arbeia Roman Fort & Museum
Fort Street
Trajan Avenue
Vespasian Av
Julian Av
Fairles Street
Roman Road
The Lawe
Hedley St
Morton St
Julian St
Cleveland St
St Aidan's Road
Henry Nelson St
George Scott St
Caer Urfa Cl
Mile End Road
MILE END ROAD B1303
Heron Dr
Wellington Dr
COSTON DR
Coston Dr
Pollard Street
James Mather St
Woodbine St
Salmon St
B1303
A183
OCEAN ROAD
Dale Street
Pier Parade
Hotel
Westovian Theatre Society
SOUTH SHIELDS
Amphitheatre
The Bents
Beach Road
Seafield Terrace
Wouldhave Court
Brigham Pl
Stannope St
Salem Street
North St
Queen Street
Ocean Rd
Museum & Art Gallery
Tyne & Wear Co Council
South Shields Station
Russell St
King St
Union Alley
Smithy St
Keppel St
Catherine St
South Tyneside Metropolitan Borough Council
South Tyneside Health Care Trust
Eleanor Street
Marine Park JMI School
Brodrick St
Belgrave Ter
Salisbury Place
Marina Drive
Nelson Av
Bents Park Road
Sea Way
Herd Sand
Saville St
Winchester St
ANDERSON ST A183
Woodbine Street
Fowler Street
Albemarle Street
Burrow Street
Thomas St
Charlotte Street
Franklin St
Mount Ter
Lane
Chapter Row
Barrington St
East St
Church Way
Doctors Surgery
Coronation Street
Old Coronation Street
Oyston St
Forest Road
Garden Lane
FERRY ST
Town Hall & Civic Offices
S Tyneside Council
Beach Road
Sydenham Ter
S Woodbine St
Bright St
Marine Approach
Broughton Road
Selbourne St
Lyndhurst St
Salisbury St
Berkely St
BEACH RD A183
St Hilda Industrial Est
STATION ROAD B1303
St Hilda Street
CROSSGATE A194
Romilly St
Erskine Road
Erskine Way
Cemetery
Claypath Lane
Percy St
St Bedes R C Primary School
South Tyneside Magistrates Court
Derby Street
Westoe Gallery
Wilson Street
Maxwell St
Candlish Street
Graham St
Wharton Street
Dunelm St
Hyde Street
Beethoven St
Handel St
Mozart St
Terrace
Rosa St
Spohr Terrace
Fitzpatrick Place
Leighton Street
Osborne Street
Aldwych St
Miller St
Eccleston Road
Mowbray
Tadema Road
Dartford Road
Kingsway
COAST
Wardle Av
Chichester Road East
Robert St
Madeira Ter
Hunter St
May St
St Michael's
Mowbray Road
Westoe Av
Lord St
Vincent Street
Westcott Ave
Wentworth Avenue
Turnberry
Gleneagles
Muirfield
Eurvalus Ct
Bamburgh
Victoria
John Clay Street
Brunswick Street
Laygate Pl
B1298
A1018
WESTOE ROAD
A194

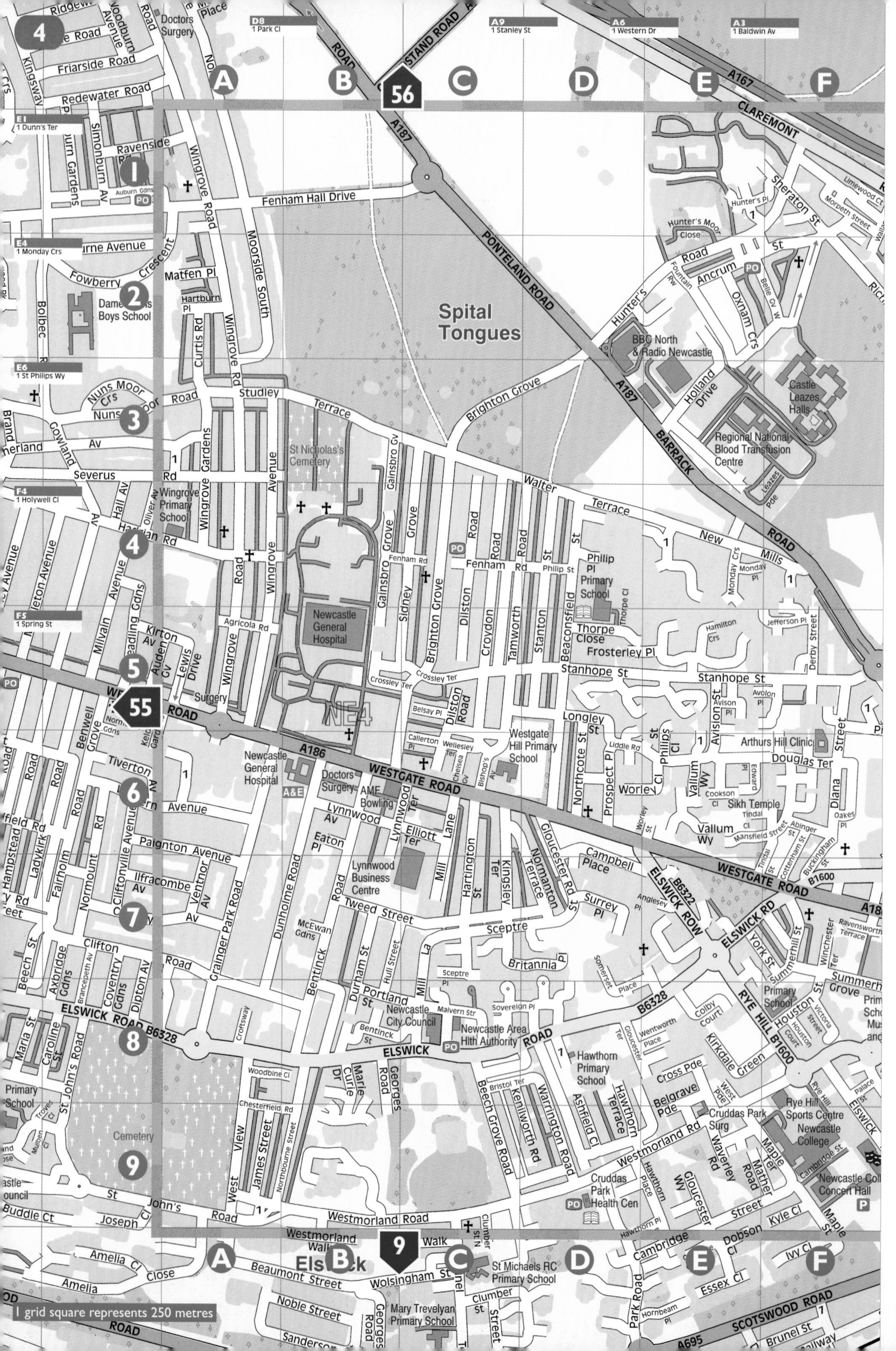
56
55
9
A
B
C
D
E
F
1
2
3
4
5
6
7
8
9
D8 1 Park Cl
A9 1 Stanley St
A6 1 Western Dr
A3 1 Baldwin Av
E1 1 Dunn's Ter
E4 1 Monday Crs
E6 1 St Philips Wy
F4 1 Holywell Cl
F5 1 Spring St
Spital Tongues
Friarside Road
Redewater Road
Ravenside
Simonburn Av
Fenham Hall Drive
Wingrove Road
Moorside South
PONTELAND ROAD
A187
CLAREMONT
Sheraton St
Hunter's Moor Close
Ancrum
Oxnam Crs
Holland Drive
BBC North & Radio Newcastle
Castle Leazes Halls
Regional National Blood Transfusion Centre
BARRACK ROAD
Fowberry Crescent
Matfen Pl
Hartburn Pl
Dame Allan's Boys School
Curtis Rd
Wingrove Rd
Studley Terrace
Brighton Grove
Nuns Moor Crs
Nuns Moor Road
Cowland
Severus Rd
Wingrove Gardens
Wingrove Avenue
St Nicholas's Cemetery
Walter Terrace
New Mills
Wingrove Primary School
Hadrian Rd
Fenham Rd
Philip Pl Primary School
Thorpe Close
Frosterley Pl
Stanhope St
Newcastle General Hospital
Gainsbro Grove
Sidney Grove
Brighton Grove
Dilston Road
Croydon Road
Tamworth Road
Stanton St
Beaconsfield St
Agricola Rd
Crossley Ter
Kirton Av
Milvain Avenue
Lewis Drive
Surgery
WESTGATE ROAD
A186
NE4
Westgate Hill Primary School
Longley St
Northcote St
Prospect Pl
Worley Cl
Philips Cl
Vallum Wy
Arthurs Hill Clinic
Douglas Ter
Sikh Temple
Diana Street
Doctors Surgery
AMF Bowling
Lynnwood Av
Eaton Pl
Elliott Ter
Lynnwood Business Centre
Mill Lane
Hartington St
Kingsley Ter
Normanton Terrace
Gloucester Rd
Campbell Place
ELSWICK ROW
B6322
Surrey Pl
ELSWICK RD
Tweed Street
Sceptre
Britannia Pl
Dunholme Road
Grainger Park Road
Bentinck Road
Durham St
Hull Street
Portland St
Newcastle City Council
Newcastle Area Hlth Authority
ELSWICK ROAD
B6328
Tiverton Av
Paignton Avenue
Ilfracombe Av
Ventnor Av
Cliftonville Avenue
Clifton Road
Fairholm
Normount Rd
Ladykirk
Hampstead Rd
Axbridge Gdns
Coventry Gdns
Dipton Av
Beech St
Maria St
Caroline St
St John's Road
Cemetery
Primary School
Woodbine Cl
Chesterfield Rd
James Street
Northbourne Street
West View
Marie Curie Dr
Georges Road
Beech Grove Road
Kenilworth Rd
Warrington Road
Hawthorn Primary School
Ashfield Cl
Hawthorn Terrace
Cross Pde
Belgrave Pde
Cruddas Park Surg
Westmorland Rd
Waverley Rd
Gloucester Wy
Cruddas Park Health Cen
Rye Hill Sports Centre
Newcastle College
Newcastle College Concert Hall
RYE HILL B1600
Houston St
Summerhill Grove
Kirkdale Green
Colby Court
St John's Road
Westmorland Road
Westmorland Walk
Joseph Cl
Buddle Ct
Amelia Cl
Amelia Close
Elswick
Beaumont Street
Wolsingham St
St Michaels RC Primary School
Mary Trevelyan Primary School
Noble Street
Clumber St
Park Road
Cambridge Street
Dobson Cl
Essex Cl
Ivy Cl
Kyle Cl
Maple St
SCOTSWOOD ROAD
A695
Brunel St
1 grid square represents 250 metres

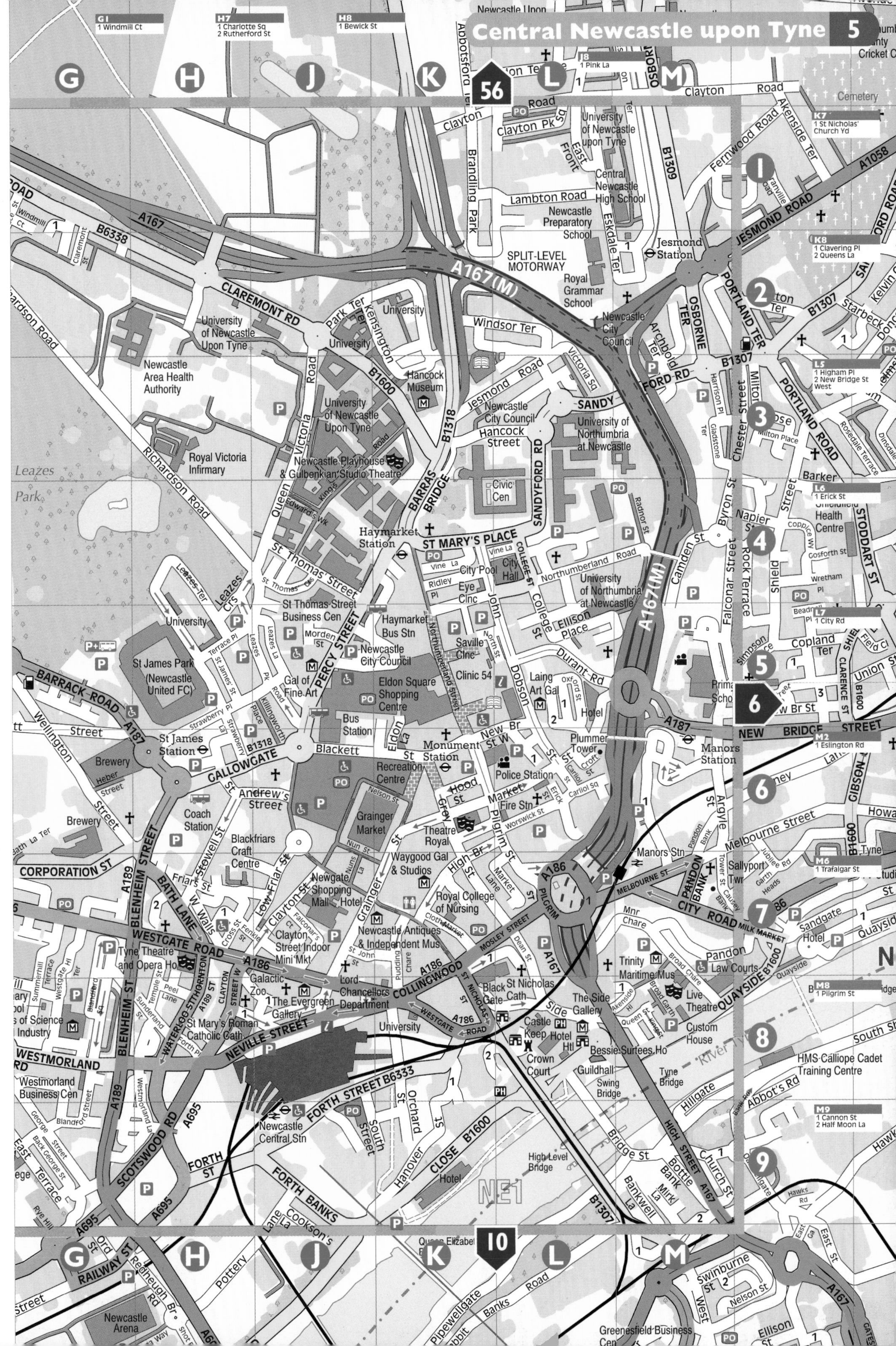

Central Newcastle upon Tyne
5
G1
1 Windmill Ct
H7
1 Charlotte Sq
2 Rutherford St
H8
1 Bewick St
J8
1 Pink La
K7
1 St Nicholas' Church Yd
K8
1 Clavering Pl
2 Queens La
L5
1 Higham Pl
2 New Bridge St West
L6
1 Erick St
L7
1 City Rd
M2
1 Eslington Rd
M6
1 Trafalgar St
M8
1 Pilgrim St
M9
1 Cannon St
2 Half Moon La
56
6
10
NE1
Clayton Road
Clayton Pk Sq
University of Newcastle upon Tyne
Central Newcastle High School
Lambton Road
Newcastle Preparatory School
Jesmond Station
Jesmond Road
Cemetery
Fernwood Road
Akenside Ter
SPLIT-LEVEL MOTORWAY
Royal Grammar School
A167(M)
A167
B6338
Claremont Rd
Richardson Road
Newcastle Area Health Authority
Royal Victoria Infirmary
Leazes Park
Queen Victoria Road
Kensington Ter
Hancock Museum
Newcastle Playhouse & Gulbenkian Studio Theatre
Barras Bridge
Windsor Ter
Jesmond Road
Newcastle City Council
Hancock Street
Sandyford Rd
University of Northumbria at Newcastle
Civic Cen
Haymarket Station
St Mary's Place
St Thomas' Street
St Thomas Street Business Cen
Haymarket Bus Stn
Newcastle City Council
City Pool
City Hall
Northumberland Road
Eye Clnc
Saville Clnc
Clinic 54
Percy Street
Gal of Fine Art
Eldon Square Shopping Centre
Bus Station
St James Park (Newcastle United FC)
University
Barrack Road
Wellington Street
Brewery
St James Station
Gallowgate
Blackett St
Monument Station
Recreation Centre
Grainger Market
Laing Art Gal
Hotel
Dobson
Durant Rd
Ellison Place
Plummer Tower
Manors Station
New Bridge Street
A187
Police Station
Fire Stn
Theatre Royal
Coach Station
Blackfriars Craft Centre
Newgate Shopping Mall
Hotel
Waygood Gal & Studios
Royal College of Nursing
Newcastle Antiques & Independent Mus
Clayton Street Indoor Mini Mkt
Corporation St
Westgate Road
Tyne Theatre and Opera Ho
Galactic Zoo
The Evergreen Gallery
Lord Chancellors Department
St Mary's Roman Catholic Cath
Neville Street
University
Collingwood
Mosley Street
Black Gate
St Nicholas Cath
Castle Keep
Hotel
Crown Court
Bessie Surtees Ho
Guildhall
Swing Bridge
Tyne Bridge
The Side Gallery
Trinity Maritime Mus
Live Theatre
Custom House
Pandon Law Courts
Quayside
Melbourne Street
City Road
Sallyport Twr
Sandgate Hotel
HMS Calliope Cadet Training Centre
Westmorland Rd
Westmorland Business Cen
Blenheim St
Scotswood Rd
Newcastle Central Stn
Forth Street B6333
Forth Banks
Close B1600
High Level Bridge
Hotel
Bridge St
High Street A167
Hanover St
Orchard St
South Street
Railway St
Newcastle Arena
Pipewellgate
Greenesfield Business Cen
Portland Road
Portland Ter
Osborne Ter
Chester Street
Falconar Street
Rock Terrace
Stoddart St
Shield Street
Copland Ter
Union St
Clarence St
Health Centre
Camden St
Byron St

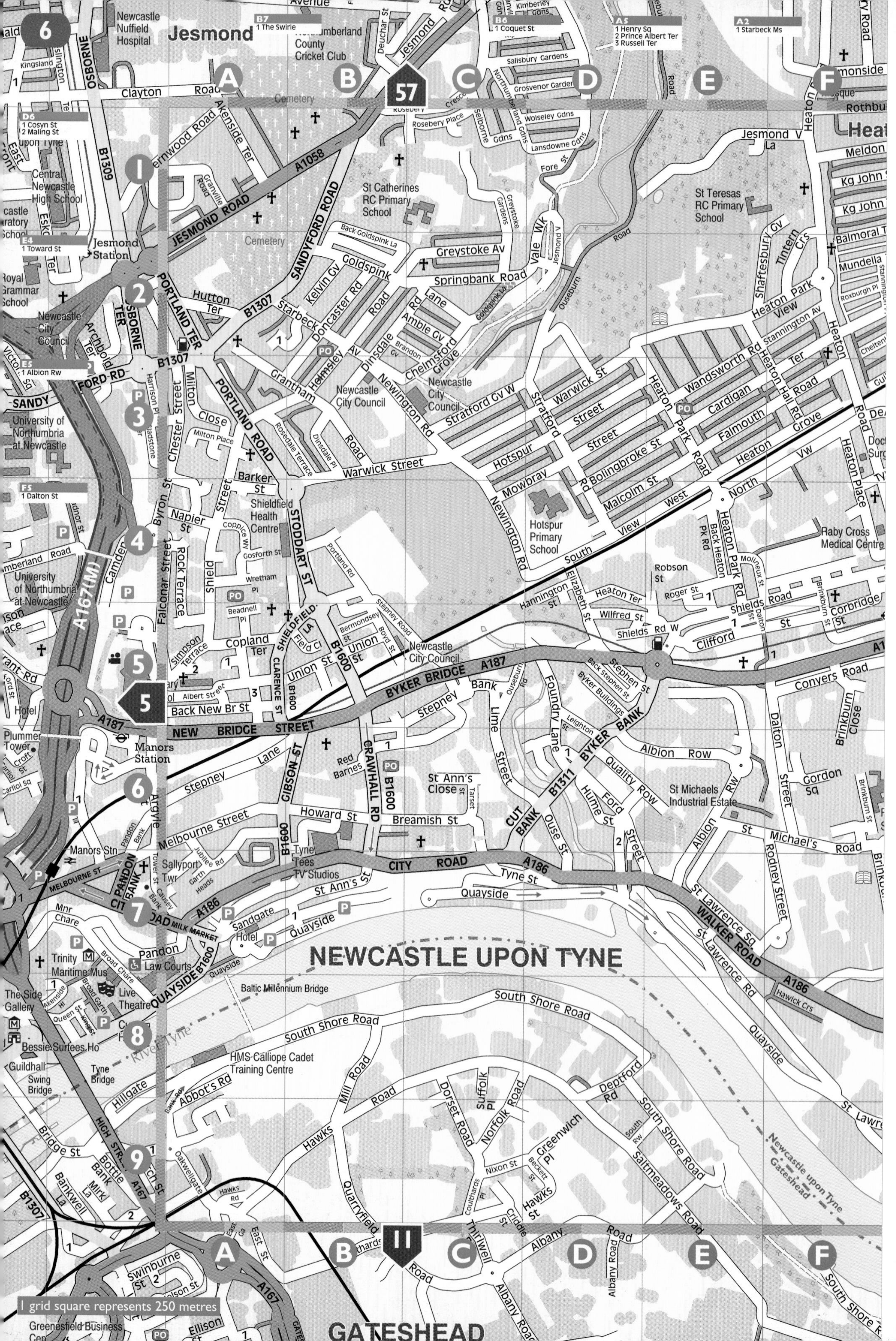
Jesmond
Newcastle Nuffield Hospital
B7 1 The Swirle
Northumberland County Cricket Club
B6 1 Coquet St
A5 1 Henry Sq 2 Prince Albert Ter 3 Russell Ter
A2 1 Starbeck Ms
A
B
C
D
E
F
57
Heaton
Cemetery
D6 1 Cosyn St 2 Maling St
Central Newcastle High School
E4 1 Toward St
Jesmond Station
Royal Grammar School
Newcastle City Council
E5 1 Albion Rw
University of Northumbria at Newcastle
F5 1 Dalton St
St Catherines RC Primary School
St Teresas RC Primary School
Shieldfield Health Centre
Newcastle City Council
Hotspur Primary School
Raby Cross Medical Centre
Manors Station
Tyne Tees TV Studios
St Michaels Industrial Estate
Sandgate Hotel
Trinity Maritime Mus
Law Courts
Live Theatre
The Side Gallery
Bessie Surtees Ho
Guildhall
Swing Bridge
Tyne Bridge
Baltic Millennium Bridge
HMS Calliope Cadet Training Centre
NEWCASTLE UPON TYNE
River Tyne
11
GATESHEAD
Greenesfield Business Centre
1 grid square represents 250 metres
JESMOND ROAD
SANDYFORD ROAD
PORTLAND ROAD
NEW BRIDGE STREET
BYKER BRIDGE
CITY ROAD
WALKER ROAD
QUAYSIDE
South Shore Road
Warwick Street
Newington Rd
Shields Road
Heaton Park Road
Stoddart St
A167(M)

G4 1 Denmark St 2 Potts St
H8 1 Till St
J2 1 Bethnell Av
J9 1 Trinity Ctyd
K8 1 Birds Nest Rd 2 Staines Rd
K9 1 Callaly Wy
L8 1 Monkchester Rd
57
58
12
NE6
Sports Club
Simonside Terrace
Rothbury Terrace
Shields Road
Chillingham Road Primary School
Spencer Street
Marleen
Walker Gate Station
Northmoor Rd
Whinneyfield Road
Infant School
Walpole St
Julian Avenue
Sutton St
Coutts Rd
Ellesmere Av
Southmoor Rd
Tenth Av
Ninth Av
Eighth Av
Seventh Av
Third Av
First Avenue
A188
A193
Chillingham Road Station
Depot Rd
Chillingham Industrial Estate
Etherley Road
Huddleston Road
Shields Road A193
Valentia Avenue
Iolanthe Crs
Trojan Av
Pembroke Av
Palmerston Av
W Farm Rd
Keebledale Av
A187
Fossway
Thorne Ter
Moorland Crs
Wall Ter
St Oswald's Gn
Ulverstone Terrace
Scrogg Road
Baret Road
Marondale Av
Calderdale Av
Kentmere
Ennerdale
Sunnycrest Av
Langley Road
Brough Park Way
Roman Avenue
Orpington Avenue
St Oswald Avenue
Vallum Rd
Lownds Ter
Alston Avenue
Ripley Ter
Musgrave Ter
Marske Ter
Farne Ter
Hurst Ter
Finsbury Avenue
Walker Comprehensive School
Medical Centre
Welbeck
Byker Terrace
Tweedy Ter
Millers Road
Shields Rd
Union Road
Union Rd
Glendale Ter
St Mark's St
Algernon Rd
Hawthorn House Medical Cen
Corbridge Road
Shields Road
Byker Station
Tunstall Av
Grace Street
Grace St
Scarborough Road
Blount St
Benson Road
Cullercoats St
Cleadon Street
Alfred Street
Ada Street
Emily St
Convers Rd
Spires Lane
Grace St
Headlam St
St Lawrence RC Primary School
Michaelgate
Chirton Wynd
Avondale Rd
B1313
Bothal St
Scarborough Ct
Gillies St
Dummorlie St
Harriet St
Morton Street
Renwick St
Canterbury St
Cresswell St
Welbeck Road
B1313 Welbeck Road
Leicester Street
Kennington Gv
Chorley Place
Adelphi Place
Lowthian Crs
Belford Ter
Denver Gdns
Parson's Av
Christie Ter
Scrogg
Avenue
Chathill Ter
Horsley Ter
Crawford Ter
Mason St
Raby St
Raby Wy
Byker
Primary School
Clydesdale Rd
Welbeck Primary School
Flodden Street
Newbold Street
Monkchester Road
Grasmere
Commercial Road
Beresford Gdns
Dunstanburgh Road
Bywell St
Lytham Pl
St Anthony's Road
Melton Avenue
Branxton Crs
Mindrum Ter
Los Terrace
Ayton St
Bolam St
Clifford Rd
Peter's Rd
Allendale Road
Clapham Av
Kingston Grove
Norbury
Wilton Avenue
Pinner Pl
Bolam
Cushat Cl
Brinkburn St
Wy
Street
Janet St
Harbottle Ct
Relton Av
Birds Nest Road
Avenue
Springwell Avenue
Burnham Grove
Lichfield Avenue
Wharrier Street
Wetheral Ter
Brampton
Lowfield Ter
A186 Walker Road
B1314
Glasshouse St
Newcastle City Council
Irthing Avenue
Chatsworth Gdns
Callaly Way
Wigmore Avenue
St Vincents RC Primary School
Monkchester Rd
Sandy Crescent
Sandy Crs
Chalfont Rd
St Peter's
Lawrence St
St Peter's Wht
Dobson Crs
Rowes Ms
Bottlehouse St
Road
The Ropery
Bakewell Terrace
A186 Walker Road
Elstob Pl
Lancefield
Chandlers Quay
Tyne
Jellicoe Rd
Portman Pl
Burstow Av
Clipstone Avenue
Evistones
Oxted Pl
Holywell Av
Belmont
Ensin St
Newcastle City Council
St Anthony's

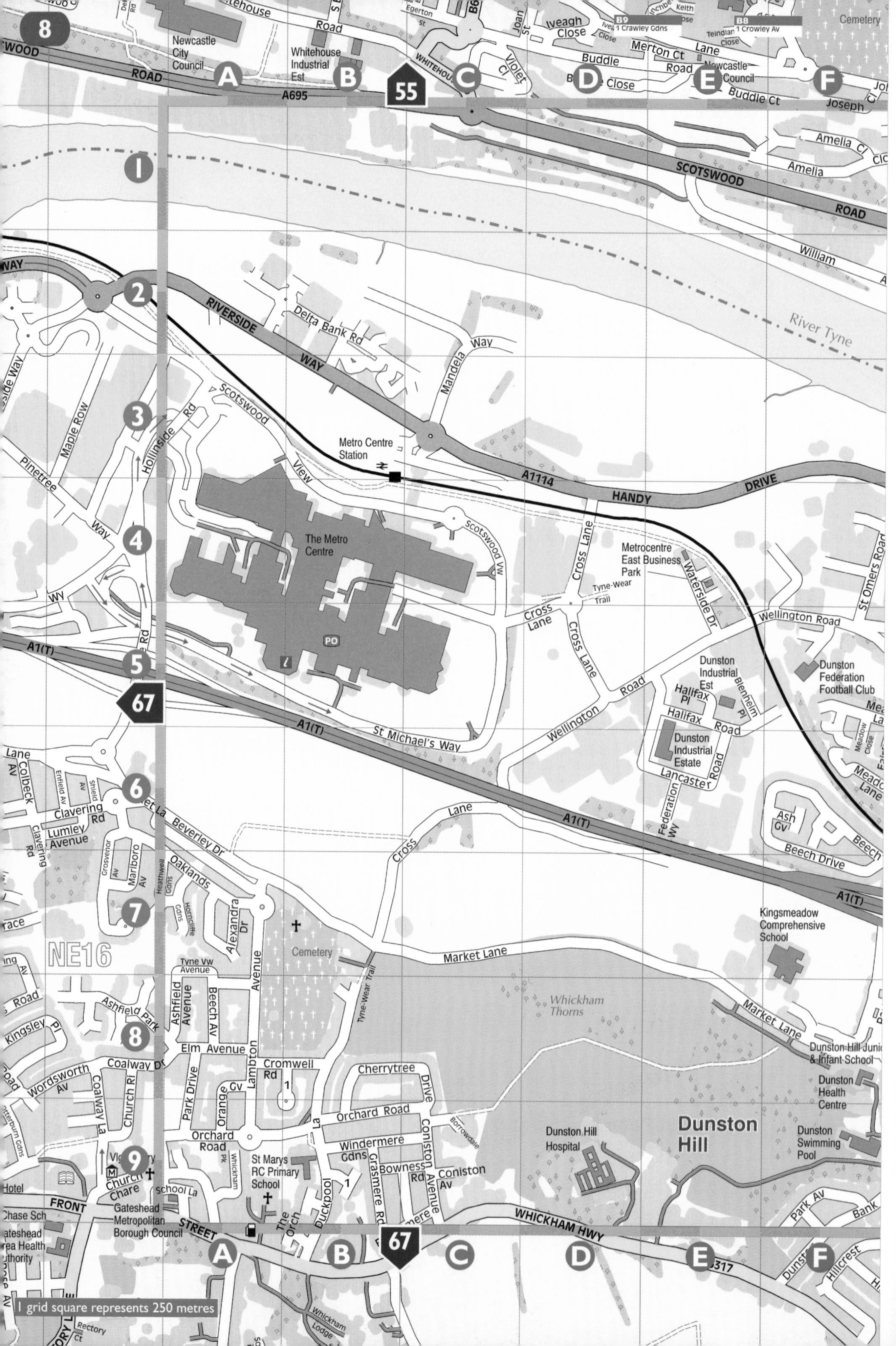
Newcastle City Council
Whitehouse Industrial Est
Whitehouse Road
A695
SCOTSWOOD ROAD
55
Iveagh Close
Buddle Road
Buddle Close
Merton Ct
Newcastle Council
Buddle Ct
Joseph
Amelia Cl
Amelia
William
Cemetery
River Tyne
RIVERSIDE WAY
Delta Bank Rd
Mandela Way
Metro Centre Station
A1114
HANDY DRIVE
Scotswood View
Scotswood Vw
The Metro Centre
Hollinside Rd
Maple Row
Pinetree Way
Cross Lane
Tyne-Wear Trail
Metrocentre East Business Park
Waterside Dr
St Omers Road
Wellington Road
Dunston Federation Football Club
A1(T)
67
St Michael's Way
Dunston Industrial Est
Halifax Pl
Halifax Road
Blenheim Pl
Dunston Industrial Estate
Lancaster Road
Federation Wy
Meadow Close
Meadow Lane
Ash Gv
Beech Drive
Colbeck Av
Enfield Av
Shield Av
Clavering Rd
Lumley Avenue
Beverley Dr
Oaklands
Grosvenor Av
Marlboro Av
Heathwell Gdns
Alexandra Dr
NE16
Cemetery
Market Lane
Kingsmeadow Comprehensive School
Whickham Thorns
Dunston Hill Junior & Infant School
Dunston Health Centre
Tyne Vw Avenue
Ashfield Avenue
Beech Av
Ashfield Park
Kingsley Pl
Wordsworth Av
Coalway Dr
Coalway La
Church Ri
Elm Avenue
Cromwell Rd
Lambton Avenue
Park Drive
Orange Gv
Cherrytree Drive
Orchard Road
Borrowdale
Coniston Avenue
Coniston Av
Windermere Gdns
Grasmere Rd
Bowness Rd
Duckpool
Dunston Hill Hospital
Dunston Hill
Dunston Swimming Pool
Park Av
St Marys RC Primary School
Church Chare
School La
Gateshead Metropolitan Borough Council
FRONT STREET
WHICKHAM HWY
Whickham Lodge
Rectory Ct
Hotel
Chase Sch
Gateshead Area Health Authority
A B C D E F
1 2 3 4 5 6 7 8 9
1 grid square represents 250 metres

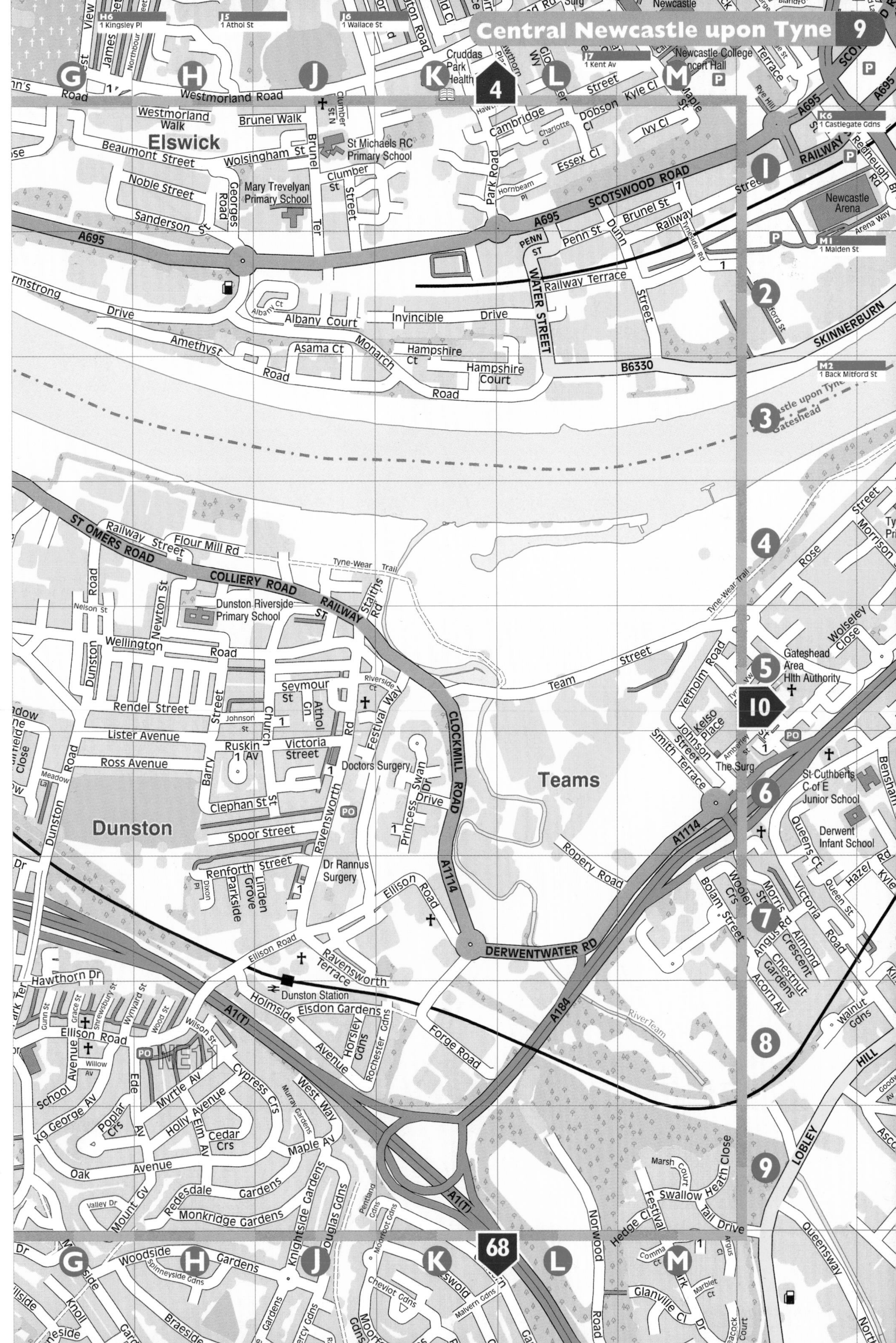

Elswick
Dunston
Teams
Westmorland Road
Westmorland Walk
Brunel Walk
Beaumont Street
Wolsingham St
Noble Street
Sanderson St
Georges Road
St Michaels RC Primary School
Mary Trevelyan Primary School
Clumber St
Cruddas Park Health
Cambridge
Dobson Cl
Kyle Cl
Ivy Cl
Essex Cl
Park Road
Hornbeam Pl
SCOTSWOOD ROAD
A695
Penn St
Brunel St
Railway Street
Newcastle Arena
Arena Way
Railway Terrace
WATER STREET
Armstrong Drive
Albany Court
Invincible Drive
Amethyst Road
Asama Ct
Monarch Road
Hampshire Ct
Hampshire Court
B6330
SKINNERBURN
Newcastle College Concert Hall
H6 1 Kingsley Pl
J5 1 Athol St
J6 1 Wallace St
J7 1 Kent Av
K6 1 Castlegate Gdns
M1 1 Maiden St
M2 1 Back Mitford St
Newcastle upon Tyne
Gateshead
ST OMERS ROAD
Railway Street
Flour Mill Rd
COLLIERY ROAD
RAILWAY ST
Tyne-Wear Trail
Staithes Rd
Dunston Riverside Primary School
Newton St
Nelson St
Wellington Road
Dunston Road
Rendel Street
Lister Avenue
Ross Avenue
Meadow La
Seymour St
Athol Gn
Riverside Ct
Festival Way
Church St
Johnson St
Ruskin Av
Victoria Street
Ravensworth Rd
Doctors Surgery
Swan Dr
Princess Drive
Barry Street
Clephan St
Spoor Street
Renforth Street
Dixon Pl
Parkside
Linden Grove
Dr Rannus Surgery
CLOCKMILL ROAD
A1114
Ellison Road
DERWENTWATER RD
Ravensworth Terrace
Dunston Station
Holmside Avenue
Elsdon Gardens
Horsley Gdns
Rochester Gdns
Forge Road
Team Street
Yetholm Road
Kelso Place
Johnson Street
Smith Terrace
Amberley St
The Surg
Gateshead Area Hlth Authority
Wolseley Close
Rose Street
Morrison St
St Cuthberts C of E Junior School
Derwent Infant School
Queens Ct
Victoria Road
Hazel Rd
Queen St
Morris St
Almond Crescent
Chestnut Gardens
Acorn Av
Angus Rd
Wooler Crs
Bolam Street
Ropery Road
River Team
A184
Walnut Gdns
HILL
LOBLEY
Queensway
Hawthorn Dr
Ellison Road
Gunn St
Grace St
Shrewsbury St
Wynyard St
Wood St
Wilson St
Willow Av
School Avenue
Ede Av
NE11
Myrtle Av
Cypress Crs
Holly Avenue
Elm Av
Cedar Crs
Poplar Crs
Kg George Av
Oak Avenue
Maple Av
Murray Gardens
West Way
A1(T)
Redesdale Gardens
Monkridge Gardens
Valley Dr
Mount Gv
Knightside Gardens
Douglas Gdns
Pentland Gdns
Moorfoot Gdns
Marsh Court
Swallow Tail Drive
Heath Close
Festival
Hedge Cl
Norwood Road
Woodside Gardens
Spinneyside Gdns
Braeside
Knoll
Cheviot Gdns
Malvern Gdns
Glanville Cl
Marblet Ct
Peacock Court
Comma Ct
Argus Cl
Percy Gdns
Moorfoot Gdns
Bensham

4
10
68

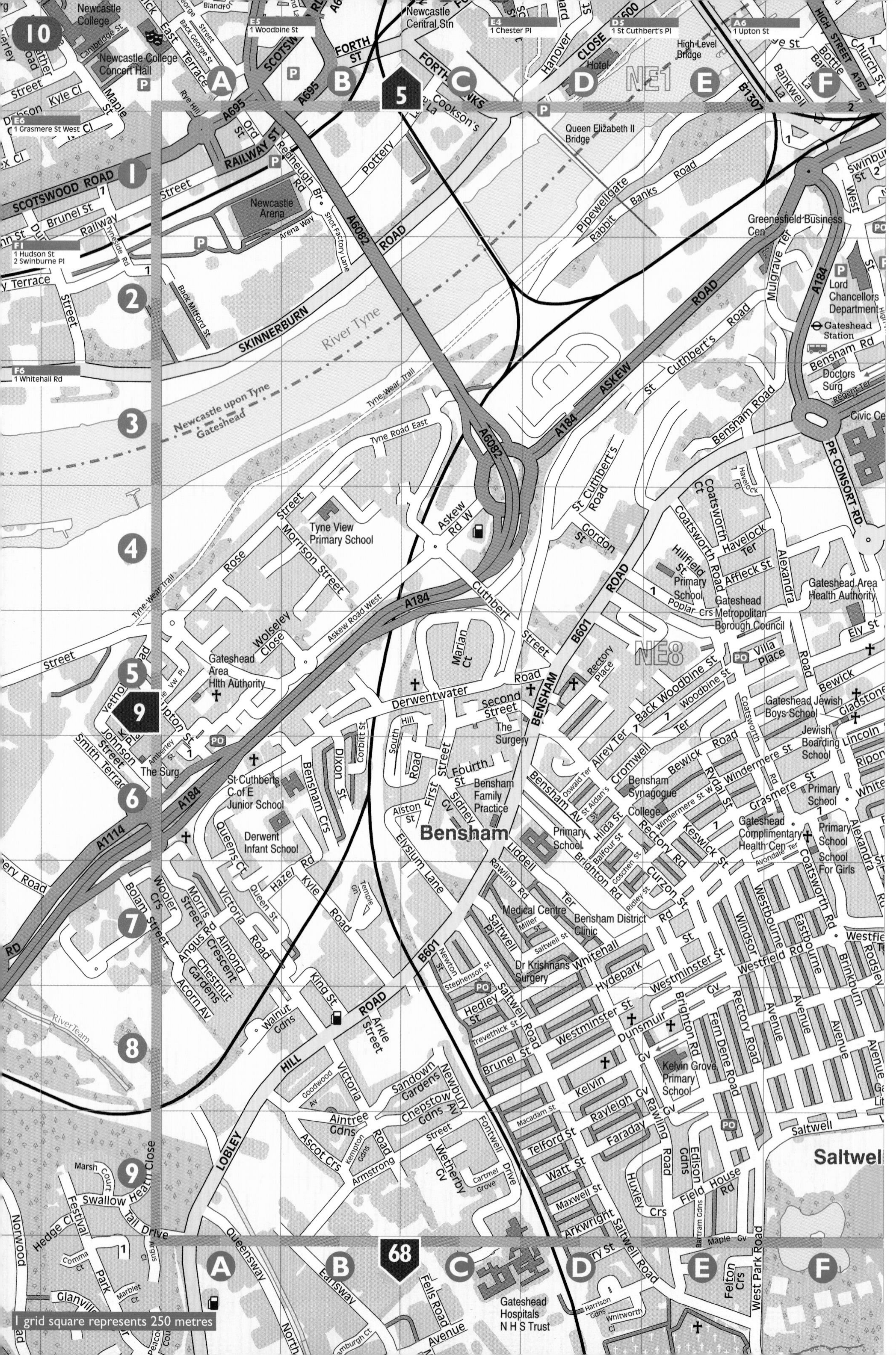
10
Newcastle College
Newcastle College Concert Hall
E5 1 Woodbine St
E4 1 Chester Pl
D5 1 St Cuthbert's Pl
A6 1 Upton St
E6 1 Grasmere St West
F1 1 Hudson St 2 Swinburne Pl
F6 1 Whitehall Rd
Newcastle Central Stn
High Level Bridge
NE1
Queen Elizabeth II Bridge
A B C D E F
5
1
2
3
4
5
6
7
8
9
9
68
SCOTSWOOD ROAD
RAILWAY ST
Newcastle Arena
Arena Way
Shot Factory Lane
A6082 ROAD
SKINNERBURN
River Tyne
Newcastle upon Tyne
Gateshead
Tyne-Wear Trail
Tyne Road East
Pipewellgate
Rabbit Banks Road
Greenesfield Business Cen
Lord Chancellors Department
Gateshead Station
ASKEW ROAD
A184
Tyne View Primary School
Morrison Street
Rose Street
Askew Road West
Wolseley Close
Gateshead Area Hlth Authority
The Surg
St Cuthberts C of E Junior School
Derwent Infant School
Derwentwater Road
Marian Ct
Cuthbert Street
Second Street
The Surgery
Bensham Family Practice
Bensham
BENSHAM ROAD B601
NE8
Hillfield St Primary School
Gateshead Metropolitan Borough Council
Gateshead Area Health Authority
Gateshead Jewish Boys School
Jewish Boarding School
Primary School
Gateshead Complimentary Health Cen
School For Girls
Bensham Synagogue
College
Primary School
Medical Centre
Bensham District Clinic
Dr Krishnans Surgery
Kelvin Grove Primary School
Saltwell
LOBLEY HILL ROAD
Queensway
Earlsway
Fells Road
Gateshead Hospitals N H S Trust
West Park Road
Saltwell Road
Swallow Heath Close
Tall Drive
Festival Park
Norwood
River Team
1 grid square represents 250 metres

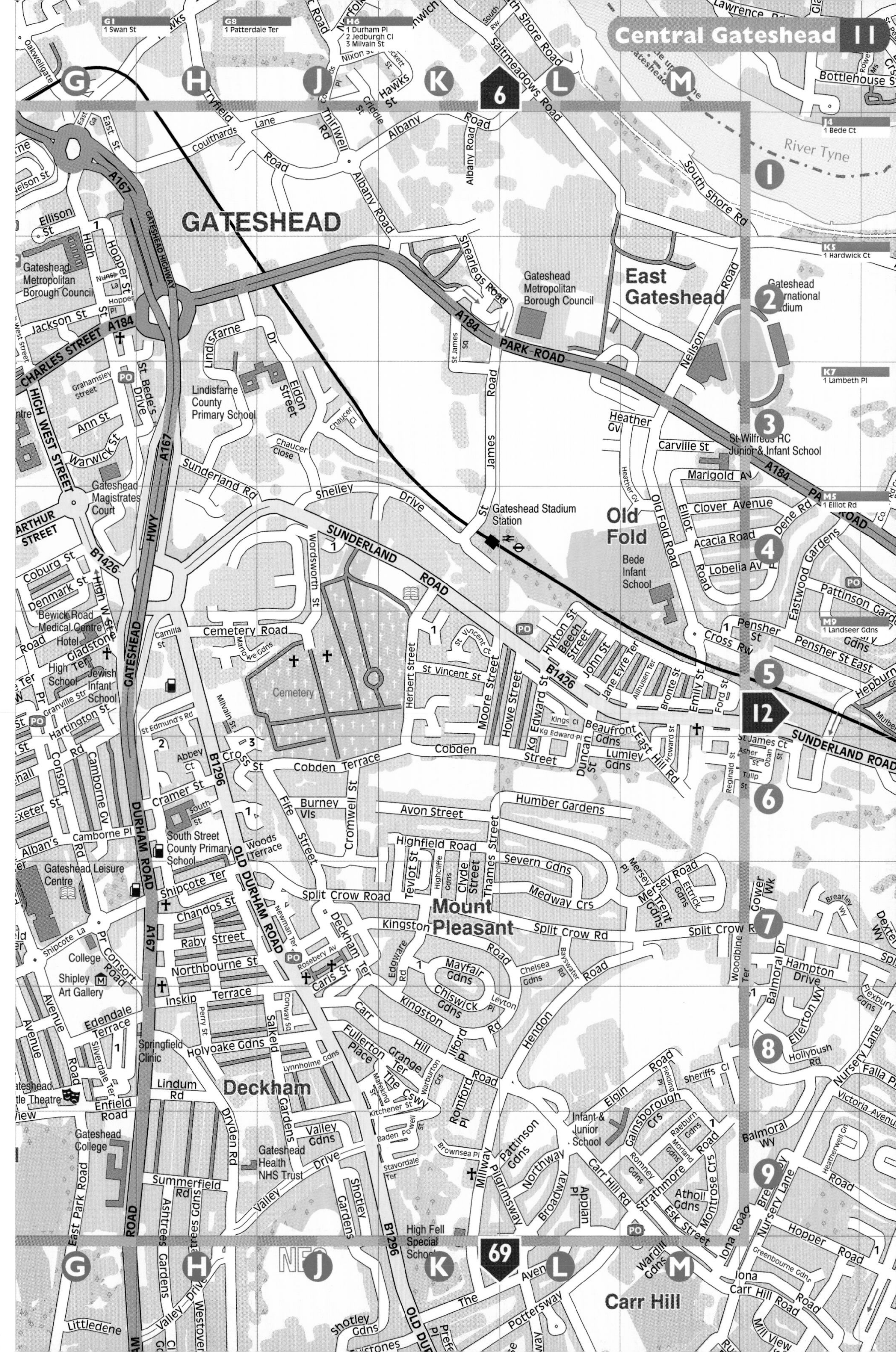
G1
1 Swan St
G8
1 Patterdale Ter
H6
1 Durham Pl
2 Jedburgh Cl
3 Milvain St
J4
1 Bede Ct
K5
1 Hardwick Ct
K7
1 Lambeth Pl
M5
1 Elliot Rd
M9
1 Landseer Gdns
GATESHEAD
East Gateshead
Old Fold
Mount Pleasant
Deckham
Carr Hill
River Tyne
Gateshead Metropolitan Borough Council
Gateshead International Stadium
St Wilfreds RC Junior & Infant School
Gateshead Stadium Station
Bede Infant School
Lindisfarne County Primary School
Gateshead Magistrates Court
Bewick Road Medical Centre
High Ter School
Jewish Infant School
South Street County Primary School
Gateshead Leisure Centre
College
Shipley Art Gallery
Springfield Clinic
Gateshead College
Gateshead Health NHS Trust
High Fell Special School
Infant & Junior School
Cemetery
PARK ROAD
SUNDERLAND ROAD
CHARLES STREET
HIGH WEST STREET
GATESHEAD HIGHWAY
DURHAM ROAD
OLD DURHAM ROAD
A167
A184
B1426
B1296
Albany Road
Saltmeadows Road
South Shore Rd
Sunderland Rd
Shelley Drive
Cemetery Road
Cobden Terrace
Split Crow Road
Kingston Road
Carr Hill Road
Hendon Road
Avon Street
Humber Gardens
Highfield Road
Severn Gdns
Medway Crs
Mersey Road
Split Crow Rd
Old Fold Road
Clover Avenue
Acacia Road
Eastwood Gardens
Pattinson Gardens
Pensher St East
Balmoral Dr
Nursery Lane
Victoria Avenue
Hopper Road
Valley Drive
Summerfield Rd
Dryden Rd
Lindum Rd
Enfield Road
Edendale Terrace
Holyoake Gdns
Inskip Terrace
Northbourne St
Raby Street
Chandos St
Shipcote Ter
Coburg St
Denmark St
Warwick St
Ann St
Jackson St
Ellison St
6
12
69

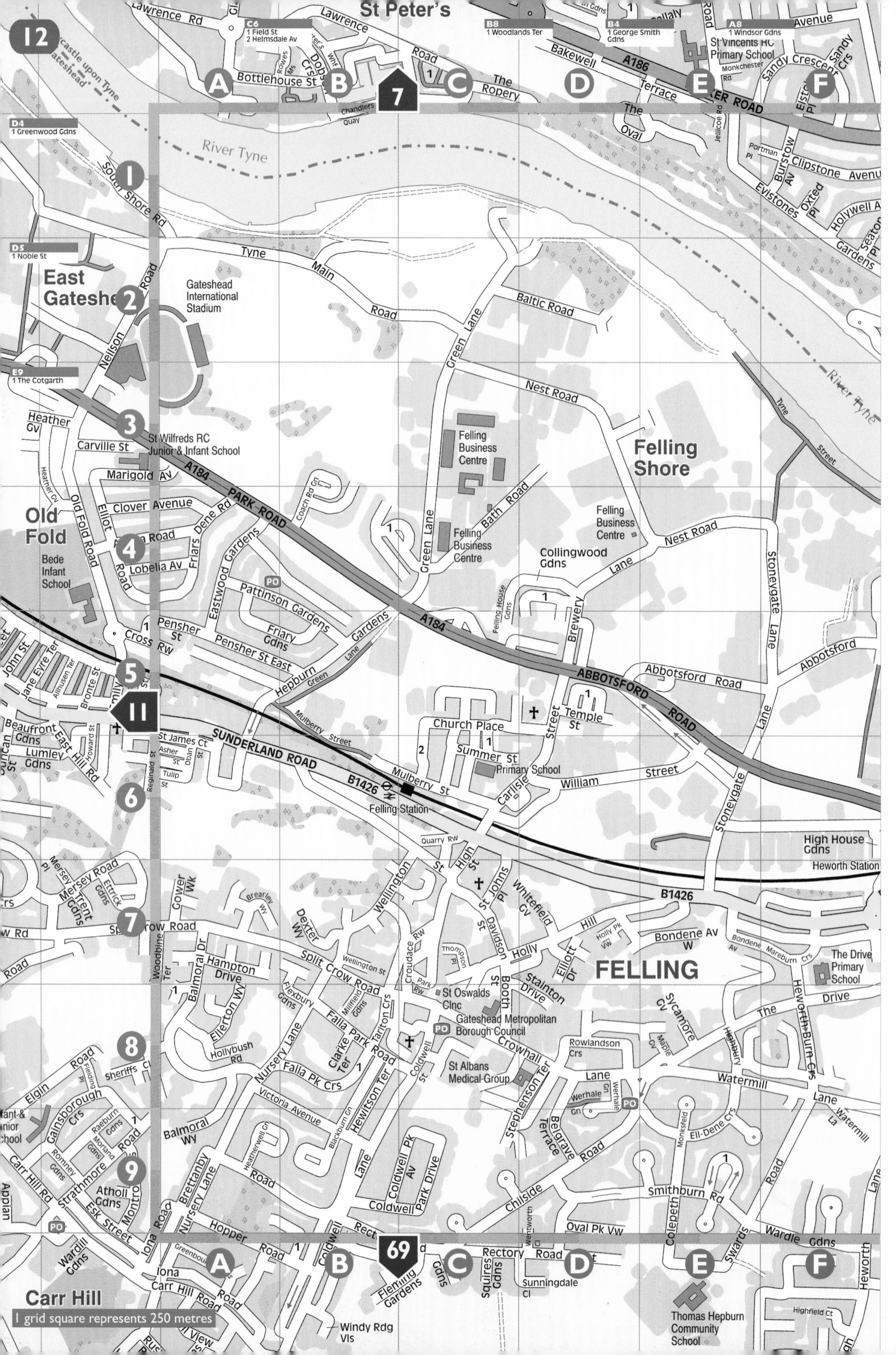
St Peter's
C6
1 Field St
2 Helmsdale Av
B8
1 Woodlands Ter
B4
1 George Smith Gdns
A8
1 Windsor Gdns
D4
1 Greenwood Gdns
D5
1 Noble St
E9
1 The Cotgarth
River Tyne
East Gateshead
Gateshead International Stadium
St Wilfreds RC Junior & Infant School
Felling Business Centre
Felling Shore
Old Fold
Bede Infant School
Felling Station
St Vincents RC Primary School
St Oswalds Clnc
Gateshead Metropolitan Borough Council
St Albans Medical Group
The Drive Primary School
Thomas Hepburn Community School
FELLING
Carr Hill
Heworth Station
High House Gdns
A184
PARK ROAD
ABBOTSFORD ROAD
SUNDERLAND ROAD
B1426
A186
Tyne Main Road
Green Lane
Baltic Road
Nest Road
Bath Road
Old Fold Road
Stoneygate Lane
Split Crow Road
Falla Park Road
Victoria Avenue
Watermill Lane
Smithburn Rd
Wardle Gdns
Rectory Road
Carr Hill Rd
Iona Road
1 grid square represents 250 metres

7
11
69

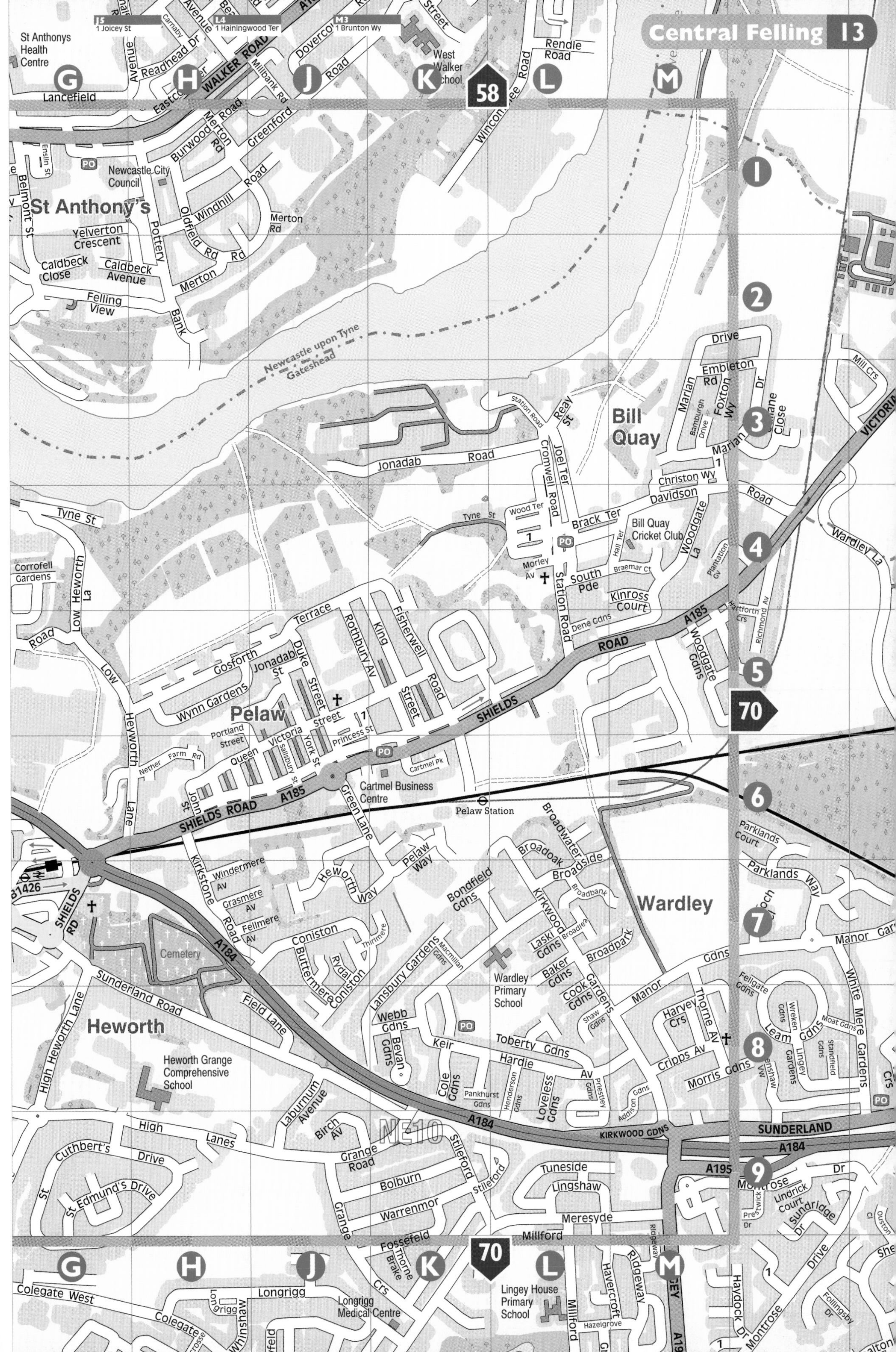
St Anthonys Health Centre
J5 1 Joicey St
L4 1 Hainingwood Ter
M3 1 Brunton Wy
West Walker School
Rendle Road
Lancefield
Readhead Dr
Walker Road
Millbank Rd
Dovercourt Road
Merton Road
Burwood Rd
Greenford
Wincomblee Road
58
Enslin St
Belmont St
Newcastle City Council
St Anthony's
Windhill
Oldfield Rd
Merton Rd
Pottery
Yelverton Crescent
Caldbeck Close
Caldbeck Avenue
Felling View
Bank
Merton
Newcastle upon Tyne
Gateshead
Station Road
Reay St
Bill Quay
Drive
Embleton Rd
Marian Dr
Bamburgh Drive
Foxton Wy
Close
Mill Crs
Jonadab Road
Joel Ter
Cromwell Road
Christon Wy
Davidson Road
Wood Ter
Tyne St
Brack Ter
Bill Quay Cricket Club
Hall Ter
Woodgate La
Plantation Gv
Wardley La
Tyne St
Corrofell Gardens
Low Heworth La
Morley Av
South Pde
Braemar Ct
Station Road
Kinross Court
Dene Gdns
Hartforth Crs
Richmond Av
Terrace
Rothbury Av
King Street
Fisherwell Road
Woodgate Gdns
Road
Gosforth
Jonadab St
Duke Street
Low Heworth Lane
Wynn Gardens
Pelaw
Street
Princess St
Shields Road
A185
Portland Street
Victoria
York St
Queen
Salisbury St
Nether Farm Rd
Cartmel Pk
Cartmel Business Centre
John St
Shields Road
Green Lane
Pelaw Station
70
Broadwater
Broadoak
Broadside
Parklands Court
Parklands Way
Kirkstone Road
Windermere Av
Grasmere Av
Fellmere Av
Heworth Way
Pelaw Way
Bondfield Gdns
Kirkwood
Broadbank
Wardley
B1426
Shields Rd
Cemetery
A184
Coniston
Buttermere
Rydal
Coniston
Thirlmere
Lansbury Gardens
Macmillan Gdns
Laski Gdns
Broadlea
Broadpark
Manor Gdns
Fellgate Gdns
White Mere Gardens
Sunderland Road
Field Lane
Wardley Primary School
Baker Gdns
Cook Gdns
Gardens
Manor
Harvey Crs
Thorne Av
Wrekin Gdns
Moat Gdns
Leam Gdns
Lingey Gardens
Standfield Gdns
High Heworth Lane
Heworth
Webb Gdns
Bevan Gdns
Keir
Toberty Gdns
Hardie
Shaw Gdns
Cripps Av
Morris Gdns
Heworth Grange Comprehensive School
Cole Gdns
Pankhurst Gdns
Henderson Gdns
Loveless Gdns
Av
Gdns
Priestley
Addison Gdns
Laburnum Avenue
Birch Av
NE10
A184
Kirkwood Gdns
Sunderland
A184
High Lanes
Cuthbert's Drive
St Edmund's Drive
St
Grange Road
Bolburn
Stileford
Stileford
Tuneside
Lingshaw
A195
Montrose Dr
Lindrick Court
Sundridge Dr
Prestwick Dr
Warrenmor
Grange
Meresyde
Millford
Fossefeld
Thorne Brake
Ridgeway
Drive
Colegate West
Longrigg
Longrigg Medical Centre
Crs
Lingey House Primary School
Havercroft
Ridgeway
Haydock Dr
Montrose
Follingsby Dr
Colegate
Whinshaw
Millford
Hazelgrove
A195
G
H
J
K
L
M
1
2
3
4
5
6
7
8
9

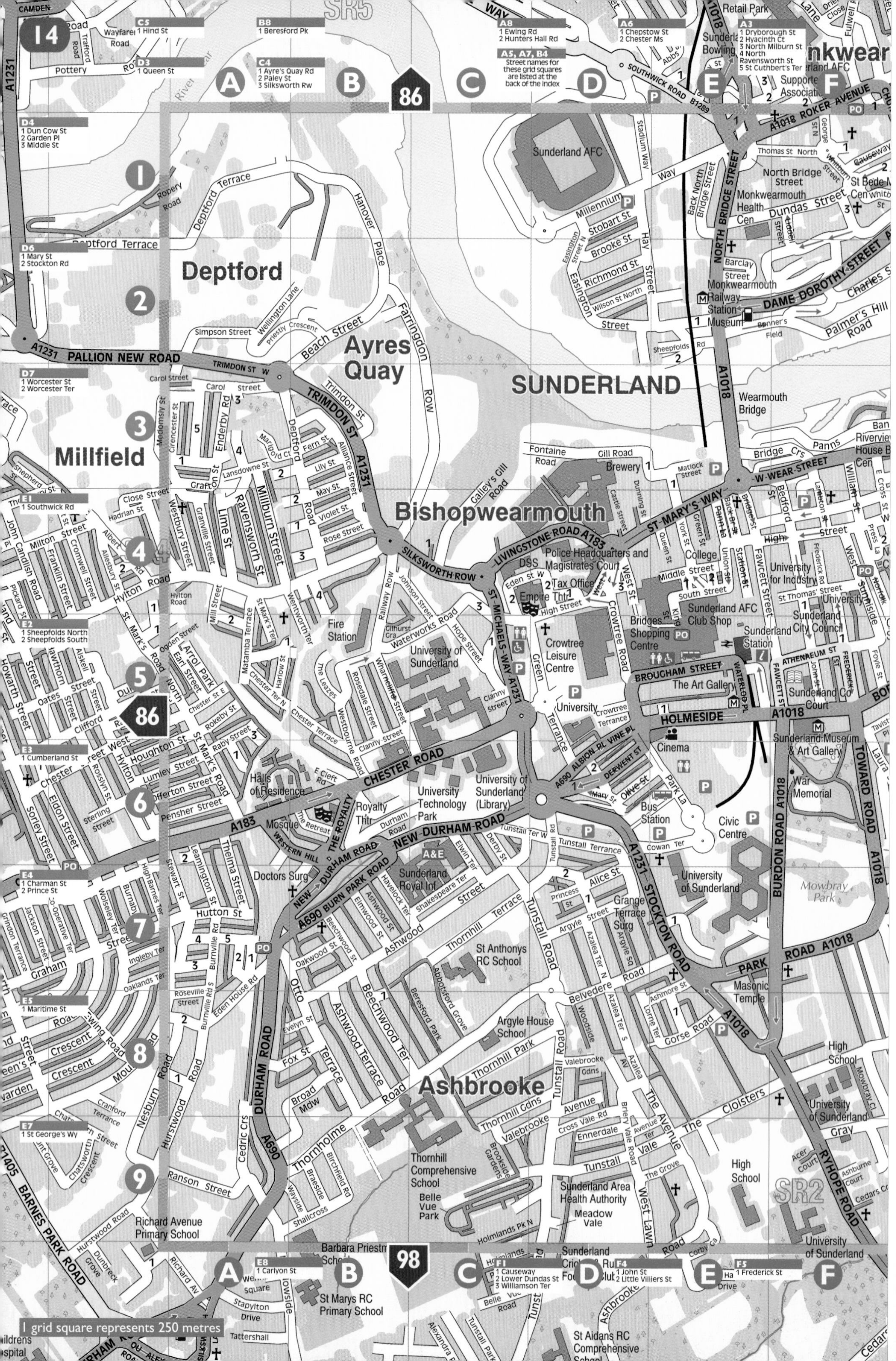

14
86
98
A
B
C
D
E
F
1
2
3
4
5
6
7
8
9
SR5
SR2
C5 1 Hind St
D3 1 Queen St
B8 1 Beresford Pk
C4 1 Ayre's Quay Rd 2 Paley St 3 Silksworth Rw
A8 1 Ewing Rd 2 Hunters Hall Rd
A5, A7, B4 Street names for these grid squares are listed at the back of the index
A6 1 Chepstow St 2 Chester Ms
A3 1 Dryborough St 2 Hyacinth Ct 3 North Milburn St 4 North Ravensworth St 5 St Cuthbert's Ter
D4 1 Dun Cow St 2 Garden Pl 3 Middle St
D6 1 Mary St 2 Stockton Rd
D7 1 Worcester St 2 Worcester Ter
E1 1 Southwick Rd
E2 1 Sheepfolds North 2 Sheepfolds South
E3 1 Cumberland St
E4 1 Charman St 2 Prince St
E5 1 Maritime St
E7 1 St George's Wy
E8 1 Carlyon St
F1 1 Causeway 2 Lower Dundas St 3 Williamson Ter
F4 1 John St 2 Little Villiers St
F5 1 Frederick St
Deptford
Ayres Quay
SUNDERLAND
Millfield
Bishopwearmouth
Ashbrooke
Sunderland AFC
Monkwearmouth Health Cen
Monkwearmouth Railway Station Museum
Wearmouth Bridge
Police Headquarters and Magistrates Court
DSS
Tax Office
Empire Thtr
Crowtree Leisure Centre
Bridges Shopping Centre
Sunderland AFC Club Shop
Sunderland Station
College
University for Industry
Sunderland City Council
University
The Art Gallery
Sunderland Co Court
Sunderland Museum & Art Gallery
War Memorial
Cinema
Bus Station
Civic Centre
University of Sunderland
Mowbray Park
Masonic Temple
High School
Fire Station
University of Sunderland
University Technology Park
University of Sunderland (Library)
Halls of Residence
Mosque
Royalty Thtr
Doctors Surg
Sunderland Royal Inf
A&E
St Anthonys RC School
Grange Terrace Surg
Argyle House School
Thornhill Comprehensive School
Belle Vue Park
Sunderland Area Health Authority
Richard Avenue Primary School
St Marys RC Primary School
St Aidans RC Comprehensive School
Sunderland Cricket & Rugby Football Club
A1231 PALLION NEW ROAD
TRIMDON ST
A1231
SILKSWORTH ROW
ST MICHAELS WAY A1231
LIVINGSTONE ROAD A183
ST MARY'S WAY
NORTH BRIDGE STREET
A1018
DAME DOROTHY STREET A1018
ROKER AVENUE
SOUTHWICK ROAD B1289
W WEAR STREET
HOLMESIDE A1018
BROUGHAM STREET
WATERLOO PL
BURDON ROAD A1018
TOWARD ROAD A1018
PARK ROAD A1018
CHESTER ROAD
A183
NEW DURHAM ROAD
A690 BURN PARK ROAD
DURHAM ROAD A690
A1231 STOCKTON ROAD
RYHOPE ROAD
B1405 BARNES PARK ROAD
A690 ALBION PL VINE PL
DERWENT ST
Hanover Place
Farringdon Row
Deptford Terrace
Beach Street
Millburn Street
Ravensworth St
Lime St
Westbury Street
Hylton Road
Crowtree Road
Tunstall Road
Thornhill Terrace
The Cloisters
The Avenue
West Lawn
Ranson Street
Ashwood Terrace
Beechwood Ter
Eden House Rd
Cedric Crs
Stadium Way
Hay Street
1 grid square represents 250 metres

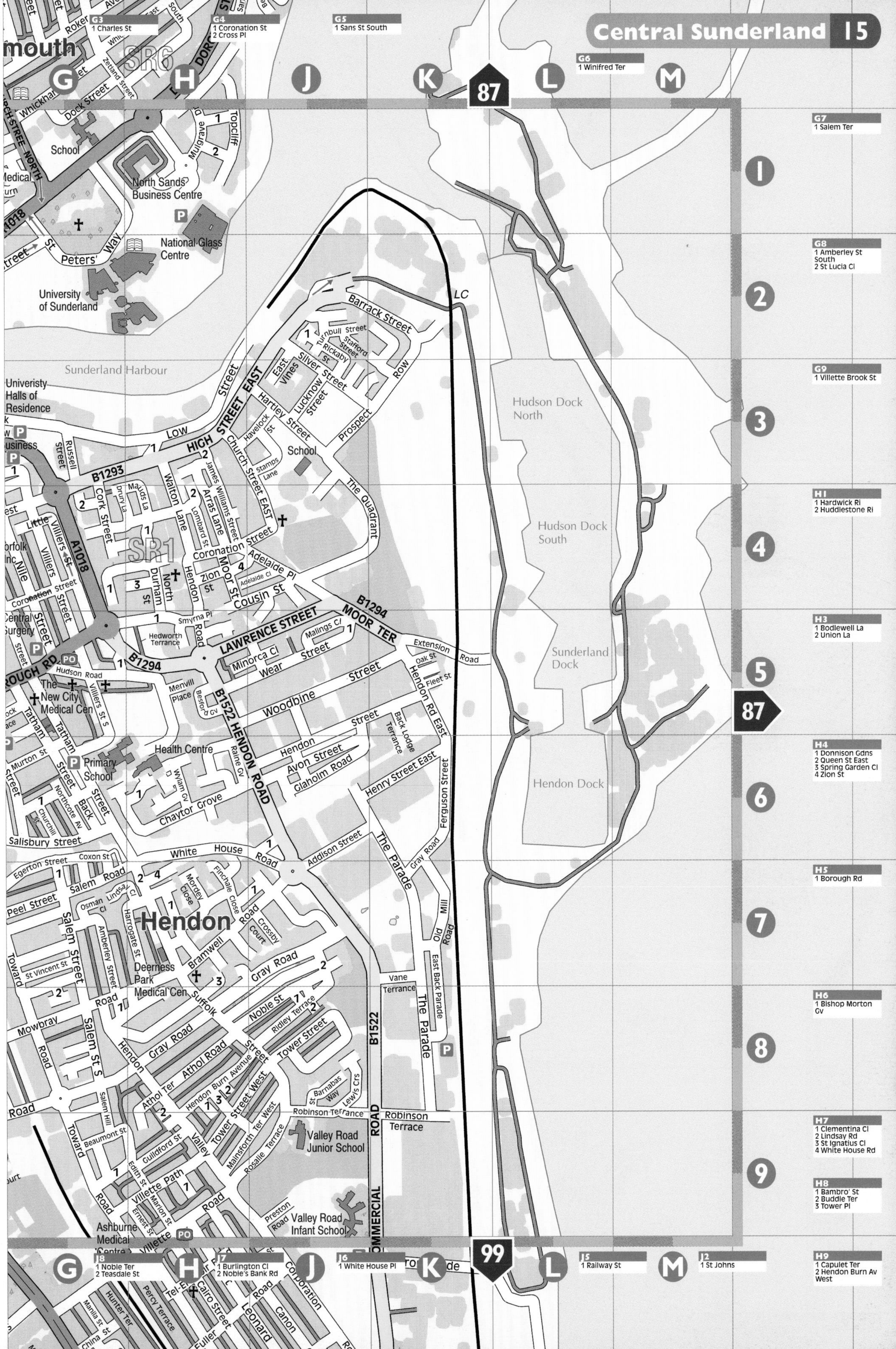
G3
1 Charles St
G4
1 Coronation St
2 Cross Pl
G5
1 Sans St South
G6
1 Winifred Ter
G7
1 Salem Ter
G8
1 Amberley St South
2 St Lucia Cl
G9
1 Villette Brook St
H1
1 Hardwick Ri
2 Huddlestone Ri
H3
1 Bodlewell La
2 Union La
H4
1 Donnison Gdns
2 Queen St East
3 Spring Garden Cl
4 Zion St
H5
1 Borough Rd
H6
1 Bishop Morton Gv
H7
1 Clementina Cl
2 Lindsay Rd
3 St Ignatius Cl
4 White House Rd
H8
1 Bambro' St
2 Buddle Ter
3 Tower Pl
H9
1 Capulet Ter
2 Hendon Burn Av West
J8
1 Noble Ter
2 Teasdale St
J7
1 Burlington Cl
2 Noble's Bank Rd
J6
1 White House Pl
J5
1 Railway St
J2
1 St Johns
87
99
SR6
SR1
North Sands Business Centre
National Glass Centre
University of Sunderland
Sunderland Harbour
University Halls of Residence
Hudson Dock North
Hudson Dock South
Sunderland Dock
Hendon Dock
Hendon
Health Centre
Primary School
The New City Medical Cen
Central Surgery
Deerness Park Medical Cen
Valley Road Junior School
Valley Road Infant School
Ashburne Medical Centre
High Street East
Low Street
Lawrence Street
Moor Ter
Hendon Road
Commercial Road
Barrack Street
The Quadrant
Robinson Terrace
The Parade

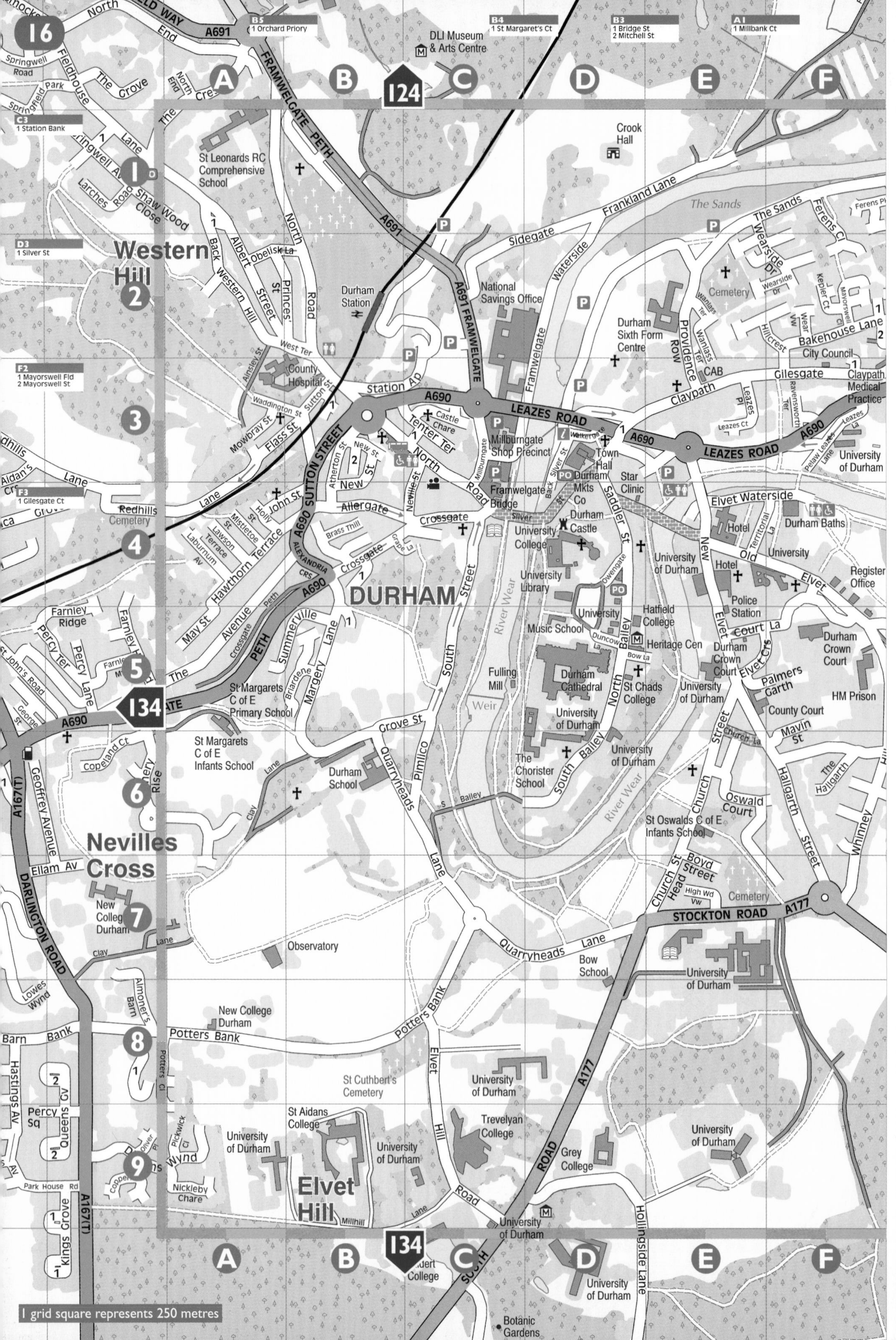
B5
1 Orchard Priory
B4
1 St Margaret's Ct
B3
1 Bridge St
2 Mitchell St
A1
1 Millbank Ct
C3
1 Station Bank
D3
1 Silver St
F2
1 Mayorswell Fld
2 Mayorswell St
F3
1 Gilesgate Ct
124
134
A
B
C
D
E
F
1
2
3
4
5
6
7
8
9
DLI Museum & Arts Centre
North End
A691
Springwell Road
Fieldhouse Lane
The Grove
The Crescent
Springwell Park
Larches Road
Shaw Wood Close
FRAMWELGATE PETH
Crook Hall
St Leonards RC Comprehensive School
Frankland Lane
The Sands
Ferens Cl
Western Hill
Back Western Hill
Albert Street
Obelisk La
Princes' St
North Road
Durham Station
Sidegate
Waterside
National Savings Office
Framwelgate
A691 FRAMWELGATE
Durham Sixth Form Centre
Providence Row
Wanlass Ter
Cemetery
Wearside Dr
Kepler Ct
Hillcrest
Bakehouse Lane
City Council
Gilesgate
Claypath Medical Practice
Claypath
CAB
West Ter
County Hospital
Ainsley St
Sutton St
Waddington St
Mowbray St
Flass St
Station App
A690
Castle Chare
Tenter Ter
LEAZES ROAD
Walkergate
Town Hall
Leazes Pl
Leazes Ct
Ravensworth Ter
University of Durham
Millburngate Shop Precinct
Durham Mkts Co
Star Clinic
Elvet Waterside
Durham Baths
Redhills Cemetery
Lane
John St
A690 SUTTON STREET
Atherton St
New St
North St
Neville St
Allergate
Crossgate
Framwelgate Bridge
Silver St
Saddler St
Back Silver St
Durham Castle
University College
Hotel
Old Elvet
Register Office
Holly St
Mistletoe St
Lawson Terrace
Laburnum Av
Hawthorn Terrace
ALEXANDRIA CRS
Brass Thill
Grape La
South Street
University Library
Owengate
Police Station
Farnley Ridge
Percy Ter
Percy Lane
May St
The Avenue
Crossgate Peth
PETH
DURHAM
Summerville
Margery Lane
Briardene
River Wear
University
Music School
Hatfield College
Dun Cow La
Bailey
Heritage Cen
Elvet
Court La
Durham Crown Court
St John's Road
George St
St Margarets C of E Primary School
Fulling Mill
Weir
Durham Cathedral
Bow La
St Chads College
North Bailey
Elvet Crs
Palmers Garth
County Court
HM Prison
Copeland Ct
Rise
Grove St
Quarryheads
Pimlico
University of Durham
Church La
Mavin St
The Hallgarth
St Margarets C of E Infants School
Durham School
Clay Lane
The Chorister School
South Bailey
Church Street
Oswald Court
Hallgarth Street
Whinney Hill
Geoffrey Avenue
A167(T)
Nevilles Cross
S Bailey
St Oswalds C of E Infants School
Ellam Av
Lane
Church St Head
Boyd Street
High Wd Vw
New College Durham
STOCKTON ROAD
A177
DARLINGTON ROAD
Clay Lane
Observatory
Quarryheads Lane
Bow School
Lowes Wynd
Almoner's Barn
New College Durham
Potters Bank
Barn Bank
Potters Cl
Hastings Av
Queens Gv
Percy Sq
St Cuthbert's Cemetery
Elvet Hill
A177
Trevelyan College
St Aidans College
Pickwick Cl
Dickens Wynd
Oliver Pl
Copperfield
Nickleby Chare
Park House Rd
Kings Grove
Elvet Hill
Grey College
Road
Lane
Millhill
ROAD
Hollingside Lane
University of Durham
SOUTH
St Cuthbert's College
Botanic Gardens
1 grid square represents 250 metres

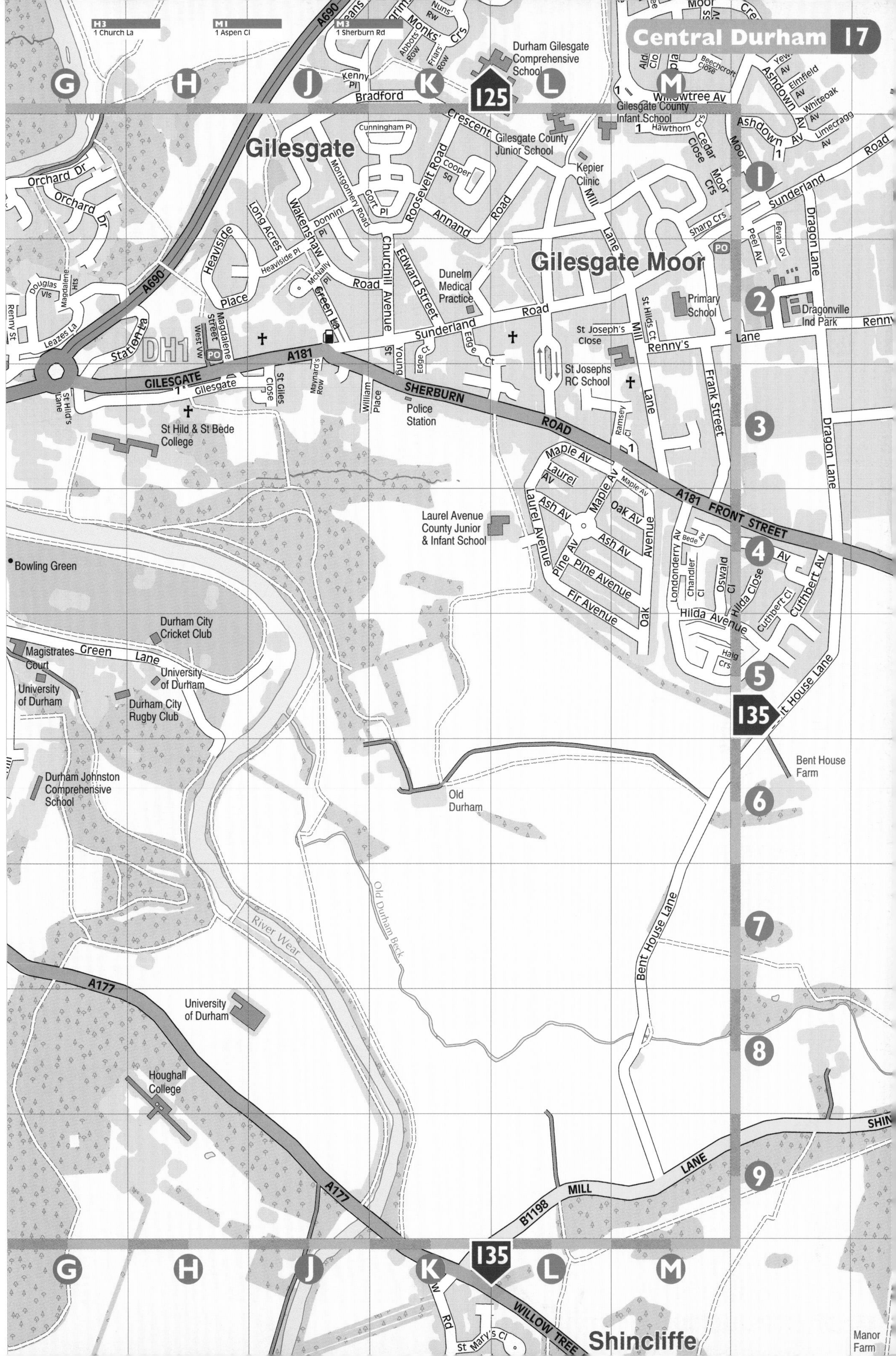
H3 1 Church La
M1 1 Aspen Cl
M3 1 Sherburn Rd
125
135
Gilesgate
Gilesgate Moor
Shincliffe
DH1
Durham Gilesgate Comprehensive School
Gilesgate County Infant School
Gilesgate County Junior School
Kepier Clinic
Dunelm Medical Practice
Primary School
Dragonville Ind Park
St Joseph's Close
St Josephs RC School
Police Station
St Hild & St Bede College
Laurel Avenue County Junior & Infant School
Bowling Green
Durham City Cricket Club
Magistrates Court
University of Durham
Durham City Rugby Club
Durham Johnston Comprehensive School
Old Durham
Bent House Farm
Houghall College
Manor Farm
River Wear
Old Durham Beck
A690
A181
A177
B1198
GILESGATE
SHERBURN ROAD
FRONT STREET
MILL LANE
WILLOW TREE
Sunderland Road
Bent House Lane
Dragon Lane
Renny's Lane
Green Lane
Orchard Dr
Heaviside Place
Long Acres
Wakenshaw Road
Churchill Avenue
Edward Street
Roosevelt Road
Annand Road
Montgomery Road
Cunningham Pl
Cooper Sq
Bradford Crescent
Mill Lane
Frank Street
Maple Av
Laurel Avenue
Ash Av
Oak Avenue
Pine Avenue
Fir Avenue
Hilda Avenue
Cuthbert Av
Londonderry Av
Ashdown Av
Willowtree Av

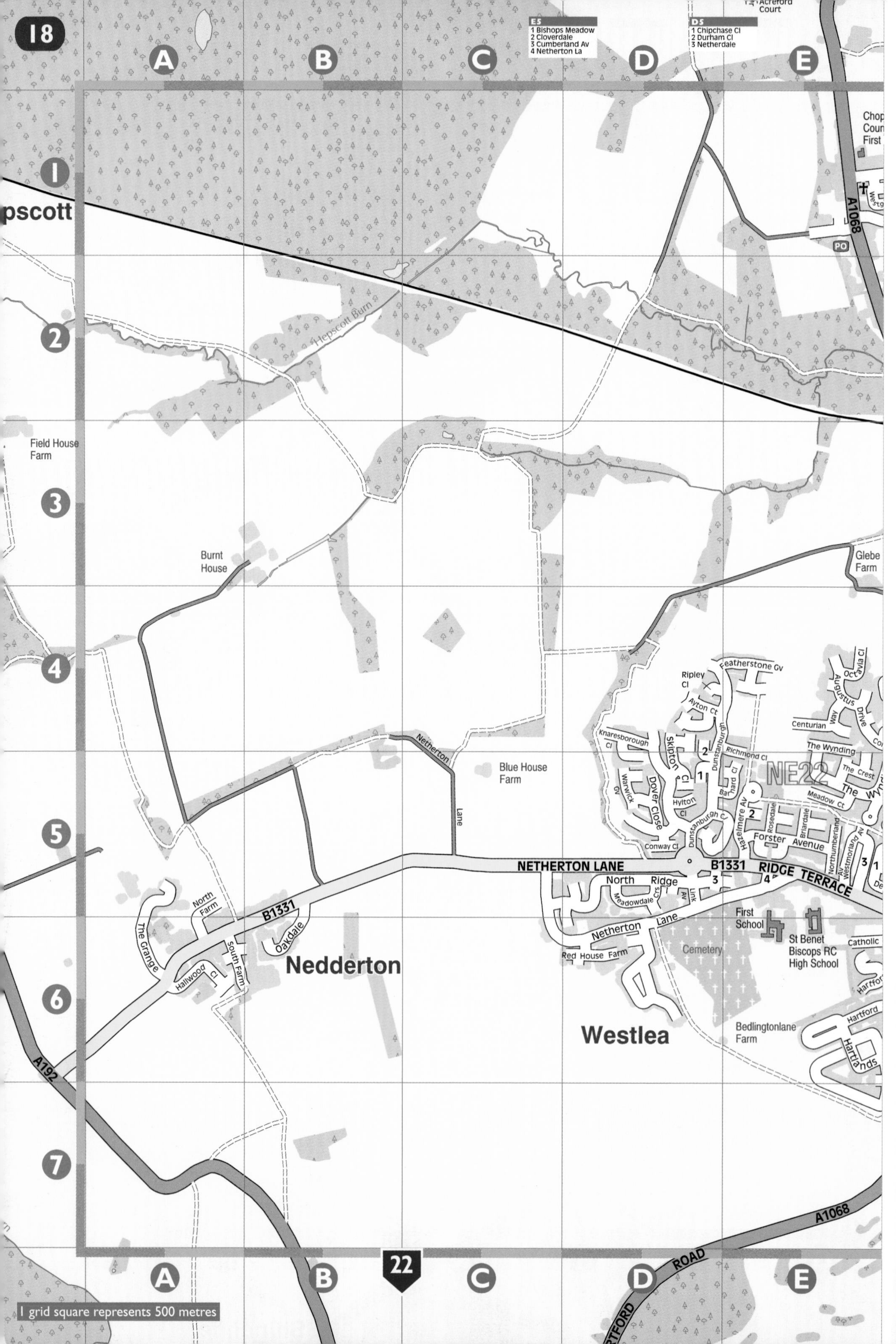
E5
1 Bishops Meadow
2 Cloverdale
3 Cumberland Av
4 Netherton La
D5
1 Chipchase Cl
2 Durham Cl
3 Netherdale
Acreford Court
A
B
C
D
E
1
2
3
4
5
6
7
pscott
A1068
PO
Hepscott Burn
Field House Farm
Burnt House
Glebe Farm
Netherton Lane
Blue House Farm
NE22
Featherstone Gv
Ripley Cl
Ayton Ct
Knaresborough Cl
Skipton Cl
Dunstanburgh
Richmond Cl
Warwick Gv
Dover Close
Hylton Cl
Barnard Cl
Dunstanburgh Cl
Hazelmere Av
Rosedale
Briardale
Conway Cl
Forster Avenue
Northumberland Av
Westmorland Av
Octavia Cl
Augustus Drive
Centurian Way
The Wynding
The Crest
Meadow Ct
NETHERTON LANE
B1331
RIDGE TERRACE
North Ridge
Meadowdale Crs
Link Av
North Farm
The Grange
South Farm
Oakdale
Hallwood Cl
Nedderton
Netherton Lane
Red House Farm
First School
Cemetery
St Benet Biscops RC High School
Catholic
Hartford
Westlea
Bedlingtonlane Farm
Hartlands
A192
A1068
ROAD
22
1 grid square represents 500 metres

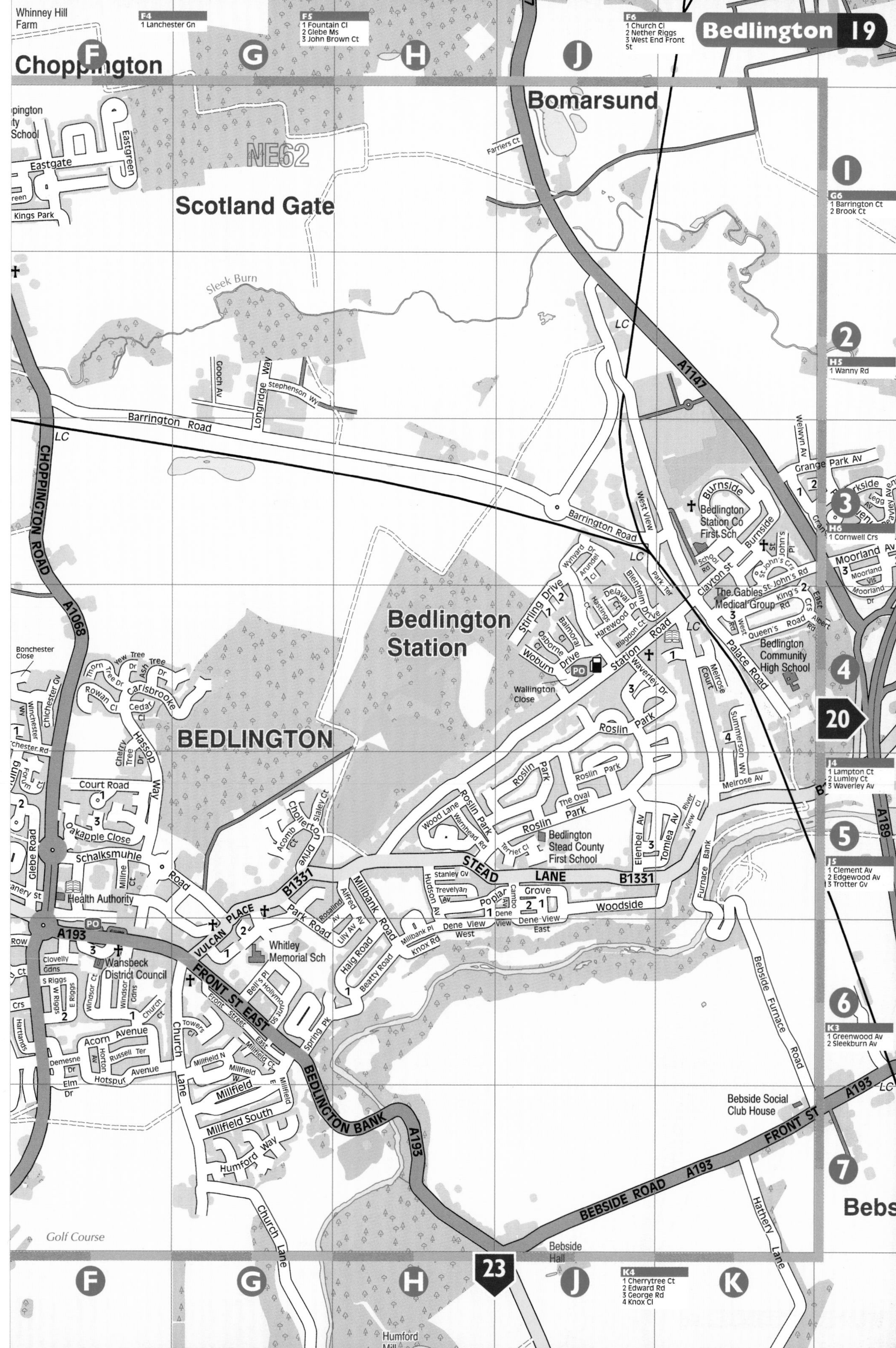
F4
1 Lanchester Gn
F5
1 Fountain Cl
2 Glebe Ms
3 John Brown Ct
F6
1 Church Cl
2 Nether Riggs
3 West End Front St
G6
1 Barrington Ct
2 Brook Ct
H5
1 Wanny Rd
H6
1 Cornwell Crs
J4
1 Lampton Ct
2 Lumley Ct
3 Waverley Av
J5
1 Clement Av
2 Edgewood Av
3 Trotter Gv
K3
1 Greenwood Av
2 Sleekburn Av
K4
1 Cherrytree Ct
2 Edward Rd
3 George Rd
4 Knox Cl
Whinney Hill Farm
Choppington
Scotland Gate
Bomarsund
NE62
Eastgate
Eastgreen
Kings Park
Sleek Burn
Farriers Ct
Gooch Av
Longridge Way
Stephenson Way
Barrington Road
CHOPPINGTON ROAD
A1068
A1147
A193
A189
B1331
Bedlington Station
BEDLINGTON
Bedlington Station Co First Sch
The Gables Medical Group
Bedlington Community High School
Wallington Close
Whitley Memorial Sch
Wansbeck District Council
Health Authority
Bedlington Stead County First School
Bebside Social Club House
Bebside Hall
Humford Mill
Golf Course
STEAD LANE
FRONT ST EAST
BEDLINGTON BANK
BEBSIDE ROAD
FRONT ST
VULCAN PLACE
Station Road
Palace Road
Stirling Drive
Woburn Drive
Roslin Park
Millbank Road
Park Road
Church Lane
Millfield
Millfield South
Humford Way
Acorn Avenue
Hotspur Avenue
Hassop Way
Carisbrooke
Court Road
Oakapple Close
Schalksmuhle Road
Glebe Road
Woodside
Dene View West
Dene View East
Furnace Bank
Bebside Furnace Road
Hathery Lane
Melrose Av
Summerson Wy
Moorland Av
Grange Park Av
Burnside
Clayton St
St John's Rd
Queen's Road
King's Rd
West View
Cholerton Drive
Beatty Road
Haig Road
Spring Pk
Wood Lane
Elenbel Av
Tomlea Av
Bebs

20
23

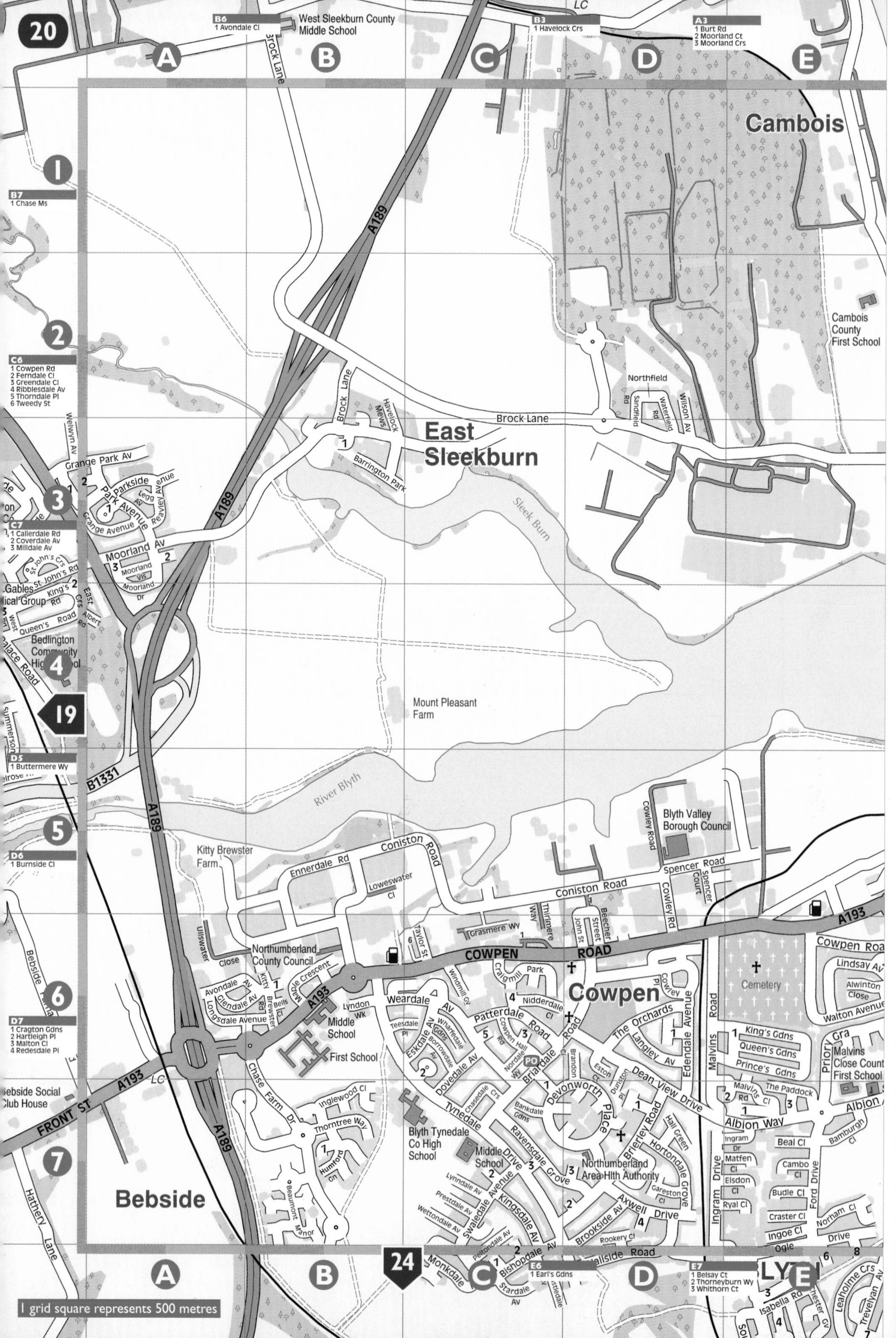

19
24

1 grid square represents 500 metres

F5
1 Grieve St
2 Millfield Gdns
F6
1 Goschen St
2 Hambledon St
3 Sweethope Av
4 Thompson St
F7
1 High St
2 Rosebery Av
F
G
H
J
K
1
2
3
4
5
6
7
G5
1 Goschen St
2 Thompson St
3 Worsdell St
G6
1 Arthur St
2 Boyne Ct
3 Cummings St
4 Davison St
5 French St
6 Gatacre St
7 Kerry Cl
8 Merton Sq
9 Seaforth St
10 Simpson St
11 Thompson St
G7
1 Aldborough St
2 Back Croft Rd
3 Barnard St
4 Crofton St
H6
Street names for this grid square are listed at the back of the index
H7
1 Carlton St
2 Coburg St
3 Crown St
4 Hawthorne Rd
5 Oxford St
6 Percy St South
7 Rosamond Pl
8 St Cuthberts Ct
9 Wellington St
North Blyth
Dale St
Gray St
Crawford St
Ann's Rw
Regent Street
Hodgson's Road
Willow Av
Poplar Av
Sycamore Av
Chestnut Av
Balfour St
Portland
Durban St
Laburnum
Lilac Av
W Salisbury St
Kimberley St
Stephen St
Station St
Burt St
Disraeli Street
Gladstone St
Beaumont St
Wright St
Waterloo Med Group
Maddison St
Regent St
Kg St
B1329
Cowpen Road
Delaval Ter
Edward St
Wolsley Rd
Wanley St
Waterloo Road
B1328
Union St
B1327
Rink St
Headway Thtr
Percy
Stanley St
Bridge St
Pol Stn
Low Quay
St Andrews RC Aided First School
Harper St
Bowes St
Bolam Avenue
Sidney St
Lynn St
Blyth Sports Centre
Marlow St
Claremont Ter
Blyth Valley Borough Council
St Wilfrids Middle School
Renwick Rd
Bondicar Ter
Marine Ter
Cypress Gdns
Middleton
Coomassie Rd
Croft Rd
Dr Reg Carrs Surg
Phoenix Thtr
Plessey Rd
Junior Sch
First School
Forster St
Ridley Avenue
Bath La
Bath Ter
Bridge St
East Pk View
Park Vw
Stannington St
Collingwood Rd
Haughton Ter
Winchester Av
Cypress Dr
Cypress Crs
Rowley St
Richard St
Maughan St
Northumberland Co Council
B1329
Prs Louise Road
Princess Louise First School
Louise Rd
Jubilee Rd
First School
William St
Victoria
Third Av
A193 Broadway
Kingsway
Blyth Spartans AFC
Plessey Rd
Plessey Av
Dalmatia Ter
Hunter Av
Briardene Rd
Roseman Ter
Grantham St
Wensley
First Av
Sixth Avenue
Road
25
PO

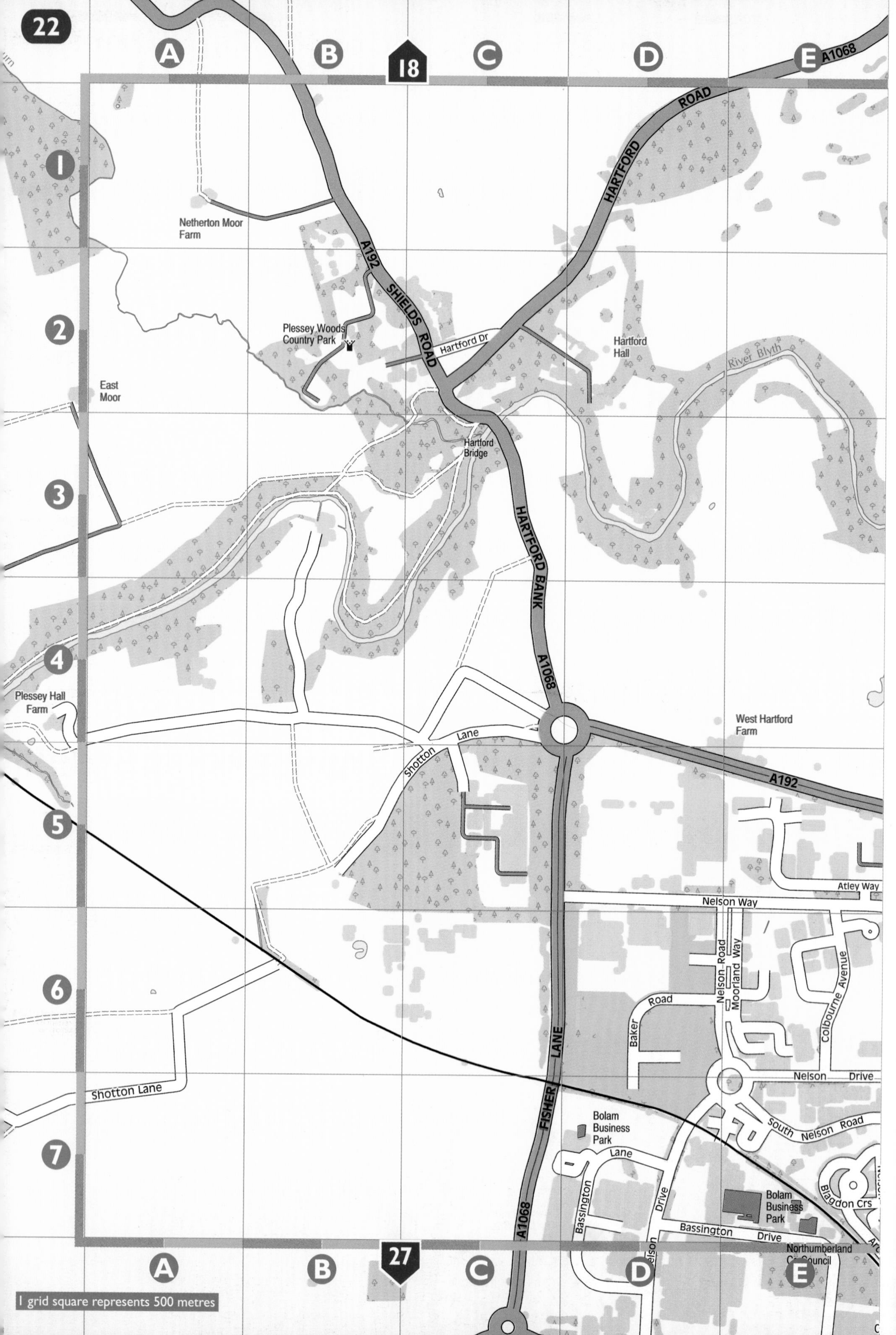

A
B
18
C
D
E
A1068
1
2
3
4
5
6
7
HARTFORD ROAD
Netherton Moor Farm
A192
SHIELDS ROAD
Plessey Woods Country Park
Hartford Dr
Hartford Hall
River Blyth
East Moor
Hartford Bridge
HARTFORD BANK
A1068
Plessey Hall Farm
West Hartford Farm
Shotton Lane
A192
Atley Way
Nelson Way
Nelson Road
Moorland Way
Colbourne Avenue
Baker Road
FISHER LANE
Nelson Drive
South Nelson Road
Shotton Lane
Bolam Business Park
Lane
Bassington
Drive
Bolam Business Park
Blagdon Crs
Bassington Drive
A1068
Northumberland Co Council
27
1 grid square represents 500 metres

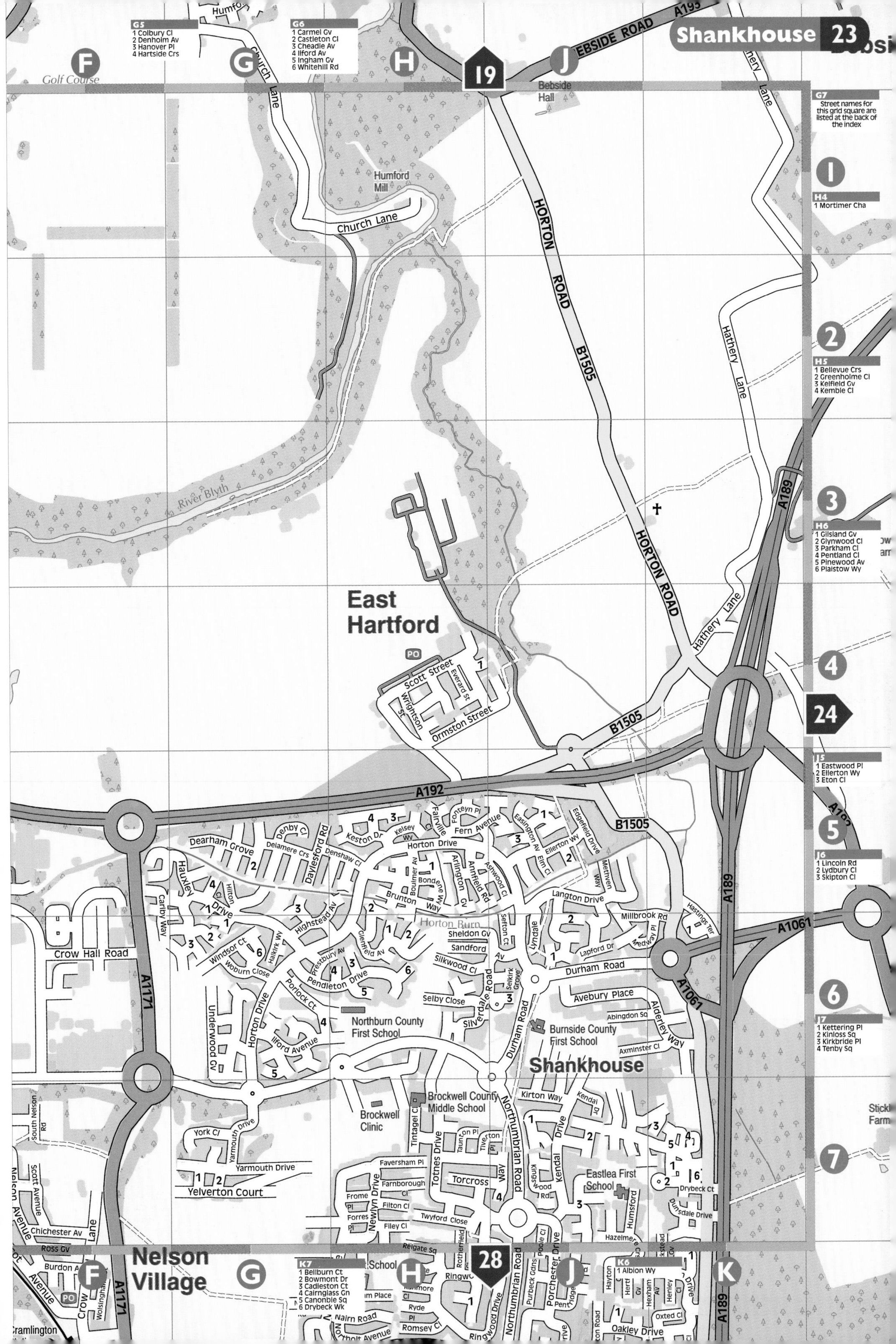
G5
1 Colbury Cl
2 Denholm Av
3 Hanover Pl
4 Hartside Crs
G6
1 Carmel Gv
2 Castleton Cl
3 Cheadle Av
4 Ilford Av
5 Ingham Gv
6 Whitehill Rd
19
BEBSIDE ROAD A193
Bebside Hall
Golf Course
Church Lane
Humford Mill
G7
Street names for this grid square are listed at the back of the index
H4
1 Mortimer Cha
HORTON ROAD
B1505
Hathery Lane
H5
1 Bellevue Crs
2 Greenholme Cl
3 Kelfield Gv
4 Kemble Cl
River Blyth
A189
H6
1 Gilsland Gv
2 Glynwood Cl
3 Parkham Cl
4 Pentland Cl
5 Pinewood Av
6 Plaistow Wy
East Hartford
PO
Scott Street
Everard St
Wrightson St
Ormston Street
24
J5
1 Eastwood Pl
2 Ellerton Wy
3 Eton Cl
A192
J6
1 Lincoln Rd
2 Lydbury Cl
3 Skipton Cl
A1061
A1171
Crow Hall Road
Dearham Grove
Delamere Crs
Denby Cl
Daylesford Rd
Denshaw Cl
Keston Dr
Kelsey Wy
Fairville
Fonteyn Pl
Fern Avenue
Horton Drive
Easington Av
Ellerton Wy
Edgefield Drive
Methven Way
Hauxley Drive
Hilton Cl
Carlby Way
Highstead Av
Boulmer Av
Bondene Way
Arlington Gv
Annfield Rd
Ashwood Cl
Elm Cl
Langton Drive
Millbrook Rd
Hastings Ter
Brunton Way
Horton Burn
Sheldon Gv
Sandford Av
Sefton Ct
Lyndale
Lapford Dr
Medway Pl
Windsor Ct
Halkirk Wy
Woburn Close
Glenfield Av
Prestbury Av
Pendleton Drive
Silkwood Cl
Selkirk Grove
Durham Road
Porlock Ct
Selby Close
Silverdale Road
Avebury Place
Abingdon Sq
Alderley Way
Underwood Gv
Horton Drive
Northburn County First School
Burnside County First School
Ilford Avenue
Axminster Cl
Shankhouse
J7
1 Kettering Pl
2 Kinloss Sq
3 Kirkbride Pl
4 Tenby Sq
Kirton Way
Kendal Dr
Brockwell County Middle School
Brockwell Clinic
Northumbrian Road
South Nelson Rd
York Cl
Yarmouth Drive
Tintagel Cl
Totnes Drive
Taunton Pl
Tiverton Pl
Kendal Drive
Stickley Farm
Scott Avenue
Nelson Avenue
Yelverton Court
Faversham Pl
Farnborough Cl
Frome Pl
Newlyn Drive
Torcross Way
Kingswood Rd
Eastlea First School
Drybeck Ct
Dunsdale Drive
Chichester Av
Lane
Forres Pl
Filton Cl
Filey Cl
Twyford Close
Humsford
Hazelmere Cr
Ross Gv
Burdon Av
Nelson Village
Reigate Sq
School
28
Rotherfield
Poole Cl
Porchester Drive
K6
1 Albion Wy
K7
1 Bellburn Ct
2 Bowmont Dr
3 Cadleston Ct
4 Cairnglass Gn
5 Canonbie Sq
6 Drybeck Wk
Ringwood Drive
Purbeck Gdns
Hayton
Hexham Av
Henley Cl
Drive
PO
Crow
Wolsingham
Cramlington
Ryde Pl
Romsey Cl
Nairn Road
Northolt Avenue
Oakley Drive
Oxted Cl
A189
A1171
F G H J K

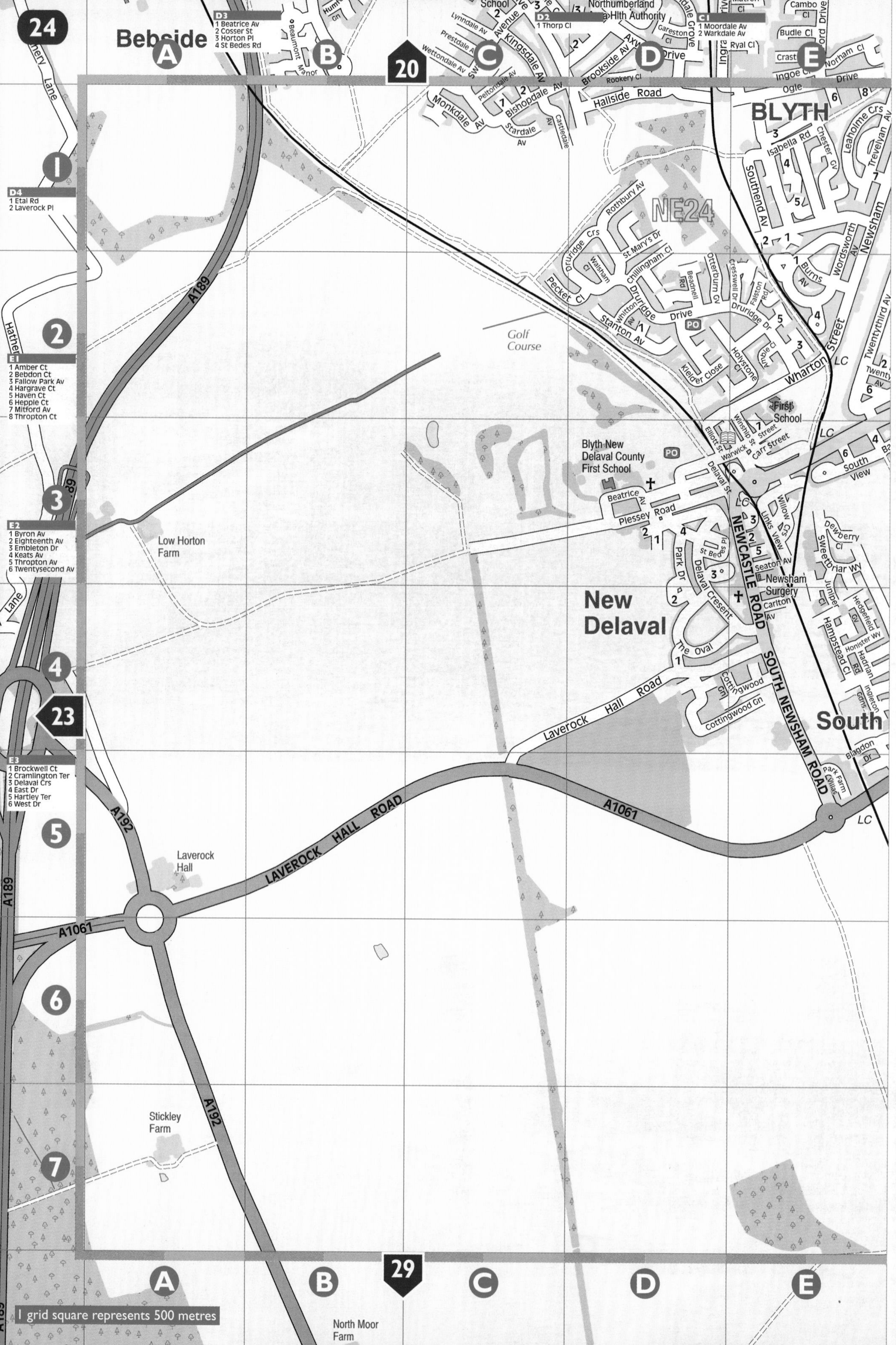

Bebside
D3
1 Beatrice Av
2 Cosser St
3 Horton Pl
4 St Bedes Rd
D2
1 Thorp Cl
C1
1 Moordale Av
2 Warkdale Av
Northumberland
Hlth Authority
20
BLYTH
NE24
D4
1 Etal Rd
2 Laverock Pl
E1
1 Amber Ct
2 Bebdon Ct
3 Fallow Park Av
4 Hargrave Ct
5 Haven Ct
6 Hepple Ct
7 Mitford Av
8 Thropton Ct
E2
1 Byron Av
2 Eighteenth Av
3 Embleton Dr
4 Keats Av
5 Thropton Av
6 Twentysecond Av
E3
1 Brockwell Ct
2 Cramlington Ter
3 Delaval Crs
4 East Dr
5 Hartley Ter
6 West Dr
Golf Course
Low Horton Farm
Blyth New Delaval County First School
First School
Newsham Surgery
New Delaval
South
23
A189
A192
A1061
LAVEROCK HALL ROAD
NEWCASTLE ROAD
SOUTH NEWSHAM ROAD
Laverock Hall
Stickley Farm
North Moor Farm
29
1 grid square represents 500 metres

Blyth 25
F1
1 Cherry Trees
2 Elm Trees
3 Fourth Av
4 Kendal Av
5 Rowan Ct
6 Second Av
F2
1 Eighth Av
2 Fenwick Av
3 Newlands Av
4 Newlands Pl
5 Twentieth Av
6 Twentyfifth Av
F3
1 Clifton Gdns
2 Glendford Pl
F4
1 Elstree Gdns
G1
1 Broadway Crs
2 Columbia Ter
3 Eleventh Av
4 George St
5 Kingsway
6 Rutherford St
G2
1 Amberley Wy
2 Ashford Cl
3 Aylesford Sq
4 Bexhill Sq
5 Coquet Av
6 Guillemot Cl
7 Seafield Rd
G3
1 Dalston Pl
2 Downe Cl
3 Redshank Dr
H1
1 Chamberlain St
2 Nixon Ter
3 Twizell St
4 Woodside
21
30
Sports Centre
Blyth Valley Borough Council
St Wilfrids Middle School
Princess Louise First School
First School
Blyth Spartans AFC
Northumberland Co Council
Isabella Pit
Middle School
Newsham
South Beach
Link House
Beachway
Cemetery
Gloucester Lodge Farm
Lysdon Farm
Seaton Red House Farm
Hartley Links
Seaton Sluice Middle School
A193 BROADWAY
A193 ROTARY WAY
ROTARY WAY A193
PLESSEY RD
PLESSEY ROAD
WENSLEYDALE TERRACE
B1329
LINKS ROAD
LINKS-ROAD
A193
NEWSHAM SOUTH ROAD
A1061
B1523
Barras Av
Barras Av West
Amersham Road
Solingen Estate
Wolmer Rd
Dent St
Grantham St
Tenth Avenue
Twelfth Avenue
Fifteenth Av
Ninth Av
Sixth Avenue
Seventh
First Av
Third Av
Eighth Av
Newlands Rd
Kingsway
Jubilee Rd
Dalmatia Ter
Hunter Av
Grimsby St
Bohemia Ter
Arcadia Ter
Briarwood Rd
Woodbine Ter
Rosemary Ter
Allendale Rd
Brinkburn
Matthew Rd
Wansbeck Av
Warkworth Av
Alconbury Cl
Appledore Rd
Addington
Burnham Cl
Banbury Way
Bromley Gdns
Carrick Dr
Melville Av
Grange Cl
Farnham Cl
Fairfield Av
Dunblane Dr
Dunkeld Cl
Pastures
Deal Cl
Dorking Close
Curlew Way
Lapwing Cl
Plover Dr
Dunlin Dr
Osprey Dr
Kingfisher Wy
Sandpiper Cl
Petrel Wy
Teal Avenue
Shearwater Wy
Cormorant
Shearwater Way
Tern Cl
Mallard Wy
Heron Close
Avocet Cl
Fulmar Drive
Elder Close
Kittiwake Close
Albatross Way
Herring Gull Cl
Earlswood Gv
Esher Gdns
Epsom Wy
Eastwood Av
Sandringham Drive
Ingleby Wy
Gosport Wy
Garasdale Cl
Gateley Av
Links Road
Conway Grove
Alston Grove
Astley Gdns

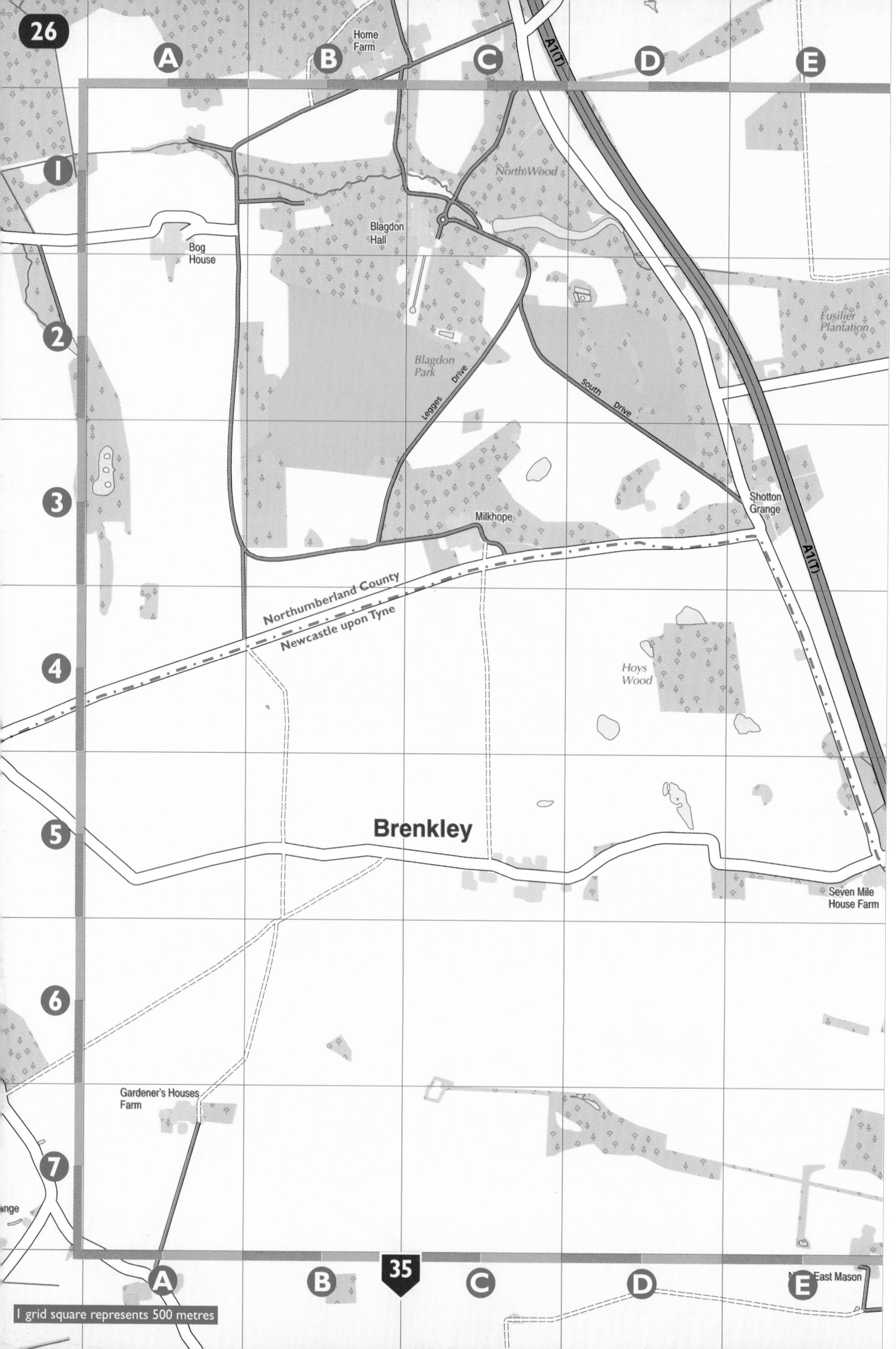
A
B
C
D
E
Home Farm
A1(T)
1
2
3
4
5
6
7
North Wood
Bog House
Blagdon Hall
Fusilier Plantation
Blagdon Park
Legges Drive
South Drive
Shotton Grange
Milkhope
Northumberland County
Newcastle upon Tyne
Hoys Wood
Brenkley
Seven Mile House Farm
Gardener's Houses Farm
East Mason
1 grid square represents 500 metres

35

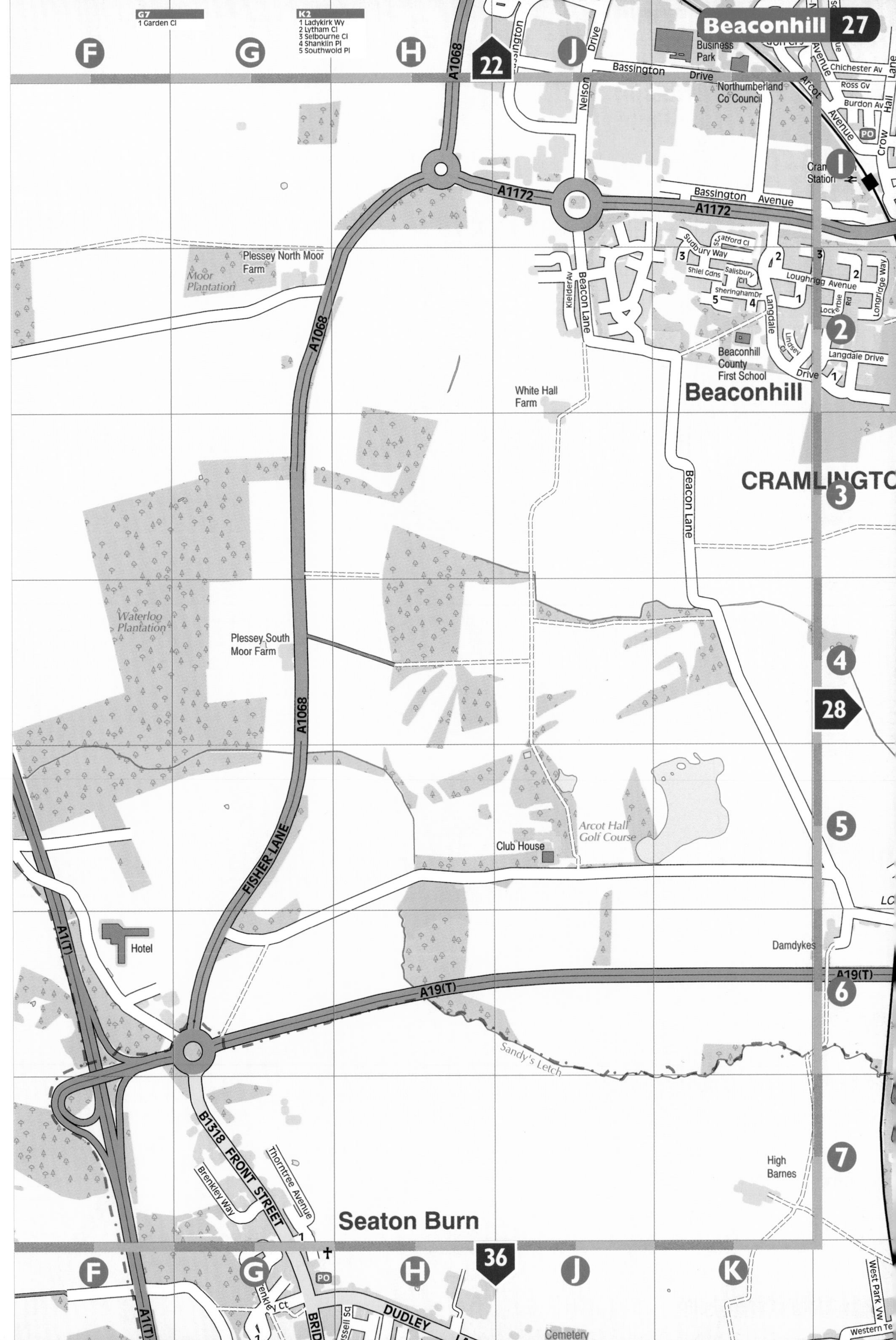
G7
1 Garden Cl
K2
1 Ladykirk Wy
2 Lytham Cl
3 Selbourne Cl
4 Shanklin Pl
5 Southwold Pl
22
28
36
Business Park
Bassington Drive
Nelson Drive
Northumberland Co Council
Chichester Av
Ross Gv
Burdon Av
Arcot Avenue
Cramlington Station
A1068
A1172
Bassington Avenue
Plessey North Moor Farm
Moor Plantation
Sudbury Way
Salisbury Cl
Shiel Gdns
Sheringham Dr
Loughrigg Avenue
Longridge Way
Lockerbie Rd
Kielder Av
Beacon Lane
Langdale
Lindsey Cl
Langdale Drive
Beaconhill County First School
Beaconhill
White Hall Farm
CRAMLINGTON
Waterloo Plantation
Plessey South Moor Farm
Arcot Hall Golf Course
Club House
FISHER LANE
A1(T)
Hotel
Damdykes
A19(T)
Sandy's Letch
High Barnes
B1318 FRONT STREET
Brenkley Way
Thorntree Avenue
Seaton Burn
DUDLEY
Cemetery
West Park Vw
Western Te
F
G
H
J
K
1
2
3
4
5
6
7

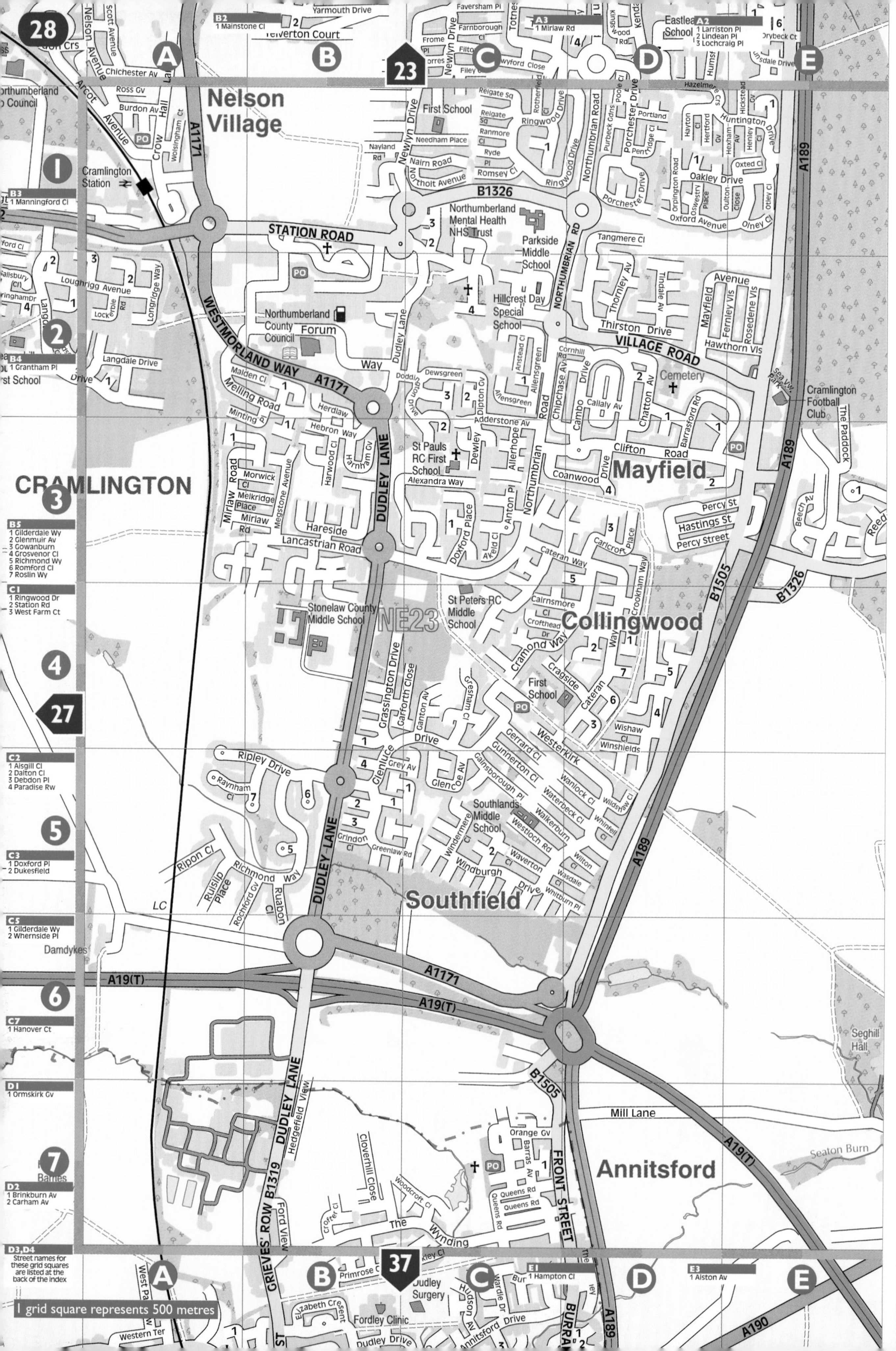

28
23
27
37
A
B
C
D
E
1
2
3
4
5
6
7
Nelson Village
CRAMLINGTON
Mayfield
Collingwood
Southfield
Annitsford
NE23
Cramlington Station
Northumberland County Council
Northumberland Mental Health NHS Trust
Parkside Middle School
Hillcrest Day Special School
First School
St Pauls RC First School
St Peters RC Middle School
Stonelaw County Middle School
Southlands Middle School
Cemetery
Cramlington Football Club
Forum
Seghill Hall
Dudley Surgery
Fordley Clinic
Damdykes
Seaton Burn
A1171
A189
A19(T)
B1326
B1505
B1319
A190
STATION ROAD
WESTMORLAND WAY
DUDLEY LANE
NORTHUMBRIAN RD
VILLAGE ROAD
FRONT STREET
GRIEVES' ROW
Mill Lane
Nelson Avenue
Scott Avenue
Arcot Avenue
Chichester Av
Ross Gv
Burdon Av
Crow Hall
Wolsingham Ct
Yarmouth Drive
Tiverton Court
Faversham Pl
Farnborough Ct
Frome
Newlyn Drive
Reigate Sq
Reigate Sq
Ranmore Cl
Ryde Pl
Romsey Cl
Nayland Rd
Needham Place
Nairn Road
Northolt Avenue
Ringwood Drive
Northumbrian Road
Porchester Drive
Portland
Purbeck Gdns
Poole Cl
Huntington Drive
Hayton Cl
Hertford Gv
Hexham Av
Henley Cl
Hickstead
Oxted Cl
Oakley Drive
Orpington Road
Oswestry Place
Oulton Close
Otley Cl
Oxford Avenue
Olney Cl
Tangmere Cl
Thornley Av
Tindale Av
Thirston Drive
Mayfield
Fernley Vls
Rosedene Vls
Hawthorn Vls
Avenue
Loughrigg Avenue
Longridge Way
Langdale Drive
Malden Cl
Melling Road
Minting Pl
Herdlaw
Hebron Way
Harwood Cl
Harnham Gv
Dewsgreen
Dipton Gv
Allensgreen
Anstead Cl
Chipchase Av
Cornhill Rd
Cambo Drive
Callaly Av
Chatton Av
Barrasford Rd
Clifton Road
Adderstone Av
Allerhope
Dewley
Alexandra Way
Coanwood Drive
Anton Pl
Doxford Place
Percy St
Hastings St
Percy Street
Beech Av
The Paddock
Mirlaw Road
Morwick Cl
Melkridge Place
Megstone Avenue
Mirlaw Rd
Hareside
Lancastrian Road
Cateran Way
Caricroft Place
Crookham Way
Cairnsmore Cl
Crofthead Dr
Cramond Way
Cragside
Cateran
Wishaw Cl
Winshields
Westerkirk
Grassington Drive
Garforth Close
Ganton Av
Gresham Cl
Gerrard Cl
Gunnerton Cl
Gainsborough Pl
Glencoe Av
Grey Av
Glenluce
Grindon Cl
Greenlaw Rd
Windermere
Windburgh Drive
Waverton Cl
Westloch Rd
Walkerburn
Waterbeck Cl
Wanlock Cl
Wildshaw Cl
Whinfell Cl
Wilton Cl
Wasdale Cl
Whitburn Pl
Ripley Drive
Raynham Cl
Ripon Cl
Ruislip Place
Richmond Way
Rochford Gv
Ruabon Cl
Hedgefield View
Clover hill Close
Woodcroft Cl
Crofter Cl
Ford View
The Wynding
Orange Gv
Barras Av
Queens Rd
Primrose Cl
Elizabeth Cresent
Hudson Av
Wardle Dr
Annitsford Drive
Dudley Drive
Western Ter
West Park
Burradon
B2 1 Mainstone Cl
A3 1 Mirlaw Rd
A2 1 Larriston Pl 2 Lindean Pl 3 Lochcraig Pl
B3 1 Manningford Cl
B4 1 Grantham Pl
B5 1 Gilderdale Wy 2 Glenmuir Av 3 Gowanburn 4 Grosvenor Cl 5 Richmond Wy 6 Romford Cl 7 Roslin Wy
C1 1 Ringwood Dr 2 Station Rd 3 West Farm Ct
C2 1 Aisgill Cl 2 Dalton Cl 3 Debdon Pl 4 Paradise Rw
C3 1 Doxford Pl 2 Dukesfield
C5 1 Gilderdale Wy 2 Whernside Pl
C7 1 Hanover Ct
D1 1 Ormskirk Gv
D2 1 Brinkburn Av 2 Carham Av
D3,D4 Street names for these grid squares are listed at the back of the index
E1 1 Hampton Cl
E3 1 Alston Av
1 grid square represents 500 metres

F3
1 Weldon Rd
F7
1 Burnside Vw
2 Hazelmere Dene
3 Warwick Cl
F
G
H
24
J
G6
Street names for this grid square are listed at the back of the index
1
H7
1 Esmaralda Gdns
2 Hazlitt Pl
North Moor Farm
A192
Montrose Close
Hastings Gdns
Melton Drive
Alston Rd
2
PO
J5
1 St Stephen's Cl
Chipchase Ct
Dorchester Ct
Bristol
Avon Court
East Cramlington
Double Row
3
K5
1 Astley Gdns
2 Rothley Gv
3 Starlight Crs
B1326
First School
SEATON DELAVAL
4
30
A192
ASTLEY ROAD
Allenheads
Middle School
Whytrigg Close
Linden Road
Western Avenue
Blyth St
Prospect Av
Mitford Av
Doctors Surg
Park Road
Park View
Blyth Valley Borough Council
A190
Ridsdale Cl
5
Middle Farm
Ancroft Road
Prospect Avenue
Glanton Av
Avenue Road
AVENUE ROAD
Astley Community High School
Elsdon
Whitfield Rd
Bavington Road
Swinburn Road
Fontburn
Atkinson House School
Whiteford Pl
Thornbury Av
Trinity Gv
Kentmere Cl
Dene Grove
Acomb Avenue
6
Front Street
Murrayfield
Twickenham Ct
Front Street
Hatfield Drive
Trevone Pl
Winton Cl
Kirkwood Cl
Deneside
Burnlea
Hill Av
A190
Newburgh Av
Ashkirk Wy
Thornhill Cl
Carrington Close
Seghill County First School
Forest Way
Front St
STATION ROAD
Barrass Av
Fox Lea Walk
The Close
Bonnivard Gdns
Barrowburn Pl
Melrose Av
The Crescent
Chester Ct
Oakfield Way
Birchwood Cl
Seghill
7
Reid's Lane
MAIN STREET NORTH
38
F
G
H
J
K
West Fie
BACKWORT

A6
1 Vanborough Ct
A5
1 Ambleside Cl
2 Kearsley Cl
3 Wallington Ct
A2
1 Maple Ct
2 Wansbeck Gv
C6
1 Bardon Crs
2 Horsley Gdns
E1
1 Hastings Av
2 Marden Ct
E2
1 Aidan Av
25
29
39
New Hartley
Seaton
SEATON DELAVAL
Holywell
Seaton Red House Farm
Seaton Sluice Middle School
Lookout Farm
Avenue Head Farm
Seaton Terrace
Astley Community High School
Holywell County First School
Crow Hall Farm
Bank Top
Hartley Links
THE AVENUE
A190
A192
FOUNTAIN HEAD
St Michael's Avenue
Lysdon Burn
Seaton Burn
Holywell Dene Road
NE25
North Tyneside
Northumberland County
1 grid square represents 500 metres

G2
1 Collywell Ct
2 Waterford Cl
G3
1 Southward Cl
Seaton Sluice
Hartley
NE26
Crag Point
St Mary's or Bait Island
St Mary's Lighthouse
Hartley West Farm
Brier Dene Farm
Whitley Lodge First School
Cemetery
BERESFORD ROAD
BLYTH ROAD
HARTLEY LANE
THE LINKS
A193
B1325
Seaton Burn
Brierdene
Gerrard Road
Garsdale Road
Westley Avenue
Gorsedene Road
Craneswater Av
Brierdene Rd
Astley Drive
Grenada Drive
Dereham Rd
Granville Av
Malvern Road
Simonside
The Rise
The Crest
St Mary's Wynd
East End
Millfield
Elwyn Close
Southward
Clarence St
Queens Road
Collywell
West Ter
Bay Rd
Albert Rd
Taylor Gdns
Millway
Park Field Ter
Easedale
Westlands
Cresswell Av
Seaburn Gv
The Links
Melton Crs
Budworth Av
Rosewood Crs
Dereham Cl
Elwin Cl
40

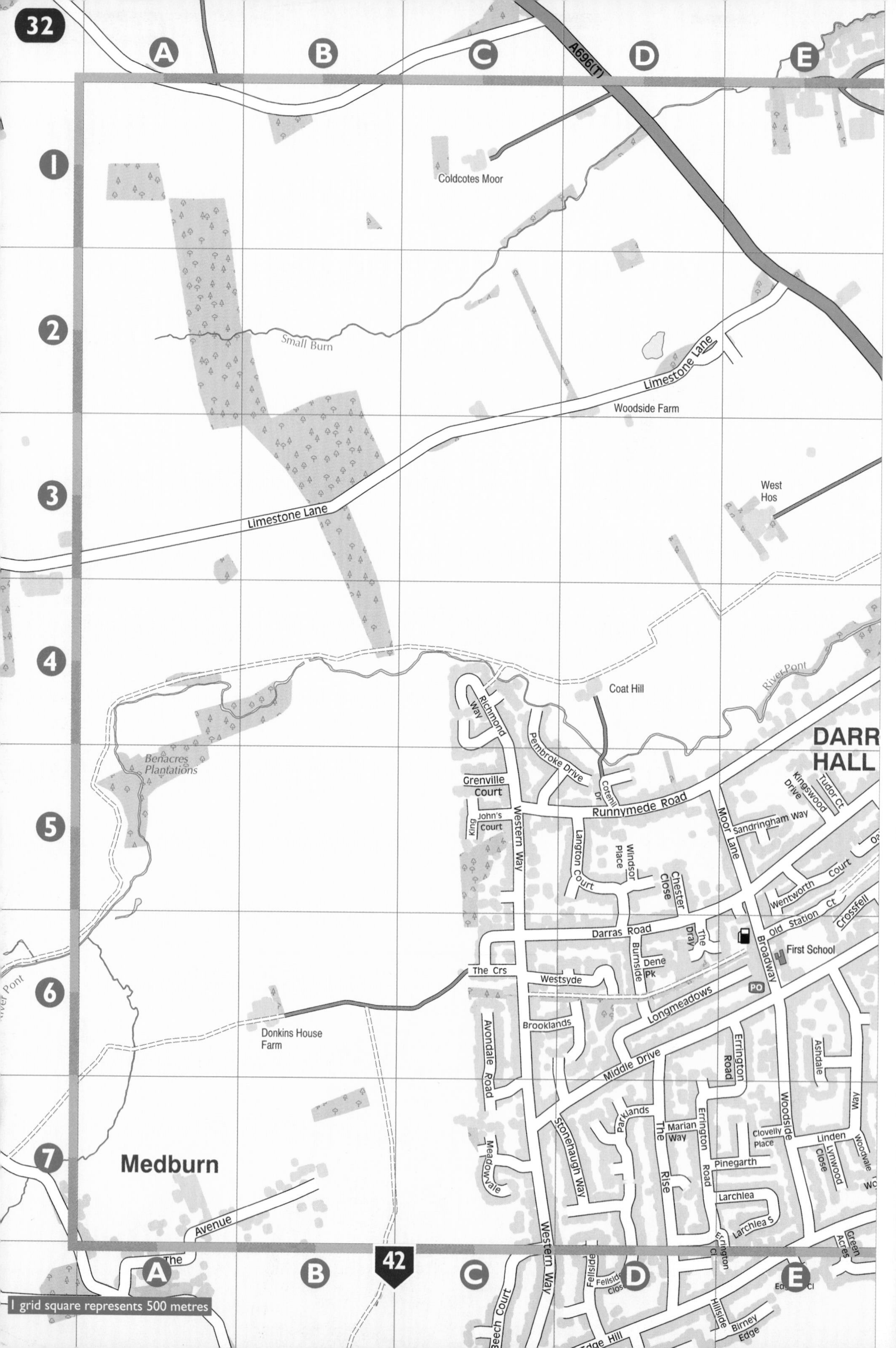
A
B
C
D
E
A696(T)
1
2
3
4
5
6
7
Coldcotes Moor
Small Burn
Limestone Lane
Woodside Farm
West Hos
Coat Hill
River Pont
DARR HALL
Benacres Plantations
Richmond Way
Pembroke Drive
Cotehill Dr
Grenville Court
King John's Court
Western Way
Runnymede Road
Moor Lane
Sandringham Way
Kingswood Drive
Tudor Ct
Langton Court
Windsor Place
Chester Close
Wentworth Court
Old Station Ct
Crossfell
Darras Road
Burnside
The Dray
Dene Pk
Broadway
First School
PO
The Crs
Westsyde
Longmeadows
Brooklands
Avondale Road
Donkins House Farm
Middle Drive
Errington Road
Ashdale
Way
Woodside
Stonehaugh Way
Parklands
The Rise
Marian Way
Clovelly Place
Linden Close
Lynwood
Woodvale
Pinegarth
Larchlea
Larchlea S
Errington Cl
Meadowvale
Medburn
Avenue
The
Green Acres
42
Fellside
Fellside Close
Beech Court
Hillside
Birney Edge
Edge Hill
1 grid square represents 500 metres

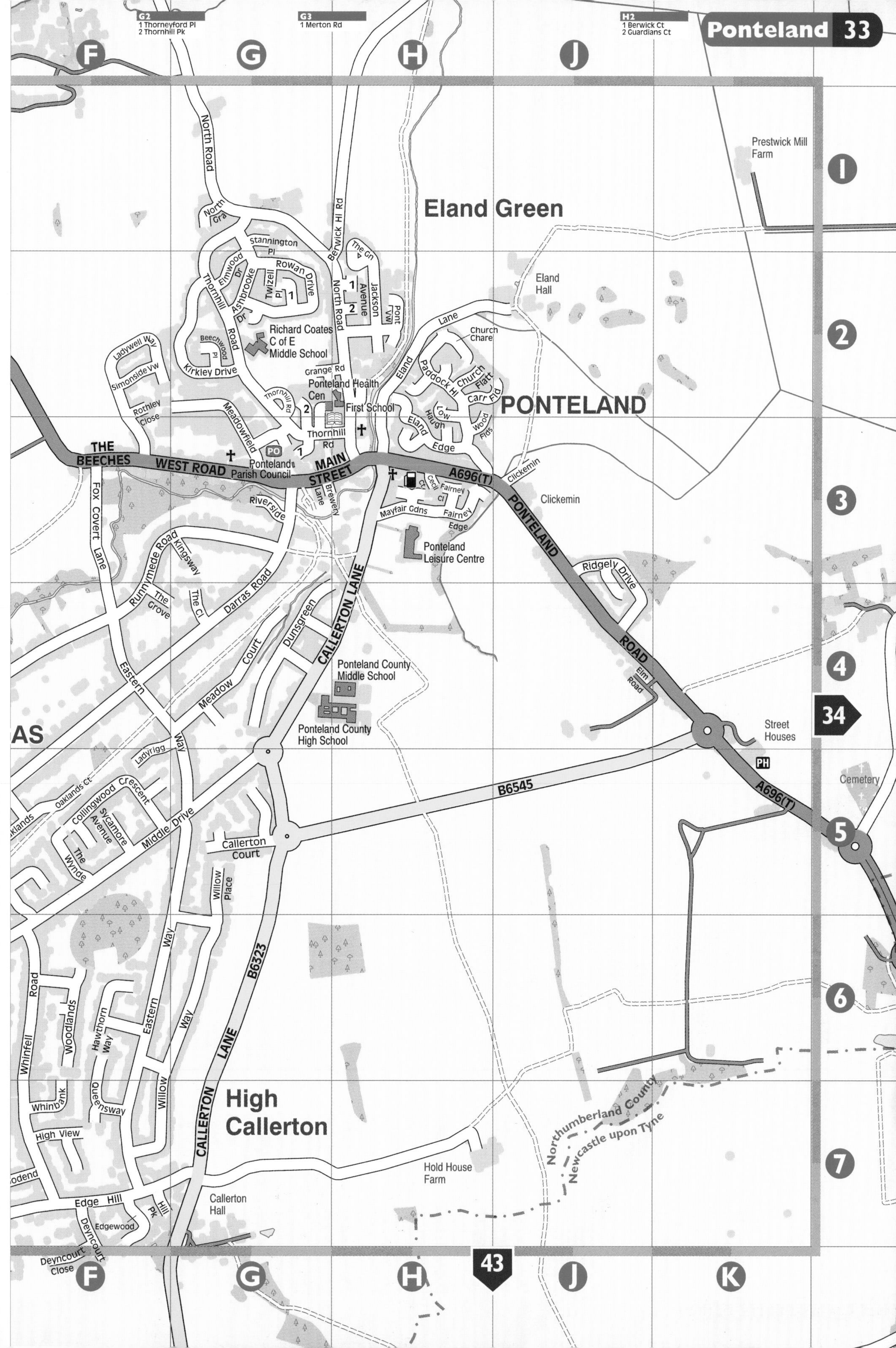
G2
1 Thorneyford Pl
2 Thornhill Pk
G3
1 Merton Rd
H2
1 Berwick Ct
2 Guardians Ct
Eland Green
PONTELAND
High Callerton
Prestwick Mill Farm
Eland Hall
Clickemin
Street Houses
Cemetery
Hold House Farm
Callerton Hall
Richard Coates C of E Middle School
Ponteland Health Cen
First School
Ponteland Parish Council
Ponteland Leisure Centre
Ponteland County Middle School
Ponteland County High School
North Road
Berwick Hl Rd
Stannington Pl
Rowan Drive
Twizell Pl
Ashbrooke Dr
Elmwood Dr
Thornhill Road
Jackson Avenue
Pont Vw
Lane
Church Chare
Paddock Hl
Church Flatt
Carr Fld
Low Haugh
Eland Edge
Wood Flds
Beechwood Pl
Kirkley Drive
Ladywell Way
Simonside Vw
Rothley Close
Meadowfield
Grange Rd
Thornhill Rd
THE BEECHES
WEST ROAD
MAIN STREET
Brewery Lane
Riverside
A696(T)
PONTELAND ROAD
Mayfair Gdns
Fairney Edge
Fairney Cl
Cecil Ct
Fox Covert Lane
Runnymede Road
Kingsway
The Grove
The Cl
Darras Road
Dunsgreen
CALLERTON LANE
Ridgely Drive
Elm Road
Eastern Way
Meadow Court
Ladyrigg
Oaklands Ct
Collingwood Crescent
Sycamore Avenue
Middle Drive
The Wynde
Callerton Court
Willow Place
B6545
B6323
Whinfell Road
Woodlands
Hawthorn Way
Willow Way
Queensway
Whinbank
High View
Edge Hill
Hill Pk
Edgewood
Deyncourt
Deyncourt Close
Northumberland County
Newcastle upon Tyne
PO
PH
34
43
F G H J K
1 2 3 4 5 6 7

A
B
C
D
E
Carr Grange Farm
Prestwick Mill Farm
1
2
3
4
5
6
7
Newcastle upon Tyne
Northumberland County
Dinnington
Moory Spot
Prestwick Whins
Prestwick Hall
Prestwick
33
Houses
PH
Cemetery
A696(T)
Prestwick Pit Houses
Newcastle International Airport
Airport Station
B6918
Woolsington Hall
Airport Freightway
Woolsington
Hall
South Drive
Hotel
LC
44
Callerton Park Station
Middle Drive
Low Luddick
1 grid square represents 500 metres

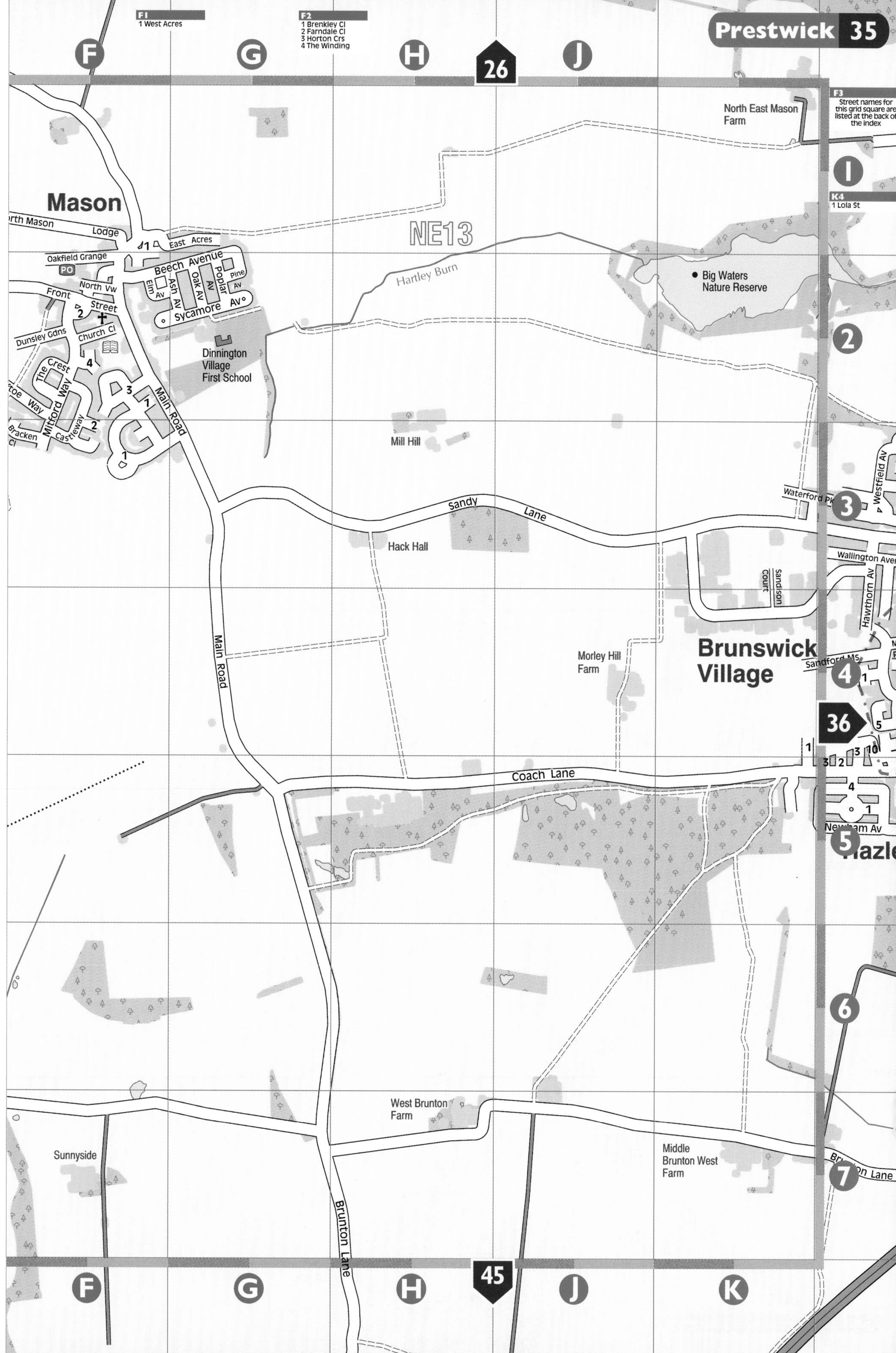
F1
1 West Acres
F2
1 Brenkley Cl
2 Farndale Cl
3 Horton Crs
4 The Winding
F3
Street names for this grid square are listed at the back of the index
K4
1 Lola St
26
36
45
Mason
North Mason
Lodge
East Acres
Oakfield Grange
PO
Beech Avenue
North Vw
Front Street
Elm Av
Ash Av
Oak Av
Poplar Av
Pine Av
Sycamore Av
Church Cl
Dunsley Gdns
The Crest
Mitford Way
Castleway
Bracken Cl
Main Road
Dinnington Village First School
NE13
Hartley Burn
North East Mason Farm
Big Waters Nature Reserve
Mill Hill
Sandy Lane
Hack Hall
Waterford Pk
Westfield Av
Wallington Avenue
Sandison Court
Hawthorn Av
Brunswick Village
Sandford Ms
Morley Hill Farm
Coach Lane
Newham Av
West Brunton Farm
Sunnyside
Middle Brunton West Farm
Brunton Lane

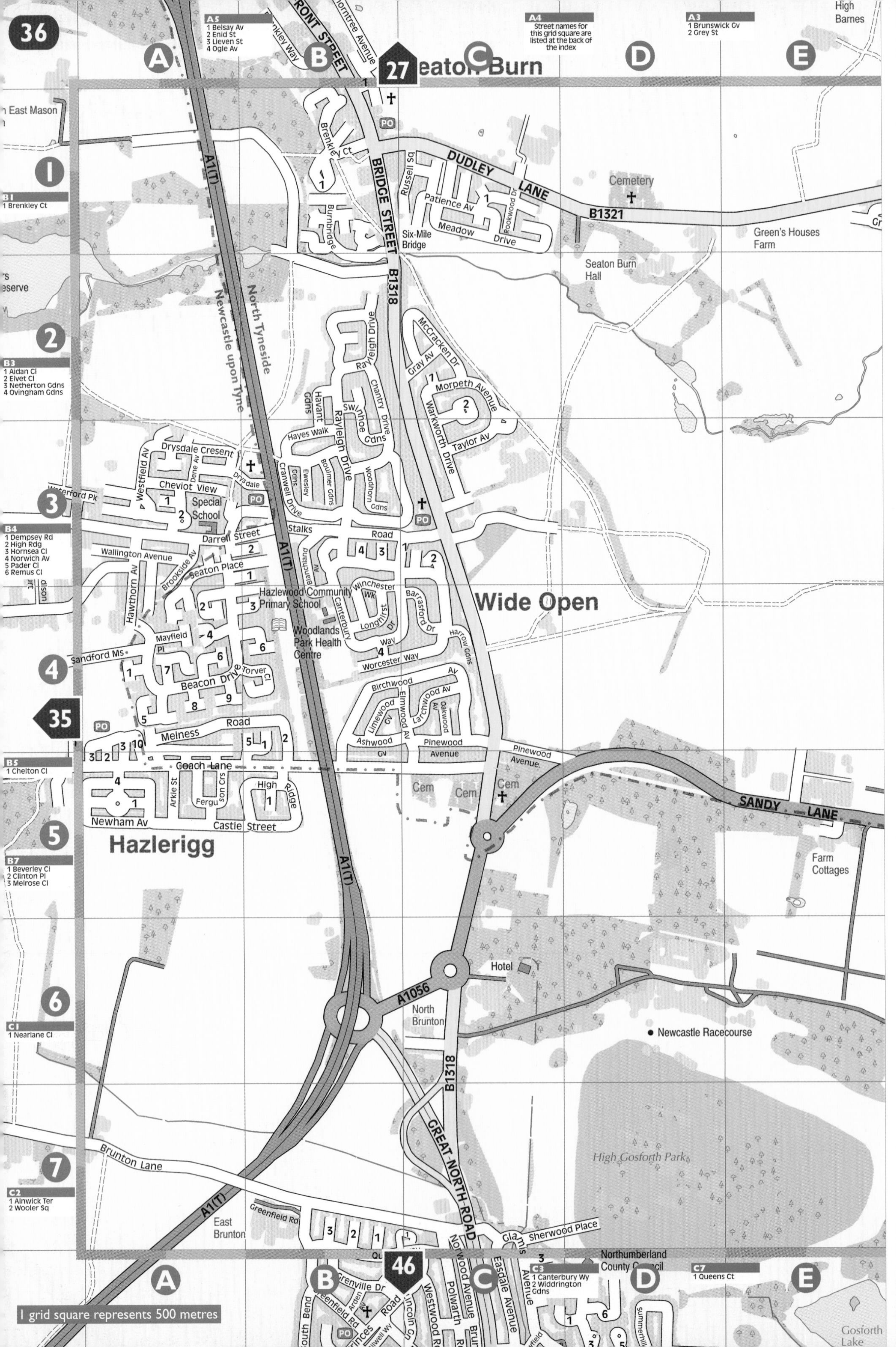
A5
1 Belsay Av
2 Enid St
3 Lieven St
4 Ogle Av
A4
Street names for this grid square are listed at the back of the index
A3
1 Brunswick Gv
2 Grey St
B1
1 Brenkley Ct
B3
1 Aidan Cl
2 Elvet Cl
3 Netherton Gdns
4 Ovingham Gdns
B4
1 Dempsey Rd
2 High Rdg
3 Hornsea Cl
4 Norwich Av
5 Pader Cl
6 Remus Cl
B5
1 Chelton Cl
B7
1 Beverley Cl
2 Clinton Pl
3 Melrose Cl
C1
1 Nearlane Cl
C2
1 Alnwick Ter
2 Wooler Sq
C3
1 Canterbury Wy
2 Widdrington Gdns
C7
1 Queens Ct
Seaton Burn
27
35
46
High Barnes
Cemetery
Green's Houses Farm
Seaton Burn Hall
Six-Mile Bridge
DUDLEY LANE
B1321
BRIDGE STREET
B1318
A1(T)
North Tyneside
Newcastle upon Tyne
Wide Open
Hazlewood Community Primary School
Woodlands Park Health Centre
Special School
Hazlerigg
SANDY LANE
Farm Cottages
Hotel
A1056
North Brunton
Newcastle Racecourse
GREAT NORTH ROAD
High Gosforth Park
Brunton Lane
East Brunton
Greenfield Rd
Sherwood Place
Northumberland County Council
Gosforth Lake
1 grid square represents 500 metres

Annitsford
F1
1 Bamborough Ct
2 Green Crs
G1
1 Southfields
G7
1 Dene Av
28
F
G
H
J
The Wynding
Queens Rd
Oakley Cl
Primrose Close
Dudley Surgery
GRIEVES' ROW
Ford View
West Park Vw
Western Ter
Elizabeth Crescent
Fordley Clinic
Hudson Av
Wardle Dr
Burnside Av
The Spinney
BURRADON ROAD
A189
A190
MAIN STREET
MARKET ST
Brookside
Dudley Drive
Craig Crs
Charles Dr
Annitsford Drive
Ashkirk
Fern Drive
Bowman Drive
Coquet Ter
Wansbeck Rd
Blyth Close
Station Rd
Fordley
Love Avenue
Ozanan Cl
Wright Dr
B1321
Seaton Burn
DUDLEY
WEETSLADE ROAD
Weetslade Crs
B1319
Ethel St
Burradon House
B1505
Cheviot Grange
GREAT LIME ROAD
High Weetslade
Means Drive
Burradon
Kirkwood
First Kirklands School
FRONT STREET
Camperdown
Hall Drive
Reed Avenue
Allanville
Greenhills
Longhirst
Locomotion Way
Mylord Crescent
Atkin St
Moor View
KILLINGWORTH WAY
A1056
Sedgemoor
Sixteen
Culloden Wk
Glencoe
Newbury
Flodden
Bosworth
Bannockburn
Garth
Bailey Green First Sch
Woodvale Road
Cherry Gv
Kenilworth
Northgate
Edge
West Bailey
STATION ROAD
Chaffinch Way
Hamsterley Dr
Mount
Citadel West
Angus Cl
Moor Edge First School
Garth Six
Swindale Drive
Deepdale Gdns
W Wynd
Derwent Way
Southgate
Citadel East
North Tyneside Area Health Authority
Garth Thirty Three
Harvey Combe
North Tyneside Council
Great Lime Road
Newcastle upon Tyne
North Tyneside
Bolam
Road
Broomlee Rd
George Stephenson High School
Station Road
LC
Whitecroft Road
Reynolds Av
Harriot Dr
KILLINGWORTH DRIVE
Killingworth Drive
Sharon Close
Arrow Cl
Northumbrian Way
Killingworth
Northfield Dr
Samson Cl
Planet Place
Comet Row
Hazel Gv
Armstrong Dr
Blucher Rd
Killingworth Middle School
West Lane
Leybourne Avenue
Elm Grove
Gosforth Wood
The Chase
Westmoor Middle School
Georgian
Chiltern
Westmoor Drive
Pentland Grove
BENTON
Greenhaugh
Lane
47
West Moor First School
Kings Road
Albert
LIME ROAD
Forest Hall
Holly Av
K
K6
1 Bolam Rd
2 East Bailey
3 West Bailey
K5
Street names for this grid square are listed at the back of the index
K4
1 Algernon
2 Callerton
3 Hauxley
4 Havanna
H1
1 Briarwood
2 Burn Vw
3 Burt Crs
4 Owen Brannigan Dr
H2
1 March Rd
H4
1 Attlee Cl
2 Front St
3 Shillaw Pl
38
H5
1 Bell Gv
2 Chestnut Cl
3 Garth Thirteen
Villa
Amberley
J1
1 Bridge Cottages
2 Seaton Cft
Longstone Ct
J5
Street names for this grid square are listed at the back of the index
J4
1 Eastwood Cl
2 Hall Dr
3 Netherton
4 Redford Pl
5 Stagshaw
Castles
West Lane
J6
1 Coniston Cl
2 Grasmere Ct
1
2
3
4
5
6
7

Seghill
29
A7 1 East Stoneycroft 2 West Stoneycroft
A6 1 Green La
A5 1 Amberley Cha
B5 1 Cragside Gdns 2 Cranham Cl 3 Darden Cl
B6 1 Applewood 2 Downswood 3 Garleigh Cl 4 Garth Twenty Five 5 Garth Twenty Four 6 Goodwood 7 Greenwood 8 Hazelwood 9 Rosewood
D5 1 Castle Sq
E4 1 Ashbourne Cl
Northumberland County
North Tyneside
BACKWORTH LANE
B1322
A19(T)
A1056
Fisher Road
B1322 BACKWORTH LANE
High Farm
Backworth County First School
Melrose Av
Church
Shrewsbury Dr
Killingworth Avenue
Ecclestone Cl
Killingworth Village
Amberley First School
Edge Mt
The Cft
Knivestone Ct
Megstone Ct
Longstone Ct
Crumstone Ct
East Bailey
Simonside Way
Blueburn Dr
Harwood Drive
KILLINGWORTH LANE B1317
Garth Twenty Seven
East House Farm
West Lane
WEST LANE B1317
KILLINGWORTH ROAD
Killingworth Moor
Holystone Farm
Holystone First School
Holystone Dr
Southgate
Denewood
Leybourne Avenue
Elm Grove
48
Palmersville
Benton Square
Laurel Av
WHITLEY ROAD
St Cuthbert's Rd
37

Bank Top
J4
1 Collingwood Rd
2 Wellington Av
K5
1 Harewood Crs
NE25
F
G
H
30
J
West Field
A192
I
Northumberland County
North Tyneside
Holywell Grange Farm
2
East Holywell
Fenwick's Close Farm
HARTLEY LANE
West Holywell
Brierdene Burn
Cemetery
Earsdon
Church Wy
Front Street
Woodlands Cl
John St
Gdn Ter
Waterloo Rd
Monkseaton Rd
Holly Av
Whitley Rd
Nelson Rd
Hesleyside Rd
Redheugh Rd
Tarset Rd
Greystead Rd
Burnbank Av
Walwick Rd
Haddon Cl
Kielder Houxty
Kielder Road
Haddon Gn
Ludlow Dr
Hatfield Gdns
Wentworth Gdns
Arundel Drive
Sandringham Drive
First School
Wilton
Otterburn Avenue
Thorntree
Marina Dr
Otterburn Av
Harewood Crs
EARSDON ROAD
40
MONKSEATON
Westgate Cl
Red House
3
The Ridings
North Ridge
Berrishill
Tolls Cl
4
Carnoustie
Church
Drive
5
kworth
NE27
Road
LC
Shamford Cl
Moor Edge Farm
Moor Edge Rd
EARSDON ROAD
Hector St
Earsdon Vw
Shiremoor Middle School
South St
Wark Av
Grange Av
Seaton Rd
PO
Shiremoor Station
Hartside Crs
Harle Rd
Havelock Rd
Harlow Av
STATION ROAD
Ford Crs
Etal Crs
Avenue
Milfield Avenue
Park Avenue
Brandon Av
Lesbury
Belford Av
Beadnell Gdns
Park Grove
Shiremoor
West Monkseaton
6
A186
Emmerson Pl
Kirkland Wk
Craster Avenue
Park Crs
Allendale Crs
Glendale Rd
Stanton Road
Felton Cl
Witton Rd
Farne Rd
Beal Rd
Park Rd
Alnwinton Rd
Langley Av
B1322
Shiremoor First School
Brenkley Av
Horsley Av
Matten
Dilston Cl
Harbottle Av
Angerton Av
Lane
Well Lane
Murton
Sherwood Close
The Bridle
7
NEW YORK ROAD
Cartington Av
Lilburn Rd
Brunton Cl
Kirkley Rd
Horton Av
Colwell Rd
St Albans View
Brunswick Rd
Holyfields
Park La
Murton Lane
BENTON ROAD
A191
NEW YORK ROAD
49
West St
Turner St
Grayfields
K
Adderstone Gdns
Warenton Place
Murton Lane
NEW YORK ROAD
New York
Link North

C4
1 Highbury
2 Holmlands
B4
1 Newsteads Cl
A3
1 Dovecote Cl
D1
1 Grenada Cl
2 Grenada Pl
3 St John's Cl
4 St John's Pl
5 St Vincent's Pl
6 St Vincent's Wy
D7
1 Quantock Cl
E3
1 Marine Av
31
39
50
Brier Dene Farm
Brierdene Burn
Whitley Lodge First School
Glebe School
Claremont Footcare Surgery
Whitley Sands
Monkseaton
Whitley Bay High School
Beaumont Park Surgery
First School
Marine Avenue Medical Cen
Doctors Surg
Doctors Surgery
Monkseaton Station
West Monkseaton Station
Monkseaton Clinic
Middle School
Medical Cen
Marden Bridge Middle School
Whitley Bay Cricket Club
Whitley Bay Rockcliff RFC
Whitley Bay Ice Rink
Whitley Bay Football Club
Police Station
West Monkseaton
Monkseaton High School
Preston Grange
Primary School
New York
THE LINKS
A193
A1148
MONKSEATON DRIVE
EARSDON ROAD
SEATONVILLE ROAD
A192
HILLHEADS ROAD
A191
SHIELDS ROAD
RAKE LANE
PRESTON RD
PARK ROAD
PROM
Well Lane
Murton Lane
1 grid square represents 500 metres

F4
1 Ocean Vw
F6
1 Cranbourne Gv
F7
Street names for this grid square are listed at the back of the index
G5
1 Simpson St
WHITLEY BAY
Cullercoats
Marden
Promenade
Esplanade
North Tyneside Council Offices
Doctors Surgery
Hotel
Whitley Bay Station
Cullercoats Station
Cullercoats Primary School
Marden High School
Monkhouse School
Long Sands
WHITLEY ROAD SOUTH
A193
THE BROADWAY
Grand Parade
Beverley Terrace
Links Road
51

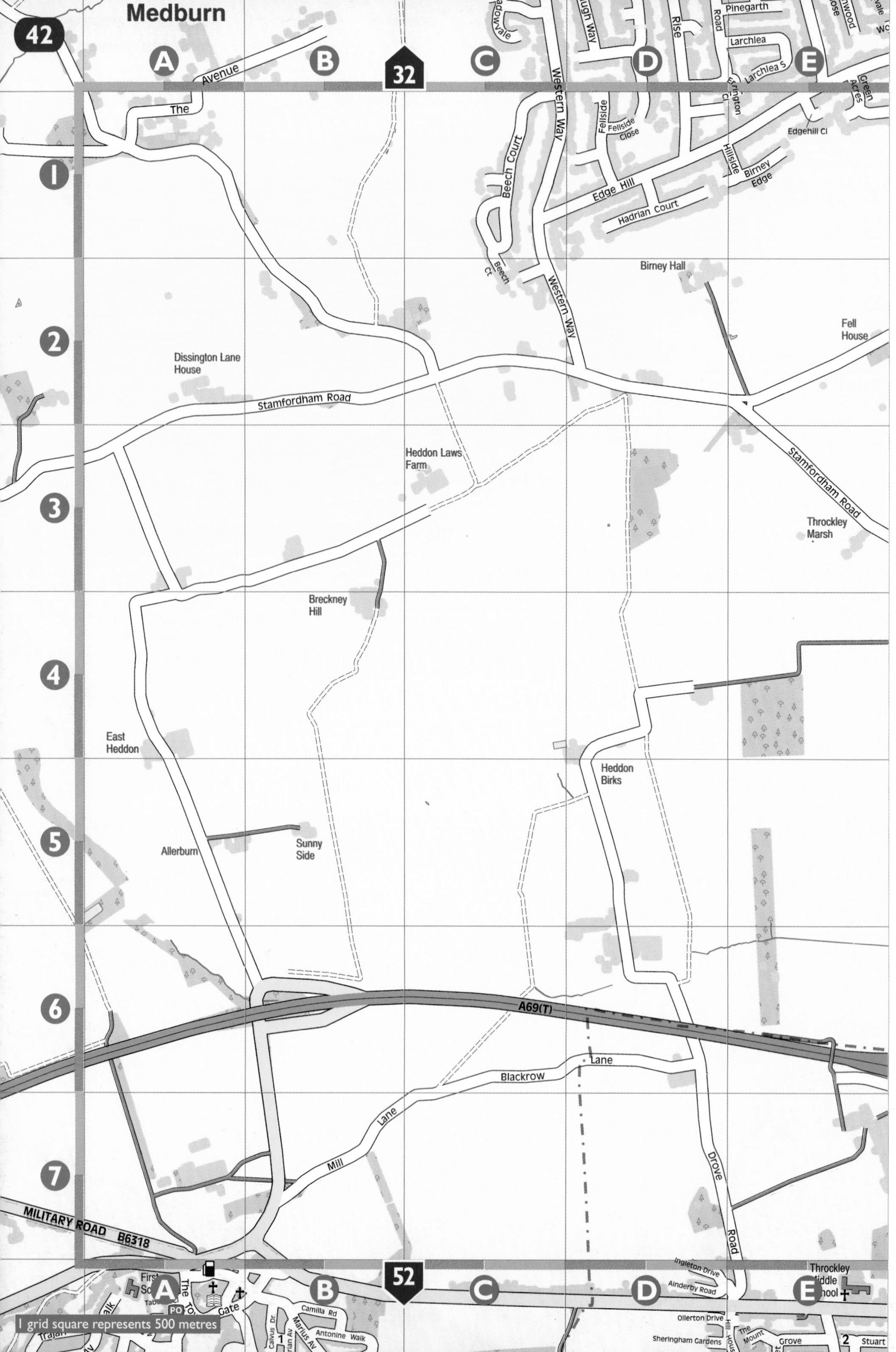

1 grid square represents 500 metres

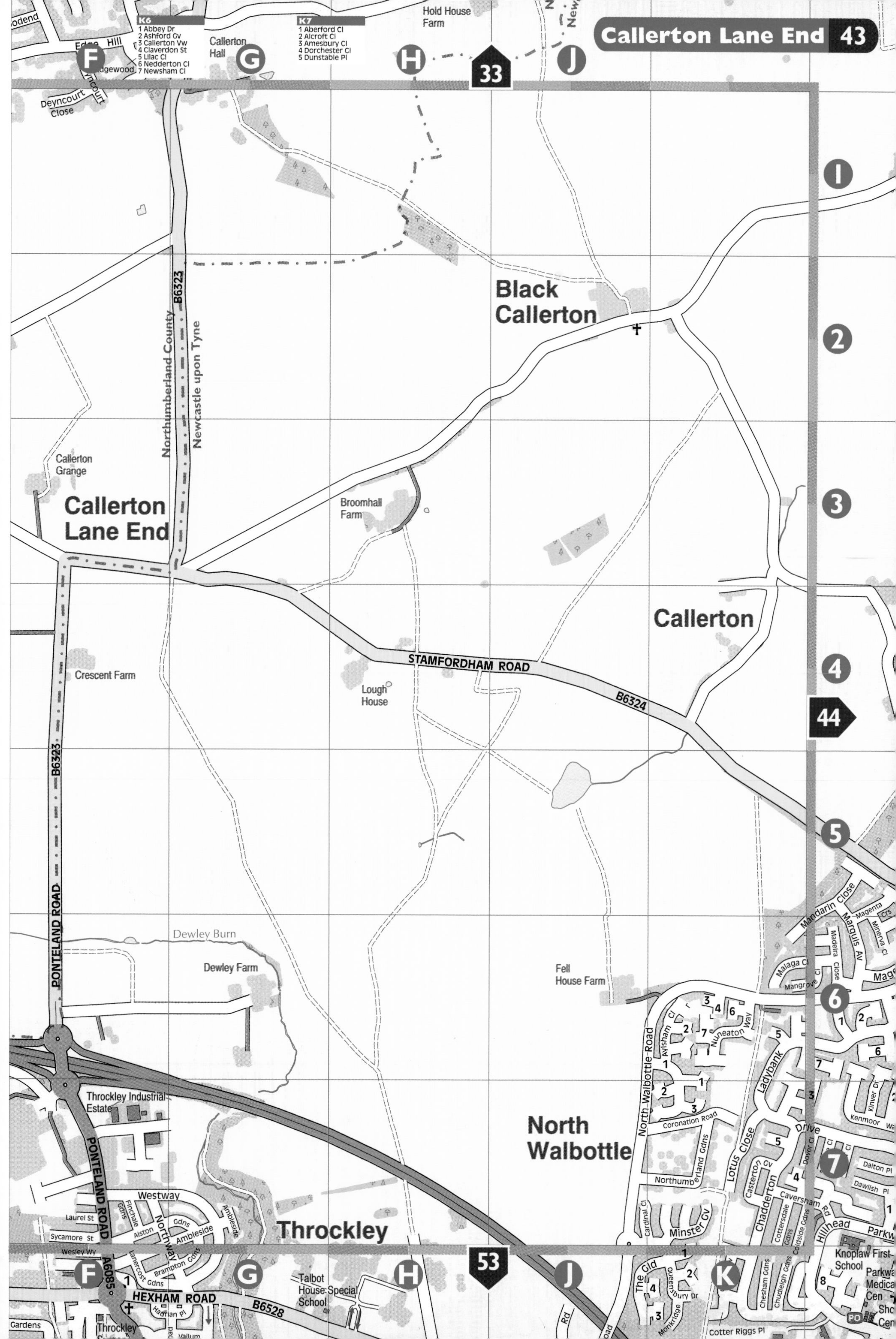
K6
1 Abbey Dr
2 Ashford Gv
3 Callerton Vw
4 Claverdon St
5 Lilac Cl
6 Nedderton Cl
7 Newsham Cl
K7
1 Aberford Cl
2 Alcroft Cl
3 Amesbury Cl
4 Dorchester Cl
5 Dunstable Pl
Hold House Farm
Callerton Hall
Edge Hill
Deyncourt Close
33
44
53
Black Callerton
Callerton Grange
Callerton Lane End
Northumberland County
Newcastle upon Tyne
B6323
Broomhall Farm
Callerton
STAMFORDHAM ROAD
B6324
Crescent Farm
Lough House
PONTELAND ROAD
Dewley Burn
Dewley Farm
Fell House Farm
Throckley Industrial Estate
North Walbottle
North Walbottle Road
Throckley
Westway
Laurel St
Sycamore St
Wesley Wy
Ambleside
Northway
Brampton Gdns
Hexham Road
B6528
A6085
Hadrian Pl
Talbot House Special School
Coronation Road
Northumberland Gdns
Lotus Close
Ladybank
Chadderton Drive
Casterton Gv
Minster Gv
Cardinal Cl
The Gld
Queensbury Dr
Monkridge
Chesham Gdns
Chudleigh Gdns
Cottersdale Gdns
Coldside Gdns
Caversham Rd
Hillhead Parkway
Knoplaw First School
Aylsham Cl
Nuneaton Way
Mandarin Close
Marquis Av
Madeira Close
Malaga Cl
Mangrove Cl
Minerva Cl
Kinver Dr
Kenmoor Way
Dover Cl
Dalton Pl
Dawlish Pl
Cotter Riggs Pl
Gardens
Vallum

B6
1 Dunford Gdns
2 West Mdw
A7
1 Dulverston Cl
2 Kidderminster Dr
3 Lobelia Cl
A6
1 Coley Hill Cl
2 Janus Cl
3 Jonquil Cl
4 Kelso Cl
5 Kelson Wy
6 Killin Cl
7 Lupin Cl
B7
1 Glebe Cl
2 Gleneagle Cl
3 Goodwood Cl
4 Gracefield Cl
5 Grosvenor Ct
C6
1 Dewley Pl
C7
1 Bamburgh Rd
2 Baybridge Rd
3 Counden Rd
4 Kendale Wk
5 Marsham Rd
6 Mitford Dr
7 Norham Dr
8 Trafford Wk
9 Westward Ct
10 Whorlton Pl
D6
1 Bardon Cl
2 Whittingham Rd
D7
1 Anson Pl
2 Bournemouth Gdns
3 Buxton Gdns
4 Chatsworth Gdns
5 Highfield Cl
6 Matlock Gdns
7 Newbiggin La
8 Wimbourne Gn
E6
1 Alwinton Cl
2 Fielding Ct
3 Kidlandlee Gn
4 Kielder Cl
5 Yetholm Pl
E7
1 Ambergate Cl
2 Denton Ga
3 Denton Gv
4 Hillary Pl
5 Kyloe Vls
34
43
54
Callerton Park Station
Low Luddick
B6918
Middle Drive
Woolsington
A696(T)
PONTELAND ROAD
Bullock Steads
Kenton Bankfoot
Butterlaw
Whorlton Hall
Low Newbiggin
Lowbiggin
Newbiggin Lane
Simonside First Sch
Whorlton Grange
Golf Course
Newbiggin Hall Estate
Cheviot First School
Chevyside Middle School
St Marks RC Primary School
Redburn Road
Westerhope Small Business Park
Westerhope
NE5
Chapel Park Shopping Cen
Newcastle City Council
STAMFORDHAM RD
Westerhope First School
Westerhope Clinic
Knoplaw First School
Parkway School
Roachburn Road
Linhope
Doctors Surg
First School
1 grid square represents 500 metres

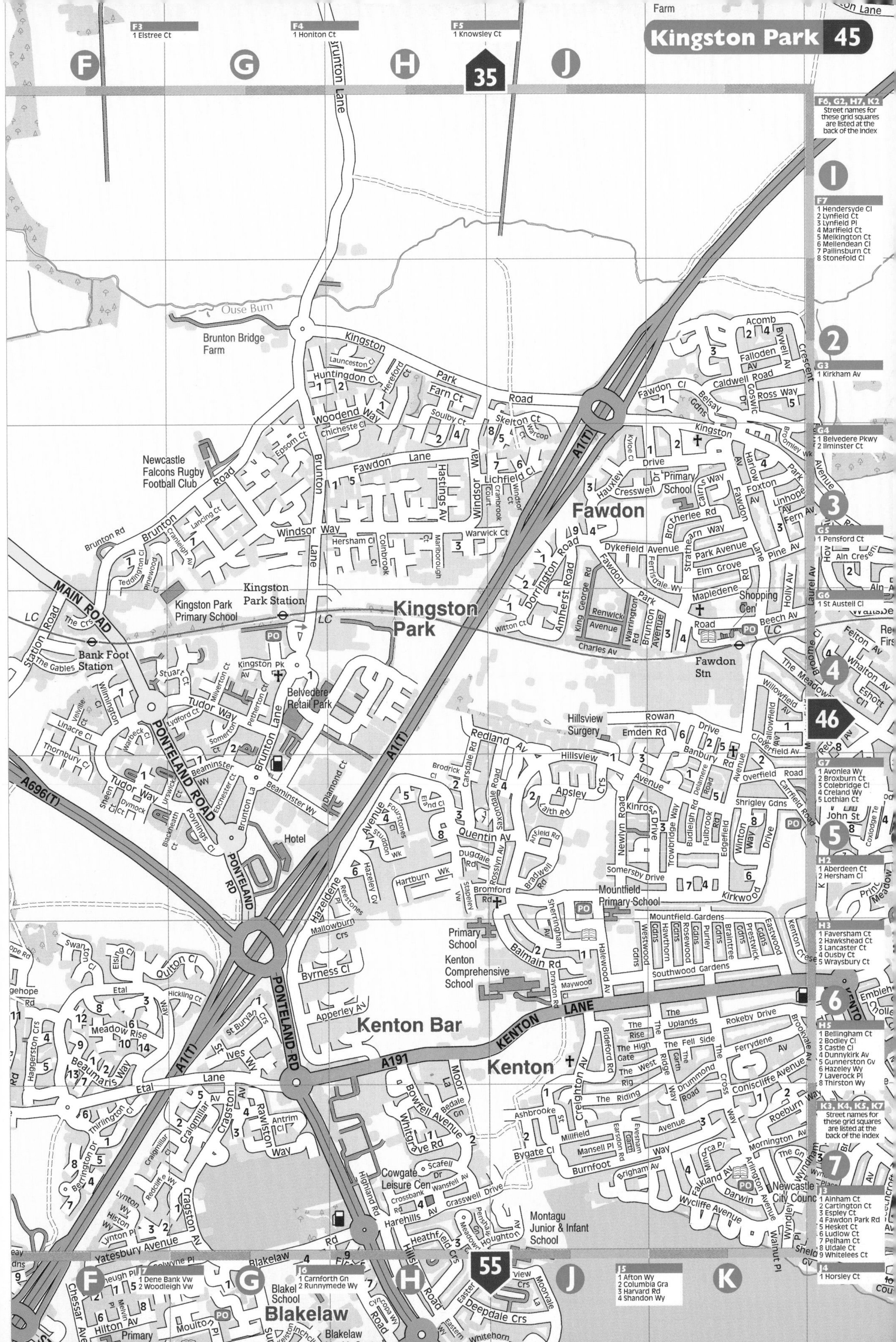
F3
1 Elstree Ct
F4
1 Honiton Ct
F5
1 Knowsley Ct
35
F
G
H
J
F6, G2, H7, K2
Street names for these grid squares are listed at the back of the index
1
F7
1 Hendersyde Cl
2 Lynfield Ct
3 Lynfield Pl
4 Marlfield Ct
5 Melkington Ct
6 Mellendean Cl
7 Pallinsburn Ct
8 Stonefold Cl
2
G3
1 Kirkham Av
G4
1 Belvedere Pkwy
2 Ilminster Ct
3
G5
1 Pensford Ct
G6
1 St Austell Cl
4
46
G7
1 Avonlea Wy
2 Broxburn Ct
3 Colebridge Cl
4 Creland Wy
5 Lothian Ct
5
H2
1 Aberdeen Ct
2 Hersham Cl
H3
1 Faversham Ct
2 Hawkshead Ct
3 Lancaster Ct
4 Ousby Ct
5 Wraysbury Ct
6
H5
1 Bellingham Ct
2 Bodley Cl
3 Castle Cl
4 Dunnykirk Av
5 Gunnerston Gv
6 Hazeley Wy
7 Laverock Pl
8 Thirston Wy
K3, K4, K5, K7
Street names for these grid squares are listed at the back of the index
7
J3
1 Alnham Ct
2 Cartington Ct
3 Espley Ct
4 Fawdon Park Rd
5 Hesket Ct
6 Ludlow Ct
7 Pelham Ct
8 Uldale Ct
9 Whitelees Ct
J4
1 Horsley Ct
J7
1 Dene Bank Vw
2 Woodleigh Vw
J6
1 Carnforth Gn
2 Runnymede Wy
J5
1 Afton Wy
2 Columbia Gra
3 Harvard Rd
4 Shandon Wy
55
K
Brunton Lane
Ouse Burn
Brunton Bridge Farm
Kingston Park Road
Launceston Cl
Huntingdon Cl
Hereford Ct
Farn Ct
Woodend Way
Chichester Cl
Soulby Ct
Skelton Ct
Warcop Ct
Newcastle Falcons Rugby Football Club
Epsom Ct
Fawdon Lane
Hastings Av
Windsor Way
Lichfield Cl
Cranbrook Court
Windsor Ct
Lancing Ct
Cranleigh Av
Brunton Road
Brunton Rd
Hersham Cl
Colnbrook
Marlborough Ct
Warwick Ct
Teddington Cl
Pinewood Cl
Kingston Park Station
Kingston Park Primary School
Kingston Park
MAIN ROAD
Station Road
The Crs
Bank Foot Station
The Gables
LC
PO
Kingston Pk Av
Stuart Ct
Milverton Ct
Belvedere Retail Park
Tudor Way
Lydford Ct
Petherton Ct
Somerton Ct
Wilmington Cl
Yelville Cl
Linacre Cl
Thornbury Cl
Warbeck Cl
PONTELAND ROAD
Beaminster Wy
Brunton Lane
Ebchester Ct
Urswick Ct
Dymock Ct
Sheen Ct
Blackheath Ct
Poynings Cl
Diamond Ct
Beaminster Wy
Brunton La
Hotel
A696(T)
A1(T)
PONTELAND RD
Acomb
Bywell Av
Falloden Av
Crescent
Caldwell Road
Ross Way
Fawdon Cl
Belsay Gdns
Goswick Dr
Kingston
Bromley Wk
Kyloe Cl
Drive
Harlow Av
Park
Avenue
Hauxley Dr
Cresswell
Primary School
Cairns Way
Fawdon
Foxton Av
Linhope Av
Fern Av
Brotherlee Rd
Strathearn Way
Dorrington Road
Dykefield Avenue
Ferndale Wy
Park Avenue
Elm Grove
Fawdon Park
Mapledene Rd
Pine Av
Holly Av
Laurel Av
Amherst Road
King George Rd
Renwick Avenue
Warrington Rd
Brunton Avenue
Witton Ct
Shopping Cen
Beech Av
Charles Av
Fawdon Stn
Aln Cres
Felton Av
Whalton Av
The Meadows
Eshott Cl
Willowfield Av
Hallowfield Av
Cloverfield Av
Hillsview Surgery
Rowan Drive
Emden Rd
Redland Av
Hillsview Avenue
Banbury Rd
Overfield Road
Carrfield Road
Brodrick Cl
Carsdale Rd
Saxondale Road
Apsley Crs
Laith Rd
Delamere Road
Shrigley Gdns
Fourstones Cl
Elland Cl
Studdon Wk
Avenue
Quentin Av
Anfield Rd
Newlyn Road
Kinross Drive
Trowbridge Way
Budleigh Rd
Fulbrook Rd
Edgefield
Winton Way
Drive
John St
Coxlodge Te
Hazeley Gv
Hartburn Wk
Dugdale Rd
Rosslyn Av
Bradwell Rd
Somersby Drive
Kirkwood
Reestones Pl
Hazeldene
Stapeley Vw
Bromford Rd
Mountfield Primary School
Mallowburn Crs
Primary School
Sheringham Av
Mountfield Gardens
Gdns
Hawthorn Gdns
Rosewood Gdns
Purley Gdns
Braintree Gdns
Prestwick Gdns
Eastwood Gdns
Westwood Gdns
Kenton Cres
Halewood Av
Southwood Gardens
Byrness Cl
Kenton Comprehensive School
Balmain Rd
Drayton Rd
Maywood Cl
Apperley Av
Kenton Bar
KENTON LANE
A191
The Uplands
Rokeby Drive
Brookvale Av
The Rise
The High Gate
The West Rig
The Ridge
The Garth
The Fell Side
The Cross Way
Ferrydene Av
Bideford Rd
Kenton
Creighton Av
Drummond Road
Coniscliffe Avenue
The Riding
Roeburn Way
Moor La
Bedale Gn
Bowfell Avenue
Whitgrave Rd
Ashbrooke St
Millfield
Earsdon Rd
Garth
Evesham Avenue
Mornington Av
Bygate Cl
Mansell Pl
Burnfoot Way
Brigham Av
Falkland Av
Arlington Avenue
Darwin
Wyndham Av
Newcastle City Council
Wycliffe Avenue
Walnut Pl
Scafell Dr
Wansfell Av
Cowgate Leisure Cen
Crossbank Rd
Harehills Av
Grasswell Drive
Highland Rd
Heathfield Crs
Meadowfield
Penshurst
Houghton Av
Montagu Junior & Infant School
Swanton Ct
Elsing Cl
Quiton Cl
Etal
Hickling Ct
Meadow Rise
Haggerston Crs
Beaumaris Way
St Ives Wy
St Buryan Crs
Etal Lane
Thirlington Cl
Craigmillar Av
Cragston Av
Rawlston Way
Antrim Cl
Berrington Dr
Redcliffe Wy
Lynton Wy
Histon Wy
Lynton Pl
Cragston Av
Yatesbury Avenue
Rd
Blakelaw
Colwyne Pl
Chessar Ave
Melvin Pl
Hilton Av
Blakelaw School
Blakelaw
Moulton Pl
Primary
Cyncopa Wy
Road
Deepdale Crs
Moorvale La
Eastern Wy
Whitehorn
Farm
Lane

E5, E6, E7 Street names for these grid squares are listed at the back of the index
A4, A5 Street names for these grid squares are listed at the back of the index
A3
1 Chatton Wynd
2 Etal Pl
3 Fern Av
4 Wansbeck Rd North
36
45
56
A6
1 Delaval Ter
2 Dunmoor Cl
3 Hownam Cl
A7
1 Carlton Cl
2 Hardwick Pl
3 Wyndsail Pl
4 Wyndtop Pl
B3
1 Berkeley Sq
2 Kielder Wy
B4
1 Amble Wy
B6
1 Bloomsbury Ct
2 The Firs
3 Meadowfield Rd
4 Thornfield Rd
B7
1 Richmond Ms
C1
1 Hartside Pl
2 Inglewood Pl
3 Linwood Pl
C3
1 Langholm Rd
2 Marlborough Ap
3 Whitebridge Ct
C5
1 Edward St
C6
1 Gordon Av
2 Linden Av
3 Roseworth Av
4 St Nicholas Av
C7
1 Leslie Crs
D1
1 Beech Cl
2 Chapel Cl
3 Heathfield Pl
4 Juniper Cl
5 Kilnshaw Pl
6 Low Gosforth Ct
D2
1 Charleswood
2 Ferriby Cl
3 Navenby Cl
4 Scalby Cl
D5
1 Cambo Cl
2 Manor Cl
3 Rothley Cl
D6
1 Grove Av
D7
1 Albemarle Av
2 Kingswood Av
3 Treherne Rd
E4
1 Turnberry Wy
East Brunton
NORTH ROAD
GREAT NORTH ROAD
Northumberland County Council
Gosforth Lake
Northern Rugby Club
Golf Course
Ouse Burn
NE3
Broadway East First School
Wansbeck Road Stn
Regent Farm First School
Grange First School
Gosforth High School
St Charles RC Primary School
Regent Centre Station
The Open University
Middle School
Archbishop Runcie C of E School
Gosforth Industrial Est
GOSFORTH
Coxlodge
Gosforth West Middle School
Archibald First School
SALTERS' ROAD
CHURCH AV
STATION ROAD
South Gosforth Station
South Gosforth
Gosforth Memorial Health Cen
Sanderson Hosp
Ascham House Sch
High School
Police Stn
The Surg
Gosforth Cricket Club
The Hobart Gallery
Eastcliffe Grammar School
South Gosforth First School
Ilford Road Stn
HADDRICKSMILL ROAD
MATTHEW BANK
Newcastle City Council
La Sagesse Convent High School
Newcastle Clinic
Newcastle Reform Synagogue
KENTON RD
Westfield School
The Avenues Medical Practice
Kenton Lodge Residential School
West Jesmond
A189
B1318
HIGH ST
Heathery
Woodlea Gardens
Hollywood Avenue
Cheswick
Broadway
Park Avenue
Regent Farm Road
Kenton Road
Graham Park Road
Moorfield
Towers Avenue
Mitchell Avenue
Doctors Surg
1 grid square represents 500 metres

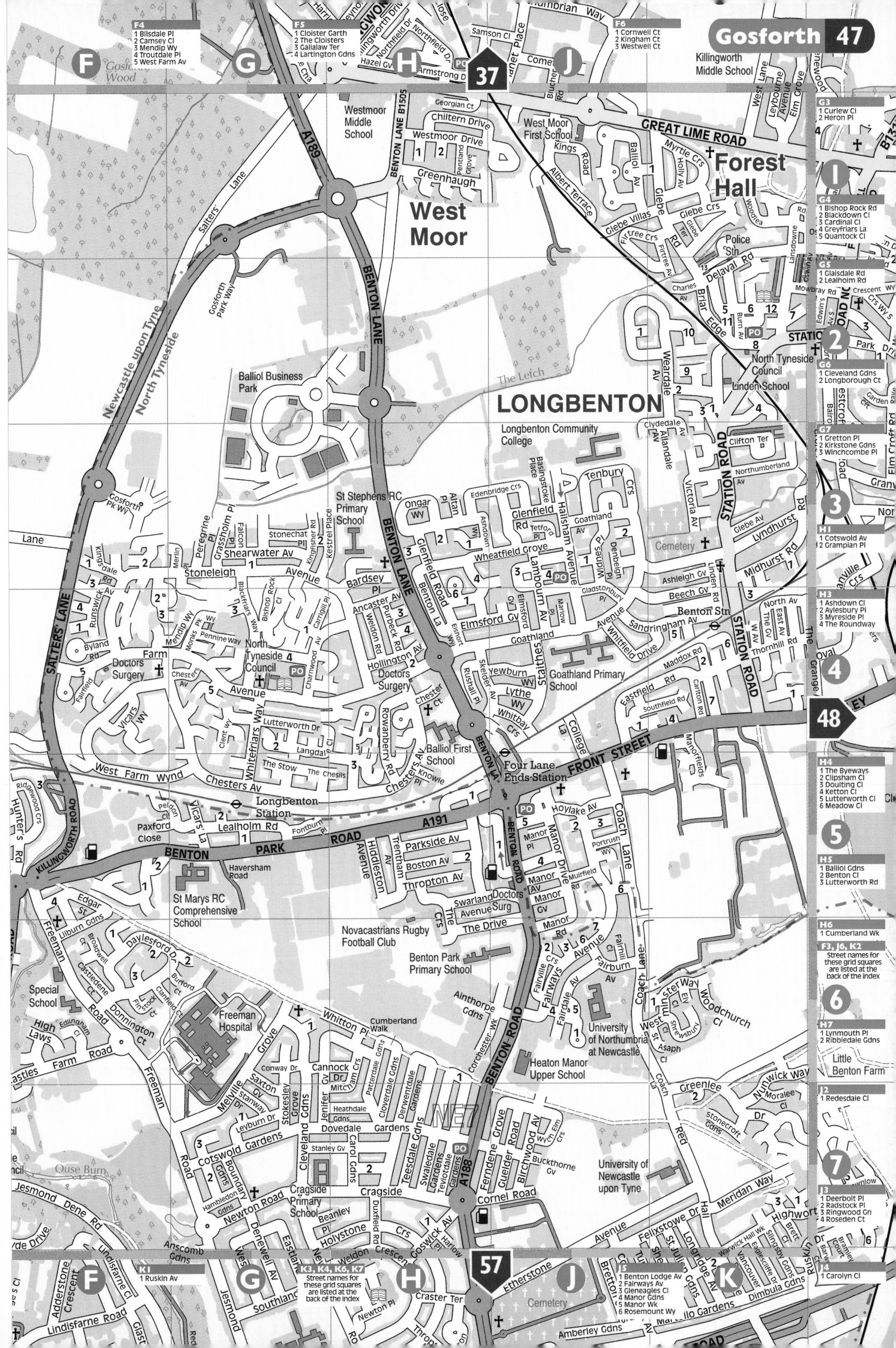
F4
1 Bilsdale Pl
2 Camsey Cl
3 Mendip Wy
4 Troutdale Pl
5 West Farm Av
F5
1 Cloister Garth
2 The Cloisters
3 Gallalaw Ter
4 Lartington Gdns
F6
1 Cornwell Ct
2 Kingham Ct
3 Westwell Ct
G3
1 Curlew Cl
2 Heron Pl
G4
1 Bishop Rock Rd
2 Blackdown Cl
3 Cardinal Cl
4 Greyfriars La
5 Quantock Cl
G5
1 Glaisdale Rd
2 Lealholm Rd
G6
1 Cleveland Gdns
2 Longborough Ct
G7
1 Gretton Pl
2 Kirkstone Gdns
3 Winchcombe Pl
H1
1 Cotswold Av
2 Grampian Pl
H3
1 Ashdown Cl
2 Aylesbury Pl
3 Myreside Pl
4 The Roundway
H4
1 The Byeways
2 Clipsham Cl
3 Doulting Cl
4 Ketton Cl
5 Lutterworth Cl
6 Meadow Cl
H5
1 Balliol Gdns
2 Benton Cl
3 Lutterworth Rd
H6
1 Cumberland Wk
F3, J6, K2
Street names for these grid squares are listed at the back of the index
H7
1 Lynmouth Pl
2 Ribbledale Gdns
J2
1 Redesdale Cl
J3
1 Deerbolt Pl
2 Radstock Pl
3 Ringwood Gn
4 Roseden Ct
J4
1 Carolyn Cl
K1
1 Ruskin Av
K3, K4, K6, K7
Street names for these grid squares are listed at the back of the index
J5
1 Benton Lodge Av
2 Fairways Av
3 Gleneagles Cl
4 Manor Gdns
5 Manor Wk
6 Rosemount Wy
37
48
57
West Moor
Forest Hall
LONGBENTON
Killingworth Middle School
Westmoor Middle School
West Moor First School
Balliol Business Park
Longbenton Community College
St Stephens RC Primary School
North Tyneside Council
Doctors Surgery
Goathland Primary School
Balliol First School
Four Lane Ends Station
Longbenton Station
Benton Stn
Cemetery
Linden School
Police Stn
St Marys RC Comprehensive School
Novacastrians Rugby Football Club
Benton Park Primary School
Freeman Hospital
Special School
University of Northumbria at Newcastle
Heaton Manor Upper School
University of Newcastle upon Tyne
Cragside Primary School
Little Benton Farm
Gosforth Wood
The Letch
Ouse Burn
NE7
Newcastle upon Tyne
North Tyneside
GREAT LIME ROAD
BENTON LANE
SALTERS' LANE
KILLINGWORTH ROAD
BENTON PARK ROAD
A191
A189
A188
FRONT STREET
STATION ROAD
BENTON ROAD
Coach Lane
Freeman Road
Newton Road
Jesmond Dene Rd
Lindisfarne Road
Meridan Way
Cornel Road

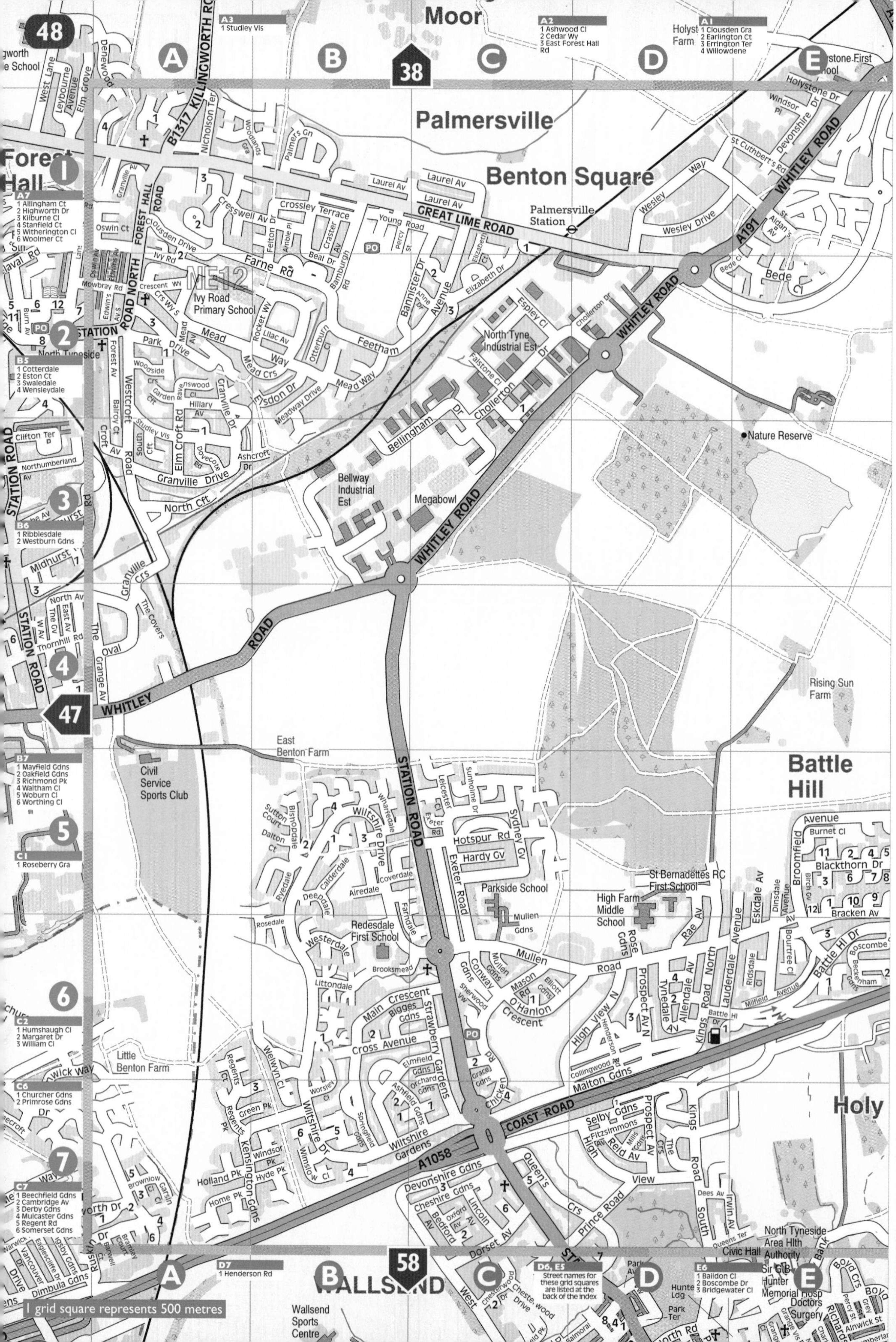
Moor
38
A B C D E
Palmersville
Benton Square
Forest Hall
Palmersville Station
GREAT LIME ROAD
WHITLEY ROAD
STATION ROAD
COAST ROAD
A1058
A191
B1317 KILLINGWORTH RD
North Tyne Industrial Est
Bellway Industrial Est
Megabowl
Ivy Road Primary School
NE12
Nature Reserve
Rising Sun Farm
East Benton Farm
Civil Service Sports Club
Battle Hill
Parkside School
St Bernadettes RC First School
High Farm Middle School
Redesdale First School
Little Benton Farm
Holy
WALLSEND
Wallsend Sports Centre
North Tyneside Area Hlth Authority
Sir G B Hunter Memorial Hosp
Doctors Surgery
Civic Hall
47
58
1 2 3 4 5 6 7
A3 1 Studley Vls
A2 1 Ashwood Cl 2 Cedar Wy 3 East Forest Hall Rd
A1 1 Clousden Gra 2 Earlington Ct 3 Errington Ter 4 Willowdene
A7 1 Allingham Ct 2 Highworth Dr 3 Kilburne Cl 4 Stanfield Ct 5 Witherington Cl 6 Woolmer Ct
B5 1 Cotterdale 2 Eston Ct 3 Swaledale 4 Wensleydale
B6 1 Ribblesdale 2 Westburn Gdns
B7 1 Mayfield Gdns 2 Oakfield Gdns 3 Richmond Pk 4 Waltham Cl 5 Woburn Cl 6 Worthing Cl
C1 1 Roseberry Gra
C2 1 Humshaugh Cl 2 Margaret Dr 3 William Cl
C6 1 Churcher Gdns 2 Primrose Gdns
C7 1 Beechfield Gdns 2 Cambridge Av 3 Derby Gdns 4 Mulcaster Gdns 5 Regent Rd 6 Somerset Gdns
D7 1 Henderson Rd
D6, E5 Street names for these grid squares are listed at the back of the index
E6 1 Baildon Cl 2 Boscombe Dr 3 Bridgewater Cl
1 grid square represents 500 metres

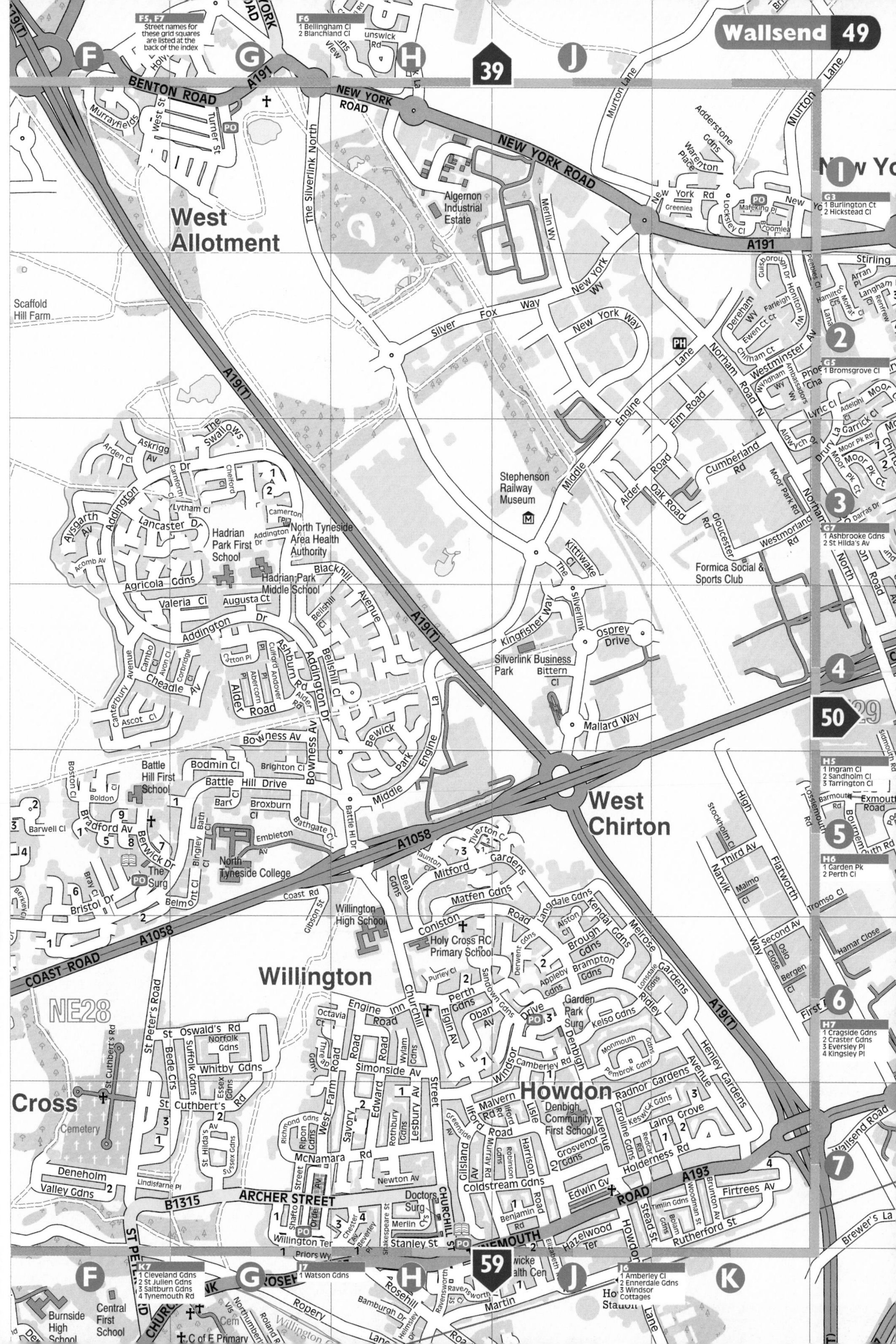
West Allotment
Willington
West Chirton
Howdon
Cross
NE28
BENTON ROAD
NEW YORK ROAD
A191
A19(T)
A1058
COAST ROAD
A193
B1315
ARCHER STREET
Silver Fox Way
Algernon Industrial Estate
Stephenson Railway Museum
Silverlink Business Park
Formica Social & Sports Club
North Tyneside Area Health Authority
Hadrian Park First School
Hadrian Park Middle School
Battle Hill First School
North Tyneside College
Willington High School
Holy Cross RC Primary School
Denbigh Community First School
Garden Park Surg
Scaffold Hill Farm
Cemetery
Burnside High School
Central First School
F5, F7 Street names for these grid squares are listed at the back of the index
F6 1 Bellingham Cl 2 Blanchland Cl
G3 1 Burlington Ct 2 Hickstead Cl
G5 1 Bromsgrove Cl
G7 1 Ashbrooke Gdns 2 St Hilda's Av
H5 1 Ingram Cl 2 Sandholm Cl 3 Tarrington Cl
H6 1 Garden Pk 2 Perth Cl
H7 1 Cragside Gdns 2 Craster Gdns 3 Eversley Pl 4 Kingsley Pl
K7 1 Cleveland Gdns 2 St Julien Gdns 3 Saltburn Gdns 4 Tynemouth Rd
J7 1 Watson Gdns
J6 1 Amberley Cl 2 Ennerdale Gdns 3 Windsor Cottages
39
50
59

50
A4
1 Humshaugh Rd
2 Norham Rd
3 Nunwick Gdns
A3
1 Alston Cl
2 Hexham Cl
3 Moorhouses Rd
A2
1 Bodmin Rd
2 Coldstream Wy
3 Elgin Cl
4 Perth Cl
A
B
40
C
D
E
A5
1 Bournemouth Rd
2 Eyemouth Rd
3 Lynmouth Rd
4 Norham Rd
D6, D7, E2, E3
Street names for these grid squares are listed at the back of the index
E4, E5, E6, E7
Street names for these grid squares are listed at the back of the index
1
B2
1 St Aidan's Cl
2 Sherborne Av
3 Somerset Gv
4 Taunton Av
B3
1 Hedgeley Rd
2 Lynn Rd
3 Netherton Gv
4 Thirston Pl
5 Whitton Gdns
2
B4
1 Bellister Rd
2 Berkley Rd
3 Glendower Av
4 Gunnerton Pl
5 Juliet Av
6 Mortimer Av
7 Surrey Rd
B5
1 Biddlestone Crs
2 Craster Rd
3 Plessey Gdns
4 Tosson Pl
3
B6
1 Chillingham Dr
B7
1 Cockburn Ter
2 Nelson Crs
3 St John's Wk
4
49
C2
1 Caynham Cl
2 Overton Rd
5
C4
1 Rutland Pl
C5
1 Millbrook
2 Mill Cl
3 Thorncliffe Pl
6
C6
1 Coventry Gdns
2 Didcot Av
3 Meadow Well Wy
4 Wincanton Pl
C7
1 Woodlea Ct
7
D1
1 Langdon Cl
2 Pentland Cl
3 Pevensey Cl
D2
1 Westbury Rd
D3
1 Hawthorn Gdns
D4
1 Glendale Gv
2 Milton Gv
3 Milton Pl
D5
1 Appleby Ct
2 Carlton Ter
3 Chirton Gn
4 Lovaine Pl West
60
1 grid square represents 500 metres
New York
Preston Grange
Preston
Billy Mill
Chirton
NE29
Percy Main
RAKE LANE
A191
A192
PRESTON RD
BEACH ROAD
A1058
COAST ROAD
BILLY ML LANE
B1316
LYNN ROAD
REGENT TER
BILLY MILL AVENUE
NORTH ROAD
B1304
WALTON AV
HAWKEY'S LA
PRESTON ROAD
FRONT ST
CHIRTON GN
SPENCE TER
ALBION RD
A1149
COACH LA
HOWDON RD
PRUDHOE ST
WALLSEND RD
A193
A187
HOWDON ROAD
York Road
Whitehouse Primary School
St Anselm's RC High School
North Shields Rugby Club
John Spence Community High School
Cemetery
Tynemouth College
North Tyneside Area Hlth Authority
Spring Terrace Hlth Centre
North Tyneside Council
North Shields Stn
Norham Community High School
Bugatti Industrial Park
Doctors Surg
Meadow Well Station
North Tyneside Metropolitan Borough Council
The Parks Sports Centre
Infant School
Primary School
Percy Main Station
Cricket Club
Chirton Dene Way
Earl Grey Way
Ballast Hill Road
Waterville Road
West Percy Road
Norham Road North
Woolsington Road

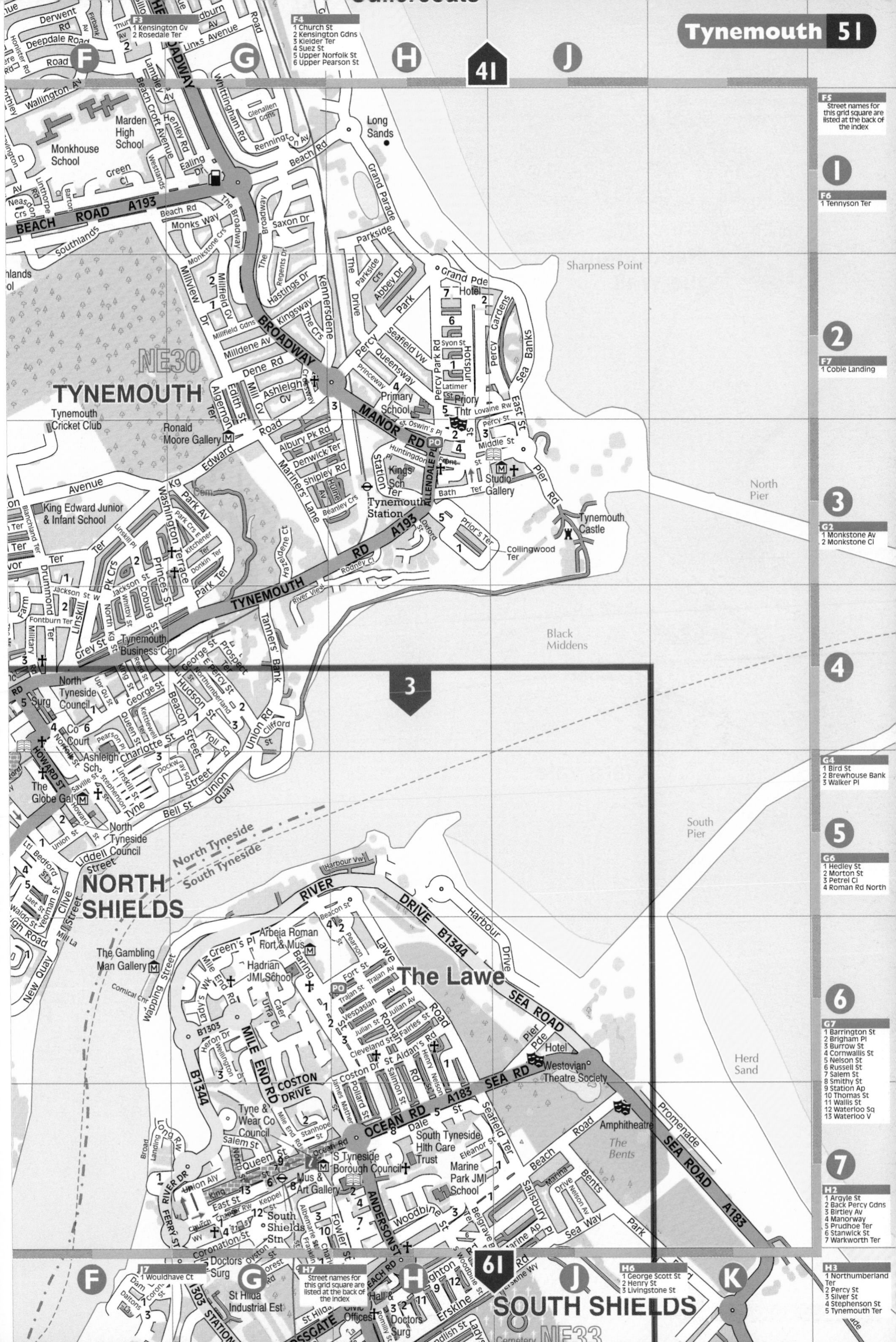
Tynemouth 51
F3
1 Kensington Gv
2 Rosedale Ter
F4
1 Church St
2 Kensington Gdns
3 Kielder Ter
4 Suez St
5 Upper Norfolk St
6 Upper Pearson St
F5
Street names for this grid square are listed at the back of the index
F6
1 Tennyson Ter
F7
1 Coble Landing
G2
1 Monkstone Av
2 Monkstone Cl
G4
1 Bird St
2 Brewhouse Bank
3 Walker Pl
G6
1 Hedley St
2 Morton St
3 Petrel Cl
4 Roman Rd North
G7
1 Barrington St
2 Brigham Pl
3 Burrow St
4 Cornwallis St
5 Nelson St
6 Russell St
7 Salem St
8 Smithy St
9 Station Ap
10 Thomas St
11 Wallis St
12 Waterloo Sq
13 Waterloo V
H2
1 Argyle St
2 Back Percy Gdns
3 Birtley Av
4 Manorway
5 Prudhoe Ter
6 Stanwick St
7 Warkworth Ter
H3
1 Northumberland Ter
2 Percy St
3 Silver St
4 Stephenson St
5 Tynemouth Ter
H6
1 George Scott St
2 Henry St
3 Livingstone St
H7
Street names for this grid square are listed at the back of the index
J7
1 Wouldhave Ct
41
3
61
TYNEMOUTH
NORTH SHIELDS
SOUTH SHIELDS
The Lawe
NE30
NE33
Long Sands
Sharpness Point
North Pier
South Pier
Black Middens
Herd Sand
Tynemouth Castle
Collingwood Ter
Tynemouth Station
Marden High School
Monkhouse School
Tynemouth Cricket Club
Ronald Moore Gallery
King Edward Junior & Infant School
Tynemouth Business Cen
North Tyneside Council
Ashleigh Sch
The Globe Gal
The Gambling Man Gallery
Arbeia Roman Fort & Mus
Hadrian JMI School
Westovian Theatre Society
Amphitheatre
The Bents
South Tyneside Hlth Care Trust
Marine Park JMI School
S Tyneside Borough Council
Mus & Art Gallery
South Shields Stn
Tyne & Wear Co Council
St Hilda Industrial Est
Studio Gallery
Kings Sch
Primary School
Priory Thtr
Hotel
North Tyneside
South Tyneside
BEACH ROAD A193
BROADWAY
MANOR RD
TYNEMOUTH RD A193
RIVER DRIVE B1344
SEA ROAD A183
OCEAN RD A183
MILE END RD
COSTON DRIVE
ANDERSON ST
Grand Parade
Sea Banks
Pier Rd
Harbour Drive
Promenade
F
G
H
J
K

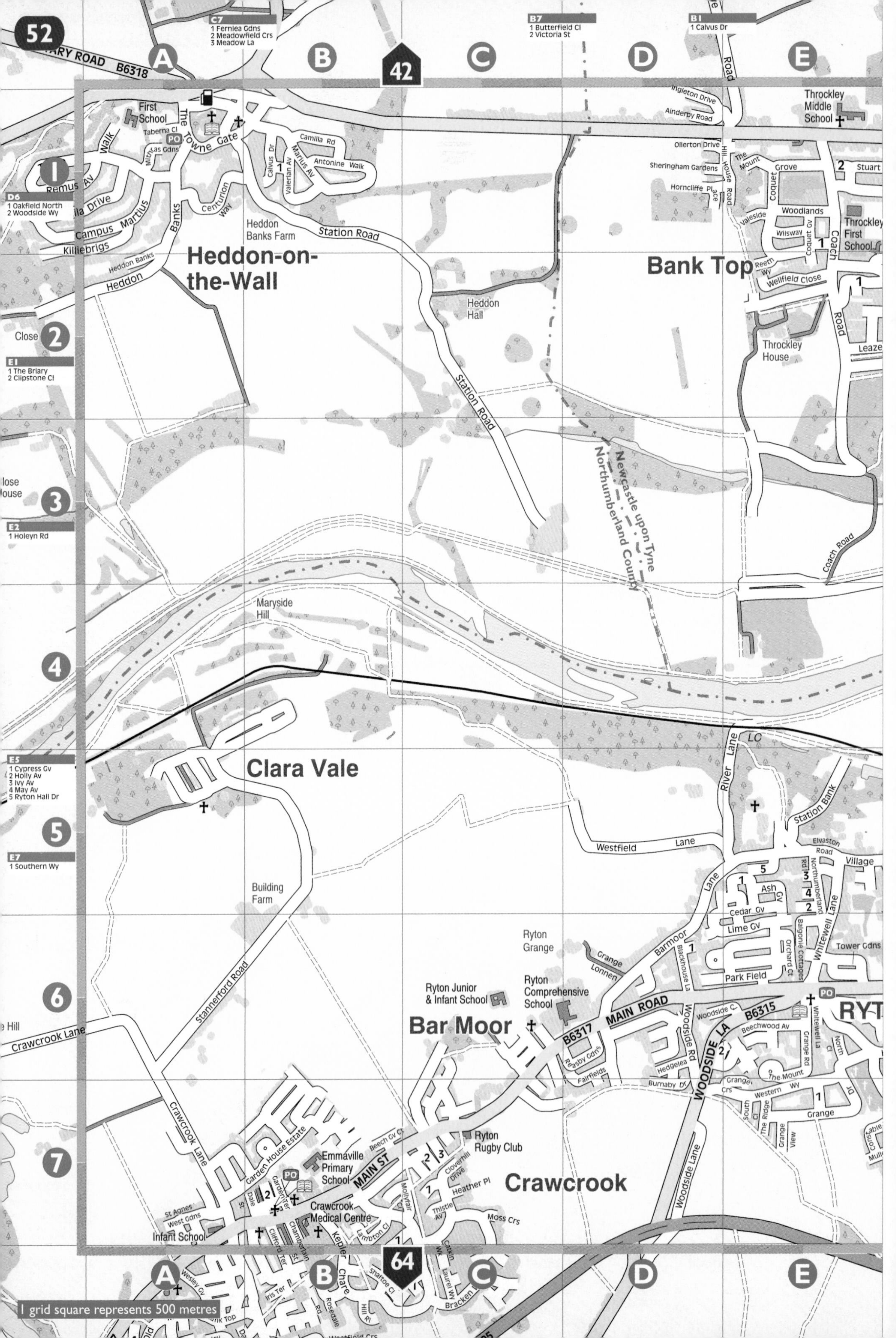
C7
1 Fernlea Gdns
2 Meadowfield Crs
3 Meadow La
B7
1 Butterfield Cl
2 Victoria St
B1
1 Calvus Dr
D6
1 Oakfield North
2 Woodside Wy
E1
1 The Briary
2 Clipstone Cl
E2
1 Holeyn Rd
E5
1 Cypress Gv
2 Holly Av
3 Ivy Av
4 May Av
5 Ryton Hall Dr
E7
1 Southern Wy
Heddon-on-the-Wall
Bank Top
Clara Vale
Bar Moor
Crawcrook
Throckley Middle School
Throckley First School
Heddon Banks Farm
Heddon Hall
Throckley House
Maryside Hill
Building Farm
Ryton Grange
Ryton Junior & Infant School
Ryton Comprehensive School
Emmaville Primary School
Crawcrook Medical Centre
Infant School
Ryton Rugby Club
Station Road
Stannerford Road
Crawcrook Lane
Westfield Lane
River Lane
Station Bank
MAIN ROAD
MAIN ST
WOODSIDE LA
Woodside Lane
Newcastle upon Tyne
Northumberland County
1 grid square represents 500 metres

42
64

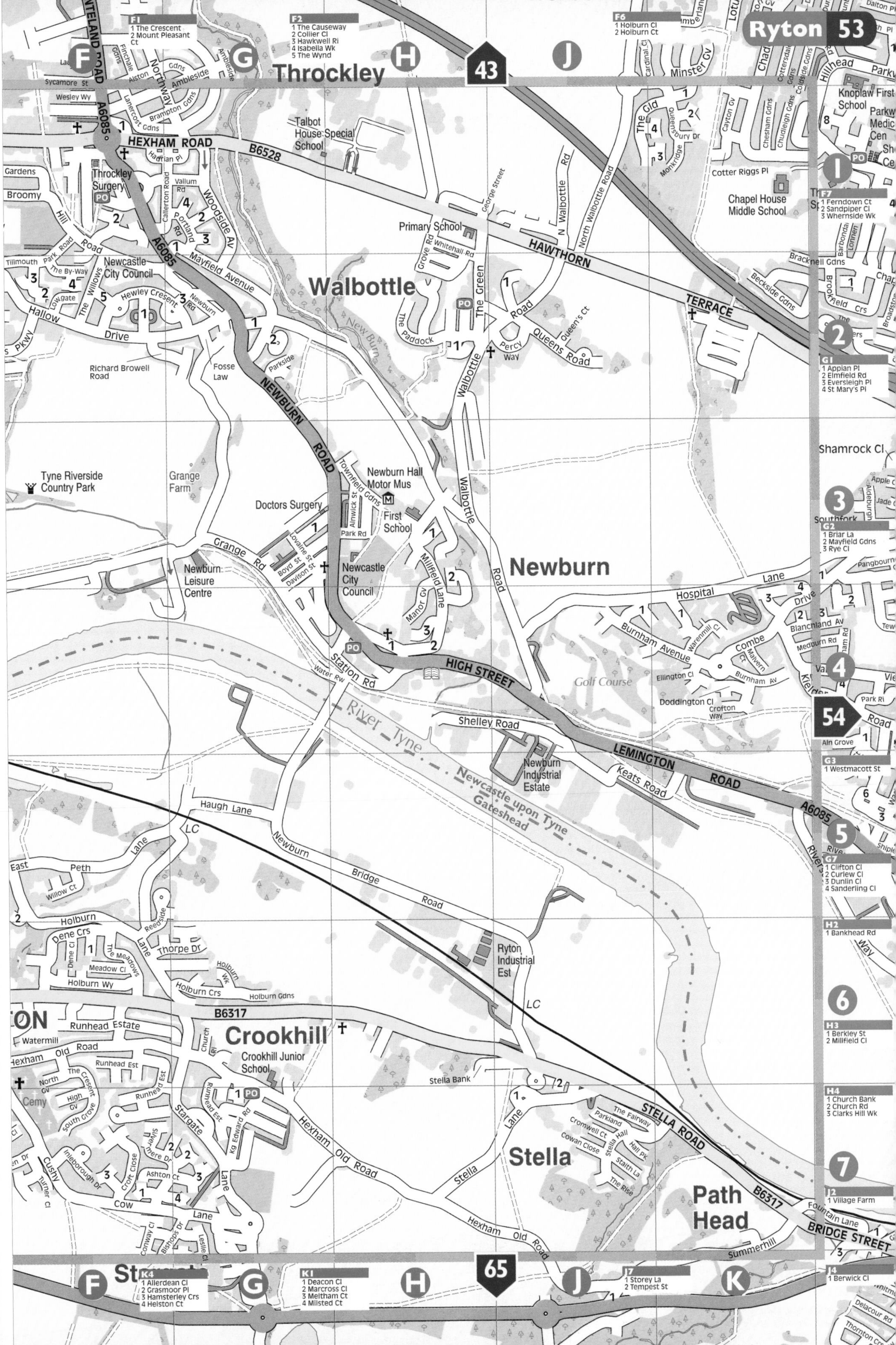
F1
1 The Crescent
2 Mount Pleasant Ct
F2
1 The Causeway
2 Collier Cl
3 Hawkwell Ri
4 Isabella Wk
5 The Wynd
F6
1 Holburn Cl
2 Holburn Ct
F7
1 Ferndown Ct
2 Sandpiper Cl
3 Whernside Wk
G1
1 Applan Pl
2 Elmfield Rd
3 Eversleigh Pl
4 St Mary's Pl
G2
1 Briar La
2 Mayfield Gdns
3 Rye Cl
G3
1 Westmacott St
G7
1 Clifton Cl
2 Curlew Cl
3 Dunlin Cl
4 Sanderling Cl
H2
1 Bankhead Rd
H3
1 Berkley St
2 Millfield Cl
H4
1 Church Bank
2 Church Rd
3 Clarks Hill Wk
J2
1 Village Farm
J4
1 Berwick Cl
J7
1 Storey La
2 Tempest St
K1
1 Deacon Cl
2 Marcross Cl
3 Meltham Ct
4 Milsted Ct
K4
1 Allerdean Cl
2 Grasmoor Pl
3 Hamsterley Crs
4 Helston Ct
43
54
65
Throckley
Walbottle
Newburn
Crookhill
Stella
Path Head
HEXHAM ROAD
B6528
HAWTHORN
TERRACE
NEWBURN ROAD
A6085
HIGH STREET
LEMINGTON ROAD
STELLA ROAD
B6317
BRIDGE STREET
River Tyne
Newcastle upon Tyne
Gateshead
Talbot House Special School
Throckley Surgery
Newcastle City Council
Primary School
Newburn Hall Motor Mus
First School
Doctors Surgery
Newburn Leisure Centre
Tyne Riverside Country Park
Grange Farm
Newburn Industrial Estate
Ryton Industrial Est
Crookhill Junior School
Chapel House Middle School
Knoplaw First School
Golf Course
Stella Bank

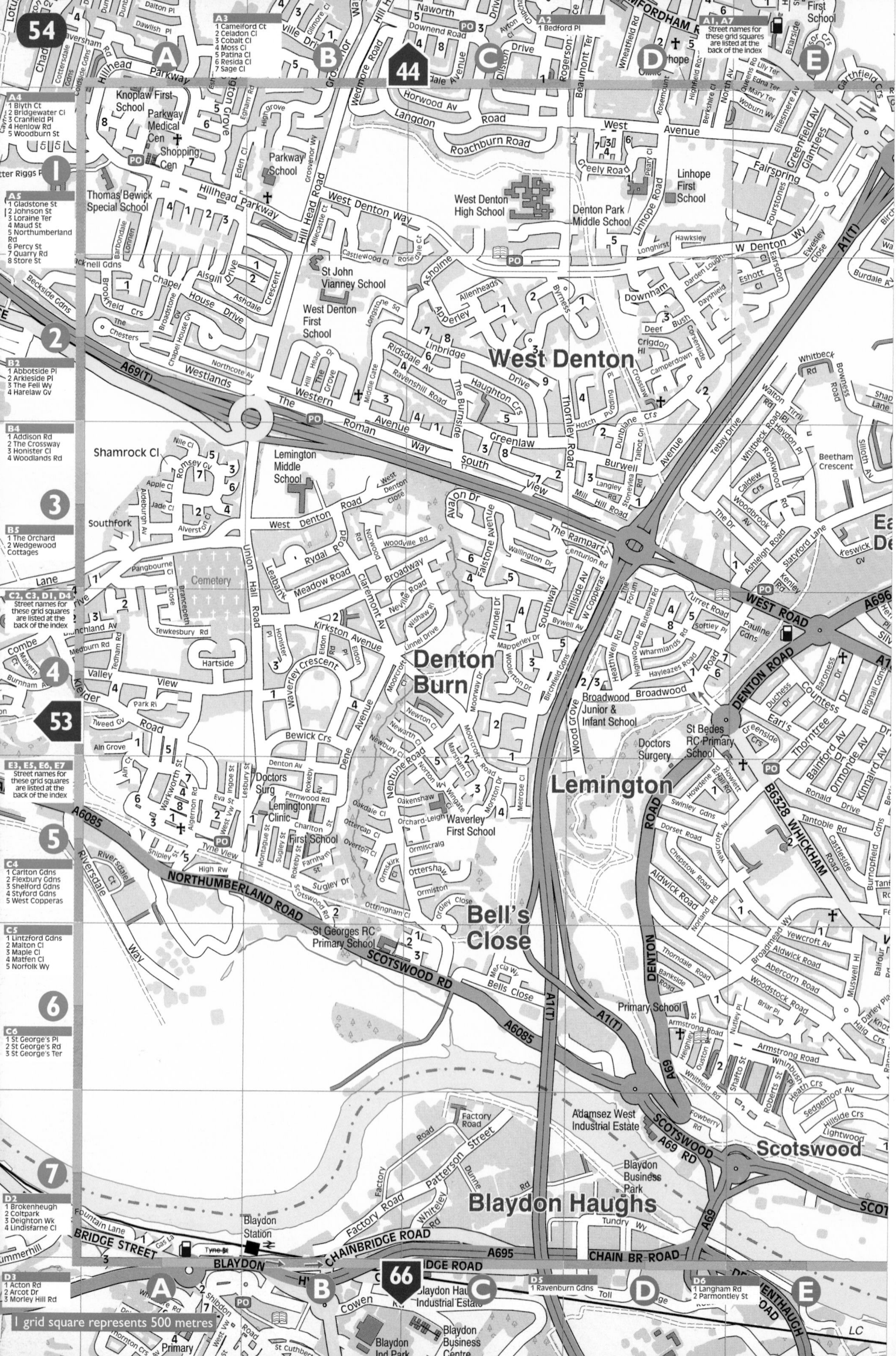
A3
1 Camelford Ct
2 Celadon Cl
3 Cobalt Cl
4 Moss Cl
5 Patina Cl
6 Resida Cl
7 Sage Cl
A2
1 Bedford Pl
A1, A7
Street names for these grid squares are listed at the back of the index
A4
1 Blyth Ct
2 Bridgewater Cl
3 Cranfield Pl
4 Henlow Rd
5 Woodburn St
A5
1 Gladstone St
2 Johnson St
3 Loraine Ter
4 Maud St
5 Northumberland Rd
6 Percy St
7 Quarry Rd
8 Store St
B2
1 Abbotside Pl
2 Arkleside Pl
3 The Fell Wy
4 Harelaw Gv
B4
1 Addison Rd
2 The Crossway
3 Honister Cl
4 Woodlands Rd
B5
1 The Orchard
2 Wedgewood Cottages
C2, C3, D1, D6
Street names for these grid squares are listed at the back of the index
E3, E5, E6, E7
Street names for these grid squares are listed at the back of the index
C4
1 Carlton Gdns
2 Flexbury Gdns
3 Shelford Gdns
4 Styford Gdns
5 West Copperas
C5
1 Lintzford Gdns
2 Malton Cl
3 Maple Cl
4 Matfen Cl
5 Norfolk Wy
C6
1 St George's Pl
2 St George's Rd
3 St George's Ter
D2
1 Brokenheugh
2 Coltpark
3 Deighton Wk
4 Lindisfarne Cl
D3
1 Acton Rd
2 Arcot Dr
3 Morley Hill Rd
D5
1 Ravenburn Gdns
D6
1 Langham Rd
2 Parmontley St
44
53
66
West Denton
Denton Burn
Lemington
Bell's Close
Blaydon Haughs
Scotswood
Knoplaw First School
Parkway Medical Cen
Shopping Cen
Thomas Bewick Special School
Parkway School
St John Vianney School
West Denton First School
West Denton High School
Denton Park Middle School
Linhope First School
Lemington Middle School
Cemetery
Broadwood Junior & Infant School
Doctors Surgery
St Bedes RC Primary School
Doctors Surg
Lemington Clinic
Charlton First School
Waverley First School
St Georges RC Primary School
Primary School
Adamsez West Industrial Estate
Blaydon Business Park
Blaydon Station
Blaydon Haughs Industrial Estate
Blaydon Ind Park
Blaydon Business Centre
Hillhead Parkway
West Denton Way
W Denton Wy
Western Avenue
Roman Way
South View
West Denton Road
West Road
Denton Road
B6328 Whickham Road
Northumberland Road
Scotswood Rd
Chainbridge Road
Bridge Street
Blaydon
A69(T)
A1(T)
A6085
A695
A69
Union Hall Road
Thornley Road
Hill Head Road
Roachburn Road
Langdon Road
West Avenue
Fordham Rd
1 grid square represents 500 metres

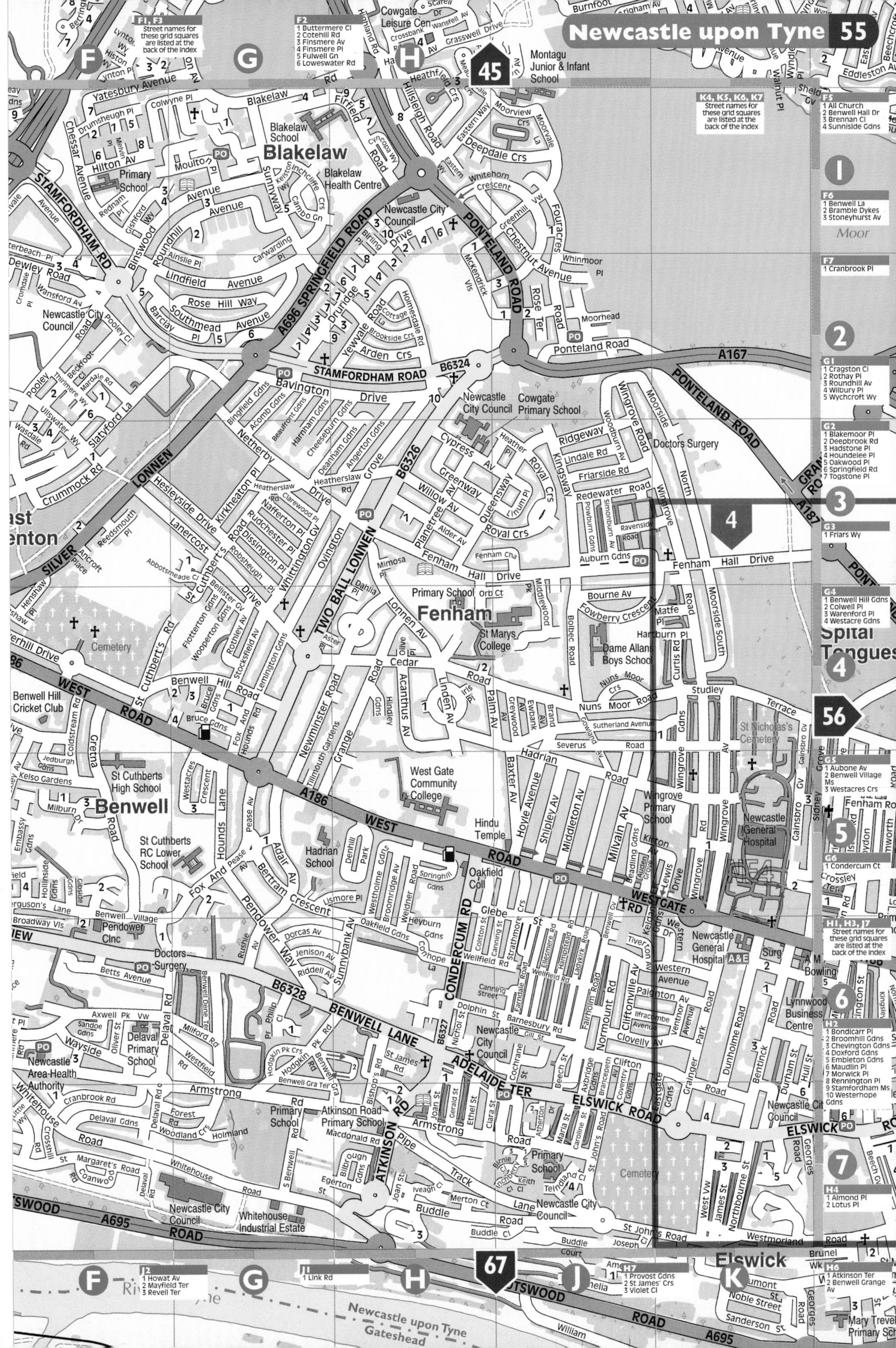
F1, F3
Street names for these grid squares are listed at the back of the index
F2
1 Buttermere Cl
2 Cotehill Rd
3 Finsmere Av
4 Finsmere Pl
5 Fulwell Gn
6 Loweswater Rd
K4, K5, K6, K7
Street names for these grid squares are listed at the back of the index
F5
1 All Church
2 Benwell Hall Dr
3 Brennan Cl
4 Sunniside Gdns
F6
1 Benwell La
2 Bramble Dykes
3 Stoneyhurst Av
F7
1 Cranbrook Pl
G1
1 Cragston Cl
2 Rothay Pl
3 Roundhill Av
4 Wilbury Pl
5 Wychcroft Wy
G2
1 Blakemoor Pl
2 Deepbrook Rd
3 Hadstone Pl
4 Houndelee Pl
5 Oakwood Pl
6 Springfield Rd
7 Togstone Pl
G3
1 Friars Wy
G4
1 Benwell Hill Gdns
2 Colwell Pl
3 Warenford Pl
4 Westacre Gdns
G5
1 Aubone Av
2 Benwell Village Ms
3 Westacres Crs
G6
1 Condercum Ct
H1, H3, J7
Street names for these grid squares are listed at the back of the index
H2
1 Bondicarr Pl
2 Broomhill Gdns
3 Chevington Gdns
4 Doxford Gdns
5 Embleton Gdns
6 Maudlin Pl
7 Morwick Pl
8 Rennington Pl
9 Stamfordham Ms
10 Westerhope Gdns
H4
1 Almond Pl
2 Lotus Pl
H6
1 Atkinson Ter
2 Benwell Grange Av
H7
1 Provost Gdns
2 St James' Crs
3 Violet Cl
J1
1 Link Rd
J2
1 Howat Av
2 Mayfield Ter
3 Revell Ter
F G H I J K
1 2 3 4 5 6 7
45
56
67
Blakelaw
Fenham
Benwell
Elswick
Spital Tongues
Moor
Cowgate Leisure Cen
Montagu Junior & Infant School
Blakelaw School
Blakelaw Health Centre
Newcastle City Council
Primary School
Cowgate Primary School
Doctors Surgery
Dame Allans Boys School
St Marys College
Cemetery
Benwell Hill Cricket Club
St Cuthberts High School
St Cuthberts RC Lower School
West Gate Community College
Hadrian School
Hindu Temple
Oakfield Coll
Wingrove Primary School
Newcastle General Hospital
St Nicholas's Cemetery
Lynnwood Business Centre
Pendower Clnc
Delaval Primary School
Newcastle Area Health Authority
Atkinson Road Primary School
Whitehouse Industrial Estate
Mary Trevelyan Primary Sch
STAMFORDHAM RD
A696 SPRINGFIELD ROAD
PONTELAND ROAD
A167
STAMFORDHAM ROAD B6324
SILVER LONNEN
TWO BALL LONNEN
B6326
A186 WEST ROAD
WESTGATE RD
CONDERCUM RD
B6328 BENWELL LANE
ADELAIDE TER
ELSWICK ROAD
ATKINSON RD
A695
SCOTSWOOD ROAD
Fenham Hall Drive
Newcastle upon Tyne
Gateshead

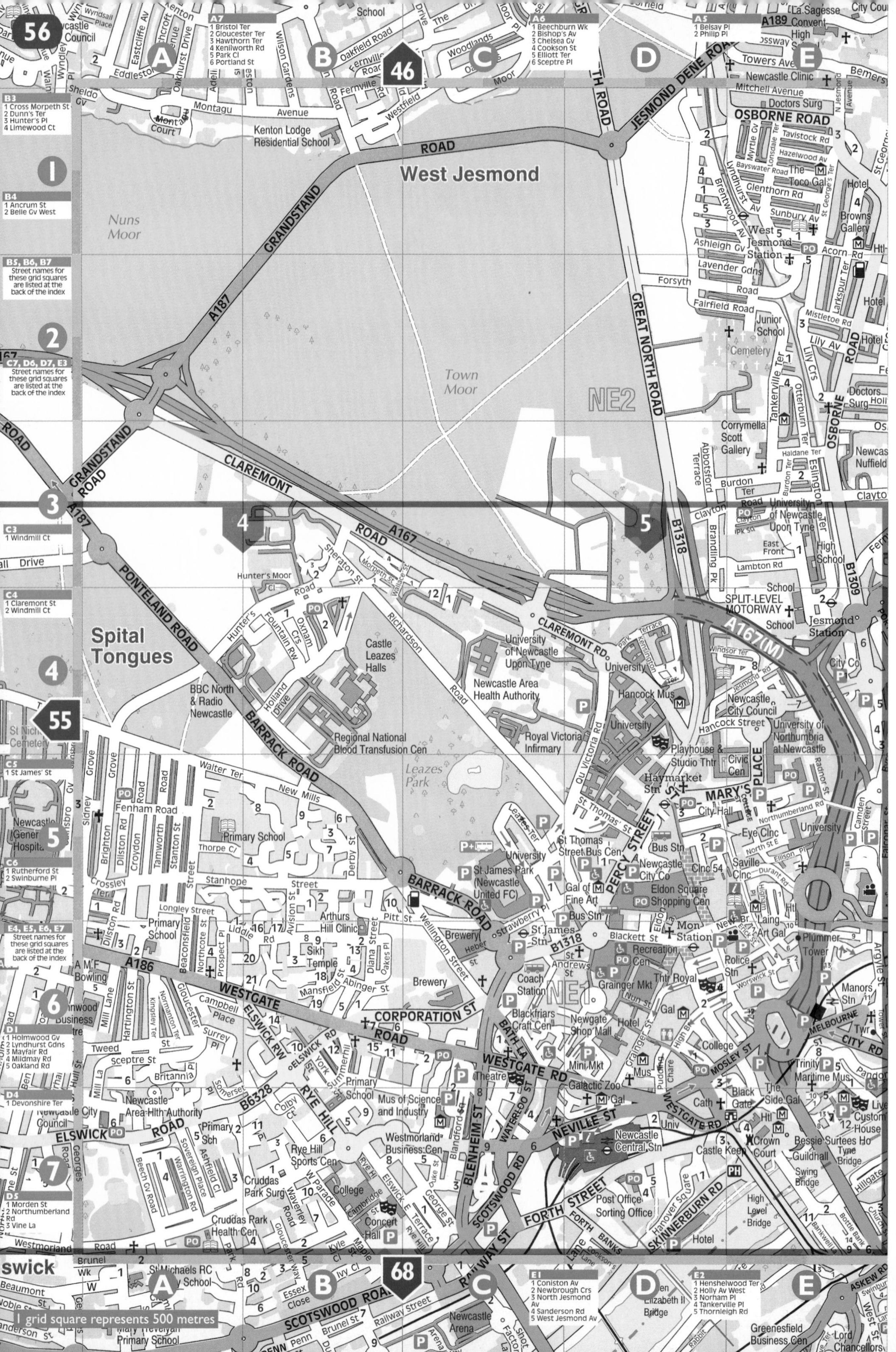
A7
1 Bristol Ter
2 Gloucester Ter
3 Hawthorn Ter
4 Kenilworth Rd
5 Park Cl
6 Portland St
A6
1 Beechburn Wk
2 Bishop's Av
3 Chelsea Gv
4 Cookson St
5 Elliott Ter
6 Sceptre Pl
A5
1 Belsay Pl
2 Philip Pl
B3
1 Cross Morpeth St
2 Dunn's Ter
3 Hunter's Pl
4 Limewood Ct
B4
1 Ancrum St
2 Belle Gv West
B5, B6, B7
Street names for these grid squares are listed at the back of the index
C7, D6, D7, E3
Street names for these grid squares are listed at the back of the index
C3
1 Windmill Ct
C4
1 Claremont St
2 Windmill Ct
C5
1 St James' St
C6
1 Rutherford St
2 Swinburne Pl
E4, E5, E6, E7
Street names for these grid squares are listed at the back of the index
D1
1 Holmwood Gv
2 Lyndhurst Gdns
3 Mayfair Rd
4 Mildmay Rd
5 Oakland Rd
D4
1 Devonshire Ter
D5
1 Morden St
2 Northumberland Rd
3 Vine La
E1
1 Coniston Av
2 Newbrough Crs
3 North Jesmond Av
4 Sanderson Rd
5 West Jesmond Av
E2
1 Henshelwood Ter
2 Holly Av West
3 Norham Pl
4 Tankerville Pl
5 Thornleigh Rd
46
4
5
55
68
West Jesmond
Nuns Moor
Town Moor
NE2
NE1
Spital Tongues
Leazes Park
GRANDSTAND ROAD
CLAREMONT ROAD
GREAT NORTH ROAD
JESMOND DENE ROAD
OSBORNE ROAD
PONTELAND ROAD
BARRACK ROAD
WESTGATE ROAD
WESTGATE RD
CORPORATION ST
ELSWICK ROAD
RYE HILL
SCOTSWOOD ROAD
SCOTSWOOD RD
BLENHEIM ST
NEVILLE ST
FORTH STREET
PERCY STREET
ST MARY'S PLACE
SKINNERBURN RD
RAILWAY ST
A167
A167(M)
A187
A186
B1318
B1309
B6328
SPLIT-LEVEL MOTORWAY
Kenton Lodge Residential School
Montagu Avenue
Castle Leazes Halls
BBC North & Radio Newcastle
Regional National Blood Transfusion Cen
University of Newcastle Upon Tyne
Newcastle Area Health Authority
Royal Victoria Infirmary
Hancock Mus
Playhouse & Studio Thtr
Haymarket Stn
St James Park (Newcastle United FC)
Eldon Square Shopping Cen
Grainger Mkt
Newgate Shop Mall
Coach Station
Blackfriars Craft Cen
Mus of Science and Industry
Newcastle Central Stn
Castle Keep
Crown Court
Bessie Surtees Ho
Guildhall
Tyne Bridge
Swing Bridge
High Level Bridge
Post Office Sorting Office
Westmorland Business Cen
Rye Hill Sports Cen
Cruddas Park Surg
Cruddas Park Health Cen
Concert Hall
Newcastle Arena
Greenesfield Business Cen
Newcastle General Hospital
Newcastle Area Hlth Authority
Newcastle City Council
Arthurs Hill Clinic
Sikh Temple
Brewery
Jesmond Station
West Jesmond Station
Junior School
Cemetery
Corrymella Scott Gallery
Newcastle Clinic
Manors Stn
Plummer Tower
Laing Art Gal
Monument Station
Theatre Royal
Maritime Mus
Custom House
Trinity
The Side Gal
Black Gate
Mary Trevelyan Primary School
St Michaels RC School
1 grid square represents 500 metres

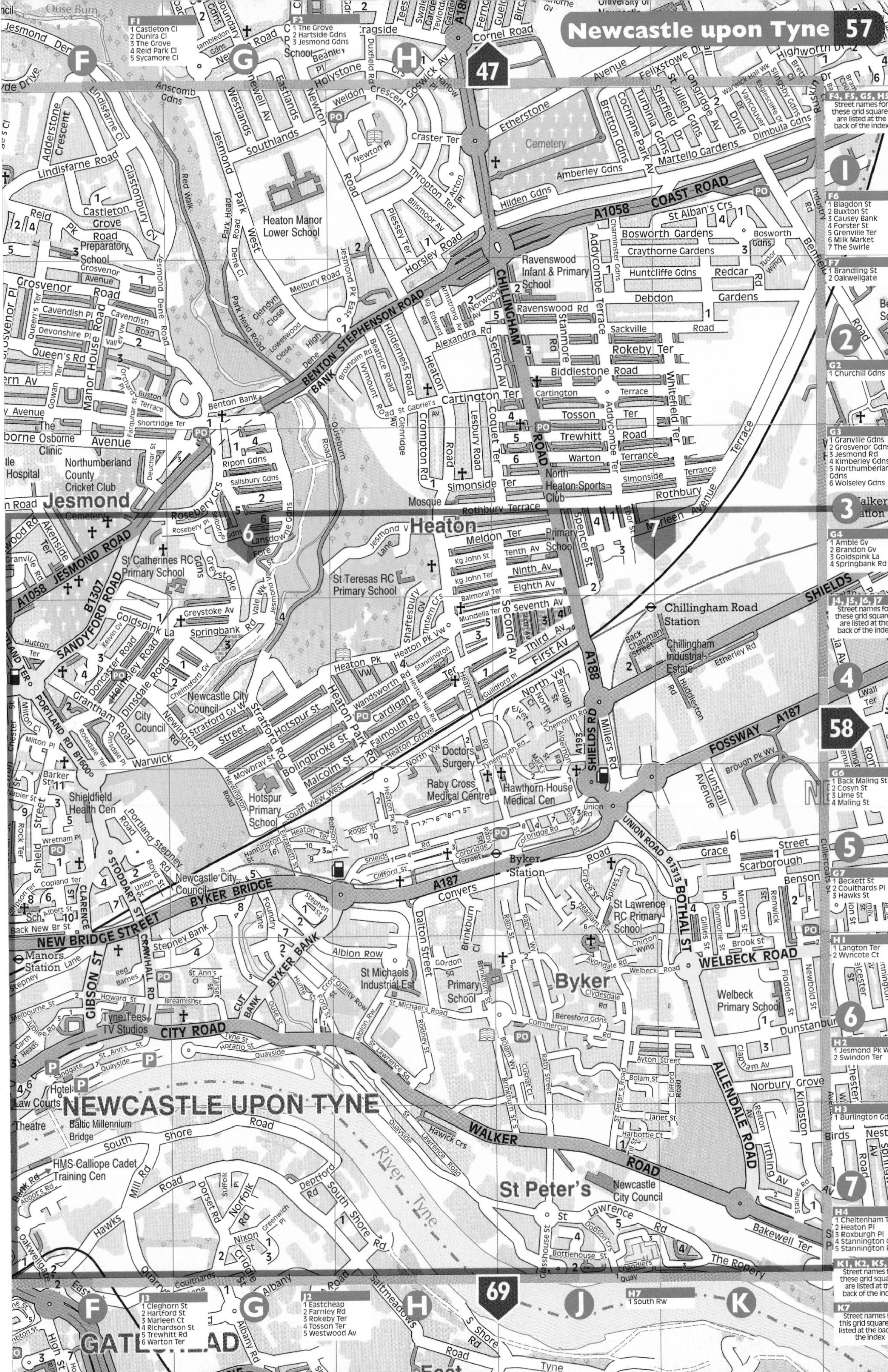
F1
1 Castleton Cl
2 Dunira Cl
3 The Grove
4 Reid Park Cl
5 Sycamore Cl
F2
1 The Grove
2 Hartside Gdns
3 Jesmond Gdns
47
F4, F5, G5, H5
Street names for these grid squares are listed at the back of the index
F6
1 Blagdon St
2 Buxton St
3 Causey Bank
4 Forster St
5 Grenville Ter
6 Milk Market
7 The Swirle
F7
1 Brandling St
2 Oakwellgate
G2
1 Churchill Gdns
G3
1 Granville Gdns
2 Grosvenor Gdns
3 Jesmond Rd
4 Kimberley Gdns
5 Northumberland Gdns
6 Wolseley Gdns
G4
1 Amble Gv
2 Brandon Gv
3 Goldspink La
4 Springbank Rd
J4, J5, J6, J7
Street names for these grid squares are listed at the back of the index
58
G6
1 Back Maling St
2 Cosyn St
3 Lime St
4 Maling St
G7
1 Beckett St
2 Coulthards Pl
3 Hawks St
H1
1 Langton Ter
2 Wyncote Ct
H2
1 Jesmond Pk West
2 Swindon Ter
H3
1 Burlington Gdns
H4
1 Cheltenham Ter
2 Heaton Pl
3 Roxburgh Pl
4 Stannington Gv
5 Stannington Pl
K1, K2, K5, K6
Street names for these grid squares are listed at the back of the index
K7
Street names for this grid square are listed at the back of the index
J3
1 Cleghorn St
2 Hartford St
3 Marleen Ct
4 Richardson St
5 Trewhitt Rd
6 Warton Ter
J2
1 Eastcheap
2 Farnley Rd
3 Rokeby Ter
4 Tosson Ter
5 Westwood Av
H7
1 South Rw
69
Jesmond
Heaton
Byker
St Peter's
NEWCASTLE UPON TYNE
GATESHEAD
Heaton Manor Lower School
Ravenswood Infant & Primary School
Northumberland County Cricket Club
St Catherines RC Primary School
St Teresas RC Primary School
Chillingham Road Station
Chillingham Industrial Estate
Newcastle City Council
Hotspur Primary School
Raby Cross Medical Centre
Hawthorn House Medical Cen
Byker Station
St Lawrence RC Primary School
St Michaels Industrial Est
Welbeck Primary School
Tyne Tees TV Studios
Manors Station
Shieldfield Health Cen
Baltic Millennium Bridge
HMS Calliope Cadet Training Cen
Law Courts
Theatre
Cemetery
A1058 COAST ROAD
BENTON BANK STEPHENSON ROAD
CHILLINGHAM ROAD
A1058 JESMOND ROAD
SANDYFORD ROAD
NEW BRIDGE STREET
BYKER BRIDGE
CITY ROAD
WALKER ROAD
FOSSWAY A187
WELBECK ROAD
ALLENDALE ROAD
BOTHAL ST
UNION ROAD B1313
River Tyne

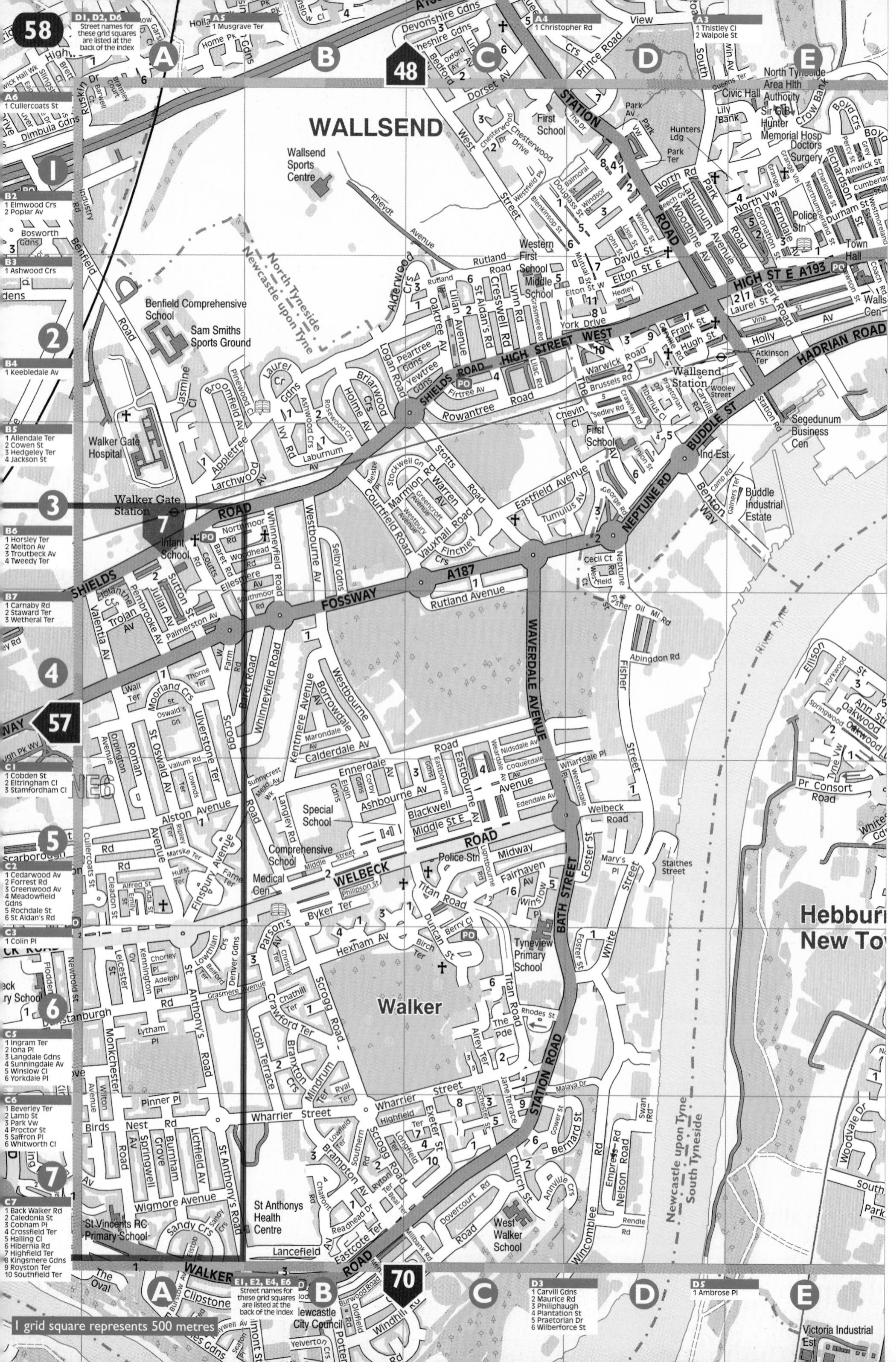
D1, D2, D6 Street names for these grid squares are listed at the back of the index
A5 1 Musgrave Ter
A4 1 Christopher Rd
A3 1 Thistley Cl 2 Walpole St
A6 1 Cullercoats St
B2 1 Elmwood Crs 2 Poplar Av
B3 1 Ashwood Crs
B4 1 Keebledale Av
B5 1 Allendale Ter 2 Cowen St 3 Hedgeley Ter 4 Jackson St
B6 1 Horsley Ter 2 Melton Av 3 Troutbeck Av 4 Tweedy Ter
B7 1 Carnaby Rd 2 Staward Ter 3 Wetheral Ter
C1 1 Cobden St 2 Eltringham Cl 3 Stamfordham Cl
C2 1 Cedarwood Av 2 Forrest Rd 3 Greenwood Av 4 Meadowfield Gdns 5 Rochdale St 6 St Aidan's Rd
C3 1 Colin Pl
C5 1 Ingram Ter 2 Iona Pl 3 Langdale Gdns 4 Sunningdale Av 5 Winslow Cl 6 Yorkdale Pl
C6 1 Beverley Ter 2 Lamb St 3 Park Vw 4 Proctor St 5 Saffron Pl 6 Whitworth Cl
C7 1 Back Walker Rd 2 Caledonia St 3 Cobham Pl 4 Crossfield Ter 5 Halling Cl 6 Hibernia Rd 7 Highfield Ter 8 Kingsmere Gdns 9 Royston Ter 10 Southfield Ter
E1, E2, E4, E6 Street names for these grid squares are listed at the back of the index
D3 1 Carvill Gdns 2 Maurice Rd 3 Philiphaugh 4 Plantation St 5 Praetorian St 6 Wilberforce St
D5 1 Ambrose Pl
48
57
70
WALLSEND
Wallsend Sports Centre
North Tyneside
Newcastle upon Tyne
Benfield Comprehensive School
Sam Smiths Sports Ground
Walker Gate Hospital
Walker Gate Station
Western First School
Middle School
First School
North Tyneside Area Hlth Authority
Civic Hall
Sir G B Hunter Memorial Hosp
Doctors Surgery
Police Stn
Town Hall
Wallsend Station
Segedunum Business Cen
Ind Est
Buddle Industrial Estate
HIGH STREET WEST
HIGH ST E A193
HADRIAN ROAD
BUDDLE ST
NEPTUNE RD
STATION ROAD
SHIELDS ROAD
FOSSWAY
A187
WAVERDALE AVENUE
WELBECK ROAD
BATH STREET
WALKER ROAD
Special School
Comprehensive School
Medical Cen
Police Stn
Tyneview Primary School
Walker
St Anthonys Health Centre
St Vincents RC Primary School
West Walker School
River Tyne
Newcastle upon Tyne
South Tyneside
Hebburn New Town
Victoria Industrial Est
Newcastle City Council
NE6
1 grid square represents 500 metres

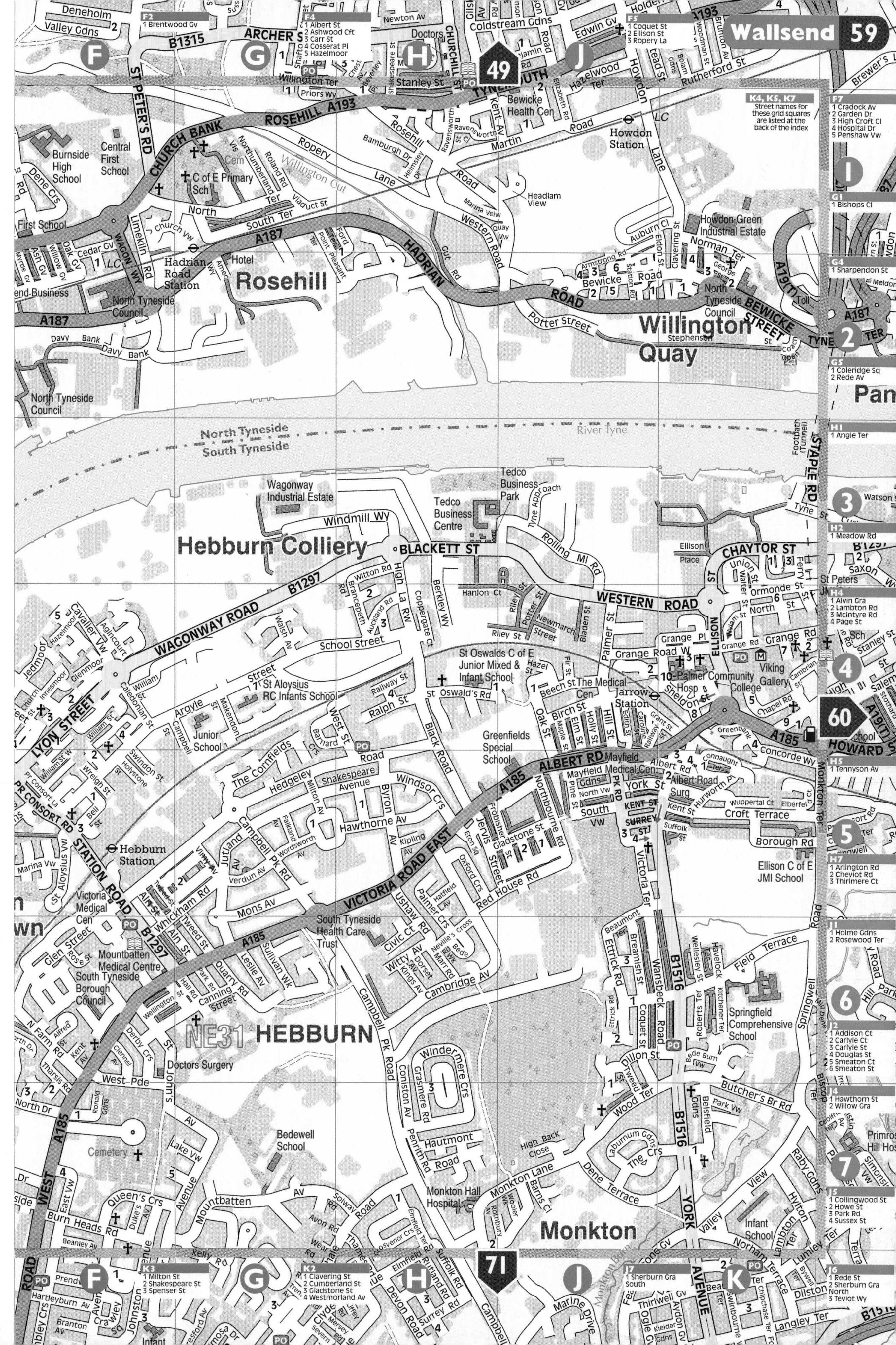
F2
1 Brentwood Gv
F4
1 Albert St
2 Ashwood Cft
3 Carr St
4 Cosserat Pl
5 Hazelmoor
F5
1 Coquet St
2 Ellison St
3 Ropery La
49
K4, K5, K7
Street names for these grid squares are listed at the back of the index
F7
1 Cradock Av
2 Garden Dr
3 High Croft Cl
4 Hospital Dr
5 Penshaw Vw
G1
1 Bishops Cl
G4
1 Sharpendon St
G5
1 Coleridge Sq
2 Rede Av
H1
1 Angle Ter
H2
1 Meadow Rd
H4
1 Alvin Gra
2 Lambton Rd
3 Mcintyre Rd
4 Page St
H5
1 Tennyson Av
H7
1 Arlington Rd
2 Cheviot Rd
3 Thirlimere Ct
J1
1 Holme Gdns
2 Rosewood Ter
J2
1 Addison Ct
2 Carlyle Ct
3 Carlyle St
4 Douglas St
5 Smeaton Ct
6 Smeaton St
J4
1 Hawthorn St
2 Willow Gra
J5
1 Collingwood St
2 Howe St
3 Park Rd
4 Sussex St
J6
1 Rede St
2 Sherburn Gra North
3 Teviot Wy
J7
1 Sherburn Gra South
K2
1 Clavering St
2 Cumberland St
3 Gladstone St
4 Westmorland Av
K3
1 Milton St
2 Shakespeare St
3 Spenser St
60
71
Rosehill
Willington Quay
Hebburn Colliery
HEBBURN
NE31
Monkton
North Tyneside
South Tyneside
River Tyne
Burnside High School
Central First School
C of E Primary Sch
Hadrian Road Station
North Tyneside Council
Howdon Station
Headlam View
Howdon Green Industrial Estate
Wagonway Industrial Estate
Tedco Business Centre
Tedco Business Park
St Oswalds C of E Junior Mixed & Infant School
St Aloysius RC Infants School
Junior School
Jarrow Station
Palmer Community Hosp
College
Viking Gallery
Greenfields Special School
Mayfield Medical Cen
Albert Road Surg
Ellison C of E JMI School
Hebburn Station
Victoria Medical Cen
Mountbatten Medical Centre
South Tyneside Borough Council
South Tyneside Health Care Trust
Springfield Comprehensive School
Doctors Surgery
Cemetery
Bedewell School
Monkton Hall Hospital
Infant School
A187
A185
A193
B1297
B1315
B1516
A19(T)
HADRIAN ROAD
VICTORIA ROAD EAST
WAGONWAY ROAD
STATION ROAD
ALBERT RD
BLACKETT ST
CHAYTOR ST
WESTERN ROAD
YORK AVENUE
HOWARD ST
STAPLE RD
CHURCH BANK
ROSEHILL
ST PETER'S RD
LYON STREET
PR CONSORT RD
WEST ROAD

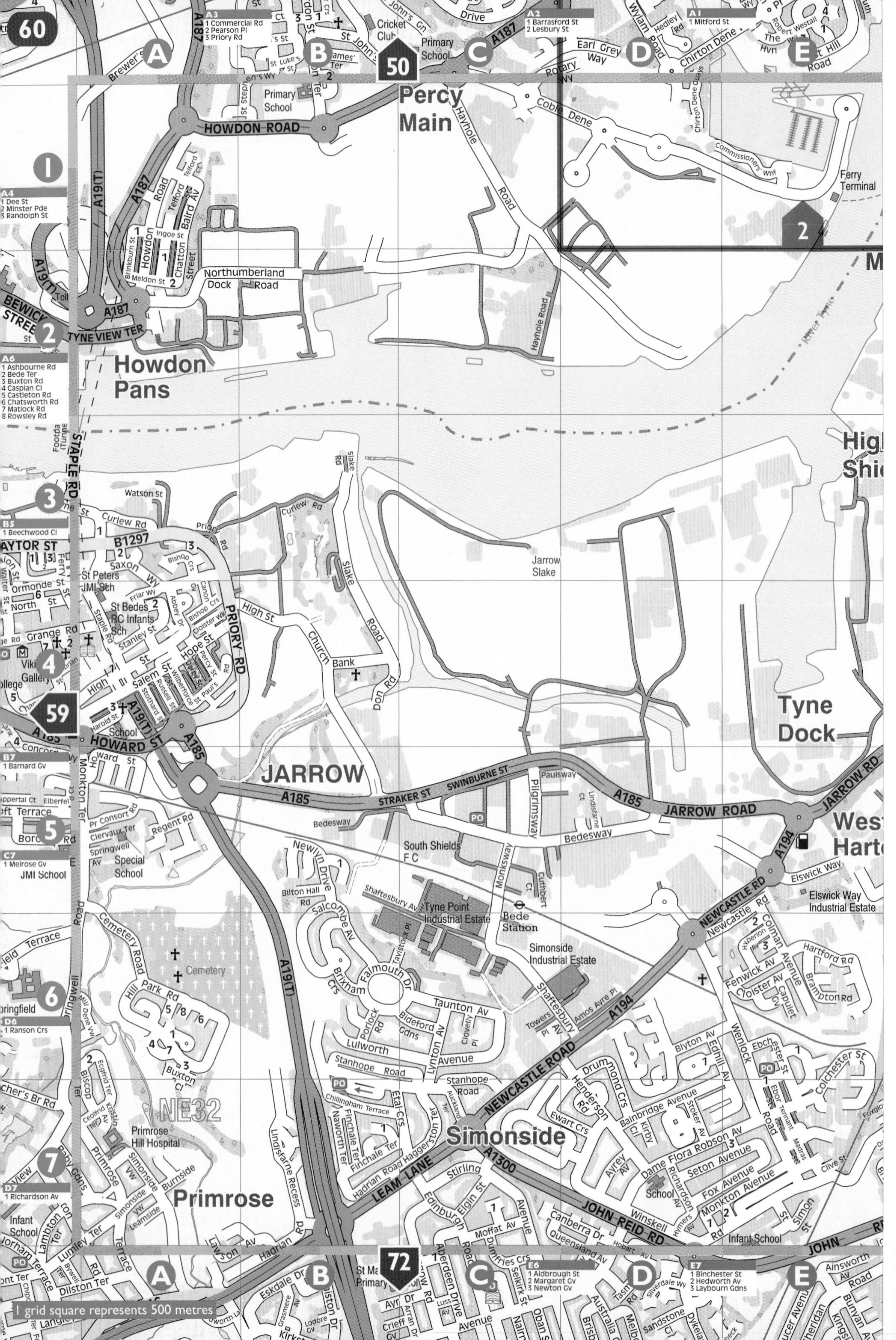
60
50
59
72
2
A
B
C
D
E
1
2
3
4
5
6
7
Percy Main
Howdon Pans
JARROW
Tyne Dock
Simonside
Primrose
Jarrow Slake
River Tyne
NE32
HOWDON ROAD
Northumberland Dock Road
Hayhole Road
Coble Dene
Commissioners' Whf
Ferry Terminal
TYNE VIEW TER
STAPLE RD
PRIORY RD
HOWARD ST
Slake Road
Church Bank
Don Rd
High St
STRAKER ST
SWINBURNE ST
JARROW ROAD
Bedesway
Pilgrimsway
Monksway
South Shields F C
Tyne Point Industrial Estate
Bede Station
Simonside Industrial Estate
Elswick Way Industrial Estate
NEWCASTLE RD
NEWCASTLE ROAD
JOHN REID RD
LEAM LANE
Cemetery
Cemetery Road
Primrose Hill Hospital
Special School
Infant School
St Peters JMI Sch
St Bedes RC Infants Sch
Primary School
Cricket Club
A3 1 Commercial Rd 2 Pearson Pl 3 Priory Rd
A2 1 Barrasford St 2 Lesbury St
A1 1 Mitford St
A4 1 Dee St 2 Minster Pde 3 Randolph St
A6 1 Ashbourne Rd 2 Bede Ter 3 Buxton Rd 4 Caspian Cl 5 Castleton Rd 6 Chatsworth Rd 7 Matlock Rd 8 Rowsley Rd
B5 1 Beechwood Cl
B7 1 Barnard Gv
C7 1 Melrose Gv
D6 1 Ranson Crs
D7 1 Richardson Av
E6 1 Aldbrough St 2 Margaret Gv 3 Newton Gv
E7 1 Binchester St 2 Hedworth Av 3 Laybourn Gdns
1 grid square represents 500 metres

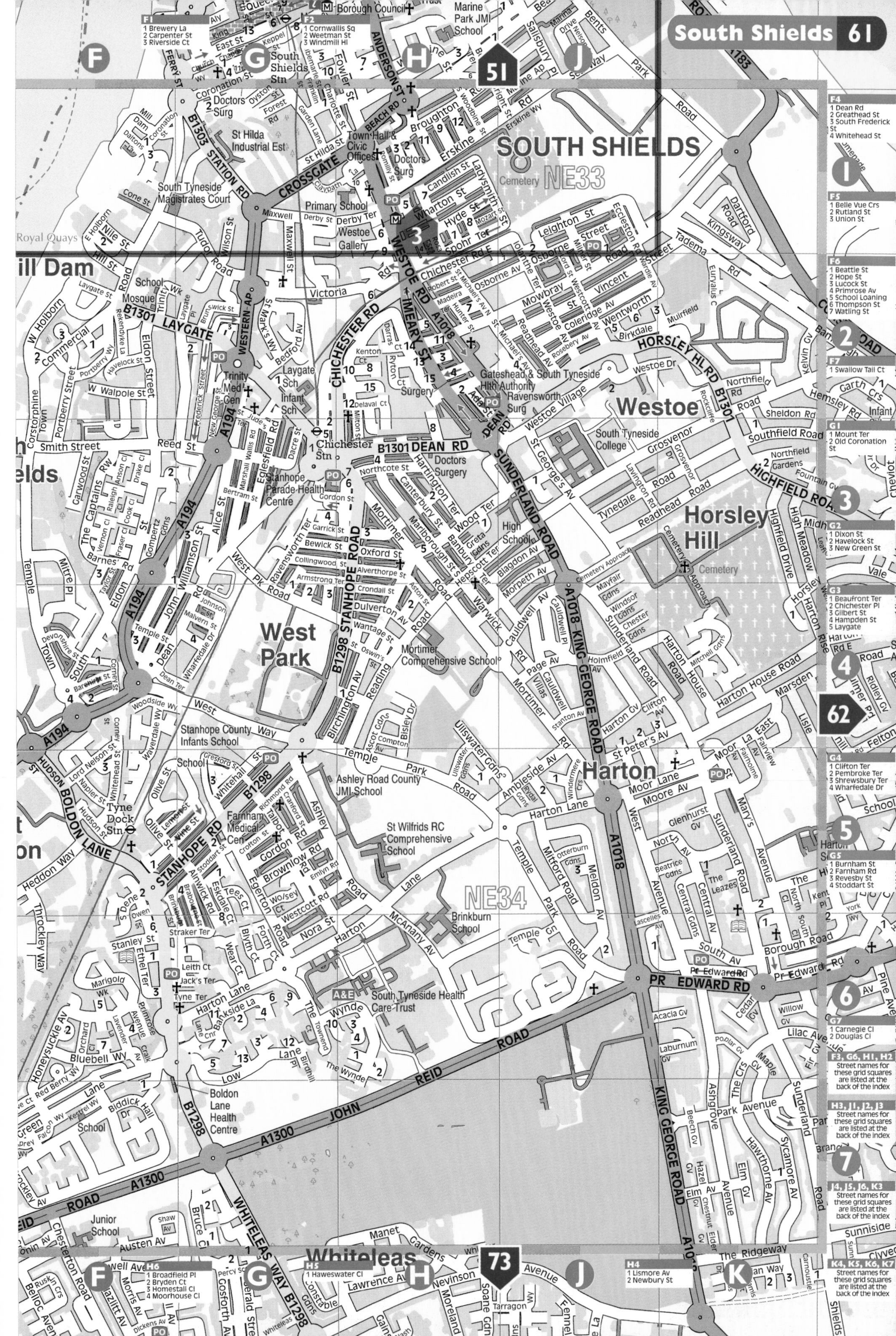

F1
1 Brewery La
2 Carpenter St
3 Riverside Ct
F2
1 Cornwallis Sq
2 Weetman St
3 Windmill Hl
F4
1 Dean Rd
2 Greathead St
3 South Frederick St
4 Whitehead St
F5
1 Belle Vue Crs
2 Rutland St
3 Union St
F6
1 Beattie St
2 Hope St
3 Lucock St
4 Primrose Av
5 School Loaning
6 Thompson St
7 Watling St
F7
1 Swallow Tail Ct
G1
1 Mount Ter
2 Old Coronation St
G2
1 Dixon St
2 Havelock St
3 New Green St
G3
1 Beaufront Ter
2 Chichester Pl
3 Gilbert St
4 Hampden St
5 Laygate
G4
1 Clifton Ter
2 Pembroke Ter
3 Shrewsbury Ter
4 Wharfedale Dr
G5
1 Burnham St
2 Farnham Rd
3 Revesby St
4 Stoddart St
G7
1 Carnegie Cl
2 Douglas Cl
F3, G6, H1, H2
Street names for these grid squares are listed at the back of the index
H3, J1, J2, J3
Street names for these grid squares are listed at the back of the index
J4, J5, J6, K3
Street names for these grid squares are listed at the back of the index
K4, K5, K6, K7
Street names for these grid squares are listed at the back of the index
H4
1 Lismore Av
2 Newbury St
H5
1 Haweswater Cl
H6
1 Broadfield Pl
2 Bryden Ct
3 Homestall Cl
4 Moorhouse Cl
51
62
73
SOUTH SHIELDS
NE33
NE34
Westoe
Horsley Hill
West Park
Harton
Whiteleas
Borough Council
Marine Park JMI School
South Shields Stn
St Hilda Industrial Est
Town Hall & Civic Offices
Doctors Surg
South Tyneside Magistrates Court
Primary School
Westoe Gallery
Cemetery
Mosque
Trinity Med Cen
Laygate Sch
Infant Sch
Chichester Stn
Surgery
Gateshead & South Tyneside Hlth Authority
Ravensworth Surg
South Tyneside College
Stanhope Parade Health Centre
Doctors Surgery
High School
Mortimer Comprehensive School
Stanhope County Infants School
Ashley Road County JMI School
St Wilfrids RC Comprehensive School
Brinkburn School
Farnham Medical Cen
Tyne Dock Stn
South Tyneside Health Care Trust
Boldon Lane Health Centre
Junior School
Royal Quays
CROSSGATE
STATION RD
WESTERN AP
B1301 LAYGATE
CHICHESTER RD
WESTOE RD
B1301 DEAN RD
SUNDERLAND ROAD
A1018 KING GEORGE ROAD
B1298 STANHOPE ROAD
STANHOPE RD
HUDSON BOLDON LANE
PR EDWARD RD
A1300 JOHN REID ROAD
WHITELEAS WAY B1298
HORSLEY HL RD B1301
HIGHFIELD ROAD

A6
1 Crossway
2 Gloucester Pl
A5
1 Bishop Ramsay Ct
2 Pinewood Vls
A2
1 Bideford Gdns
B3
1 Craster Av
B4
1 Horsley Hill Sq
B5
1 Charles Baker Wk
B6
1 Ashridge Cl
2 Carden Av
3 Flaunden Cl
4 Shilton Cl
5 Watson Pl
C4
1 Hampshire Wy
2 Redwell Ct
C5
1 White Horse Vw
D5
1 Quarry La
Trow Point
The Leas
Frenchman's Bay
Promenade
COAST ROAD
A183
Marsden
Cleadon Park
Cheviot County Junior Mixed School
South Tyneside Area Hlth Authority
South Tyneside Metropolitan Borough Council
Harton School
Infant School
MARSDEN LANE
B1301
CHEVIOT RD
HIGHFIELD ROAD
PRINCE EDWARD ROAD
PRINCE EDWARD ROAD EAST
A1300
Marsden Hall
Lizard Lane
Great North Forest Trail
Sunniside Farm
Cleador Hills Farm
Lizards Farm
61
74
1 grid square represents 500 metres

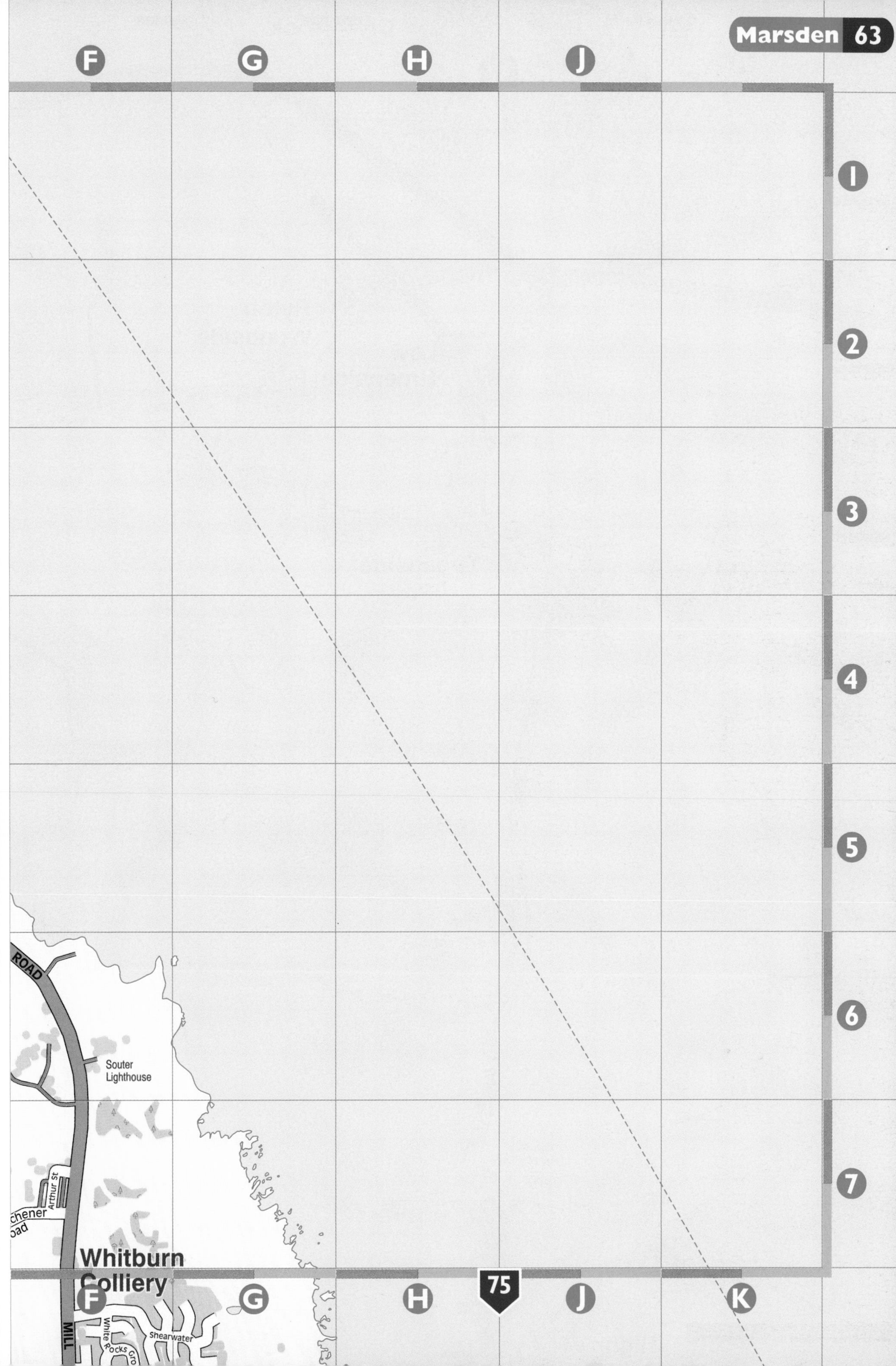
F
G
H
J
1
2
3
4
5
6
7
ROAD
Souter
Lighthouse
Arthur St
chener
oad
Whitburn
Colliery
MILL
White Rocks Gro
Shearwater
75
K

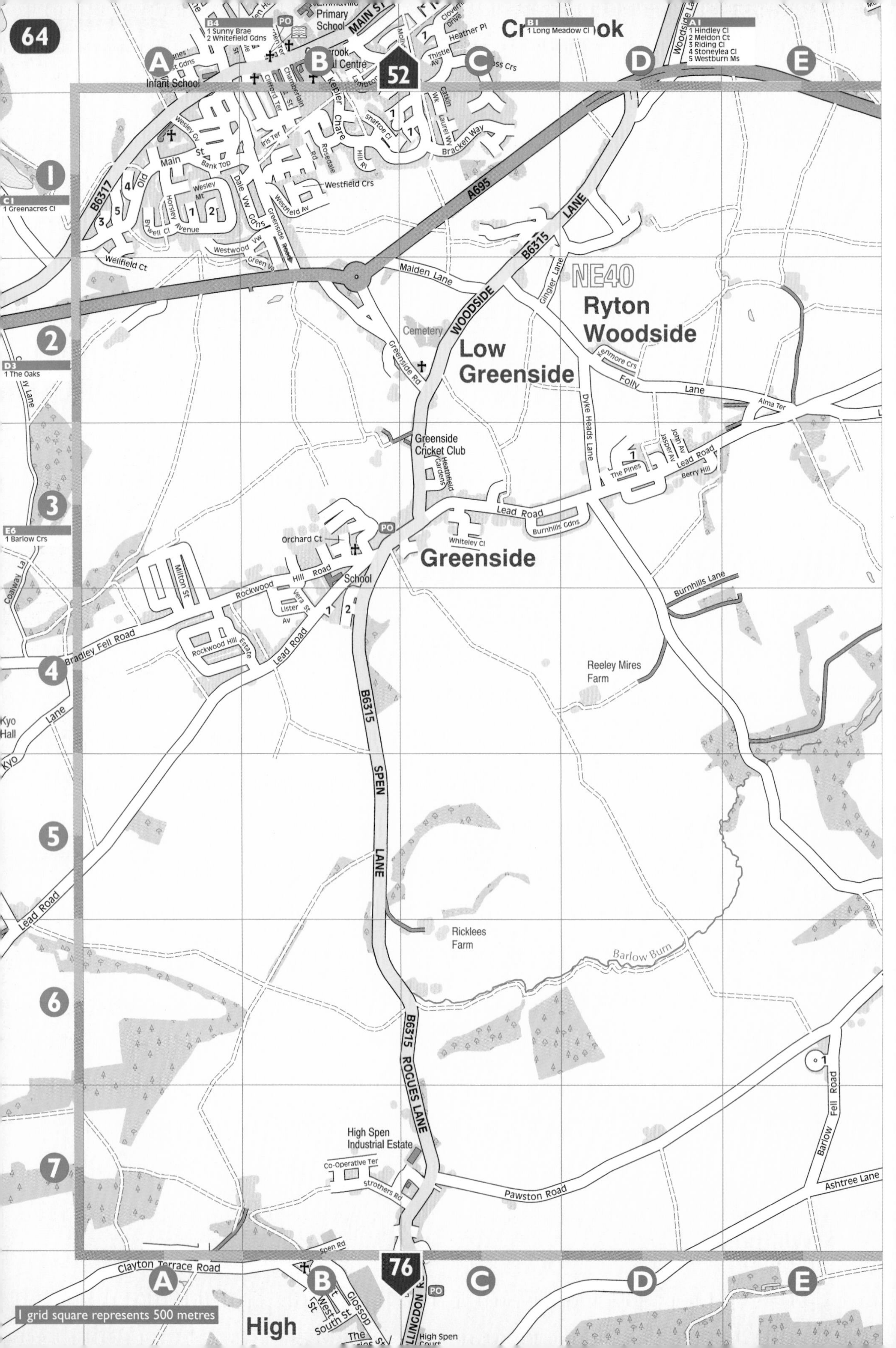
52
76
B4
1 Sunny Brae
2 Whitefield Gdns
B1
1 Long Meadow Cl
A1
1 Hindley Cl
2 Meldon Ct
3 Riding Cl
4 Stoneylea Cl
5 Westburn Ms
C1
1 Greenacres Cl
D3
1 The Oaks
E6
1 Barlow Crs
Primary School
Infant School
MAIN ST
A695
B6317
B6315
WOODSIDE LANE
NE40
Ryton Woodside
Low Greenside
Greenside
Cemetery
Greenside Cricket Club
Heathfield Gardens
Lead Road
Burnhills Gdns
Whiteley Cl
Orchard Ct
School
Rockwood Hill Road
Milton St
Lister Av
Vera St
Rockwood Hill Estate
Bradley Fell Road
Maiden Lane
Gingler Lane
Kenmore Crs
Folly Lane
Alma Ter
Dyke Heads Lane
John Av
Jasper Av
The Pines
Berry Hill
Burnhills Lane
Reeley Mires Farm
Kyo Lane
Kyo Hall
Coalway La
SPEN LANE
B6315 ROGUES LANE
Ricklees Farm
Barlow Burn
High Spen Industrial Estate
Co-Operative Ter
Strothers Rd
Pawston Road
Barlow Fell Road
Ashtree Lane
Spen Rd
Clayton Terrace Road
High
Glossop
West St
South St
High Spen Court
Westfield Crs
Westfield Av
Wesley Gv
Wesley Mt
Horsley Avenue
Bywell Cl
Wellfield Ct
Westwood Vw
Green Va
Greenside Road
Dale Vw Gdns
Bank Top
Old Main St
Kepler Chare
Rosedale Rd
Hill Rl
Iris Ter
Shaftoe Cl
Chamberlain St
Clifford Ter
Catkin Wk
Laurel Wy
Bracken Way
Thistle Av
Heather Pl
Clover Drive
Greenside Rd
1 grid square represents 500 metres

Stargate
Blaydon Burn
Winlaton
Barlow
Low Thornley
Stephen's Hall
Norman's Riding Farm
Thornley Bank
St Thomas More RC (aided) Comprehensive School
Hollyhurst Medical Cen
West Lane Junior & Infant School
Winlaton Mill
Derwent Walk Country Park
Stargate Lane
Beweshill Lane
Herd House La
Ridge Road
Burn Road
Barlow Lane
Garesfield Lane
Thornley Lane
Mill Lane
Scotland Head
Church Street
North Street
Hollinhill
A694
H4 1 Farndale Cl 2 Waverley Cl
J1 1 Beweshill La
J3 Street names for this grid square are listed at the back of the index
I4 1 Barlowfield Cl 2 Brandon Cl 3 Burnthouse Cl 4 Cresswell Cl 5 Lyndhurst Cl 6 Stampley Cl 7 Whinney Cl 8 Woodburn Cl
K2 1 Lanercost Av 2 Westway
K3 1 Back St 2 Branch St 3 Mount Pleasant 4 Northlands 5 Ramsay St 6 Weatherside
K4 Street names for this grid square are listed at the back of the index
53
66
77

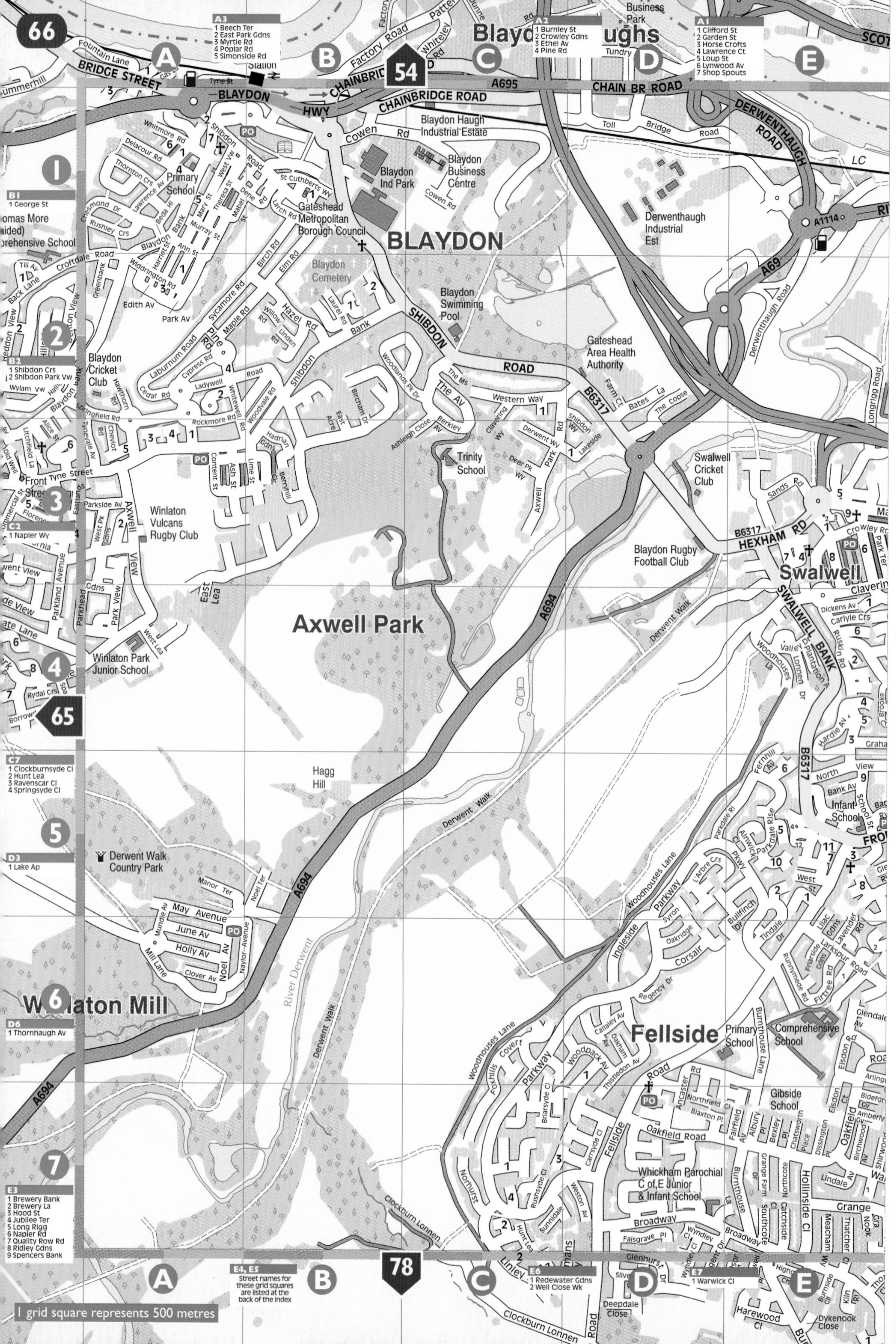

66
A3
1 Beech Ter
2 East Park Gdns
3 Myrtle Rd
4 Poplar Rd
5 Simonside Rd
A2
1 Burnley St
2 Crowley Gdns
3 Ethel Av
4 Pine Rd
A1
1 Clifford St
2 Garden St
3 Horse Crofts
4 Lawrence Ct
5 Loup St
6 Lynwood Av
7 Shop Spouts
54
A
B
C
D
E
Blaydon Haughs
Blaydon Business Park
Fountain Lane
BRIDGE STREET
Station
Tyne St
BLAYDON HWY
CHAINBRIDGE ROAD
A695
CHAIN BR ROAD
DERWENTHAUGH ROAD
Toll Bridge Road
Cowen Rd
Blaydon Haugh Industrial Estate
Blaydon Ind Park
Blaydon Business Centre
Derwenthaugh Industrial Est
A1114
A69
Derwenthaugh Road
LC
1
B1
1 George St
Thomas More (Aided) Comprehensive School
Gateshead Metropolitan Borough Council
BLAYDON
Blaydon Cemetery
Primary School
Blaydon Swimming Pool
SHIBDON ROAD
Gateshead Area Health Authority
B6317
2
B2
1 Shibdon Crs
2 Shibdon Park Vw
Blaydon Cricket Club
Trinity School
Swalwell Cricket Club
HEXHAM RD
Blaydon Rugby Football Club
Swalwell
SWALWELL BANK
3
C2
1 Napier Wy
Winlaton Vulcans Rugby Club
Axwell View
Axwell Park
A694
Derwent Walk
4
Winlaton Park Junior School
65
C7
1 Clockburnsyde Cl
2 Hunt Lea
3 Ravenscar Cl
4 Springsyde Cl
Hagg Hill
5
D3
1 Lake Ap
Derwent Walk Country Park
Manor Ter
May Avenue
June Av
Holly Av
Clover Av
Noel Av
Naylor Avenue
Mill Lane
River Derwent
Woodhouses Lane
Parkway
Ingleside
Corsair
Regency Dr
Infant School
6
Winlaton Mill
D6
1 Thornhaugh Av
Fellside
Primary School
Comprehensive School
Gibside School
Oakfield Road
Whickham Parochial C of E Junior & Infant School
Broadway
Clockburn Lonnen
7
E3
1 Brewery Bank
2 Brewery La
3 Hood St
4 Jubilee Ter
5 Long Rigg
6 Napier Rd
7 Quality Row Rd
8 Ridley Gdns
9 Spencers Bank
78
E4, E5
Street names for these grid squares are listed at the back of the index
E6
1 Redewater Gdns
2 Well Close Wk
E7
1 Warwick Cl
1 grid square represents 500 metres

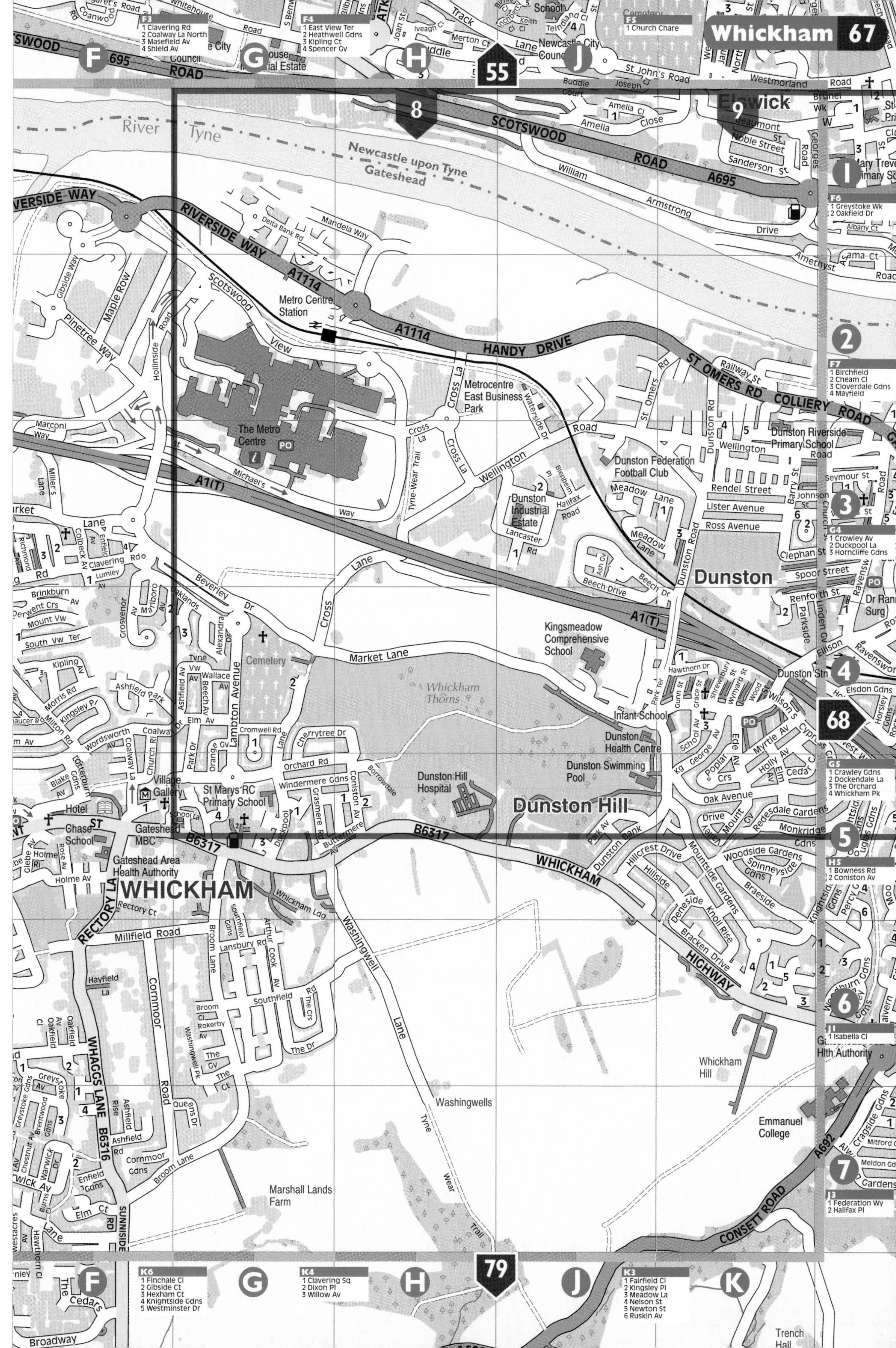
F3
1 Clavering Rd
2 Coalway La North
3 Masefield Av
4 Shield Av
F4
1 East View Ter
2 Heathwell Gdns
3 Kipling Ct
4 Spencer Gv
F5
1 Church Chare
F6
1 Greystoke Wk
2 Oakfield Dr
F7
1 Birchfield
2 Cheam Cl
3 Cloverdale Gdns
4 Mayfield
G4
1 Crowley Av
2 Duckpool La
3 Horncliffe Gdns
G5
1 Crawley Gdns
2 Dockendale La
3 The Orchard
4 Whickham Pk
H5
1 Bowness Rd
2 Coniston Av
J1
1 Isabella Cl
J3
1 Federation Wy
2 Halifax Pl
K6
1 Finchale Cl
2 Gibside Ct
3 Hexham Ct
4 Knightside Gdns
5 Westminster Dr
K4
1 Clavering Sq
2 Dixon Pl
3 Willow Av
K3
1 Fairfield Cl
2 Kingsley Pl
3 Meadow La
4 Nelson St
5 Newton St
6 Ruskin Av
55
8
9
68
79
F
G
H
J
K
1
2
3
4
5
6
7
River Tyne
Newcastle upon Tyne
Gateshead
Elswick
SCOTSWOOD ROAD A695
William Armstrong Drive
RIVERSIDE WAY A1114
HANDY DRIVE
ST OMERS RD
COLLIERY ROAD
Metro Centre Station
The Metro Centre
Metrocentre East Business Park
Dunston Federation Football Club
Dunston Industrial Estate
Dunston
Kingsmeadow Comprehensive School
Dunston Riverside Primary School
Whickham Thorns
Cemetery
Market Lane
Dunston Hill Hospital
Dunston Health Centre
Dunston Swimming Pool
Dunston Hill
Infant School
St Marys RC Primary School
Village Gallery
Gateshead MBC
Chase School
Gateshead Area Health Authority
WHICKHAM
B6317
WHICKHAM HIGHWAY
Millfield Road
Cornmoor Road
Broom Lane
Washingwell Lane
Washingwells
Tyne Wear Trail
Marshall Lands Farm
Whickham Hill
Emmanuel College
CONSETT ROAD
A692
WHAGGS LANE B6316
RECTORY LA
SUNNISIDE RD
A1(T)
Broadway
Trench Hall

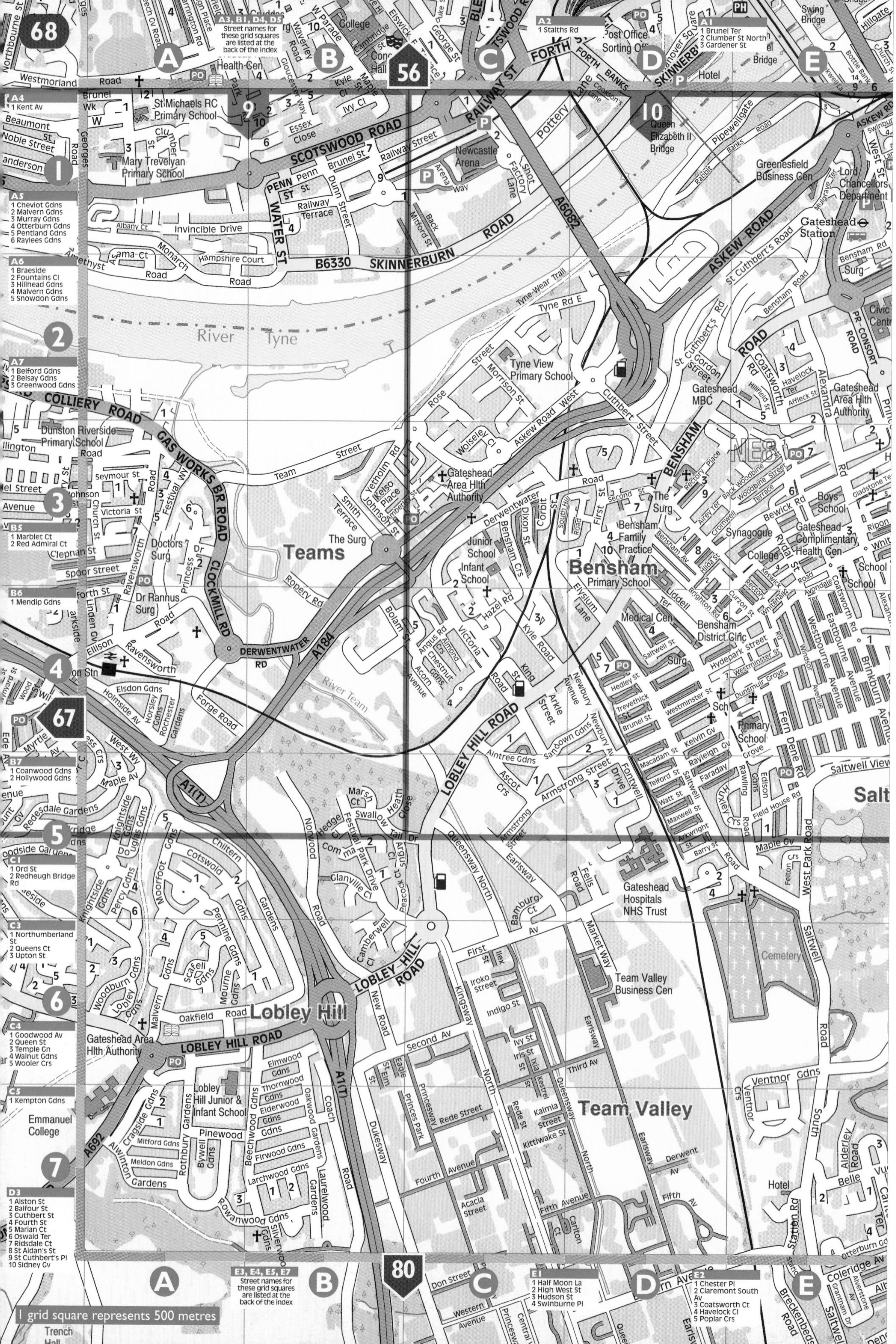

68
56
9
10
67
80
A
B
C
D
E
1
2
3
4
5
6
7
A3, B1, D4, D5
Street names for these grid squares are listed at the back of the index
A2
1 Staiths Rd
A1
1 Brunel Ter
2 Clumber St North
3 Gardener St
A4
1 Kent Av
A5
1 Cheviot Gdns
2 Malvern Gdns
3 Murray Gdns
4 Otterburn Gdns
5 Pentland Gdns
6 Raylees Gdns
A6
1 Braeside
2 Fountains Cl
3 Hillhead Gdns
4 Malvern Gdns
5 Snowdon Gdns
A7
1 Belford Gdns
2 Belsay Gdns
3 Greenwood Gdns
B5
1 Marblet Ct
2 Red Admiral Ct
B6
1 Mendip Gdns
B7
1 Coanwood Gdns
2 Hollywood Gdns
C1
1 Ord St
2 Redheugh Bridge Rd
C3
1 Northumberland St
2 Queens Ct
3 Upton St
C4
1 Goodwood Av
2 Queen St
3 Temple Gn
4 Walnut Gdns
5 Wooler Crs
C5
1 Kempton Gdns
D3
1 Alston St
2 Balfour St
3 Cuthbert St
4 Fourth St
5 Marian Ct
6 Oswald Ter
7 Ridsdale Ct
8 St Aidan's St
9 St Cuthbert's Pl
10 Sidney Gv
E3, E4, E5, E7
Street names for these grid squares are listed at the back of the index
E1
1 Half Moon La
2 High West St
3 Hudson St
4 Swinburne Pl
E2
1 Chester Pl
2 Claremont South Av
3 Coatsworth Ct
4 Havelock Cl
5 Poplar Crs
1 grid square represents 500 metres
Westmorland Road
College
Health Cen
St Michaels RC Primary School
Mary Trevelyan Primary School
SCOTSWOOD ROAD
Railway Street
RAILWAY ST
FORTH BANKS
Post Office Sorting Off
Newcastle Arena
Queen Elizabeth II Bridge
Swing Bridge
Greenesfield Business Cen
Lord Chancellors Department
Gateshead Station
Invincible Drive
Hampshire Court
WATER ST
B6330 SKINNERBURN ROAD
A6082
ASKEW ROAD
River Tyne
COLLIERY ROAD
GAS WORKS BR ROAD
CLOCKMILL RD
Dunston Riverside Primary School
Tyne View Primary School
Askew Road West
Team Street
Teams
The Surg
Gateshead Area Hlth Authority
Gateshead MBC
Gateshead Area Hlth Authority
BENSHAM
Bensham
Bensham Family Practice
Primary School
Medical Cen
Bensham District Clnc
Synagogue
College
Boys School
Gateshead Complimentary Health Cen
School
Primary School
Junior School
Infant School
Doctors Surg
Dr Rannus Surg
DERWENTWATER RD
A184
River Team
LOBLEY HILL ROAD
A1(T)
Lobley Hill
Gateshead Area Hlth Authority
Lobley Hill Junior & Infant School
Emmanuel College
A692
Gateshead Hospitals NHS Trust
Team Valley Business Cen
Team Valley
Kingsway
Queensway North
Cemetery
Saltwell Road
Saltwell View
Ventnor Gdns
Hotel
Trench Hall

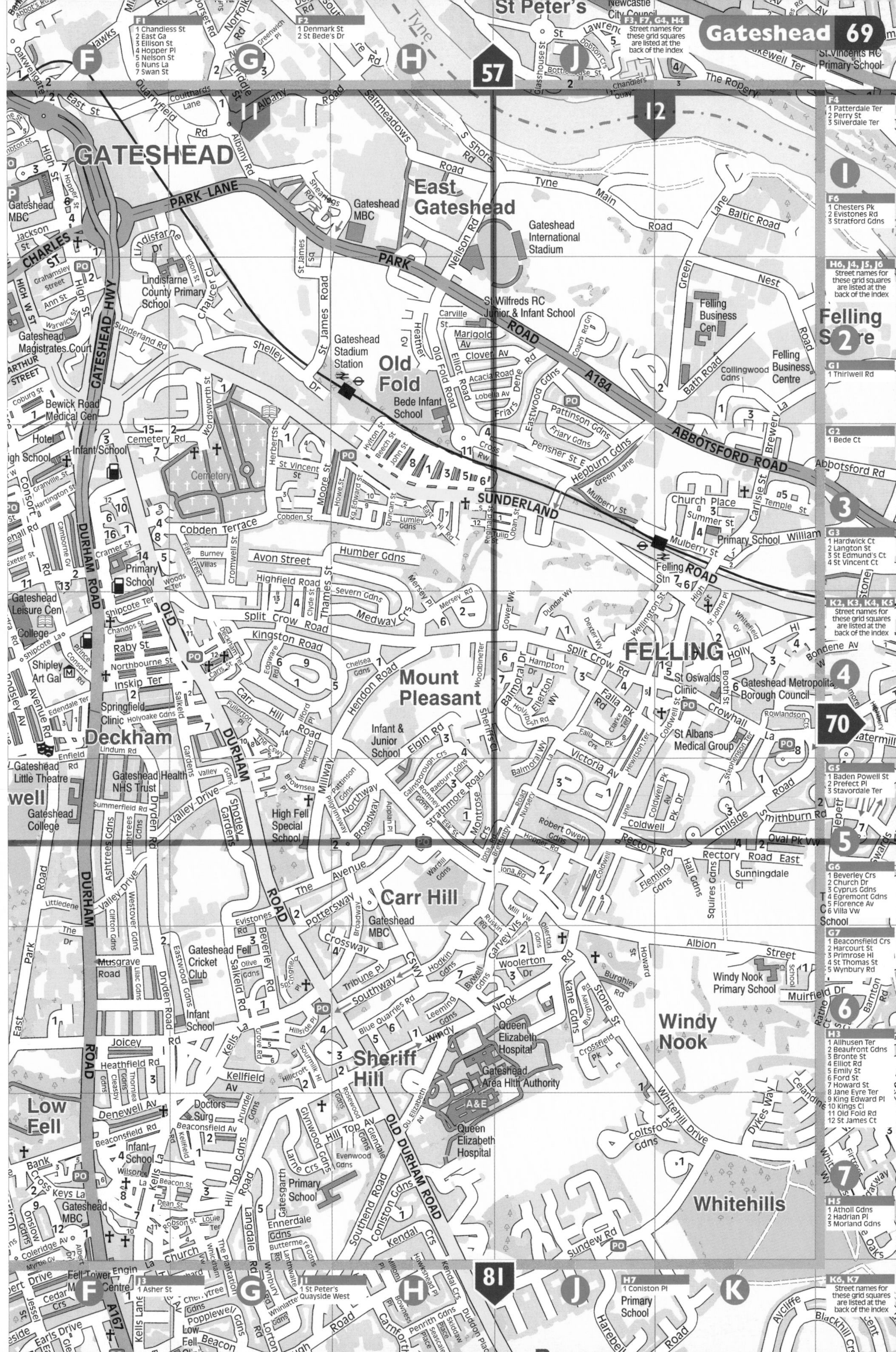
F1
1 Chandless St
2 East Ga
3 Ellison St
4 Hopper Pl
5 Nelson St
6 Nuns La
7 Swan St
F2
1 Denmark St
2 St Bede's Dr
F3, F7, G4, H4
Street names for these grid squares are listed at the back of the index
St Peter's
Newcastle City Council
57
12
11
70
81
GATESHEAD
East Gateshead
Gateshead MBC
Gateshead International Stadium
PARK LANE
PARK ROAD
A184
ABBOTSFORD ROAD
SUNDERLAND ROAD
Tyne Main Road
Baltic Road
Nest Road
Felling Business Cen
Felling Business Centre
Felling Square
St Wilfreds RC Junior & Infant School
Gateshead Stadium Station
Old Fold
Bede Infant School
Lindisfarne County Primary School
Gateshead MBC
Gateshead Magistrates Court
GATESHEAD HWY
CHARLES ST
HIGH W ST
ARTHUR STREET
Bewick Road Medical Cen
Infant School
Cemetery
Cemetery Rd
Cobden Terrace
Avon Street
Humber Gdns
Highfield Road
Split Crow Road
Kingston Road
Medway Crs
Hendon Road
Mount Pleasant
Infant & Junior School
High Fell Special School
Gateshead Leisure Cen
College
Shipley Art Gal
Springfield Clinic
Deckham
Gateshead Little Theatre
Gateshead Health NHS Trust
Gateshead College
DURHAM ROAD
OLD DURHAM ROAD
Valley Drive
FELLING
St Oswalds Clinic
Gateshead Metropolitan Borough Council
St Albans Medical Group
Felling Stn
Church Place
Primary School
Victoria Av
Rectory Rd
Rectory Road East
Carr Hill
Gateshead MBC
Gateshead Fell Cricket Club
Infant School
Albion Street
Windy Nook Primary School
Windy Nook
Queen Elizabeth Hospital
Gateshead Area Hlth Authority
A&E
Sheriff Hill
Low Fell
Doctors Surg
Infant School
Gateshead MBC
Primary School
Whitehills
Whitehill Drive
Coltsfoot Gdns
Sundew Rd
Fell Tower Centre
A167
Primary School
F4
1 Patterdale Ter
2 Perry St
3 Silverdale Ter
F6
1 Chesters Pk
2 Evistones Rd
3 Stratford Gdns
H6, J4, J5, J6
Street names for these grid squares are listed at the back of the index
G1
1 Thirlwell Rd
G2
1 Bede Ct
G3
1 Hardwick Ct
2 Langton St
3 St Edmund's Ct
4 St Vincent Ct
K2, K3, K4, K5
Street names for these grid squares are listed at the back of the index
G5
1 Baden Powell St
2 Prefect Pl
3 Stavordale Ter
G6
1 Beverley Crs
2 Church Dr
3 Cyprus Gdns
4 Egremont Gdns
5 Florence Av
6 Villa Vw
G7
1 Beaconsfield Crs
2 Harcourt St
3 Primrose Hl
4 St Thomas St
5 Wynbury Rd
H3
1 Allhusen Ter
2 Beaufront Gdns
3 Bronte St
4 Elliot Rd
5 Emily St
6 Ford St
7 Howard St
8 Jane Eyre Ter
9 King Edward Pl
10 Kings Cl
11 Old Fold Rd
12 St James Ct
H5
1 Atholl Gdns
2 Hadrian Pl
3 Morland Gdns
J3
1 Asher St
J1
1 St Peter's Quayside West
H7
1 Coniston Pl
K6, K7
Street names for these grid squares are listed at the back of the index

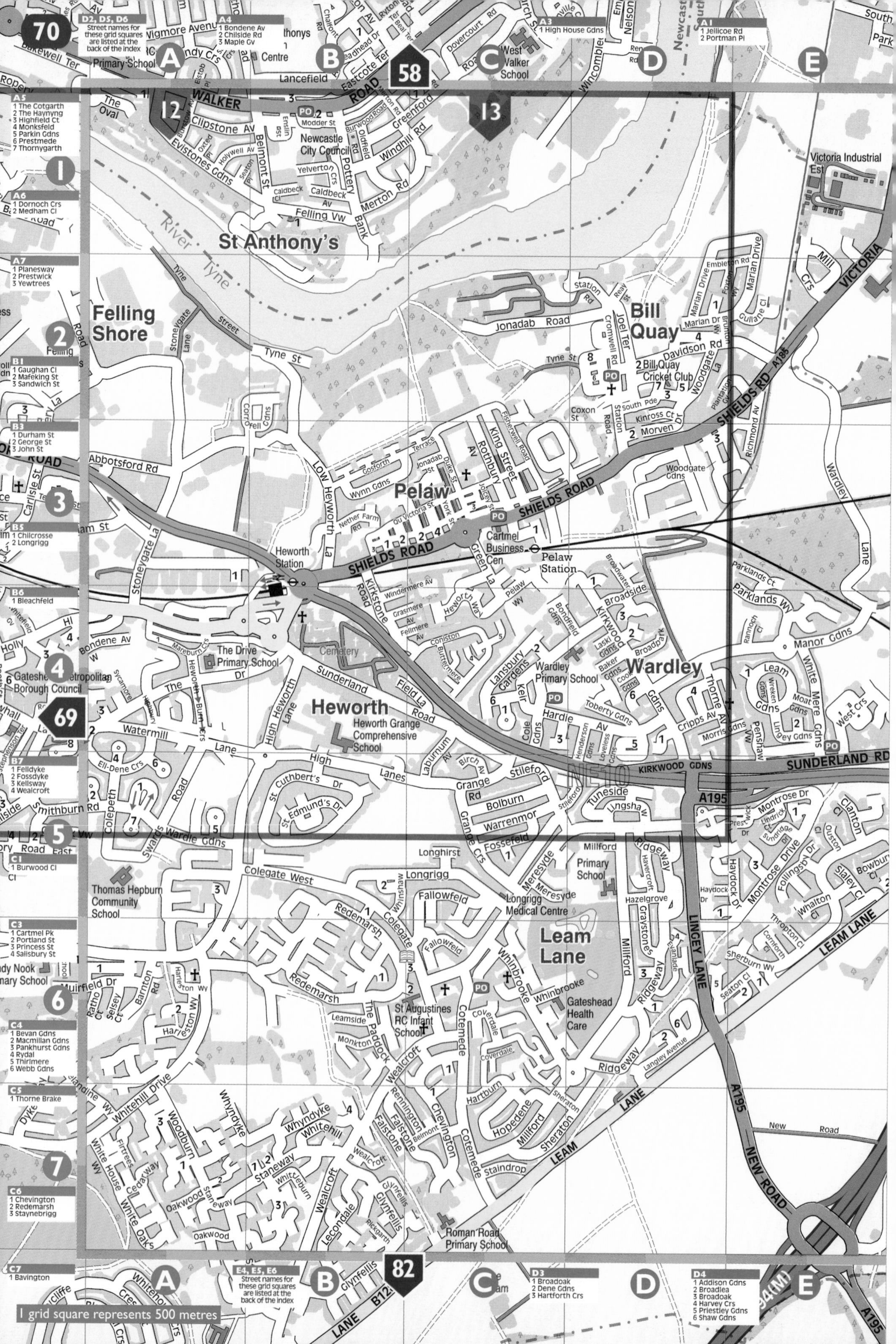

70
D2, D5, D6 Street names for these grid squares are listed at the back of the index
A4 1 Bondene Av 2 Chilside Rd 3 Maple Gv
A3 1 High House Gdns
A1 1 Jellicoe Rd 2 Portman Pl
58
12
13
A
B
C
D
E
A5 1 The Cotgarth 2 The Haynyng 3 Highfield Ct 4 Monksfeld 5 Parkin Gdns 6 Prestmede 7 Thornygarth
A6 1 Dornoch Crs 2 Medham Cl
A7 1 Planesway 2 Prestwick 3 Yewtrees
B1 1 Gaughan Cl 2 Mafeking St 3 Sandwich St
B3 1 Durham St 2 George St 3 John St
B5 1 Chilcrosse 2 Longrigg
B6 1 Bleachfeld
B7 1 Felldyke 2 Fossdyke 3 Kellsway 4 Wealcroft
C1 1 Burwood Cl
C3 1 Cartmel Pk 2 Portland St 3 Princess St 4 Salisbury St
C4 1 Bevan Gdns 2 Macmillan Gdns 3 Pankhurst Gdns 4 Rydal 5 Thirlmere 6 Webb Gdns
C5 1 Thorne Brake
C6 1 Chevington 2 Redemarsh 3 Staynebrigg
C7 1 Bavington
E4, E5, E6 Street names for these grid squares are listed at the back of the index
D3 1 Broadoak 2 Dene Gdns 3 Hartforth Crs
D4 1 Addison Gdns 2 Broadlea 3 Broadoak 4 Harvey Crs 5 Priestley Gdns 6 Shaw Gdns
69
82
1
2
3
4
5
6
7
1 grid square represents 500 metres
Walker Road
Wigmore Avenue
Primary School
Centre
Lancefield
Eastcote Ter
West Walker School
Wincomblee
Victoria Industrial Est
The Oval
Clipstone Av
Evistones Gdns
Belmont St
Newcastle City Council
Pottery Bank
Windhill Rd
Merton Rd
Greenford
Felling Vw
River Tyne
St Anthony's
Felling Shore
Tyne St
Jonadab Road
Station Rd
Bill Quay
Bill Quay Cricket Club
Davidson Rd
Marian Drive
Woodgate La
Victoria
Shields Road
Shields Rd A185
Abbotsford Rd
Low Heworth La
Pelaw
King Street
Rothbury Av
Heworth Station
Cartmel Business Cen
Pelaw Station
Kirkstone Road
Broadside
Wardley
Wardley Lane
Parklands Wy
Manor Gdns
The Drive Primary School
Cemetery
Gateshead Metropolitan Borough Council
Heworth
Heworth Grange Comprehensive School
Sunderland Road
Field La Road
Wardley Primary School
Hardie Av
Thorne Av
Cripps Av
Leam Gdns
White Mere Gdns
West Crs
Sunderland Rd
Kirkwood Gdns
NE10
Watermill Lane
High Heworth Lane
High Lanes
St Cuthbert's Dr
St Edmund's Dr
Grange Rd
Stileford
Bolburn
Warrenmor
Tuneside
Lingshaw
A195
Montrose Dr
Clanton
Smithburn Rd
Colepeth
Swards Road
Wardle Gdns
Colegate West
Thomas Hepburn Community School
Longhirst
Longrigg
Fallowfeld
Redemarsh
Colegate
Millford Primary School
Longrigg Medical Centre
Leam Lane
Hazelgrove
Graystones
Ridgeway
Lingey Lane
Haydock Dr
Montrose Drive
Leam Lane
Muirfield Dr
Barnton Rd
Harleston Wy
St Augustines RC Infant School
The Paddock
Cotemede
Whinbrooke
Gateshead Health Care
Langley Avenue
Whitehill Drive
Whyndyke
Woodburn
Wealcroft
Chevington
Hartburn
Hopedene
Millford
Sheraton
Leam Lane
New Road
A195
Staneway
Oakwood
White House
White Oaks
Cedarway
Glynfells
Lecondale
Staindrop
Roman Road Primary School
A194(M)

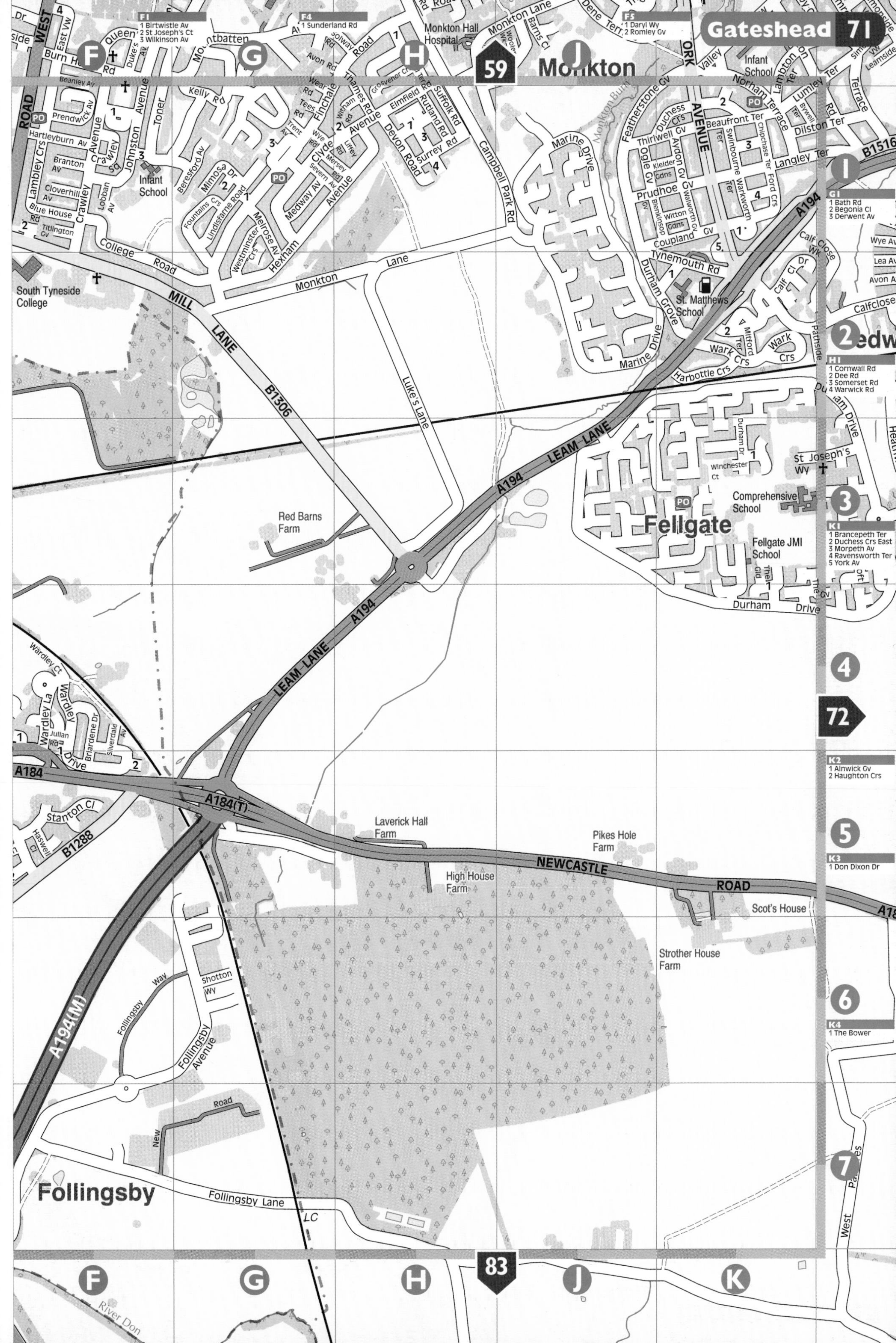
Monkton
Fellgate
Follingsby
Monkton Hall Hospital
South Tyneside College
Infant School
St. Matthews School
Comprehensive School
Fellgate JMI School
Red Barns Farm
Laverick Hall Farm
Pikes Hole Farm
High House Farm
Scot's House
Strother House Farm
MILL LANE
B1306
LEAM LANE
A194
A194(M)
A184
A184(T)
B1288
NEWCASTLE ROAD
B1516
Luke's Lane
Monkton Lane
College Road
Campbell Park Rd
Marine Drive
Durham Drive
Follingsby Lane
Follingsby Avenue
Follingsby Way
Shotton Wy
New Road
West Pastures
River Don
Monkton Burn
F1 1 Birtwistle Av 2 St Joseph's Ct 3 Wilkinson Av
F4 1 Sunderland Rd
F5 1 Daryl Wy 2 Romley Gv
G1 1 Bath Rd 2 Begonia Cl 3 Derwent Av
H1 1 Cornwall Rd 2 Dee Rd 3 Somerset Rd 4 Warwick Rd
K1 1 Brancepeth Ter 2 Duchess Crs East 3 Morpeth Av 4 Ravensworth Ter 5 York Av
K2 1 Alnwick Gv 2 Haughton Crs
K3 1 Don Dixon Dr
K4 1 The Bower
59
72
83

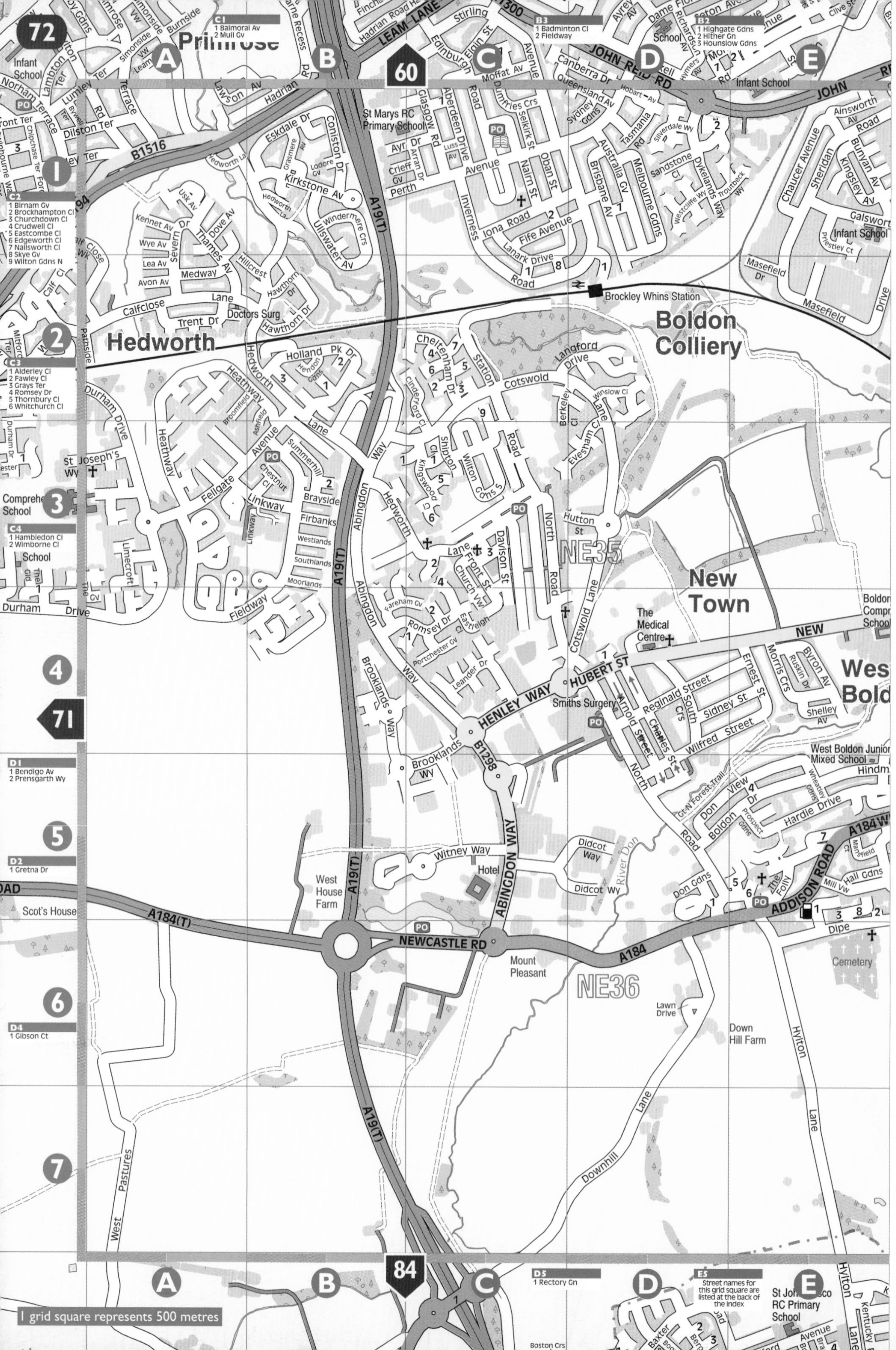
72
60
71
84
Primrose
Hedworth
Boldon Colliery
New Town
West Boldon
NE35
NE36
C1
1 Balmoral Av
2 Muil Gv
B3
1 Badminton Cl
2 Fieldway
B2
1 Highgate Gdns
2 Hither Gn
3 Hounslow Gdns
C2
1 Birnam Gv
2 Brockhampton Cl
3 Churchdown Cl
4 Crudwell Cl
5 Eastcombe Cl
6 Edgeworth Cl
7 Nailsworth Cl
8 Skye Gv
9 Wilton Gdns N
C3
1 Alderley Cl
2 Fawley Cl
3 Grays Ter
4 Romsey Dr
5 Thornbury Cl
6 Whitchurch Cl
C4
1 Hambledon Cl
2 Wimborne Cl
D1
1 Bendigo Av
2 Prensgarth Wy
D2
1 Gretna Dr
D4
1 Gibson Ct
D5
1 Rectory Gn
E5
Street names for this grid square are listed at the back of the index
Brockley Whins Station
St Marys RC Primary School
Infant School
Doctors Surg
The Medical Centre
Smiths Surgery
West Boldon Junior Mixed School
Hotel
West House Farm
Scot's House
Mount Pleasant
Down Hill Farm
Cemetery
St John Bosco RC Primary School
A19(T)
A184(T)
A184
B1516
B1298
JOHN REID RD
LEAM LANE
NEWCASTLE RD
HENLEY WAY
HUBERT ST
ABINGDON WAY
ADDISON ROAD
River Don
1 grid square represents 500 metres

61
F4
1 Wilson Dr
F5
1 Alpine Gv
2 Claremount Ct
3 Everest Gv
4 Grampian Gv
5 Rosemount Ct
6 Snowdon Gv
7 Stewart Dr
Whiteleas
Biddick Hall
King George Comprehensive School
G1
Street names for this grid square are listed at the back of the index
G4
1 Borrowdale Cl
Cleadon Grange
G5
1 Bowness Cl
2 The Fairways
3 Patterdale Cl
Cleadon Village County JM School
H1
1 Romney Av
2 Sandalwood
Albert Elliott County Junior Mixed School
East Boldon
Boldon North Bridge
Boker Lane Health Centre
Junior School
East Boldon Station
74
H2
1 Sutherland Ct
H5
1 Beatrice Gdns
2 Charlcote Crs
3 Coulton Dr
4 Grange Ter
5 St Chad's Vls
Blue House Farm
Low House Farm
J3
1 Celtic Crs
2 Kelvin Gv
3 Paddock Cl
4 Saxon Cl
Belle Vue Villa
Field House
J4
1 Beckenham Cl
Mundles
85
K3
1 East Boldon Rd
2 South Dr
K1
1 Carnoustie Dr
2 Ganton Ct
3 Heartsbourne Dr
J5
1 Bede Ter
2 Crossways
Witherwack
GALSWORTHY ROAD
BENTON ROAD
BOLDON LANE
WHITELEAS WAY B1298
B1298
FRONT STREET
A184
SUNDERLAND ROAD
WHITBURN ROAD
A1018 SHIELDS
STATION AP
Tileshed Lane
Moor Lane
Blue House Lane
Bell House Road
Mundles Lane
River Don

74
62
73
86
A4
1 Old Course Rd
A3
1 Low Meadow
2 Sandgrove
3 Windermere
A2
1 Heather Cl
2 Oakleigh Gdns
A5
1 Moorfield Gdns
B4
1 Mayfield Dr
C7
1 Barton Ct
2 Cumbrian Av
3 Dalegarth Gv
4 Gatesgarth Gv
5 Skiddaw Dr
6 Threlkeld Gv
7 Troutbeck Rd
8 Wasdale Ct
E3
1 Highcroft Dr
E4
1 Moor Vw
E6
1 Hawthorn Ter
E7
1 Cuthbertson Cl
2 Princes Gdns
Cleadon
South Bents
Fulwell
SR6
Sunniside Farm
Cleadon Hills Farm
Lizards Farm
Cleadon Grange
Oakleigh Gardens School
Wellands Farm
Undercliff
Cleadon Village County JM School
Cleadon Village C of E Infant School
Little Theatre
West Hall
Whitburn Junior Mixed School
Sea View Park
Moor Farm
Blue House Farm
Seaburn Dene Primary School
Mere Knolls Cemetery
Fulwell Medical Centre
Junior School
SHIELDS ROAD
SUNDERLAND ROAD
A1018 SHIELDS ROAD
NEWCASTLE ROAD
A184
MOOR LANE
B1299
WHITBURN ROAD
DYKELANDS ROAD
Cleadon Lane
Chick's Lane
Lizard Lane
Moor Lane
Dene Lane
Blue House Lane
Bell House Road
Woodlands Road
Sunniside Lane
1 grid square represents 500 metres

F3
1 Buckingham Cl
2 Marina Ter
3 Robinson Gdns
F4
1 Cornthwaite Dr
2 Staffords La
F5
1 Whitburn Bents Rd
F6
1 Hart Ter
G4
1 Ash Gv
63
87
Whitburn Colliery
WHITBURN
Shearwater
White Rocks Grove
Lilac Av
Lily Crs
Marsden Av
Rose Crs
Fern Avenue
Wheatall Drive
Fulmar Wk
Cedar Gv
Poplar Drive
Birch Av
Geoffrey St
Rupert St
Sycamore Rd
Maple Gv
Bryers St
Bowman St
Whitburn Cem
Myrtle Avenue
Myrtle Av
Larch Av
Oak Crs
Elm Dr
Beech Av
Croftside Av
Rackly Wy
Adolphus Street
Holly Av
Guards
Front St
STREET
Church Lane
East Flds
EAST STREET
Whitburn Comprehensive School
Whitburn Cricket Club
Markham Av
Newark Dr
Nicholas Av
Hill Vw
MILL LANE
A183
WHITBURN BENTS ROAD
Bilsdale
Swaledale
Ryedale
Farndale Av
Eskdale Rd
Whitby Av
Bents Av
Hotel

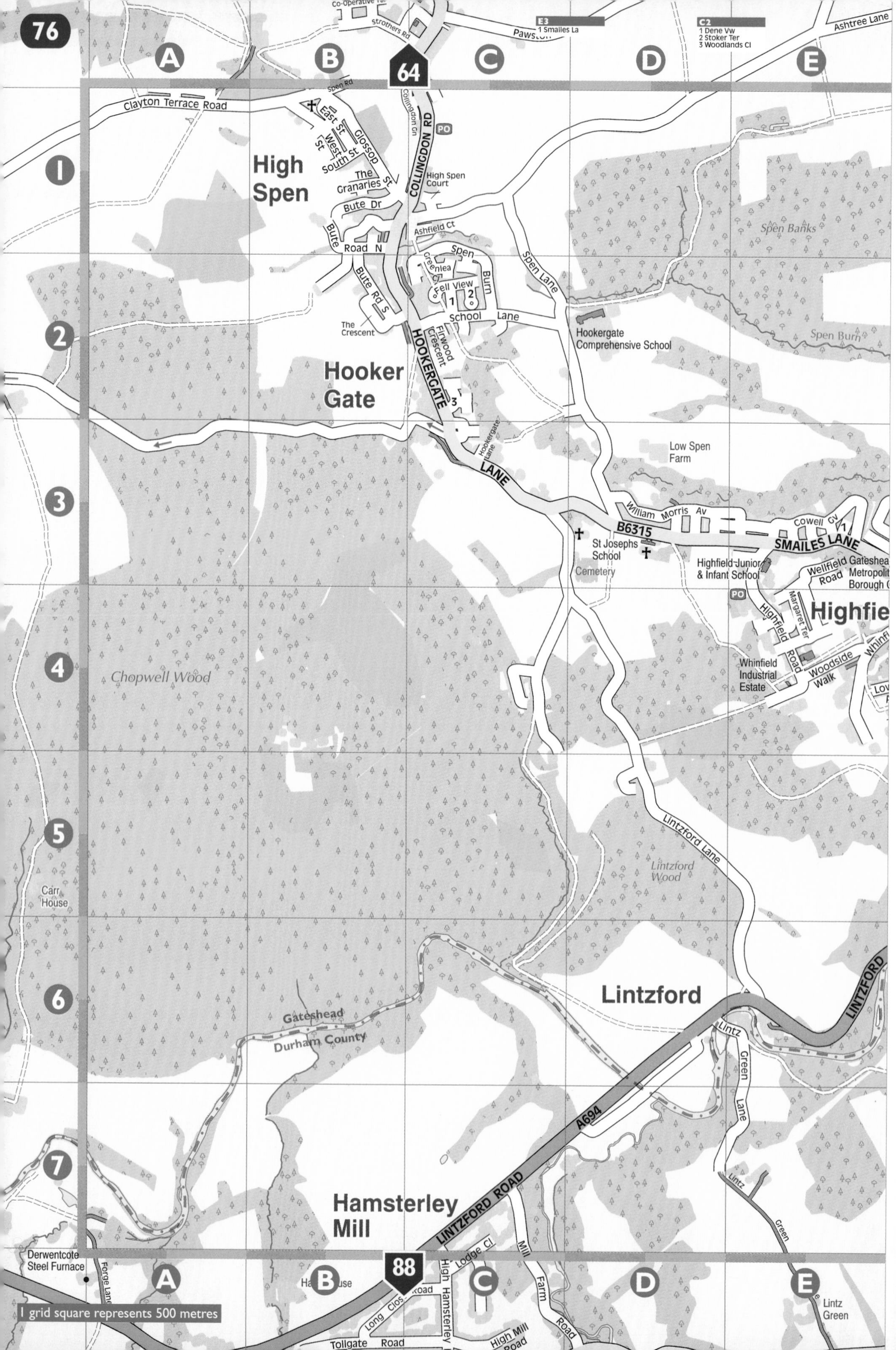

E3
1 Smailes La
C2
1 Dene Vw
2 Stoker Ter
3 Woodlands Cl
64
88
A
B
C
D
E
1
2
3
4
5
6
7
Co-operative Ter
Strothers Rd
Pawston Rd
Ashtree Lane
Spen Rd
Clayton Terrace Road
East St
West St
Glossop St
South St
Collingdon Gn
COLLINGDON RD
PO
High Spen
The Granaries
High Spen Court
Bute Dr
Bute Road N
Ashfield Ct
Greenlea Cl
Fell View
Spen Burn
Bute Rd S
The Crescent
School Lane
Spen Lane
Firwood Crescent
HOOKERGATE
Hooker Gate
Hookergate Lane
LANE
Hookergate Comprehensive School
Spen Banks
Spen Burn
Low Spen Farm
William Morris Av
B6315
Cowell Gv
SMAILES LANE
St Josephs School
Cemetery
Highfield Junior & Infant School
Wellfield Road
Gateshead Metropolitan Borough Council
Highfield
Highfield Road
Margaret Ter
Whinfield Industrial Estate
Woodside Walk
Chopwell Wood
Lintzford Lane
Lintzford Wood
Carr House
Lintzford
Gateshead
Durham County
LINTZFORD
Lintz Green Lane
A694
LINTZFORD ROAD
Hamsterley Mill
Lintz Green
Lodge Cl
Mill Farm Road
High Hamsterley Road
Derwentcote Steel Furnace
Forge Lane
Long Close Road
Tollgate Road
High Mill Road
Lintz Green
1 grid square represents 500 metres

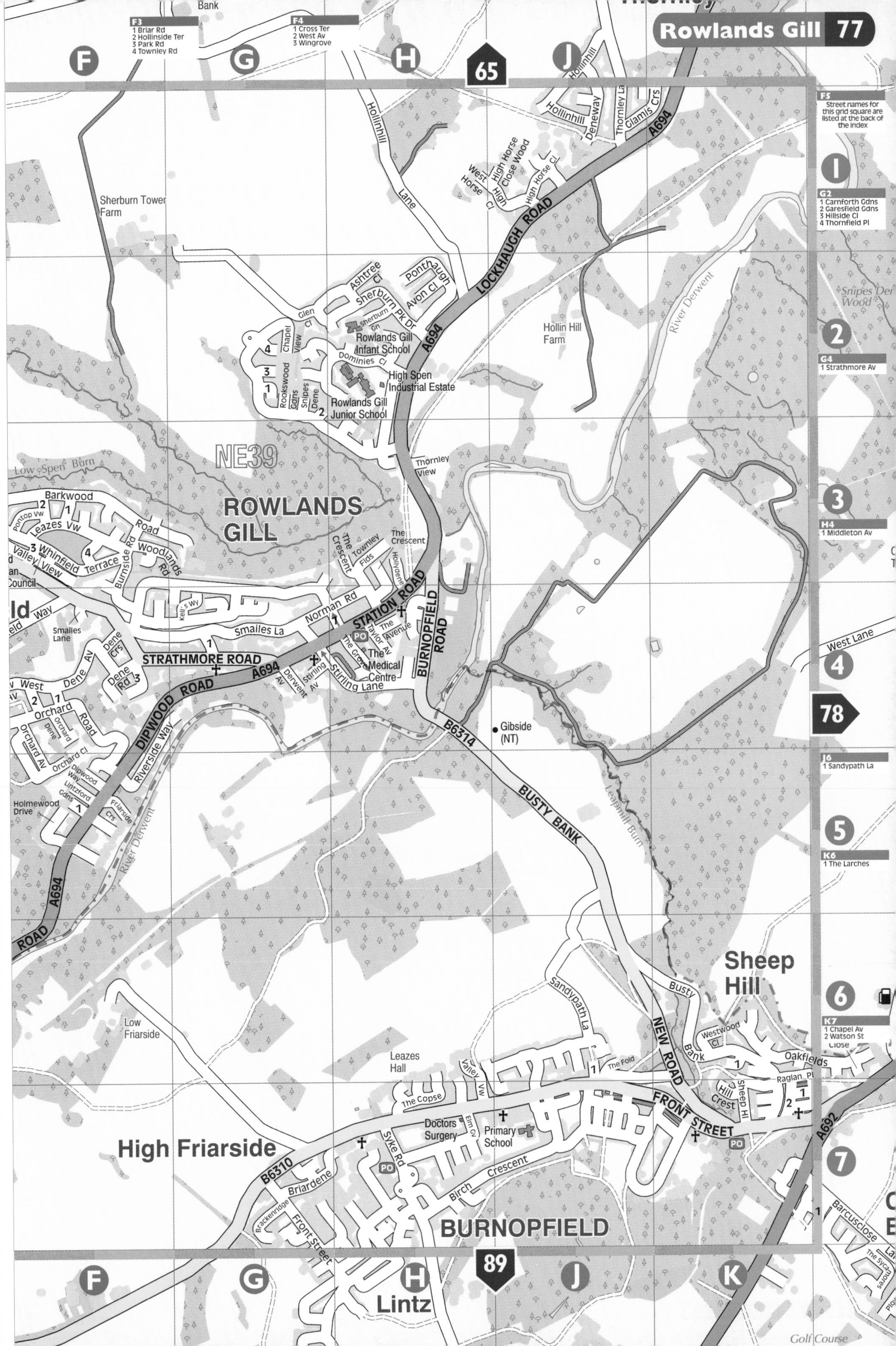
F3
1 Briar Rd
2 Hollinside Ter
3 Park Rd
4 Townley Rd
F4
1 Cross Ter
2 West Av
3 Wingrove
F5
Street names for this grid square are listed at the back of the index
G2
1 Carnforth Gdns
2 Garesfield Gdns
3 Hillside Cl
4 Thornfield Pl
G4
1 Strathmore Av
H4
1 Middleton Av
J6
1 Sandypath La
K6
1 The Larches
K7
1 Chapel Av
2 Watson St
65
78
89
ROWLANDS GILL
NE39
Sherburn Tower Farm
Hollin Hill Farm
Snipes Dene Wood
River Derwent
Rowlands Gill Infant School
Rowlands Gill Junior School
High Spen Industrial Estate
LOCKHAUGH ROAD
A694
STATION ROAD
BURNOPFIELD ROAD
STRATHMORE ROAD
DIPWOOD ROAD
B6314
BUSTY BANK
Gibside (NT)
Leapmill Burn
Low Spen Burn
The Medical Centre
Sheep Hill
NEW ROAD
FRONT STREET
High Friarside
Low Friarside
Leazes Hall
Doctors Surgery
Primary School
B6310
BURNOPFIELD
Lintz
A692
Golf Course

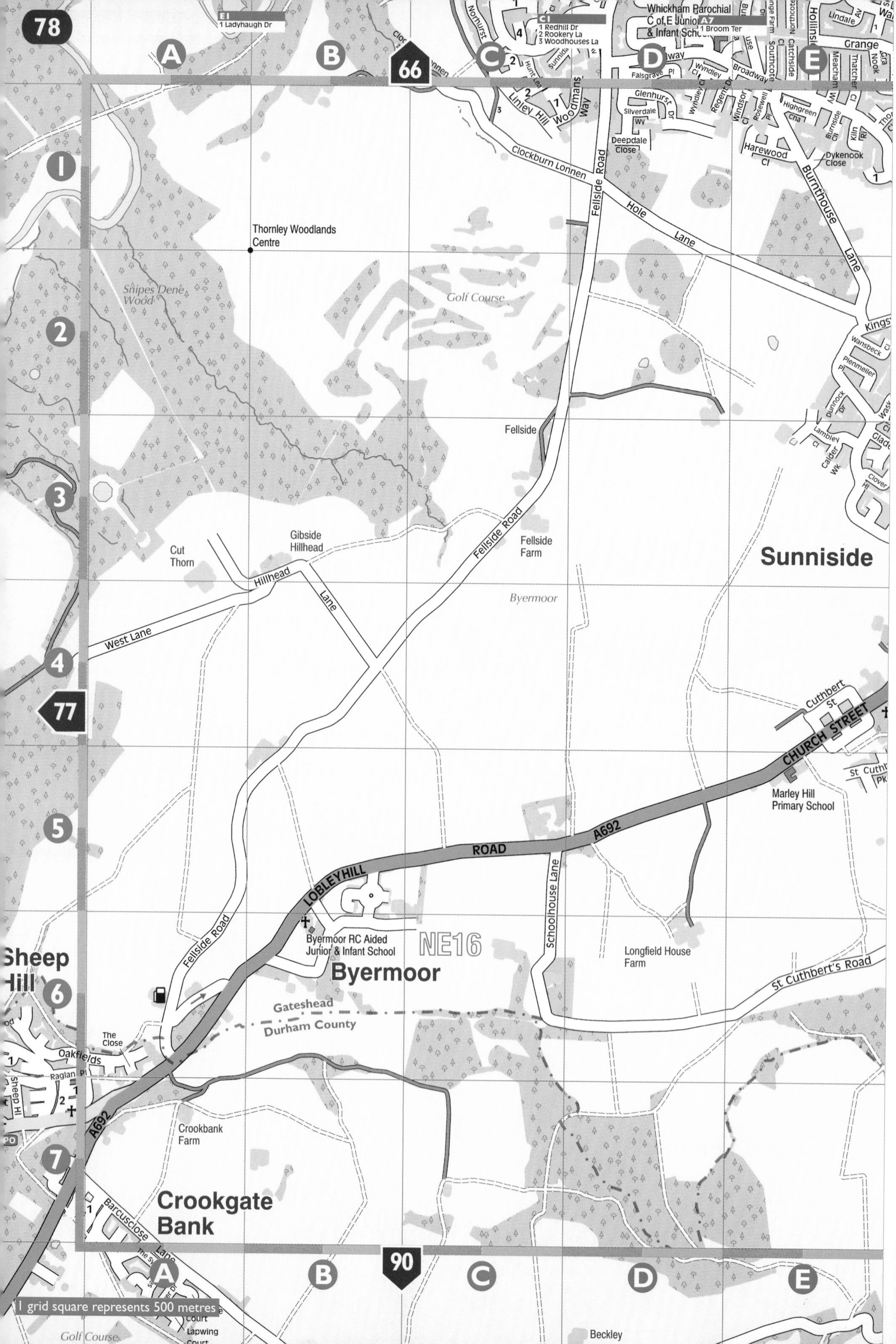

66
77
90
A
B
C
D
E
1
2
3
4
5
6
7
E1 1 Ladyhaugh Dr
C1 1 Redhill Dr 2 Rookery La 3 Woodhouses La
A7 1 Broom Ter
Whickham Parochial C of E Junior & Infant School
Clockburn Lonnen
Fellside Road
Hole Lane
Burnthouse Lane
Thornley Woodlands Centre
Snipes Dene Wood
Golf Course
Fellside
Fellside Farm
Gibside Hillhead
Cut Thorn
Hillhead Lane
West Lane
Byermoor
Sunniside
Cuthbert St
CHURCH STREET
Marley Hill Primary School
LOBLEYHILL ROAD
A692
Schoolhouse Lane
Longfield House Farm
St Cuthbert's Road
Byermoor RC Aided Junior & Infant School
NE16
Gateshead
Durham County
Sheep Hill
The Close
Oakfields
Raglan Pl
Crookbank Farm
Crookgate Bank
Barcusclose Lane
Lapwing Court
Golf Course
Beckley
Linley Hill
Woodmans Way
Glenhurst Dr
Silverdale Wy
Deepdale Close
Harewood Cl
Dykenook Close
Broadway
Grange
Wansbeck
Plenmeller Pl
Dunnock Dr
Lambley Cl
Calder Wk

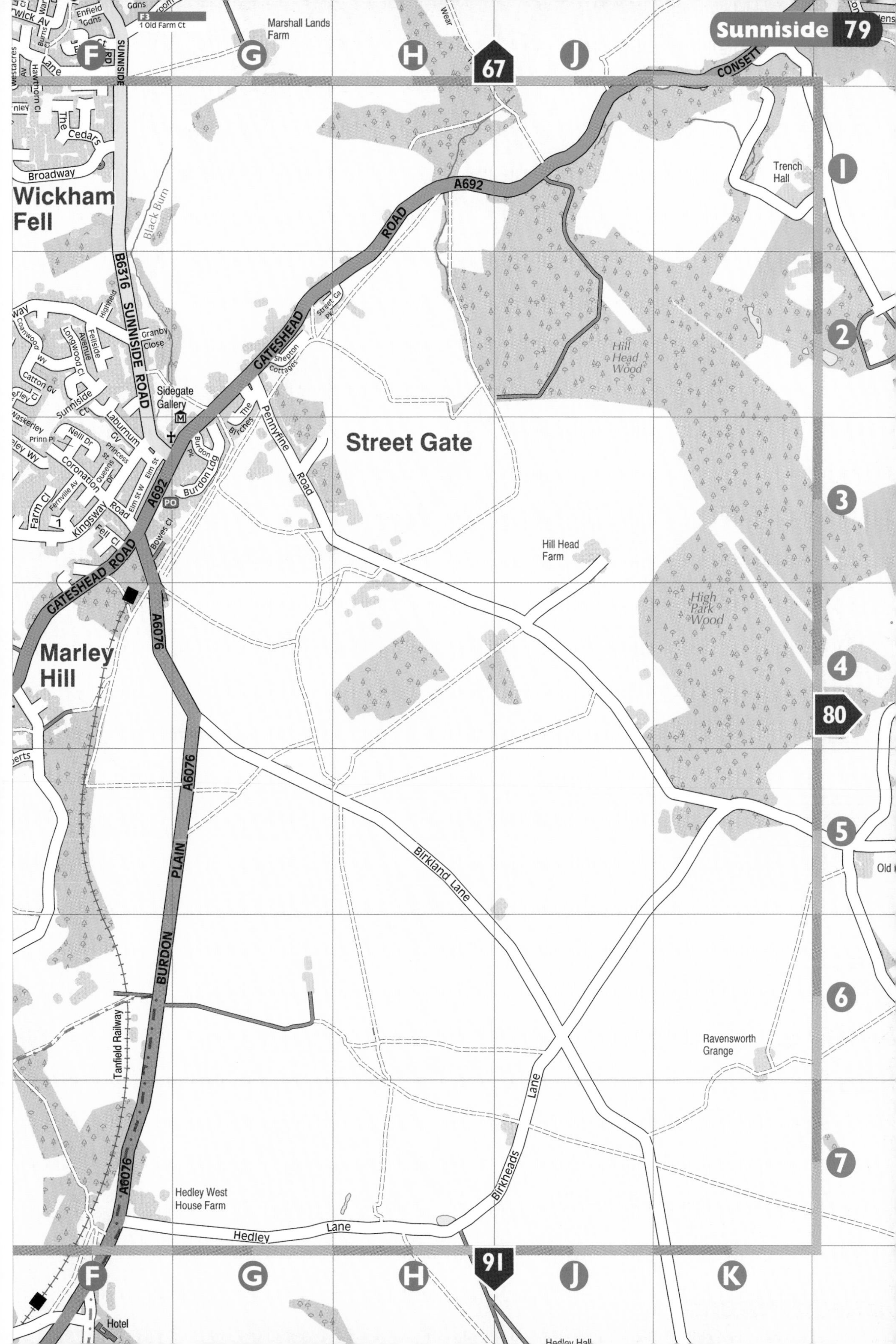
Wickham Fell
Street Gate
Marley Hill
Marshall Lands Farm
Trench Hall
Hill Head Wood
High Park Wood
Hill Head Farm
Ravensworth Grange
Hedley West House Farm
Sidegate Gallery
Black Burn
Tanfield Railway
A692
GATESHEAD ROAD
CONSETT
B6316 SUNNISIDE ROAD
A6076
BURDON PLAIN
Birkland Lane
Birkheads Lane
Hedley Lane
Pennyfine Road
Broadway
The Cedars
Kingsway
Coronation Road
Laburnum Gv
Sunniside Ct
Granby Close
Shepton Cottages
Burdon Lodge
The Birches
Street Gate Pk
Bowes Cl
Fell Cl
Farm Cl
Longwood Avenue
Fellside
Highfield
Catton Gv
Neill Dr
Prinn Pl
Princess St
Queens Dr
Elm St
Elm St W
Fernville Av
Hawthorn Cl
Enfield Gdns
1 Old Farm Ct
Hotel
Hedley Hall
Old
F G H J K
1 2 3 4 5 6 7
67
80
91

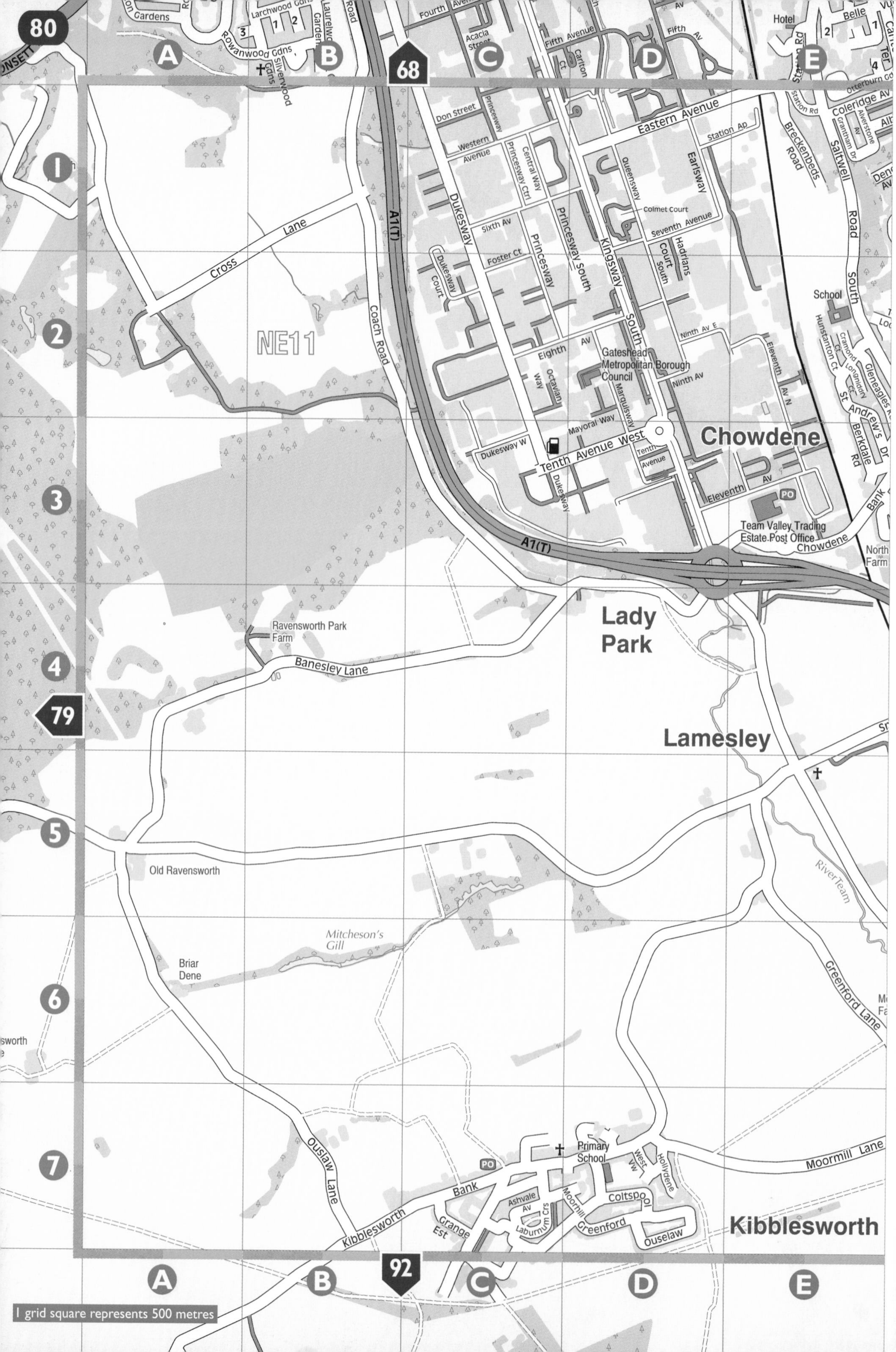
80
68
79
92
A
B
C
D
E
1
2
3
4
5
6
7
Cross Lane
Coach Road
A1(T)
NE11
Dukesway
Princesway
Kingsway South
Eastern Avenue
Earlsway
Queensway
Colmet Court
Seventh Avenue
Hadrians
Court South
Eighth Av
Ninth Av
Ninth Av E
Eleventh Av
Tenth Avenue West
Mayoral Way
Marquisway
Gateshead Metropolitan Borough Council
Chowdene
Team Valley Trading Estate Post Office
School
Lady Park
Lamesley
Ravensworth Park Farm
Banesley Lane
Old Ravensworth
Mitcheson's Gill
Briar Dene
Ouslaw Lane
Kibblesworth Bank
Primary School
Moormill Lane
Greenford Lane
River Team
Kibblesworth
1 grid square represents 500 metres

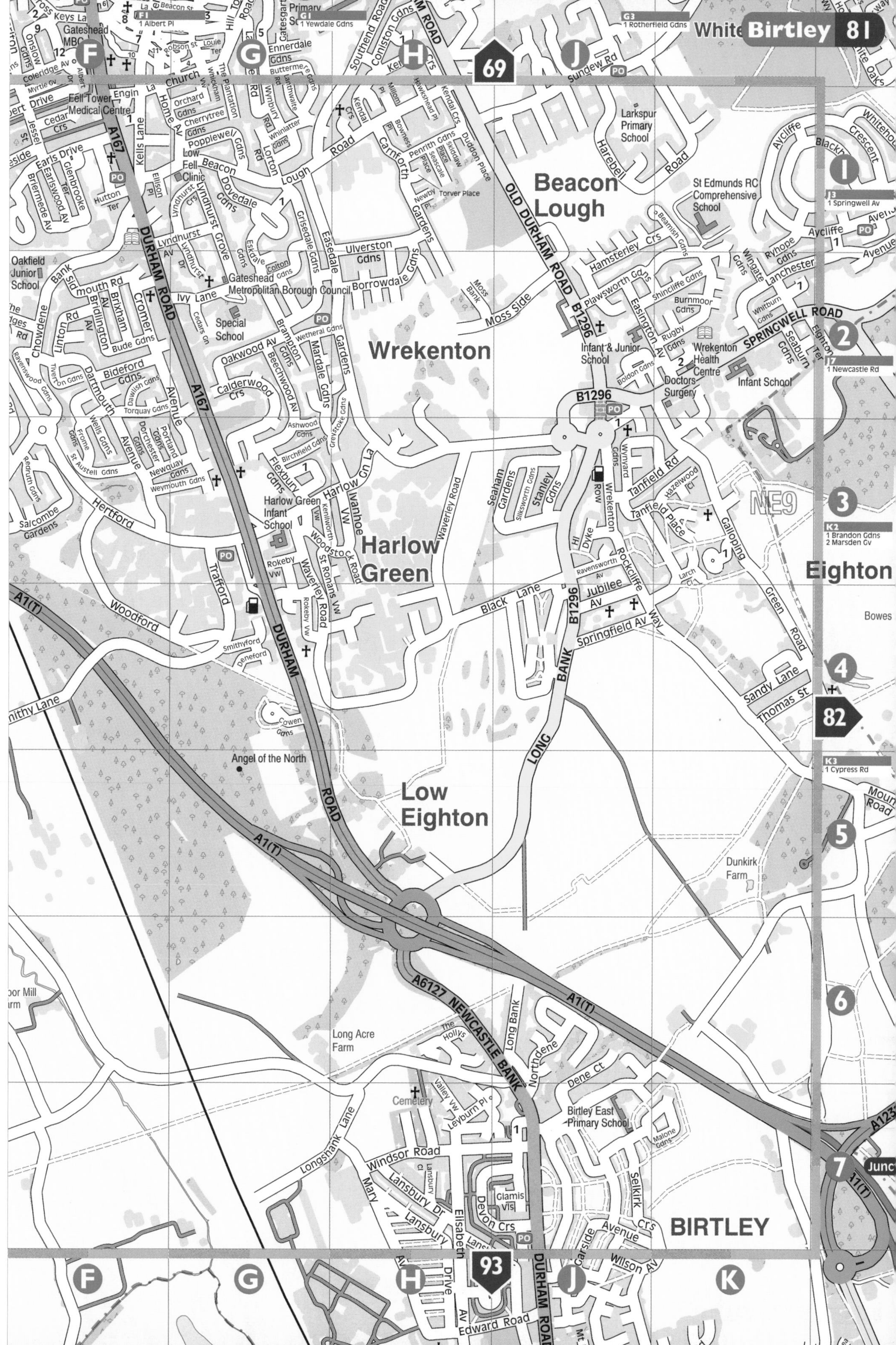
69
93
82
F
G
H
J
I
K
1
2
3
4
5
6
7
NE9
F1 1 Albert Pl
G1 1 Yewdale Gdns
G3 1 Rotherfield Gdns
J3 1 Springwell Av
J7 1 Newcastle Rd
K2 1 Brandon Gdns 2 Marsden Gv
K3 1 Cypress Rd
Beacon Lough
Wrekenton
Harlow Green
Low Eighton
Eighton
BIRTLEY
Bowes
Gateshead MBC
Fell Tower Medical Centre
Low Fell Clinic
Oakfield Junior School
Special School
Gateshead Metropolitan Borough Council
Harlow Green Infant School
Larkspur Primary School
St Edmunds RC Comprehensive School
Infant & Junior School
Wrekenton Health Centre
Doctors Surgery
Infant School
Angel of the North
Long Acre Farm
Dunkirk Farm
Cemetery
Birtley East Primary School
DURHAM ROAD
A167
OLD DURHAM ROAD
B1296
LONG BANK
A1(T)
A6127 NEWCASTLE BANK
SPRINGWELL ROAD
Black Lane
Waverley Road
Kells Lane
Ivy Lane
Lough Road
Beacon Lough
Moss Side
Sundew Rd
Harebell Road
Hertford
Woodford
Trafford
Smithy Lane
Smithyford
Deneford
Cowen Gdns
Tanfield Rd
Tanfield Place
Galloping Green Road
Sandy Lane
Thomas St
Jubilee Av
Springfield Av
Way
Rockcliffe
Wrekenton Row
Dyke Hl
Ravensworth Av
Larch Cl
Hazelwood Cl
Seaham Gardens
Silksworth Gdns
Stanley Gdns
Wynyard Gdns
Ivanhoe Vw
Harlow Gn La
Kenilworth Vw
Woodstock Road
St Ronans Vw
Rokeby Vw
Flexbury Gdns
Birchfield Gdns
Ashwood Gdns
Greystoke Gdns
Calderwood Crs
Oakwood Av
Beechwood Av
Brampton Gdns
Wetheral Gdns
Mardale Gdns
Gardens
Borrowdale Gdns
Ulverston Gdns
Easedale
Grisedale Gdns
Carnforth Gardens
Torver Place
Newby Pl
Penrith Gdns
Skiddaw Place
Seascale Place
Duddon Place
Kendal Crs
Hawkshead Pl
Bowness Pl
Millom Pl
Whinlatter Gdns
Lorton Rd
Wynbury Rd
Coniston Gdns
Southend Road
Ennerdale Gdns
Buttermere Gdns
Hamsterley Crs
Beamish Gdns
Plawsworth Gdns
Shincliffe Gdns
Burnmoor Gdns
Easington Av
Rugby Gdns
Boldon Gdns
Wingate Gdns
Ryhope Gdns
Lanchester
Whitburn Gdns
Seaburn Gdns
Eighton Ter
Aycliffe
Aycliffe Crescent
Avenue
Whitehouse Crescent
White Oaks
Mount Road
A1231
Junction
Cromer Avenue
Brixham Av
Bridlington Av
Linton Rd
Chowdene Bank
Bude Gdns
Bideford Gdns
Dartmouth Avenue
Dawlish Gdns
Torquay Gdns
Tiverton Gdns
Ravenswood Gdns
Frome Gdns
Wells Gdns
Dorchester Gdns
Portland Gdns
Newquay Gdns
Weymouth Gdns
St Austell Gdns
Redruth Gdns
Salcombe Gardens
Lyndhurst Grove
Lyndhurst Av
Lyndhurst Dr
Lyndhurst Crs
Dovedale Gdns
Eskdale Gdns
Colton Gdns
Popplewell Gdns
Cherrytree Gdns
Orchard Gdns
Ellison Pl
Hutton Ter
Glenbrooke Ter
Earls Drive
Eastwood Av
Briermede Av
Jessel
Cedar Crs
Church
Engine La
Home Av
Coleridge Av
Myrtle Gv
Keys La
Onslow
Robson St
Louie Ter
Whickham Vw
The Plantation
Hill Top Road
Beacon St
Long Bank
Northdene
Dene Ct
The Hollys
Valley Vw
Leyburn Pl
Longshank Lane
Windsor Road
Lansbury Ct
Lansbury Dr
Lansbury
Mary Av
Elisabeth Drive
Devon Crs
Glamis Vls
Malone Gdns
Selkirk Crs
Garside Avenue
Wilson Av
Edward Road
DURHAM ROAD
PO

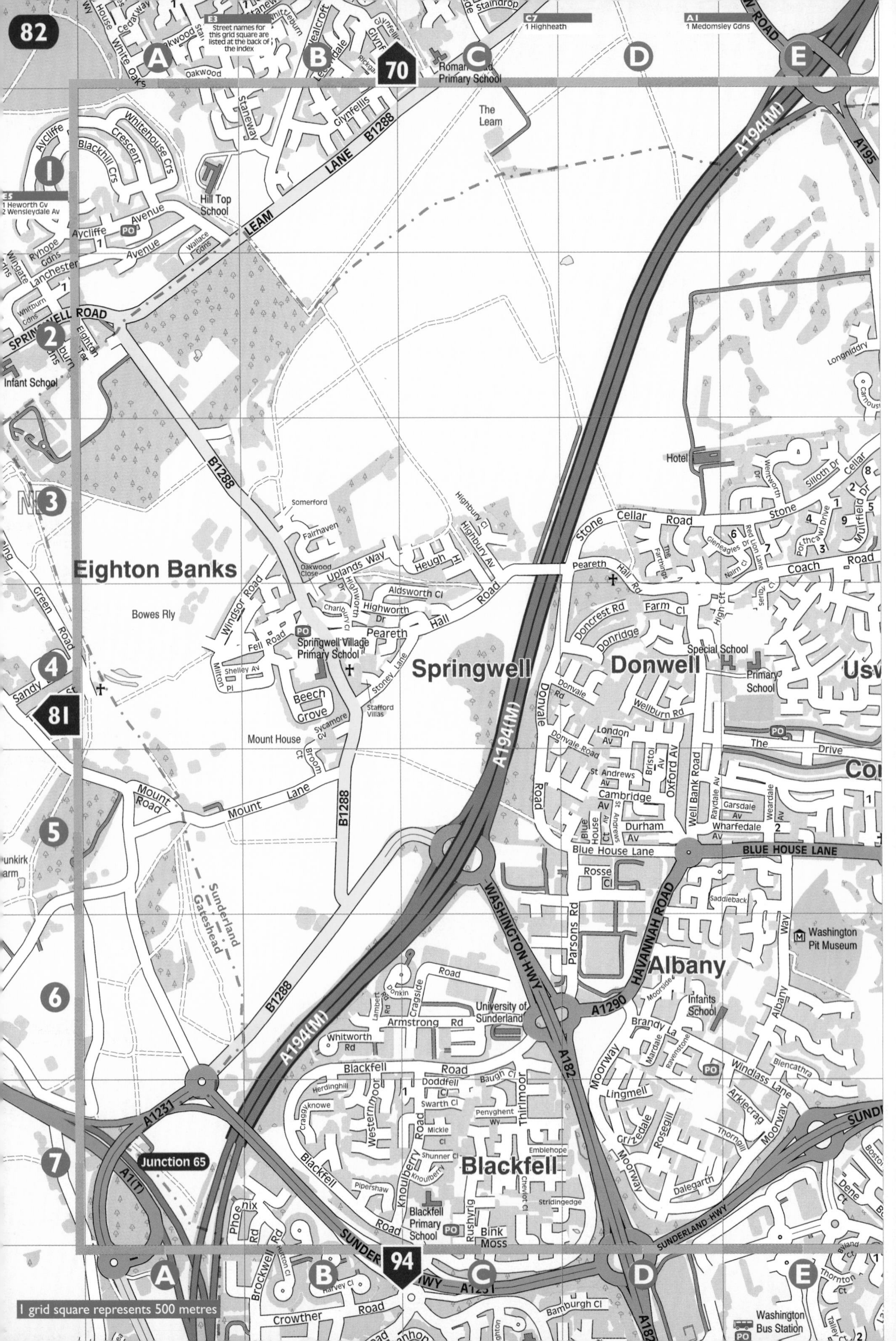
70
81
94
Street names for this grid square are listed at the back of the index
E3
C7 1 Highheath
A1 1 Medomsley Gdns
E5 1 Heworth Gv 2 Wensleydale Av
Eighton Banks
Springwell
Donwell
Albany
Blackfell
Bowes Rly
Mount House
The Leam
Hill Top School
Springwell Village Primary School
Roman Road Primary School
Special School
Primary School
Infants School
Blackfell Primary School
Infant School
University of Sunderland
Washington Pit Museum
Washington Bus Station
Hotel
Junction 65
A194(M)
A1(T)
A1231
A1290
A182
A195
B1288
LEAM LANE
SPRINGWELL ROAD
WASHINGTON HWY
HAVANNAH ROAD
BLUE HOUSE LANE
SUNDERLAND HWY
Stone Cellar Road
Coach Road
Peareth Hall Road
Uplands Way
Mount Lane
Mount Road
Windsor Road
Fell Road
Green Road
Beech Grove
Blackfell Road
Armstrong Rd
Whitworth Rd
Windlass Lane
Moorway
Lingmell
Dalegarth
Rosegill
Thirlmoor
Knoulberry Road
Crowther Road
Bamburgh Cl
Sunderland Gateshead
1 grid square represents 500 metres

Follingsby
F2 1 Downfield
F3 1 Cumberland Wy 2 Rutland Pl
Follingsby Lane
LC
F
G
H
71
J
F4 Street names for this grid square are listed at the back of the index
River Don
South Tyneside
Sunderland
I
F5 1 Laurens Ct
East House
Waterloo Road
2
F7 1 Trenton Av
North Moor Farm
NORTHUMBERLAND WAY
Dalmahoy
Gullane
The Fairway
Foxton Hall
Northumbria Sports Centre
Road
Merevale Cl
Barton Cl
Usworth Secondary School
Heworth Road
Stephenson Road
Marwell Dr
Stedham Cl
Usworth Hall Road
Waterloo Road
3
G3 1 Marwell Dr 2 Whitbourne Cl 3 Wimpole Cl
West Moor Farm
Wiltshire Pl
Norfolk Dr
Warwick Dr
Baird Cl
Westmorland Av
Essex
St Bedes RC Primary School
Drive
Rutherford
Rainhill Road
Rainhill Cl
NE37
Sulgrave Road
Monterey
Usworth
Inkerman Road
A1290
4
84
Usworth Colliery Junior School
Gayton Rd
Waterloo Rd
Brackley
Usworth Grange Primary School
Tyne Gardens
Park Gv
Vernon St
Cherry Blossom Way
G4 1 Wylam Cl
Concord
Sulgrave
Marlborough Road
Road
Viola St
Helmdon
Silverstone Road
House Ter
Manor
Foxley
Barmston Lane
Victoria Road Health Centre
Manor Vw
Mnr Vw E
Banbury
Usworth Station Rd
Edgecote
5
G5 1 Front St 2 Hall Rd 3 Usworth Station Rd
Victoria Rd
Cherwell
LC
Mandeville
Spout La
VERMONT
GLOVER ROAD
Washington Football Club
Industrial Road
Tower Rd
Spire Road
Nissan Way
6
H3 1 Watcombe Cl
Washington Secondary School
Spout Lane
Bridgewater Rd
Glover Industrial Estate
Brindley Road
WASHINGTON
Barmston
NORTHUMBERLAND HIGHWAY
A1231
SUNDERLAND HIGHWAY
A1231
Washington Village Primary School
Richmond Av
Hill Rise
Spout Lane
Barmston Way
Horsley Road
Valley Forge
Autumn Cl
Village Lane
Burnhope Road
Stockley Rd
Pattinson Road
Barmston Lane
7
Crs
St Josephs School
Cemetery
Glebe
Barmston Medical Centre
Alston Road
Lee Cl
Faraday Cl
Barmston
Abbey Cl
Rd
F
G
H7 1 Thornhope Cl
H
95
J
H4 1 Shalstone 2 Trafalgar Rd
K
Primary School
The
Westerhope
Primary School
Washington Village
Parkway
Crescent
Road
Walton Road

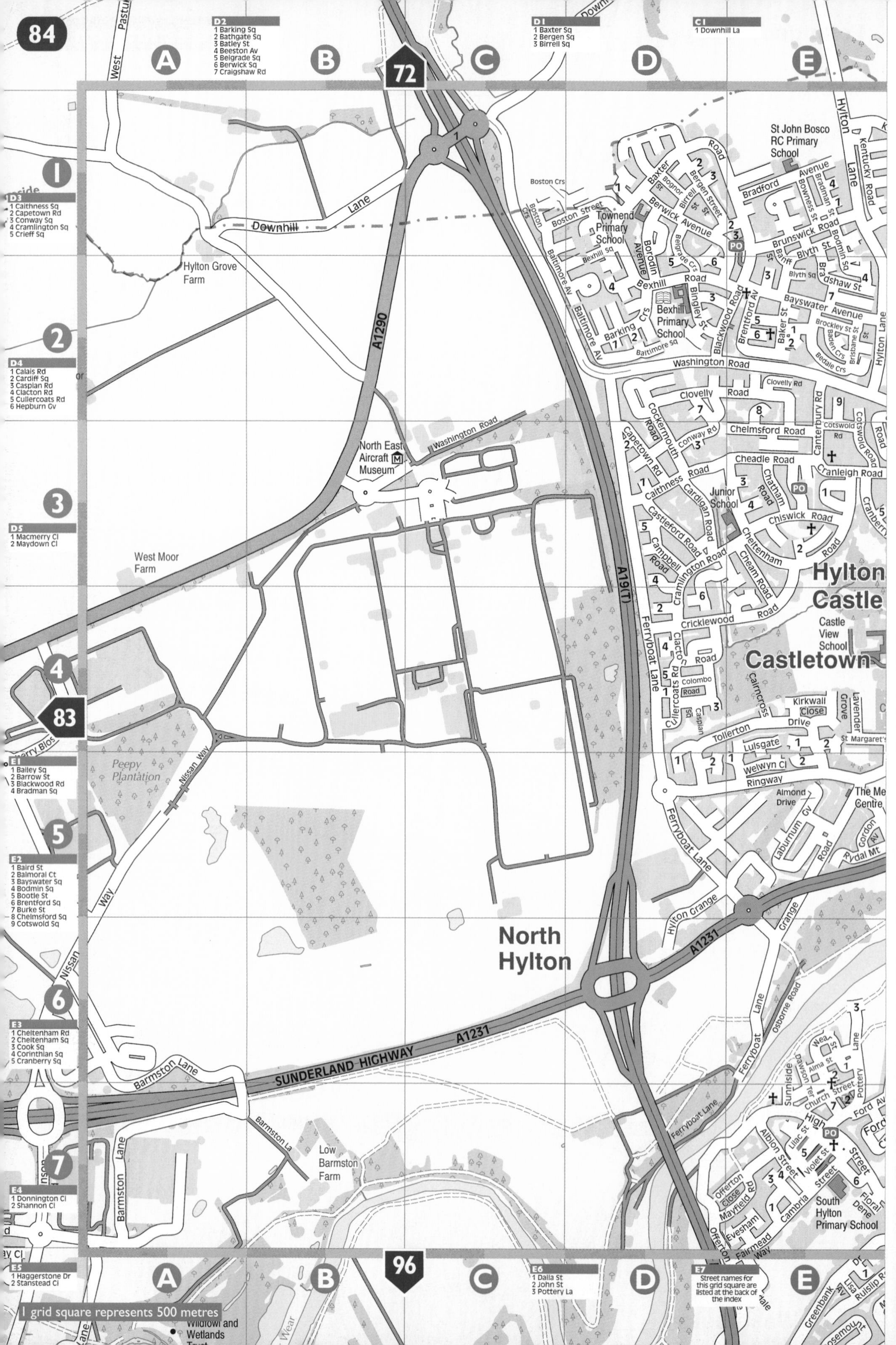

D2
1 Barking Sq
2 Bathgate Sq
3 Batley St
4 Beeston Av
5 Belgrade Sq
6 Berwick Sq
7 Craigshaw Rd
D1
1 Baxter Sq
2 Bergen Sq
3 Birrell Sq
C1
1 Downhill La
A
B
C
D
E
72
D3
1 Caithness Sq
2 Capetown Rd
3 Conway Sq
4 Cramlington Sq
5 Crieff Sq
D4
1 Calais Rd
2 Cardiff Sq
3 Caspian Rd
4 Clacton Rd
5 Cullercoats Rd
6 Hepburn Gv
D5
1 Macmerry Cl
2 Maydown Cl
E1
1 Bailey Sq
2 Barrow St
3 Blackwood Rd
4 Bradman Sq
E2
1 Baird St
2 Balmoral Ct
3 Bayswater Sq
4 Bodmin Sq
5 Bootle St
6 Brentford Sq
7 Burke St
8 Chelmsford Sq
9 Cotswold Sq
E3
1 Cheltenham Rd
2 Cheltenham Sq
3 Cook Sq
4 Corinthian Sq
5 Cranberry Sq
E4
1 Donnington Cl
2 Shannon Cl
E5
1 Haggerstone Dr
2 Stanstead Cl
E6
1 Dalla St
2 John St
3 Pottery La
E7
Street names for this grid square are listed at the back of the index
1
2
3
4
5
6
7
83
96
Downhill Lane
Hylton Grove Farm
A1290
North East Aircraft Museum
Washington Road
West Moor Farm
Peepy Plantation
Nissan Way
A19(T)
North Hylton
A1231
SUNDERLAND HIGHWAY
Barmston Lane
Barmston La
Low Barmston Farm
St John Bosco RC Primary School
Townend Primary School
Bexhill Primary School
Junior School
Hylton Castle
Castle View School
Castletown
Washington Road
Clovelly Road
Chelmsford Road
Cheadle Road
Cranleigh Road
Chiswick Road
Cricklewood Road
Ferryboat Lane
Tollerton Drive
Lulsgate
Welwyn Cl
Ringway
Almond Drive
Laburnum Gv
Hylton Grange
Osborne Road
Sunniside
South Hylton Primary School
Offerton Close
Mayfield Rd
Evesham
Cambria
Fairmead Way
Greenbank Av
Ruislip Rd
1 grid square represents 500 metres
Wildfowl and Wetlands Trust

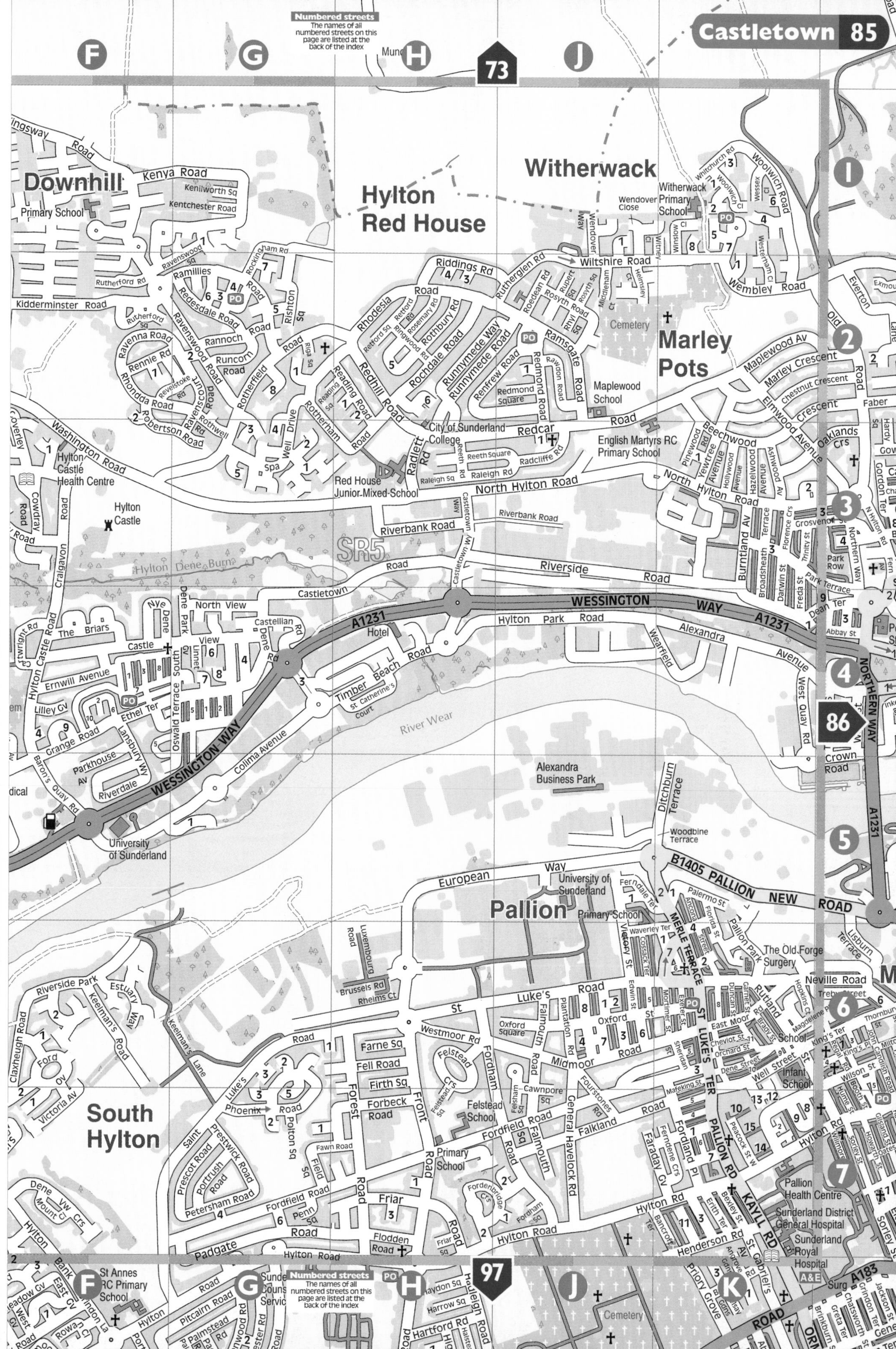
Numbered streets
The names of all numbered streets on this page are listed at the back of the index
73
Downhill
Hylton Red House
Witherwack
Marley Pots
Kenya Road
Kenilworth Sq
Kentchester Road
Primary School
Rutherford Rd
Kidderminster Road
Ramillies
Redesdale Road
Ravenswood Road
Rannoch Road
Runcorn Road
Rotherfield Road
Ravenna Road
Rennie Rd
Rhondda Road
Robertson Road
Washington Road
Hylton Castle Health Centre
Hylton Castle
Cowdray Road
Craigavon Road
Rishton Sq
Riga Sq
Reading Road
Rotherham Road
Well Drive
Spa
Redhill Road
Rhodesia Road
Rochdale Road
Rothbury Rd
Runnymede Way
Runnymede Road
Renfrew Road
Redmond Road
Redmond Square
Ramsgate Road
Rosyth Road
Roedean Rd
Rutherglen Rd
Riddings Rd
Wiltshire Road
Wendover Way
Wendover Close
Witherwack Primary School
Woolwich Road
Wembley Road
Cemetery
Maplewood School
Maplewood Av
Marley Crescent
Chestnut Crescent
Elmwood Avenue
Beechwood
Oaklands Crs
City of Sunderland College
Redcar Road
Reeth Square
Raleigh Rd
Radcliffe Rd
Radlett Rd
Red House Junior Mixed School
English Martyrs RC Primary School
North Hylton Road
Riverbank Road
Castletown Way
SR5
Hylton Dene Burn
Riverside Road
Castletown Road
WESSINGTON WAY
A1231
Hylton Park Road
Alexandra Avenue
Wearfield
North View
Dene Park
Castellian Rd
Hotel
Timber Beach Road
St Catherine's Court
Castle View
Ernwill Avenue
Oswald Terrace South
Lansbury Way
Grange Road
Lilley Gv
Parkhouse Av
Riverdale
Baron's Quay Rd
Colima Avenue
River Wear
University of Sunderland
Alexandra Business Park
Ditchburn Terrace
Woodbine Terrace
European Way
B1405 PALLION NEW ROAD
Pallion
University of Sunderland Primary School
MERLE TERRACE
Pallion Park
The Old Forge Surgery
Neville Road
Luxembourg Road
Brussels Rd
Rheims Ct
St Luke's Road
Oxford Square
Oxford St
Midmoor Road
Westmoor Rd
Felstead Crs
Felstead School
Fordham Road
Falmouth Road
Cawnpore Sq
General Havelock Rd
Fordfield Road
Falkland Road
ST LUKE'S TER
PALLION RD
KAYLL RD
Pallion Health Centre
Sunderland District General Hospital
Sunderland Royal Hospital
A&E
Riverside Park
Estuary Way
Keelman's Road
Keelman's Lane
Claxheugh Road
Ford Ov
Victoria Av
South Hylton
Phoenix Road
Polton Sq
Prestwick Road
Portrush Road
Prescot Road
Petersham Road
Forest Road
Front Road
Farne Sq
Fell Road
Firth Sq
Forbeck Road
Field Sq
Friar Road
Flodden Road
Primary School
Hylton Road
Padgate Road
Henderson Rd
Priory Grove
Dene Vw Crs
Mount Cl
Hylton Bank
St Annes RC Primary School
Ashfield
86
97
A183
Cemetery
Numbered streets
The names of all numbered streets on this page are listed at the back of the index

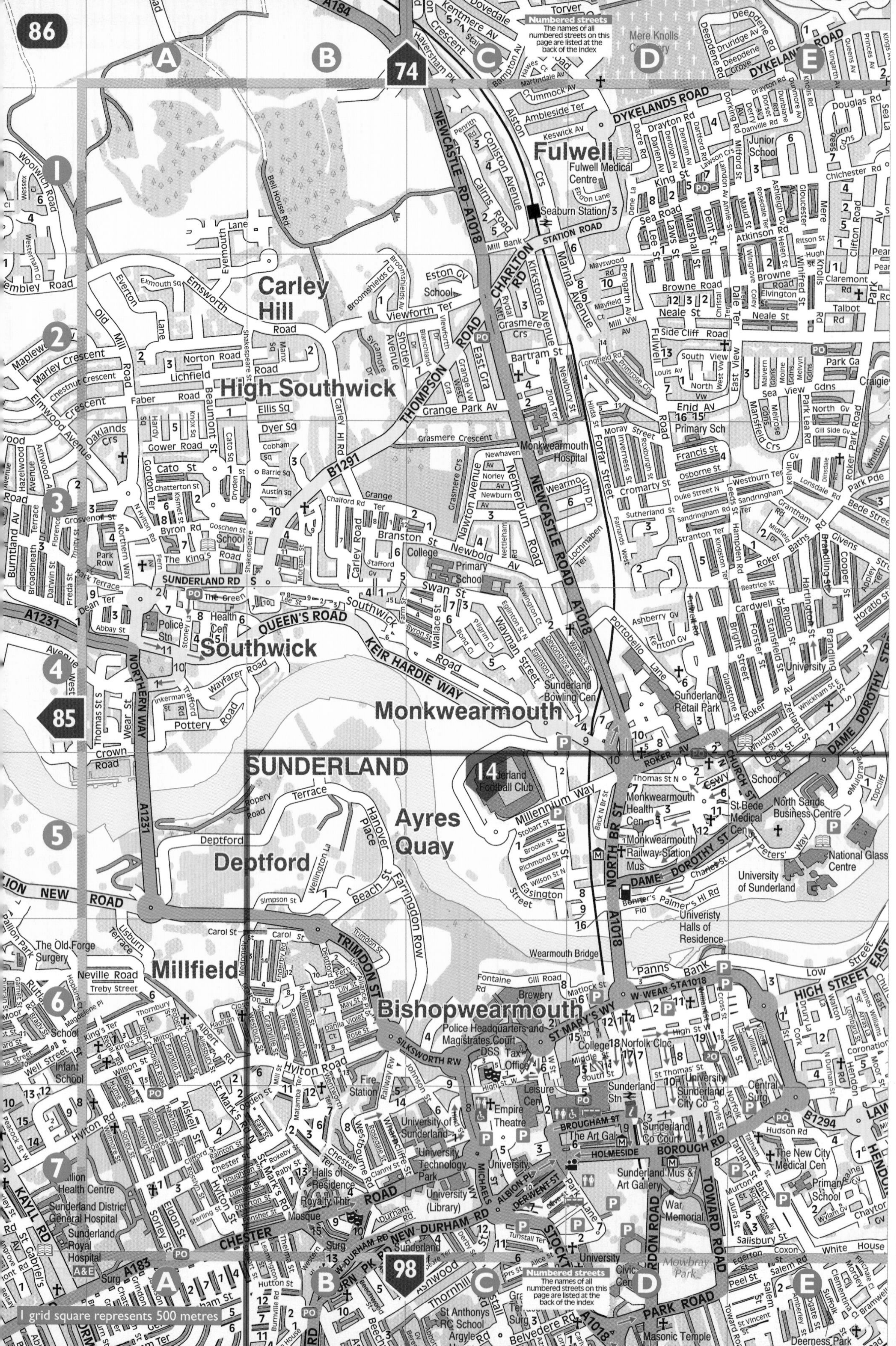

Numbered streets
The names of all numbered streets on this page are listed at the back of the index
74
85
98
A
B
C
D
E
1
2
3
4
5
6
7
Fulwell
Carley Hill
High Southwick
Southwick
Monkwearmouth
SUNDERLAND
Ayres Quay
Deptford
Millfield
Bishopwearmouth
Mere Knolls Cemetery
Seaburn Station
Fulwell Medical Centre
Monkwearmouth Hospital
Sunderland Bowling Cen
Sunderland Retail Park
Sunderland Football Club
Monkwearmouth Health Cen
Monkwearmouth Railway Station Mus
St Bede Medical Cen
North Sands Business Centre
National Glass Centre
University of Sunderland
University Halls of Residence
Wearmouth Bridge
Police Headquarters and Magistrates Court
DSS Tax Office
Leisure Cen
Empire Theatre
Sunderland Stn
Sunderland City Co
Central Surg
The New City Medical Cen
University Technology Park
University (Library)
Halls of Residence
Royalty Thtr
Mosque
The Art Gal
Sunderland Co Court
Sunderland Mus & Art Gallery
War Memorial
Mowbray Park
Masonic Temple
St Anthonys RC School
Deerness Park
The Old Forge Surgery
Pallion Health Centre
Sunderland District General Hospital
Sunderland Royal Hospital
Infant School
Fire Station
College
Primary School
Junior School
Primary Sch
NEWCASTLE RD A1018
NEWCASTLE ROAD A1018
NORTH BR ST A1018
THOMPSON ROAD B1291
NORTHERN WAY A1231
A1231
QUEEN'S ROAD
KEIR HARDIE WAY
DYKELANDS ROAD
STATION ROAD
TRIMDON ST
SILKSWORTH RW
ST MARY'S WY
W WEAR ST A1018
DAME DOROTHY ST
CHESTER ROAD
NEW DURHAM RD
HOLMESIDE
BOROUGH RD
TOWARD ROAD
PARK ROAD
HIGH STREET EAST
B1294
A183
A184
1 grid square represents 500 metres

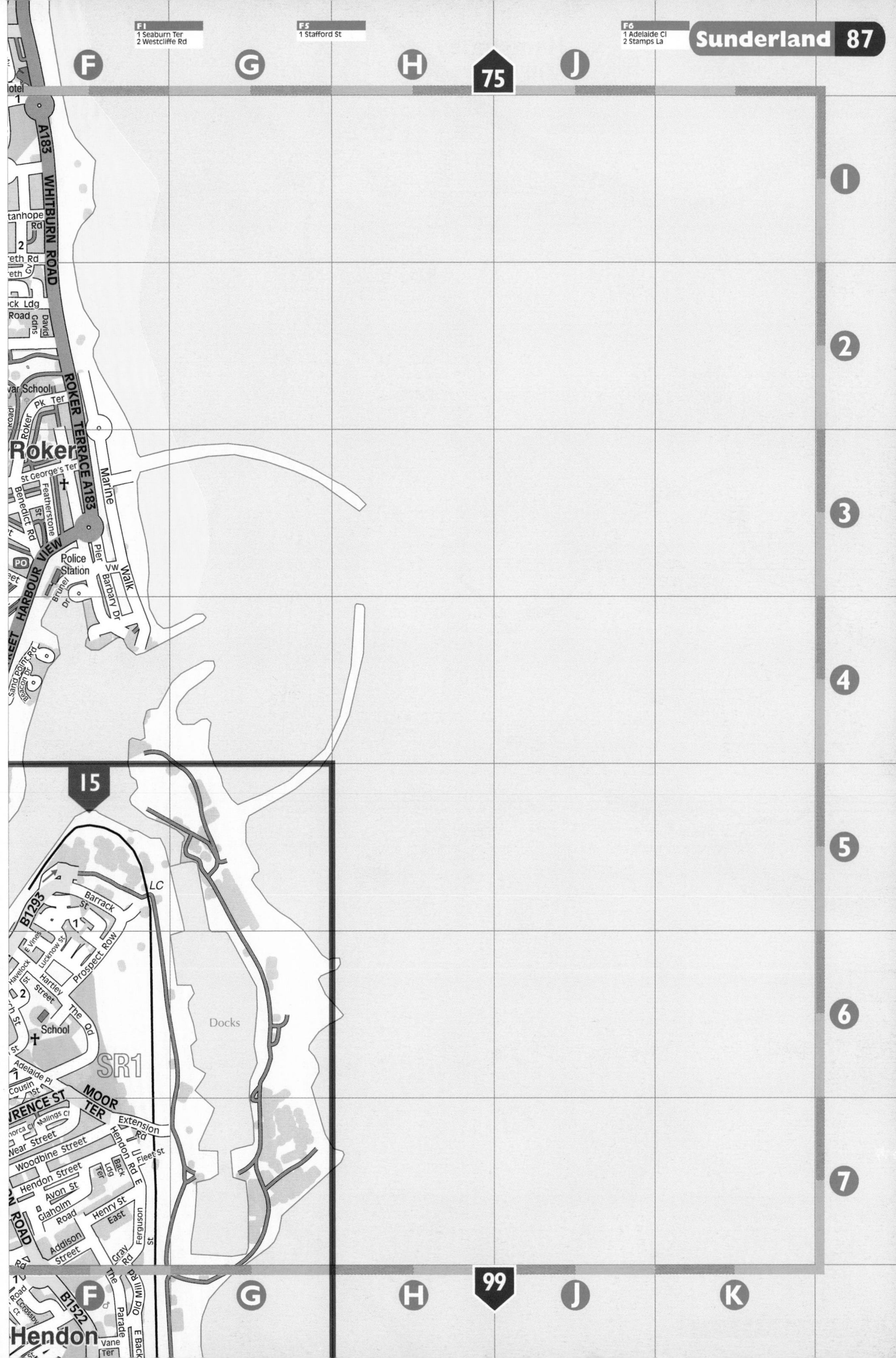
F1
1 Seaburn Ter
2 Westcliffe Rd
F5
1 Stafford St
F6
1 Adelaide Cl
2 Stamps La
75
99
15
F
G
H
J
K
1
2
3
4
5
6
7
WHITBURN ROAD
A183
ROKER TERRACE A183
Roker
Marine Walk
Pier Vw
Barbary Dr
Brunel Dr
Police Station
HARBOUR VIEW
Benedict Rd
Featherstone St
St George's Ter
Pk Ter
Roker
Stanhope Rd
David Gdns
Sand Point Rd
Beacon Dr
Docks
SR1
B1293
Barrack St
Prospect Row
Lucknow St
Hartley Street
Havelock St
The Od
School
Adelaide Pl
Cousin St
MOOR TER
Extension Rd
Malings Cl
Wear Street
Woodbine Street
Hendon Street
Hendon Rd
Avon St
Back Ldg Ter
Fleet St
Henry St East
Ferguson St
Glaholm Road
Addison Street
Gray Rd
B1522
The Parade
Old Mill Rd
Hendon
Vane Ter
E Back
LC

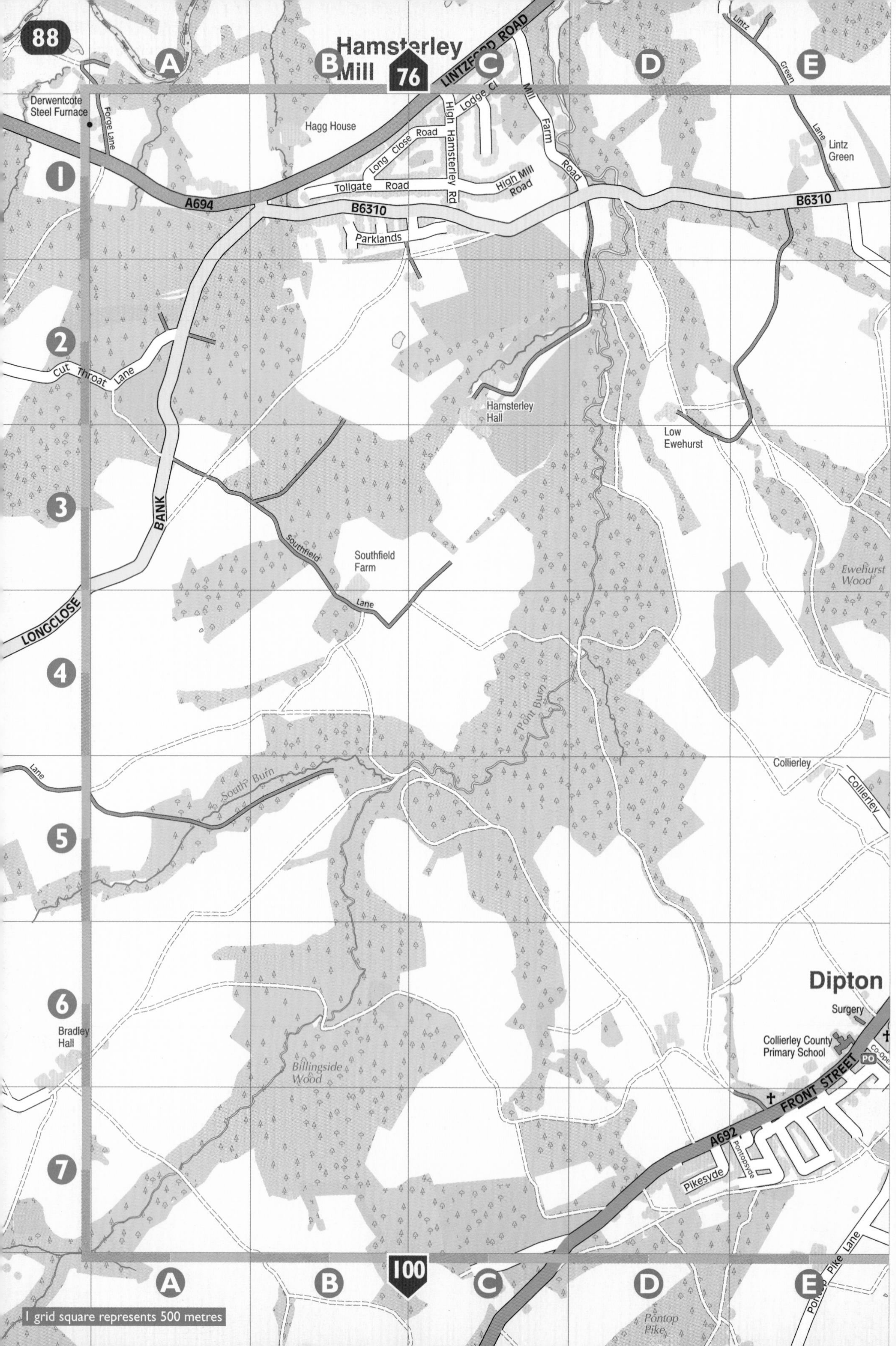
Hamsterley Mill
76
LINTZFORD ROAD
A
B
C
D
E
Derwentcote Steel Furnace
Forge Lane
Hagg House
Lodge Cl
High Hamsterley Rd
Long Close Road
Mill Farm Road
Lintz Green
Lane
Lintz Green
Tollgate Road
High Mill Road
A694
B6310
B6310
Parklands
1
2
Cut Throat Lane
Hamsterley Hall
Low Ewehurst
3
BANK
Southfield Lane
Southfield Farm
Ewehurst Wood
LONGCLOSE
4
Pont Burn
Lane
South Burn
Collierley
Collierley
5
6
Dipton
Surgery
Bradley Hall
Collierley County Primary School
PO
Co-Op
FRONT STREET
Billingside Wood
A692
Pontopsyde
Pikesyde
7
Pontop Pike Lane
100
Pontop Pike
1 grid square represents 500 metres

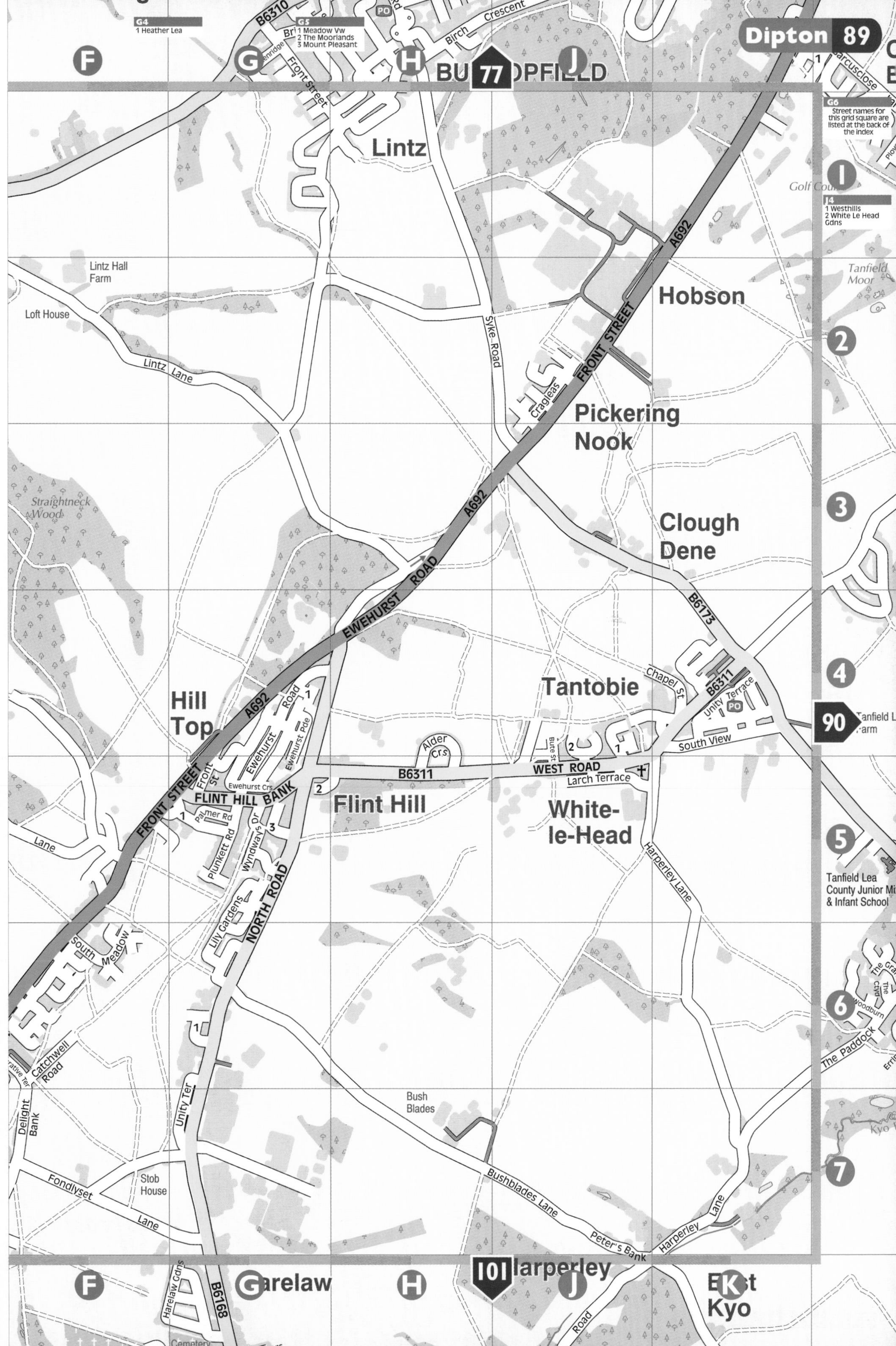
G4
1 Heather Lea
G5
1 Meadow Vw
2 The Moorlands
3 Mount Pleasant
G6
Street names for this grid square are listed at the back of the index
J4
1 Westhills
2 White Le Head Gdns
B6310
Birch Crescent
Front Street
Lintz
Lintz Hall Farm
Loft House
Lintz Lane
Syke Road
A692
Hobson
Golf Course
Tanfield Moor
Cragleas
FRONT STREET
Pickering Nook
Straightneck Wood
Clough Dene
EWEHURST ROAD
B6173
Tantobie
Chapel St
B6311
Unity Terrace
PO
South View
Tanfield Lea Farm
Hill Top
Ewehurst Road
Ewehurst Pde
Ewehurst Crs
Front St
FLINT HILL BANK
Alder Crs
Bute St
WEST ROAD
Larch Terrace
Flint Hill
White-le-Head
Palmer Rd
Plunkett Rd
Wyndways Dr
NORTH ROAD
Harperley Lane
Tanfield Lea County Junior Mix & Infant School
Lane
South Meadow
Lilly Gardens
The Paddock
Woodburn
Catchwell Road
Delight Bank
Unity Ter
Bush Blades
Fondlyset Lane
Stob House
Bushblades Lane
Peter's Bank
Harperley Lane
Harperley
Harelaw Gdns
B6168
Garelaw
East Kyo
Road
Cemetery
F
G
H
J
I
K
2
3
4
5
6
7
77
90
101

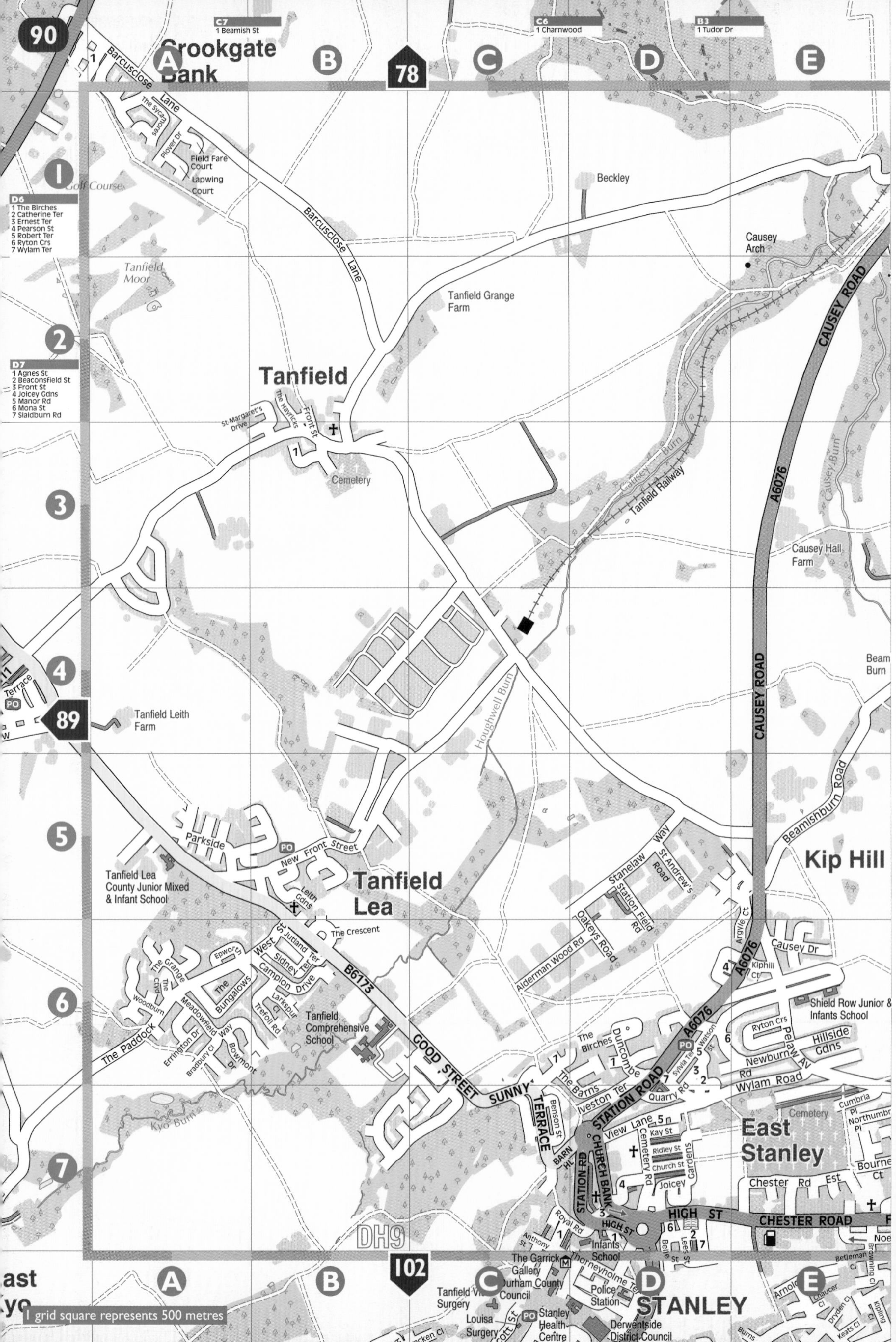

90
78
89
102
C7 1 Beamish St
C6 1 Charnwood
B3 1 Tudor Dr
D6 1 The Birches 2 Catherine Ter 3 Ernest Ter 4 Pearson St 5 Robert Ter 6 Ryton Crs 7 Wylam Ter
D7 1 Agnes St 2 Beaconsfield St 3 Front St 4 Joicey Gdns 5 Manor Rd 6 Mona St 7 Slaidburn Rd
Crookgate Bank
Barcusclose Lane
Field Fare Court
Lapwing Court
Plover Dr
Golf Course
Tanfield Moor
Beckley
Causey Arch
Tanfield Grange Farm
Tanfield
St Margaret's Drive
The Havricks
Front St
Cemetery
Causey Burn
Tanfield Railway
CAUSEY ROAD
A6076
Causey Hall Farm
Tanfield Leith Farm
Houghwell Burn
Beamish Burn
Beamishburn Road
Kip Hill
Parkside
New Front Street
Tanfield Lea
Tanfield Lea County Junior Mixed & Infant School
Leith Gdns
The Crescent
Stanelaw Way
St Andrew's Road
Station Field Rd
Oakeys Road
Alderman Wood Rd
Argyle Ct
Causey Dr
Kiphill Ct
Shield Row Junior & Infants School
Ryton Crs
Pelaw Av
Hillside Gdns
Newburn Rd
Wylam Road
Epworth
The Grange
West St
Jutland Ter
Sidney Ter
Campion Drive
The Bungalows
Larkspur Cl
Trefoil Rd
Woodburn
Meadowfield Way
Errington Dr
Bradbury Cl
Bowmont Dr
The Paddock
Tanfield Comprehensive School
B6173
GOOD STREET
SUNNY TERRACE
Benson St
The Birches
Duncombe
The Barns
Iveston Ter
STATION ROAD
Quarry Rd
Sylvia Ter
Watson St
Kyo Burn
View Lane
Kay St
Ridley St
Church St
Cemetery Rd
Gardens
Joicey
CHURCH BANK
STATION RD
BARN HL
Cemetery
East Stanley
Cumbria Pl
Northumbria Pl
Bourne Ct
Chester Rd Est
HIGH ST
CHESTER ROAD
Royal Rd
Anthony St
Infants School
Belle St
Lees St
DH9
The Garrick Gallery
Durham County Council
Thorneyholme Ter
Police Station
STANLEY
Tanfield View Surgery
Louisa Surgery
Stanley Health Centre
Derwentside District Council
Bracken Cl
Arnold
Chaucer Cl
Dryden Cl
Keats Cl
Kipling
Betjeman Cl
Browning Cl
Burns
Noel
1 grid square represents 500 metres

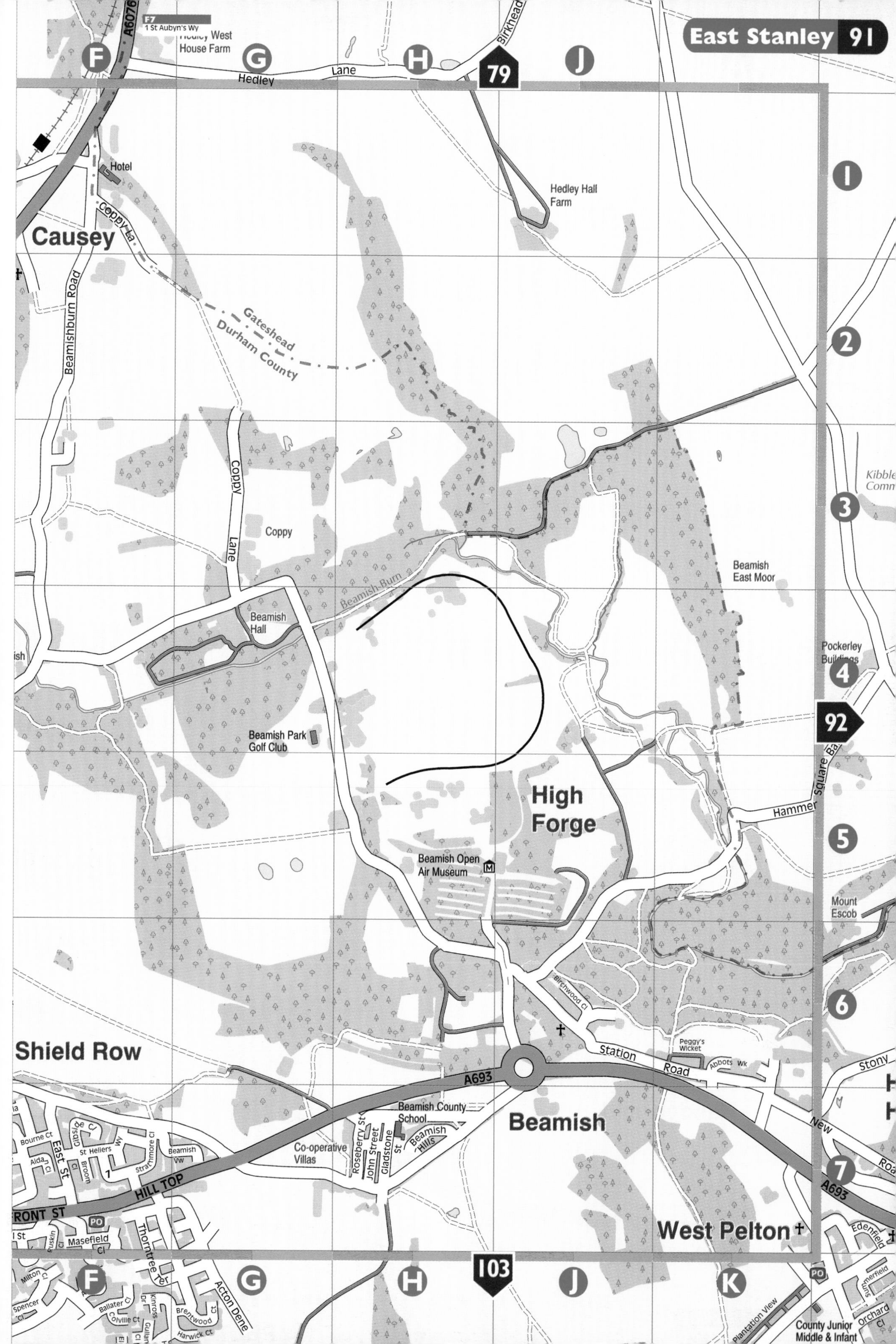
F7
1 St Aubyn's Wy
Hedley West House Farm
A6076
F
G
H
J
79
Birkhead
Hedley
Lane
Hotel
Causey
Coppy La
Hedley Hall Farm
1
Gateshead
Durham County
Beamishburn Road
2
Coppy
Lane
Coppy
3
Kibble Comm
Beamish East Moor
Beamish-Burn
Beamish Hall
Pockerley Buildings
4
92
Beamish Park Golf Club
Square Ba
Hammer
High Forge
5
Beamish Open Air Museum
Mount Escob
Birchwood Cl
6
Shield Row
Station
Road
Peggy's Wicket
Abbots Wk
Stony
A693
Beamish County School
Beamish
New
Roa
Bourne Ct
Gibside Cl
East St
Alda
Broom
St Heliers
Wy
Strathmore Cl
Beamish Vw
Co-operative Villas
Roseberry St
John Street
Gladstone St
Beamish Hills
7
A693
HILL TOP
FRONT ST
PO
Ruskin
St
Masefield Cl
Thorntree Ter
West Pelton
Edenfield
F
G
103
H
J
K
Milton Cl
Spencer Cl
Ballater Cl
Colville Ct
Kinross Dr
Brentwood Ct
Acton Dene
Harwick Ct
PO
Plantation View
Orchard Cl
County Junior Middle & Infant

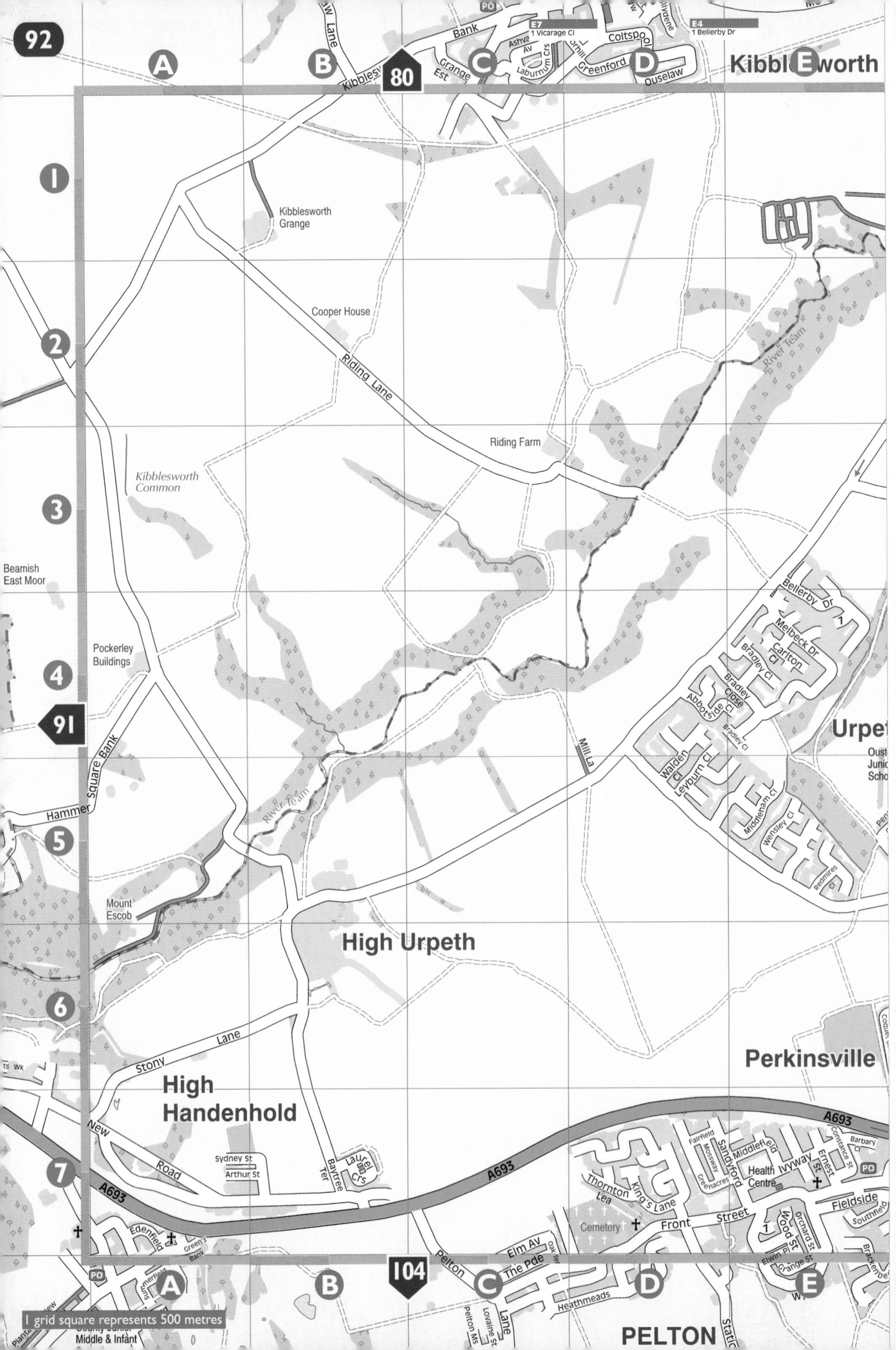

Kibblesworth
Kibblesworth Grange
Cooper House
Riding Lane
Riding Farm
River Team
Kibblesworth Common
Beamish East Moor
Pockerley Buildings
Square Bank
Hammer
Mount Escob
Mill La
High Urpeth
Urpeth
Perkinsville
Stony Lane
High Handenhold
New Road
Sydney St
Arthur St
Baytree Ter
Laurel Crs
A693
Bellerby Dr
Melbeck Dr
Carlton Cl
Bradley Cl
Bradley Close
Abbotside Cl
Walden Cl
Leyburn Cl
Middleham Cl
Wensley Cl
Redmires Cl
Thornton Lea
King's Lane
Cemetery
Front Street
Health Centre
Fairfield
Mossway
Greenacres
Sandyford
Middlefield
Ivyway
Ernest St
Constance St
Barbary Cl
Fieldside
Southfield
Wood St
Orchard St
Elwin Pl
Grange St
Elm Av
The Pde
Oak Ter
Pelton Lane
Heathmeads
Lovaine St
Pelton Ms
Edenfield
Green's Bank
PELTON
Middle & Infant
Coltspool
Greenford
Ouselaw
Grange Est
Laburnum Crs
E7 1 Vicarage Cl
E4 1 Bellerby Dr
1 grid square represents 500 metres

80
91
104

J2
1 Birtley La
2 Holyoake Gdns
3 Ruskin Rd
F
G
H
J
81
BIRTLEY
Lansbury Dr
Ellisabeth Drive Av
Glamis Vls
Garside Avenue
Selkirk Crs
Wilson Av
Rutland Sq
Edward Road
DURHAM ROAD
St Josephs Infant School
Mt Pleasant
Mount Rd
Gateshead Metropolitan Borough Council
Poplar Crs
Ravensworth Road
Pine St
May St
Primrose Ter
The Uplands
B1288
FELL BANK
Birtley Lane Surg
Orchard St
Orchard Pk
King St
George St
Jones St
Morris St
West St
The Av
South Vw
Hillside
Hi Top
Portmeads Road
Penshaw Way
Station Lane
Rowletch Burn
Rowletch Burn Industrial Estate
A6127
St John's Pl
St John's St
School St
Birtley Lane
Primary School
Portobello
Shadon Way
Low Urpeth
Birtley St Josephs RC School
Harras Bank
Lord Lawson of Beamish Secondary School
Birtley Medical Group Practice
Birtley Swimming Baths
Radcliffe St
Wilfrid St
Leafield House School
Springs
Birtley La
Glenluce
Lydford Wy
Polpero Cl
Hartland Dr
Tamerton Dr
Portobello County Junior Infant School
Dunvegan
Abernethy
Athull
Alford
Angus
Turnberry
The Oval
The Viola Crs
Coldstream
Ross
Callander
Cannock
Cromarty
Ouston
Barley Mow
A6127 DURHAM ROAD
Colebrooke
Enderdale
Thirlmere
94
Errol Pl
Kirkstone
Iris Crs
Arisaig
Aberfoyle
Ouston County Infant School
Coldstream Close
Barley Mow Primary School
Dorset Avenue
Pembroke Av
Athlone Pl
Nairn Cl
Scafell
Coniston
Hartside
Sandray Close
Moray Cl
York Rd
Ardrossan
Aberdeen
Carnoustie
Rothsay
Byron
Milbanke Close
St Benets Primary RC School
Norfolk Avenue
Suffolk Pl
The Dr
Knaresdale
Cambridge Pl
Oxford Pl
Cumberland Pl
Cheshire Av
Durham Pl
Bedford Avenue
Vigo La
Lodge
Picktree
Institute Ter
Lyne Cl
Alice St
Conway Pl
Brecon Pl
Ouston Lane
Ascot Pl
Gairloch Dr
Wansbeck Cl
Drum Road
First Av
Second Av
Third Av
Drum Road
Pelaw Gra Ct
Sinclair Drive
Park View Comprehensive School
Leander Av
Hampton Ct
Merlin Dr
Kingsmere
Lombard Drive
Picktree Lane
Ash Mdw
North Dr
Linford
Pelton Health Clinic
Pelton County Junior & Infant School
Queensmere
Wear Lodge
NORTH ROAD
Drum Rd
105
A693
Low Flatts Rd
Lyndhurst Avenue
Long Dean Pk
K
Pelton La
Vigo Lane
A1(M)
1
2
3
4
5
6
7

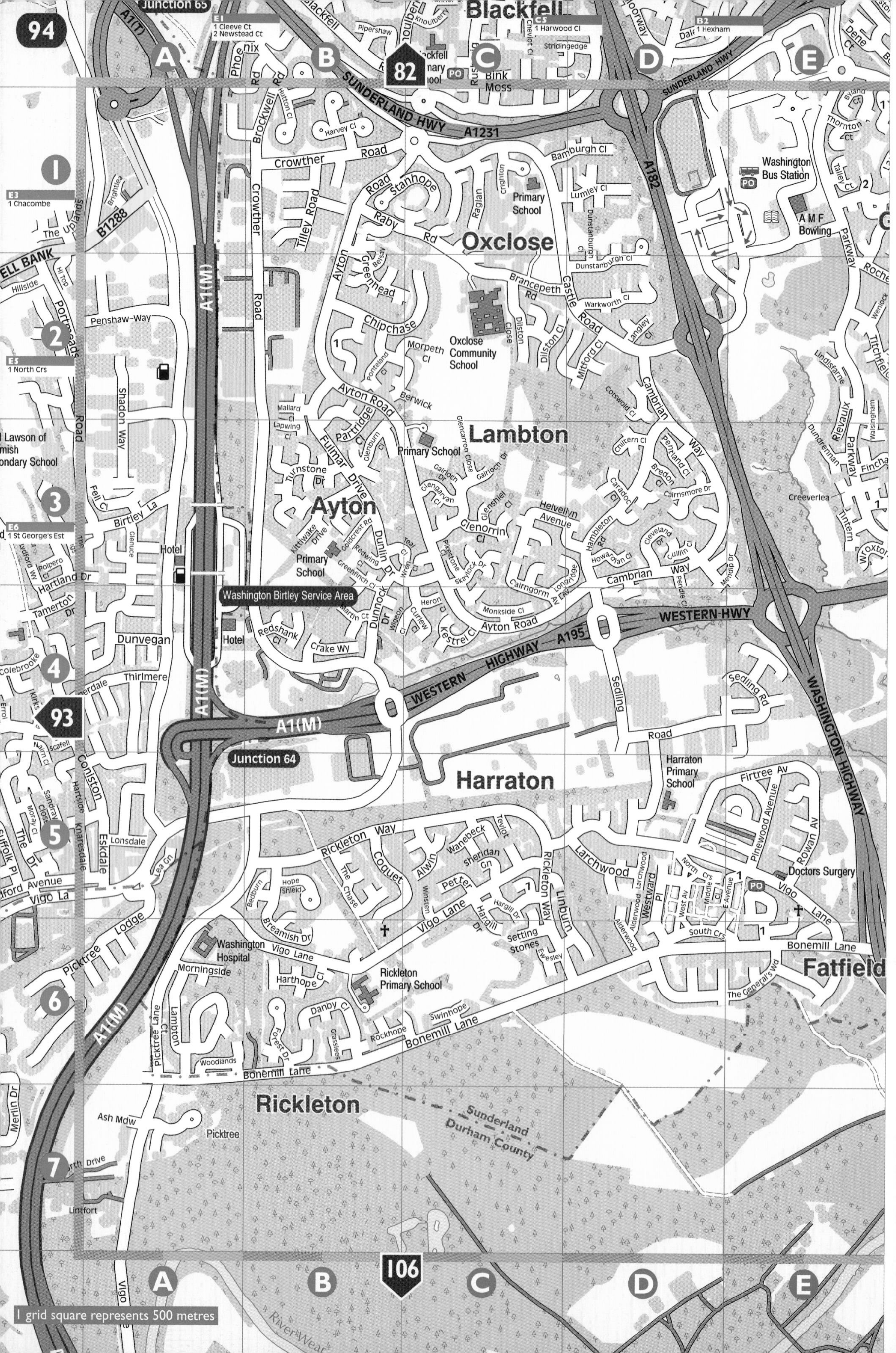
Junction 65
Blackfell
Oxclose
Lambton
Ayton
Harraton
Rickleton
Fatfield
Washington Birtley Service Area
Junction 64
Washington Bus Station
A M F Bowling
Oxclose Community School
Primary School
Harraton Primary School
Rickleton Primary School
Washington Hospital
Doctors Surgery
Sunderland
Durham County
SUNDERLAND HWY
WESTERN HWY
WESTERN HIGHWAY
WASHINGTON HIGHWAY
A1(M)
A1231
A182
A195
B1288
82
93
106
1 grid square represents 500 metres

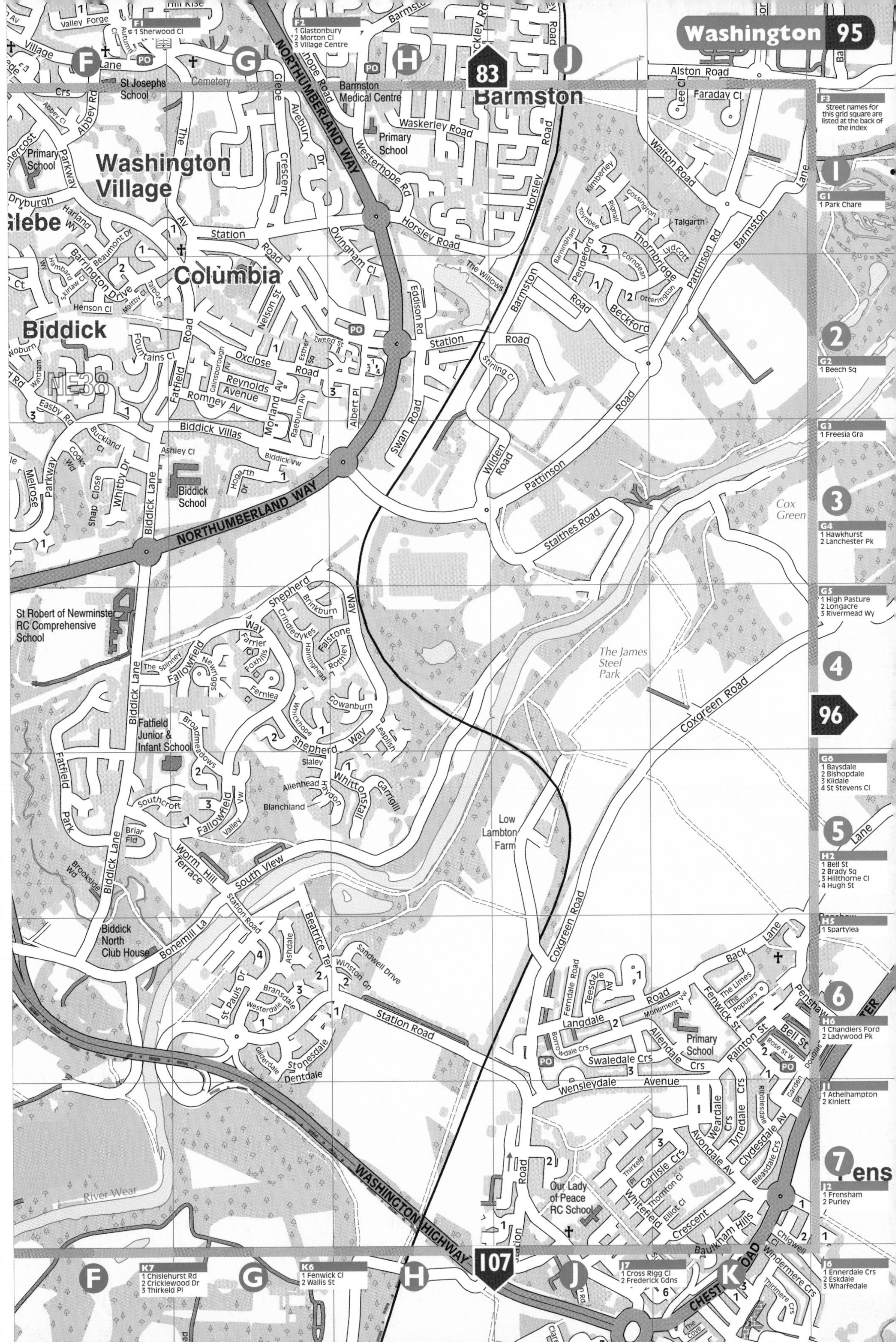

Washington 95
83
Barmston
Washington Village
Glebe
Columbia
Biddick
NE38
F1
1 Sherwood Cl
F2
1 Glastonbury
2 Morton Cl
3 Village Centre
F3
Street names for this grid square are listed at the back of the index
G1
1 Park Chare
G2
1 Beech Sq
G3
1 Freesia Gra
G4
1 Hawkhurst
2 Lanchester Pk
G5
1 High Pasture
2 Longacre
3 Rivermead Wy
G6
1 Baysdale
2 Bishopdale
3 Kildale
4 St Stevens Cl
H2
1 Bell St
2 Brady Sq
3 Hillthorne Cl
4 Hugh St
H5
1 Spartylea
H6
1 Chandlers Ford
2 Ladywood Pk
J1
1 Athelhampton
2 Kinlett
J2
1 Frensham
2 Purley
J6
1 Ennerdale Crs
2 Eskdale
3 Wharfedale
J7
1 Cross Rigg Cl
2 Frederick Gdns
K6
1 Fenwick Cl
2 Wallis St
K7
1 Chislehurst Rd
2 Cricklewood Dr
3 Thirkeld Pl
96
107
Northumberland Way
Washington Highway
St Josephs School
Cemetery
Barmston Medical Centre
Primary School
St Robert of Newminster RC Comprehensive School
Biddick School
Fatfield Junior & Infant School
Biddick North Club House
Our Lady of Peace RC School
The James Steel Park
Low Lambton Farm
Cox Green
River Wear
Station Road
Horsley Road
Waskerley Road
Westerhope Rd
Pattinson Rd
Barmston Road
Staithes Road
Coxgreen Road
Biddick Lane
Biddick Villas
Fatfield Park
Shepherd Way
Fallowfield Way
Worm Hill Terrace
South View
Bonemill La
Wensleydale Avenue
Swaledale Crs
Langdale
Whitefield Crescent
Baulkham Hills
Chester Road
Pens

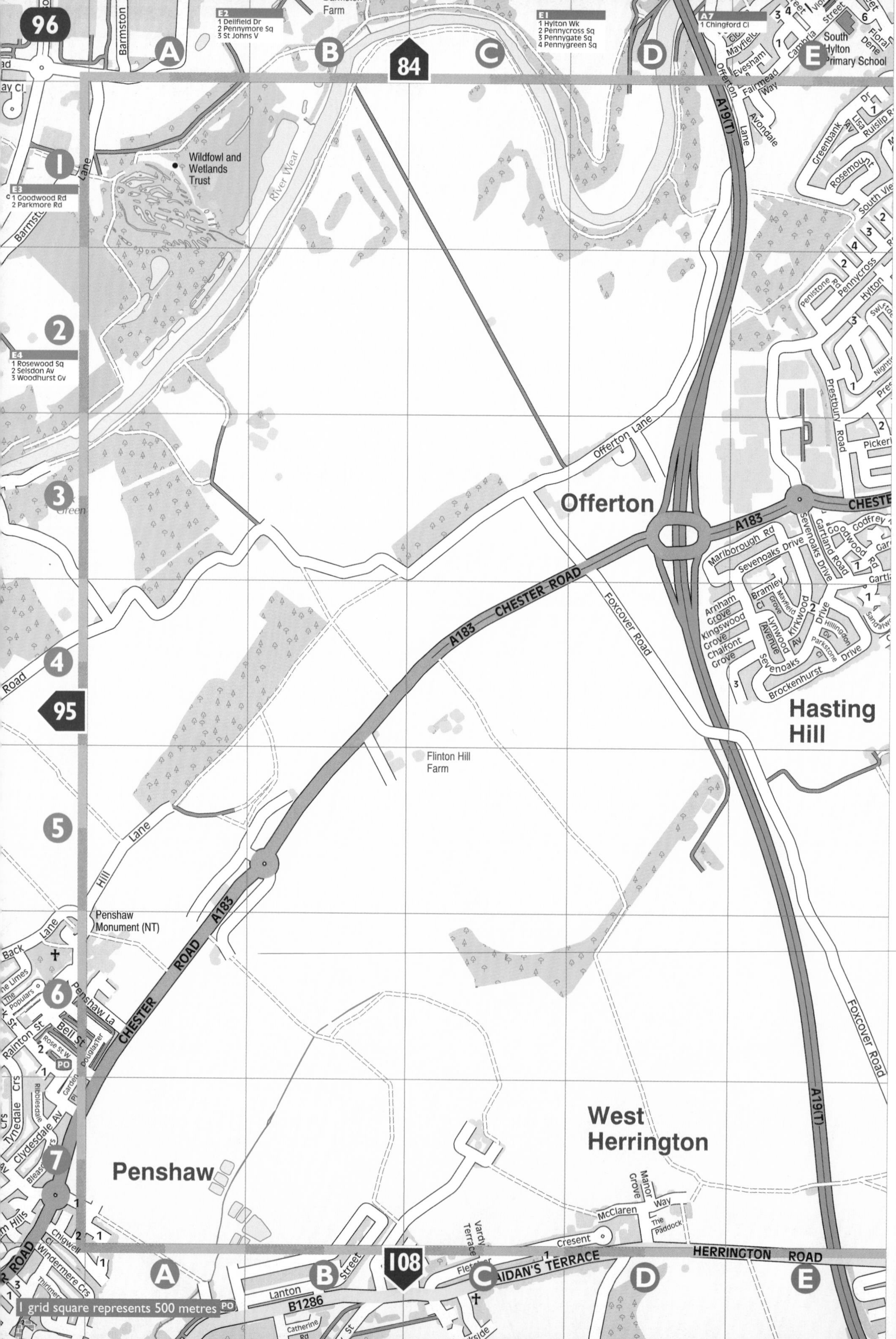

96
84
95
108
E2 1 Dellfield Dr 2 Pennymore Sq 3 St Johns V
E1 1 Hylton Wk 2 Pennycross Sq 3 Pennygate Sq 4 Pennygreen Sq
A7 1 Chingford Cl
E3 1 Goodwood Rd 2 Parkmore Rd
E4 1 Rosewood Sq 2 Selsdon Av 3 Woodhurst Gv
Barmston Farm
Wildfowl and Wetlands Trust
River Wear
South Hylton Primary School
Offerton Lane
Offerton
Hasting Hill
Chester Road
A183
A19(T)
Foxcover Road
Flinton Hill Farm
Penshaw Monument (NT)
Hill Lane
Penshaw
West Herrington
Herrington Road
Aidan's Terrace
B1286
Lanton Street
Manor Grove
McClaren Way
The Paddock
Cresent
Marlborough Rd
Sevenoaks Drive
Gartland Road
Goodwood Rd
Godfrey
Arnham Grove
Kingswood Grove
Chalfont Grove
Bramley Cl
Lynwood Avenue
Kirkwood Av
Parkstone Cl
Brockenhurst
Prestbury Road
Penistone Rd
Pennycross
Greenbank Av
Rosemount
Avondale
Evesham
Mayfield
Fairmead Way
Camoria Street
Penshaw La
Bell St
Rainton St
Clydesdale Av
Tynedale Crs
Ribblesdale
Chigwell
Windermere Crs
Back Lane
Barmston Lane
1 grid square represents 500 metres

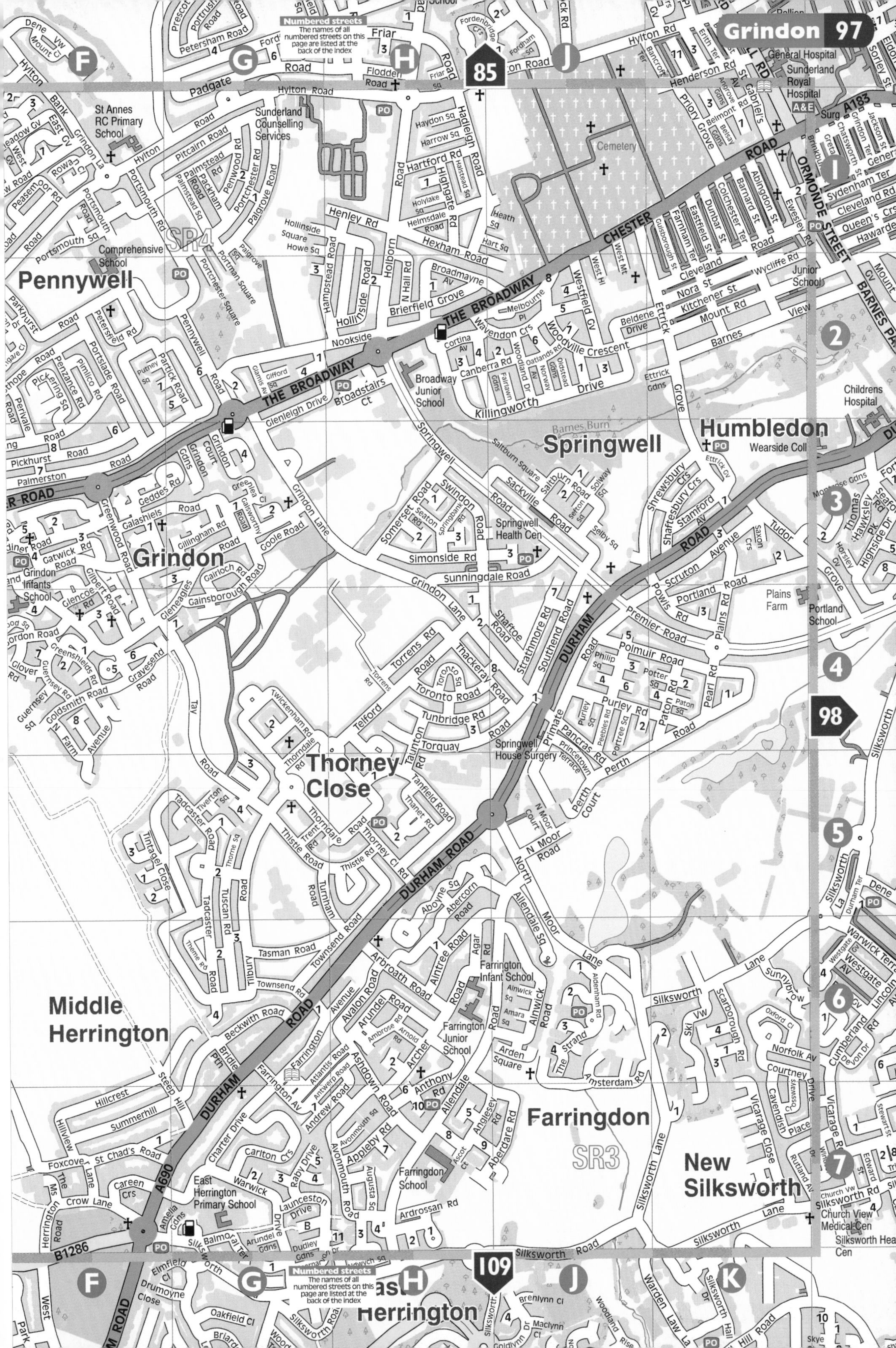
Numbered streets
The names of all numbered streets on this page are listed at the back of the index
85
98
109
F
G
H
J
I
K
2
3
4
5
6
7
Pennywell
Grindon
Springwell
Humbledon
Thorney Close
Middle Herrington
Farringdon
New Silksworth
East Herrington
SR4
SR3
St Annes RC Primary School
Comprehensive School
Sunderland Counselling Services
Cemetery
General Hospital
Sunderland Royal Hospital
A&E
Childrens Hospital
Wearside Coll
Junior School
Broadway Junior School
Springwell Health Cen
Springwell House Surgery
Plains Farm
Portland School
Grindon Infants School
Farrington Infant School
Farrington Junior School
Farringdon School
East Herrington Primary School
Church View Medical Cen
Silksworth Health Cen
Barnes Burn
THE BROADWAY
CHESTER ROAD
DURHAM ROAD
A690
A183
B1286
ORMONDE STREET
Hylton Road
Padgate Road
Pennywell Road
Grindon Lane
Springwell Road
Sackville Road
Shaftoe Road
Southend Road
Premier Road
Polmuir Road
Perth Road
Tudor Grove
Barnes View
Mount Rd
Kitchener St
Nora St
Cleveland Rd
Woodville Crescent
Killingworth Drive
Hexham Road
Henley Rd
Holborn Rd
Hadleigh Road
Thorndale Road
Thistle Road
Telford Road
Torquay Rd
Toronto Road
Tunbridge Rd
Tadcaster Road
Tuscan Rd
Tilbury Road
Tasman Road
Townsend Road
Turnham Road
Arbroath Road
Aintree Road
Agar Rd
North Moor Lane
Allendale Sq
Ashdown Road
Avonmouth Road
Appleby Rd
Anthony Rd
Aberdare Rd
Arden Square
The Strand
Amsterdam Rd
Silksworth Lane
Silksworth Road
Scarborough Rd
Vicarage Close
Vicarage Rd
Cavendish Place
Courtney Drive
Norfolk Av
Cumberland Rd
Westgate Av
Warwick Terr
Sunnybrow
Ski Vw
Silksworth Rd
Hillcrest
Summerhill
St Chad's Road
Foxcove
Crow Lane
Herrington Road
Careen Crs
Charter Drive
Carlton Crs
Warwick
Launceston Drive
Raby Drive
Ardrossan Rd
Beckwith Road
Bridle Pth
Steep Hill
Hillview
Palmerston Road
Pickhurst Road
Greenwood Road
Gilbert Road
Gleneagles Road
Gainsborough Road
Goole Road
Galashiels Road
Gillingham Rd
Goldsmith Road
Gravesend Road
Guernsey Sq
Farm Avenue
Portsmouth Road
Portchester Road
Palgrove Road
Pitcairn Road
Partick Road
Portslade Road
Penzance Rd
Pimlico Rd
Perivale Road
Parkhurst Road
Hylton Bank
Grindon La
Henderson Rd
Priory Grove
Abingdon St
Barnard St
Colchester Ter
Dunbar St
Eastfield St
Farnham Ter
Gabriel's
Westfield Gv
Ettrick Grove
Shrewsbury Crs
Shaftesbury Crs
Stamford Av
Scruton Avenue
Portland Road
Plains Rd
Powis Rd
Purley Rd
Paton Rd
Pearl Rd
Pancras Rd
Princetown Terrace
Primate Rd
Perth Court
N Moor Court
N Moor Road
Strathmore Rd
Thackeray Road
Torrens Rd
Sunningdale Road
Simonside Rd
Somerset Road
Swindon Road
Saltburn Road
Nookside
Broadstairs Ct
Glenleigh Drive
Brierfield Grove
Hollinside Road
Hampstead Road
Wavendon Crs
Canberra Rd
Silksworth Hall Dr
Warden Law La
Woodland Rise
Hill Road
Oakfield Cl
Drumoyne Close
Silksworth Road
West Park

98
86
97
110
A
B
C
D
E
1
2
3
4
5
6
7
Numbered streets
The names of all numbered streets on this page are listed at the back of the index
1 grid square represents 500 metres
Ashbrooke
Hillview
Tunstall
Humbledon
Ryhope Colliery
Pallion Health Centre
Sunderland District General Hospital
Sunderland Royal Hospital
A&E
Halls of Residence
Royalty Thtr
University (Library)
Technology Park
Sunderland Mus & Art Gallery
War Memorial
Mowbray Park
University
Civic Centre
Masonic Temple
Royal Inf
St Anthonys RC School
Argyle House School
Grange Terrace Surg
Deerness Park Medical Cen
Primary School
Medical Cen
Junior School
Thornhill Comprehensive School
Barbara Priestman School
St Marys RC Primary School
Sunderland Cricket & Rugby Football Club
University of Sunderland
St Aidans RC Comprehensive School
High School
Ashburne Medical Cen
Childrens Hospital
Wearside Coll
Plains Farm
Portland School
Sunderland Eye Infirmary
Belford House Sports Club
Southmoor School
Hillview Clinic
Hillview Infant School
City of Sunderland College
Infants School
Church View Medical Cen
Silksworth Health Cen
CHESTER ROAD
DURHAM ROAD
A183
A690
A1018
B1405
B1286
STOCKTON RD
BURDON RD
TOWARD ROAD
PARK ROAD
RYHOPE ROAD
QUEEN ALEXANDRA RD
QU ALEXANDRA RD
ORMONDE STREET
BARNES PARK ROAD
TUNSTALL BANK
TUNSTALL VILLAGE GN
BURDON ROAD
RYHOPE ST
Tunstall Road
Silksworth Lane
Leechmere Road
Toll Bar Road
Essen Way
Crosslea Avenue
Newlands Avenue
Tunstall Rd
Ashwood Ter
Thornhill Ter
Thornholme
Ashbrooke Rd
Ashbrooke Range
Nilverton Avenue
Glen Path
Stannington Grove
Laurel Grove
Helvellyn Rd
Westheath Av
Silksworth Terrace
Silksworth Rd
Vicarage Road
Warwick Terrace
Westgate Av
Cumberland Rd
Blind Lane
Hawthorn Av
Regency Dr
Paddock La
Ryemount Rd
Ravensworth
Shaftesbury Av
Western Hl
Edmond Court
Hewitt Avenue
Leechmere
Lansdowne

F1
1 Burlington Cl
2 St Barnabas Wy
F4
1 Carnegie St
2 Hemming St
3 Markham St
F5
Street names for this grid square are listed at the back of the index
F6
1 Burlawn Cl
2 Ouseburn Cl
3 Padstow Cl
F7
1 Nelson St
G5
1 Askern Av
2 Millthorp Cl
G6
1 Ladock Cl
87
111
Hendon
Grangetown
SR2
Valley Road Junior School
Valley Road Infant School
Grangetown Junior & Infant School
Cemetery
Ryhope Health Centre
Ryhope Cemetery
Promenade
COMMERCIAL ROAD
OCEAN RD
RYHOPE ROAD A1018
B1522
Salterfen Lane
Rosslyn Avenue
Station Road

88
A
B
C
D
E
1
2
3
4
5
6
7
Pikesyde
Pontop Pike
Pontop Pike Lane
A692
A693
East Castle
Eden Avenue
Tweed Avenue
Pont Lane
Went Crs
Avenue
Grassmere Ms
Annaside Mews
Ives' Road
Redwell Hills Clinic
Redwell Hills Farm
Brooms Primary School
LEADGATE
Low Brooms Farm
Brooms Lane
Stonyheap Lane
Stony Heap
Dunelm Way
Dunelm Walk
Dunelm Cl
DURHAM RD
Willow Crs
Lilac Pl
Hanging Stone
Hangings
Sunniside Farm
Leadgate Industrial Estate
Back Lane
A691
Iveston Lane
Iveston
Durham Hill
Gorecock
Moorside
Lund's Lane
WOODSIDE BANK
Woodside
Esp Green
1 grid square represents 500 metres

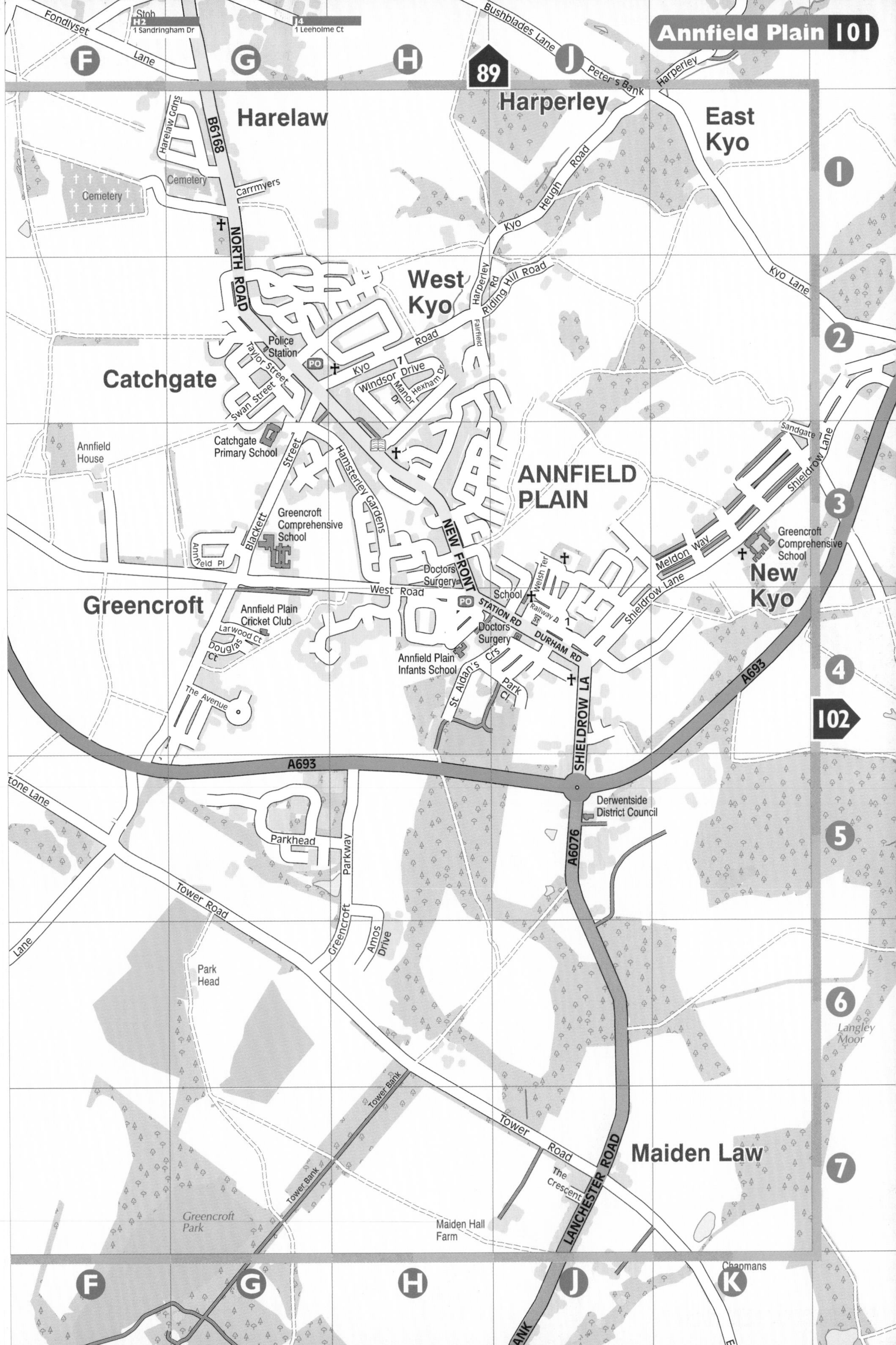
Stob
H2
1 Sandringham Dr
J4
1 Leeholme Ct
Fondlyset
Lane
F
G
H
J
K
89
102
Bushblades Lane
Peter's Bank
Harperley
Harperley
East Kyo
Harelaw
Harelaw Gdns
B6168
Cemetery
Cemetery
Carrmyers
NORTH ROAD
Kyo
Heugh
Road
West Kyo
Harperley Rd
Riding Hill Road
Fairfield
Kyo Lane
Police Station
PO
Kyo
Road
Windsor Drive
Manor Dr
Hexham Dr
Taylor Street
Swan Street
Catchgate
Catchgate Primary School
Annfield House
Street
Hamsterley Gardens
ANNFIELD PLAIN
Sandgate
Shieldrow Lane
Greencroft Comprehensive School
Blackett
Annfield Pl
NEW FRONT
Doctors Surgery
West Road
School
Welsh Ter
Railway
Meldon Way
Shieldrow Lane
Greencroft Comprehensive School
New Kyo
Greencroft
Annfield Plain Cricket Club
Larwood Ct
Douglas Ct
STATION RD
DURHAM RD
Doctors Surgery
Annfield Plain Infants School
St Aidan's Crs
Park Cl
The Avenue
SHIELDROW LA
A693
A693
A693
Derwentside District Council
A6076
Parkhead
Parkway
Tower Road
Greencroft
Amos Drive
Lane
Park Head
Langley Moor
Tower Bank
Tower Bank
Tower
Road
The Crescent
LANCHESTER ROAD
Maiden Law
Greencroft Park
Maiden Hall Farm
Chapmans
1
2
3
4
5
6
7

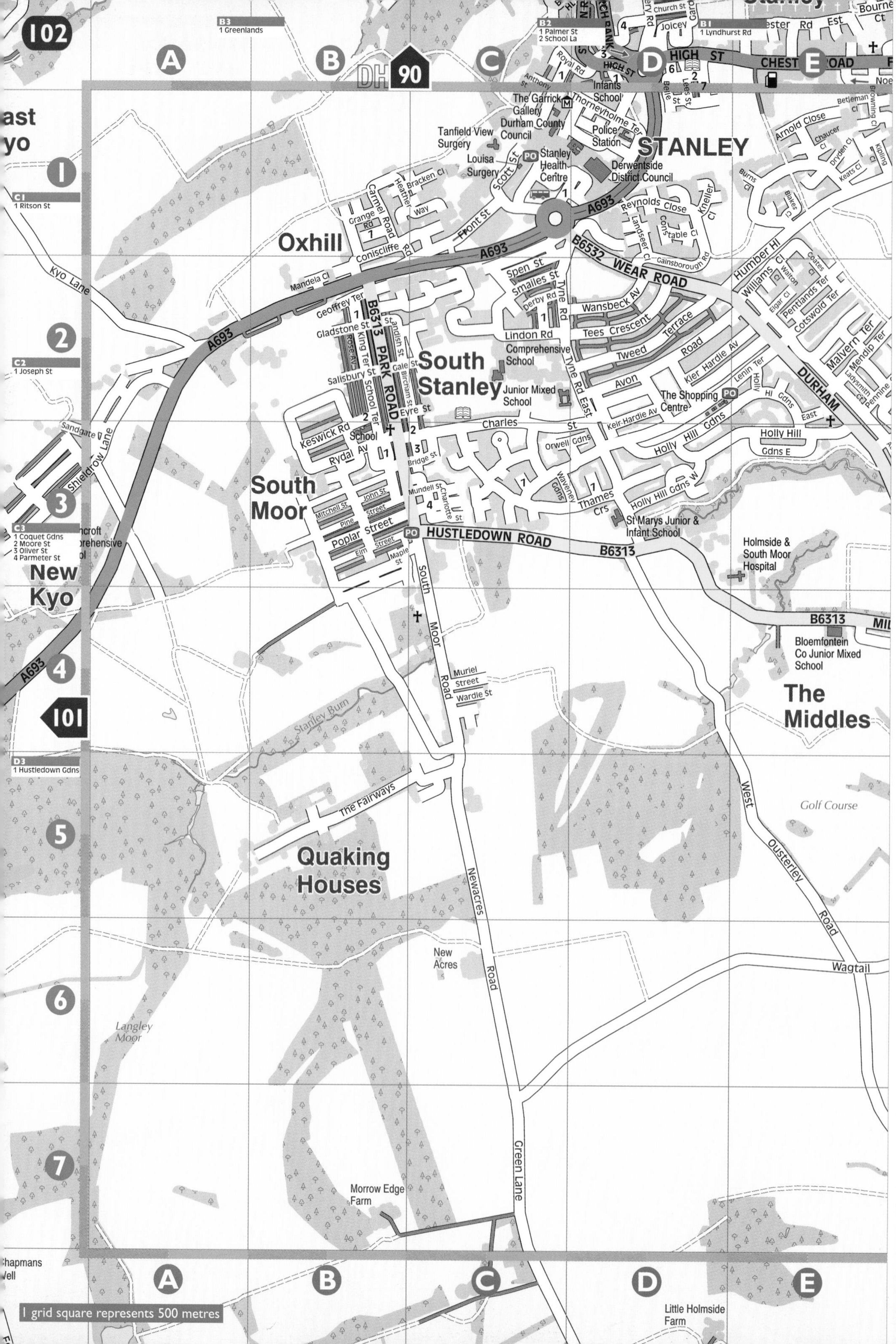
STANLEY
Oxhill
South Stanley
South Moor
New Kyo
Quaking Houses
The Middles
Holmside & South Moor Hospital
Bloemfontein Co Junior Mixed School
St Marys Junior & Infant School
Comprehensive School
Junior Mixed School
Derwentside District Council
Stanley Health Centre
Police Station
The Garrick Gallery
Durham County Council
Tanfield View Surgery
Louisa Surgery
The Shopping Centre
Golf Course
New Acres
Langley Moor
Morrow Edge Farm
Little Holmside Farm
Chapmans Well
HUSTLEDOWN ROAD
B6313
B6532 WEAR ROAD
A693
B6513 PARK ROAD
South Moor Road
Newacres Road
Green Lane
West Ousterley Road
Wagtail
Kyo Lane
Shieldrow Lane
Sandgate
The Fairways
Stanley Burn
Muriel Street
Wardle St
Charles St
HIGH ST
CHESTER ROAD
DURHAM
B3 1 Greenlands
B2 1 Palmer St 2 School La
B1 1 Lyndhurst Rd
C1 1 Ritson St
C2 1 Joseph St
C3 1 Coquet Gdns 2 Moore St 3 Oliver St 4 Parmeter St
D3 1 Hustledown Gdns
1 grid square represents 500 metres

DH 90

101

West Pelton
Craghead
Holmside
91
104
112
F
G
H
J
I
K
2
3
4
5
6
7
FRONT ST
Masefield Cl
Thorntree Ter
Acton Dene
Ballater Cl
Colville Ct
Kinross Dr
Gullane Ct
Brentwood Ct
Harwick Ct
Hawick Ct
Elgin Gv
Girvan Cl
Forres Court
Spencer Cl
Milton Cl
Ruskin Cl
1 Pankhurst Pl
Burnside JMI School
Fonteyn
Nightingale
Potter Pl
Bronte Pl
Stanley Wood
Stanley Burn
ROAD
B6532
Woodside
Gardens
Oak Terrace
Dr Dhuny's Surgery
Hazel Ter
Palm Ter
Beech Ter
Front St
B6313
CRAGHEAD
LANE
BLUEHOUSE BANK
Thomas St
John St
EDWARD ST
Wagtail Lane
Wylam St
Railway St
Ousterley
Ousterley Ter
Wagtail Ter
Lane
LOWERY LANE
White House Farm
Humbleburn Lane
B6532
BLACK HOUSE LANE
Wheatley Green Lane
Wheatley Green Farm
Beech Grove Farm
Humble Burn
Twizell Hall
Twizell Lane
Twizell Burn
Eden Hill Farm
Plantation View
County Middle School
Orchard Cl
Edenfield
Holmside Hall
Holmside
Hag Wood
Cong Burn
PO

104
92
103
113
A
B
C
D
E
1
2
3
4
5
6
7
A693
Arthur St
Edenfield
Green's Bank
Summerfield
Orchard Cl
Plantation View
County Junior Middle & Infant School
Golf Course
Grange Villa
Stone Row
Pine St
Queen St
Albert St
West Street
East Street
Newbridge Banks
Pelton Lane
Pelton Ms
Lovaine St
Holyoake St
Alexandra St
Provident St
Industrial St
Roseberry Primary School
Roseberry Vls
Elm Av
The Pde
Oak Ter
Heathmeads
Thornton Lea
King's Lane
Greenacres
Cemetery
Front Street
Health Centre
Fieldside
Southfield
Wood St
Elwin Pl
Grange St
The Wynd
Brackenbed
PELTON
Station Lane
Newfield
Front Street
Blindy Burn
Twizell Burn
New Grange Terrace
Plunkett Ter
Miller Gdns
Fellrose Surgery
Pelton Fell Surgery
Valley Rd
Fell Rd
Briarwood Av
Whitehill Crs
Tennyson Rd
Byron Avenue
Shakespere Ter
Ruskin Av
Henley Av
Wordsworth Avenue
DH2
B6313
BEAMISH VIEW
BLUEHOUSE BANK
Hett Hills
White Hall Farm
Tribley Farm
Waldridge
Olive St
Waldridge Lane
Little Burn
Broomy Holm
Beech Grove Farm
Humble Burn
OUSE LANE
Congburn Bridge
CONGBURN BANK
Cong Burn
Edmondsley JMI School
1 grid square represents 500 metres

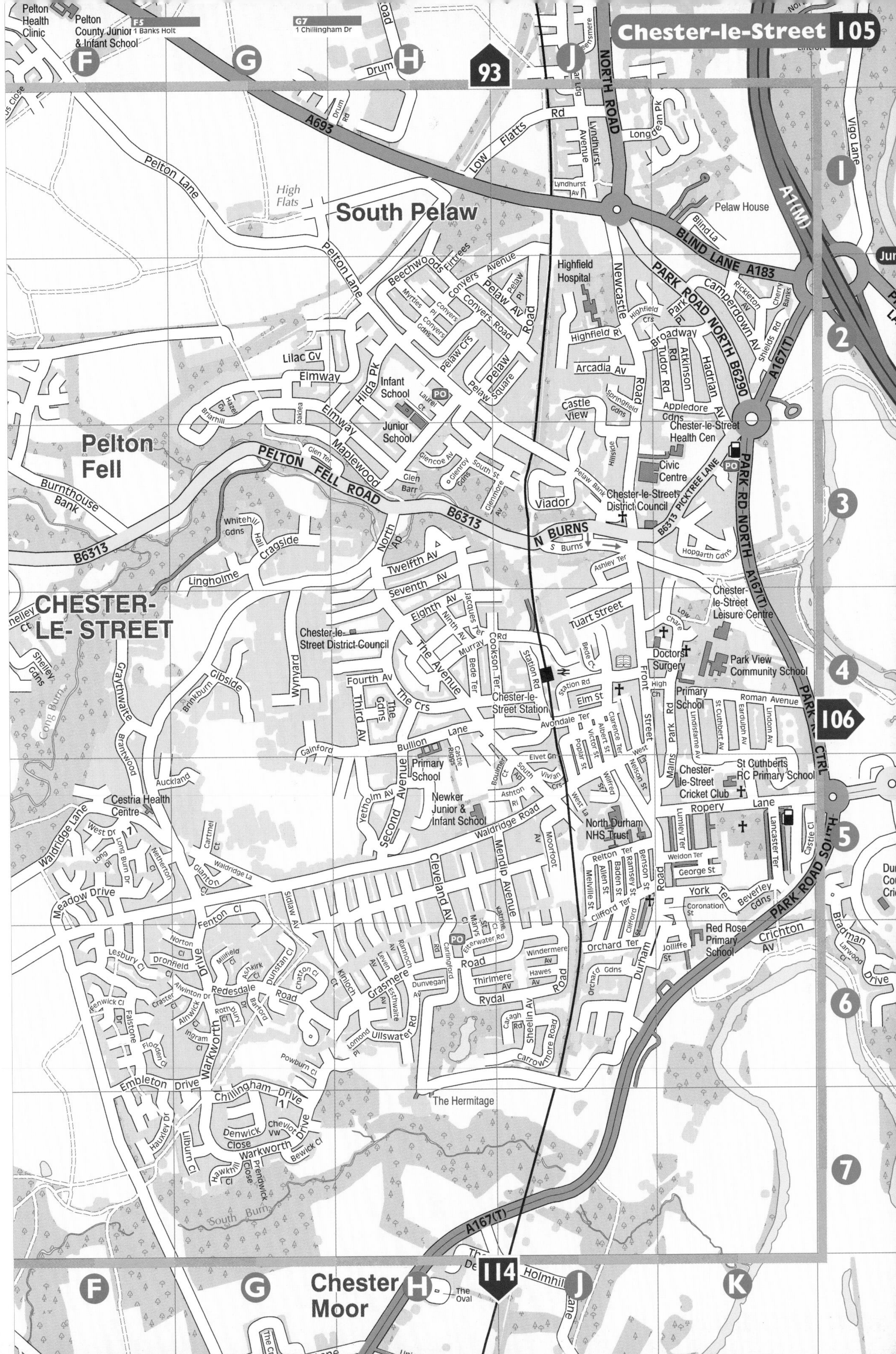
South Pelaw
Pelton Fell
CHESTER-LE-STREET
Chester Moor
A693
A1(M)
B6313
A167(T)
PELTON FELL ROAD
BLIND LANE A183
PARK ROAD NORTH B6290
NORTH ROAD
PARK ROAD SOUTH
Pelaw House
Highfield Hospital
Chester-le-Street District Council
Chester-le-Street Station
Chester-le-Street Leisure Centre
Park View Community School
Chester-le-Street Cricket Club
North Durham NHS Trust
Red Rose Primary School
Cestria Health Centre
The Hermitage
93
106
114

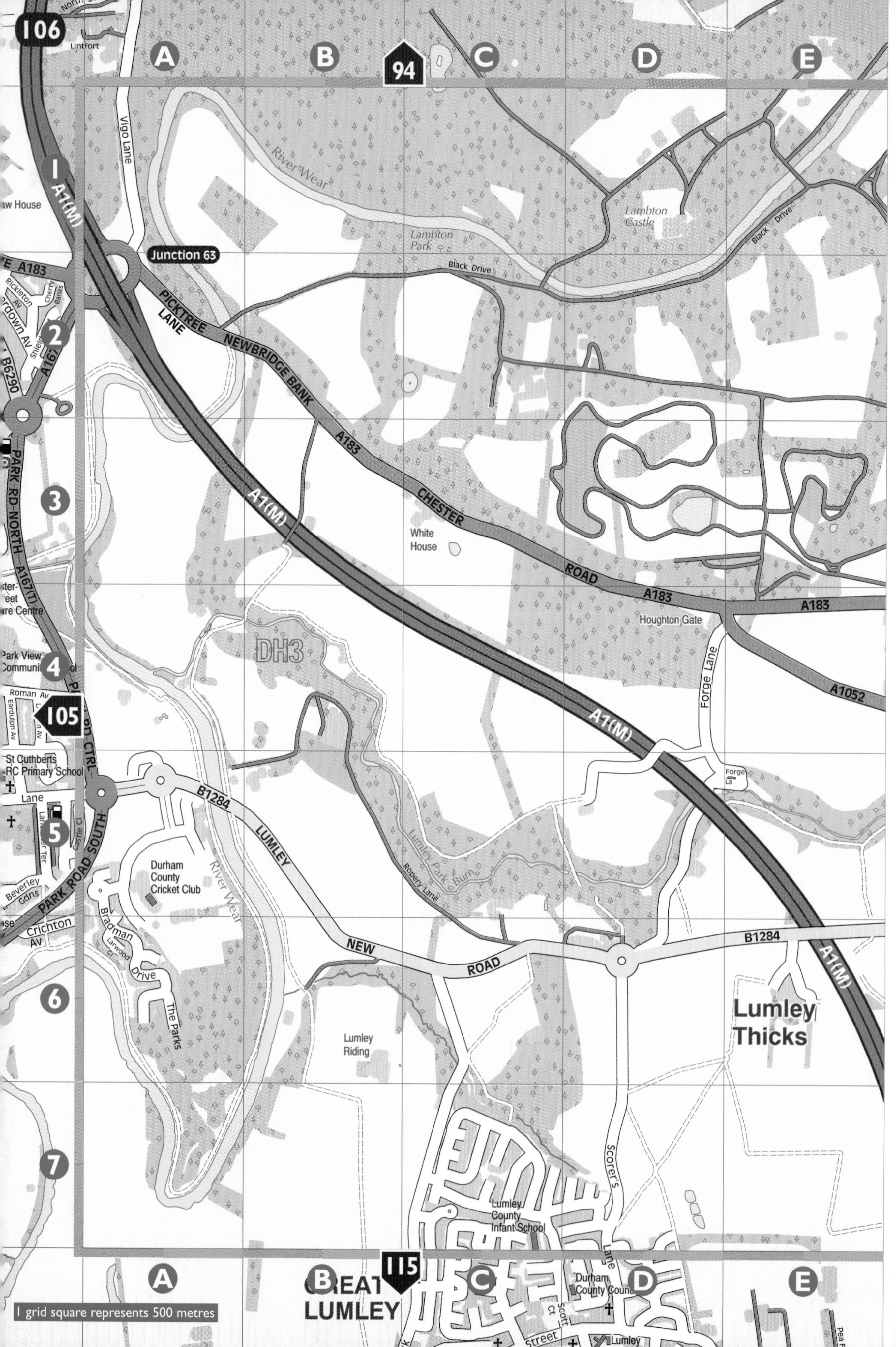

106
Lintfort
A
B
94
C
D
E
Vigo Lane
River Wear
Lambton Castle
Lambton Park
Black Drive
Black Drive
Junction 63
A183
Rickleton Av
Cherry Banks
PICKTREE LANE
NEWBRIDGE BANK
A183
CHESTER ROAD
A183
A183
A1(M)
A1(M)
A1(M)
A1(M)
White House
Houghton Gate
Forge Lane
A1052
DH3
B6290
A167
PARK-RD-NORTH
A167(T)
Park View
Roman Av
105
St Cuthberts RC Primary School
Lane
PARK ROAD SOUTH
Castle Cl
Beverley Gdns
Crichton Av
B1284
LUMLEY
NEW ROAD
B1284
Durham County Cricket Club
River Wear
Bradman Drive
Larwood Cl
The Parks
Lumley Park Burn
Ropery Lane
Forge La
Lumley Riding
Lumley Thicks
Scorer's Lane
Lumley County Infant School
115
GREAT LUMLEY
Durham County Council
Scott Ct
Street
Lumley
1 grid square represents 500 metres
1
2
3
4
5
6
7

J1
1 Craighill
2 Kelso Gv
3 Station Rd
J2
1 Larkfield Crs
River Wear
95
Our Lady of Peace RC Prim Sch
Washington Highway
Station Road
Carlisle Cl
Whitefield Crescent
Baulkham Hills
Chester Road
Windermere Crs
J6
1 Brancepeth Av
2 Murray Av
3 Raby Cl
J7
1 Chilton Gdns
2 Cross St
Westbourne Surg
Grangewood Surg
Primary School
Shiney Row
Westbourne Drive
Princes St
The Crs
Lowerson Av
Maple Ter
Wright Ter
Claremont Dr
Collingwood Dr
Highfield Rd
Brentwood Rd
Gainsborough Crescent
Burnden Grove
Paddock Close
Larkfield Crescent
Hunter St
Herrington Burn
City of Sunderland College
Philadelphia Cricket
K1
1 Council Av
2 The Harbour
3 The Haven
4 Jedburgh Rd
5 Mill Pit
6 Oakmere Cl
Trinity Park
Success
Blossom Gv
Bradwell Wy
West Vw
Bourn Lea
Ross Lea
Golf Course Road
Bowes Lea
Briar Cl
Briar Lea
Birkdale Dr
Woodhall Spa
The Belfry
Lytham Grange
K2
1 Beaufort Cl
2 Coldstream Cl
3 Galashiels Gv
Durham County
Sunderland
The Avenue
Fence
Road
Bowes House
Chester Road
Burnmoor Cricket Club
Blind Lane
Bournmoor
Castlereigh Cl
The Mdw
St Barnabas
Carnation Av
Ellesmere
Beumaris
Marigold Crs
Lilac Sq
Alwin Cl
Lambourne Cl
Primrose Crs
Meadow Gra
New Lambton
Mill Ct
108
K5
1 Holystone Cl
Thorneyburn
Newminster Close
Burnside
K7
1 Churchill Sq
Lindisfarne Cl
Ellesmere
Breckon Hill
Lumley New Road
Sydney St
Fence Houses Surg
Woodlea County Primary School
Oak St
Pinewood St
Maplewood St
Elmwood St
Woodland Gra
Avenue
Vivian
Ravensworth Av
Rose Avenue
Acacia Av
Grange Av
Fence Houses
DH4
Blackthorn Way
Sedgeletch Road
Cherry Way
Moors Burn
Otterburn
Burnside
Sherburn Grove
Houghton Welfare Cricket
A1052
LC
Morton House
Durham St
Dubmire County Junior & Infant School
Morley Ter
Bankhead Ter
Dubmire Ct
High Dubmire
Moorsfield
Kelr
Hardie St
Parnell St
Disraeli St
Gladstone Street
Dairy Lane
South View Ter
St Michaels
St Andrews
Wynyard Street
Chilton Gdns
John Street
James Ter
Dubmire Cottages
Thames Crs
Avon Crs
Front Street
Highfield Drive
Colliery Row
Dairy
Longacre
Aireys Close
Morton Grange Farm
116
Newcastle Lane
Wear Street
Syston Close
Relton Cl
Atherton Dr
Chilton Moor
PH
F
G
H
J
K
1
2
3
4
5
6
7

108
Penshaw
A3
1 Bigbury Cl
2 Elfordleigh
3 Fowler Cl
4 Honiton Cl
5 Sidmouth Cl
6 Torrington Cl
7 Warren Cl
A
B
96
C
A2
1 Connaught Cl
2 Goodrich Cl
D
A1
1 Cricklewood Dr
E
Manor Grove
Way
McClaren
The Paddock
Herrington Road
Cresent
Fletcher
St Aidan's Terrace
Hardy Terrace
Lanton
Street
B1286
Catherine Rd
Langley St
Freezemoor Road
Kirkside
New Herrington
Chigwell
Windermere Crs
Thirlmere Crs
Road
Marne St
A4
1 Bickington Ct
2 Lydford Ct
3 Saunton Ct
4 Tavistock Ct
Herrington Medical Centre
iney Row
City of Sunderland
A5
1 Byland Cl
2 Littleburn Cl
3 Rosedale Crs
4 Thorneyburn Cl
Road
Philadelphia Cricket Club
Chapel Rw
Philadelphia
Herrington Hill Ho
Tilbury Cl
Granville Dr
Bradwell Wy
Romney Cl
Success
Trinity Park
Blossom
Bradwell Wy
West Vw
Philadelphia Lane
A6
1 Stoneleigh Cl
Stony Gate
Dainton Cl
Okehampton Drive
The Crs
A182
North St
Front St
Sunderland Road
High Lane
Road
A7
1 Redburn Cl
2 Southburn Cl
Lynton Ct
Westleigh Rd
Devonport
Grange View
South Street
Over the Hill Farm
Coaley Lane
The Dell
The Leas
Cathedral View
Newbottle
Durham
Houghton Road
107
Sunniside
Coaley Lane
Ter
Newbottle Primary School
Beechwood
A690
B1
1 Sutherland Gra
Railway St
Thornhurn
Newminster Close
Buckland Cl
Newstead Rd
Tintern Close
Fountains Crs
Blind Lane
Chester St
Lumley St
Ruby St
Grasswell
B3
1 Green Av
2 Sparkwell Cl
3 Voltage Ter
Close
Lindisfarne Cl
Newbottle Street
B4
Street names for this grid square are listed at the back of the index
Otterburn Crs
Brinkburn
Burnside Avenue
Woodburn Dr
Moorsburn Dr
Newburn Crs
Burnside Primary School
Gas House Lane
Halliwell St
Station Rd
Houghton Cut
Hillside Way
Sunderland St
Baker St
Balfour St
Outram St
Ironside St
Elizabeth St
Edwin St
Market Place Industrial Estate
Sherburn Grove
B5
1 Gertrude St
2 Hylton St
Houghton Colliery Welfare Cricket Club
Leyburn Gv
Leyburn Cl
Grey St
Newbottle St
The Green
Lake Road
Market Place
B1404
B6
1 Cross St
High Dubmire
Lime Av
Seaburn Dr
Larch Av
Briar Av
Beech Av
Burn Park Road
Greenwood Av
Bernard St
Gilpin St
Violet St
Dickens St
Burn Prom
Vine St
Broadway
The Church Street
Nesham Pl
Mt Pleasant
Windsor Crs
Ryhope Street
Seaham Road
Dairy Lane
Thornhill Street
Wallace
Sunderland City Council
Dairy La
Durham Road
Houghton Health Cen
John Street
Longacre
Longacre
The Oval
Ferrand Dr
A1052
Holly Av
Kirklea Road
Earsdon Rd
New Town
B7
1 Linden Gv
Michaels
Andrews
Airey Close
Hutton Close
Nine Lands
Willow Road
Finchale Cl
Whickham Cl
Castle Dene Grove
Houghton Kepier Sch
Bernard Gilpin Primary Sch
Windsor Crs
The Rigg
Kirkstone Cl
Kingsway
Colliery Row
Marsden Close
Durham
Wingate Close
Stanhope Close
Houghton-le-Spring
117
Martindale Park
Normandy Crs
Queensway
Burdon Av
Seaton Av
Villas Lane
C1
1 Hill Ter
Witton Grove
C6
1 Mautland St
Dunelm Drive
Longlands Drive
Road
Thistlecroft
C7
1 Church St
2 Pottery Yd
3 Sunderland St
Burns
Shakespeare
Moore
Lawnswood
Lane
Dunelm
Dunkirk Av
Dene Gdns
D7
1 Alamein Av
2 The Close
3 Earsdon Rd
4 Edlingham Ct
5 Kirknewton Cl
6 Queensway
Chilton Moor
1 grid square represents 500 metres
PO

East Herrington
Farringdon School
Primary School
Benedict Biscop C of E School
Church View Medical Cen
Silksworth He
New
Durham Road
B1286
City Way
A19(T)
B1404
Doxford Pk Wy
Doxford Park Way
Silksworth Road
Silksworth Lane
Crow Lane
Herrington Road
Warden Law La
Mill Hill Road
Hall Farm Road
Moorside Road
Camberwell Way
Glanville Rd
Hangmans Lane
Salter's Lane
Low Haining
Haining
Warden Law North Farm
Warden Law
Thristley House Farm
Clubhouse
Golf Course
High Sharpley
G1 1 Braemar Gdns
G2 1 Grayling Ct
H1 Street names for this grid square are listed at the back of the index
H2 1 Maplebeck Cl 2 Maxton Cl 3 Midsomer Cl 4 Milsted Cl 5 Minskip Cl 6 Montford Cl
J1 1 Aspen Ct 2 Bordeaux Cl 3 Bowlynn Cl 4 Dunnlynn Cl 5 Plane Tree Ct
J2 1 Bristlecone 2 Cottonwood 3 Elsdonburn Rd 4 Markby Cl 5 Mayo Dr 6 Medina Cl 7 Meltham Dr 8 Membury Cl 9 Milrig Cl 10 Monterey
J3 1 Whitebark
K1 1 Crawford Ct 2 Hawkins Ct
K2 1 Abbotsfield Cl 2 Cardinals Cl 3 Deaconsfield Cl 4 Deansfield Cl 5 Harvest Cl 6 Hightree Cl 7 Honeycomb Cl 8 Monksfield Cl
97
110
118

Tunstall
Doxford Park
Burdon
Old Burdon
Seaton
DOXFORD PARK WAY
BURDON ROAD
B1286
Burdon Lane
Nettles Lane
Tunstall Lodge Farm
Lodgeside Meadow
East Farm
Burn Hall Farm
Pacific Hall Farm
Sharpley Hall Farm
A19(T)
A1018
B1404
SEATON LANE
Sunderland
Durham County
Seaton Grove
Westlea Junior School
Seaton Moor House
A3
1 Aylsham Ct
2 Chandos
3 Perrycrofts
4 Sheringham Cl
5 Thornbank Cl
A2
1 Fairgreen Cl
2 Fernwood Cl
3 Hightree Cl
4 Katrine Ct
A1
Street names for this grid square are listed at the back of the index
B1
1 Closeburn Sq
2 Danby Cl
3 Drybeck Sq
4 Monkswood Sq
B2
1 Leyfield Cl
C1
1 Rodney Cl
E1
1 Stafford Gv
E7
1 Pacific Hall
2 Slingley Cl
98
109
119
1 grid square represents 500 metres

F1
1 Aldbrough Cl
2 Hemlington Cl
F2
1 Ellington Cl
2 Greenhow Cl
G1
1 Fawcett Ter
2 Hedley Ter
H7
1 Clara St
2 Hambleton Dr
3 Newlands Rd E
J7
1 Antrim Gdns
2 Camelot Cl
3 Church Gn
K7
1 Henry St
2 Vane Ter
99
120
Ryhope
Ryhope Cemetery
Ryhope General Hospital
STOCKTON ROAD
A1018
THE VILLAGE
SEA VIEW
B1287
Rossiyn Avenue
Primary School
School
Station Road
Brewer Terrace
Arthur Av
Regent Road
Mariville W
Mariville E
Viewforth Rd
Sunderland
Durham County
Seaham Grange
Seaham Hall
Lord Byrons Walk
LC
B1285
Northlea
New Seaham School Primary
Seaham Comprehensive School
Burnhall Drive
Neasham Rd
Norfolk Close
Norton Avenue
Napier Road
Northlea Road
STATION ROAD
Church Court
Kingfisher Industrial Est
B1404
Cheviot Gdns
Cheviot Court
Stockton St
Durham St
Seaham Station
Station Road
Harbour Walk
NORTH ROAD
Promenade
New Drive
Dene Way
Derwent Close
Tintagel Drive
Merlin Cl
Dalden Grove
House Road
Northdene Av
Primary School
Community College
TEMPEST ROAD
North Terrace
Police Station
Adelaide Row Med Cen
Enfield Road
Windsor Road
Milton Close
Malvern Crescent
Portland Avenue
STRANGFORD RD
Deneside Medical Centre
Marlborough Clnc
Seaham College
B1287

Wheatley Green Farm
Holmside Hall
103
Cong Burn
Hag Wood
Holmside
Holmside Hall Road
Ash Tree Terrace
Warland Green
West Edmondsley
Holmside Lane
Warland
Holmside Lane
Whiteside Farm
Whiteside Burn
Charlaw Plantation
Charlaw Lane
Long Edge
Long Edge
Broom House
Acornclose Lane
Norburn Lane
West Hall Cottage
Horn's House
Coalpark Gill
Langley Lane
Langley
Kay's Burn
Langley Lane
Norburn Lane
122
A691
A691
1 grid square represents 500 metres

G1 1 Stobart St
H5 1 Graham Ct
H6 1 Fynway
104
114
123
Congburn Bridge
Waldridge Fell Country Park
Edmondsley JMI School
CONGBURN BANK
B6532
Tyzack Street
Jubilee Cl
Edmondsley
Sacriston Wood
Bruce St
Hamilton Terrace
EDMONDSLEY LANE
Nettlesworth West House
Westhills
Close
Daleside
Ashford Dr
Cross Lane
Deneside
Black Burn
Nettlesworth
Ugly Lane
PARK VW
Hillheads
Tan Hills
Charlaw Close
SACRISTON
Acorn Close
B6312
RC JMI School
Derwent Cl
Coniston Dr
Church Street
FRONT STREET
Morningside
Brookside
Parkside
Witton Av
Findon Avenue
Gregson St
Springside
Plawsworth Road County Infant School
Barras Hill
Rydal Close
St Cuthberts Dr
Sacriston Swimming Baths
Cemetery
Ripon Ct
Coldingham Ct
Sacriston Cricket Club
Water St
John St
PLAWSWORTH ROAD
Rose Crs
Fern Rd
Lavender Gardens
Kimblesworth
Industrial Est
PO
Iveson St
Highfield
Lilac Av
Viola Crs
Holly Crescent
Crossfield
Valley View
WITTON ROAD
DURHAM ROAD
Sacriston Junior School
Priory Ct
Penshaw Vw
Hill Crest
Redhouse Close
Eastwood
Browbank
FINDON HILL
Cathedral View
Fulforth
Fyndoune Community College
Kimblesworth Grange
The Crescent
Rose Lea
Norburn Park
Hillside
Briar Lea
May Lea
Gn Lea
Findon Av
Fyndoune Wy
Oak Lea
Waterson Crs
Dene Ct
Witton Gilbert
Wellsprings Farm
Durham Gdns
Fair View
LANE
South
Brookside
Witton Gilbert County School
Friarside
Glebeside
SACRISTON
Chapel Ct
Burnside
Fyndoun Cottage
Potter House
F
G
H
J
K
1
2
3
4
5
6
7

114
105
A
B
C
D
E
A167(T)
1 Church Vw
South Burn
Chester Moor
The Dene
The Oval
Holmhill Lane
The Crs
Waldridge Lane
Union Lane
The Gallery
Beaney Lane
Holmhill Lane
Wheatleywell Lane
Darley Court
Southill Hall
Ugly Lane
Nettlesworth Primary School
Plawsworth
PARK VIEW
B6312
Hillmeads
113
Tanmeads
Mill Lane
Mill House
Mill Lane
Tan Hills
Hawthorn Close
Cedar Avenue
Oak Crescent
Sycamore Rd
Briar Cl
Elm Crescent
Kimblesworth
Cocken Road
Viewly Grange
Nag's Fold Farm
Bishop's Grange
Kimblesworth Grange
Finchale Abbey Training Centre
Hag House
Red House
124
Beaver Cl
Oatlands Way
Rosemount
Imex Business Centre
Smithfield
Ryelands
Newton Grange
Finchale R
House
1 grid square represents 500 metres
1
2
3
4
5
6
7

H2
1 Canterbury Cl
2 Lichfield Cl
J1
1 Eggleston Cl
2 Hamsterley Cl
3 Mickleton Cl
4 Startforth Cl
J2
Street names for this grid square are listed at the back of the index
GREAT LUMLEY
Lumley County Infant School
Durham County Council
Lumley JMI School
Fenton Well Lane
Lumley Grange
Back Lane
Front Street
Scott Ct
Winchester Cl
Hazel Cl
Salisbury Cl
Gloucester Cl
Exeter Cl
Worcester Cl
Norwich Cl
St Alban's
Frosterley Cl
Nenthead Cl
Brignall Cl
Stainmore Drive
Lartington Close
Cambridge Drive
George Pit Lane
Pea Flatts Lane
Old Mill Lane
Cocken Lane
River Wear
Harbour House Farm
Charles Pit Cottages
Prior's Close
Cocken White House Farm
Low Cocken Farm
Finchale Priory
Finchale Banks
Cocken Road
Broom House
Raintonpark Wood
East Moor Leazes
Union Hall
Rowan Dr
Finchale Avenue
Beech Close
A1(M)
106
116
125
F
G
H
J
K
1
2
3
4
5
6
7

D6
1 Lea Riggs
2 St Mary's Dr
3 Sheen Cl
D1
1 Maiden Law
2 The Mews
3 Stretton Cl
C7
1 School Vw
2 Tollgate Flds
E1
1 Highfield Gra
A
B
C
D
E
107
115
126
1
2
3
4
5
6
7
Chilton Moor
West Rainton
Leamside
Rainton Gate
Morton Grange Farm
Lumley Moor Farm
Stables Farm
Broom House
Wood Side Farm
Field House Farm
Pitfield House
Moor House Farm
Nature Reserve
Black Boy Road
Newbottle Lane
Mark's Lane
Pithouse Lane
Cocken Road
Low Station Road
Station Road
Adventure Lane
Benridge Bank
Finchale View
Crescent
Rainton View
Hall Lane
Church Street
Meadows Lane
Woodside Lane
Dairy Lane
Front Street
Wear Street
Thames Cr
Avon Crs
Syston Close
Atherton Dr
Sunderland
Durham County
A1(M)
A690
PH
PO
LC
Hotel
The Surgery
West Rainton Primary School
Cem
Raintonpark Wood
1 grid square represents 500 metres

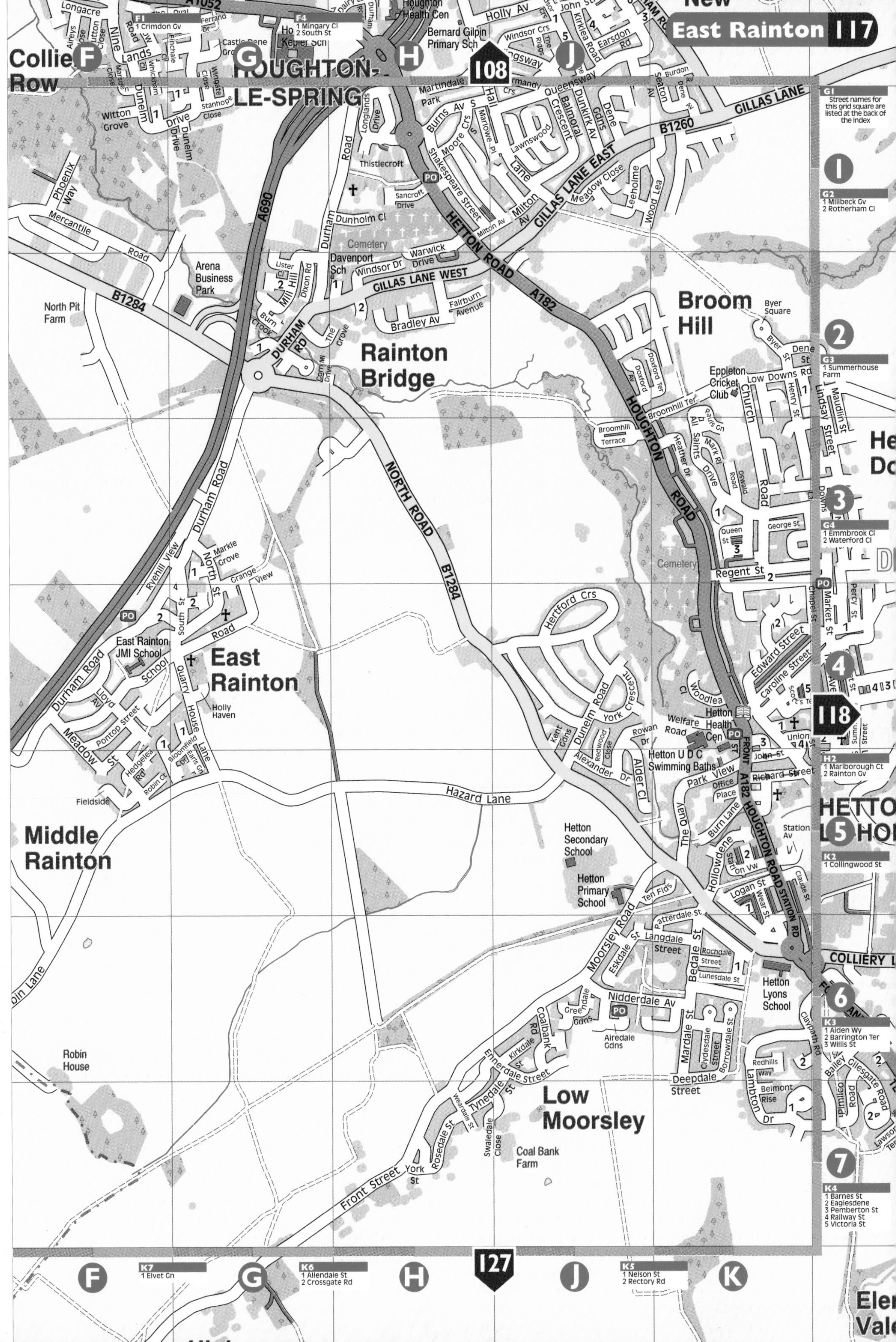

HOUGHTON-LE-SPRING
Rainton Bridge
Broom Hill
East Rainton
Middle Rainton
Low Moorsley
HETTON-LE-HOLE
Collier Row
North Pit Farm
Arena Business Park
Robin House
Coal Bank Farm
Holly Haven
Fieldside
Houghton Health Cen
Bernard Gilpin Primary Sch
Kepier Sch
Davenport Sch
East Rainton JMI School
Eppleton Cricket Club
Hetton Health Cen
Hetton U D C Swimming Baths
Hetton Secondary School
Hetton Primary School
Hetton Lyons School
Cemetery
A690
A182
B1284
B1260
A1052
HETTON ROAD
HOUGHTON ROAD
NORTH ROAD
GILLAS LANE WEST
GILLAS LANE EAST
GILLAS LANE
Hazard Lane
Front Street
COLLIERY LANE
108
118
127
G1 Street names for this grid square are listed at the back of the index
F1 1 Crimdon Gv
F4 1 Mingary Cl 2 South St
G2 1 Millbeck Gv 2 Rotherham Cl
G3 1 Summerhouse Farm
G4 1 Emmbrook Cl 2 Waterford Cl
H2 1 Marlborough Ct 2 Rainton Gv
K2 1 Collingwood St
K3 1 Alden Wy 2 Barrington Ter 3 Willis St
K4 1 Barnes St 2 Eaglesdene 3 Pemberton St 4 Railway St 5 Victoria St
K7 1 Elvet Gn
K6 1 Allendale St 2 Crossgate Rd
K5 1 Nelson St 2 Rectory Rd
F G H J K
1 2 3 4 5 6 7

A6
1 Gelt Crs
2 White Gates Dr
A5
1 John St
A4
1 Eppleton Rw
2 Stephenson Cl
3 Victory St East
4 Victory St West
A7
1 Hornsey Ter
2 Peth Gn
B7
1 Jubilee Sq
C7
1 Frosterley Cl
109
117
128
Clubhouse
GILLAS LANE
B1404
Golf Course
Durham County
Sunderland
High Sharpley
Green Lane
Salter's Lane
Byer Square
Dene St
Low Downs
Church
Henry St
Lindsay Street
Maudlin St
Hetton Downs
Oswald Road
Downs La
Nicholas Street
North Lane
Downs Pit Lane
DH5
Great Eppleton
Carrhouse Lane
Market St
Chapel St
Percy St
Edward Street
S Market St
The Avenue
Summerson Street
Urwin Street
John St
Richard Street
FRONT ST
A182 HOUGHTON ROAD
STATION RD
HETTON-LE-HOLE
Carr House Farm
Salter's Lane
Logan St
Wear St
Claude St
COLLIERY LANE
B1285
Lyons
Murton Moor Farm
Eppleton Hall
FOUR LANE ENDS
Claypath Rd
Castle Way
Bailey
Gilesgate Road
Pimlico Road
Derwent Street
Caldew Ct
Lyons Avenue
Bowes Av
Lyons La
Redhills Way
Belmont Rise
Lambton Dr
LILYWHITE TER
PEMBERTON BANK
Lawson Ter
Seymour Ter
Walter Terrace
Neil St
Hartside Gdns
Murton Lane
Cemetery
Bradley Ter
Blindy La
Brick Garth
Elemore Leisure Cen
The Poplars
The Lawns
North View
Willow Crescent
The Elms
Easington Lane
Murton Moor
HIGH STREET SOUTH
Dorset St
Prospect Crs
Thames St
Tyne
Trent St
Tamar St
Elemore Vale
Rydal Av
Coniston Av
Grasmere Avenue
Windermere Av
Thirlmere Av
Ullswater Av
Easington Lane Primary School
A
B
C
D
E
1
2
3
4
5
6
7
1 grid square represents 500 metres

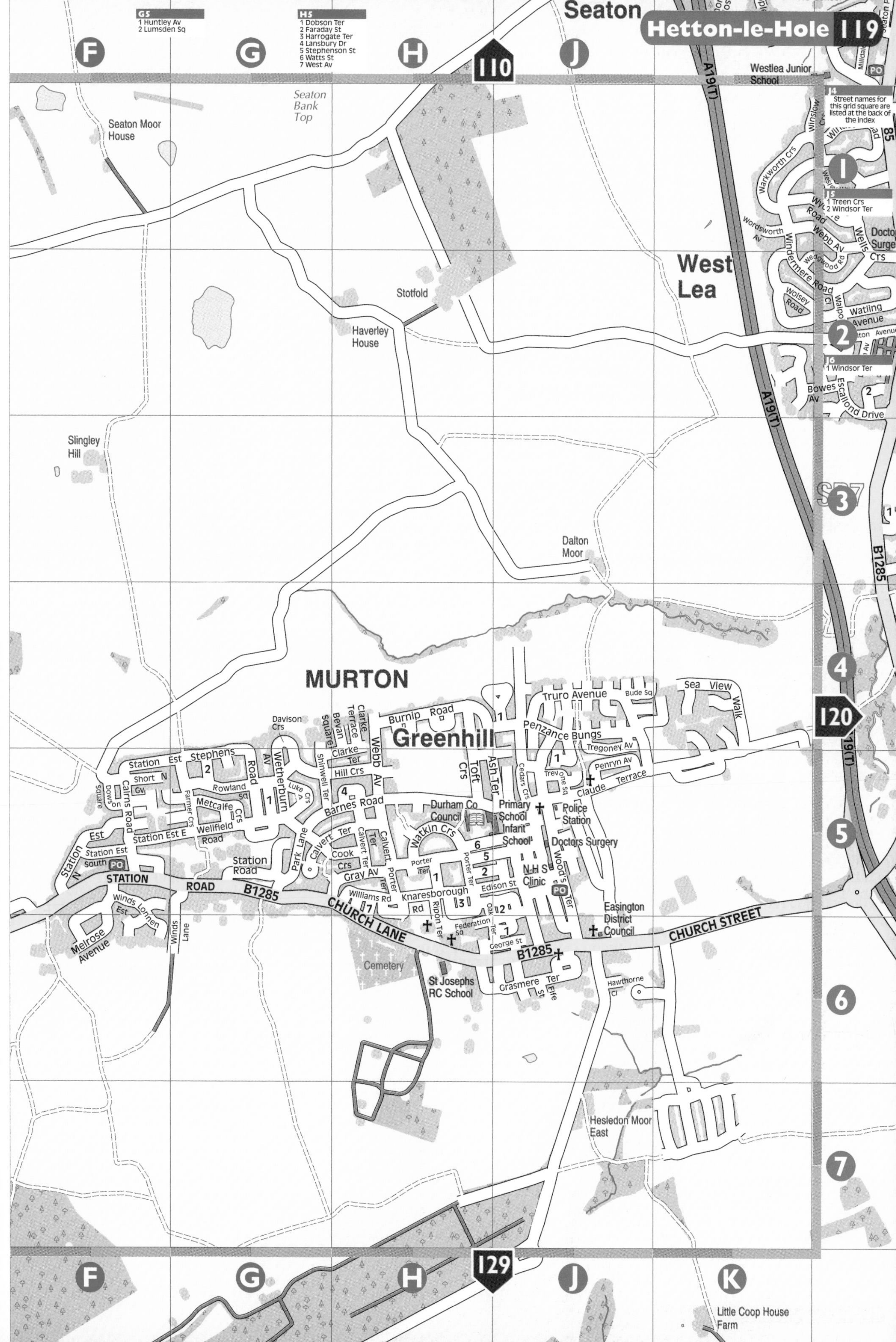
G5
1 Huntley Av
2 Lumsden Sq
H5
1 Dobson Ter
2 Faraday St
3 Harrogate Ter
4 Lansbury Dr
5 Stephenson St
6 Watts St
7 West Av
J4
Street names for this grid square are listed at the back of the index
J5
1 Treen Crs
2 Windsor Ter
J6
1 Windsor Ter
Seaton
Seaton Bank Top
Seaton Moor House
Westlea Junior School
West Lea
Stotfold
Haverley House
Slingley Hill
Dalton Moor
MURTON
Greenhill
Durham Co Council
Primary School
Infant School
Police Station
Doctors Surgery
N H S Clinic
Easington District Council
St Josephs RC School
Cemetery
Hesleden Moor East
Little Coop House Farm
Station Road
Church Lane
Church Street
B1285
A19(T)
Truro Avenue
Sea View Walk
Penzance Bungs
Burnip Road
Barnes Road
Watkin Crs
Knaresborough Rd
Melrose Avenue
Winds Lane
Claude Terrace
Wellfield Road
Grasmere Ter
Watling Avenue
Escallond Drive
Windermere Road
Webb Av
110
120
129
F
G
H
J
K
1
2
3
4
5
6
7

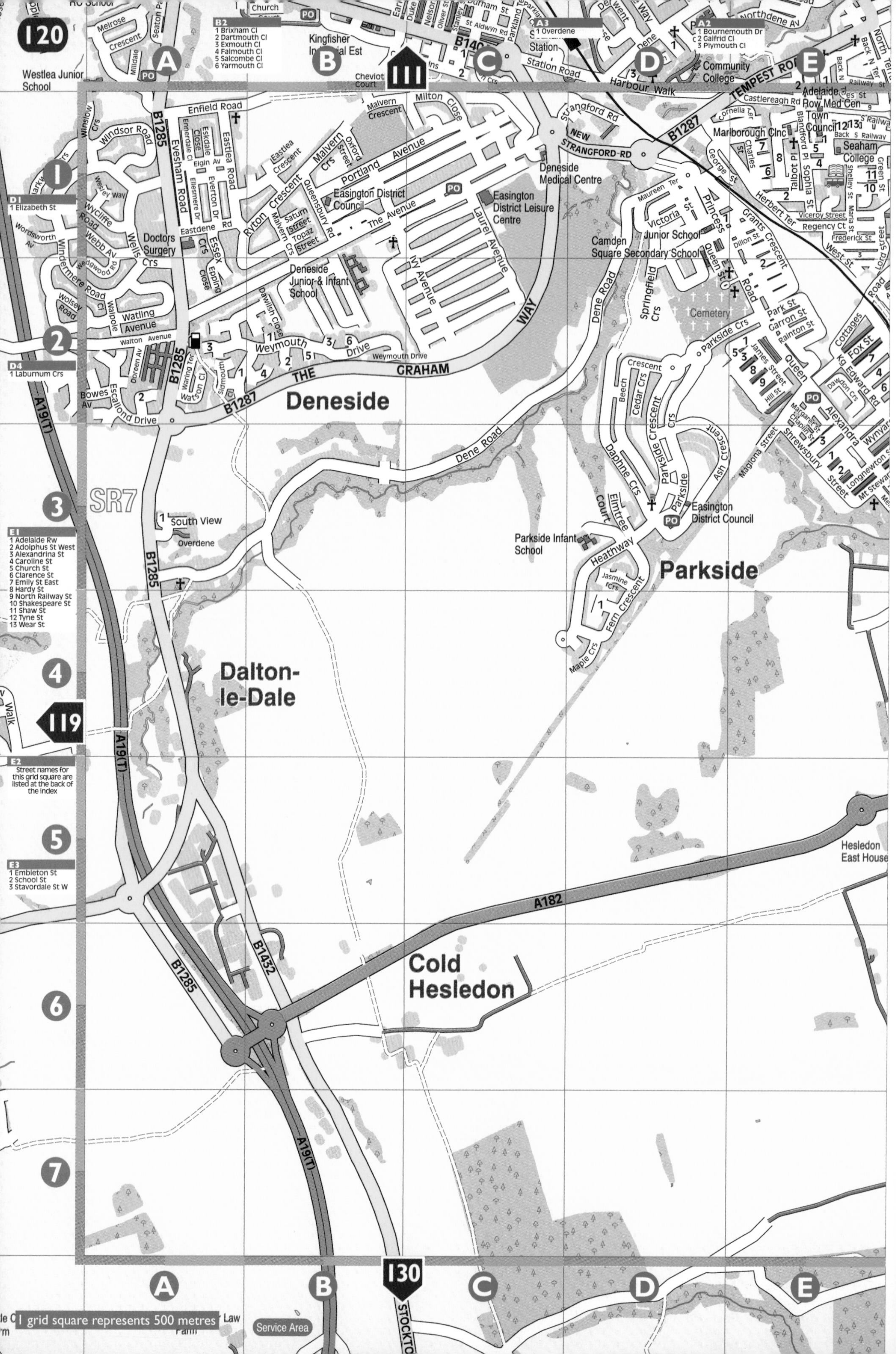

B2
1 Brixham Cl
2 Dartmouth Cl
3 Exmouth Cl
4 Falmouth Cl
5 Salcombe Cl
6 Yarmouth Cl
A3
1 Overdene
A2
1 Bournemouth Dr
2 Galfrid Cl
3 Plymouth Cl
D1
1 Elizabeth St
D4
1 Laburnum Crs
E1
1 Adelaide Rw
2 Adolphus St West
3 Alexandrina St
4 Caroline St
5 Church St
6 Clarence St
7 Emily St East
8 Hardy St
9 North Railway St
10 Shakespeare St
11 Shaw St
12 Tyne St
13 Wear St
E2
Street names for this grid square are listed at the back of the index
E3
1 Embleton St
2 School St
3 Stavordale St W
Westlea Junior School
Kingfisher Industrial Est
Cheviot Court
Station
Station Road
Harbour Walk
Community College
TEMPEST ROAD
Enfield Road
Windsor Road
Evesham Road
Eastlea Road
Eastlea Crescent
Malvern Crescent
Milton Close
Portland Avenue
Oxford Street
Ryton Crescent
Queensbury Rd
Easington District Council
The Avenue
Easington District Leisure Centre
Laurel Avenue
Ivy Avenue
Deneside Medical Centre
Strangford Rd
NEW STRANGFORD RD
B1287
B1285
Doctors Surgery
Wells Crs
Webb Av
Wycliffe Road
Windermere Road
Wordsworth Av
Watling Avenue
Walpole
Walton Avenue
Deneside Junior & Infant School
Dawlish Close
Weymouth Drive
THE GRAHAM WAY
Deneside
Escallond Drive
Bowes Av
Doreen Av
Waring Ter
Watson Cl
Sidmouth
Dene Road
Camden Square Secondary School
Victoria St
Junior School
Princess
Maureen Ter
Marlborough Clnc
Grants Crescent
Herbert Ter
Cemetery
Springfield Crs
Parkside Crs
Park St
Garron St
Rainton St
James Street
Queen
Hill St
Cedar Crs
Beech
Crescent
Parkside Crescent
Daphne Crs
Ash Crescent
Parkside
Easington District Council
Elmtree Court
Heathway
Parkside Infant School
Parkside
Jasmine Crs
Fern Crescent
Maple Crs
Castlereagh Rd
Adelaide Row Med Cen
Town Council
Seaham College
Viceroy Street
Regency Ct
Frederick St
West St
Alexandra
Shrewsbury Street
Magona Street
Kg Edward Rd
Fox St
Cottages
Longnewton St
SR7
South View
Overdene
A19(T)
Dalton-le-Dale
A182
Hesledon East House
Cold Hesledon
B1432
STOCKTON
Service Area
1 grid square represents 500 metres

111
119
130

F1
1 Aline St
2 Mary St
3 South Ter
F2
1 Robert St
2 Ropery Wk
F3
1 Londonderry St
2 Seaham St
SEAHAM
Police Station
PO
Foundry Road
Primary School
Bottle Works Rd
Robert St
Alfred St
Stewart St
Candlish Ter
Gas Works Road
Embankment
Hill Crs
Dawdon
Edith Street
LC
Nose's Point
A182
Kinley Hill
Chourdon Point
Hawthorn Hive
131
F
G
H
J
K
1
2
3
4
5
6
7

B3
1 Hazelwood Ct
2 Springwell Cl
B2
1 Brownney Ct
2 Oak St
A3
1 Beamish Cl
2 Elemore Cl
3 Meadowbank
4 Penshaw Cl
5 Whitburn Cl
112
Norburn Lane
A691
Hedley's Wood
Stobbilee Farm
Wall Nook
Wallnook Lane
River Browney
Langley Park
Hill Top
Derwentside College
Garden Avenue
The Crescent
Low Moor Road
Dale St
Hawthorne Ter
Bridge St
Palm St
Pine St
Elm St
Bridge Wy
Drive
Park Close
Kingsway
Esh Hillside
Netherton Cl
Eppleton Cl
Hospital Road
Cherrytree Drive
Maplewood Court
Beech Court
Middridge Road
Phoenix Cl
Hylton Cl
Cedar Ct
Eastern Av
Crossways
Hilltop View
Springwell Av
East Clere
Langley Park Primary School
Front Street
College Road
Ushaw Farm
Ushaw College
Broadgate Road
East Flass Farm
B6302
COCKHOUSE LANE
Flasshall Lane
Arthur St
Surgery
Temperance Ter
Ushaw Moor Infant School
Ushaw Moor
Whitehouse
Ushaw Moor Cricket Club
Flass Hall
Hare Holme Farm
132
1 grid square represents 500 metres

Witton Gilbert
Wellsprings Farm
Fyndoune Cottage
Witton Gilbert County School
SACRISTON
LANE
Brookside
Cragside
Friarside
Glebeside
FRONT ST
Chapel Ct
Newton St
Burnside
A691
F5
1 Fulforth Cl
2 Hartside Vw
G1
1 Deneside
G6
Street names for this grid square are listed at the back of the index
Potterhouse La
Hartside Farm
Trout's Lane
Trouts Lane School
Durham County N H S Trust
Earls House Hospital
Sniperley Hall
Lodge Farm
Aden Cottage
Stotgate
Hedley Ct
Hilltop Road
Blackcliffe Way
College Vw
Park Wd Av
Beaurepaire
Woodside Av
East Side Av
Quarry Crs
Woodland Close
Cook Avenue
Ritson Avenue
Kingston Avenue
Taylor Avenue
Bearpark Colliery Road
County Junior & Infant School
Bearpark
River Browney
Auton Stile
Dunelm Medical Practice
Deerness Valley Comprehensive School
Aldin Grange
Arbour House
Aldridge Ct
New Acres
Oakridge Road
Ash Av
Broom Hall
Ushaw Moor Junior School
St. Josephs RC School
Holly Pk
Lilac Park
Fir Pk
Maple Pk
Broom Crescent
Chestnut Gv
B6302
Cemetery
Deerness Sports Cen
Valley View
Hollywell Court
Beech Gv
Elder Ct
Brancpeth
Baxter Wood
Toll
113
124
133

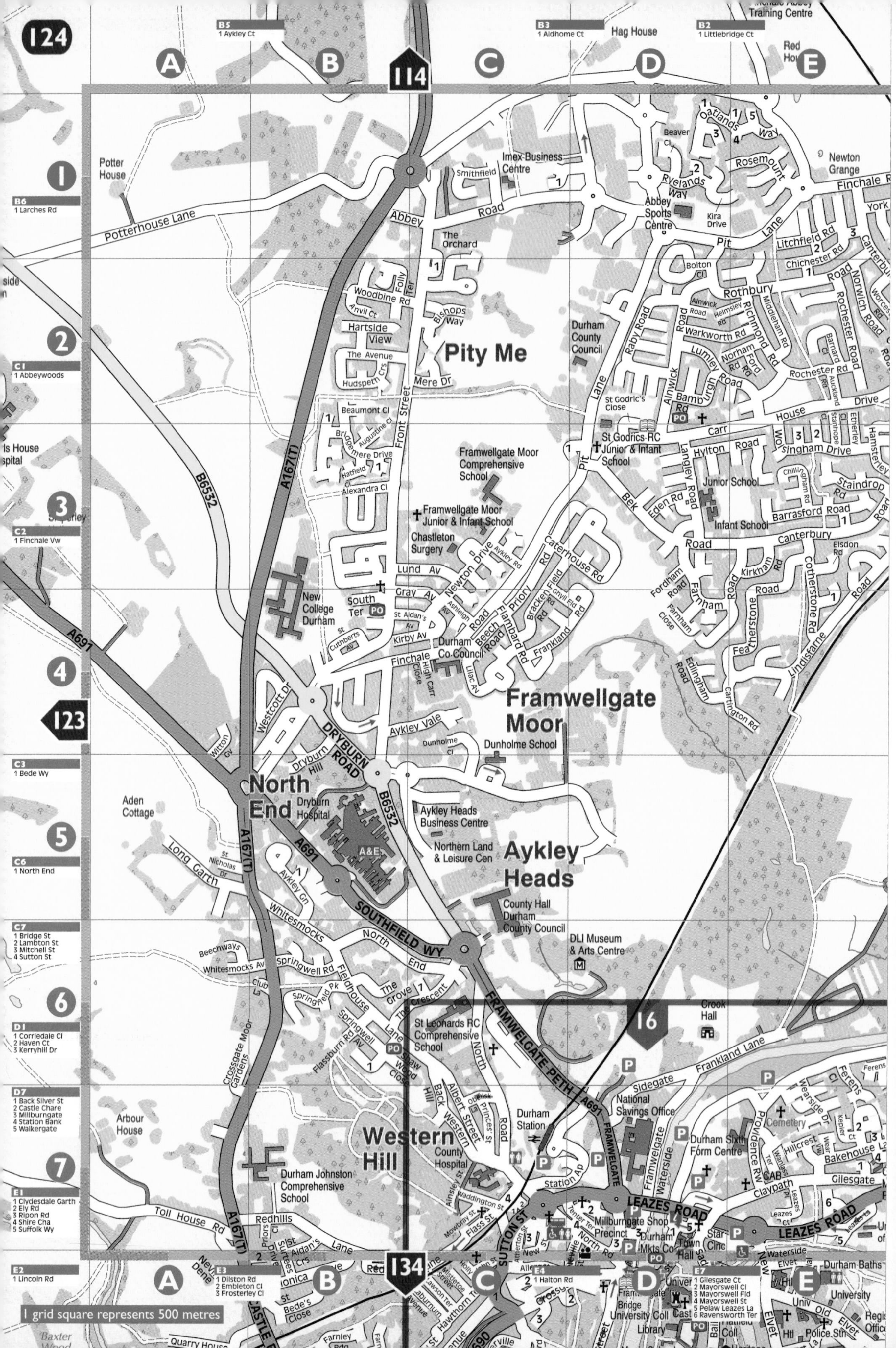

124
114
123
134
16
A
B
C
D
E
1
2
3
4
5
6
7
B5 1 Aykley Ct
B3 1 Aldhome Ct
B2 1 Littlebridge Ct
B6 1 Larches Rd
C1 1 Abbeywoods
C2 1 Finchale Vw
C3 1 Bede Wy
C6 1 North End
C7 1 Bridge St 2 Lambton St 3 Mitchell St 4 Sutton St
D1 1 Corriedale Cl 2 Haven Ct 3 Kerryhill Dr
D7 1 Back Silver St 2 Castle Chare 3 Millburngate 4 Station Bank 5 Walkergate
E1 1 Clydesdale Garth 2 Ely Rd 3 Ripon Rd 4 Shire Cha 5 Suffolk Wy
E2 1 Lincoln Rd
E3 1 Dilston Rd 2 Embleton Cl 3 Frosterley Cl
E4 1 Halton Rd
E7 1 Gilesgate Ct 2 Mayorswell Cl 3 Mayorswell Fld 4 Mayorswell St 5 Pelaw Leazes La 6 Ravensworth Ter
1 grid square represents 500 metres
Hag House
Potter House
Potterhouse Lane
Imex Business Centre
Smithfield
Abbey Road
The Orchard
Abbey Sports Centre
Newton Grange
Finchale Rd
Pit Lane
Pity Me
Durham County Council
Woodbine Rd
Anvil Ct
Hartside View
The Avenue
Hudspeth Crs
Mere Dr
Bishops Way
Front Street
Beaumont Cl
Bridgemere Drive
Alexandra Cl
Framwellgate Moor Comprehensive School
Framwellgate Moor Junior & Infant School
Chastleton Surgery
St Godrics RC Junior & Infant School
Junior School
Infant School
Carr House Drive
Canterbury Road
Rochester Road
New College Durham
South Ter
Lund Av
Gray Av
Kirby Av
Newton Drive
Caterhouse Rd
Framwellgate Moor
Dunholme School
Aykley Vale
Westcott Dr
Dryburn Road
Dryburn Hill
Dryburn Hospital
North End
Aden Cottage
Long Garth
Aykley Heads Business Centre
Northern Land & Leisure Cen
Aykley Heads
County Hall Durham County Council
DLI Museum & Arts Centre
Southfield Wy
Whitesmocks
Springwell Rd
Crook Hall
Frankland Lane
St Leonards RC Comprehensive School
National Savings Office
Durham Station
Western Hill
County Hospital
Arbour House
Durham Johnston Comprehensive School
Durham Sixth Form Centre
Cemetery
Bakehouse La
Gilesgate
Claypath
Leazes Road
Millburngate Shop Precinct
Durham Mkts Co
Town Hall
Toll House Rd
Redhills Lane
Durham Baths
University
Police Stn
University Coll
Library
A167(T)
A691
B6532
Framwellgate Peth
Framwellgate
Sutton St
North Road

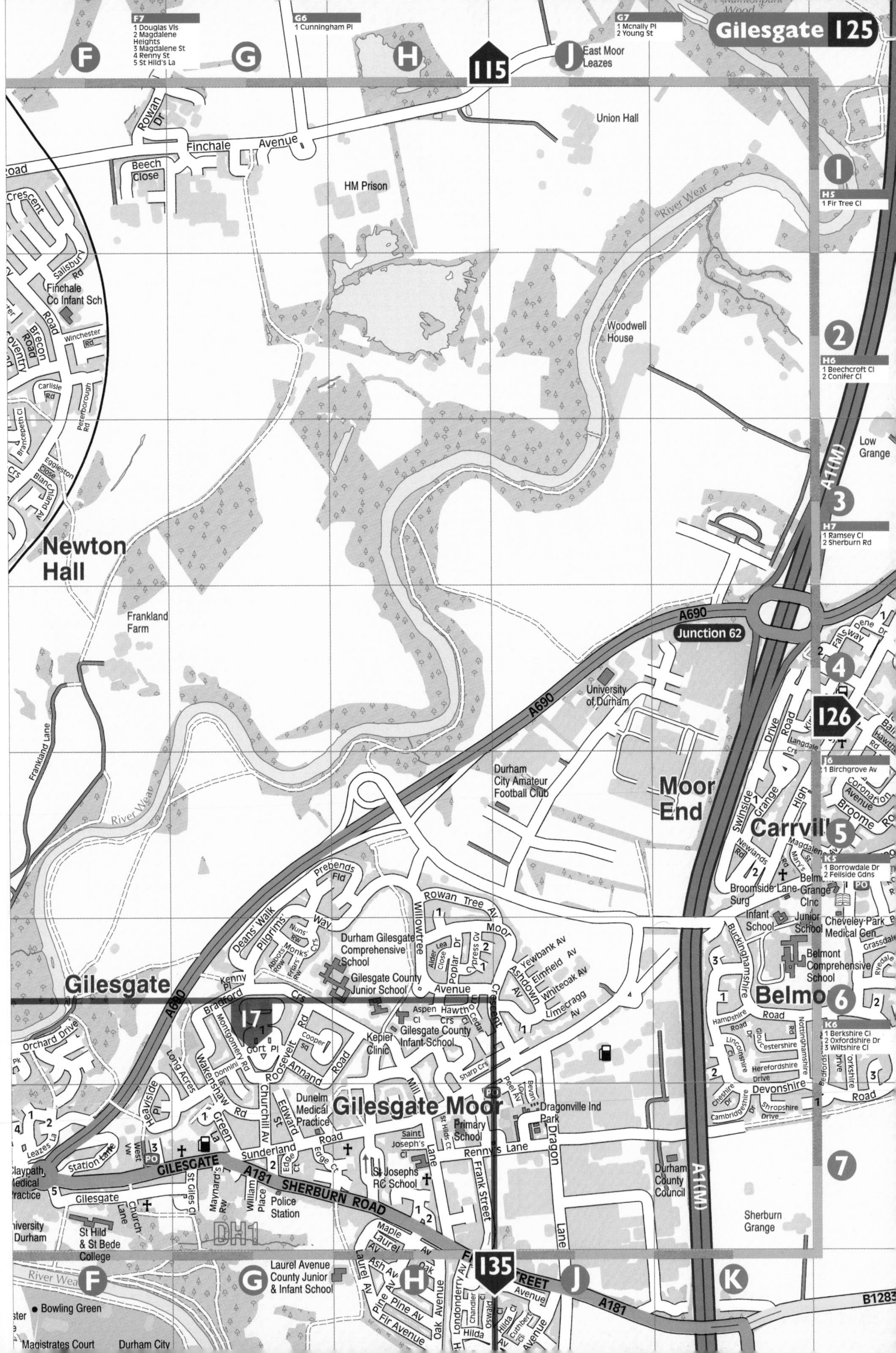
F7
1 Douglas Vls
2 Magdalene Heights
3 Magdalene St
4 Renny St
5 St Hild's La
G6
1 Cunningham Pl
G7
1 Mcnally Pl
2 Young St
H5
1 Fir Tree Cl
H6
1 Beechcroft Cl
2 Conifer Cl
H7
1 Ramsey Cl
2 Sherburn Rd
J6
1 Birchgrove Av
K5
1 Borrowdale Dr
2 Fellside Gdns
K6
1 Berkshire Cl
2 Oxfordshire Dr
3 Wiltshire Cl
115
126
135
East Moor Leazes
Union Hall
HM Prison
Finchale Avenue
Rowan Dr
Beech Close
Woodwell House
River Wear
Low Grange
A1(M)
Junction 62
A690
Newton Hall
Frankland Farm
Frankland Lane
Finchale Co Infant Sch
University of Durham
Durham City Amateur Football Club
Moor End
Carrvill
Belmont Grange Clnc
Broomside Lane
Cheveley Park Medical Cen
Belmont Comprehensive School
Durham Gilesgate Comprehensive School
Gilesgate County Junior School
Gilesgate County Infant School
Gilesgate
Gilesgate Moor
Kepier Clinic
Dunelm Medical Practice
Primary School
St Josephs RC School
Police Station
Dragonville Ind Park
Durham County Council
Sherburn Grange
St Hild & St Bede College
Laurel Avenue County Junior & Infant School
Sherburn Road
A181
Renny's Lane
Frank Street
Dragon Lane
Claypath Medical Practice
Bowling Green
Magistrates Court
Durham City
DH1
B1283

126
Rainton Gate
116
125
A6
1 Gorsedale Gv
2 Huntingdonshire Dr
3 Leicestershire Dr
4 Nthamptonshire Dr
A5
1 The Links
2 Poplar Rd
A4
1 Carrsdale
2 Carrsway
3 Ramside Vw
A7
1 Warwickshire Dr
B5
1 Borrowdale Cl
2 Ennerdale Cl
3 Patterdale Cl
C7
1 Harrison Garth
2 Liddle Av
3 Park House Cl
Wood Side Farm
Moor House Farm
Pitfield House
Pittington Road
A690
A1(M)
The Rift Farm
Low Grange
Station Rd
Front Street
High Street
Lady's Piece Lane
Pittington
Ramside Hall Hotel
Coalford Lane
Elemore St
Fatfield House
Pittington Lane
Priors Grange
Hallgarth Lane
Hallgarth
Broomside House
Coalford Beck
Cookshold Lane
Gray Avenue
Cummings Avenue
Dowsey Rd
Usher Av
Forster Av
Kidd Avenue
Beech Road
Hallgarth Street
Sports Centre
King St
George St
Mitford
Sherburn
FRONT
B1283
Sherburn Grange
Belmont
Belmont Comprehensive School
Cheveley Park Medical Cen
Cheveley Park Primary School
Broomside Lane Surg
Infant School
Junior School
Belmont Grange Clnc
Wantage Road
Grinstead Way
Bainbridge Street
Broome Road
Broomside
Brackendale Rd
Thorndale Road
Cheveley Walk
Coniston Close
Dinsdale Drive
Ullerdale Cl
Devonshire Road
Lancashire Dr
Yorkshire Drive
Staffordshire Drive
Derbyshire Drive
Shropshire Drive
Herefordshire Drive
Gloucestershire
Bedfordshire Dr
Nottinghamshire Rd
Buckinghamshire Road
Coronation Avenue
Hawthorn Rd
Briar Rd
Oakham Dr
Kinley Road
Filby Dr
Romney Dr
Falls Way
Dene Dr
Swinside
Grange
High Street
Newlands Rd
Magdalene Av
Rosedale Road
Grassdale
Riverdale
Lingdale
Ferndale
Mossdale
Brookdale
Scardale Way
Bedale Cl
Birkdale Gdns
School
1 grid square represents 500 metres

Farm
Front Street
York St
F
G
H
117
J
Ele
Vale
1
High Moorsley
Moorsley Road
Lorne St
2
Hetton le Hill
Sunderland
Durham County
Elemore Lane
Hillside
3
St Lawrence Ct
Newby Lane
PO
4
Elemore Hall School
128
Elemore Grange
Church Vale
5
Littletown
Coalford Lane
Cross Street
Plantation Avenue
Hastings House Farm
Green Lane
Littletown House
Littleton Lane
6
Cook's Hold
7
Haswell Moor Farm
F
G
H
J
K
Kell Crs
Sherburn Hill
The Croft
Local Avenue

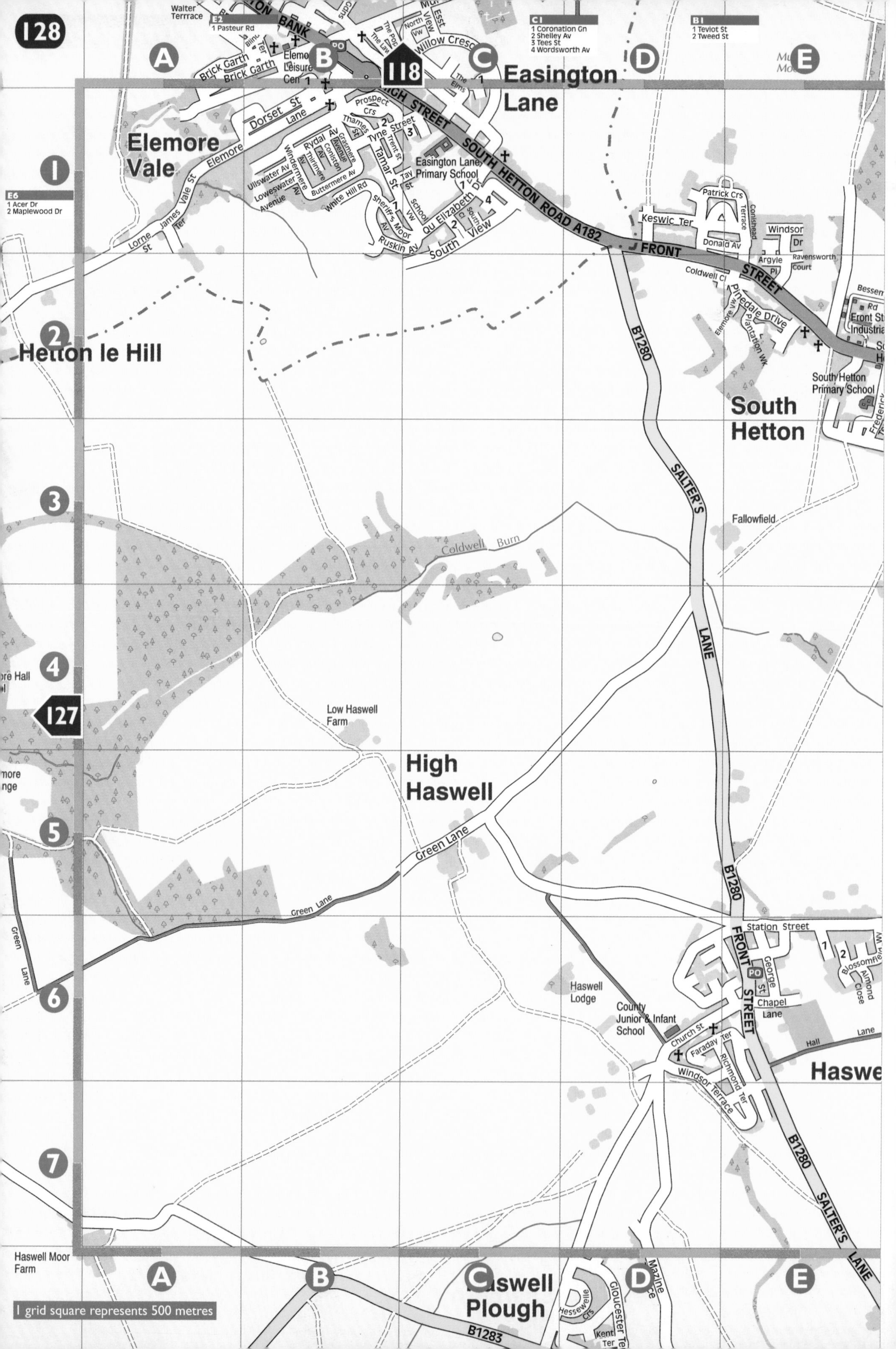

E2
1 Pasteur Rd
C1
1 Coronation Gn
2 Shelley Av
3 Tees St
4 Wordsworth Av
B1
1 Teviot St
2 Tweed St
E6
1 Acer Dr
2 Maplewood Dr
118
127
Easington Lane
Elemore Vale
Hetton le Hill
South Hetton
High Haswell
Haswell Plough
Easington Lane Primary School
South Hetton Primary School
County Junior & Infant School
Low Haswell Farm
Haswell Lodge
Haswell Moor Farm
Fallowfield
Coldwell Burn
HIGH STREET
SOUTH HETTON ROAD A182
FRONT STREET
SALTER'S LANE
B1280
B1283
Green Lane
Station Street
Chapel Lane
Hall Lane
Church St
Windsor Terrace
Patrick Crs
Keswic Ter
Donald Av
Pinedale Drive
1 grid square represents 500 metres

G2
1 Grasmere Ter
F
G
H
J
119
I
2
3
4
5
6
7
130
K
Little Coop House Farm
Windermere Road
Hawthorn Cottages
Coronation Sq
Bevin Sq
Greencroft
A182
PO
Ashwood
Oakwood
Maythorne Drive
South Hetton Health Centre
West Lane
Great Coop House Farm
Hallfield
West Moor House Farm
Duncombe Moor
Holy Cross
Pesspool Lane
Chestnut Drive
Pesspool Hall
Low Ling Close
High Ling Close
Moor House Farm
B1283
DURHAM LANE

D5
1 Comet Dr
2 Jupiter Ct
3 Saturn Cl
C6
1 Brampton Ct
2 Church Wk
3 East Grange Ct
4 Thorpe Rd
B6
1 St Mary's Cl
2 St Thomas Cl
3 Westcliff Cl
120
E4
1 Easington St
2 Oswald Ter
E5
1 St Nicholas Ter
2 Tennyson Rd
3 Whickham St
East Batter Law Farm
Service Area
West Batter Law Farm
Hawthorn
Stockton Road
West Lane
Eagle Hall
Hawthorn Burn
Thorpe Lea West
Hallfield Burn
Sunderland Road
B1432
Lea Lane
A19(T)
Hallfield
Petwell Lane
Holme Hill Farm
Holmhill
Cavell Square
Crawlaw
129
EASINGTON
Hall Walks
Rosemary Lane
Seaside Lane
Easington District Council
Glen Dene School
The Grove
Cadwell Lane
Police Station
Primary School
Rydal Mount
Manisty Terrace
Moncreiff Terrace
Davis Terrace
North Crescent
Oak Road
Durham Lane
Cemetery
Easington Comprehensive School
Thorpe Road
Stockton Road
A1086
Little Thorpe
Thorpe Burn
Andrew's Lane
136
Kitching Road
Cemetery

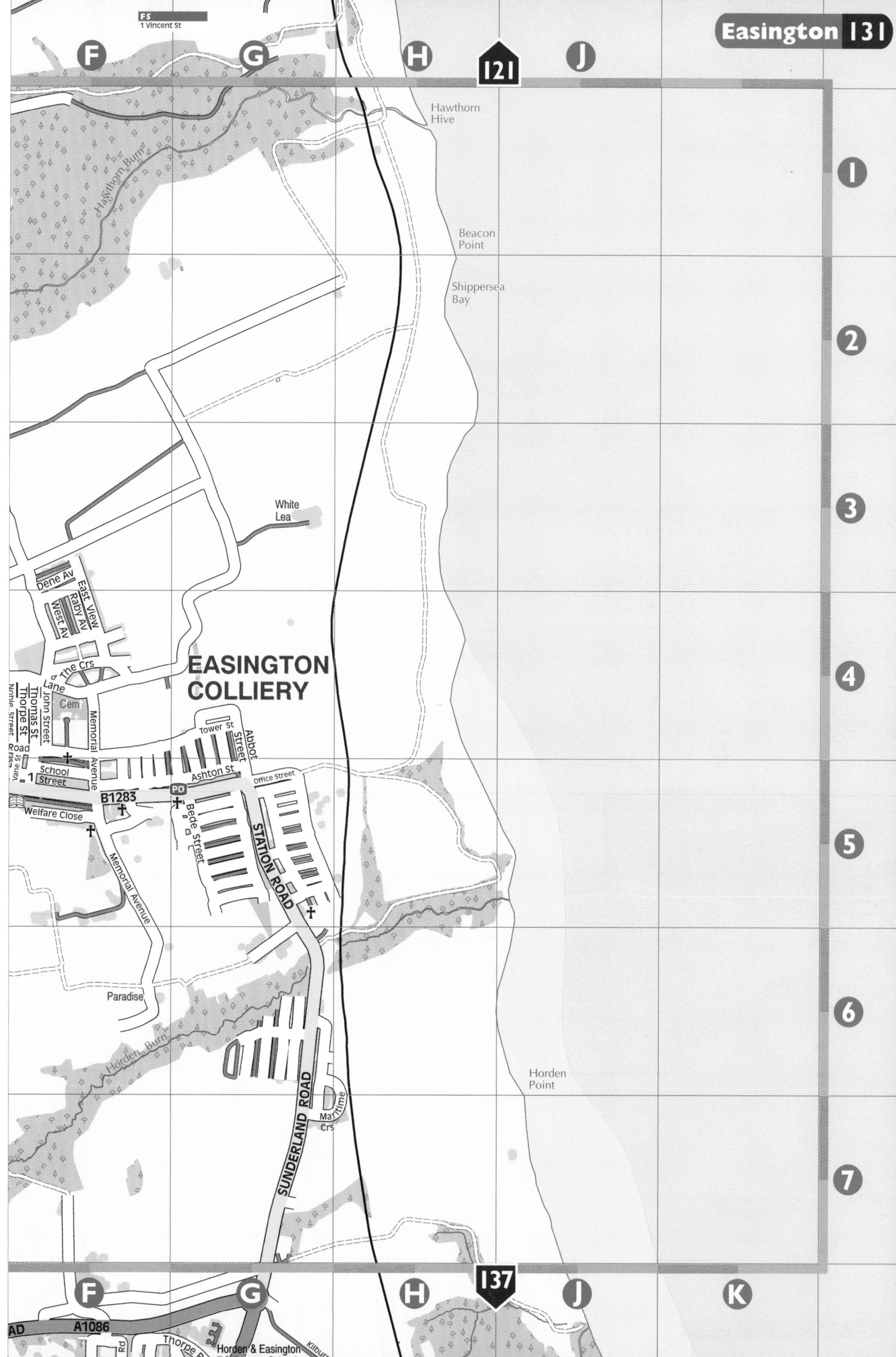
FS
1 Vincent St
F
G
H
121
J
Hawthorn Hive
Hawthorn Burn
Beacon Point
Shippersea Bay
White Lea
Dene Av
East View
Raby Av
West Av
The Crs
Lane
EASINGTON COLLIERY
Cem
John Street
Thomas St
Thorpe St
Noble Street
Memorial Avenue
Tower St
Abbot Street
Road
School Street
Ashton St
Office Street
PO
B1283
Welfare Close
Bede Street
STATION ROAD
Memorial Avenue
Paradise
Horden Burn
SUNDERLAND ROAD
Maritime Crs
Horden Point
137
K
A1086
Thorpe R
Horden & Easington
Kilburn
1
2
3
4
5
6
7

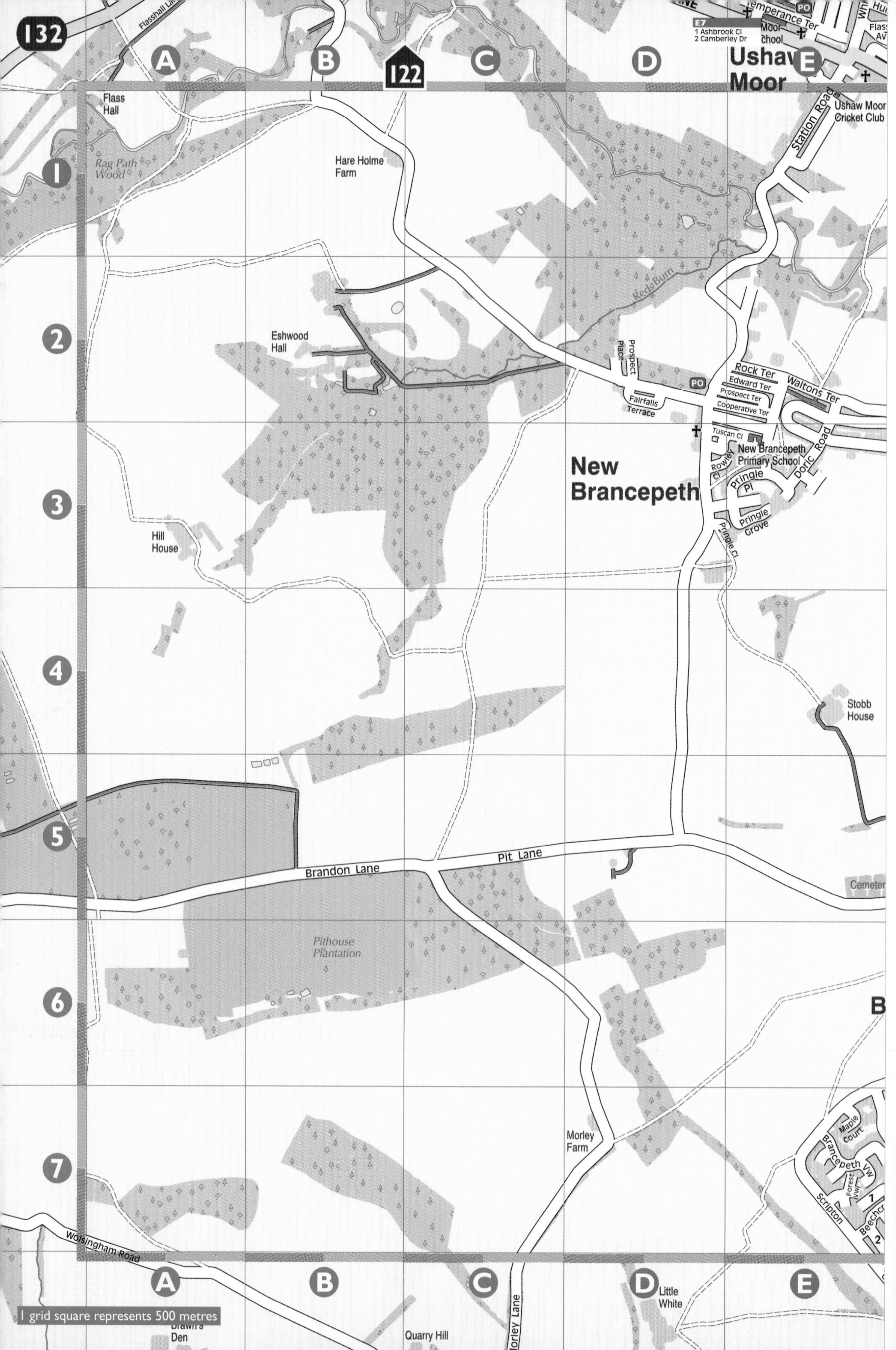
132
122
A
B
C
D
E
Flasshall La
1 Ashbrook Cl
2 Camberley Dr
Temperance Ter
Ushaw Moor
Flass Hall
Rag Path Wood
Hare Holme Farm
Station Road
Ushaw Moor Cricket Club
Red Burn
Eshwood Hall
Prospect Place
Fairfalls Terrace
Rock Ter
Edward Ter
Prospect Ter
Cooperative Ter
Waltons Ter
Tuscan Cl
Rowley Cl
New Brancepeth Primary School
Doric Road
Pringle Pl
Pringle Grove
Pringle Cl
New Brancepeth
Hill House
Stobb House
Brandon Lane
Pit Lane
Cemetery
Pithouse Plantation
Morley Farm
Maple Court
Brancepeth Vw
Forest Vw
Scripton
Beechcr
Wolsingham Road
Little White
Morley Lane
Quarry Hill
Drawn's Den
1
2
3
4
5
6
7
1 grid square represents 500 metres

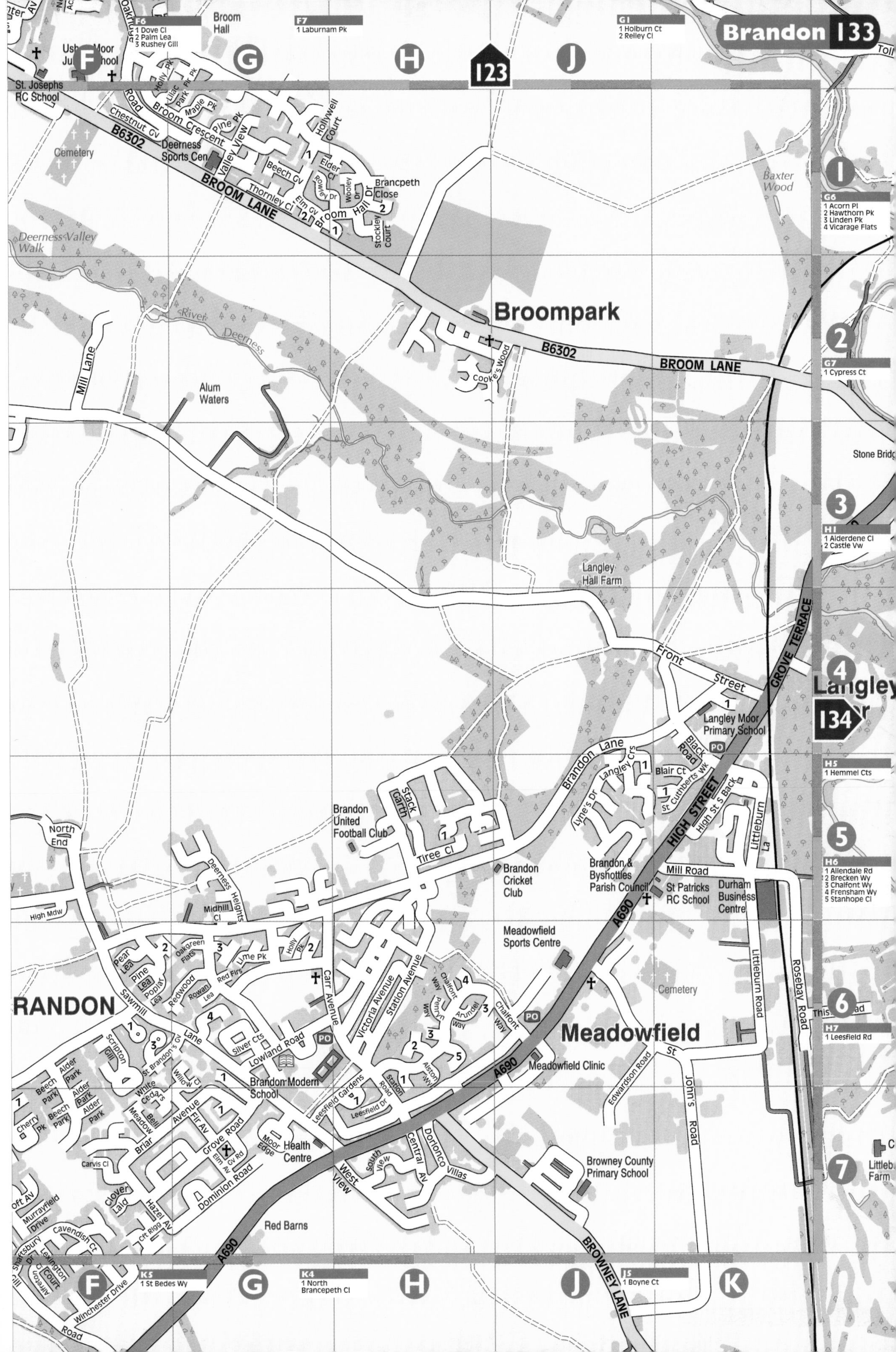

F6
1 Dove Cl
2 Palm Lea
3 Rushey Gill
F7
1 Laburnam Pk
G1
1 Holburn Ct
2 Relley Cl
Broom Hall
123
St. Josephs RC School
Cemetery
Chestnut Gv
Broom Crescent
Deerness Sports Cen
Valley View
Beech Gv
Thornley Cl
Elm Gv
Broom Hall Dr
Brancpeth Close
Stockley Court
Hollywell Court
Elder Cl
Rowley Dr
Wooley Dr
B6302
BROOM LANE
Deerness Valley Walk
River Deerness
Baxter Wood
G6
1 Acorn Pl
2 Hawthorn Pk
3 Linden Pk
4 Vicarage Flats
Broompark
Cooke's Wood
G7
1 Cypress Ct
Mill Lane
Alum Waters
Stone Bridg
H1
1 Alderdene Cl
2 Castle Vw
Langley Hall Farm
GROVE TERRACE
Front Street
Langley Moor Primary School
Langley
134
Brandon Lane
Langley Crs
Blair Ct
Black Road
St Cuthberts Wk
High St S Back
H5
1 Hemmel Cts
Stack Garth
Brandon United Football Club
Tiree Cl
Lyne's Dr
HIGH STREET
Littleburn La
North End
Deerness Heights
Brandon Cricket Club
Brandon & Byshottles Parish Council
Mill Road
St Patricks RC School
Durham Business Centre
H6
1 Allendale Rd
2 Brecken Wy
3 Chalfont Wy
4 Frensham Wy
5 Stanhope Cl
High Mdw
Midhill Cl
Meadowfield Sports Centre
A690
Oakgreen Flats
Lime Pk
Holly Pk
Carr Avenue
Victoria Avenue
Station Avenue
Chalfont Way
Penryn Way
Arundel Way
Cemetery
Littleburn Road
Rosebay Road
BRANDON
Pear Lea
Pine Lea
Poplar Lea
Redwood
Rowan Lea
Red Firs
Sawmill Lane
Silver Cts
Lowland Road
PO
Meadowfield
H7
1 Leesfield Rd
Scripton Gill
St Brandon's Gv
Alder Park
Beech Park
White Cedars
Willow Cl
Brandon Modern School
Alston Wy
Meadowfield Clinic
Edwardson Road
St John's Road
Cherry Pk
Bell Meadow
Briar
Avenue
Fir Av
Grove Road
Elm Gv Rd
Leesfield Gardens
Leesfield Dr
Station Road
Moor Edge
Health Centre
Carvis Cl
Clover Laid
Hazel Av
Dominion Road
South View
West View
Central Av
Dorlonco Villas
Browney County Primary School
Littleb Farm
Murrayfield Drive
Cavendish Ct
Cft Rigg
Red Barns
Shaftsbury
Lexington Court
Winchester Drive
Road
K5
1 St Bedes Wy
K4
1 North Brancepeth Cl
J5
1 Boyne Ct
BROWNEY LANE
F G H J K
1 2 3 4 5 6 7

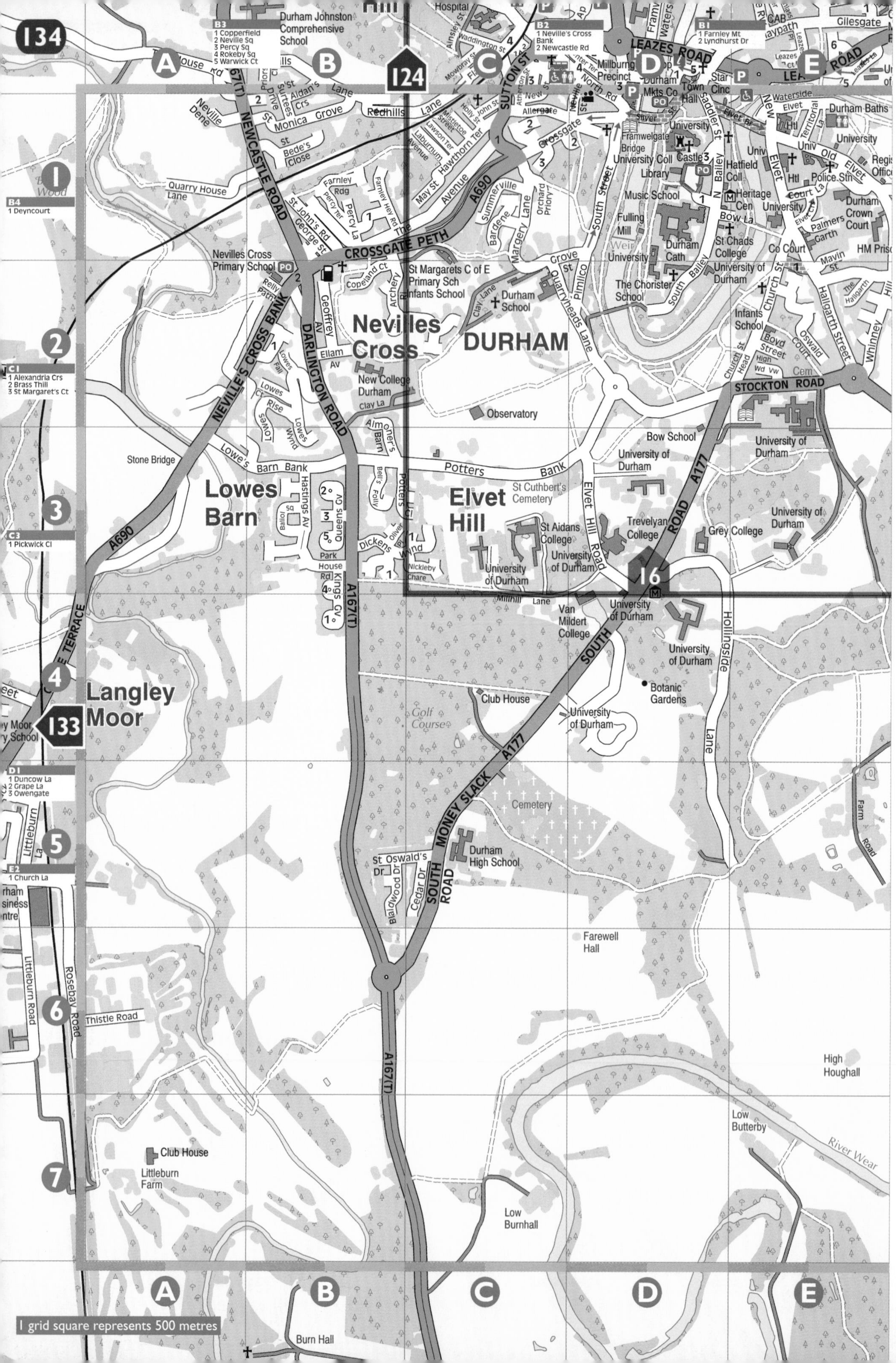
B3
1 Copperfield
2 Neville Sq
3 Percy Sq
4 Rokeby Sq
5 Warwick Ct
Durham Johnston Comprehensive School
124
B2
1 Neville's Cross Bank
2 Newcastle Rd
B1
1 Farnley Mt
2 Lyndhurst Dr
LEAZES ROAD
Gilesgate
B4
1 Deyncourt
C1
1 Alexandria Crs
2 Brass Thill
3 St Margaret's Ct
C3
1 Pickwick Cl
D1
1 Duncow La
2 Grape La
3 Owengate
E2
1 Church La
NEWCASTLE ROAD
CROSSGATE PETH
SUTTON ST
Crossgate
North Rd
Neville Dene
Monica Grove
Redhills Lane
St Bede's Close
Quarry House Lane
Nevilles Cross Primary School
St Margarets C of E Primary Sch Infants School
Nevilles Cross
DURHAM
Durham School
Framwelgate Bridge
University Coll
Castle
Library
Music School
Fulling Mill
Durham Cath
Hatfield Coll
Heritage Cen
St Chads College
University of Durham
The Chorister School
Durham Baths
Police Stn
Durham Crown Court
HM Prison
Co Court
Palmers Garth
Hallgarth Street
Infants School
Boyd Street
STOCKTON ROAD
New College Durham
Observatory
Bow School
University of Durham
NEVILLE'S CROSS BANK
DARLINGTON ROAD
Stone Bridge
Lowe's Barn Bank
Potters Bank
Lowes Barn
Elvet Hill
St Cuthbert's Cemetery
St Aidans College
Trevelyan College
Grey College
Elvet Hill Road
ROAD A177
16
Van Mildert College
Hollingside Lane
Botanic Gardens
Club House
Golf Course
A690
A167(T)
Langley Moor
133
Cemetery
Durham High School
SOUTH MONEY SLACK A177
SOUTH ROAD
St Oswald's Dr
Farewell Hall
Thistle Road
Littleburn Road
Rosebay Road
High Houghall
Low Butterby
River Wear
Club House
Littleburn Farm
Low Burnhall
Burn Hall
A B C D E
1 2 3 4 5 6 7
1 grid square represents 500 metres

Claypath Medical Practice
Gilesgate
GILESGATE
A181
SHERBURN ROAD
G4 1 Hall Farm
H4 1 Jubilee Pl
J5 1 Lindesfarne 2 Thropton Cl
J6 1 Bromley Cl
K5 1 Langton Lea
St Josephs RC School
Police Station
University of Durham
St Hild & St Bede College
Laurel Avenue County Junior & Infant School
River Wear
Bowling Green
Magistrates Court
Durham City Cricket Club
Green Lane
University of Durham
Durham City Rugby Club
Durham Johnston Comprehensive School
FRONT STREET
Bede Avenue
Oak Avenue
Londonderry Av
Pine Av
Fir Avenue
Hilda
Cuthbert Avenue
Haig Crs
Sherburn Grange
B1283
A1(M)
125
Bent House Lane
Bent House Farm
Old Durham
Old Durham Beck
University of Durham
A177
Houghall College
17
SHINCLIFFE LANE
MILL LANE
B1198
Shincliffe Lane
Shincliffe
WILLOW TREE AVENUE A177
Low Road
St Mary's Cl
Low Gn
High Street
Hall Lane
PH
Manor Farm
LC
High Shincliffe
Hillcrest
Heathways
Hill Mdw
Beal Wk
Foxton Wy
Meldon Wy
Mitford Cl
Whitwell Acres
Shincliffe C of E Junior & Infant School
The Orc
Ancroft Garth
Apperley Av
Telford Close
Houghall Farm
West Grange
Strawberry Lane
Low Grange
High Grange
South Grange
High Butterby Farm
Marlene Avenue
Dallymore Dri
F
G
H
I
J
K
1
2
3
4
5
6
7

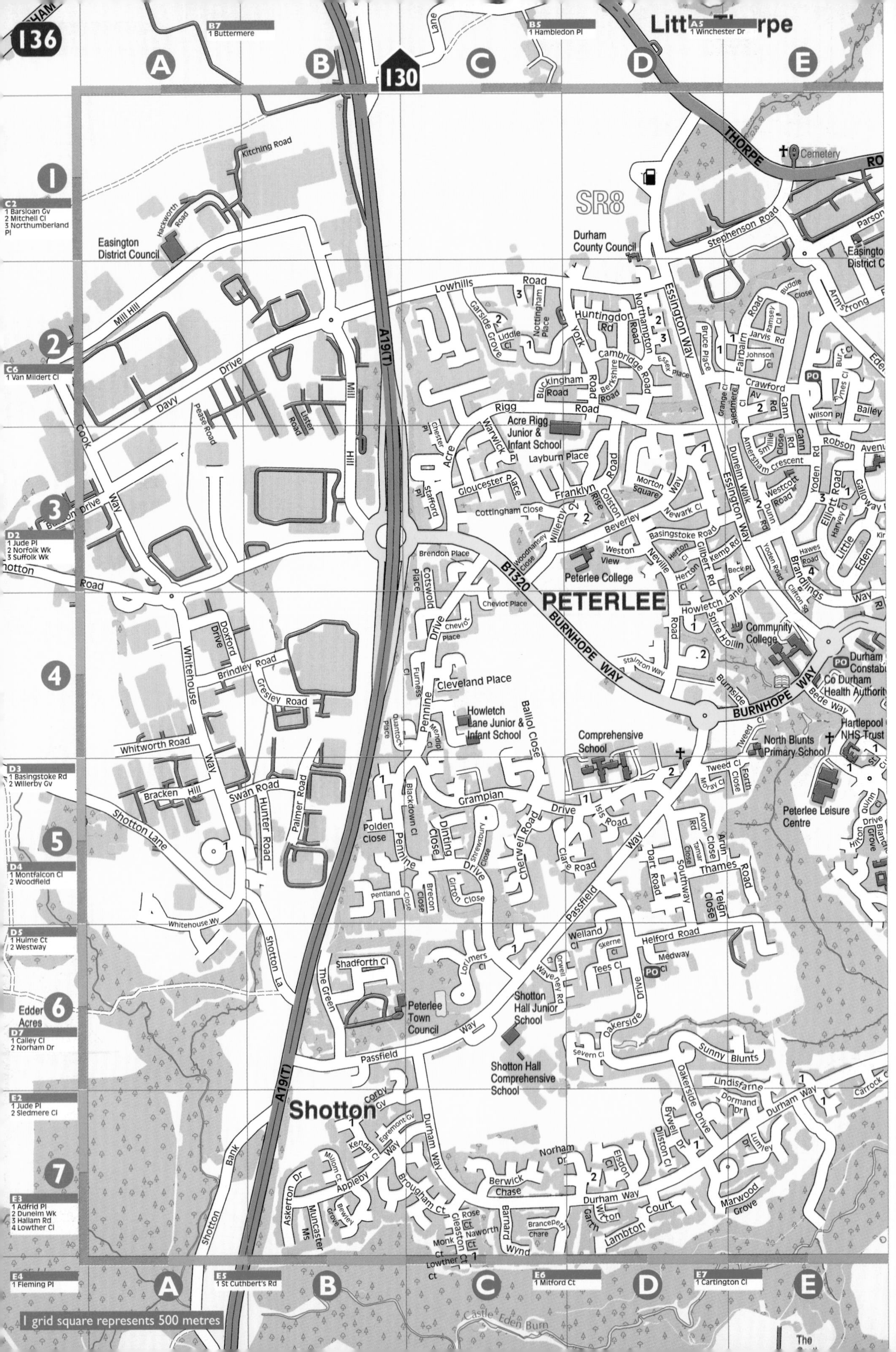
130
A
B
C
D
E
1
2
3
4
5
6
7
B7
1 Buttermere
B5
1 Hambledon Pl
A5
1 Winchester Dr
Little Thorpe
C2
1 Barsloan Gv
2 Mitchell Cl
3 Northumberland Pl
C6
1 Van Mildert Cl
D2
1 Jude Pl
2 Norfolk Wk
3 Suffolk Wk
D3
1 Basingstoke Rd
2 Willerby Gv
D4
1 Montfalcon Cl
2 Woodfield
D5
1 Hulme Ct
2 Westway
D7
1 Calley Cl
2 Norham Dr
E2
1 Jude Pl
2 Sledmere Cl
E3
1 Adfrid Pl
2 Dunelm Wk
3 Hallam Rd
4 Lowther Cl
E4
1 Fleming Pl
E5
1 St Cuthbert's Rd
E6
1 Mitford Ct
E7
1 Cartington Cl
SR8
PETERLEE
Shotton
Edder Acres
A19(T)
B1320
BURNHOPE WAY
THORPE ROAD
Cemetery
Easington District Council
Durham County Council
Acre Rigg Junior & Infant School
Peterlee College
Community College
Howletch Lane Junior & Infant School
Comprehensive School
North Blunts Primary School
Peterlee Leisure Centre
Durham Constabulary
Co Durham Health Authority
Hartlepool NHS Trust
Peterlee Town Council
Shotton Hall Junior School
Shotton Hall Comprehensive School
Castle Eden Burn
Kitching Road
Hackworth Road
Mill Hill
Davy Drive
Cook Way
Pease Road
Lister Road
Shotton Road
Whitehouse Way
Doxford Drive
Brindley Road
Gresley Road
Whitworth Road
Bracken Hill
Swan Road
Hunter Road
Palmer Road
Shotton Lane
Whitehouse Wy
Shotton La
Shotton Bank
Lowhills Road
Garside Grove
Liddle Cl
Nottingham Place
Huntingdon Rd
York Road
Northampton Road
Cambridge Road
Berkshire Road
Essex Place
Essington Way
Buckingham Road
Rigg Road
Acre Rigg
Warwick Pl
Chester Pl
Stafford Pl
Gloucester Place
Layburn Place
Franklyn Rise
Colston Road
Morton Square
Newark Cl
Cottingham Close
Willerby Gv
Woodmansey Close
Beverley Way
Weston View
Basingstoke Road
Neville Road
Herton Cl
Gilbert Rd
Kemp Rd
Beck Pl
Howletch Lane
Spire Hollin
Stainton Way
Burnside
Brendon Place
Cotswold Place
Cheviot Place
Pennine Drive
Furness Cl
Cleveland Place
Balliol Close
Quantock Place
Mendip Cl
Grampian Drive
Blackdown Cl
Polden Close
Dinting Close
Shrewsbury Close
Cherwell Road
Isis Road
Clare Road
Pentland Close
Brecon Close
Girton Close
Passfield Way
Dart Road
Southway
Thames Road
Avon Rd
Tamar Close
Arun Close
Teign Close
Tweed Cl
Moray Cl
Forth Close
Welland Cl
Skerne Cl
Helford Road
Medway Cl
Tees Cl
Orwell Cl
Waveney Rd
Lorimers Cl
Shadforth Cl
The Green
Oakerside Drive
Severn Cl
Sunny Blunts
Lindisfarne
Dormand Dr
Durham Way
Carrock Ct
Bywell Dr
Dilston Cl
Elsdon Cl
Norham Dr
Lumley Dr
Marwood Grove
Berwick Chase
Wilton Ct
Lambton Court
Garth
Brancepeth Chare
Barnard Wynd
Rose Ct
Naworth Ct
Gleaston Ct
Monk Ct
Lowther Ct
Brougham Ct
Appleby Way
Kendal Cl
Egremont Gv
Corby Gv
Askerton Dr
Millom Ct
Muncaster Ms
Bewley Grove
Stephenson Road
Parson
Armstrong
Buddle Close
Ramsey Cl
Fairbairn Road
Jarvis Rd
Johnson Cl
Bruce Place
Crawford Av
Grange Cl
Sledmere Cl
Cann Rd
Wilson Pl
Bailey
Robson Avenue
Smillie Close
Amersham Crescent
Dunelm Walk
Westcott Road
Yoden Rd
Elliott Road
Galloway
Harvey Cl
Little Eden
Hawes Road
Brandlings Way
Clifton Sq
Yoden Road
Bede Way
Hilton Drive
Quinn Grove
Eden
Burt Cl
Innes Cl
1 grid square represents 500 metres

F3
1 Alston Wk
2 Ambleside Cl
3 Bowness Cl
4 Troutbeck Wy
F4
Street names for this grid square are listed at the back of the index
F5
1 Beaumont Pl
131
G3
1 Cowell St
2 Hamilton St
3 Handley St
4 North Av
G4
1 Edendale Ter
2 Kell Rd
G5
1 Delavale Cl
2 Thornes Cl
H3
1 Edward Cain Ct
2 Grant St
3 John Wilson Ct
4 Nelson Cl
5 Ninth St
6 Thorpe St
H4
1 Dene Bank Av
2 Rogers Cl
J4
1 Adam St
2 Eve St
3 Paradise St
4 Reynolds Ct
K6
1 Shaftesbury Crs
A1086
Horden & Easington RC Primary School
Thorpe Road
Kilburn
Timber Rd
Drive
Webb Sq
Wilkinson Rd
Beaumont Crs
Faraday Road
Bruce
Kirkup Road
Moutter Cl
Naisbitt Av
Yoden Crs
Belford St
Alnwick St
Rothbury Av
Morpeth St
Newcastle Av
Sunderland Av
Northumberland St
Durham Av
Blackhills Road
Durham County Council
Park Road
Yoden Avenue
SUNDERLAND ROAD
Horden
Eden Hall Infant School
Edenhill Road
Pickard Close
Ashton Rise
Mansell Crs
Lakeland Dr
Keswick Road
Grasmere Rd
Ellison Road
Shotton Road
Greenside Avenue
South Terrace
Thirlmere Rd
Kirkstone Avenue
Rydal Crs
Chapel-Hill Road
Rosedale Terrace
Roseby Road
Edward Av
Skiddaw Cl
Staveley Rd
Scafell Close
Grisedale Rd
Wasdale Cl
SURTEES ROAD
County
Cumbrian Way
Matterdale Road
Braithwaite Road
Community Care
B1320
YODEN WAY
Leazes
Granville Road
Nesbit Road
Hovingham Close
Harrison Close
Heath Cl
Heath Close
Fulwell Road
Dean Cl
Church Close
O'Neil Drive
Manor Way
Bede Way
Chilton Garth
Eastdene Way
White Lea Close
Garth Cornfield
Eastfield
Hawthorns Hospital
Thompson St
Sea View Gdns
Park La
Nelson Cl
Doctors Surg
First Street
Eden Street
Clayton Street
Seventh Street
Eighth St
Tees St
Tenth St
Eleventh St
Twelfth St
Warren St
Fourth St
Third St
Dene St
Dr Chandys Surg
Cotsford Junior School
Fifth Street
Sixth St
SHOTTON RD
Park Terrace
Hardwick St
COTSFORD LA
Cem
Beach Gv
Windsor Ter
Cedar St
Acacia Av
Bay Av
Alder Rd
Cotsford
Yoden Primary School
Murray St
Seymour St
Horden Cotsford County Infant School
Lane
Dixon Rise
Dene House County Mixed Modern School
Cresswell Av
Burnside Av
Dene Vis
Willow Gv
COAST ROAD
Shaftesbury Road
Shaftesbury Av
Castle Eden Burn
Bellister Pk
Welfare Crs
Eleventh St
Tenth
Hardwick St
West St
North St
Blackhall Primary School
Hardwick Hall Farm
Hotel
Hales Cl
Kenber Dr
Laider Cl
Keating Cl
Stuart Cl
B1281
Dene Leazes
Castle Eden Dene Nature Reserve
HESLEDEN ROAD
F G H J K
1 2 3 4 5 6 7

Albany 82 D6
Annfield Plain 101 J3
Annitsford 28 D7
Axwell Park 66 B4
Aykley Heads 124 C5
Ayres Quay 14 B2
Ayton 94 B3
Backworth 38 E5
Bank Top 52 D2
Barley Mow 93 J4
Barlow 65 F6
Bar Moor 52 C6
Barmston 95 H1
Battle Hill 48 E5
Beaconhill 27 K2
Beacon Lough 81 J1
Beamish 91 J7
Bearpark 123 H6
Bebside 20 A7
Bedlington 19 G4
Bedlington Station 19 H4
Bell's Close 54 C5
Belmont 125 K6
Bensham 10 C6
Benton Square 48 C1
Benwell 55 F5
Biddick 95 F2
Biddick Hall 73 F2
Bill Quay 13 L3
Billy Mill 50 B3
Birtley 81 K7
Bishopwearmouth 14 B4
Black Callerton 43 J2
Blackfell 82 C7
Blakelaw 55 G1
Blaydon 66 B1
Blaydon Burn 65 G3
Blaydon Haughs 54 C7
Blyth 24 E1
Boldon Colliery 72 D2
Bomarsund 19 J1
Bournmoor 107 G4
Brandon 132 E6
Brenkley 26 B5
Broom Hill 117 K2
Broompark 133 J2
Brunswick Village 35 K4
Burdon 110 B4
Burnopfield 77 H7
Burnside 107 K5
Burradon 37 H4
Byermoor 78 B6
Byker 7 G6
Callerton 43 K4
Callerton Lane End 43 F3
Cambois 20 E1
Camperdown 37 J4
Carley Hill 86 B2
Carr Hill 69 H5
Carrville 125 K5
Castletown 84 E4
Catchgate 101 F2
Causey 91 F1
Chester-le-Street 105 F4
Chester Moor 114 B1
Chilton Moor 116 E1
Chirton 2 A2
Chowdene 80 E3
Clara Vale 52 B5
Cleadon 74 A4
Cleadon Park 62 A6
Clough Dene 89 K3
Cold Hesledon 120 C6
Colliery Row 108 A7
Collingwood 28 C4
Columbia 95 G2
Concord 82 E5
Cowpen 20 D6
Coxlodge 46 A5
Craghead 103 H5
Cramlington 27 K3
Crawcrook 52 C7
Crookgate Bank 78 A7
Crookhill 53 G6
Cullercoats 41 H7
Dalton-le-Dale 120 A4
Darras Hall 32 E4
Dawdon 121 F3
Deckham 11 H8
Deneside 120 B2
Denton Burn 54 C4
Deptford 14 A2
Deptford 86 A5
Dinnington 34 E2
Dipton 88 E6
Donwell 82 D4
Downhill 85 F1
Doxford Park 110 A3
Dudley 37 G2
Dunston 9 G6
Dunston Hill 8 E9
Durham 16 B4
Earsdon 39 J3
Easington 130 B5
Easington Colliery 131 G4
Easington Lane 118 C7
East Boldon 73 G4
East Cramlington 29 F3
East Denton 54 E3
East Gateshead 11 M2
East Hartford 23 H4
East Herrington 109 H1
East Holywell 39 F2
East Kyo 101 K1
East Rainton 117 G4
East Sleekburn 20 C3
East Stanley 90 E7
Edmondsley 113 F2
Eighton Banks 81 K3
Eland Green 33 H1
Elemore Vale 128 A1
Elswick 9 H1
Elvet Hill 16 B9
Farringdon 97 J7
Fatfield 94 E6
Fawdon 45 J3
Fellgate 71 J3
Felling 12 D7
Felling Shore 12 D3
Fellside 66 D6
Fence Houses 107 J6
Fenham 55 H4
Flint Hill 89 H5
Follingsby 71 F7
Fordley 37 H2
Forest Hall 47 K1
Framwellgate Moor 124 C4
Fulwell 86 C1
Gateshead 11 H1
Gilesgate 17 H1
Gilesgate 125 F6
Gilesgate Moor 17 L2
Glebe 94 E1
Gosforth 46 B5
Grangetown 98 E5
Grange Villa 104 A2
Grasswell 108 B5
Great Eppleton 118 C3
Great Lumley 115 G1
Greencroft 101 F4
Greenhill 119 H4
Greenside 64 C3
Grindon 97 F3
Hallgarth 126 D5
Harelaw 101 G1
Harlow Green 81 H3
Harperley 101 J1
Harraton 94 C5
Hartley 31 H4
Harton 61 J5
Hasting Hill 96 E4
Haswell 128 E6
Hawthorn 130 C2
Hazlerigg 36 A5
Heaton 6 F1
Hebburn 59 G6
Hebburn Colliery 59 G3
Hebburn New Town 58 E5
Heddon-on-the-Wall 52 A2
Hedworth 72 A2
Hendon 15 H7
Hetton Downs 118 A3
Hetton-le-Hill 127 K2
Hetton-le-Hole 118 A5
Heworth 13 G8
High Callerton 33 G7
High Dubmire 107 K7
Highfield 76 E4
High Forge 91 J5
High Friarside 77 F7
High Handenhold 92 A7
High Haswell 128 C5
High Moorsley 127 G1
High Shields 60 E3
High Shincliffe 135 H5
High Southwick 86 A2
High Spen 76 B1
High Urpeth 92 B6
Hill Top 89 G4
Hill Top 122 C4
Hillview 98 C5
Hobson 89 K2
Holmside 112 C1
Holy Cross 48 E7
Holywell 30 C6
Hooker Gate 76 B2
Horden 137 F3
Horsley Hill 61 K3
Houghton-le-Spring 108 B7
Howdon 49 J7
Howdon Pans 60 A2
Humbledon 97 K3
Hylton Castle 84 E3
Hylton Red House 85 H1
Isabella Pit 25 F2
Iveston 100 B6
Jarrow 60 B5
Jesmond 57 F3
Kenton 45 H6
Kenton Bankfoot 44 E4
Kenton Bar 45 H6
Kibblesworth 80 E7
Killingworth 37 K7
Killingworth Moor 38 C7
Killingworth Village 38 A5
Kimblesworth 113 K5
Kingston Park 45 H4
Kip Hill 90 E5
Lady Park 80 D4
Lambton 94 C3
Lamesley 80 D4
Langley Moor 134 A4
Langley Park 122 C3
The Lawe 3 J4
Leam Lane 70 C6
Leamside 116 B6
Lemington 54 C5
Lintz 89 H1
Lintzford 76 D6
Little Thorpe 130 D7
Littletown 127 H5
Lobley Hill 68 B6
Longbenton 47 J2
Low Eighton 81 H5
Lowes Barn 134 A3
Low Fell 69 F7
Low Greenside 64 C2
Low Moorsley 117 J7
Low Thornley 65 J7
Lumley Thicks 106 E6
Lyons 118 B6
Maiden Law 101 J7
Marden 40 E7
Marley Hill 79 F4
Marley Pots 85 K2
Marsden 62 C6
Mason 35 F1
Mayfield 28 D3
Meadowfield 133 J6
Medburn 32 A7
Middle Herrington 97 F6
Middle Rainton 117 F5
The Middles 102 E4
Mill Dam 60 E2
Millfield 86 A6
Monkseaton 40 B3
Monkton 59 J7
Monkwearmouth 86 B4
Moor End 125 K5
Mount Pleasant 11 K7
Murton 39 K7
Murton 119 G4
Nedderton 18 B6
Nelson Village 28 A1
Nettlesworth 113 K4
Nevilles Cross 134 B2
Newbiggin Hall Estate 44 D6
Newbottle 108 C4
New Brancepeth 132 D3
Newburn 53 J3
Newcastle upon Tyne 6 B7
New Delaval 24 D4
Newfield 104 C2
New Hartley 30 B2
New Herrington 108 C1
New Kyo 101 K3
Newsham 24 C2
Newsham 25 F3
New Silksworth 97 K7
Newton Hall 125 F3
New Town 72 D3
New Town 108 E7
New York 50 A1
North Blyth 21 G4
North End 124 A5
North Hylton 84 C6
Northlea 111 H6
North Shields 2 A4
North Walbottle 43 J7
Offerton 96 C3
Old Burdon 110 A5
Old Fold 11 L4
Ouston 93 G4
Oxclose 94 C1
Oxhill 102 B1
Pallion 85 H5
Palmersville 48 C1
Parkside 120 D3
Path Head 53 K7
Pelaw 13 H5
Pelton 104 D1
Pelton Fell 105 F3
Pennywell 97 F2
Penshaw 96 A7
Percy Main 60 C1
Perkinsville 92 E6
Peterlee 136 C4
Philadelphia 108 B2
Pickering Nook 89 J2
Pittington 126 E3
Pity Me 124 C2
Plawsworth 114 B4
Ponteland 33 J2
Portobello 93 J2
Preston 50 E2
Preston Grange 40 D7
Prestwick 34 B4
Primrose 60 A7
Quaking Houses 102 B5
Rainton Bridge 117 H2
Rainton Gate 116 B7
Rickleton 94 B7
Roker 87 F3
Rosehill 59 G2
Rowlands Gill 77 G3
Ryhope 111 F1
Ryhope Colliery 98 E7
Ryton 52 E6
Ryton Woodside 64 D2
Sacriston 113 G4
St Anthony's 13 G1
St Peter's 7 H9
Saltwell 10 F9
Scotland Gate 19 G1
Scotswood 54 E7
Seaham 121 F1
Seaton 30 D3
Seaton 110 D7
Seaton Burn 27 H7
Seaton Delaval 29 K4
Seaton Sluice 31 F3
Seghill 29 G7
Shankhouse 23 J6
Sheep Hill 77 K6
Sheriff Hill 69 H6
Shield Row 91 F6
Shincliffe 135 H4
Shiney Row 107 K2
Shiremoor 39 J6
Shotton 136 B7
Simonside 60 C7
South Beach 25 J3
South Bents 74 E6
Southfield 28 C5
South Gosforth 46 D6
South Hetton 128 E2
South Hylton 85 F7
South Moor 102 B3
South Newsham 24 E4
South Pelaw 105 H1
South Shields 3 L6
South Stanley 102 C2
Southwick 86 A4
Spital Tongues 4 C2
Springwell 82 C4
Springwell 97 J3
Stanley 102 D1
Stargate 65 F1
Stella 53 J7
Stony Gate 108 E3
Stony Heap 100 C4
Street Gate 79 H3
Sulgrave 83 G5
Sunderland 14 C3
Sunderland 86 A5
Sunniside 78 E3
Sunniside 108 A4
Swalwell 66 E3
Tanfield 90 B2
Tanfield Lea 90 B5
Tan Hills 114 A4
Tantobie 89 J4
Teams 9 L6
Team Valley 68 D7
Thorney Close 97 G5
Throckley 43 G7
Tunstall 98 C7
Tyne Dock 60 E4
Tynemouth 51 F2
Urpeth 92 E4
Ushaw Moor 122 E7
Usworth 82 E4
Walbottle 53 G2
Waldridge 104 E6
Walker 58 B6
Wall Nook 122 C2
Wallsend 58 B1
Wardley 13 M7
Washington 83 J7
Washington Village 95 F1
West Allotment 49 G1
West Boldon 72 E4
West Chirton 49 J5
West Denton 54 C2
Westerhope 44 B6
Western Hill 124 B7
West Harton 60 E5
West Herrington 96 D7
West Holywell 39 F3
West Jesmond 56 B1
West Kyo 101 H2
Westlea 18 D6
West Lea 119 K2
West Monkseaton 40 A6
West Moor 47 H1
Westoe 61 J2
West Park 61 G4
West Pelton 91 K7
West Rainton 116 D5
Whickham 67 F5
Whitburn 75 F3
Whitburn Colliery 63 F7
Whitehills 69 K7
Whiteleas 73 G1
White-le-Head 89 J5
Whitley Bay 41 G4
Whitley Sands 40 E2
Wickham Fell 79 F1
Wide Open 36 C4
Willington 49 G6
Willington Quay 59 J2
Windy Nook 69 K6
Winlaton 65 J2
Winlaton Mill 65 K6
Witherwack 85 J1
Witton Gilbert 113 H7
Woolsington 44 B2
Woolsington Hall 34 C7
Wrekenton 81 H2

USING THE STREET INDEX

Street names are listed alphabetically. Each street name is followed by its postal town or area locality, the Postcode District, the page number, and the reference to the square in which the name is found.

Example: **Abbey Cl** *FAWY* SO45 .... **155** L5 1

Some entries are followed by a number in a blue box. This number indicates the location of the street within the referenced grid square. The full street name is listed at the side of the map page.

GENERAL ABBREVIATIONS

Abbreviation	Meaning
ACC	ACCESS
ALY	ALLEY
AP	APPROACH
AR	ARCADE
ASS	ASSOCIATION
AV	AVENUE
BCH	BEACH
BLDS	BUILDINGS
BND	BEND
BNK	BANK
BR	BRIDGE
BRK	BROOK
BTM	BOTTOM
BUS	BUSINESS
BVD	BOULEVARD
BY	BYPASS
CATH	CATHEDRAL
CEM	CEMETERY
CEN	CENTRE
CFT	CROFT
CH	CHURCH
CHA	CHASE
CHYD	CHURCHYARD
CIR	CIRCLE
CIRC	CIRCUS
CL	CLOSE
CLFS	CLIFFS
CMP	CAMP
CNR	CORNER
CO	COUNTY
COLL	COLLEGE
COM	COMMON
COMM	COMMISSION
CON	CONVENT
COT	COTTAGE
COTS	COTTAGES
CP	CAPE
CPS	COPSE
CR	CREEK
CREM	CREMATORIUM
CRS	CRESCENT
CSWY	CAUSEWAY
CT	COURT
CTRL	CENTRAL
CTS	COURTS
CTYD	COURTYARD
CUTT	CUTTINGS
CV	COVE
CYN	CANYON
DEPT	DEPARTMENT
DL	DALE
DM	DAM
DR	DRIVE
DRO	DROVE
DRY	DRIVEWAY
DWGS	DWELLINGS
E	EAST
EMB	EMBANKMENT
EMBY	EMBASSY
ESP	ESPLANADE
EST	ESTATE
EX	EXCHANGE
EXPY	EXPRESSWAY
EXT	EXTENSION
F/O	FLYOVER
FC	FOOTBALL CLUB
FK	FORK
FLD	FIELD
FLDS	FIELDS
FLS	FALLS
FLS	FLATS
FM	FARM
FT	FORT
FWY	FREEWAY
FY	FERRY
GA	GATE
GAL	GALLERY
GDN	GARDEN
GDNS	GARDENS
GLD	GLADE
GLN	GLEN
GN	GREEN
GND	GROUND
GRA	GRANGE
GRG	GARAGE
GT	GREAT
GTWY	GATEWAY
GV	GROVE
HGR	HIGHER
HL	HILL
HLS	HILLS
HO	HOUSE
HOL	HOLLOW
HOSP	HOSPITAL
HRB	HARBOUR
HTH	HEATH
HTS	HEIGHTS
HVN	HAVEN
HWY	HIGHWAY
IMP	IMPERIAL
IN	INLET
IND EST	INDUSTRIAL ESTATE
INF	INFIRMARY
INFO	INFORMATION
INT	INTERCHANGE
IS	ISLAND
JCT	JUNCTION
JTY	JETTY
KG	KING
KNL	KNOLL
L	LAKE
LA	LANE
LDG	LODGE
LGT	LIGHT
LK	LOCK
LKS	LAKES
LNDG	LANDING
LTL	LITTLE
LWR	LOWER
MAG	MAGISTRATE
MAN	MANSIONS
MD	MEAD
MDW	MEADOWS
MEM	MEMORIAL
MKT	MARKET
MKTS	MARKETS
ML	MALL
ML	MILL
MNR	MANOR
MS	MEWS
MSN	MISSION
MT	MOUNT
MTN	MOUNTAIN
MTS	MOUNTAINS
MUS	MUSEUM
MWY	MOTORWAY
N	NORTH
NE	NORTH EAST
NW	NORTH WEST
O/P	OVERPASS
OFF	OFFICE
ORCH	ORCHARD
OV	OVAL
PAL	PALACE
PAS	PASSAGE
PAV	PAVILION
PDE	PARADE
PH	PUBLIC HOUSE
PK	PARK
PKWY	PARKWAY
PL	PLACE
PLN	PLAIN
PLNS	PLAINS
PLZ	PLAZA
POL	POLICE STATION
PR	PRINCE
PREC	PRECINCT
PREP	PREPARATORY
PRIM	PRIMARY
PROM	PROMENADE
PRS	PRINCESS
PRT	PORT
PT	POINT
PTH	PATH
PZ	PIAZZA
QD	QUADRANT
QU	QUEEN
QY	QUAY
R	RIVER
RBT	ROUNDABOUT

RD ROAD
RDG RIDGE
REP REPUBLIC
RES RESERVOIR
RFC RUGBY FOOTBALL CLUB
RI RISE
RP RAMP
RW ROW
S SOUTH
SCH SCHOOL
SE SOUTH EAST
SER SERVICE AREA
SH SHORE
SHOP SHOPPING
SKWY SKYWAY
SMT SUMMIT
SOC SOCIETY
SP SPUR
SPR SPRING
SQ SQUARE
ST STREET
STN STATION
STR STREAM
STRD STRAND
SW SOUTH WEST
TDG TRADING
TER TERRACE
THWY THROUGHWAY
TNL TUNNEL
TOLL TOLLWAY
TPK TURNPIKE
TR TRACK
TRL TRAIL
TWR TOWER
U/P UNDERPASS
UNI UNIVERSITY
UPR UPPER
V VALE
VA VALLEY
VIAD VIADUCT
VIL VILLA
VIS VISTA
VLG VILLAGE
VLS VILLAS
VW VIEW
W WEST
WD WOOD
WHF WHARF
WK WALK
WKS WALKS
WLS WELLS
WY WAY
YD YARD
YHA YOUTH HOSTEL

POSTCODE TOWNS AND AREA ABBREVIATIONS

ASHBK/HED/RY Ashbrooke/Hedon/Ryhope
BDLGTN Bedlington
BDN/LAN/SAC Brandon/Lanchester/Sacriston
BLAY Blaydon
BLYTH Blyth
BOL Boldon
BOLCOL Boldon Colliery
BW/LEM/TK/HW Benwell/Lemington/Throckley/Heddon-on-the-Wall
BYK/HTN/WLK Byker/Heaton/Walker
CHPW Chopwell
CLDN/WHIT/ROK Cleadon/Whitburn/Roker
CLS/BIR/GTL Chester-le-Street/Birtley/Great Lumley
CLSW/PEL Chester-le-Street west/Pelton
CNUT Central Newcastle upon Tyne
CON/LDGT Consett/Leadgate
CRAM Cramlington
DHAM Durham
DIN/WO Dinnington/Wide Open
DUN/TMV Dunston/Team Valley
ELS/FEN Elswick/Fenham
FELL Felling
GATE Gateshead
GOS/KPK Gosforth/Kingston Park
HAR/WTLS Harton/Whiteleas
HEBB Hebburn
HLH Hetton-le-Hole
HLS Houghton-le-Spring
JES Jesmond
JRW Jarrow
LGB/HTN Longbenton/Heaton
LGB/KIL Longbenton/Killingworth
LWF/SPW/WRK Low Fell/Springwell/Wrekenton
MLFD/PNYW Millfield/Pennywell
MONK Monkseaton
MPTH Morpeth
NSHW North Shields west
PLEE/EAS Peterlee/Easington
PONT/DH Ponteland/Darras Hall
RDHAMSE Rural Durham south & east
RHTLP Rural Hartlepool
ROWG Rowlands Gill
RYTON Ryton
SEA/MUR Seaham/Murton
SMOOR Shiremoor
SSH South Shields
STKFD/GP Stakefold/Guide Post
STLY/ANP Stanley/Annfield Plain
STMFDH Stamfordham
SUND Sunderland
SUNDSW Sunderland southwest
SWCK/CAS Southwick/Castletown
TYNE/NSHE Tynemouth/North Shields east
WASHN Washington north
WASHS Washington south
WBAY Whitley Bay
WD/WHPE/BLK West Denton/Westerhope/Blakelaw
WICK/BNPF Wickham/Burnopfield
WLSD/HOW Wallsend/Howdon
WYLAM Wylam

Index - streets

A

Abbay St *SWCK/CAS* SR5 86 A4
Abbey Cl *MONK* NE25 40 B5
WASHS NE38 95 F1
Abbey Ct *GATE* NE8 11 H6
Abbey Dr *JRW* NE32 60 A4
TYNE/NSHE NE30 51 H2
WD/WHPE/BLK NE5 43 K6 1
Abbey Rd *DHAM* DH1 124 B1
WASHS NE38 95 F1
Abbeywoods *DHAM* DH1 124 C1 1
Abbotsfield Cl *SUNDSW* SR3 109 K2 1
Abbotsford Gv
ASHBK/HED/RY SR2 14 C7
Abbotsford Pk *MONK* NE25 40 D5
Abbotsford Rd *FELL* NE10 12 C5
Abbotsford Ter *JES* NE2 56 D3
Abbotside Cl *CLSW/PEL* DH2 92 D4
Abbotside Pl
WD/WHPE/BLK NE5 54 B2 1
Abbotsmeade Cl
WD/WHPE/BLK NE5 55 F3
Abbot's Rd *GATE* NE8 6 A9
Abbots' Rw *DHAM* DH1 125 G6
Abbot St *PLEE/EAS* SR8 131 G4
Abbots Wk *STLY/ANP* DH9 91 K6
Abbots Wy *NSHW* NE29 50 B1
Abbs St *SWCK/CAS* SR5 86 D4 1
Abercorn Pl *WLSD/HOW* NE28 49 G4
Abercorn Rd
BW/LEM/TK/HW NE15 54 E6
SUNDSW SR3 97 H5
Abercrombie Pl
WD/WHPE/BLK NE5 55 F1 1
Aberdare Rd *SUNDSW* SR3 97 H7
Aberdeen *CLSW/PEL* DH2 93 F5
Aberdeen Ct *DIN/WO* NE13 45 H2 1
Aberdeen Dr *JRW* NE32 60 C7
Aberford Cl
WD/WHPE/BLK NE5 43 K7 1
Aberfoyle *CLSW/PEL* DH2 93 F5
Aberfoyle Ct *STLY/ANP* DH9 103 F1
Abernethy *CLSW/PEL* DH2 93 F4
Abingdon Rd *BYK/HTN/WLK* NE6 58 D4
Abingdon Sq *CRAM* NE23 23 J6
Abingdon St *MLFD/PNYW* SR4 97 K1
Abingdon Wy *BOL* NE36 72 C5
BOLCOL NE35 72 B3
Abinger St *ELS/FEN* NE4 4 F6
Aboyne Sq *SUNDSW* SR3 97 H5
Acacia Av *HLS* DH4 107 J6
PLEE/EAS SR8 137 J4
Acacia Gv *HAR/WTLS* NE34 61 J6
Acacia Rd *FELL* NE10 11 M4
Acacia St *DUN/TMV* NE11 68 C7
Acanthus Av *ELS/FEN* NE4 55 H4
Acer Ct *ASHBK/HED/RY* SR2 14 F9
Acer Dr *RDHAMSE* DH6 128 E6 1
Acklam Av *ASHBK/HED/RY* SR2 99 F5
Acomb Av *MONK* NE25 30 A6
WLSD/HOW NE28 49 F3
Acomb Ct *ASHBK/HED/RY* SR2 99 F5 1
BDLGTN NE22 19 G5
Acomb Crs *GOS/KPK* NE3 45 K2
Acomb Gdns
WD/WHPE/BLK NE5 55 G3
Acorn Av *BDLGTN* NE22 19 F6
GATE NE8 10 A7
Acorn Cl *BDN/LAN/SAC* DH7 113 G4
Acornclose La
BDN/LAN/SAC DH7 112 E4
Acorn Pl *BDN/LAN/SAC* DH7 133 G6 1
Acorn Rd *JES* NE2 56 E1
Acre Rigg Rd *PLEE/EAS* SR8 136 C3
Acton Dene *STLY/ANP* DH9 103 G1
Acton Dr *NSHW* NE29 50 B2
Acton Pl *LGB/HTN* NE7 57 H1
Acton Rd *WD/WHPE/BLK* NE5 54 D3 1
Adair Av *BW/LEM/TK/HW* NE15 55 G5
Adam St *PLEE/EAS* SR8 137 J4 1
Ada St *BYK/HTN/WLK* NE6 7 L5
SSH NE33 61 H2
Adderstone Av *CRAM* NE23 28 C3
Adderstone Crs *JES* NE2 57 F1
Adderstone Gdns *NSHW* NE29 49 K1
Addington Crs *NSHW* NE29 50 C4
Addington Dr *BLYTH* NE24 25 G2
WLSD/HOW NE28 49 F3
Addison Ct *WLSD/HOW* NE28 59 J2 1
Addison Gdns *FELL* NE10 13 M9
Addison Rd *BOL* NE36 72 E5
BW/LEM/TK/HW NE15 54 B4 1
Addison St *ASHBK/HED/RY* SR2 15 J7
NSHW NE29 2 D4
Addycombe Ter
BYK/HTN/WLK NE6 57 J2
Adelaide Cl *SUND* SR1 15 H4
Adelaide Pl *SUND* SR1 15 J4
Adelaide Rw *SEA/MUR* SR7 120 E1 1
Adelaide Ter *ELS/FEN* NE4 55 H6
Adeline Gdns *GOS/KPK* NE3 56 A1
Adelphi Cl *NSHW* NE29 50 A2
Adelphi Pl *BYK/HTN/WLK* NE6 7 L6
Adfrid Pl *PLEE/EAS* SR8 136 E3 1
Admiral Wy *SUNDSW* SR3 109 G2
Adolphus St
CLDN/WHIT/ROK SR6 75 F4
Adolphus St West
SEA/MUR SR7 120 E1 2
Adventure La *HLS* DH4 116 C5
Affleck St *GATE* NE8 10 E4
Afton Ct *HAR/WTLS* NE34 61 G6 1
Afton Wy *GOS/KPK* NE3 45 J5 1
Agar Rd *SUNDSW* SR3 97 H6
Agincourt *HEBB* NE31 59 F4
LGB/KIL NE12 37 K5 1
Agnes Maria St *GOS/KPK* NE3 46 A5 1
Agnes St *STLY/ANP* DH9 90 D7 1
Agricola Gdns *WLSD/HOW* NE28 49 F4
Agricola Rd *ELS/FEN* NE4 4 A5
Aidan Av *WBAY* NE26 30 E2 1
Aidan Cl *DIN/WO* NE13 36 B3 1
STLY/ANP DH9 91 F7
Aidan Wk *GOS/KPK* NE3 46 D5
Aiden Wy *HLH* DH5 117 K3 1
Ailesbury St *MLFD/PNYW* SR4 86 A6
Ainderby Rd
BW/LEM/TK/HW NE15 52 D1
Ainsdale Gdns
WD/WHPE/BLK NE5 54 A1 1
Ainsley St *DHAM* DH1 16 A3
Ainslie Pl *BYK/HTN/WLK* NE6 55 F2
Ainsworth Av *HAR/WTLS* NE34 72 E1
Ainthorpe Cl *SUNDSW* SR3 98 B7 1
Ainthorpe Gdns *LGB/HTN* NE7 47 H6
Aintree Gdns *GATE* NE8 10 B9
Aintree Rd *SUNDSW* SR3 97 H6
Airedale *WLSD/HOW* NE28 48 B5
Airedale Gdns *HLH* DH5 117 J6
Aireys Cl *HLS* DH4 108 A7
Airey Ter *BYK/HTN/WLK* NE6 58 C6
GATE NE8 10 D6
Airport Freightway
DIN/WO NE13 34 C7
Airville Mt *SUNDSW* SR3 110 A3
Aisgill Cl *CRAM* NE23 28 C2 1
Aisgill Dr *WD/WHPE/BLK* NE5 54 A2
Aiskell St *MLFD/PNYW* SR4 86 A7
Akeld Cl *CRAM* NE23 28 C3
Akenside Hl *CNUT* NE1 5 L8
Alamein Av *HLH* DH5 108 D7 1
Alansway Gdns *SSH* NE33 61 H3 1
Albany Av *LGB/KIL* NE12 47 K2 1
Albany Ct *ELS/FEN* NE4 9 H2
Albany Rd *GATE* NE8 11 K1
Albany St East *SSH* NE33 61 H3 2
Albany St West *SSH* NE33 61 H3 1
Albany Wy *WASHN* NE37 82 E6
Albatross Wy *BLYTH* NE24 25 G4
Albemarle Av *JES* NE2 46 D7 1
Albemarle St *SSH* NE33 3 H7
Albert Av *WLSD/HOW* NE28 58 D1 1
Albert Dr *LWF/SPW/WRK* NE9 69 F7 1
Albert Pl *LWF/SPW/WRK* NE9 81 F1 1
WASHS NE38 95 H3
Albert Rd *BDLGTN* NE22 19 K4
JRW NE32 59 K4 1
MLFD/PNYW SR4 86 A6
WBAY NE26 31 G2
Albert St *CLS/BIR/GTL* DH3 105 J4
CLSW/PEL DH2 104 A2
DHAM DH1 16 A2
HEBB NE31 59 F4 1
JES NE2 6 A5
SEA/MUR SR7 120 E2
Albert Ter *LGB/KIL* NE12 47 J1
Albion Pl *SUND* SR1 14 D6
Albion Rd *TYNE/NSHE* NE30 2 E1 1
Albion Rd West *NSHW* NE29 2 C2
Albion Rw *BYK/HTN/WLK* NE6 6 E5 1
Albion St *FELL* NE10 69 K6
MLFD/PNYW SR4 84 E7
Albion Ter *NSHW* NE29 2 D1
Albion Wy *BLYTH* NE24 20 E7
CRAM NE23 23 K6 1
Albury Park Rd
TYNE/NSHE NE30 51 G3
Albury Pl *WICK/BNPF* NE16 66 E7
Albury Rd *JES* NE2 46 D7
Albyn Gdns *SUNDSW* SR3 98 A3 1
Alconbury Cl *BLYTH* NE24 25 G2
Alcroft Cl *WD/WHPE/BLK* NE5 43 K7 2
Aldborough St *BLYTH* NE24 21 G7 1
Aldbrough Cl
ASHBK/HED/RY SR2 111 F1 1
Aldbrough St *HAR/WTLS* NE34 60 E6 1
Aldeburgh Av
BW/LEM/TK/HW NE15 54 A3
Aldenham Rd *SUNDSW* SR3 97 J6
Alder Av *ELS/FEN* NE4 55 H3
Alder Cl *HLH* DH5 117 J5
Alder Crs *STLY/ANP* DH9 89 H4
Alderdene Cl
BDN/LAN/SAC DH7 133 H1 1
Alder Gv *MONK* NE25 40 C3
Alder Lea Cl *DHAM* DH1 125 H6
Alderley Cl *ASHBK/HED/RY* SR2 99 F4
BOLCOL NE35 72 C3 1
Alderley Dr *LGB/KIL* NE12 38 B5
Alderley Rd *LWF/SPW/WRK* NE9 68 E7
Alderley Wy *CRAM* NE23 23 K6
Alderman Wood Rd
STLY/ANP DH9 90 C6
Alderney Gdns
WD/WHPE/BLK NE5 54 A1 2
Alder Pk *BDN/LAN/SAC* DH7 133 F7
Alder Rd *NSHW* NE29 49 J3
PLEE/EAS SR8 137 J4
WLSD/HOW NE28 49 G4
Aldershot Rd *SUNDSW* SR3 97 H7 1
Aldershot Sq *SUNDSW* SR3 97 H7 2
Alder St *SWCK/CAS* SR5 85 F4 1
Alder Wy *LGB/KIL* NE12 37 J5 1
Alderwood *WASHS* NE38 94 D6
Alderwood Crs
BYK/HTN/WLK NE6 58 B2
Alderwyk *FELL* NE10 70 D6 1
Aldhome Ct *DHAM* DH1 124 B3 1
Aldridge Ct *BDN/LAN/SAC* DH7 123 F7
Aldsworth Cl
LWF/SPW/WRK NE9 82 B4
Aldwick Rd
BW/LEM/TK/HW NE15 54 D5
Aldwych Dr *NSHW* NE29 49 K3
Aldwych Rd *SUNDSW* SR3 97 H7 1
Aldwych Sq *SUNDSW* SR3 109 H1
Aldwych St *SSH* NE33 3 M9
Alexander Dr *HLH* DH5 117 J5
Alexander Ter
CLDN/WHIT/ROK SR6 86 D2 1
Alexandra Av *SWCK/CAS* SR5 85 K4
Alexandra Cl *DHAM* DH1 124 B3
Alexandra Dr *WICK/BNPF* NE16 8 A7
Alexandra Gdns *NSHW* NE29 50 C4
Alexandra Pk
ASHBK/HED/RY SR2 98 C2
SUNDSW SR3 98 B2
Alexandra Rd
BYK/HTN/WLK NE6 57 H2
GATE NE8 10 F6
Alexandra St *CLSW/PEL* DH2 104 C1
WLSD/HOW NE28 58 E1 1
Alexandra Wy *CRAM* NE23 28 C3
Alexandria Crs *DHAM* DH1 16 B4
Alexandrina St
SEA/MUR SR7 120 E1 3
Alford *CLSW/PEL* DH2 93 F4
Alfred Av *BDLGTN* NE22 19 H5
Alfred St *BYK/HTN/WLK* NE6 7 L5
HEBB NE31 59 F6
SEA/MUR SR7 121 F2
Algernon *LGB/KIL* NE12 37 K4 1
Algernon Pl *WBAY* NE26 41 F5
Algernon Rd
BW/LEM/TK/HW NE15 54 A5
BYK/HTN/WLK NE6 7 G4
Algernon Ter *TYNE/NSHE* NE30 51 G2
Algiers Rd *SUNDSW* SR3 97 G7 1
Alice St *ASHBK/HED/RY* SR2 14 D7
BLAY NE21 65 K3
CLSW/PEL DH2 93 F6
SSH NE33 61 G3
Aline St *SEA/MUR* SR7 121 F1 1
SUNDSW SR3 98 B7
Alison Dr *BOL* NE36 73 H5
Allandale Av *LGB/KIL* NE12 47 K3
Allanville *LGB/KIL* NE12 37 J5
All Church
BW/LEM/TK/HW NE15 55 F5 1
Allendale Av *WLSD/HOW* NE28 48 D6
Allendale Crs *HLS* DH4 95 J6
SMOOR NE27 39 J6
Allendale Dr *HAR/WTLS* NE34 62 A3
Allendale Pl *TYNE/NSHE* NE30 51 H3
Allendale Rd
BDN/LAN/SAC DH7 133 H6 1
BLYTH NE24 25 H1
BYK/HTN/WLK NE6 7 J7
SUNDSW SR3 97 H7 1
Allendale Sq *SUNDSW* SR3 97 J5
Allendale St *HLH* DH5 117 K6 1
Allendale Ter
BYK/HTN/WLK NE6 58 B5 1
Allenhead *WASHS* NE38 95 G5
Allenheads *MONK* NE25 29 K4
WD/WHPE/BLK NE5 54 C2
Allensgreen *CRAM* NE23 28 C2
Allen St *CLS/BIR/GTL* DH3 105 J5
Allerdean Cl
BW/LEM/TK/HW NE15 53 K4 1
Allergate *DHAM* DH1 16 B4
Allerhope *CRAM* NE23 28 C3
Allerton Gdns
BYK/HTN/WLK NE6 57 K1 1
Allerwash
WD/WHPE/BLK NE5 54 C2 1
Allhusen Ter *GATE* NE8 11 M5
Alliance St *MLFD/PNYW* SR4 14 B3 1
Allingham Ct *LGB/HTN* NE7 48 A7 1
Alloa Rd *SUNDSW* SR3 97 H6 1
Allonby Wy
WD/WHPE/BLK NE5 55 F3 1
All Saints Dr *HLH* DH5 117 K2
Alma Pl *NSHW* NE29 50 E4
WBAY NE26 41 F5
Alma St *MLFD/PNYW* SR4 84 E6
Alma Ter *RYTON* NE40 64 E2
Almond Cl *RDHAMSE* DH6 128 E6
Almond Crs *GATE* NE8 10 A7
Almond Dr *SWCK/CAS* SR5 84 E5
Almond Pl *ELS/FEN* NE4 55 H4 1
Almoner's Barn *DHAM* DH1 134 B2
Aln Av *GOS/KPK* NE3 46 A4
Aln Ct *BW/LEM/TK/HW* NE15 54 A5
Aln Crs *GOS/KPK* NE3 46 A3
Aln Gv *BW/LEM/TK/HW* NE15 54 A4
Alnham Ct *GOS/KPK* NE3 45 J3 1
Alnmouth Av *NSHW* NE29 50 B6
Alnmouth Dr *GOS/KPK* NE3 46 E6 1
Aln St *HEBB* NE31 59 F5
Aln Wk *GOS/KPK* NE3 46 A4 1
Alnwick Av *NSHW* NE29 50 B6
Alnwick Cl *CLSW/PEL* DH2 105 G6
WICK/BNPF NE16 66 E5
Alnwick Gv *JRW* NE32 71 K2 1
Alnwick Rd *DHAM* DH1 124 D2
HAR/WTLS NE34 61 G5
SUNDSW SR3 97 J6
Alnwick Sq *SUNDSW* SR3 97 J6
Alnwick St
BW/LEM/TK/HW NE15 53 H3
PLEE/EAS SR8 137 G1
WLSD/HOW NE28 58 E1
Alnwick Ter *DIN/WO* NE13 36 C2 1
Alpine Gv *BOL* NE36 73 F5 1
Alpine Wy *SUNDSW* SR3 98 A3 2
Alresford *LGB/KIL* NE12 37 K5 2
Alston Av *BYK/HTN/WLK* NE6 7 M4
CRAM NE23 28 E3 1
Alston Cl *NSHW* NE29 50 A3 1
WLSD/HOW NE28 49 J6
Alston Crs *CLDN/WHIT/ROK* SR6 74 C7
Alston Gdns
BW/LEM/TK/HW NE15 43 F7
Alston Gv *WBAY* NE26 30 E1
Alston Rd *MONK* NE25 30 A2
WASHS NE38 83 K7
Alston St *GATE* NE8 10 B6
Alston Wk *PLEE/EAS* SR8 137 F3 1
Alston Wy *BDN/LAN/SAC* DH7 133 H6
Altan Pl *LGB/KIL* NE12 47 H3
Alum Well Rd
LWF/SPW/WRK NE9 68 E7 1
LWF/SPW/WRK NE9 69 F7 2
Alverston Cl
BW/LEM/TK/HW NE15 54 A3
Alverstone Av
LWF/SPW/WRK NE9 80 E1
Alverthorpe St *SSH* NE33 61 H3
Alvin Gra *JRW* NE32 59 H4 1
Alwin *WASHS* NE38 94 C5
Alwin Cl *HLS* DH4 107 G4
Alwinton Av *NSHW* NE29 50 B2
Alwinton Cl *BLYTH* NE24 20 E6
WD/WHPE/BLK NE5 44 E6 1
Alwinton Dr *CLSW/PEL* DH2 105 G6
Alwinton Gdns *DUN/TMV* NE11 68 A7
Alwinton Rd *SMOOR* NE27 39 J6
Alwinton Ter *GOS/KPK* NE3 46 D5
Amara Sq *SUNDSW* SR3 97 J6
Ambassadors Wy *NSHW* NE29 49 K2
Amber Ct *BLYTH* NE24 24 E1 1
Ambergate Cl
WD/WHPE/BLK NE5 44 E7 1
Amberley Cha *LGB/KIL* NE12 38 A5 1
Amberley Cl *WLSD/HOW* NE28 49 J6 1
Amberley Gdns *LGB/HTN* NE7 57 J1
Amberley St *ASHBK/HED/RY* SR2 15 G7
GATE NE8 9 M6
Amberley St South
ASHBK/HED/RY SR2 15 G8 1
Amberley Wy *BLYTH* NE24 25 G2 1
Amberly Gv *WICK/BNPF* NE16 66 E7
Amble Av *HAR/WTLS* NE34 62 B3
MONK NE25 41 F6
Amble Cl *BLYTH* NE24 24 E2
Amble Gv *JES* NE2 6 B2
Amble Pl *LGB/KIL* NE12 48 B1
Ambleside
BW/LEM/TK/HW NE15 43 G7
Ambleside Av *HAR/WTLS* NE34 61 J5
SEA/MUR SR7 110 E7
Ambleside Cl *MONK* NE25 30 A5 1
PLEE/EAS SR8 137 F3 2
Ambleside Ter
CLDN/WHIT/ROK SR6 86 C1
Amble Wy *GOS/KPK* NE3 46 B4 1
Ambridge Wy *GOS/KPK* NE3 45 K5 1
Ambrose Pl
BYK/HTN/WLK NE6 58 D5 1
Ambrose Rd *SUNDSW* SR3 97 H6
Amec Wy *WLSD/HOW* NE28 59 G2
Amelia Cl *ELS/FEN* NE4 8 F1
Amelia Gdns *SUNDSW* SR3 97 F7
Amersham Crs *PLEE/EAS* SR8 136 E3
Amersham Pl
WD/WHPE/BLK NE5 55 F1 2
Amersham Rd *BLYTH* NE24 25 F3
Amesbury Cl
WD/WHPE/BLK NE5 43 K7 3
Amethyst Rd *ELS/FEN* NE4 9 H2
Amethyst St *MLFD/PNYW* SR4 85 K6 1
Amherst Rd *GOS/KPK* NE3 45 J4
Amos Ayre Pl *HAR/WTLS* NE34 60 D6
Amos Dr *STLY/ANP* DH9 101 H6
Amsterdam Rd *SUNDSW* SR3 97 J6
Amy St *SWCK/CAS* SR5 86 B3 1
Ancaster Av *LGB/KIL* NE12 47 H4
Ancaster Rd *WICK/BNPF* NE16 66 D7
Ancona St *MLFD/PNYW* SR4 85 K5
Ancroft Av *NSHW* NE29 50 D3
Ancroft Garth *DHAM* DH1 135 J6
Ancroft Pl *WD/WHPE/BLK* NE5 55 F3
Ancroft Rd *MONK* NE25 29 J5
Ancroft Wy *GOS/KPK* NE3 45 K2 1
Ancrum St *JES* NE2 4 E2
Anderson St *SSH* NE33 3 J7
Andover Pl *WLSD/HOW* NE28 49 G4
Andrew Rd *SUNDSW* SR3 97 G7
Andrew's La *PLEE/EAS* SR8 130 B7
Anfield Rd *GOS/KPK* NE3 45 J5
Angerton Av *SMOOR* NE27 39 H7
TYNE/NSHE NE30 50 E1
Angerton Gdns
WD/WHPE/BLK NE5 55 H3
Anglesey Gdns
WD/WHPE/BLK NE5 54 A1 3
Anglesey Pl *ELS/FEN* NE4 4 D7
Anglesey Rd *SUNDSW* SR3 97 H7
Anglesey Sq *SUNDSW* SR3 97 H7 3
Angle Ter *WLSD/HOW* NE28 59 H1 1
Angram Dr *ASHBK/HED/RY* SR2 99 G5
Angrove Gdns *MLFD/PNYW* SR4 85 K7
Angus *CLSW/PEL* DH2 93 F4
Angus Cl *LGB/KIL* NE12 37 J6
Angus Crs *NSHW* NE29 50 B6
Angus Rd *GATE* NE8 10 A7
Annand Rd *DHAM* DH1 17 K1
Anne Dr *LGB/KIL* NE12 48 C2
Annfield Pl *STLY/ANP* DH9 101 G3
Annfield Rd *CRAM* NE23 23 H5
Annie St *CLDN/WHIT/ROK* SR6 86 D1
Annitsford Dr *CRAM* NE23 37 H1
Ann's Rw *BLYTH* NE24 21 G5
Ann St *BLAY* NE21 66 A1
GATE NE8 11 G3
HEBB NE31 58 E4

Annville Crs BYK/HTN/WLK NE6 58 C7
Anscomb Gdns LGB/HTN NE7 47 F7
Anson Cl SSH NE33 61 F3
Anson Pl WD/WHPE/BLK NE5 44 D7 1
Anstead Cl CRAM NE23 28 C2
Anthony Rd SUNDSW SR3 97 H7 6
Anthony St STLY/ANP DH9 90 C7
Antonine Wk
BW/LEM/TK/HW NE15 52 B1
Anton Pl CRAM NE23 28 C3
Antrim Cl WD/WHPE/BLK NE5 45 G7
Antrim Gdns SEA/MUR SR7 111 J7 1
Antwerp Rd SUNDSW SR3 97 G7
Anvil Ct DHAM DH1 124 B2
Apperley WD/WHPE/BLK NE5 54 C2
Apperley Av DHAM DH1 135 K6
GOS/KPK NE3 45 G6
Appian Pl
BW/LEM/TK/HW NE15 53 G1 1
LWF/SPW/WRK NE9 11 L9
Appleby Ct NSHW NE29 2 B1
Appleby Gdns WLSD/HOW NE28 49 J6
Appleby Pk NSHW NE29 50 D4
Appleby Rd SUNDSW SR3 97 H7
Appleby Sq SUNDSW SR3 97 H7 7
Appleby St NSHW NE29 2 D5
Appleby Wy PLEE/EAS SR8 136 B7
Apple Cl BW/LEM/TK/HW NE15 54 A3
Appledore Gdns
CLS/BIR/GTL DH3 105 K2
Appledore Rd BLYTH NE24 25 G2
Appleforth Av
ASHBK/HED/RY SR2 99 G5
Appletree Gdns
BYK/HTN/WLK NE6 58 A3
MONK NE25 40 C6
Applewood LGB/KIL NE12 38 B6 1
Appley Ter CLDN/WHIT/ROK SR6 86 E4
Apsley Crs GOS/KPK NE3 45 J5
Arbroath Rd SUNDSW SR3 97 H6
Arcadia Av CLS/BIR/GTL DH3 105 J2
Arcadia Ter BLYTH NE24 25 G1
Archbold Ter JES NE2 5 M2
Archer Rd SUNDSW SR3 97 H6
Archer Sq SUNDSW SR3 97 H6 2
Archer St WLSD/HOW NE28 49 G7
Archery Ri DHAM DH1 134 B2
Archibald St GOS/KPK NE3 46 C5
Arcot Av CRAM NE23 22 E7
MONK NE25 40 C6
Arcot Dr MONK NE25 40 C7
WD/WHPE/BLK NE5 54 D3 2
Arden Av GOS/KPK NE3 46 B1
Arden Cl WLSD/HOW NE28 49 F3
Arden Crs WD/WHPE/BLK NE5 55 H2
Arden Sq SUNDSW SR3 97 J6
Ardrossan CLSW/PEL DH2 93 F5
Ardrossan Rd SUNDSW SR3 97 H7
Arena Wy ELS/FEN NE4 10 A2
Argus Cl DUN/TMV NE11 68 B5
Argyle Ct STLY/ANP DH9 90 E6
Argyle Pl NSHW NE29 50 E2 1
RDHAMSE DH6 128 E2
Argyle Sq ASHBK/HED/RY SR2 14 D7
Argyle St ASHBK/HED/RY SR2 14 D7
CNUT NE1 5 M6
HEBB NE31 59 G4
TYNE/NSHE NE30 51 H2 1
Arisaig CLSW/PEL DH2 93 F4
Arklecrag WASHN NE37 82 E7
Arkleside Pl
WD/WHPE/BLK NE5 54 B2 2
Arkle St DIN/WO NE13 36 A5
GATE NE8 10 B8
Arkwright St GATE NE8 68 D5
Arlington Av GOS/KPK NE3 45 K7
Arlington Gv CRAM NE23 23 H5
WICK/BNPF NE16 66 E6
Arlington Rd HEBB NE31 59 H7 1
Arlington St MLFD/PNYW SR4 85 K7 1
Armstrong Av
BYK/HTN/WLK NE6 57 H2
HAR/WTLS NE34 61 J4 1
Armstrong Dr LGB/KIL NE12 37 H7
Armstrong Rd
BW/LEM/TK/HW NE15 54 D6
ELS/FEN NE4 55 H7
PLEE/EAS SR8 136 E2
WASHN NE37 82 B6
WLSD/HOW NE28 59 J2
Armstrong St DUN/TMV NE11 68 C5
GATE NE8 10 B9
Armstrong Ter SSH NE33 61 G3
Arncliffe Av MLFD/PNYW SR4 97 J2 1
Arncliffe Gdns
WD/WHPE/BLK NE5 54 A1 3
Arnham Gv MLFD/PNYW SR4 96 D4
Arnold Cl STLY/ANP DH9 102 E1
Arnold Rd SUNDSW SR3 97 H6
Arnold St BOLCOL NE35 72 D4
Arran Ct SUNDSW SR3 110 A1 1
Arran Dr JRW NE32 72 C1
Arran Pl NSHW NE29 50 A2
Arras La SUND SR1 15 H4
Arrol Pk MLFD/PNYW SR4 14 A5
Arrow Cl LGB/KIL NE12 37 H7
Arthur Av ASHBK/HED/RY SR2 111 G1
Arthur Cook Av
WICK/BNPF NE16 67 G5
Arthur St BLYTH NE24 21 G6 1
CLDN/WHIT/ROK SR6 63 F7
GATE NE8 11 G4
JRW NE32 59 K5 1
STLY/ANP DH9 92 A7
Arun Cl PLEE/EAS SR8 136 D5
Arundel Cl BDLGTN NE22 19 J3
DIN/WO NE13 36 A4 1
Arundel Dr
BW/LEM/TK/HW NE15 54 C4
MONK NE25 39 K5
Arundel Gdns
LWF/SPW/WRK NE9 69 G7
SUNDSW SR3 97 G7
Arundel Rd SUNDSW SR3 97 H6
Arundel Wy BDN/LAN/SAC DH7 133 H6
Asama Ct ELS/FEN NE4 9 J2
Ascot Cl WLSD/HOW NE28 49 F4
Ascot Ct SUNDSW SR3 97 H7
Ascot Crs GATE NE8 10 B9
Ascot Gdns HAR/WTLS NE34 61 H5
Ascot Pl CLSW/PEL DH2 93 F7
Ash Av BDN/LAN/SAC DH7 123 F7
DHAM DH1 17 L4
DIN/WO NE13 35 F2
Ashberry Gv
CLDN/WHIT/ROK SR6 86 D4
Ashbourne Av
BYK/HTN/WLK NE6 58 B5
Ashbourne Cl SMOOR NE27 38 E4 1
Ashbourne Rd JRW NE32 60 A6 1
Ashbrook Cl
BDN/LAN/SAC DH7 132 E7 1
Ashbrooke MONK NE25 40 C4
Ashbrooke Cross
ASHBK/HED/RY SR2 98 C3 1
Ashbrooke Dr PONT/DH NE20 33 G2
Ashbrooke Gdns
WLSD/HOW NE28 49 G7 1
Ashbrooke Range
ASHBK/HED/RY SR2 98 C3 2
Ashbrooke Rd
ASHBK/HED/RY SR2 98 C3
Ashbrooke St
WD/WHPE/BLK NE5 45 J7
Ashburne Ct
ASHBK/HED/RY SR2 14 F9
Ashburn Rd WLSD/HOW NE28 49 G4
Ashburton Rd GOS/KPK NE3 46 A6
Ashbury MONK NE25 40 A3
Ashby St ASHBK/HED/RY SR2 99 F3
Ash Crs SEA/MUR SR7 120 D3
Ashcroft Dr LGB/KIL NE12 48 A3
Ashdale HLS DH4 95 G6
PONT/DH NE20 32 E6
Ashdale Crs WD/WHPE/BLK NE5 54 A2
Ashdown Av DHAM DH1 125 J6
Ashdown Cl LGB/KIL NE12 47 H3 1
Ashdown Rd SUNDSW SR3 97 H6
Ashdown Wy LGB/KIL NE12 47 H3
Asher St GATE NE8 11 M6
Ashfield JRW NE32 72 B3
Ashfield Av WICK/BNPF NE16 8 A8
Ashfield Cl ELS/FEN NE4 4 D8
Ashfield Ct ROWG NE39 76 C1
Ashfield Gdns WLSD/HOW NE28 48 B7
Ashfield Gv NSHW NE29 2 C1
WBAY NE26 40 E3
Ashfield Pk WICK/BNPF NE16 67 F4
Ashfield Ri WICK/BNPF NE16 67 F7
Ashfield Rd GOS/KPK NE3 46 A6
WICK/BNPF NE16 67 F7
Ashford Cl BLYTH NE24 25 G2 2
Ashford Dr BDN/LAN/SAC DH7 113 G4
Ashford Gv
WD/WHPE/BLK NE5 43 K6 2
Ashford Rd SUNDSW SR3 97 H7 8
Ash Gv CLDN/WHIT/ROK SR6 75 G4 1
DUN/TMV NE11 8 F6
RYTON NE40 52 E5
WLSD/HOW NE28 59 F1
Ashgrove Av HAR/WTLS NE34 61 K7
Ashkirk CRAM NE23 37 G1
Ashkirk Cl CLSW/PEL DH2 105 G6
Ashkirk Wy MONK NE25 30 A6
Ashleigh Av DHAM DH1 124 C4
Ashleigh Cl BLAY NE21 66 B3
Ashleigh Crs
WD/WHPE/BLK NE5 54 E3 1
Ashleigh Gv
CLDN/WHIT/ROK SR6 86 E1
JES NE2 56 D1
LGB/KIL NE12 47 K3
TYNE/NSHE NE30 51 G2
Ashleigh Rd WD/WHPE/BLK NE5 54 E3
Ashley Cl LGB/KIL NE12 38 B5
WASHS NE38 95 F3
Ashley Rd HAR/WTLS NE34 61 G5
Ashley Ter CLS/BIR/GTL DH3 105 J3
Ashmead Cl LGB/KIL NE12 38 A5
Ash Mdw CLS/BIR/GTL DH3 94 A7
Ashmore St ASHBK/HED/RY SR2 14 E8
Asholme WD/WHPE/BLK NE5 54 C2
Ashridge Cl HAR/WTLS NE34 62 B6 1
Ashridge Ct FELL NE10 70 D5 1
Ash St BLAY NE21 66 A3
Ash Ter SEA/MUR SR7 119 H5
Ashton Ct RYTON NE40 53 F7
Ashton Ri CLSW/PEL DH2 105 J5
PLEE/EAS SR8 137 F3
Ashton St PLEE/EAS SR8 131 G5
Ashton Wy SUNDSW SR3 109 G1
WBAY NE26 40 B2
Ashtree Cl ROWG NE39 77 H2
Ash Tree Dr BDLGTN NE22 19 F4
Ashtree La BLAY NE21 64 E7
Ashtrees Gdns
LWF/SPW/WRK NE9 11 H9
Ash Tree Ter BDN/LAN/SAC DH7 112 C1
Ashvale Av DUN/TMV NE11 80 C7
Ashwell Rd SUNDSW SR3 97 H7 9
Ashwood RDHAMSE DH6 129 F3
Ashwood Av SWCK/CAS SR5 85 K3
Ashwood Cl CRAM NE23 23 H5
LGB/KIL NE12 48 A2 1
Ashwood Crs
BYK/HTN/WLK NE6 58 B3 1
Ashwood Cft HEBB NE31 59 F4 2
Ashwood Gdns
LWF/SPW/WRK NE9 81 G3
Ashwood Gv DIN/WO NE13 36 B4
SWCK/CAS SR5 85 F4 2
Ashwood St ASHBK/HED/RY SR2 14 B7
Ashwood Ter
ASHBK/HED/RY SR2 14 B8
Askern Av
ASHBK/HED/RY SR2 99 G5 1
Askerton Dr PLEE/EAS SR8 136 B7
Askew Rd GATE NE8 10 D3
Askew Rd West GATE NE8 10 C4
Askrigg Av ASHBK/HED/RY SR2 99 F5
WLSD/HOW NE28 49 F3
Aspen Cl DHAM DH1 17 M1 1
Aspen Ct SUNDSW SR3 109 J1 1
Aspley Cl SUNDSW SR3 110 A1
Association Rd
CLDN/WHIT/ROK SR6 86 E3 1
Aster Pl ELS/FEN NE4 55 G4
Astley Dr WBAY NE26 40 C1
Astley Gdns MONK NE25 29 K5 1
WBAY NE26 30 E1
Astley Gv WBAY NE26 30 E1
Astley Rd MONK NE25 29 K4
Aston Sq SUNDSW SR3 97 H7 10
Aston St SSH NE33 61 H4
Athelhampton WASHS NE38 95 J1 1
Athelstan Rigg
ASHBK/HED/RY SR2 99 G7
Athenaeum St SUND SR1 14 F5
Atherton Dr ELS/FEN NE4 55 J7
HLS DH4 116 D1
Atherton St DHAM DH1 16 B4
Athlone Pl CLS/BIR/GTL DH3 93 K5
Athol Gdns ASHBK/HED/RY SR2 111 G1
MONK NE25 40 B6
Athol Gn DUN/TMV NE11 9 J5
Athol Gv SUNDSW SR3 98 A7 1
Atholl Gdns LWF/SPW/WRK NE9 11 M9
Athol Rd ASHBK/HED/RY SR2 15 H8
Athol St DUN/TMV NE11 9 J5 1
Athol Ter ASHBK/HED/RY SR2 15 H8
Athull CLSW/PEL DH2 93 F4
Atkinson Gdns NSHW NE29 2 D7
Atkinson Rd
CLDN/WHIT/ROK SR6 86 D1 1
CLS/BIR/GTL DH3 105 K2
ELS/FEN NE4 55 H7
Atkinson St WLSD/HOW NE28 58 D2 1
Atkinson Ter ELS/FEN NE4 55 H6 1
WLSD/HOW NE28 58 D2
Atkin St LGB/KIL NE12 37 H4
Atlantis Rd SUNDSW SR3 97 G6
Atley Wy CRAM NE23 22 E5
Attlee Cl CRAM NE23 37 H4 1
Attlee Gv ASHBK/HED/RY SR2 98 E6
Attwood Gv SWCK/CAS SR5 86 B4 1
Aubone Av
BW/LEM/TK/HW NE15 55 G5 1
Auburn Cl WLSD/HOW NE28 59 J1
Auburn Gdns ELS/FEN NE4 55 J3
Auckland CLSW/PEL DH2 105 F5
Auckland Av HAR/WTLS NE34 62 B5
Auckland Rd DHAM DH1 124 E2
HEBB NE31 59 H4
Auckland Ter JRW NE32 60 C7
Auden Gv ELS/FEN NE4 55 J5
Audley Gdns SUNDSW SR3 98 B3
Audley Rd GOS/KPK NE3 46 E6
Augusta Ct WLSD/HOW NE28 49 G4
Augusta Sq SUNDSW SR3 97 H7
Augustine Cl DHAM DH1 124 B3
August Pl SSH NE33 3 K9
SSH NE33 61 J2 1
Augustus Dr BDLGTN NE22 18 E4
Austen Av HAR/WTLS NE34 73 F1
Austen Pl STLY/ANP DH9 102 E3
Austin Sq SWCK/CAS SR5 86 B3
Australia Gv HAR/WTLS NE34 72 D1
Austral Pl DIN/WO NE13 36 A4 2
Auton Stile BDN/LAN/SAC DH7 123 F6
Autumn Cl WASHS NE38 83 F7
Avalon Dr BW/LEM/TK/HW NE15 54 C3
Avalon Rd SUNDSW SR3 97 H6
Avebury Dr WASHS NE38 95 G1
Avebury Pl CRAM NE23 23 J6
Avenue Rd GATE NE8 11 G8
MONK NE25 29 K6
Avenue Ter ASHBK/HED/RY SR2 14 D9
The Avenue ASHBK/HED/RY SR2 14 D8
BLAY NE21 66 C2
CLS/BIR/GTL DH3 93 J2
CLS/BIR/GTL DH3 107 G2
CLSW/PEL DH2 105 H4
DHAM DH1 16 A5
DHAM DH1 124 B2
DHAM DH1 134 B1
HLH DH5 118 A4
LWF/SPW/WRK NE9 69 G5
MONK NE25 30 A4
PONT/DH NE20 42 A1
ROWG NE39 77 H4
SEA/MUR SR7 120 B1
STLY/ANP DH9 101 G4
WASHS NE38 95 G1
WBAY NE26 40 D4
WLSD/HOW NE28 58 D2
Avenue Vivian HLS DH4 107 H6
Aviemore Rd BOL NE36 73 F5
Avision St ELS/FEN NE4 4 E6
Avison Pl ELS/FEN NE4 4 E5
Avocet Cl BLYTH NE24 25 G4
Avolon Pl ELS/FEN NE4 4 E5
Avon Av JRW NE32 72 A2
NSHW NE29 50 C6
Avon Cl ROWG NE39 77 H2
WLSD/HOW NE28 49 F4
Avon Ct MONK NE25 30 A3
Avon Crs HLS DH4 107 J7
Avoncroft Cl SEA/MUR SR7 110 D7
Avondale MLFD/PNYW SR4 96 E1
Avondale Av BLYTH NE24 20 A6
HLS DH4 95 K7
LGB/KIL NE12 47 K2 2
Avondale Cl BLYTH NE24 20 B6 1
Avondale Gdns BOL NE36 72 E5 1
Avondale Rd BYK/HTN/WLK NE6 7 H6
PONT/DH NE20 32 C6
Avondale Ter CLSW/PEL DH2 105 J4
GATE NE8 10 F7
Avonlea Wy
WD/WHPE/BLK NE5 45 G7 1
Avonmouth Rd SUNDSW SR3 97 G7
Avonmouth Sq SUNDSW SR3 97 H7
Avon Rd HEBB NE31 59 G7
PLEE/EAS SR8 136 D5
STLY/ANP DH9 102 D2
Avon St GATE NE8 11 K6
SUND SR1 15 J6
Awnless Ct HAR/WTLS NE34 61 G6 2
Axbridge Gdns ELS/FEN NE4 55 J7
Axminster Cl CRAM NE23 23 J6
Axwell Dr BLYTH NE24 20 D7
Axwell Park Rd BLAY NE21 66 C3
Axwell Park Vw
BW/LEM/TK/HW NE15 55 F6
Axwell Vw BLAY NE21 66 A3
WICK/BNPF NE16 66 E5 1
Aycliffe Av LWF/SPW/WRK NE9 81 K1
Aycliffe Crs LWF/SPW/WRK NE9 81 K1
Aydon Gv JRW NE32 71 K1
Aykley Ct DHAM DH1 124 B5 1
Aykley Gn DHAM DH1 124 B5
Aykley Rd DHAM DH1 124 C3
Aykley V DHAM DH1 124 B4
Aylesbury Dr SUNDSW SR3 110 A2
Aylesbury Pl LGB/KIL NE12 47 H3 2
Aylesford Sq BLYTH NE24 25 G2 3
Aylsham Cl WD/WHPE/BLK NE5 43 K6
Aylsham Ct SUNDSW SR3 110 A3 1
Aylyth Pl GOS/KPK NE3 45 K7 1
Ayr Dr JRW NE32 72 B1
Ayre's Quay Rd SUND SR1 14 C4 1
Ayre's Ter NSHW NE29 2 C1 1
Ayrey Av HAR/WTLS NE34 60 D7
Aysgarth Av ASHBK/HED/RY SR2 99 F4
WLSD/HOW NE28 49 F3
Ayton Av ASHBK/HED/RY SR2 99 F5
Ayton Cl WD/WHPE/BLK NE5 44 C7
Ayton Ct BDLGTN NE22 18 D4
Ayton Rd WASHS NE38 94 B2
Ayton St BYK/HTN/WLK NE6 7 H7
Azalea Av ASHBK/HED/RY SR2 14 D8
Azalea Ter North
ASHBK/HED/RY SR2 14 D7
Azalea Ter South
ASHBK/HED/RY SR2 14 D8

B

Back Bridge St SUND SR1 14 E4
Back Croft Rd BLYTH NE24 21 G7 2
Back George St ELS/FEN NE4 5 G9
Back Goldspink La JES NE2 6 B1
Back Heaton Park Rd
BYK/HTN/WLK NE6 6 E4
Back La BLAY NE21 65 K2
CLS/BIR/GTL DH3 115 H1
CON/LDGT DH8 100 B5
HLS DH4 95 K6
MONK NE25 40 C4
Back Lodge Ter SUND SR1 15 K5
Back Mitford St ELS/FEN NE4 9 M2 1
Back New Bridge St CNUT NE1 6 A5
Back North Bridge St
SWCK/CAS SR5 14 E1
Back North Railway St
SEA/MUR SR7 111 K7
Back North Ter SEA/MUR SR7 111 K7
Back Percy Gdns
TYNE/NSHE NE30 51 H2 2
Back Rw WICK/BNPF NE16 66 E5
Back Ryhope St
ASHBK/HED/RY SR2 98 E7
Back Silver St DHAM DH1 16 D4
Back South Railway St
SEA/MUR SR7 120 E1
Back Stephen St
BYK/HTN/WLK NE6 6 D5
Back St BLAY NE21 65 K3 1
Back Walker Rd
BYK/HTN/WLK NE6 58 C7 1
Back Western Hl DHAM DH1 16 A2
Back Woodbine St GATE NE8 10 D5
Backworth La CRAM NE23 38 B1
Baden Crs SWCK/CAS SR5 84 E2
Baden Powell St
LWF/SPW/WRK NE9 11 J9
Baden St CLS/BIR/GTL DH3 105 J5
Badger Cl SUNDSW SR3 110 A2
Badminton Cl BOLCOL NE35 72 B3 1
Baffin Ct SUNDSW SR3 109 K1
Baildon Cl WLSD/HOW NE28 48 E6 1
Bailey Ri PLEE/EAS SR8 136 E2
Bailey Sq SWCK/CAS SR5 84 E1 1
Bailey Wy HLH DH5 118 A6
Bainbridge Av HAR/WTLS NE34 60 D7
SUNDSW SR3 98 B3
Bainbridge Holme Cl
SUNDSW SR3 98 B3
Bainbridge Holme Rd
SUNDSW SR3 98 C3
Bainbridge St DHAM DH1 126 A4
Bainford Av
BW/LEM/TK/HW NE15 54 E5
Baird Av WLSD/HOW NE28 60 A1
Baird Cl WASHN NE37 83 G3
Baird St SWCK/CAS SR5 84 E2 1
Bakehouse La DHAM DH1 16 F2
Baker Gdns FELL NE10 13 L7
Baker Rd CRAM NE23 22 D6
Baker St HLH DH5 108 C6
SWCK/CAS SR5 84 E2
Bakewell Ter BYK/HTN/WLK NE6 7 K9
Baldersdale Gdns SUNDSW SR3 98 B4
Baldwin Av BOL NE36 73 H5
ELS/FEN NE4 4 A3 1
Balfour Rd
BW/LEM/TK/HW NE15 54 E6
Balfour St BLYTH NE24 21 F5
GATE NE8 10 D7
HLH DH5 108 C6
Balgonie Cottages RYTON NE40 52 E6
Baliol Sq DHAM DH1 134 B3
Balkwell Av NSHW NE29 50 B5
Balkwell Gn NSHW NE29 50 C4
Ballast Hl BLYTH NE24 21 H6 1
Ballast Hill Rd NSHW NE29 2 D7
Ballater Cl STLY/ANP DH9 103 F1
Balliol Av LGB/KIL NE12 47 J1
Balliol Cl PLEE/EAS SR8 136 C4
Balliol Gdns LGB/HTN NE7 47 H5 1
Balmain Rd GOS/KPK NE3 45 J6
Balmoral Av GOS/KPK NE3 46 E6 2
JRW NE32 72 C1 1
Balmoral Cl BDLGTN NE22 19 J4
Balmoral Ct SWCK/CAS SR5 84 E2 2
Balmoral Crs HLH DH5 117 J1
Balmoral Dr FELL NE10 12 A8
Balmoral Gdns NSHW NE29 50 D3
Balmoral St WLSD/HOW NE28 58 D1
Balmoral Ter
ASHBK/HED/RY SR2 99 F4
BYK/HTN/WLK NE6 6 F2
GOS/KPK NE3 46 E6
SUNDSW SR3 97 G7
Balmoral Wy FELL NE10 12 A9
Balroy Ct LGB/KIL NE12 48 A2
Baltic Millennium Br CNUT NE1 6 A8
Baltic Rd FELL NE10 12 C2
Baltimore Av SWCK/CAS SR5 84 C1
Baltimore Sq SWCK/CAS SR5 84 D2
Bamborough Ct CRAM NE23 37 F1 1
Bamborough Ter
TYNE/NSHE NE30 50 E3
Bambro' St
ASHBK/HED/RY SR2 15 H8 1
Bamburgh Av SSH NE33 61 K2
Bamburgh Cl BLYTH NE24 20 E7
WASHS NE38 94 C1
Bamburgh Ct DUN/TMV NE11 68 C6
Bamburgh Dr FELL NE10 13 M3
WLSD/HOW NE28 59 H1
Bamburgh Gdns SUNDSW SR3 98 B3 1
Bamburgh Gv HAR/WTLS NE34 62 B3
Bamburgh Rd DHAM DH1 124 D2
LGB/KIL NE12 48 B2
WD/WHPE/BLK NE5 44 C7 1
Bampton Av
CLDN/WHIT/ROK SR6 74 C7
Banbury WASHN NE37 83 G5
Banbury Gdns
WLSD/HOW NE28 49 F5 1
Banbury Rd GOS/KPK NE3 45 K4
Banbury Ter SSH NE33 61 H3
Banbury Wy BLYTH NE24 25 F2
NSHW NE29 50 B6
Bancroft Ter MLFD/PNYW SR4 85 K7
Banesley La DUN/TMV NE11 80 B4
Banff St SWCK/CAS SR5 84 E1
Bank Av WICK/BNPF NE16 66 E5
Bankdale Gdns BLYTH NE24 20 C7
Bankhead Rd
BW/LEM/TK/HW NE15 53 H2 1
Bankhead Ter HLS DH4 107 J6
Bank Rd GATE NE8 6 A9
Banks Holt CLSW/PEL DH2 105 F5 1
Bankside Cl ASHBK/HED/RY SR2 98 E7
Bankside La HAR/WTLS NE34 61 G6
Bankside Rd
BW/LEM/TK/HW NE15 54 D6
Bank Top RYTON NE40 64 A1
Bankwell La GATE NE8 5 M9
Bannister Dr LGB/KIL NE12 48 B2
Bannockburn LGB/KIL NE12 37 K5 1
Barbara St ASHBK/HED/RY SR2 99 F3
Barbary Cl CLSW/PEL DH2 92 E7
Barbary Dr CLDN/WHIT/ROK SR6 87 F3
Barbondale Lonnen
WD/WHPE/BLK NE5 54 A2
Barbour Av HAR/WTLS NE34 62 A4
Barclay Pl WD/WHPE/BLK NE5 55 F2
Barclay St SWCK/CAS SR5 14 E2
Barcusclose La
WICK/BNPF NE16 78 A7
Bardolph Rd NSHW NE29 50 B4
Bardon Cl
WD/WHPE/BLK NE5 44 D6 1
Bardon Crs MONK NE25 30 C6 1
Bardsey Pl LGB/KIL NE12 47 H4
Barehirst St SSH NE33 61 F4
Barents Cl
WD/WHPE/BLK NE5 54 D1 1
Baret Rd BYK/HTN/WLK NE6 7 M1
Barford Dr CLSW/PEL DH2 105 G6
Baring St SSH NE33 3 H4
Barker St JES NE2 6 A4
Barking Crs SWCK/CAS SR5 84 D2
Barking Sq SWCK/CAS SR5 84 D2 1
Barkwood Rd ROWG NE39 77 F3
Barlow Crs BLAY NE21 64 E6 1
Barlow Fell Rd BLAY NE21 64 E7
Barlowfield Cl BLAY NE21 65 J4 1
Barlow La BLAY NE21 65 F6
Barmoor La RYTON NE40 52 D6
Barmouth Cl
WLSD/HOW NE28 49 F5 2
Barmouth Rd NSHW NE29 50 A5
Barmouth Wy NSHW NE29 50 B6
Barmston La WASHN NE37 84 A7
WASHS NE38 95 K1
Barmston Rd WASHS NE38 95 J2
Barmston Wy WASHS NE38 83 H7
Barnard Cl BDLGTN NE22 18 D5
DHAM DH1 124 E2
Barnard Crs HEBB NE31 59 G4
Barnard Gv JRW NE32 60 B7 1
Barnard St BLYTH NE24 21 G7 3
MLFD/PNYW SR4 97 K1
Barnard Wynd PLEE/EAS SR8 136 C7
Barnesbury Rd ELS/FEN NE4 55 J6
Barnes Park Rd
MLFD/PNYW SR4 98 A2
Barnes Rd SEA/MUR SR7 119 G5
SSH NE33 61 F3 1
Barnes St HLH DH5 117 K4 1
Barnes Vw MLFD/PNYW SR4 97 K2
Barn Hl STLY/ANP DH9 90 C7
Barn Hollows SEA/MUR SR7 130 D2
Barningham WASHS NE38 95 J2
Barningham Cl SUNDSW SR3 98 B4
Barns Cl JRW NE32 59 J7
Barnstaple Cl
WLSD/HOW NE28 49 F5 3
Barnstaple Rd NSHW NE29 50 A2
The Barns STLY/ANP DH9 90 C6
Barnton Rd FELL NE10 70 A6
Barnwood Cl
WLSD/HOW NE28 48 E5 1
Baroness Dr
BW/LEM/TK/HW NE15 54 E4
Baron's Quay Rd SWCK/CAS SR5 85 F5
Baronswood GOS/KPK NE3 46 B6
Barrack Rd ELS/FEN NE4 4 E3
Barrack St SUND SR1 15 J2
Barras Av BLYTH NE24 25 F2
CRAM NE23 28 C7
Barras Av West BLYTH NE24 24 E3
Barras Br CNUT NE1 5 K4

Barras Dr SUNDSW SR3 98 B4
Barrasford Cl GOS/KPK NE3 46 A6
Barrasford Dr DIN/WO NE13 36 C4
Barrasford Rd CRAM NE23 28 D3 1
DHAM DH1 124 E3
Barrasford St
WLSD/HOW NE28 60 A2 1
Barrass Av CRAM NE23 29 F7
Barr Cl WLSD/HOW NE28 49 G5
Barrie Sq SWCK/CAS SR5 86 B3
Barrington Av TYNE/NSHE NE30 40 D7
Barrington Ct BDLGTN NE22 19 G6 1
Barrington Dr WASHS NE38 95 F1
Barrington Pk BDLGTN NE22 20 B3
Barrington Rd BDLGTN NE22 19 J3
STKFD/GP NE62 19 F3
Barrington St SSH NE33 3 G7
Barrington Ter HLH DH5 117 K3 2
Barron St South
SWCK/CAS SR5 85 G4 1
Barrowburn Pl CRAM NE23 29 H7
Barrow St SWCK/CAS SR5 84 E1 2
Barry St DUN/TMV NE11 9 H6
GATE NE8 68 D5
Barsloan Gv PLEE/EAS SR8 136 C2 1
Barton Cl TYNE/NSHE NE30 51 F1
WASHN NE37 83 G3
WLSD/HOW NE28 49 F5 4
Barton Ct
CLDN/WHIT/ROK SR6 74 C7 1
Bartram St SWCK/CAS SR5 86 C2
Barwell Cl WLSD/HOW NE28 49 F5
Barwell Ct LGB/HTN NE7 48 A7
Basildon Gdns
WLSD/HOW NE28 48 E5 2
Basil Wy HAR/WTLS NE34 73 J1
Basingstoke Pl LGB/KIL NE12 47 J3
Basingstoke Rd
PLEE/EAS SR8 136 D3 1
Baslow Gdns SUNDSW SR3 98 B3
Bassington Av CRAM NE23 27 K1
Bassington Dr CRAM NE23 22 D7
Bassington La CRAM NE23 22 D7
Bates La BLAY NE21 66 D2
Bath Cl WLSD/HOW NE28 49 G5
Bathgate Cl WLSD/HOW NE28 49 G5
Bathgate Sq SWCK/CAS SR5 84 D2 2
Bath La BLYTH NE24 21 H7
CNUT NE1 5 H7
Bath Lane Ter ELS/FEN NE4 4 F7
Bath Rd FELL NE10 12 C4
HEBB NE31 71 G1 1
Bath St BYK/HTN/WLK NE6 58 C6
Bath Ter BLYTH NE24 21 H7
GOS/KPK NE3 46 D5
TYNE/NSHE NE30 51 H3
Batley St SWCK/CAS SR5 84 D2 3
Battle Hill Dr WLSD/HOW NE28 48 D6
WLSD/HOW NE28 49 H5
Baugh Cl WASHN NE37 82 C7
Baulkham Hills HLS DH4 107 K1
Bavington FELL NE10 70 C7 1
Bavington Dr
WD/WHPE/BLK NE5 55 G2
Bavington Gdns
TYNE/NSHE NE30 50 E1
Bavington Rd MONK NE25 30 A5
Bawtry Gv NSHW NE29 50 C5
Baxter Av ELS/FEN NE4 55 J5
Baxter Rd SWCK/CAS SR5 84 D1
Baxter Sq SWCK/CAS SR5 84 D1 1
Bay Av PLEE/EAS SR8 137 J4
Baybridge Rd
WD/WHPE/BLK NE5 44 C7 2
Baysdale HLS DH4 95 G6 1
Bayswater Av SWCK/CAS SR5 84 E2
Bayswater Rd GATE NE8 11 L7
JES NE2 56 E1
Bayswater Sq SWCK/CAS SR5 84 E2 2
Baytree Gdns MONK NE25 40 C6
Baytree Ter STLY/ANP DH9 92 B7
Baywood Gv
WLSD/HOW NE28 48 E5 3
Beach Av WBAY NE26 40 E4
Beach Croft Av
TYNE/NSHE NE30 41 F7
Beachcross Rd
MLFD/PNYW SR4 14 A7 1
Beach Gv PLEE/EAS SR8 137 H4
Beach Rd NSHW NE29 50 C3
SSH NE33 3 K8
TYNE/NSHE NE30 50 E2
Beach St MLFD/PNYW SR4 14 B2
Beachville St
MLFD/PNYW SR4 14 A7 2
Beachway BLYTH NE24 25 H3
Beach Wy TYNE/NSHE NE30 50 E1
Beacon Dr CLDN/WHIT/ROK SR6 87 F4
DIN/WO NE13 36 A4
Beacon Gld HAR/WTLS NE34 62 C5
Beacon La CRAM NE23 27 J2
Beacon Lough Rd
LWF/SPW/WRK NE9 81 G1
Beaconsfield Av
LWF/SPW/WRK NE9 69 G7
Beaconsfield Cl MONK NE25 40 B2
Beaconsfield Crs
LWF/SPW/WRK NE9 69 G7 1
Beaconsfield Rd
LWF/SPW/WRK NE9 69 F7
Beaconsfield St BLYTH NE24 21 H6 2
ELS/FEN NE4 4 D5
STLY/ANP DH9 90 D7 2
Beaconside HAR/WTLS NE34 62 C5
Beacon St LWF/SPW/WRK NE9 69 F7
SSH NE33 3 H3
TYNE/NSHE NE30 2 F1
Beadling Gdns ELS/FEN NE4 55 J5
Beadnell Av NSHW NE29 50 B6
Beadnell Cl BLAY NE21 65 J4
Beadnell Gdns SMOOR NE27 39 H6
Beadnell Pl JES NE2 6 A5
Beadnell Rd BLYTH NE24 24 D2
Beadnell Wy GOS/KPK NE3 46 A4 2
Beal Cl BLYTH NE24 20 E7
Beal Dr LGB/KIL NE12 48 B2
Beal Gdns WLSD/HOW NE28 49 H5
Beal Rd SMOOR NE27 39 H6
Beal Ter BYK/HTN/WLK NE6 58 B7
Beal Wk DHAM DH1 135 J5
Beal Wy GOS/KPK NE3 46 B5
Beaminster Wy GOS/KPK NE3 45 G5
WD/WHPE/BLK NE5 45 G5
Beamishburn Rd STLY/ANP DH9 90 E5
Beamish Cl
BDN/LAN/SAC DH7 122 A3 1
WLSD/HOW NE28 48 E5 4
Beamish Gdns
LWF/SPW/WRK NE9 81 K1
Beamish Hills STLY/ANP DH9 91 H7
Beamish St STLY/ANP DH9 90 C7 1
Beamish Vw CLSW/PEL DH2 104 B4
STLY/ANP DH9 91 F7
Beaney La CLSW/PEL DH2 114 A2
Beanley Av HEBB NE31 59 F7
Beanley Crs TYNE/NSHE NE30 51 G3
Beanley Pl LGB/HTN NE7 47 G7
Bearpark Colliery Rd
BDN/LAN/SAC DH7 123 G6
Beatrice Av BLYTH NE24 24 D3 1
Beatrice Gdns BOL NE36 73 H5 1
HAR/WTLS NE34 61 J5
Beatrice St CLDN/WHIT/ROK SR6 86 E4
Beatrice Ter HLS DH4 95 G5
Beattie St HAR/WTLS NE34 61 F6 1
Beatty Av JES NE2 46 E7
Beatty Rd BDLGTN NE22 19 H6
Beaufort Cl HLS DH4 107 K2 1
WD/WHPE/BLK NE5 45 H7 1
Beaufort Gdns
WLSD/HOW NE28 48 E5 5
Beaufront Cl FELL NE10 70 D6 2
Beaufront Gdns GATE NE8 11 L5
WD/WHPE/BLK NE5 55 G3
Beaufront Ter JRW NE32 71 K1
SSH NE33 61 G3 1
Beauly WASHS NE38 95 F3 1
Beaumaris Gdns SUNDSW SR3 97 G7
Beaumaris Wy
WD/WHPE/BLK NE5 45 F6
Beaumont Cl DHAM DH1 124 B2
Beaumont Crs PLEE/EAS SR8 137 F1
Beaumont Dr MONK NE25 40 A2
WASHS NE38 95 F2
Beaumont Mnr BLYTH NE24 20 B7
Beaumont Pl PLEE/EAS SR8 137 F5 1
Beaumont St
ASHBK/HED/RY SR2 15 G9
BLYTH NE24 21 F6
ELS/FEN NE4 9 G1
NSHW NE29 2 C2 1
SEA/MUR SR7 120 E2 1
SWCK/CAS SR5 86 A2
Beaumont Ter GOS/KPK NE3 46 D5
JRW NE32 59 J6
WD/WHPE/BLK NE5 54 D1
Beaurepaire BDN/LAN/SAC DH7 123 F6
Beaver Cl DHAM DH1 124 D1
Bebdon Ct BLYTH NE24 24 E1 2
Bebside Furnace Rd
BLYTH NE24 19 K6
Bebside Rd BLYTH NE24 19 J7
Beckenham Av BOL NE36 73 H4
Beckenham Cl BOL NE36 73 J4 1
Beckenham Gdns
WLSD/HOW NE28 48 E6
Beckett St GATE NE8 6 D9
Beckfoot Cl WD/WHPE/BLK NE5 55 F2
Beckford WASHS NE38 95 J2
Beckford Cl WLSD/HOW NE28 48 E5 6
Beck Pl PLEE/EAS SR8 136 E3
Beckside Gdns
WD/WHPE/BLK NE5 53 K2
Beckwith Rd SUNDSW SR3 97 G6
Beda Hl BLAY NE21 66 A1
Bedale Cl DHAM DH1 126 A5
WLSD/HOW NE28 48 E5 7
Bedale Crs SWCK/CAS SR5 84 E2
Bedale Dr MONK NE25 40 D6
Bedale Gn WD/WHPE/BLK NE5 45 H7
Bedale St HLH DH5 117 K6
Bedburn WASHS NE38 94 B5
Bede Burn Rd JRW NE32 59 K5 2
Bedeburn Rd
WD/WHPE/BLK NE5 44 D5
Bede Burn Vw JRW NE32 59 K6
Bede Cl LGB/KIL NE12 48 D2
Bede Ct CLS/BIR/GTL DH3 105 J4
GATE NE8 11 J4 1
Bede Crs WASHS NE38 82 E7
WLSD/HOW NE28 49 F6
Bede St CLDN/WHIT/ROK SR6 86 E3
PLEE/EAS SR8 131 G5
Bedesway JRW NE32 60 B5
Bede Ter BOL NE36 73 J5 1
CLSW/PEL DH2 105 H4
JRW NE32 60 A6 2
Bede Wk HEBB NE31 59 H6
Bede Wy DHAM DH1 124 C3 1
PLEE/EAS SR8 136 E4
Bedford Av CLS/BIR/GTL DH3 93 K5
SSH NE33 61 G2
WLSD/HOW NE28 48 C7
Bedford Pl SUNDSW SR3 98 A6 1
WD/WHPE/BLK NE5 54 A2 1
Bedfordshire Dr DHAM DH1 126 A7
Bedford St NSHW NE29 2 D2 1
SUND SR1 14 F3
Bedford Wy NSHW NE29 2 D2
Bedlington Bank BDLGTN NE22 19 G6
Beech Av CLDN/WHIT/ROK SR6 75 G3
CRAM NE23 28 E3
DIN/WO NE13 35 F2
GOS/KPK NE3 45 K4
HLS DH4 108 B6
WICK/BNPF NE16 8 A8
Beech Cl DHAM DH1 125 F1
GOS/KPK NE3 46 D1 1
Beech Ct BDN/LAN/SAC DH7 122 B3
BW/LEM/TK/HW NE15 42 C2
PONT/DH NE20 42 C1
Beech Crs SEA/MUR SR7 120 D2
Beechcroft Av
BDN/LAN/SAC DH7 132 E7
GOS/KPK NE3 46 A7
Beechcroft Cl DHAM DH1 125 H6 1
Beech Dr DUN/TMV NE11 8 F6
Beecher St BLYTH NE24 20 D5
The Beeches PONT/DH NE20 33 F3
Beechfield Gdns
WLSD/HOW NE28 48 C7 1
Beechfield Rd GOS/KPK NE3 46 B6
Beech Gv BDN/LAN/SAC DH7 133 G1
HAR/WTLS NE34 61 K7
LGB/KIL NE12 47 K4
LWF/SPW/WRK NE9 82 B4
WBAY NE26 40 D4
WLSD/HOW NE28 58 D1
Beech Grove Ct RYTON NE40 52 B7
Beech Grove Rd ELS/FEN NE4 4 C8
Beech Pk BDN/LAN/SAC DH7 133 F7
Beech Rd DHAM DH1 124 C4
RDHAMSE DH6 126 C7
Beech Sq WASHS NE38 95 G2 1
Beech St ELS/FEN NE4 55 J7
GATE NE8 11 L5
JRW NE32 59 J4
Beech Ter BLAY NE21 66 A3 1
STLY/ANP DH9 103 F4
Beech Wy LGB/KIL NE12 37 J5 2
Beechways DHAM DH1 124 A6
Beechwood Av
LWF/SPW/WRK NE9 81 G2
MONK NE25 40 B5
RYTON NE40 52 E6
Beechwood Cl JRW NE32 60 B5 1
Beechwood Crs SWCK/CAS SR5 85 K3
Beechwood Gdns
DUN/TMV NE11 68 B7
Beechwood Pl PONT/DH NE20 33 G2
Beechwoods CLSW/PEL DH2 105 H2
Beechwood St
ASHBK/HED/RY SR2 14 B7
Beechwood Ter
ASHBK/HED/RY SR2 14 B7
HLS DH4 108 A5
Beeston Av SWCK/CAS SR5 84 D2 4
Beetham Crs
WD/WHPE/BLK NE5 54 E3
Beethoven St SSH NE33 3 K9
Begonia Cl HEBB NE31 71 G1 2
Bek Rd DHAM DH1 124 D3
Beldene Dr MLFD/PNYW SR4 97 J2
Belford Av SMOOR NE27 39 H6
Belford Cl ASHBK/HED/RY SR2 98 D3
WLSD/HOW NE28 48 E5 8
Belford Gdns DUN/TMV NE11 68 A7 1
Belford Rd ASHBK/HED/RY SR2 98 E3
Belford St PLEE/EAS SR8 137 G2
Belford Ter BYK/HTN/WLK NE6 7 M6
TYNE/NSHE NE30 50 E3
The Belfry HLS DH4 107 J3
Belgrade Crs SWCK/CAS SR5 84 D1
Belgrade Sq SWCK/CAS SR5 84 D2 5
Belgrave Crs BLYTH NE24 21 H7
Belgrave Pde ELS/FEN NE4 4 E9
Belgrave Ter FELL NE10 12 D9
SSH NE33 3 K7
Bellburn Ct CRAM NE23 23 K7 1
Belle Gv West JES NE2 4 E2
Bellerby Dr CLSW/PEL DH2 92 E4 1
Belle St STLY/ANP DH9 90 D7
Belle Vue Av GOS/KPK NE3 46 D5
Belle Vue Bank
LWF/SPW/WRK NE9 68 E7
Bellevue Crs CRAM NE23 23 H5 1
Belle Vue Crs SSH NE33 61 F5 1
Belle Vue Gv
LWF/SPW/WRK NE9 69 F7 3
Belle Vue Pk ASHBK/HED/RY SR2 14 C9
Belle Vue Rd
ASHBK/HED/RY SR2 98 C2
Bellfield Av GOS/KPK NE3 45 K4 1
Bellgreen Av GOS/KPK NE3 46 D1
Bell Gv LGB/KIL NE12 37 H5 1
Bell House Rd SWCK/CAS SR5 74 A7
Bellingham Cl
WLSD/HOW NE28 49 F6 1
Bellingham Ct GOS/KPK NE3 45 H5 1
Bellingham Dr LGB/KIL NE12 48 B3
Bellister Gv WD/WHPE/BLK NE5 55 G3
Bellister Pk PLEE/EAS SR8 137 F6
Bellister Rd NSHW NE29 50 B4 1
Bell Meadow
BDN/LAN/SAC DH7 133 F7
Belloc Av HAR/WTLS NE34 73 F1
Bells Cl BLYTH NE24 20 B6
BW/LEM/TK/HW NE15 54 C6
Bell's Folly DHAM DH1 134 B3
Bellshill Cl WLSD/HOW NE28 49 G4
Bell's Pl BDLGTN NE22 19 G6
Bell St HEBB NE31 59 F5
HLS DH4 95 K6
MLFD/PNYW SR4 85 K7 2
WASHS NE38 95 H2 1
Belmont FELL NE10 70 C7
Belmont Av MONK NE25 40 B5
SEA/MUR SR7 130 C1
Belmont Cl WLSD/HOW NE28 49 F5
Belmont Ri HLH DH5 117 K7
Belmont Rd MLFD/PNYW SR4 97 K1
Belmont St BYK/HTN/WLK NE6 13 G1
Belmount Av GOS/KPK NE3 46 D1
Belper Cl WLSD/HOW NE28 48 E5 9
Belsay WASHS NE38 94 B4
Belsay Av DIN/WO NE13 36 A5 1
HAR/WTLS NE34 62 A4
MONK NE25 41 F5
Belsay Cl WLSD/HOW NE28 48 E5 10
Belsay Ct BLYTH NE24 20 E7 1
Belsay Gdns DUN/TMV NE11 68 A7 2
GOS/KPK NE3 45 K2
MLFD/PNYW SR4 97 K1
Belsay Pl ELS/FEN NE4 4 C5
Belsfield Gdns JRW NE32 59 K7
Belsize Pl BYK/HTN/WLK NE6 58 B3
Beltingham
WD/WHPE/BLK NE5 54 C2 2
Belvedere NSHW NE29 50 D3
Belvedere Av MONK NE25 40 C5
Belvedere Gdns LGB/KIL NE12 47 K4 1
Belvedere Pkwy
GOS/KPK NE3 45 G4 1
Belvedere Rd
ASHBK/HED/RY SR2 14 D8
Bemersyde Dr JES NE2 46 E7
Benbrake Av NSHW NE29 30 C1
Bendigo Av HAR/WTLS NE34 72 D1 1
Benedict Rd
CLDN/WHIT/ROK SR6 87 F3
Benevente St SEA/MUR SR7 120 E2 2
Benfield Gv WBAY NE26 30 E1
Benfield Rd BYK/HTN/WLK NE6 57 K1
Benjamin Rd WLSD/HOW NE28 49 J7
Benridge Bank HLS DH4 116 C6
Bensham Av GATE NE8 10 D6
Bensham Ct HAR/WTLS NE34 61 G6 3
Bensham Crs GATE NE8 10 B6
Bensham Rd GATE NE8 10 E3
Benson Rd BYK/HTN/WLK NE6 7 K5
Benson St CLS/BIR/GTL DH3 105 J5
STLY/ANP DH9 90 C7
Bent House La DHAM DH1 17 M7
Bentinck Rd ELS/FEN NE4 4 B8
Bentinck St ELS/FEN NE4 4 B8
Benton Bank BYK/HTN/WLK NE6 57 G2
JES NE2 57 G2
Benton Cl LGB/HTN NE7 47 H5 2
Benton Hall Wk LGB/HTN NE7 57 K1 2
Benton La LGB/KIL NE12 47 H3
Benton Lodge Av
LGB/HTN NE7 47 J5 1
Benton Park Rd LGB/HTN NE7 47 F5
Benton Rd HAR/WTLS NE34 73 G2
LGB/HTN NE7 47 J5
SMOOR NE27 39 F7
Benton Wy WLSD/HOW NE28 58 D2 2
Bents Park Rd SSH NE33 3 M7
Benwell Dene Ter
BW/LEM/TK/HW NE15 55 G6
Benwell Grange Av
BW/LEM/TK/HW NE15 55 H6 2
Benwell Grange Rd
BW/LEM/TK/HW NE15 55 G6
Benwell Grange Ter
BW/LEM/TK/HW NE15 55 G6
Benwell Gv ELS/FEN NE4 55 J6
Benwell Hall Dr
BW/LEM/TK/HW NE15 55 F5 2
Benwell Hill Gdns
WD/WHPE/BLK NE5 55 G4 1
Benwell Hill Rd
WD/WHPE/BLK NE5 55 F4
Benwell La
BW/LEM/TK/HW NE15 55 F6 1
Benwell Village
BW/LEM/TK/HW NE15 55 F5
Benwell Village Ms
BW/LEM/TK/HW NE15 55 G5 2
Beresford Av HEBB NE31 71 G1
Beresford Gdns
BYK/HTN/WLK NE6 7 G7
Beresford Pk
ASHBK/HED/RY SR2 14 B8 1
Beresford Rd TYNE/NSHE NE30 40 E6
WBAY NE26 31 G3
Bergen Cl NSHW NE29 49 K6
Bergen Sq SWCK/CAS SR5 84 D1 2
Bergen St SWCK/CAS SR5 84 D1
Berkdale Rd LWF/SPW/WRK NE9 80 E3
Berkeley Cl BOLCOL NE35 72 C3
LGB/KIL NE12 38 A5
SUNDSW SR3 97 G7 2
Berkeley Sq GOS/KPK NE3 46 B3 1
Berkely St SSH NE33 3 J8
Berkhamstead Ct FELL NE10 70 E5 1
Berkley Av BLAY NE21 66 C2
Berkley Cl WLSD/HOW NE28 49 F5
Berkley Rd NSHW NE29 50 B4 2
Berkley St
BW/LEM/TK/HW NE15 53 H3 1
Berkley Wy HEBB NE31 59 H3
Berkshire Cl DHAM DH1 125 K6 1
WD/WHPE/BLK NE5 54 D1
Berkshire Rd PLEE/EAS SR8 136 D2
Bermondsey St JES NE2 6 B5
Bernard St BYK/HTN/WLK NE6 58 C7
HLS DH4 108 B7
Berrington Dr
WD/WHPE/BLK NE5 45 F7
Berrishill Gv MONK NE25 40 A3
Berry Cl BYK/HTN/WLK NE6 58 C6
WLSD/HOW NE28 48 E5 11
Berryfield Cl SUNDSW SR3 110 A2
Berry Hl RYTON NE40 64 D3
Berryhill Cl BLAY NE21 66 B3
Bertram Crs
BW/LEM/TK/HW NE15 55 G5
Bertram St SSH NE33 61 G3
Berwick WASHS NE38 94 B2
Berwick Av SWCK/CAS SR5 84 D1
Berwick Cha PLEE/EAS SR8 136 C7
Berwick Cl
BW/LEM/TK/HW NE15 53 J4 1
Berwick Ct PONT/DH NE20 33 H2 1
Berwick Dr WLSD/HOW NE28 49 F5
Berwick Hill Rd PONT/DH NE20 33 H2
Berwick Sq SWCK/CAS SR5 84 D2 6
Berwick Ter NSHW NE29 50 B6
Besford Gv SUND SR1 15 H5
Bethnell Av BYK/HTN/WLK NE6 7 J2 1
Betjeman Cl STLY/ANP DH9 102 E1
Betts Av BW/LEM/TK/HW NE15 55 F6
Beumaris HLS DH4 107 F4
Bevan Av ASHBK/HED/RY SR2 110 E1
Bevan Gdns FELL NE10 13 K8
Bevan Gv DHAM DH1 125 J6
Bevan Sq SEA/MUR SR7 119 H4
Beverley Cl GOS/KPK NE3 36 B7 1
Beverley Crs
LWF/SPW/WRK NE9 69 G6 1
Beverley Dr BLAY NE21 65 H4
WICK/BNPF NE16 8 A6
Beverley Gdns
CLS/BIR/GTL DH3 105 K5
TYNE/NSHE NE30 41 G6
Beverley Pk MONK NE25 40 C5
Beverley Pl WLSD/HOW NE28 59 H1
Beverley Rd ASHBK/HED/RY SR2 99 F4
LWF/SPW/WRK NE9 69 G6
MONK NE25 40 D5
Beverley Ter
BYK/HTN/WLK NE6 58 C6 1
TYNE/NSHE NE30 41 G6
Beverley Wy PLEE/EAS SR8 136 D3
Bevin Sq RDHAMSE DH6 129 G2
Beweshill Crs BLAY NE21 65 J3
Beweshill La BLAY NE21 65 J1 1
Bewick Cl CLSW/PEL DH2 105 G7
Bewick Crs
BW/LEM/TK/HW NE15 54 B4
Bewicke Rd WLSD/HOW NE28 59 J2
Bewicke St WLSD/HOW NE28 59 K2
Bewick Pk WLSD/HOW NE28 49 H4
Bewick Rd GATE NE8 10 E6
Bewick St CNUT NE1 5 H8 1
SSH NE33 61 G3
Bewley Gdns
WLSD/HOW NE28 49 F5 5
Bewley Gv PLEE/EAS SR8 136 B7
Bexhill Rd SWCK/CAS SR5 84 D2
Bexhill Sq BLYTH NE24 25 G2 4
SWCK/CAS SR5 84 D2
Bexley Av BW/LEM/TK/HW NE15 54 E5
Bexley Pl WICK/BNPF NE16 66 E7
Bexley St MLFD/PNYW SR4 85 K7
Bickington Ct HLS DH4 108 A4 1
Biddick Hall Dr HAR/WTLS NE34 61 F7
Biddick La WASHS NE38 95 F3
Biddick Vw WASHS NE38 95 G3
Biddick Vls WASHS NE38 95 G3
Biddlestone Crs NSHW NE29 50 B5 1
Biddlestone Rd
BYK/HTN/WLK NE6 57 J2
Bideford Gdns
HAR/WTLS NE34 62 A2 1
JRW NE32 60 B6
LWF/SPW/WRK NE9 81 F2
WBAY NE26 40 D3
Bideford Gv WICK/BNPF NE16 66 E7
Bideford Rd GOS/KPK NE3 45 J6
Bideford St ASHBK/HED/RY SR2 99 F4
Bigbury Cl HLS DH4 108 A3 1
Bigges Gdns WLSD/HOW NE28 48 B6
Bilbrough Gdns ELS/FEN NE4 55 H7
Billy Mill Av NSHW NE29 50 C4
Billy Mill La NSHW NE29 50 B3
Bilsdale CLDN/WHIT/ROK SR6 75 F5
Bilsdale Pl LGB/KIL NE12 47 F4 1
Bilsmoor Av LGB/HTN NE7 57 H1
Bilton Hall Rd JRW NE32 60 B5
Binchester St HAR/WTLS NE34 60 E7 1
Bingfield Gdns
WD/WHPE/BLK NE5 55 G3
Bingley Cl WLSD/HOW NE28 49 G5
Bingley St SWCK/CAS SR5 84 D2
Bink Moss WASHN NE37 82 C7
Binswood Av
WD/WHPE/BLK NE5 55 F2
Bircham Dr BLAY NE21 66 B2
Bircham St STLY/ANP DH9 102 B2
Birch Av CLDN/WHIT/ROK SR6 75 F3
FELL NE10 13 J9
Birch Ct SUNDSW SR3 109 J1
Birch Crs WICK/BNPF NE16 77 H7
The Birches STLY/ANP DH9 90 D6 1
WICK/BNPF NE16 79 G2
Birchfield WICK/BNPF NE16 67 F7 1
Birchfield Gdns
BW/LEM/TK/HW NE15 54 C4
LWF/SPW/WRK NE9 81 G3
Birchfield Rd
ASHBK/HED/RY SR2 14 B9
Birchgate Cl BLAY NE21 65 J3 1
Birch Gv WLSD/HOW NE28 48 E5
Birchgrove Av DHAM DH1 125 J6 1
Birchington Av SSH NE33 61 G4
Birch Rd BLAY NE21 66 B2
Birch St JRW NE32 59 J4
Birch Ter BYK/HTN/WLK NE6 58 C6
Birchvale Av
WD/WHPE/BLK NE5 54 E1
Birchwood Av DIN/WO NE13 36 B4
LGB/HTN NE7 47 J7
WICK/BNPF NE16 66 E7
Birchwood Cl CRAM NE23 29 F7
STLY/ANP DH9 91 J6
Birdhill Pl HAR/WTLS NE34 61 G6
Birds Nest Rd
BYK/HTN/WLK NE6 7 K8 1
Bird St TYNE/NSHE NE30 3 G1
Birkdale MONK NE25 40 B4
SSH NE33 61 J2
Birkdale Av
CLDN/WHIT/ROK SR6 74 E5
Birkdale Cl LGB/HTN NE7 47 J6 1
WLSD/HOW NE28 48 D6 1
Birkdale Dr HLS DH4 107 J3
Birkdale Gdns DHAM DH1 126 A6
Birkheads La DUN/TMV NE11 79 J7
Birkland La WICK/BNPF NE16 79 H5
Birling Pl WD/WHPE/BLK NE5 55 H1
Birnam Gv JRW NE32 72 C2 1
Birney Edge PONT/DH NE20 42 E1
Birnie Cl ELS/FEN NE4 55 J7
Birrell Sq SWCK/CAS SR5 84 D1 3
Birrell St SWCK/CAS SR5 84 D1
Birtley Av TYNE/NSHE NE30 51 H2 3
Birtley Cl GOS/KPK NE3 46 A6
Birtley La CLS/BIR/GTL DH3 93 J2 1
Birtwistle Av HEBB NE31 71 F1 1
Biscop Ter JRW NE32 59 K6
Bishop Crs JRW NE32 60 A3
Bishopdale HLS DH4 95 G6 2
WLSD/HOW NE28 48 B5
Bishopdale Av BLYTH NE24 24 C1
Bishop Morton Gv SUND SR1 15 H6 1
Bishop Ramsay Ct
HAR/WTLS NE34 62 A5 1
Bishop Rock Cl LGB/KIL NE12 47 G4
Bishop Rock Rd LGB/KIL NE12 47 G4 1
Bishop's Av ELS/FEN NE4 4 C6
Bishops Cl WLSD/HOW NE28 59 G1 1
Bishops Dr RYTON NE40 65 F1
Bishops Meadow
BDLGTN NE22 18 E5 1
Bishop's Rd ELS/FEN NE4 55 H7
Bishops Wy DHAM DH1 124 C2
SUNDSW SR3 109 K2

Bisley Dr HAR/WTLS NE34 61 H4
Bittern Cl WLSD/HOW NE28 49 J4
Black Boy Rd HLS DH4 116 B1
Blackburn Gn FELL NE10 12 B9
Blackcliffe Wy
BDN/LAN/SAC DH7 123 F5
Blackdown Cl LGB/KIL NE12 47 G4 2
PLEE/EAS SR8 136 C5
Black Dr CLS/BIR/GTL DH3 106 C2
Blackett St CNUT NE1 5 J6
HEBB NE31 59 H3
STLY/ANP DH9 101 G3
Blackfell Rd WASHN NE37 82 B6
Blackfriars Wy LGB/KIL NE12 47 G3
Blackheath Cl WASHN NE37 82 E3 1
Blackheath Ct
WD/WHPE/BLK NE5 45 F5
Blackhill Av WLSD/HOW NE28 49 G3
Blackhill Crs LWF/SPW/WRK NE9 81 K1
Blackhills Rd PLEE/EAS SR8 137 H2
Black House La
BDN/LAN/SAC DH7 103 K7
Blackhouse La RYTON NE40 52 D6
Black La BLAY NE21 65 J2
LWF/SPW/WRK NE9 81 H4
Black Rd ASHBK/HED/RY SR2 99 F7
BDN/LAN/SAC DH7 133 K4
HEBB NE31 59 H4
Blackrow La
BW/LEM/TK/HW NE15 42 C6
Blackstone Ct BLAY NE21 65 J2
Blackthorn Dr WLSD/HOW NE28 48 E5
Blackthorn Wy HLS DH4 107 J5
Blackwell Av BYK/HTN/WLK NE6 58 C5
Blackwood Rd SWCK/CAS SR5 84 E1 3
Bladen St JRW NE32 59 J4
Blagdon Av HAR/WTLS NE34 61 J3
Blagdon Ct BDLGTN NE22 19 J4
Blagdon Crs CRAM NE23 22 E7
Blagdon Dr BLYTH NE24 24 E5
Blaidwood Dr DHAM DH1 134 B5
Blair Ct BDN/LAN/SAC DH7 133 B5
Blake Av WICK/BNPF NE16 67 F5
Blakelaw Rd
WD/WHPE/BLK NE5 55 F1 3
Blakemoor Pl
WD/WHPE/BLK NE5 55 G2 1
Blakes Cl STLY/ANP DH9 102 E1
Blanche Gv PLEE/EAS SR8 136 E5
Blanchland WASHS NE38 95 G5
Blanchland Av
BW/LEM/TK/HW NE15 53 K4
DHAM DH1 125 F3
DIN/WO NE13 36 B3
Blanchland Cl
WLSD/HOW NE28 49 F6 2
Blanchland Dr MONK NE25 30 C6
SWCK/CAS SR5 86 C2
Blanchland Ter
TYNE/NSHE NE30 51 F3
Blandford Pl SEA/MUR SR7 120 E1
Blandford Rd NSHW NE29 50 B2
Blandford Sq CNUT NE1 5 G8
Blandford St CNUT NE1 5 G9
Blaxton Pl WICK/BNPF NE16 66 D7
Blaydon Bank BLAY NE21 65 K2
Blaydon Hwy BLAY NE21 66 A1
Blaykeston Cl SEA/MUR SR7 110 E6
Bleachfeld FELL NE10 70 B6 1
Bleasdale Crs HLS DH4 95 K7
Blencathra WASHN NE37 82 E6
Blenheim LGB/KIL NE12 37 K5 4
Blenheim Dr BDLGTN NE22 19 J3
Blenheim Pl DUN/TMV NE11 8 E5
Blenheim St CNUT NE1 5 C8
Blenkinsop Gv JRW NE32 71 J1
Blenkinsop St WLSD/HOW NE28 58 C1
Blind La CLS/BIR/GTL DH3 105 K1
HLS DH4 107 K4
SUNDSW SR3 98 A6
Blindy La HLH DH5 118 B7
Bloomfield Dr HLH DH5 117 G5
Bloomsbury Ct GOS/KPK NE3 46 B6 1
Blossomfield Wy
RDHAMSE DH6 128 E6
Blossom Gv HLS DH4 107 K3
Blount St BYK/HTN/WLK NE6 7 K5
Blucher Rd LGB/KIL NE12 47 J1
NSHW NE29 2 B6
Bluebell Dene
WD/WHPE/BLK NE5 44 E5
Bluebell Wy HAR/WTLS NE34 61 F6
Blueburn Dr LGB/KIL NE12 38 B5
Bluehouse Bank STLY/ANP DH9 103 K4
Blue House Ct WASHN NE37 82 D5
Blue House La
CLDN/WHIT/ROK SR6 73 K5
WASHN NE37 82 D5
Blue House Rd HEBB NE31 71 F1
Blue Quarries Rd
LWF/SPW/WRK NE9 69 H6
Blyth Cl CRAM NE23 37 F1
Blyth Ct
BW/LEM/TK/HW NE15 54 A4 1
HAR/WTLS NE34 61 G6
Blyth Rd WBAY NE26 31 H5
Blyth Sq SWCK/CAS SR5 84 E2
Blyth St MONK NE25 29 K4
SWCK/CAS SR5 84 E2
Blyton Av ASHBK/HED/RY SR2 99 F7
HAR/WTLS NE34 60 D6
Bodlewell La SUND SR1 15 H3 1
Bodley Cl GOS/KPK NE3 45 H5 2
Bodmin Cl WLSD/HOW NE28 49 G5
Bodmin Rd NSHW NE29 50 A2 1
Bodmin Sq SWCK/CAS SR5 84 E2 4
Bodmin Wy GOS/KPK NE3 45 K4 2
Bognor St SWCK/CAS SR5 84 D1
Bohemia Ter BLYTH NE24 25 G1
Boker La BOL NE36 73 F4
Bolam Av BLYTH NE24 21 F7
TYNE/NSHE NE30 50 E1
Bolam Gdns WLSD/HOW NE28 49 K7
Bolam Gv TYNE/NSHE NE30 50 E1
Bolam Rd LGB/KIL NE12 37 K6 1
Bolam St BYK/HTN/WLK NE6 7 H7
GATE NE8 9 M7
Bolam Wy BYK/HTN/WLK NE6 7 G7
MONK NE25 29 K5
Bolbec Rd ELS/FEN NE4 55 J4
Bolburn FELL NE10 13 K9
Boldon Cl WLSD/HOW NE28 49 F5
Boldon Dr BOL NE36 72 D5
Boldon Gdns
LWF/SPW/WRK NE9 81 J2
Boldon La CLDN/WHIT/ROK SR6 73 J3
HAR/WTLS NE34 61 G7
Boldon North Br BOL NE36 73 G4
Bolingbroke Rd NSHW NE29 50 B4
Bolingbroke St
BYK/HTN/WLK NE6 6 D4
SSH NE33 3 J8 1
Bollihope Dr SUNDSW SR3 98 B4
Bolton Cl DHAM DH1 124 D2
Bonchester Cl BDLGTN NE22 19 F4
Bond Cl SWCK/CAS SR5 86 C4
Bondene Av FELL NE10 12 E7
Bondene Av West FELL NE10 12 E7
Bondene Wy CRAM NE23 23 H5
Bondfield Gdns FELL NE10 13 K7
Bondicarr Pl
WD/WHPE/BLK NE5 55 H2 1
Bondicar Ter BLYTH NE24 21 F7
Bonemill La CLS/BIR/GTL DH3 94 A6
WASHS NE38 94 E6
Bonington Wy
WD/WHPE/BLK NE5 55 F1 4
Bonner's Fld
CLDN/WHIT/ROK SR6 14 E2
Bonnivard Gdns CRAM NE23 29 H7
Booth St FELL NE10 12 C7
MLFD/PNYW SR4 86 A6
Bootle St SWCK/CAS SR5 84 E2 3
Bordeaux Cl SUNDSW SR3 109 J1 2
Border Rd WLSD/HOW NE28 58 D2 3
Boreham Cl WLSD/HOW NE28 49 F5 6
Borodin Av SWCK/CAS SR5 84 D1
Borough Rd HAR/WTLS NE34 61 K6
JRW NE32 59 K5
NSHW NE29 2 D3
SUND SR1 14 F5
SUND SR1 15 H5 1
Borrowdale WICK/BNPF NE16 8 C9
Borrowdale Av BLYTH NE24 20 C6
BYK/HTN/WLK NE6 58 B4
CLDN/WHIT/ROK SR6 74 C7
Borrowdale Cl BOL NE36 73 G4 1
DHAM DH1 126 B5 1
Borrowdale Crs BLAY NE21 65 K4
HLS DH4 95 J6
Borrowdale Dr DHAM DH1 125 K5 1
Borrowdale Gdns
LWF/SPW/WRK NE9 81 H2
Borrowdale St HLH DH5 117 K6
Boscombe Dr
WLSD/HOW NE28 48 E6 2
Boston Av LGB/HTN NE7 47 H5
WASHS NE38 82 E7
Boston Cl WLSD/HOW NE28 49 F5
Boston Crs BOL NE36 84 C1
SWCK/CAS SR5 84 C1
Boston St SWCK/CAS SR5 84 C1
Boswell Av HAR/WTLS NE34 73 F1
Bosworth LGB/KIL NE12 37 K5
Bosworth Gdns
BYK/HTN/WLK NE6 57 J1
Bothal St BYK/HTN/WLK NE6 7 J5
Bottle Bank GATE NE8 5 M9
Bottlehouse St
BYK/HTN/WLK NE6 7 G9
Bottle Works Rd SEA/MUR SR7 121 F1
Boulby Cl SUNDSW SR3 98 C7 1
Boulmer Av CRAM NE23 23 H5
Boulmer Cl GOS/KPK NE3 45 K2 2
Boulmer Ct CLSW/PEL DH2 105 J5
Boulmer Gdns DIN/WO NE13 36 B3
Boulsworth Rd NSHW NE29 50 C1
Boundary Gdns LGB/HTN NE7 47 G7
Boundary St SWCK/CAS SR5 86 C3 1
Bourne Av ELS/FEN NE4 55 J4
Bourne Ct STLY/ANP DH9 90 E7
Bournemouth Dr
SEA/MUR SR7 120 A2 1
Bournemouth Gdns
WBAY NE26 40 D3
WD/WHPE/BLK NE5 44 D7 2
Bournemouth Rd NSHW NE29 50 A5 1
Bourn Lea HLS DH4 107 J2
Bourtree Cl WLSD/HOW NE28 48 E6
Bowbank Cl SUNDSW SR3 98 B3 2
Bowburn Av SWCK/CAS SR5 85 G3 1
Bowburn Cl FELL NE10 70 E5
Bower St
CLDN/WHIT/ROK SR6 86 D1 2
The Bower JRW NE32 71 K4 1
Bowes Av SEA/MUR SR7 119 K2
Bowes Cl WICK/BNPF NE16 79 F3
Bowes Lea HLS DH4 107 H3
Bowes Lyon Cl ROWG NE39 77 F5 1
Bowes St BLYTH NE24 21 F7
GOS/KPK NE3 46 E5 1
Bowfell Av WD/WHPE/BLK NE5 45 H7
Bowfell Cl
WD/WHPE/BLK NE5 45 H7 2
Bowfield Av GOS/KPK NE3 46 C1
Bow La DHAM DH1 16 D5
Bowlynn Cl SUNDSW SR3 109 J1 3
Bowman Dr CRAM NE23 37 H1
Bowman St
CLDN/WHIT/ROK SR6 75 F3
Bowmont Dr CRAM NE23 23 K7 2
STLY/ANP DH9 90 A6
Bowness Av WLSD/HOW NE28 49 G4
Bowness Cl BOL NE36 73 G5 1
PLEE/EAS SR8 137 F3 3
Bowness Pl LWF/SPW/WRK NE9 81 H1
Bowness Rd
WD/WHPE/BLK NE5 54 E2
WICK/BNPF NE16 8 B9
Bowness St SWCK/CAS SR5 84 E1
Bowsden Ct GOS/KPK NE3 46 E5 2
Bowsden Ter GOS/KPK NE3 46 E5
Boyd Crs WLSD/HOW NE28 58 E1
Boyd Rd WLSD/HOW NE28 58 E1
Boyd St BW/LEM/TK/HW NE15 53 G3
DHAM DH1 16 E7
JES NE2 6 B5
Boyne Ct BDN/LAN/SAC DH7 133 J5 1
BLYTH NE24 21 G6 2
Brabourne St HAR/WTLS NE34 61 G5
Bracken Av WLSD/HOW NE28 48 E5
Brackenbeds Cl CLSW/PEL DH2 92 E7
Bracken Cl DIN/WO NE13 34 E3
STLY/ANP DH9 102 B1
Brackendale Rd DHAM DH1 126 A6
Brackendene Dr
LWF/SPW/WRK NE9 68 E7 2
Bracken Dr DUN/TMV NE11 67 K6
Bracken Field Rd DHAM DH1 124 C4
Brackenfield Rd GOS/KPK NE3 46 B6
Bracken Hl PLEE/EAS SR8 136 A5
Brackenridge WICK/BNPF NE16 77 G7
Brackenside GOS/KPK NE3 46 C1
Bracken Wy RYTON NE40 64 C1
Brackenwood Gv
ASHBK/HED/RY SR2 98 C4 1
Brackley WASHN NE37 83 G4
Bracknell Cl SUNDSW SR3 98 C6
Bracknell Gdns
WD/WHPE/BLK NE5 53 K2
Brack Ter FELL NE10 13 L4
Bradbury Cl FELL NE10 70 E5 2
STLY/ANP DH9 90 A6
Bradbury Ct MONK NE25 30 A2
Bradford Av SWCK/CAS SR5 84 E1
WLSD/HOW NE28 49 F5
Bradley Av HAR/WTLS NE34 62 A6
HLH DH5 117 H2
Bradley Cl CLSW/PEL DH2 92 D4
Bradley Lodge Dr
STLY/ANP DH9 89 G6 1
Bradley Ter HLH DH5 118 A7
Bradman Dr CLS/BIR/GTL DH3 106 A5
Bradman Sq SWCK/CAS SR5 84 E1 4
Bradman St SWCK/CAS SR5 84 E1
Bradshaw St SWCK/CAS SR5 84 E2
Bradwell Rd GOS/KPK NE3 45 J5
Bradwell Wy HLS DH4 107 K3
Brady Sq WASHS NE38 95 H2 2
Brady St MLFD/PNYW SR4 85 K6
Braebridge Pl GOS/KPK NE3 45 K7 2
Braemar Ct FELL NE10 13 M4
Braemar Dr HAR/WTLS NE34 62 A3
Braemar Gdns SUNDSW SR3 98 B3 3
SUNDSW SR3 109 G1 1
Braeside ASHBK/HED/RY SR2 14 B9
DUN/TMV NE11 68 A6 1
Brahman Av NSHW NE29 50 B6
Braintree Gdns GOS/KPK NE3 45 K6
Braithwaite Rd PLEE/EAS SR8 137 G4
Bramble Dykes
BW/LEM/TK/HW NE15 55 F6 2
Bramley Cl MLFD/PNYW SR4 96 E4
Bramley Ct LGB/HTN NE7 48 A7
Brampton Av
BYK/HTN/WLK NE6 58 B7
Brampton Ct PLEE/EAS SR8 130 C6 1
Brampton Gdns
BW/LEM/TK/HW NE15 53 F1
LWF/SPW/WRK NE9 81 G2
WLSD/HOW NE28 49 J6
Brampton Pl NSHW NE29 50 B5
Brampton Rd HAR/WTLS NE34 60 E6
Bramwell Rd
ASHBK/HED/RY SR2 15 H7
Brancepeth Av ELS/FEN NE4 55 J7
HLS DH4 107 J6 1
Brancepeth Chare
PLEE/EAS SR8 136 C7
Brancepeth Cl
BW/LEM/TK/HW NE15 54 A3
DHAM DH1 125 F3
Brancepeth Rd HEBB NE31 59 H3
WASHS NE38 94 C2
Brancepeth Ter JRW NE32 71 K1 1
Brancepeth Vw
BDN/LAN/SAC DH7 132 E7
Branch St BLAY NE21 65 K3 2
Brancpeth Cl
BDN/LAN/SAC DH7 133 H1
Brand Av ELS/FEN NE4 55 J4
Brandling Ct HAR/WTLS NE34 61 K7
Brandling Pk JES NE2 5 K1
Brandling St
CLDN/WHIT/ROK SR6 86 E3
Brandling St South
CLDN/WHIT/ROK SR6 86 E4 1
Brandlings Wy PLEE/EAS SR8 136 E3
Brandon Av SMOOR NE27 39 G6
Brandon Cl BLAY NE21 65 J4 2
BLYTH NE24 20 D6
HLS DH4 117 G1 1
Brandon Gdns
LWF/SPW/WRK NE9 81 K2 1
Brandon Gv JES NE2 6 B2
Brandon La BDN/LAN/SAC DH7 132 B5
BDN/LAN/SAC DH7 133 J5
Brandon Rd GOS/KPK NE3 45 K4 3
NSHW NE29 50 B4
Brandy La WASHN NE37 82 D6
Brannen St NSHW NE29 2 C3 1
Bransdale HLS DH4 95 G6
Bransdale Av
CLDN/WHIT/ROK SR6 74 E5
Branston St SWCK/CAS SR5 86 B3
Branton Av HEBB NE31 71 F1
Brantwood CLSW/PEL DH2 105 F4
Brantwood Av MONK NE25 40 B5
Branxton Crs
BYK/HTN/WLK NE6 58 B6
Brass Thill DHAM DH1 16 B4
Bray Cl WLSD/HOW NE28 49 F5
Braydon Dr NSHW NE29 50 B7
Brayside JRW NE32 70 B3
Breamish Dr WASHS NE38 94 B6
Breamish St CNUT NE1 6 B6
JRW NE32 59 J6
Brearley Wy FELL NE10 12 A7
Breckenbeds Rd
LWF/SPW/WRK NE9 80 E1
Brecken Wy
BDN/LAN/SAC DH7 133 H6 2
Brecon Cl PLEE/EAS SR8 136 C5
WD/WHPE/BLK NE5 45 F6 1
Brecon Pl CLSW/PEL DH2 93 F6
Brecon Rd DHAM DH1 125 F2
Bredon Cl WASHS NE38 94 D3
Brendale Av WD/WHPE/BLK NE5 44 B7
Brendon Pl PLEE/EAS SR8 136 C3
Brenkley Av SMOOR NE27 39 G7
Brenkley Cl DIN/WO NE13 35 F2 1
Brenkley Ct DIN/WO NE13 36 B1 1
Brenkley Wy DIN/WO NE13 27 G7
Brenlynn Cl SUNDSW SR3 109 J1
Brennan Cl
BW/LEM/TK/HW NE15 55 F5 3
Brentford Av SWCK/CAS SR5 84 E2
Brentford Sq SWCK/CAS SR5 84 E2 6
Brentwood Av JES NE2 56 D1
Brentwood Cl MONK NE25 30 B7
Brentwood Ct STLY/ANP DH9 103 G1
Brentwood Gdns SUNDSW SR3 98 B3 4
WICK/BNPF NE16 67 F7
Brentwood Gv
WLSD/HOW NE28 59 F2 1
Brentwood Rd HLS DH4 107 J2
Brettanby Rd FELL NE10 12 A9
Brett Cl LGB/HTN NE7 47 K7
Bretton Gdns LGB/HTN NE7 57 J1
Brewer's La NSHW NE29 50 A7
Brewer Ter ASHBK/HED/RY SR2 111 G1
Brewery Bank
WICK/BNPF NE16 66 E3 1
Brewery La FELL NE10 12 D5
PONT/DH NE20 33 G3
SSH NE33 2 F8 1
WICK/BNPF NE16 66 E3 2
Briar Av BDN/LAN/SAC DH7 133 F7
HLS DH4 108 B7
WBAY NE26 40 D2
Briar Cl CLSW/PEL DH2 114 A5
HLS DH4 107 H3
WLSD/HOW NE28 48 E5 12
Briardale BDLGTN NE22 18 E5
Briardale Rd BLYTH NE24 20 C7
Briardene DHAM DH1 16 B5
WICK/BNPF NE16 77 G7
Briardene Cl SUNDSW SR3 109 G1
Briardene Crs GOS/KPK NE3 46 A7
Briardene Dr FELL NE10 71 F5
Briar Edge LGB/KIL NE12 47 K2
Briar Fld WASHS NE38 95 F5
Briarfield Rd GOS/KPK NE3 46 B6
Briarhill CLSW/PEL DH2 105 G2
Briar La
BW/LEM/TK/HW NE15 53 G2 1
Briar Lea BDN/LAN/SAC DH7 113 G7
HLS DH4 107 H3
Briar Pl BW/LEM/TK/HW NE15 54 E6
Briar Rd DHAM DH1 126 A5
ROWG NE39 77 F3 1
Briarside WD/WHPE/BLK NE5 44 E7
The Briars SWCK/CAS SR5 85 F4
Briarsyde Cl WICK/BNPF NE16 66 C7
Briarwood CRAM NE23 37 H1 1
Briarwood Av CLSW/PEL DH2 104 E4
GOS/KPK NE3 46 E4
Briarwood Crs
BYK/HTN/WLK NE6 58 B2
Briarwood Rd BLYTH NE24 25 H1
The Briary
BW/LEM/TK/HW NE15 52 E1 1
Brick Garth HLH DH5 118 A7
Brick Rw ASHBK/HED/RY SR2 98 E7
Bridge Cottages CRAM NE23 37 J1 1
Bridge Crs SUND SR1 14 E3
Bridgemere Dr DHAM DH1 124 B3
Bridge Pk GOS/KPK NE3 46 C2
Bridge Rd South NSHW NE29 50 C6
Bridge St BDN/LAN/SAC DH7 122 B2
BLAY NE21 53 K7
BLYTH NE24 21 H7
DHAM DH1 16 B3 1
DIN/WO NE13 36 B1
GATE NE8 5 L9
STLY/ANP DH9 102 B3
SUND SR1 14 E4
Bridgewater Cl
BW/LEM/TK/HW NE15 54 A4 2
WLSD/HOW NE28 48 E6 3
Bridgewater Rd WASHN NE37 83 G6
Bridge Wy BDN/LAN/SAC DH7 122 C2
Bridle Pth BOL NE36 73 G5
SUNDSW SR3 97 G6
The Bridle SMOOR NE27 39 K7
Bridlington WLSD/HOW NE28 49 F5 7
Bridlington Av
LWF/SPW/WRK NE9 81 F2
Bridport Rd NSHW NE29 50 B1
Brier Dene Crs WBAY NE26 40 C1
Brierdene Rd WBAY NE26 31 J7
Brierfield Gv MLFD/PNYW SR4 97 H2
Brierley Rd BLYTH NE24 20 D7
Briermede Av
LWF/SPW/WRK NE9 81 F1
Brieryside
WD/WHPE/BLK NE5 55 H1 1
Briery Vale Rd
ASHBK/HED/RY SR2 14 D8
Brigham Av GOS/KPK NE3 45 J7
Brigham Pl SSH NE33 3 H6
Brightlea CLS/BIR/GTL DH3 94 A1
Brightman Rd NSHW NE29 2 C1
Brighton Cl WLSD/HOW NE28 49 G5
Brighton Gv ELS/FEN NE4 4 C5
NSHW NE29 2 A1
WBAY NE26 40 D2
Brighton Rd GATE NE8 10 D6
Bright St CLDN/WHIT/ROK SR6 86 E4
SSH NE33 3 K7
Brignall Cl CLS/BIR/GTL DH3 115 J2
Brignall Gdns
BW/LEM/TK/HW NE15 54 E4
Brignall Ri SUNDSW SR3 98 B4 1
Brindley Rd PLEE/EAS SR8 136 A4
WASHN NE37 83 G7
Brinkburn CLSW/PEL DH2 105 G4
WASHS NE38 95 G4
Brinkburn Av BLYTH NE24 25 H1
CRAM NE23 28 D2 1
GATE NE8 10 F7
GOS/KPK NE3 46 B4
WICK/BNPF NE16 66 E4 1
Brinkburn Cl BLAY NE21 65 J4
BYK/HTN/WLK NE6 6 F5
Brinkburn Crs HLS DH4 108 A5
Brinkburn St BYK/HTN/WLK NE6 6 F4
HAR/WTLS NE34 61 F5
MLFD/PNYW SR4 98 A1
WLSD/HOW NE28 60 A2
Brinkburn St South
BYK/HTN/WLK NE6 7 G7
Brisbane Av HAR/WTLS NE34 72 D1
Brisbane St SWCK/CAS SR5 84 E2
Bristlecone SUNDSW SR3 109 J2 1
Bristol Av WASHN NE37 82 D5
Bristol Dr WLSD/HOW NE28 49 F5
Bristol St MONK NE25 29 K3
Bristol Ter ELS/FEN NE4 4 C8
Britannia Pl ELS/FEN NE4 4 C7
Britannia Rd SUNDSW SR3 98 A7 2
Brixham Av LWF/SPW/WRK NE9 81 F2
Brixham Cl SEA/MUR SR7 120 B2 1
Brixham Crs JRW NE32 60 B6
Brixham Gdns SUNDSW SR3 98 B4
Broadbank FELL NE10 13 L7
Broad Chare CNUT NE1 5 M7
Broadfield Pl HAR/WTLS NE34 61 H6 1
Broad Garth CNUT NE1 5 M8
Broadgate Rd
BDN/LAN/SAC DH7 122 B6
Broad Landing SSH NE33 2 F6
Broadlands
CLDN/WHIT/ROK SR6 74 A5
Broadlea FELL NE10 13 L7
Broadmayne Av
MLFD/PNYW SR4 97 H2
Broadmayne Gdns
MLFD/PNYW SR4 97 H2 1
Broad Mdw ASHBK/HED/RY SR2 14 B8
Broadmeadows SUNDSW SR3 109 F1
WASHS NE38 95 G4
Broadmead Wy
BW/LEM/TK/HW NE15 54 E6
Broadoak FELL NE10 13 L6
Broadpark FELL NE10 13 L7
Broadsheath Ter SWCK/CAS SR5 85 K4
Broadside FELL NE10 13 L7
Broadstairs Ct MLFD/PNYW SR4 97 H2
Broadstone Gv
WD/WHPE/BLK NE5 54 A2
Broadwater FELL NE10 13 L6
Broadway BLYTH NE24 25 G1
BW/LEM/TK/HW NE15 54 B3
CLS/BIR/GTL DH3 105 K2
LWF/SPW/WRK NE9 11 L9
PONT/DH NE20 32 E6
TYNE/NSHE NE30 51 G2
WICK/BNPF NE16 66 D7
Broadway Cl MONK NE25 41 F6
Broadway Crs BLYTH NE24 25 G1 1
Broadway East GOS/KPK NE3 46 C3
The Broadway HLS DH4 108 C7
MLFD/PNYW SR4 97 G2
TYNE/NSHE NE30 41 F6
Broadway Vls
BW/LEM/TK/HW NE15 55 F6
Broadway West GOS/KPK NE3 46 B3
Broadwell Ct GOS/KPK NE3 47 F6
Broadwood Rd
BW/LEM/TK/HW NE15 54 D4
Brockenhurst Dr
MLFD/PNYW SR4 96 E4
Brock Farm Ct TYNE/NSHE NE30 50 E4
Brockhampton Cl
BOLCOL NE35 72 C2 2
Brock La BDLGTN NE22 20 B3
Brockley Av HAR/WTLS NE34 60 E7
Brockley St SWCK/CAS SR5 84 E2
Brockwell Cl BLAY NE21 65 J3 2
Brockwell Ct BLYTH NE24 24 E3 1
Brockwell Rd WASHS NE38 94 B1
Brodie Cl HAR/WTLS NE34 73 G1 1
Brodrick Cl GOS/KPK NE3 45 H5
Brodrick St SSH NE33 3 K7
Brokenheugh
WD/WHPE/BLK NE5 54 D2 1
Bromford Rd GOS/KPK NE3 45 H5
Bromley Av MONK NE25 40 C6
Bromley Ct DHAM DH1 135 J6 1
Bromley Gdns BLYTH NE24 25 G2
WLSD/HOW NE28 49 F5 8
Bromsgrove Cl
WLSD/HOW NE28 49 G5 1
Bronte Pl STLY/ANP DH9 103 F3
Bronte St GATE NE8 11 M5
Brookbank Cl SUNDSW SR3 109 K2
Brook Ct BDLGTN NE22 19 G6 2
Brookdale DHAM DH1 126 B6
Brooke Av BOLCOL NE35 73 F4
WICK/BNPF NE16 66 E4
Brooke St SWCK/CAS SR5 14 D2
Brookfield Crs
WD/WHPE/BLK NE5 54 A2
Brookland Dr LGB/KIL NE12 38 A6
Brookland Rd
MLFD/PNYW SR4 85 K7 3
Brooklands PONT/DH NE20 32 C6
Brooklands Wy BOLCOL NE35 72 B4
Brookside BDN/LAN/SAC DH7 113 H4
BDN/LAN/SAC DH7 123 G1
CRAM NE23 37 G1
Brookside Av BLYTH NE24 20 D7
DIN/WO NE13 36 A4
Brookside Crs
WD/WHPE/BLK NE5 55 H2
Brookside Gdns
ASHBK/HED/RY SR2 14 C9
Brookside Wd WASHS NE38 95 F5
Brooksmead WLSD/HOW NE28 48 B6
Brook St WBAY NE26 41 F4
Brookvale Av GOS/KPK NE3 45 K6
Broom Cl STLY/ANP DH9 91 F7
WICK/BNPF NE16 67 G6
Broom Ct LWF/SPW/WRK NE9 82 B4
Broom Crs BDN/LAN/SAC DH7 133 F1
Broome Cl GOS/KPK NE3 46 A4
Broome Rd DHAM DH1 126 A5
Broomfield JRW NE32 72 A3

Broomfield Av
BYK/HTN/WLK NE6 .... 58 A2
WLSD/HOW NE28 .... 48 E5
Broomfield Rd GOS/KPK NE3 .... 46 B6
Broom Hall Dr
BDN/LAN/SAC DH7 .... 133 G1
Broomhill Gdns
WD/WHPE/BLK NE5 .... 55 H2 2
Broomhill Ter HLH DH5 .... 117 J3
Broom La BDN/LAN/SAC DH7 .... 133 G1
WICK/BNPF NE16 .... 67 F7
Broomlea NSHW NE29 .... 49 K1
Broomlee Rd LGB/KIL NE12 .... 37 K6
Broomley Wk GOS/KPK NE3 .... 45 K3
Broomridge Av
BW/LEM/TK/HW NE15 .... 55 H6
Broomshields Av SWCK/CAS SR5 .... 86 B2
Broomshields Cl SWCK/CAS SR5 .... 86 B2
Broomside La DHAM DH1 .... 126 A5
Brooms La CON/LDGT DH8 .... 100 C4
Broom Ter WICK/BNPF NE16 .... 78 A7 1
Broomy Hill Rd
BW/LEM/TK/HW NE15 .... 53 F1
Brotherlee Rd GOS/KPK NE3 .... 45 K3
Brougham Ct PLEE/EAS SR8 .... 136 B7
Brougham St SUND SR1 .... 14 D5
Brough Gdns WLSD/HOW NE28 .... 49 J6
Brough Park Wy
BYK/HTN/WLK NE6 .... 7 K4
Brough St BYK/HTN/WLK NE6 .... 7 G3
Broughton Rd SSH NE33 .... 3 K8
Browbank BDN/LAN/SAC DH7 .... 113 J6
Browne Rd CLDN/WHIT/ROK SR6 .... 86 D2
Browney La BDN/LAN/SAC DH7 .... 133 J7
Browning Cl HAR/WTLS NE34 .... 73 F2
STLY/ANP DH9 .... 90 E7
Brownlow Cl LGB/HTN NE7 .... 48 A7
Brownlow Rd HAR/WTLS NE34 .... 61 G5
Brownney Ct
BDN/LAN/SAC DH7 .... 122 B2 1
Brownrigg Dr CRAM NE23 .... 28 D3 2
Brownsea Pl
LWF/SPW/WRK NE9 .... 11 K9
Browntop Pl HAR/WTLS NE34 .... 61 G6 4
Broxburn Cl WLSD/HOW NE28 .... 49 G5
Broxburn Ct
WD/WHPE/BLK NE5 .... 45 G7 2
Broxholm Rd
BYK/HTN/WLK NE6 .... 57 H2
Bruce Cl HAR/WTLS NE34 .... 61 G7
WD/WHPE/BLK NE5 .... 54 D1 2
Bruce Gdns WD/WHPE/BLK NE5 .... 55 G4
Bruce Kirkup Rd PLEE/EAS SR8 .... 137 F2
Bruce Pl PLEE/EAS SR8 .... 136 D2
Bruce St BDN/LAN/SAC DH7 .... 113 G2
Brundon Av WBAY NE26 .... 40 D2
Brunel Dr CLDN/WHIT/ROK SR6 .... 87 F4
Brunel St ELS/FEN NE4 .... 9 M1
GATE NE8 .... 10 C8
Brunel Ter ELS/FEN NE4 .... 9 J1
Brunel Wk ELS/FEN NE4 .... 9 H1
Brunswick Gv DIN/WO NE13 .... 36 A3 1
Brunswick Rd SMOOR NE27 .... 39 H7
SWCK/CAS SR5 .... 84 E1
Brunswick St SSH NE33 .... 61 G2
Brunton Av GOS/KPK NE3 .... 45 K4
WLSD/HOW NE28 .... 49 K7
Brunton Cl SMOOR NE27 .... 39 H7
Brunton Gv GOS/KPK NE3 .... 45 K4 4
Brunton La DIN/WO NE13 .... 35 H7
GOS/KPK NE3 .... 45 G5
GOS/KPK NE3 .... 46 C1
Brunton Rd DIN/WO NE13 .... 45 F3
Brunton St NSHW NE29 .... 50 B7
Brunton Ter MLFD/PNYW SR4 .... 86 A7 1
Brunton Wy CRAM NE23 .... 23 H5
FELL NE10 .... 13 M3 1
Brussels Rd MLFD/PNYW SR4 .... 85 H6
WLSD/HOW NE28 .... 58 D2
Bryden Ct HAR/WTLS NE34 .... 61 H6 2
Bryers St CLDN/WHIT/ROK SR6 .... 75 F3
Buckingham SUNDSW SR3 .... 97 J6 1
Buckingham Cl
CLDN/WHIT/ROK SR6 .... 75 F3 1
Buckingham Rd PLEE/EAS SR8 .... 136 C2
Buckinghamshire Rd
DHAM DH1 .... 125 K6
Buckingham St ELS/FEN NE4 .... 4 F7
Buckland Cl HLS DH4 .... 108 A5
WASHS NE38 .... 95 F3
Buckthorne Gv LGB/HTN NE7 .... 47 J7
Buddle Cl ELS/FEN NE4 .... 55 H7
PLEE/EAS SR8 .... 136 E2
Buddle Ct ELS/FEN NE4 .... 55 J7
Buddle Rd ELS/FEN NE4 .... 55 H7
Buddle St WLSD/HOW NE28 .... 58 D3
Buddle Ter
ASHBK/HED/RY SR2 .... 15 H8 2
Bude Gdns LWF/SPW/WRK NE9 .... 81 F2
Bude Gv NSHW NE29 .... 50 B1
Bude Sq SEA/MUR SR7 .... 119 J4
Budle Cl BLYTH NE24 .... 20 E7
Budleigh Rd GOS/KPK NE3 .... 45 K5
Budworth Av WBAY NE26 .... 31 G3
Bullfinch Dr WICK/BNPF NE16 .... 66 E6
Bullion La CLSW/PEL DH2 .... 105 H4
Bulman's La NSHW NE29 .... 50 E2 2
Bulmer Rd HAR/WTLS NE34 .... 62 A4
The Bungalows STLY/ANP DH9 .... 90 A6
Bunyan Av HAR/WTLS NE34 .... 72 E1
Burdale Av WD/WHPE/BLK NE5 .... 54 E2
Burdon Av CRAM NE23 .... 28 A1
HLH DH5 .... 108 E7
Burdon Cl CLDN/WHIT/ROK SR6 .... 73 J3
Burdon Crs CLDN/WHIT/ROK SR6 .... 73 J3
SEA/MUR SR7 .... 111 F6
Burdon Gv SUNDSW SR3 .... 98 B7
Burdon La ASHBK/HED/RY SR2 .... 110 E1
SUNDSW SR3 .... 110 A3
Burdon Ldg WICK/BNPF NE16 .... 79 G3
Burdon Main Rw NSHW NE29 .... 2 C5
Burdon Pk WICK/BNPF NE16 .... 79 G3
Burdon Pl PLEE/EAS SR8 .... 137 F4 1
Burdon Pln WICK/BNPF NE16 .... 79 F6
Burdon Rd ASHBK/HED/RY SR2 .... 14 F7
CLDN/WHIT/ROK SR6 .... 73 J3
SUNDSW SR3 .... 110 B2
Burdon St NSHW NE29 .... 50 B7
Burdon Ter JES NE2 .... 56 D3
Burford Ct LGB/HTN NE7 .... 47 G6
Burford Gdns SUNDSW SR3 .... 98 B4
Burghley Rd FELL NE10 .... 69 J6
Burke St SWCK/CAS SR5 .... 84 E2 7
Burlawn Cl
ASHBK/HED/RY SR2 .... 99 F6 1
Burleigh St SSH NE33 .... 3 K9 1
Burlington Cl
ASHBK/HED/RY SR2 .... 15 J7 1
Burlington Ct
WLSD/HOW NE28 .... 49 G3 1
Burlington Gdns
BYK/HTN/WLK NE6 .... 57 H3 1
Burnaby Dr RYTON NE40 .... 52 D7
Burnaby St MLFD/PNYW SR4 .... 98 A1 1
Burn Av LGB/KIL NE12 .... 47 K2
Burnbank Av MONK NE25 .... 39 K4
Burnbridge DIN/WO NE13 .... 36 B1
Burn Crook HLH DH5 .... 117 G2
Burnden Gv HLS DH4 .... 107 H2
Burnet Cl WLSD/HOW NE28 .... 48 E5
Burney Vls GATE NE8 .... 11 J6
Burnfoot Wy GOS/KPK NE3 .... 45 J7
Burn Gdns PLEE/EAS SR8 .... 130 D5
Burnhall Dr SEA/MUR SR7 .... 111 G6
Burnham Av
BW/LEM/TK/HW NE15 .... 53 J4
Burnham Cl BLYTH NE24 .... 25 G2
Burnham Gv BOL NE36 .... 73 H5
BYK/HTN/WLK NE6 .... 7 M8
Burnham St HAR/WTLS NE34 .... 61 G5 1
Burn Heads Rd HEBB NE31 .... 59 F7
Burnhills Gdns RYTON NE40 .... 64 C3
Burnhills La RYTON NE40 .... 64 D4
Burnhope Dr SWCK/CAS SR5 .... 86 B2 1
Burnhope Rd WASHS NE38 .... 83 G7
Burnhope Wy PLEE/EAS SR8 .... 136 C4
Burnip Rd SEA/MUR SR7 .... 119 H4
Burn La HLH DH5 .... 117 K5
Burnlea Gdns CRAM NE23 .... 29 H6
Burnley St BLAY NE21 .... 66 A2 1
Burnmoor Gdns
LWF/SPW/WRK NE9 .... 81 K2
Burnopfield Gdns
BW/LEM/TK/HW NE15 .... 54 E5
Burnopfield Rd ROWG NE39 .... 77 H4
Burn Park Rd
ASHBK/HED/RY SR2 .... 14 B7
HLS DH4 .... 108 A7
Burn Prom HLS DH4 .... 108 B7
Burn Rd BLAY NE21 .... 65 H3
Burns Av BLYTH NE24 .... 24 E2
BOLCOL NE35 .... 73 F4
Burns Av South HLH DH5 .... 117 H1
Burns Cl HAR/WTLS NE34 .... 73 F1
HLS DH4 .... 116 D6
STLY/ANP DH9 .... 102 E1
WICK/BNPF NE16 .... 67 F7
Burns Crs WICK/BNPF NE16 .... 66 E4 2
Burnside BDLGTN NE22 .... 19 K3
BDN/LAN/SAC DH7 .... 123 G1
BOL NE36 .... 73 J5
JRW NE32 .... 60 A7
PLEE/EAS SR8 .... 136 D4
PONT/DH NE20 .... 32 D6
Burnside Av CRAM NE23 .... 37 H1
HLS DH4 .... 108 A6
PLEE/EAS SR8 .... 137 H4
Burnside Cl BLYTH NE24 .... 20 D6 1
WICK/BNPF NE16 .... 78 E1
Burnside Rd GOS/KPK NE3 .... 46 C3
ROWG NE39 .... 77 F4
TYNE/NSHE NE30 .... 41 F6
The Burnside
WD/WHPE/BLK NE5 .... 54 C2
Burnside Vw CRAM NE23 .... 29 F7 1
Burns St JRW NE32 .... 59 K4 2
Burnstones
WD/WHPE/BLK NE5 .... 54 C2 3
Burnthouse Bank
CLSW/PEL DH2 .... 105 F3
Burnthouse Cl BLAY NE21 .... 65 J4 3
Burnthouse La WICK/BNPF NE16 .... 66 E7
Burnt House Rd MONK NE25 .... 40 C6
Burntland Av SWCK/CAS SR5 .... 85 K3
Burn Vw CRAM NE23 .... 37 H1 2
Burnville Rd MLFD/PNYW SR4 .... 14 A7
Burnville Rd South
MLFD/PNYW SR4 .... 14 A8
Burradon Rd CRAM NE23 .... 37 H3
Burrow St SSH NE33 .... 3 H7
Burscough Crs
CLDN/WHIT/ROK SR6 .... 86 D3 1
Burstow Av BYK/HTN/WLK NE6 .... 12 F1
Burt Av NSHW NE29 .... 50 C5
Burt Cl PLEE/EAS SR8 .... 136 E2
Burt Crs CRAM NE23 .... 37 H1 3
Burt Rd BDLGTN NE22 .... 20 A3 1
Burt St BLYTH NE24 .... 21 G6
Burwell Av WD/WHPE/BLK NE5 .... 54 D3
Burwood Rd BYK/HTN/WLK NE6 .... 13 J1
NSHW NE29 .... 50 A2
Bushblades La STLY/ANP DH9 .... 89 H7
Buston Ter JES NE2 .... 57 F2
Busty Bank WICK/BNPF NE16 .... 77 J5
Butcher's Bridge Rd JRW NE32 .... 59 K7
Bute Ct SUNDSW SR3 .... 109 K1
Bute Dr ROWG NE39 .... 76 B1
Buteland Rd
BW/LEM/TK/HW NE15 .... 54 D4
Bute Rd North ROWG NE39 .... 76 B1
Bute Rd South ROWG NE39 .... 76 B2
Bute St STLY/ANP DH9 .... 89 J4
Butsfield Gdns SUNDSW SR3 .... 98 B4 2
Butterfield Cl RYTON NE40 .... 52 B7 1
Buttermere
CLDN/WHIT/ROK SR6 .... 74 A3
FELL NE10 .... 13 J7
PLEE/EAS SR8 .... 136 B7 1
Buttermere Av HLH DH5 .... 128 B1
WICK/BNPF NE16 .... 67 G5
Buttermere Cl
WD/WHPE/BLK NE5 .... 55 F2 1
Buttermere Crs BLAY NE21 .... 65 K4 1
Buttermere Gdns
HAR/WTLS NE34 .... 61 J5 1
LWF/SPW/WRK NE9 .... 69 G7
Buttermere Rd
TYNE/NSHE NE30 .... 40 E7
Buttermere St
ASHBK/HED/RY SR2 .... 98 E4
Buttermere Wy BLYTH NE24 .... 20 D5 1
Buxton Cl JRW NE32 .... 60 A6
WLSD/HOW NE28 .... 49 F5 3
Buxton Gdns SUNDSW SR3 .... 98 B3
WD/WHPE/BLK NE5 .... 44 D7 3
Buxton Rd JRW NE32 .... 60 A6 3
Byers Ct SUNDSW SR3 .... 98 B6
Byer Sq HLH DH5 .... 117 K2
Byer St HLH DH5 .... 117 K2
The Byeways LGB/KIL NE12 .... 47 H4 1
Bygate Cl WD/WHPE/BLK NE5 .... 45 J7
Bygate Rd MONK NE25 .... 40 C5
Byker Bank BYK/HTN/WLK NE6 .... 6 D6
Byker Br CNUT NE1 .... 6 B5
Byker Buildings
BYK/HTN/WLK NE6 .... 6 D5
Byker Ter BYK/HTN/WLK NE6 .... 58 B5
Byland Cl HLS DH4 .... 108 A5 1
Byland Ct BDN/LAN/SAC DH7 .... 123 G6 1
WASHS NE38 .... 94 E1
Byland Rd LGB/KIL NE12 .... 47 F4
Byony Toft ASHBK/HED/RY SR2 .... 99 G7
Byrness WD/WHPE/BLK NE5 .... 54 C2
Byrness Cl GOS/KPK NE3 .... 45 G6
Byron Av BLYTH NE24 .... 24 E2 1
BOLCOL NE35 .... 72 E4
CLSW/PEL DH2 .... 104 E4
HEBB NE31 .... 59 H5
Byron Cl CLSW/PEL DH2 .... 93 G5
Byron Rd SWCK/CAS SR5 .... 86 A3
Byron St JES NE2 .... 5 M4
SWCK/CAS SR5 .... 86 B4
The By-way
BW/LEM/TK/HW NE15 .... 53 F2
Bywell Av
BW/LEM/TK/HW NE15 .... 54 C4
GOS/KPK NE3 .... 45 K2
HAR/WTLS NE34 .... 62 A4
SWCK/CAS SR5 .... 86 C2 1
Bywell Cl RYTON NE40 .... 64 A1
Bywell Dr PLEE/EAS SR8 .... 136 D7
Bywell Gdns DUN/TMV NE11 .... 68 A7
LWF/SPW/WRK NE9 .... 69 H6
Bywell Rd CLDN/WHIT/ROK SR6 .... 73 K4
Bywell St BYK/HTN/WLK NE6 .... 7 K6
Bywell Ter JRW NE32 .... 71 K1

C

Cadleston Ct CRAM NE23 .... 23 K7 3
Cadwell La PLEE/EAS SR8 .... 130 C5
Caernarvon Cl
WD/WHPE/BLK NE5 .... 45 F6 2
Caernarvon Dr SUNDSW SR3 .... 109 G1
Caer Urfa Cl SSH NE33 .... 3 H4
Cairncross SWCK/CAS SR5 .... 84 E4
Cairnglass Gn CRAM NE23 .... 23 K7 3
Cairngorm Av WASHS NE38 .... 94 C3
Cairnsmore Cl CRAM NE23 .... 28 C4
Cairnsmore Dr WASHS NE38 .... 94 D3
Cairns Rd SEA/MUR SR7 .... 119 F5
SWCK/CAS SR5 .... 86 C1 1
Cairns Sq SWCK/CAS SR5 .... 86 C1 2
Cairns Wy GOS/KPK NE3 .... 45 K3
Cairo St ASHBK/HED/RY SR2 .... 98 E2
Caithness Rd SWCK/CAS SR5 .... 84 D3
Caithness Sq SWCK/CAS SR5 .... 84 D3 1
Calais Rd SWCK/CAS SR5 .... 84 D4 1
Caldbeck Av BYK/HTN/WLK NE6 .... 13 G2
Caldbeck Cl BYK/HTN/WLK NE6 .... 13 G2
Calderbourne Av
CLDN/WHIT/ROK SR6 .... 86 E1 1
Calderdale WLSD/HOW NE28 .... 48 B5
Calderdale Av
BYK/HTN/WLK NE6 .... 58 B5
Calder Wk WICK/BNPF NE16 .... 78 E3
Calderwood Crs
LWF/SPW/WRK NE9 .... 81 G2
Caldew Ct HLH DH5 .... 118 A6
Caldew Crs WD/WHPE/BLK NE5 .... 54 E3
Caldwell Rd GOS/KPK NE3 .... 45 K2
Caledonian St HEBB NE31 .... 59 F4
Caledonia St
BYK/HTN/WLK NE6 .... 58 C7 2
Calf Close Dr JRW NE32 .... 71 K2
Calfclose La JRW NE32 .... 72 A2
Calf Close Wk JRW NE32 .... 71 K1
California BLAY NE21 .... 65 K3
Callaley Av WICK/BNPF NE16 .... 66 D6
Callaly Av CRAM NE23 .... 28 D2
Callaly Wy BYK/HTN/WLK NE6 .... 7 K9 1
Callander CLSW/PEL DH2 .... 93 G4
Callerdale Rd BLYTH NE24 .... 20 C7 1
Callerton LGB/KIL NE12 .... 37 K4 2
Callerton Av NSHW NE29 .... 50 A3
Callerton Ct PONT/DH NE20 .... 33 G5
Callerton La PONT/DH NE20 .... 33 G4
WD/WHPE/BLK NE5 .... 43 G2
Callerton Pl ELS/FEN NE4 .... 4 C6
Callerton Rd
BW/LEM/TK/HW NE15 .... 53 G1
Callerton Vw
WD/WHPE/BLK NE5 .... 43 K6 3
Calley Cl PLEE/EAS SR8 .... 136 D7 1
Callington Dr
ASHBK/HED/RY SR2 .... 99 F7
Calvert Ter SEA/MUR SR7 .... 119 G5
Calvus Dr
BW/LEM/TK/HW NE15 .... 52 B1 1
Camberley Cl SUNDSW SR3 .... 98 C6 1
Camberley Dr
BDN/LAN/SAC DH7 .... 132 E7 2
Camberley Rd WLSD/HOW NE28 .... 49 J6
Camberwell Cl DUN/TMV NE11 .... 68 B6
Camberwell Wy SUNDSW SR3 .... 109 H2
Cambo Av BDLGTN NE22 .... 19 J5
MONK NE25 .... 40 B6
Cambo Cl BLYTH NE24 .... 20 E7
GOS/KPK NE3 .... 46 D5 1
WLSD/HOW NE28 .... 49 F4
Cambo Dr CRAM NE23 .... 28 D3
Cambo Gn WD/WHPE/BLK NE5 .... 55 G1
Cambo Pl TYNE/NSHE NE30 .... 50 E1
Camborne Gv GATE NE8 .... 11 G6
Camborne Pl GATE NE8 .... 11 G6
Cambourne Av
CLDN/WHIT/ROK SR6 .... 86 E1 2
Cambria Gn MLFD/PNYW SR4 .... 84 E7 1
Cambrian St JRW NE32 .... 59 K4
Cambrian Wy WASHS NE38 .... 94 D2
Cambria St MLFD/PNYW SR4 .... 84 E7
Cambridge Av HEBB NE31 .... 59 H6
LGB/KIL NE12 .... 47 K2 3
WASHN NE37 .... 82 D5
WLSD/HOW NE28 .... 48 C7 2
Cambridge Dr
CLS/BIR/GTL DH3 .... 115 H2
Cambridge Pl CLS/BIR/GTL DH3 .... 93 J5
Cambridge Rd PLEE/EAS SR8 .... 136 D2
SUNDSW SR3 .... 98 A7
Cambridgeshire Dr DHAM DH1 .... 125 K7
Cambridge St ELS/FEN NE4 .... 9 K1
Camden St JES NE2 .... 5 M4
SWCK/CAS SR5 .... 86 A4 1
TYNE/NSHE NE30 .... 2 E2
Camelford Ct
BW/LEM/TK/HW NE15 .... 54 A3 1
Camelot Cl SEA/MUR SR7 .... 111 J7 2
Cameron Cl HAR/WTLS NE34 .... 73 G1 2
Camerton Pl WLSD/HOW NE28 .... 49 G3
Camilla Rd
BW/LEM/TK/HW NE15 .... 52 B1
Camilla St GATE NE8 .... 11 H5
Campbell Park Rd HEBB NE31 .... 59 G5
Campbell Pl ELS/FEN NE4 .... 4 D6
Campbell Rd SWCK/CAS SR5 .... 84 D3
Campbell St HEBB NE31 .... 59 F4
Camperdown
WD/WHPE/BLK NE5 .... 54 D2
Camperdown Av
CLS/BIR/GTL DH3 .... 105 K2
Campion Dr STLY/ANP DH9 .... 90 B6
Campion Gdns FELL NE10 .... 69 K7 1
Camp Rd WLSD/HOW NE28 .... 58 D3
Campsie Crs TYNE/NSHE NE30 .... 50 E1
Camp Ter NSHW NE29 .... 50 E4
Campville NSHW NE29 .... 50 E4
Camsey Cl LGB/KIL NE12 .... 47 F4 2
Canberra Av MONK NE25 .... 40 B6
Canberra Dr HAR/WTLS NE34 .... 60 C7
Canberra Rd MLFD/PNYW SR4 .... 97 H2
Candelford Cl LGB/HTN NE7 .... 47 K7 1
Candlish St SSH NE33 .... 3 K9
Candlish Ter SEA/MUR SR7 .... 121 F2
Canning St ELS/FEN NE4 .... 55 H6
HEBB NE31 .... 59 G6
Cannock CLSW/PEL DH2 .... 93 F4
LGB/KIL NE12 .... 37 K5 3
Cannock Dr LGB/HTN NE7 .... 47 G6
Cannon St GATE NE8 .... 5 M9 1
Cann Rd PLEE/EAS SR8 .... 136 E2
Canonbie Sq CRAM NE23 .... 23 K7 3
Canon Gv JRW NE32 .... 60 A4
Canonsfield Cl SUNDSW SR3 .... 109 K2
Canterbury Av WLSD/HOW NE28 .... 49 F4
Canterbury Cl
CLS/BIR/GTL DH3 .... 115 H2 1
Canterbury Rd DHAM DH1 .... 124 E1
SWCK/CAS SR5 .... 84 E3
Canterbury St BYK/HTN/WLK NE6 .... 7 K5
SSH NE33 .... 61 H3
Canterbury Wy DIN/WO NE13 .... 36 C3 1
Capetown Rd SWCK/CAS SR5 .... 84 D3 2
The Captains Rw SSH NE33 .... 61 F3
Capulet Gv HAR/WTLS NE34 .... 60 E6
Capulet Ter
ASHBK/HED/RY SR2 .... 15 H9 1
Caradoc Cl WASHS NE38 .... 94 D3
Caragh Rd CLSW/PEL DH2 .... 105 J6
Caraway Wk HAR/WTLS NE34 .... 73 J1
Carden Av HAR/WTLS NE34 .... 62 B6 2
Cardiff Sq SWCK/CAS SR5 .... 84 D4 2
Cardigan Gv MONK NE25 .... 40 E6
Cardigan Rd SWCK/CAS SR5 .... 84 D3
Cardigan Ter BYK/HTN/WLK NE6 .... 6 E3
Cardinal Cl LGB/KIL NE12 .... 47 G4 3
WD/WHPE/BLK NE5 .... 43 K7
Cardinals Cl SUNDSW SR3 .... 109 K2 2
Cardonnel St NSHW NE29 .... 2 C4
Cardwell St
CLDN/WHIT/ROK SR6 .... 86 E4
Careen Crs SUNDSW SR3 .... 97 F7
Carham Av CRAM NE23 .... 28 D2 2
Carham Cl GOS/KPK NE3 .... 46 D4
Carisbrooke BDLGTN NE22 .... 19 F4
Caris St GATE NE8 .... 11 J8
Carlby Wy CRAM NE23 .... 23 F5
Carlcroft Pl CRAM NE23 .... 28 D3 3
Carley Hill Rd SWCK/CAS SR5 .... 86 B2
Carley Rd SWCK/CAS SR5 .... 86 B3
Carlingford Rd CLSW/PEL DH2 .... 105 H6
Carliol Sq CNUT NE1 .... 5 L6
Carliol St CNUT NE1 .... 5 L6
Carlisle Crs HLS DH4 .... 95 J7
Carlisle Rd DHAM DH1 .... 125 F2
Carlisle St FELL NE10 .... 12 C6
Carlton Av BLYTH NE24 .... 24 E4
Carlton Cl CLSW/PEL DH2 .... 92 E4
GOS/KPK NE3 .... 46 A7 1
Carlton Ct DUN/TMV NE11 .... 68 D7
Carlton Crs SUNDSW SR3 .... 97 G7
Carlton Gdns
BW/LEM/TK/HW NE15 .... 54 C4 1
Carlton Rd LGB/KIL NE12 .... 47 K4
Carlton St BLYTH NE24 .... 21 H7 1
Carlton Ter LWF/SPW/WRK NE9 .... 68 E7
NSHW NE29 .... 2 A2
Carlyle Ct WLSD/HOW NE28 .... 59 J2 2
Carlyle Crs WICK/BNPF NE16 .... 66 E4
Carlyle St WLSD/HOW NE28 .... 59 J2 3
Carlyon St
ASHBK/HED/RY SR2 .... 14 E8 1
Carmel Gv CRAM NE23 .... 23 G6 1
Carmel Rd STLY/ANP DH9 .... 102 B1
Carnaby Rd
BYK/HTN/WLK NE6 .... 58 B7 1
Carnation Av HLS DH4 .... 107 F4
Carnegie Cl HAR/WTLS NE34 .... 61 G7 1
Carnegie St
ASHBK/HED/RY SR2 .... 99 F4 1
Carnforth Cl WLSD/HOW NE28 .... 49 F3
Carnforth Gdns
LWF/SPW/WRK NE9 .... 81 H1
ROWG NE39 .... 77 G2 1
Carnforth Gn GOS/KPK NE3 .... 45 J6 1
Carnoustie CLSW/PEL DH2 .... 93 F5
HAR/WTLS NE34 .... 73 K1
WASHN NE37 .... 82 E2
Carnoustie Cl LGB/HTN NE7 .... 47 J6 2
Carnoustie Ct MONK NE25 .... 40 A4
Carnoustie Dr
HAR/WTLS NE34 .... 73 K1 1
Carol Gdns LGB/HTN NE7 .... 47 H7
Caroline Gdns WLSD/HOW NE28 .... 49 J7
Caroline St ELS/FEN NE4 .... 55 J7
HLH DH5 .... 117 K4
JRW NE32 .... 59 J4
SEA/MUR SR7 .... 120 E1 4
Carol St MLFD/PNYW SR4 .... 14 A3
Carolyn Cl LGB/KIL NE12 .... 47 J4 1
Carolyn Crs WBAY NE26 .... 40 C2
Carolyn Wy WBAY NE26 .... 40 C2
Carpenter St SSH NE33 .... 2 F9
Carr Av BDN/LAN/SAC DH7 .... 133 G6
Carr Fld PONT/DH NE20 .... 33 H2
Carrfield Rd GOS/KPK NE3 .... 45 K5 2
Carr Hill Rd LWF/SPW/WRK NE9 .... 11 J8
Carr House Dr DHAM DH1 .... 124 D3
Carrhouse La HLH DH5 .... 118 D3
Carrick Dr BLYTH NE24 .... 25 F3
Carrigill Pl LGB/KIL NE12 .... 47 G4
Carrington Cl CRAM NE23 .... 29 G7
Carrmere Rd
ASHBK/HED/RY SR2 .... 98 E5
Carrmyers STLY/ANP DH9 .... 101 G1
Carrock Cl PLEE/EAS SR8 .... 136 E7
Carrowmore Rd
CLSW/PEL DH2 .... 105 J6
Carrsdale DHAM DH1 .... 126 A4 1
Carr St BLYTH NE24 .... 24 E3
HEBB NE31 .... 59 F4 3
Carrsway DHAM DH1 .... 126 A4 2
Carrsyde Cl WICK/BNPF NE16 .... 66 D7
Carsdale Rd GOS/KPK NE3 .... 45 H5
Cartington Av SMOOR NE27 .... 39 G7
Cartington Cl PLEE/EAS SR8 .... 136 E7 1
Cartington Ct GOS/KPK NE3 .... 45 J3 2
Cartington Rd DHAM DH1 .... 124 D4
NSHW NE29 .... 50 C5
Cartington Ter
BYK/HTN/WLK NE6 .... 57 J2
Cartmel Ct CLSW/PEL DH2 .... 105 G5
Cartmel Gv GATE NE8 .... 10 C9
Cartmel Pk FELL NE10 .... 13 K6
Cartwright Rd SWCK/CAS SR5 .... 85 F4
Carville Rd WLSD/HOW NE28 .... 58 D2
Carville St FELL NE10 .... 11 M3
Carvill Gdns WLSD/HOW NE28 .... 58 D3 1
Carvis Cl BDN/LAN/SAC DH7 .... 133 F7
Carwarding Pl
WD/WHPE/BLK NE5 .... 55 G2
Caseton Cl MONK NE25 .... 40 A3
Caspian Cl JRW NE32 .... 60 A6 4
Caspian Rd SWCK/CAS SR5 .... 84 D4 3
Caspian Sq SWCK/CAS SR5 .... 84 D4
Castellian Rd SWCK/CAS SR5 .... 85 G4
Casterton Gv
WD/WHPE/BLK NE5 .... 43 K7
Castle Chare DHAM DH1 .... 16 C3
Castle Cl CLS/BIR/GTL DH3 .... 105 K5
GOS/KPK NE3 .... 45 H5 3
HLH DH5 .... 118 A6
WICK/BNPF NE16 .... 66 E5 2
Castledale Av BLYTH NE24 .... 24 C1
Castledene Ct GOS/KPK NE3 .... 47 F6
Castle Dene Gv HLS DH4 .... 108 B7
Castleford Rd SWCK/CAS SR5 .... 84 D3
Castlegate Gdns GATE NE8 .... 9 K6 1
Castlenook Pl
BW/LEM/TK/HW NE15 .... 54 D4 1
Castlereagh Cl SEA/MUR SR7 .... 111 J7
Castlereagh Rd SEA/MUR SR7 .... 120 E1
Castlereagh St SUNDSW SR3 .... 98 A7
Castlereigh Cl HLS DH4 .... 107 F4
Castle Riggs CLSW/PEL DH2 .... 105 H4
Castle Rd WASHS NE38 .... 94 C2
Castles Farm Rd LGB/HTN NE7 .... 46 E6
Castles Gn LGB/KIL NE12 .... 38 A6
Castleside Rd
BW/LEM/TK/HW NE15 .... 54 E5
Castle Sq SMOOR NE27 .... 38 D5 1
Castle St DIN/WO NE13 .... 36 A5
SUND SR1 .... 14 D4
Castle St South
SWCK/CAS SR5 .... 85 G4 2
Castleton Cl CRAM NE23 .... 23 G6 2
JES NE2 .... 57 F1 1
Castleton Gv JES NE2 .... 57 F1
Castleton Rd JRW NE32 .... 60 A6 2
Castletown Rd SWCK/CAS SR5 .... 85 G4
Castletown Wy SWCK/CAS SR5 .... 85 H3
Castle Vw
BDN/LAN/SAC DH7 .... 133 H1 2
CLS/BIR/GTL DH3 .... 105 J2
SWCK/CAS SR5 .... 85 F4
Castleway DIN/WO NE13 .... 35 F3
Castlewood Cl
WD/WHPE/BLK NE5 .... 54 B1
Catchside Cl WICK/BNPF NE16 .... 66 E7
Catchwell Rd STLY/ANP DH9 .... 89 F6
Cateran Wy CRAM NE23 .... 28 D4
Caterhouse Rd DHAM DH1 .... 124 C3
Catharine St West
MLFD/PNYW SR4 .... 86 A7 2
Cathedral Vw
BDN/LAN/SAC DH7 .... 113 J6
HLS DH4 .... 108 B4
Catherine Cookson Ct
SSH NE33 .... 61 J2 2
Catherine Rd HLS DH4 .... 108 B1
Catherine St SSH NE33 .... 3 J7
Catherine Ter STLY/ANP DH9 .... 90 D6 2
Catholic Rw BDLGTN NE22 .... 18 E6
Catkin Wk RYTON NE40 .... 52 C7
Cato Sq SWCK/CAS SR5 .... 86 A3
Cato St SWCK/CAS SR5 .... 86 A3 1
Catton Gv WICK/BNPF NE16 .... 79 F2
Catton Pl WLSD/HOW NE28 .... 49 G4

Cauldwell Av HAR/WTLS NE34 61 J4
MONK NE25 40 B6
Cauldwell Cl MONK NE25 40 C5
Cauldwell La MONK NE25 40 B5
Cauldwell Pl HAR/WTLS NE34 61 J4
Cauldwell Vls HAR/WTLS NE34 61 J4
Causeway
CLDN/WHIT/ROK SR6 14 F1 1
LWF/SPW/WRK NE9 69 H6
The Causeway
BW/LEM/TK/HW NE15 53 F2 1
LWF/SPW/WRK NE9 11 K8
Causey Bank CNUT NE1 5 M7
Causey Dr STLY/ANP DH9 90 E6
Causey Rd STLY/ANP DH9 90 E4
Causey St GOS/KPK NE3 46 C6
Cavalier Vw HEBB NE31 59 F4
Cavalier Wy SUNDSW SR3 97 K7 1
Cavell Sq PLEE/EAS SR8 130 E4
Cavendish Ct
BDN/LAN/SAC DH7 133 F7
Cavendish Pl JES NE2 57 F2
SUNDSW SR3 97 K7
Cavendish Rd JES NE2 57 F2
Caversham Rd
WD/WHPE/BLK NE5 43 K7
Cawnpore Sq MLFD/PNYW SR4 85 J7
Caynham Cl NSHW NE29 50 C2 1
Cayton Gv WD/WHPE/BLK NE5 53 K1
Cecil Ct PONT/DH NE20 33 H3
WLSD/HOW NE28 58 D3
Cecil St NSHW NE29 2 C2
Cedar Av CLSW/PEL DH2 114 A4
Cedar Cl BDLGTN NE22 19 F4
DHAM DH1 17 M1
Cedar Crs DUN/TMV NE11 9 H9
LWF/SPW/WRK NE9 81 F1
SEA/MUR SR7 120 D2
Cedar Dr DHAM DH1 134 C5
Cedar Gv CLDN/WHIT/ROK SR6 75 F2
HAR/WTLS NE34 61 K6
RYTON NE40 52 E6
WLSD/HOW NE28 59 F2
Cedar Rd BLAY NE21 66 A2
ELS/FEN NE4 55 H4
Cedars Ct ASHBK/HED/RY SR2 14 F9
Cedars Crs SEA/MUR SR7 119 J5
Cedars Gn LWF/SPW/WRK NE9 81 G2
Cedars Pk ASHBK/HED/RY SR2 98 E3
The Cedars ASHBK/HED/RY SR2 98 D2
WICK/BNPF NE16 79 F1
Cedar St PLEE/EAS SR8 137 J4
Cedartree Gdns MONK NE25 40 C6
Cedarway FELL NE10 70 A7
Cedar Wy LGB/KIL NE12 48 A2 2
Cedarwood Av
BYK/HTN/WLK NE6 58 C2 1
Cedarwood Gv
ASHBK/HED/RY SR2 98 C4
Cedric Crs ASHBK/HED/RY SR2 14 A9
Celadon Cl
BW/LEM/TK/HW NE15 54 A3 2
Celandine Cl GOS/KPK NE3 46 D3
Celandine Wy FELL NE10 69 K6
Celtic Cl CLDN/WHIT/ROK SR6 73 J3
Celtic Crs
CLDN/WHIT/ROK SR6 73 J3 1
Cemetery Ap HAR/WTLS NE34 61 J3
Cemetery Rd GATE NE8 11 H5
JRW NE32 60 A6
STLY/ANP DH9 90 D7
Centenary Av HAR/WTLS NE34 62 A5
Central Av BDN/LAN/SAC DH7 133 H7
CLDN/WHIT/ROK SR6 74 E4
HAR/WTLS NE34 61 K5
NSHW NE29 50 C5
Central Gdns HAR/WTLS NE34 61 K5 1
Centurian Wy BDLGTN NE22 18 E4
Centurion Rd
BW/LEM/TK/HW NE15 54 C3
Centurion Wy
BW/LEM/TK/HW NE15 52 A1
LWF/SPW/WRK NE9 69 H6 1
Ceolfrid Ter JRW NE32 60 A7
Chacombe WASHS NE38 94 E3 1
Chadderton Dr
WD/WHPE/BLK NE5 43 K7
Chadwick St
WLSD/HOW NE28 58 D2 4
Chaffinch Wy LGB/KIL NE12 37 J5
Chainbridge Rd BLAY NE21 66 B1
Chain Bridge Rd BLAY NE21 66 D1
Chalfont Gv MLFD/PNYW SR4 96 D4
Chalfont Rd BYK/HTN/WLK NE6 58 B7
Chalfont Wy
BDN/LAN/SAC DH7 133 H6 3
Chalford Rd SWCK/CAS SR5 86 B3
Chamberlain St BLYTH NE24 25 H1 1
RYTON NE40 52 B7
Chandler Cl DHAM DH1 17 M4
Chandlers Ford HLS DH4 95 H6 1
Chandlers Quay
BYK/HTN/WLK NE6 12 B1
Chandos SUNDSW SR3 110 A3 2
Chandos St GATE NE8 11 H7
Chandra Pl
WD/WHPE/BLK NE5 55 F1 5
Chantry Cl SUNDSW SR3 109 J2
Chantry Dr DIN/WO NE13 36 B2
Chapel Av WICK/BNPF NE16 77 K7 1
Chapel Cl GOS/KPK NE3 46 D1 2
Chapel Ct BDN/LAN/SAC DH7 123 F1
Chapel Hill Rd PLEE/EAS SR8 137 F3
Chapel House Dr
WD/WHPE/BLK NE5 54 A2
Chapel House Gv
BW/LEM/TK/HW NE15 54 A2
Chapel La RDHAMSE DH6 128 E6
Chapel Rd JRW NE32 59 K4
Chapel Rw HLS DH4 108 A2
Chapel St HLH DH5 117 K4
NSHW NE29 50 C5
STLY/ANP DH9 89 J4
Chapel Vw HLS DH4 116 C7
ROWG NE39 77 G2
Chaplin St SEA/MUR SR7 120 E2
Chapman St
CLDN/WHIT/ROK SR6 86 E1 3
Chapter Rw SSH NE33 3 G7
Charlaw Cl BDN/LAN/SAC DH7 113 G4
Charlaw La BDN/LAN/SAC DH7 112 D3
Charlbury Cl LWF/SPW/WRK NE9 82 B4
Charlcote Crs BOL NE36 73 H5 2
Charles Av GOS/KPK NE3 45 J4
LGB/KIL NE12 47 K2
Charles Baker Wk
HAR/WTLS NE34 62 B5 1
Charles Dr CRAM NE23 37 H1
Charles St BOLCOL NE35 72 D4
CLDN/WHIT/ROK SR6 14 F2
DIN/WO NE13 36 A4 3
GATE NE8 11 G3
SEA/MUR SR7 120 E1
STLY/ANP DH9 102 C3
SUND SR1 15 G3 1
Charleswood GOS/KPK NE3 46 D2 1
Charlotte Cl ELS/FEN NE4 9 L1
Charlotte Sq CNUT NE1 5 H7 1
Charlotte St SSH NE33 3 H7
STLY/ANP DH9 102 C3
TYNE/NSHE NE30 2 F2
WLSD/HOW NE28 58 E1
Charlton Gv
CLDN/WHIT/ROK SR6 74 A4
Charlton Rd SWCK/CAS SR5 86 C2
Charlton St
BW/LEM/TK/HW NE15 54 B5
Charman St SUND SR1 14 E4 1
Charminster Gdns
BYK/HTN/WLK NE6 57 J1
Charnwood STLY/ANP DH9 90 C6 1
Charnwood Av LGB/KIL NE12 47 G4
Charter Dr SUNDSW SR3 97 G7
Chasedale Crs BLYTH NE24 20 C7
Chase Farm Dr BLYTH NE24 20 B6
Chase Ms BLYTH NE24 20 B7 1
The Chase LGB/KIL NE12 37 G7
NSHW NE29 2 B1
WASHS NE38 94 B5
Chatham Cl MONK NE25 30 A7
Chatham Rd SWCK/CAS SR5 84 E3
Chathill Cl MONK NE25 40 A4
Chathill Ter BYK/HTN/WLK NE6 58 B6
Chatsworth Crs
MLFD/PNYW SR4 98 A2 1
Chatsworth Gdns
BYK/HTN/WLK NE6 7 K9
WD/WHPE/BLK NE5 44 D7 4
Chatsworth Pl WICK/BNPF NE16 66 E7
Chatsworth Rd JRW NE32 60 A6 3
Chatsworth St MLFD/PNYW SR4 98 A1
Chatsworth St South
MLFD/PNYW SR4 98 A2 2
Chatterton St SWCK/CAS SR5 86 A3
Chatton Av CRAM NE23 28 D3
HAR/WTLS NE34 62 B3
Chatton Cl CLSW/PEL DH2 105 G6
Chatton St WLSD/HOW NE28 60 A2
Chatton Wynd GOS/KPK NE3 46 A3 1
Chaucer Av HAR/WTLS NE34 72 E1
Chaucer Cl GATE NE8 11 J3
STLY/ANP DH9 102 E1
Chaucer Rd WICK/BNPF NE16 66 E4
Chaytor Gv SUND SR1 15 H6
Chaytor St JRW NE32 59 K3
Cheadle Av CRAM NE23 23 G6 3
WLSD/HOW NE28 49 F4
Cheadle Rd SWCK/CAS SR5 84 E3
Cheam Cl WICK/BNPF NE16 67 F7 2
Cheam Rd SWCK/CAS SR5 84 E3
Cheeseburn Gdns
WD/WHPE/BLK NE5 55 G3
Cheldon Cl MONK NE25 40 A3
Chelford Cl WLSD/HOW NE28 49 G3
Chelmsford Gv JES NE2 6 C3
Chelmsford Rd SWCK/CAS SR5 84 E3
Chelmsford Sq SWCK/CAS SR5 84 E2 2
Chelsea Gdns GATE NE8 11 L7
Chelsea Gv ELS/FEN NE4 4 C6
Cheltenham Dr BOLCOL NE35 72 C2
Cheltenham Rd
SWCK/CAS SR5 84 E3 1
Cheltenham Sq
SWCK/CAS SR5 84 E3 2
Cheltenham Ter
BYK/HTN/WLK NE6 6 F2
Chelton Cl DIN/WO NE13 36 B5 1
Chepstow Gdns GATE NE8 10 C9
Chepstow Rd
BW/LEM/TK/HW NE15 54 D5
Chepstow St
MLFD/PNYW SR4 14 A6 1
Cherry Banks CLS/BIR/GTL DH3 105 K2
Cherry Blossom Wy
WASHN NE37 83 K5
Cherry Gv LGB/KIL NE12 37 J5
Cherry Pk BDN/LAN/SAC DH7 133 F7
Cherrytree Cl LGB/KIL NE12 38 B7
Cherrytree Ct BDLGTN NE22 19 K4 1
Cherry Tree Dr BDLGTN NE22 19 F5
Cherrytree Dr
BDN/LAN/SAC DH7 122 A3
WICK/BNPF NE16 8 B8
Cherrytree Gdns
LWF/SPW/WRK NE9 81 G1
MONK NE25 40 D6
Cherry Trees BLYTH NE24 25 F1 1
Cherry Wy HLS DH4 107 K6
Cherwell WASHN NE37 83 H5
Cherwell Rd PLEE/EAS SR8 136 C5
Chesham Gdns
WD/WHPE/BLK NE5 53 K1
Cheshire Av CLS/BIR/GTL DH3 93 J5
Cheshire Dr DHAM DH1 125 K7
Cheshire Gdns WLSD/HOW NE28 48 C7
Cheshire Gv HAR/WTLS NE34 62 B4
The Chesils LGB/KIL NE12 47 G5
Chesmond Dr BLAY NE21 65 K1
Chessar Av WD/WHPE/BLK NE5 55 F1
Chester Av WLSD/HOW NE28 49 H7
Chester Cl PONT/DH NE20 32 D5
Chester Ct LGB/KIL NE12 47 H4
Chesterfield Rd ELS/FEN NE4 4 A9
Chester Gdns HAR/WTLS NE34 61 J4
Chester Gv BLYTH NE24 24 E1
CRAM NE23 29 F7
Chester Ms MLFD/PNYW SR4 14 A6 2
Chester Pl GATE NE8 10 E4 1
PLEE/EAS SR8 136 C2
Chester Rd CLS/BIR/GTL DH3 106 C3
HLS DH4 107 F4
MLFD/PNYW SR4 96 C4
STLY/ANP DH9 90 E7
Chester Road Est STLY/ANP DH9 90 E7
Chesters Av LGB/KIL NE12 47 G4
Chesters Pk
LWF/SPW/WRK NE9 69 F6 1
The Chesters MONK NE25 40 B3
WD/WHPE/BLK NE5 54 A2
Chester St HLS DH4 108 B5
JES NE2 6 A3
MLFD/PNYW SR4 86 A7
Chester St East
MLFD/PNYW SR4 14 A5
Chester St West
MLFD/PNYW SR4 86 A7 3
Chester Ter SUND SR1 14 B5
Chester Ter North
MLFD/PNYW SR4 14 A5
Chesterton Rd HAR/WTLS NE34 61 F7
Chesterwood Dr
WLSD/HOW NE28 58 C1
Chestnut Av BLYTH NE24 21 F5
MONK NE25 40 D5
WD/WHPE/BLK NE5 55 J1
WICK/BNPF NE16 67 F7
Chestnut Cl JRW NE32 72 B3
LGB/KIL NE12 37 H5 2
Chestnut Crs SWCK/CAS SR5 85 K2
Chestnut Dr RDHAMSE DH6 129 F6
Chestnut Gdns GATE NE8 10 A7
Chestnut Gv BDN/LAN/SAC DH7 133 F1
HAR/WTLS NE34 61 K7
Chestnut St WLSD/HOW NE28 58 E2 1
Cheswick Dr GOS/KPK NE3 46 D4
Cheveley Wk DHAM DH1 126 A6
Chevin Cl BYK/HTN/WLK NE6 58 C2
Chevington FELL NE10 70 C6 1
Chevington Gdns
WD/WHPE/BLK NE5 55 H2 3
Chevington Gv MONK NE25 40 B2
Cheviot Cl WASHN NE37 82 C7
Cheviot Ct SEA/MUR SR7 111 G7
Cheviot Gdns DUN/TMV NE11 68 A5 1
SEA/MUR SR7 111 G7
Cheviot Gra CRAM NE23 37 J3
Cheviot La ASHBK/HED/RY SR2 98 D7
Cheviot Pl PLEE/EAS SR8 136 C4
Cheviot Rd BLAY NE21 66 A3
HAR/WTLS NE34 62 A3
JRW NE32 59 H7 2
Cheviot St MLFD/PNYW SR4 85 K6
Cheviot Vw CLSW/PEL DH2 105 G7
DIN/WO NE13 36 A3
The Cheyne SUNDSW SR3 110 A2
Chichester Av CRAM NE23 23 F7
Chichester Cl GOS/KPK NE3 45 G3
Chichester Gv BDLGTN NE22 19 F4
Chichester Pl SSH NE33 61 G3 2
Chichester Rd
CLDN/WHIT/ROK SR6 86 E1
DHAM DH1 124 E2
SSH NE33 61 H2 1
Chichester Rd East SSH NE33 61 H2
Chicken Rd WLSD/HOW NE28 48 C7
Chick's La CLDN/WHIT/ROK SR6 74 E3
Chigwell Cl HLS DH4 95 K7
Chilcrosse FELL NE10 70 B5 1
Chilham Ct NSHW NE29 49 K2
Chillingham Cl BLYTH NE24 24 D2
Chillingham Dr
CLSW/PEL DH2 105 G7 1
NSHW NE29 50 B6 1
Chillingham Rd
BYK/HTN/WLK NE6 57 J2
DHAM DH1 124 E3
Chillingham Ter JRW NE32 60 B7
Chilside Rd FELL NE10 12 C9
Chiltern Cl WASHS NE38 94 D3
Chiltern Dr LGB/KIL NE12 47 H1
Chiltern Gdns DUN/TMV NE11 68 A5
Chiltern Rd NSHW NE29 40 D7
Chilton Gdns HLS DH4 107 J7 1
Chilton Garth PLEE/EAS SR8 137 G5
Chilton St SWCK/CAS SR5 86 C4 1
China St ASHBK/HED/RY SR2 98 E2
Chingford Cl HLS DH4 96 A7 1
Chipchase WASHS NE38 94 B2
Chipchase Av CRAM NE23 28 C3
Chipchase Cl BDLGTN NE22 18 D5 1
Chipchase Ct MONK NE25 29 K2
Chipchase Crs
WD/WHPE/BLK NE5 44 C7
Chipchase Ter JRW NE32 71 K1
Chirton Av HAR/WTLS NE34 62 C5
NSHW NE29 2 A3
Chirton Dene Quays NSHW NE29 2 B8
Chirton Dene Wy NSHW NE29 2 B7
Chirton Gn NSHW NE29 2 A2
Chirton Gv HAR/WTLS NE34 62 C5
Chirton Hill Dr NSHW NE29 50 A3
Chirton La NSHW NE29 50 C4
Chirton West Vw NSHW NE29 2 B2
Chirton Wynd BYK/HTN/WLK NE6 7 H6
Chislehurst Rd HLS DH4 95 K7 1
Chiswick Gdns GATE NE8 11 K8
Chiswick Rd MONK NE25 30 A6
SWCK/CAS SR5 84 E3
Chollerford Av MONK NE25 41 F5
NSHW NE29 50 A4
Chollerford Cl GOS/KPK NE3 46 A6
Chollerford Ms MONK NE25 30 C6
Chollerton Dr BDLGTN NE22 19 G5
LGB/KIL NE12 48 C3
Choppington Rd
STKFD/GP NE62 19 F3
Chorley Pl BYK/HTN/WLK NE6 7 L6
Chowdene Bank
DUN/TMV NE11 80 E3
LWF/SPW/WRK NE9 81 F2
Christal Ter CLDN/WHIT/ROK SR6 86 D2
Christie Ter BYK/HTN/WLK NE6 58 B6
Christon Cl GOS/KPK NE3 46 E5 3
Christon Rd GOS/KPK NE3 46 C5
Christon Wy FELL NE10 13 M4
Chudleigh Gdns
WD/WHPE/BLK NE5 53 K1
Church Av GOS/KPK NE3 46 D5
Church Bank
BW/LEM/TK/HW NE15 53 H4 1
JRW NE32 60 B4
STLY/ANP DH9 90 D7
SWCK/CAS SR5 86 A4 2
WLSD/HOW NE28 59 F1
Church Chare PONT/DH NE20 33 H2
WICK/BNPF NE16 67 F5 1
Church Cl BDLGTN NE22 19 F6 1
DIN/WO NE13 35 F2
MONK NE25 40 A5
PLEE/EAS SR8 137 F5
SEA/MUR SR7 111 J7
Church Ct BDLGTN NE22 19 F6
SEA/MUR SR7 111 G7
Churchdown Cl BOLCOL NE35 72 C2 3
Church Dr
LWF/SPW/WRK NE9 69 G6 2
Churcher Gdns
WLSD/HOW NE28 48 C6 1
Church Flatt PONT/DH NE20 33 H2
Church Gn SEA/MUR SR7 111 J7 3
Churchill Av DHAM DH1 17 K1
MONK NE25 40 C6
SWCK/CAS SR5 86 A3 2
Churchill Gdns JES NE2 57 G2 1
Churchill Sq HLS DH4 107 K7 1
Churchill St SUND SR1 15 G6
WLSD/HOW NE28 49 H6
Church La BDLGTN NE22 19 G6
CLDN/WHIT/ROK SR6 75 F4
DHAM DH1 16 E6
DHAM DH1 17 H3 1
GOS/KPK NE3 46 D5
LWF/SPW/WRK NE9 69 H6 2
SEA/MUR SR7 119 G5
Church Pl FELL NE10 12 C5
Church Ri RYTON NE40 53 G6
WICK/BNPF NE16 67 F5
Church Rd
BW/LEM/TK/HW NE15 53 H4 2
GOS/KPK NE3 46 D5
HLH DH5 117 K2
LWF/SPW/WRK NE9 81 F1
SMOOR NE27 38 E4
Church St BDN/LAN/SAC DH7 113 G5
BLAY NE21 65 J3
BYK/HTN/WLK NE6 58 C7
DHAM DH1 16 E6
DUN/TMV NE11 9 J5
GATE NE8 5 M9
HEBB NE31 59 F4
HLH DH5 108 C7 1
HLS DH4 108 C7
HLS DH4 116 D6
MLFD/PNYW SR4 84 E7
RDHAMSE DH6 128 D6
SEA/MUR SR7 119 J6
SEA/MUR SR7 120 E1 5
STLY/ANP DH9 90 D7
SWCK/CAS SR5 86 B3 2
TYNE/NSHE NE30 2 F1 1
WICK/BNPF NE16 78 E5
Church St East SUND SR1 15 H3
Church Street Head DHAM DH1 16 E7
Church St North
CLDN/WHIT/ROK SR6 86 D4
Church V RDHAMSE DH6 127 F5
Church Vw BOLCOL NE35 72 C3
CLSW/PEL DH2 114 B5 1
SUNDSW SR3 98 A7
WLSD/HOW NE28 59 F1
Church Wk PLEE/EAS SR8 130 C6 2
Church Wy MONK NE25 39 J3
NSHW NE29 2 D1 1
SSH NE33 3 G7
Cinderford Cl BOLCOL NE35 72 B2
Cirencester St MLFD/PNYW SR4 14 A3
Citadel East LGB/KIL NE12 37 K6
Citadel West LGB/KIL NE12 37 K6
City Rd CNUT NE1 5 L7 1
City Wy SUNDSW SR3 109 G1
Civic Ct HEBB NE31 59 H6
Clacton Rd SWCK/CAS SR5 84 D4 4
Clanfield Ct LGB/HTN NE7 47 F6
Clanny St SUND SR1 14 B6
Clanton Cl FELL NE10 70 E5
Clapham Av BYK/HTN/WLK NE6 7 K7
Clappersgate PLEE/EAS SR8 130 B6
Clara St ELS/FEN NE4 55 H7
SEA/MUR SR7 111 H7 1
Claremont Av
BW/LEM/TK/HW NE15 54 B3
CLDN/WHIT/ROK SR6 86 E2 1
Claremont Crs WBAY NE26 40 C1
Claremont Dr HLS DH4 107 J1
Claremont Gdns BOL NE36 73 H5
WBAY NE26 40 D3
Claremont Rd
CLDN/WHIT/ROK SR6 86 E2
JES NE2 56 A3
WBAY NE26 40 C1
Claremont St JES NE2 5 G2
Claremont Ter BLYTH NE24 21 F7
Claremount Ct BOL NE36 73 F5 2
Clarence St JES NE2 6 A5
SEA/MUR SR7 120 E1 6
SWCK/CAS SR5 86 A3 3
WBAY NE26 31 G3
Clarence Ter CLS/BIR/GTL DH3 105 J4
Clarendon Sq SWCK/CAS SR5 86 B2 2
Clare Rd PLEE/EAS SR8 136 C5
Clarewood Av HAR/WTLS NE34 62 A3
Clarewood Pl
WD/WHPE/BLK NE5 55 G3
Clarke Ter FELL NE10 12 B8
SEA/MUR SR7 119 H4
Clarks Hill Wk
BW/LEM/TK/HW NE15 53 H4 3
Claude St HLH DH5 117 K5
Claude Ter SEA/MUR SR7 119 J5
Claverdon St
WD/WHPE/BLK NE5 43 K6 4
Clavering Pl CNUT NE1 5 K8 1
Clavering Rd
WICK/BNPF NE16 67 F3 1
Clavering St WLSD/HOW NE28 59 K2 1
Clavering Wy BLAY NE21 66 C3
Claverley Dr SMOOR NE27 38 E4
Claxheugh Rd
MLFD/PNYW SR4 85 F6 1
Claxton St PLEE/EAS SR8 137 H3
Clay La DHAM DH1 134 B2
Claymere Rd
ASHBK/HED/RY SR2 98 E5
Claypath DHAM DH1 16 E3
Claypath La SSH NE33 3 H9
Claypath Rd HLH DH5 117 K6
Claypool Ct HAR/WTLS NE34 61 G6 5
Clayton Park Sq JES NE2 5 L1
Clayton Rd JES NE2 5 K1
Clayton St BDLGTN NE22 19 K4
CNUT NE1 5 J7
JRW NE32 59 K4 3
Clayton St West CNUT NE1 5 H8
Clayworth Rd GOS/KPK NE3 46 B1
Cleadon Hill Dr HAR/WTLS NE34 74 A1
Cleadon Hill Rd HAR/WTLS NE34 62 B7
Cleadon La BOL NE36 73 J4
CLDN/WHIT/ROK SR6 74 C3
Cleadon Mdw
CLDN/WHIT/ROK SR6 74 A3
Cleadon St BYK/HTN/WLK NE6 7 L5
Cleasby Gdns
LWF/SPW/WRK NE9 69 F6
Cleaside Av HAR/WTLS NE34 62 A7
Cleehill Dr NSHW NE29 50 C2
Cleeve Ct WASHS NE38 94 E1 1
Clement Av BDLGTN NE22 19 J5 1
Clementina Cl
ASHBK/HED/RY SR2 15 H7 1
Clement St
LWF/SPW/WRK NE9 69 F7 4
Clennel Av HEBB NE31 59 F6
Clent Wy LGB/KIL NE12 47 G4
Clephan St DUN/TMV NE11 9 H6
Clervaux Ter JRW NE32 60 A5
Cleveland Av CLSW/PEL DH2 105 H5
NSHW NE29 50 D3
Cleveland Crs NSHW NE29 50 E4 5
Cleveland Dr WASHS NE38 94 D3
Cleveland Gdns LGB/HTN NE7 47 G6 1
WLSD/HOW NE28 49 K7 1
Cleveland Pl PLEE/EAS SR8 136 C4
Cleveland Rd MLFD/PNYW SR4 97 K2
Cleveland St SSH NE33 3 J5
Cleveland Ter NSHW NE29 50 E4 6
Cleveland Vw
CLDN/WHIT/ROK SR6 74 E6
Clickemin PONT/DH NE20 33 J3
Clifford Rd BYK/HTN/WLK NE6 7 J7
Clifford St BLAY NE21 66 A1 1
BYK/HTN/WLK NE6 6 E5
CLS/BIR/GTL DH3 105 J6
MLFD/PNYW SR4 86 A7
TYNE/NSHE NE30 3 H1
Clifford Ter CLS/BIR/GTL DH3 105 J6
RYTON NE40 52 B7
Cliff Rd ASHBK/HED/RY SR2 111 G1
Cliff Rw WBAY NE26 41 G5
Cliffside HAR/WTLS NE34 62 C5
Clifton Av HAR/WTLS NE34 61 J4
WLSD/HOW NE28 58 D1 2
Cliftonbourne Av
CLDN/WHIT/ROK SR6 86 E1 4
Clifton Cl RYTON NE40 53 G7 1
Clifton Gdns BLYTH NE24 25 F3 1
LWF/SPW/WRK NE9 69 F5
NSHW NE29 50 C7
Clifton Gv MONK NE25 40 C3
Clifton Rd CLDN/WHIT/ROK SR6 86 E2
CRAM NE23 28 D3
ELS/FEN NE4 55 J6
Clifton Sq PLEE/EAS SR8 136 E3
Clifton Ter LGB/KIL NE12 47 K3
SSH NE33 61 G4 1
WBAY NE26 41 F4
Cliftonville Av ELS/FEN NE4 55 J6
Cliftonville Gdns WBAY NE26 40 E3
Clinton Pl GOS/KPK NE3 36 B7 2
Clipsham Cl LGB/KIL NE12 47 H4 2
Clipstone Av BYK/HTN/WLK NE6 12 F1
Clipstone Cl
BW/LEM/TK/HW NE15 52 E1 2
Clive St HAR/WTLS NE34 60 E7
NSHW NE29 2 E4
Clockburn Lonnen
WICK/BNPF NE16 66 B7
Clockburnsyde Cl
WICK/BNPF NE16 66 C7 1
Clockmill Rd GATE NE8 9 K5
Clockstand Cl
CLDN/WHIT/ROK SR6 86 E3 2
Clockwell St SWCK/CAS SR5 85 K4 1
Cloister Av HAR/WTLS NE34 60 E6
Cloister Garth LGB/HTN NE7 47 F5 1
The Cloisters
ASHBK/HED/RY SR2 14 E9
LGB/HTN NE7 47 F5 2
Cloister Wk JRW NE32 60 A4
Close CNUT NE1 5 K9
Closeburn Sq SUNDSW SR3 110 B1 1
Closefield Gv MONK NE25 40 C5
Close St MLFD/PNYW SR4 86 A6
SWCK/CAS SR5 86 B4 2
The Close BLAY NE21 65 J3 3
CLDN/WHIT/ROK SR6 73 K3
CRAM NE23 29 G7
HLH DH5 108 D7 2
PONT/DH NE20 33 G4
WD/WHPE/BLK NE5 54 C3 1
WICK/BNPF NE16 78 A6
Cloth Market CNUT NE1 5 K7
Clousden Dr LGB/KIL NE12 48 A1
Clousden Gra LGB/KIL NE12 48 A1 1
Clovelly Av ELS/FEN NE4 55 J6
Clovelly Gdns BDLGTN NE22 19 F6
WBAY NE26 40 E3
Clovelly Pl JRW NE32 60 C6
PONT/DH NE20 32 E7
Clovelly Rd SWCK/CAS SR5 84 D2
Clover Av BLAY NE21 66 A6

FELL NE10 11 M4
Cloverdale BDLGTN NE22 18 E5 2
Cloverdale Gdns LGB/HTN NE7 47 H7
WICK/BNPF NE16 67 F7 3
Cloverfield Av GOS/KPK NE3 45 K4
Clover Hl WICK/BNPF NE16 78 E3
Cloverhill Av HEBB NE31 71 F1
Cloverhill Cl CRAM NE23 28 B7
Cloverhill Dr RYTON NE40 52 C7
Clover Laid BDN/LAN/SAC DH7 133 F7
Club La DHAM DH1 124 B6
Clumber St ELS/FEN NE4 9 J1
Clumber St North ELS/FEN NE4 4 C9
Clyde Av HEBB NE31 71 G1
Clydedale Av LGB/KIL NE12 47 J3
Clydesdale Av HLS DH4 95 K7
Clydesdale Garth DHAM DH1 124 E1 1
Clydesdale Rd BYK/HTN/WLK NE6 7 H6
Clydesdale St HLH DH5 117 K6
Clyde St GATE NE8 11 K7
Clyvedon Ri HAR/WTLS NE34 74 A1
Coach La DIN/WO NE13 35 J5
LGB/HTN NE7 47 J5
NSHW NE29 2 C3
Coach Open WLSD/HOW NE28 59 K2
Coach Rd BW/LEM/TK/HW NE15 52 E1
DUN/TMV NE11 68 B7
WASHN NE37 82 E3
WLSD/HOW NE28 58 E2
Coach Road Gn FELL NE10 12 B4
Coalbank Rd HLH DH5 117 J6
Coaley La HLS DH4 108 A4
Coalford La RDHAMSE DH6 126 E3
Coalford Rd RDHAMSE DH6 126 C7
Coalway Dr WICK/BNPF NE16 67 F4
Coalway La WICK/BNPF NE16 67 F4
Coalway La North
WICK/BNPF NE16 67 F3 2
Coanwood Dr CRAM NE23 28 C3
Coanwood Gdns
DUN/TMV NE11 68 B7 1
Coanwood Rd
BW/LEM/TK/HW NE15 55 F7
Coanwood Wy WICK/BNPF NE16 79 F2
Coast Rd BYK/HTN/WLK NE6 57 J1
HAR/WTLS NE34 62 D4
NSHW NE29 50 B4
PLEE/EAS SR8 137 J4
SSH NE33 61 K2
WLSD/HOW NE28 49 F6
Coates Cl STLY/ANP DH9 102 E1
Coatsworth Ct GATE NE8 10 E3
Coatsworth Rd GATE NE8 10 E4
Cobalt Cl
BW/LEM/TK/HW NE15 54 A3 3
Cobbett Crs HAR/WTLS NE34 73 F1
Cobden Rd CRAM NE23 28 D4 2
Cobden St GATE NE8 11 K6
WLSD/HOW NE28 58 C1 1
Cobden Ter GATE NE8 11 J6
Cobham Pl
BYK/HTN/WLK NE6 58 C7 3
Cobham Sq SWCK/CAS SR5 86 B3
Coble Dene NSHW NE29 60 C1
Coburg St BLYTH NE24 21 H7 2
GATE NE8 11 G4
TYNE/NSHE NE30 51 F4
Cochrane Park Av LGB/HTN NE7 57 J1
Cochrane St ELS/FEN NE4 55 J6
Cochran St BLAY NE21 54 A7 1
Cockburn Ter NSHW NE29 50 B7 1
Cocken La CLS/BIR/GTL DH3 115 J2
DHAM DH1 115 J5
Cocken Rd CLS/BIR/GTL DH3 114 E5
DHAM DH1 115 K5
Cockermouth Rd SWCK/CAS SR5 84 D2
Cockhouse La
BDN/LAN/SAC DH7 122 C7
Colbeck Av WICK/BNPF NE16 67 F3
Colbourne Av CRAM NE23 22 E6
Colbury Cl CRAM NE23 23 G5 1
Colby Ct ELS/FEN NE4 4 E8
Colchester St HAR/WTLS NE34 60 E7
Colchester Ter MLFD/PNYW SR4 97 K1
Coldbeck Ct CRAM NE23 28 D3 4
Coldingham Ct
BDN/LAN/SAC DH7 113 G5
Coldingham Gdns
WD/WHPE/BLK NE5 55 H1 2
Coldside Gdns
WD/WHPE/BLK NE5 53 K1
Coldstream CLSW/PEL DH2 93 F4
Coldstream Av SWCK/CAS SR5 86 B3 3
Coldstream Cl HLS DH4 107 K2 2
Coldstream Dr BLAY NE21 65 J4
Coldstream Gdns
WLSD/HOW NE28 49 H7
Coldstream Rd
BW/LEM/TK/HW NE15 55 F5
Coldstream Wy NSHW NE29 50 A2 2
Coldwell Cl RDHAMSE DH6 128 D2
Coldwell La FELL NE10 69 J5
Coldwell Park Av FELL NE10 12 B9
Coldwell Park Dr FELL NE10 12 B9
Coldwell St FELL NE10 12 C8
Colebridge Cl
WD/WHPE/BLK NE5 45 G7 3
Colebrooke CLS/BIR/GTL DH3 93 K4
Cole Gdns FELL NE10 13 K8
Colegate FELL NE10 70 B5
Colegate West FELL NE10 70 A5
Coleridge Av
LWF/SPW/WRK NE9 80 E1
SSH NE33 61 J2
Coleridge Rd SWCK/CAS SR5 85 F3 1
Coleridge Sq HEBB NE31 59 G5 1
Coley Hill Cl
WD/WHPE/BLK NE5 44 A6 1
Coley Ter CLDN/WHIT/ROK SR6 86 E2
Colgrove Wy GOS/KPK NE3 45 K5 3
Colima Av SWCK/CAS SR5 85 G4 3
Colin Pl BYK/HTN/WLK NE6 58 C3 1
Colin Ter ASHBK/HED/RY SR2 111 F1
College Burn Rd SUNDSW SR3 109 J2
College Cl FELL NE10 69 K6 1
College Dr SSH NE33 61 J3 1
College La LGB/HTN NE7 47 J4
College Rd HEBB NE31 71 F1
College St CNUT NE1 5 L4
College Vw BDN/LAN/SAC DH7 123 F6
Collier Cl
BW/LEM/TK/HW NE15 53 F2 2
Collierley La STLY/ANP DH9 88 E5
Colliery La HLH DH5 118 A6
Colliery Rd DUN/TMV NE11 9 H4
Collin Av HAR/WTLS NE34 62 B6
Collingdon Gn ROWG NE39 64 B7
Collingdon Rd ROWG NE39 76 C1
Collingwood Av
WLSD/HOW NE28 48 D6
Collingwood Crs PONT/DH NE20 33 F5
Collingwood Dr HLS DH4 107 J1
Collingwood Gdns FELL NE10 12 D4
Collingwood Rd MONK NE25 39 J4 1
Collingwood St CNUT NE1 5 K8
HEBB NE31 59 J5 1
HLH DH5 117 K2 1
SSH NE33 61 G3
SWCK/CAS SR5 86 B3 4
Collingwood Ter BLYTH NE24 21 G7
TYNE/NSHE NE30 51 J3
Collingwood Vw NSHW NE29 2 B3
Collywell Bay Rd WBAY NE26 31 G2
Collywell Ct WBAY NE26 31 G2 1
Colman Av HAR/WTLS NE34 60 E6
Colnbrook Cl GOS/KPK NE3 45 H3
Colombo Rd SWCK/CAS SR5 84 D4
Colston Ri PLEE/EAS SR8 136 D3
Colston St ELS/FEN NE4 55 H6
Colston Wy MONK NE25 40 B2
Coltere Av BOL NE36 73 J5
Colton Gdns LWF/SPW/WRK NE9 81 G2
Coltpark WD/WHPE/BLK NE5 54 D2 2
Coltsfoot Gdns FELL NE10 69 J7
Coltspool DUN/TMV NE11 80 D7
Columba St SWCK/CAS SR5 86 B3 3
Columba Wk GOS/KPK NE3 46 D5
Columbia Gra GOS/KPK NE3 45 J5 2
Columbia Ter BLYTH NE24 25 G1 2
Colville Ct STLY/ANP DH9 103 F1
Colwell Pl WD/WHPE/BLK NE5 55 G4 2
Colwell Rd SMOOR NE27 39 H7
Colwyne Pl WD/WHPE/BLK NE5 55 F1
Combe Dr
BW/LEM/TK/HW NE15 53 K4
Comet Dr PLEE/EAS SR8 130 D5 1
Comet Rw LGB/KIL NE12 37 J7
Comet Sq SUNDSW SR3 98 A7 3
Comical Cnr SSH NE33 2 F5
Comma Ct DUN/TMV NE11 68 B5
Commercial Rd
ASHBK/HED/RY SR2 99 F2
BYK/HTN/WLK NE6 7 G7
GOS/KPK NE3 46 E5 4
JRW NE32 60 A3 1
SSH NE33 61 F2
Commercial St BLAY NE21 65 K3
Commissioners' Whf NSHW NE29 2 B8
Compton Av HAR/WTLS NE34 61 H4
Compton Rd NSHW NE29 2 A3
Concorde Wy JRW NE32 59 K5
Condercum Ct
BW/LEM/TK/HW NE15 55 G6 1
Condercum Rd ELS/FEN NE4 55 H6
Cone St SSH NE33 2 F9
Congburn Bank
BDN/LAN/SAC DH7 104 B7
Conhope La
BW/LEM/TK/HW NE15 55 H6
Conifer Cl DHAM DH1 125 H6 2
Coniscliffe Av GOS/KPK NE3 45 K7
Coniscliffe Rd STLY/ANP DH9 102 B2
Conishead Ter RDHAMSE DH6 128 E1
Coniston CLS/BIR/GTL DH3 93 K5
FELL NE10 13 J7
Coniston Av HEBB NE31 59 H6
HLH DH5 128 B1
JES NE2 56 E1 1
SWCK/CAS SR5 86 C1
WICK/BNPF NE16 8 C9
Coniston Cl DHAM DH1 126 B5
LGB/KIL NE12 37 J6 1
PLEE/EAS SR8 137 F4 1
Coniston Crs BLAY NE21 65 K4 2
Coniston Dr BDN/LAN/SAC DH7 113 G4
JRW NE32 72 B1
Coniston Gdns
LWF/SPW/WRK NE9 69 H7
Coniston Pl
LWF/SPW/WRK NE9 69 H7 1
Coniston Rd BLYTH NE24 20 B5
TYNE/NSHE NE30 40 D7
WLSD/HOW NE28 49 H6
Connaught Cl HLS DH4 108 A2 1
Connaught Ter JRW NE32 59 K5
Conningsby Cl GOS/KPK NE3 46 D2
Consett Rd DUN/TMV NE11 67 K7
Constable Cl RYTON NE40 52 E7
STLY/ANP DH9 102 D1
Constable Gdns HAR/WTLS NE34 73 G1
Constance St CLSW/PEL DH2 92 E7
Content St BLAY NE21 66 A3
Conway Cl BDLGTN NE22 18 D5
RYTON NE40 65 F1
Conway Dr LGB/HTN NE7 47 G6
Conway Gdns SUNDSW SR3 97 H7 11
WLSD/HOW NE28 48 C6
Conway Gv WBAY NE26 30 E1
Conway Pl CLSW/PEL DH2 93 F6
Conway Rd SWCK/CAS SR5 84 D3
Conway Sq LWF/SPW/WRK NE9 11 J8
SWCK/CAS SR5 84 D3 3
Conyers Av CLSW/PEL DH2 105 H2
Conyers Gdns CLSW/PEL DH2 105 H2
Conyers Pl CLSW/PEL DH2 105 H2
Conyers Rd BYK/HTN/WLK NE6 6 F5
CLSW/PEL DH2 105 H2
Cook Av BDN/LAN/SAC DH7 123 F6
Cook Cl SSH NE33 61 F3
Cook Crs SEA/MUR SR7 119 G5
Cooke's Wd BDN/LAN/SAC DH7 133 H2
Cook Gdns FELL NE10 13 L8
Cookshold La RDHAMSE DH6 126 E7
Cookson Cl ELS/FEN NE4 4 E6
Cookson's La CNUT NE1 5 J9
Cookson Ter CLSW/PEL DH2 105 H4
Cook Sq SWCK/CAS SR5 84 E3 3
Cooks Wd WASHS NE38 95 F3
Coomassie Rd BLYTH NE24 21 G7
Coomside CRAM NE23 28 D4 2
Cooperative Ter
BDN/LAN/SAC DH7 132 D2
Co-operative Ter
MLFD/PNYW SR4 98 A1 2
ROWG NE39 64 B7
STLY/ANP DH9 88 E6
Cooper Sq DHAM DH1 17 K1
Cooper St
CLDN/WHIT/ROK SR6 86 E4 2
Copeland Ct DHAM DH1 134 B2
Copland Ter JES NE2 6 A5
Copley Av HAR/WTLS NE34 73 G2
Copley Dr SUNDSW SR3 98 B4
Copperas La
BW/LEM/TK/HW NE15 54 D4 2
Copperfield DHAM DH1 134 B3 1
Coppergate Ct HEBB NE31 59 H4
Coppice Wy JES NE2 6 A4
Coppy La STLY/ANP DH9 91 G3
WICK/BNPF NE16 91 F1
The Copse BLAY NE21 66 D2
WICK/BNPF NE16 77 H7
Coquet WASHS NE38 94 B5
Coquet Av BLYTH NE24 25 G2 3
GOS/KPK NE3 46 B4
HAR/WTLS NE34 62 A3
WBAY NE26 40 E4
Coquetdale Av
BYK/HTN/WLK NE6 58 C5
Coquet Dr CLSW/PEL DH2 92 E6
Coquet Gdns STLY/ANP DH9 102 C3 1
Coquet Gv
BW/LEM/TK/HW NE15 52 E2
Coquet St CNUT NE1 6 B6 1
HEBB NE31 59 F5 1
JRW NE32 59 J6
Coquet Ter BYK/HTN/WLK NE6 57 H2
CRAM NE23 37 F1
Corbiere Cl SUNDSW SR3 109 J1
Corbitt St GATE NE8 10 B6
Corbridge Cl WLSD/HOW NE28 49 G4
Corbridge Rd BYK/HTN/WLK NE6 7 G4
Corbridge St BYK/HTN/WLK NE6 6 F5
Corby Gdns BYK/HTN/WLK NE6 58 B5
Corby Ga ASHBK/HED/RY SR2 98 D2 2
Corby Gv PLEE/EAS SR8 136 B7
Corby Hall Dr
ASHBK/HED/RY SR2 98 D2 3
Corchester Rd BDLGTN NE22 18 E4
Corchester Wk LGB/HTN NE7 47 H6
Corinthian Sq SWCK/CAS SR5 84 E3 4
Cork St SUND SR1 15 G4
Cormorant Cl BLYTH NE24 25 H3
Cornbank Cl SUNDSW SR3 110 A2
Corndean WASHS NE38 95 J2
Cornelia Ter SEA/MUR SR7 120 D1
Cornel Rd LGB/HTN NE7 47 H7
Corney St SSH NE33 61 F4
The Cornfields HEBB NE31 59 G5
Cornforth Cl FELL NE10 70 E6
Cornhill Av GOS/KPK NE3 45 K3 1
Cornhill Crs NSHW NE29 50 B3
Cornhill Rd CRAM NE23 28 C2
SWCK/CAS SR5 86 B3 3
Corn Mill Dr HLH DH5 117 G2
Cornmoor Gdns
WICK/BNPF NE16 67 F7
Cornmoor Rd WICK/BNPF NE16 67 F6
Cornthwaite Dr
CLDN/WHIT/ROK SR6 75 F4 1
Cornwallis Sq SSH NE33 61 F2 2
Cornwallis St SSH NE33 3 G7 1
Cornwall Rd HEBB NE31 71 H1 1
Cornwell Ct LGB/HTN NE7 47 F6 1
Cornwell Crs BDLGTN NE22 19 H6 1
Coronation Av DHAM DH1 126 A5
Coronation Gn HLH DH5 128 C1 1
Coronation Rd
WD/WHPE/BLK NE5 43 K7
WICK/BNPF NE16 79 F3
Coronation Sq RDHAMSE DH6 129 G2
Coronation St
CLS/BIR/GTL DH3 105 K5
NSHW NE29 2 D4
SSH NE33 2 F8
SUND SR1 15 G4 1
WLSD/HOW NE28 58 E1
Coronation Ter
MLFD/PNYW SR4 85 F7 1
Corporation Rd
ASHBK/HED/RY SR2 99 F2
Corporation St ELS/FEN NE4 5 G7
Corriedale Cl DHAM DH1 124 D1 1
Corrofell Gdns FELL NE10 13 G4
Corry Ct MLFD/PNYW SR4 97 J2 2
Corsair WICK/BNPF NE16 66 D6
Corsenside WD/WHPE/BLK NE5 54 D2
Corstorphine Town SSH NE33 61 F3
Cortina Av MLFD/PNYW SR4 97 H2
Cossack Ter MLFD/PNYW SR4 85 J6
Cosserat Pl HEBB NE31 59 F4 4
Cosser St BLYTH NE24 24 D3 2
Coston Dr SSH NE33 3 H6
Cosyn St BYK/HTN/WLK NE6 6 D6 1
Cotehill Dr PONT/DH NE20 32 D5
Cotehill Rd
WD/WHPE/BLK NE5 55 F2 2
Cotemede FELL NE10 70 C7
The Cotgarth FELL NE10 12 E9 1
Cotherstone Ct SUNDSW SR3 98 B4
Cotherstone Rd DHAM DH1 124 E3
Cotman Gdns HAR/WTLS NE34 73 H1
Cotsford La PLEE/EAS SR8 137 J4
Cotswold Av LGB/KIL NE12 47 H1 1
Cotswold Cl WASHS NE38 94 D2
Cotswold Dr MONK NE25 40 D6
Cotswold Gdns DUN/TMV NE11 68 A5
LGB/HTN NE7 47 G7
Cotswold La BOLCOL NE35 72 C2
Cotswold Pl PLEE/EAS SR8 136 C3
Cotswold Rd NSHW NE29 40 C7
SWCK/CAS SR5 84 E3
Cotswold Sq SWCK/CAS SR5 84 E2 1
Cotswold Ter STLY/ANP DH9 102 E2
Cottage La WD/WHPE/BLK NE5 55 H2
Cottages Rd SEA/MUR SR7 120 E2
Cottenham St ELS/FEN NE4 4 F7
Cotterdale WLSD/HOW NE28 48 B5 1
Cotter Riggs Pl
WD/WHPE/BLK NE5 53 K1
Cottersdale Gdns
WD/WHPE/BLK NE5 43 K7
Cottingham Cl PLEE/EAS SR8 136 C3
Cottingwood Gn BLYTH NE24 24 D4
Cottonwood SUNDSW SR3 109 J2 2
Coulthards La GATE NE8 11 H1
Coulthards Pl GATE NE8 6 C9
Coulton Dr BOL NE36 73 H5 3
Council Av HLS DH4 107 K1 1
Counden Rd
WD/WHPE/BLK NE5 44 C7 3
Countess Av WBAY NE26 40 E4
Countess Dr
BW/LEM/TK/HW NE15 54 E4
Coupland Gv JRW NE32 71 J1
Courtfield Rd
BYK/HTN/WLK NE6 58 B3
Court La DHAM DH1 16 E5
Courtney Dr SUNDSW SR3 97 K6
Court Rd BDLGTN NE22 19 F5
The Court WICK/BNPF NE16 67 G6
The Courtyard STLY/ANP DH9 90 A6
Cousin St SUND SR1 15 H4
Coutts Rd BYK/HTN/WLK NE6 7 M1
Coventry Gdns ELS/FEN NE4 55 J7
NSHW NE29 50 C6 1
Coventry Rd DHAM DH1 124 E2
Coverdale FELL NE10 70 C6
WLSD/HOW NE28 48 B5
Coverdale Av BLYTH NE24 20 C7 2
Coverley Rd SWCK/CAS SR5 84 E2
The Covers LGB/KIL NE12 48 A4
The Cove HLS DH4 107 K1
Cowan Cl BLAY NE21 53 J7
Cowans Av LGB/KIL NE12 37 J5 3
Cowan Ter ASHBK/HED/RY SR2 14 D6
Cowdray Rd SWCK/CAS SR5 85 F3
Cowell Gv ROWG NE39 76 E3
Cowell St PLEE/EAS SR8 137 G3 1
Cowen Gdns
LWF/SPW/WRK NE9 81 G4
Cowen Rd BLAY NE21 66 B1
Cowen St BYK/HTN/WLK NE6 58 B5 2
Cowley Pl BLYTH NE24 20 D6
Cowley Rd BLYTH NE24 20 D5
Cowpen Hall Rd BLYTH NE24 20 C6
Cowpen Rd BLYTH NE24 20 C6 1
Coxfoot Cl HAR/WTLS NE34 61 G6 3
Coxgreen Rd HLS DH4 95 J6
Coxlodge Rd GOS/KPK NE3 46 A5
Coxlodge Ter GOS/KPK NE3 46 A5
Coxon St ASHBK/HED/RY SR2 15 G6
Cradock Av HEBB NE31 59 F7 1
Craggyknowe WASHN NE37 82 B7
Craghall Dene GOS/KPK NE3 46 E6 3
Craghall Dene Av JES NE2 46 E6 1
Craghead La STLY/ANP DH9 103 J4
Cragleas WICK/BNPF NE16 89 J2
Cragside BDN/LAN/SAC DH7 123 G1
CLSW/PEL DH2 105 G3
CRAM NE23 28 C4
HAR/WTLS NE34 62 B6
LGB/HTN NE7 47 H7
WBAY NE26 40 C2
Cragside Av NSHW NE29 50 B2
Cragside Gdns DUN/TMV NE11 68 A7
LGB/KIL NE12 38 B5 1
WLSD/HOW NE28 49 H7 1
Cragside Rd WASHN NE37 82 C6
Cragston Av WD/WHPE/BLK NE5 45 G7
Cragston Cl
WD/WHPE/BLK NE5 55 G1 1
Cragton Gdns BLYTH NE24 20 D7 1
Craigavon Rd SWCK/CAS SR5 85 F4
Craig Crs CRAM NE23 37 G1
Craighill HLS DH4 107 J1 1
Craigmillar Av
WD/WHPE/BLK NE5 45 G7
Craigmillar Cl
WD/WHPE/BLK NE5 45 F7
Craigmill Pk BLYTH NE24 20 C6
Craigshaw Rd SWCK/CAS SR5 84 D2 2
Craigwell Dr SUNDSW SR3 110 A3
Craik Av HAR/WTLS NE34 61 F6
Crake Wy WASHS NE38 94 B4
Cramer St GATE NE8 11 H6
Cramlington Rd SWCK/CAS SR5 84 D3
Cramlington Sq
SWCK/CAS SR5 84 D3 4
Cramlington Ter BLYTH NE24 24 E3 2
Cramond Ct LWF/SPW/WRK NE9 80 E2
Cramond Wy CRAM NE23 28 C4
Cranberry Rd SWCK/CAS SR5 84 E3
Cranberry Sq SWCK/CAS SR5 84 E3 3
Cranborne SUNDSW SR3 109 G1
Cranbourne Gv
TYNE/NSHE NE30 41 F6 1
Cranbrook Av GOS/KPK NE3 46 C3
Cranbrook Ct GOS/KPK NE3 45 J3
Cranbrook Pl
BW/LEM/TK/HW NE15 55 F7 1
Cranbrook Rd
BW/LEM/TK/HW NE15 55 F7
Craneswater Av WBAY NE26 31 J7
Cranfield Pl
BW/LEM/TK/HW NE15 54 A4 3
Cranford St HAR/WTLS NE34 61 G5
Cranford Ter
MLFD/PNYW SR4 98 A1 3
Cranham Cl LGB/KIL NE12 38 B5 2
Cranleigh Av DIN/WO NE13 45 F3
Cranleigh Pl MONK NE25 40 B2
Cranleigh Rd SWCK/CAS SR5 84 E3
Cranshaw Pl CRAM NE23 28 D3 3
Crantock Rd GOS/KPK NE3 45 K5 4
Cranwell Dr DIN/WO NE13 36 B3
Craster Av HAR/WTLS NE34 62 B3 1
LGB/KIL NE12 48 B1
SMOOR NE27 39 G6
Craster Cl BLYTH NE24 20 E7
CLSW/PEL DH2 105 F6
MONK NE25 40 B3
Craster Gdns
WLSD/HOW NE28 49 H7 2
Craster Rd NSHW NE29 50 B5 2
Craster Sq GOS/KPK NE3 46 A4
Craster Ter LGB/HTN NE7 57 H1
Crawford Av PLEE/EAS SR8 136 E2
Crawford Ct SUNDSW SR3 109 K1 1
Crawford Pl MONK NE25 40 C5
Crawford St BLYTH NE24 21 F5
Crawford Ter
BYK/HTN/WLK NE6 58 B6
Crawhall Rd CNUT NE1 6 B6
Crawlaw Rd PLEE/EAS SR8 130 E4
Crawley Av HEBB NE31 71 F1
Crawley Gdns
WICK/BNPF NE16 8 B9 1
Crawley Rd WLSD/HOW NE28 58 D2
Crawley Sq HEBB NE31 71 F1
Craythorne Gdns
BYK/HTN/WLK NE6 57 J1
Creeverlea WASHS NE38 94 E3
Creighton Av GOS/KPK NE3 45 J7
Creland Wy
WD/WHPE/BLK NE5 45 G7 4
The Crescent
BDN/LAN/SAC DH7 101 J7
BDN/LAN/SAC DH7 113 G7
BW/LEM/TK/HW NE15 53 F1 1
CLDN/WHIT/ROK SR6 73 K4
CLSW/PEL DH2 105 H4
CLSW/PEL DH2 114 B1
CRAM NE23 29 G7
DHAM DH1 124 B6
DIN/WO NE13 45 F4
HAR/WTLS NE34 61 K7
HLS DH4 107 J2
HLS DH4 108 B3
HLS DH4 116 C6
JRW NE32 59 J7
LGB/HTN NE7 47 H5
PLEE/EAS SR8 131 F4
PONT/DH NE20 32 C6
ROWG NE39 76 B2
ROWG NE39 77 H3
RYTON NE40 53 F6
STLY/ANP DH9 90 B6
SUNDSW SR3 98 A5
TYNE/NSHE NE30 51 G2
WICK/BNPF NE16 67 G6
WLSD/HOW NE28 48 D7
Crescent Wy North
LGB/KIL NE12 48 A2
Crescent Wy South
LGB/KIL NE12 48 A2
Cressbourne Av
CLDN/WHIT/ROK SR6 86 E1 3
Cresswell Av LGB/KIL NE12 48 A1
NSHW NE29 50 D3
PLEE/EAS SR8 137 H4
WBAY NE26 31 F2
Cresswell Cl BLAY NE21 65 J4 4
MONK NE25 40 C6
Cresswell Dr BLYTH NE24 24 D2
GOS/KPK NE3 45 J3
Cresswell Rd WLSD/HOW NE28 58 C2
Cresswell St BYK/HTN/WLK NE6 7 K5
The Crest BDLGTN NE22 18 E5
DIN/WO NE13 35 F2
WBAY NE26 31 G4
Crichton Av CLS/BIR/GTL DH3 105 K6
Cricklewood Dr HLS DH4 95 K7 2
HLS DH4 108 A1 1
Cricklewood Rd SWCK/CAS SR5 84 D4
Criddle St GATE NE8 6 C9
Crieff Gv JRW NE32 72 B1
Crieff Sq SWCK/CAS SR5 84 D3 3
Crigdon Hl WD/WHPE/BLK NE5 54 D2
Crighton WASHS NE38 94 C1
Crimdon Gv HLS DH4 117 F1 1
Crindledykes WASHS NE38 95 G4
Cripps Av FELL NE10 13 M8
Croft Av LGB/KIL NE12 48 A3
WLSD/HOW NE28 58 E1 2
Croft Cl RYTON NE40 53 F7
Croftdale Rd BLAY NE21 65 K2
Crofter Cl CRAM NE23 28 B7
Crofthead Dr CRAM NE23 28 C4
Crofton St BLYTH NE24 21 G7 4
HAR/WTLS NE34 61 G5
Crofton Wy
BW/LEM/TK/HW NE15 53 K4
Croft Rigg BDN/LAN/SAC DH7 133 F7
Croft Rd BLYTH NE24 21 G7
Croftside Av
CLDN/WHIT/ROK SR6 75 F4
Croft St CNUT NE1 5 L6
Croftsway ELS/FEN NE4 4 A8
Croft Ter JRW NE32 59 K5
The Croft GOS/KPK NE3 46 A6
LGB/KIL NE12 38 A5
Cromarty CLSW/PEL DH2 93 F4
Cromarty St
CLDN/WHIT/ROK SR6 86 D3
Cromdale Pl WD/WHPE/BLK NE5 55 F2
Cromer Av LWF/SPW/WRK NE9 81 F2
Cromer Gdns WBAY NE26 40 E3
Crompton Rd
BYK/HTN/WLK NE6 57 H2
Cromwell Av BLAY NE21 65 K2
Cromwell Ct BLAY NE21 53 J7
Cromwell Rd FELL NE10 13 L3
WICK/BNPF NE16 8 A8
Cromwell St GATE NE8 11 J6
MLFD/PNYW SR4 86 A6
Cromwell Ter GATE NE8 10 D6
Crondall St SSH NE33 61 H4
Cronin Av HAR/WTLS NE34 60 E7
Crookham Wy CRAM NE23 28 D4
Cropthorne FELL NE10 70 D6 3
Cross Av WLSD/HOW NE28 48 B6
Crossbank Rd
WD/WHPE/BLK NE5 45 H7
Crossbrook Rd
WD/WHPE/BLK NE5 55 H1 3
Crossby Ct ASHBK/HED/RY SR2 15 J7
Crossfell PONT/DH NE20 32 E6
Crossfield BDN/LAN/SAC DH7 113 H6
Crossfield Pk FELL NE10 69 J6

Crossfield Ter
BYK/HTN/WLK NE6 58 C7 4
Crossgate DHAM DH1 16 C4
SSH NE33 3 H9
Crossgate Moor Gdns
DHAM DH1 124 A7
Crossgate Peth DHAM DH1 16 A5
Crossgate Rd HLH DH5 117 K6 2
Crosshill Rd
BW/LEM/TK/HW NE15 55 F7
Cross Keys La
LWF/SPW/WRK NE9 69 F7
Cross La BDN/LAN/SAC DH7 113 H4
DUN/TMV NE11 8 D5
DUN/TMV NE11 80 A2
WICK/BNPF NE16 8 B7
Crosslaw WD/WHPE/BLK NE5 54 D2
Crosslea Av SUNDSW SR3 98 B3
Crossley Ter ELS/FEN NE4 4 B5
LGB/KIL NE12 48 B1
Cross Pde ELS/FEN NE4 4 E8
Cross Pl SUND SR1 15 G4 2
Cross Rigg Cl HLS DH4 95 J7 1
Cross Rw GATE NE8 11 M5
Cross St CNUT NE1 5 H7
GATE NE8 11 H6
HLS DH4 107 J7 2
HLS DH4 108 B6 1
RDHAMSE DH6 127 G6
Cross Ter ROWG NE39 77 F4 1
Cross Vale Rd
ASHBK/HED/RY SR2 14 D9
Crossway HAR/WTLS NE34 62 A6 1
JES NE2 46 E7
LWF/SPW/WRK NE9 69 G6
TYNE/NSHE NE30 51 G2
Crossways BDN/LAN/SAC DH7 122 B3
BOL NE36 73 J5 2
SUNDSW SR3 97 K7
The Crossway
BW/LEM/TK/HW NE15 54 B4 2
The Cross Wy GOS/KPK NE3 45 K6
Croudace Rw FELL NE10 12 C7
Crow Bank WLSD/HOW NE28 58 E1
Crow Hall La CRAM NE23 28 A1
Crowhall La FELL NE10 12 C8
Crow Hall Rd CRAM NE23 23 F6
Crow La SUNDSW SR3 97 F7
Crowley Av WICK/BNPF NE16 8 B8 1
Crowley Gdns BLAY NE21 66 A2 2
Crowley Rd WICK/BNPF NE16 66 E3
Crown Rd SWCK/CAS SR5 86 A5
Crown St BLYTH NE24 21 H7 3
Crowther Rd WASHS NE38 94 B1
Crowtree Rd SUND SR1 14 D4
Crowtree Ter SUND SR1 14 D5
Croydon Rd ELS/FEN NE4 4 C5
Crozier St SWCK/CAS SR5 86 C4 2
Crudwell Cl BOLCOL NE35 72 C2 4
Crummock Av
CLDN/WHIT/ROK SR6 86 C1
Crummock Rd
WD/WHPE/BLK NE5 55 F3
Crumstone Ct LGB/KIL NE12 38 A5
Cuba St ASHBK/HED/RY SR2 98 E3
Cuillin Cl WASHS NE38 94 D3
Culford Pl WLSD/HOW NE28 49 G4
Cullercoats Rd SWCK/CAS SR5 84 D4 5
Cullercoats St BYK/HTN/WLK NE6 7 L5
Culloden Wk LGB/KIL NE12 37 K5 6
Cumberland Av BDLGTN NE22 18 E5 3
Cumberland Pl CLS/BIR/GTL DH3 93 K5
HAR/WTLS NE34 62 B4
Cumberland Rd NSHW NE29 49 K3
SUNDSW SR3 98 A6
Cumberland St SUND SR1 14 E3 1
WLSD/HOW NE28 58 E1
WLSD/HOW NE28 59 K2 2
Cumberland Wk
LGB/HTN NE7 47 H6 1
Cumberland Wy WASHN NE37 83 F3 1
Cumbrian Av
CLDN/WHIT/ROK SR6 74 C7 2
Cumbrian Wy PLEE/EAS SR8 137 F4
Cumbria Pl STLY/ANP DH9 90 E7
Cummings Av RDHAMSE DH6 126 C7
Cummings St BLYTH NE24 21 G6 3
Cunningham Pl DHAM DH1 17 J1
Curlew Cl LGB/KIL NE12 47 G3 1
RYTON NE40 53 G7 2
WASHS NE38 94 C4
Curlew Rd JRW NE32 60 A3
Curlew Wy BLYTH NE24 25 G3
Curtis Rd ELS/FEN NE4 4 A3
Curzon Pl WD/WHPE/BLK NE5 55 F1 6
Curzon Rd West
WLSD/HOW NE28 58 D2 5
Curzon St GATE NE8 10 E7
Cushat Cl BYK/HTN/WLK NE6 7 G7
Cushy Cow La RYTON NE40 53 F7
Cut Bank CNUT NE1 6 C6
Cuthbert Cl DHAM DH1 135 J1
Cuthbert Ct JRW NE32 60 C5
Cuthbertson Cl
CLDN/WHIT/ROK SR6 74 E7 1
Cuthbert St GATE NE8 10 C4
WICK/BNPF NE16 78 E4
Cygnet Cl WD/WHPE/BLK NE5 44 B6
Cyncopa Wy
WD/WHPE/BLK NE5 55 H1
Cypress Av ELS/FEN NE4 55 H3
Cypress Ct
BDN/LAN/SAC DH7 133 G7 1
Cypress Crs BLYTH NE24 21 G7
DUN/TMV NE11 9 H8
Cypress Dr BLYTH NE24 21 G7
Cypress Gdns BLYTH NE24 21 G7
Cypress Gv DHAM DH1 125 H6
RYTON NE40 52 E5 1
Cypress Rd BLAY NE21 66 A2
LWF/SPW/WRK NE9 81 K3 1
Cypress Sq SUNDSW SR3 98 A6 2
Cyprus Gdns
LWF/SPW/WRK NE9 69 G6 3

D

Dachet Rd MONK NE25 40 B2
Dacre Rd CLDN/WHIT/ROK SR6 86 D1
Dacre St SSH NE33 61 G3
Dahlia Ct MLFD/PNYW SR4 14 B4 1
Dahlia Pl ELS/FEN NE4 55 H3
Dainton Cl HLS DH4 108 A3
Dairy La HLS DH4 108 B7
Dalden Gv SEA/MUR SR7 111 K7
Dalegarth WASHN NE37 82 D7
Dalegarth Gv
CLDN/WHIT/ROK SR6 74 C7 3
Dale Rd MONK NE25 40 B5
Daleside BDN/LAN/SAC DH7 113 H4
Dale St BDN/LAN/SAC DH7 122 B2
BLYTH NE24 21 G5
RYTON NE40 52 B7
SSH NE33 3 J6
Dale Ter CLDN/WHIT/ROK SR6 86 E2
Dale Top MONK NE25 30 B7
Dale View Gdns RYTON NE40 64 A1
Dalla St MLFD/PNYW SR4 84 E6 1
Dalmahoy WASHN NE37 83 F2
Dalmatia Ter BLYTH NE24 25 G1
Dalston Pl BLYTH NE24 25 G3 1
Dalton Cl CRAM NE23 28 C2 2
Dalton Ct WLSD/HOW NE28 48 B5
Dalton Pl WD/WHPE/BLK NE5 44 A7
Daltons La SSH NE33 2 F8
Dalton St BYK/HTN/WLK NE6 6 F5 1
Dame Dorothy St
CLDN/WHIT/ROK SR6 14 E2
Dame Flora Robson Av
HAR/WTLS NE34 60 D7
Danby Cl SUNDSW SR3 110 B1 2
WASHS NE38 94 B6
Danby Gdns
BYK/HTN/WLK NE6 57 K2 1
Danville Rd
CLDN/WHIT/ROK SR6 86 E1
Daphne Crs SEA/MUR SR7 120 D3
Darden Cl LGB/KIL NE12 38 B5 3
Darden Lough
WD/WHPE/BLK NE5 54 D2
Darien Av CLDN/WHIT/ROK SR6 86 D1
Darley Ct CLSW/PEL DH2 114 B3
Darley Pl BW/LEM/TK/HW NE15 54 E6
Darlington Rd DHAM DH1 134 B2
Darras Ct SSH NE33 61 H2
Darras Dr NSHW NE29 50 A3
Darras Rd PONT/DH NE20 32 D6
Darrell St DIN/WO NE13 36 A3
Dartford Rd
CLDN/WHIT/ROK SR6 86 D1
SSH NE33 61 K1
Dartmouth Av
LWF/SPW/WRK NE9 81 F2
Dartmouth Cl SEA/MUR SR7 120 B2 2
Dart Rd PLEE/EAS SR8 136 D5
Darvall Cl MONK NE25 40 B2
Darwin Crs GOS/KPK NE3 45 K7
Darwin St SWCK/CAS SR5 85 K4
Daryl Cl BLAY NE21 65 J3 4
Daryl Wy FELL NE10 71 F5 1
Davenport Dr GOS/KPK NE3 46 B1
David Gdns
CLDN/WHIT/ROK SR6 87 F2
Davidson Rd FELL NE10 13 M4
Davidson St FELL NE10 12 C7
David St WLSD/HOW NE28 58 D2
Davison Av SUNDSW SR3 98 B7
WBAY NE26 40 D3
Davison Crs SEA/MUR SR7 119 G4
Davison St BLYTH NE24 21 G6 4
BOLCOL NE35 72 C3
BW/LEM/TK/HW NE15 53 G3
Davis Ter PLEE/EAS SR8 130 E6
Davy Bank WLSD/HOW NE28 59 F2
Davy Dr PLEE/EAS SR8 136 A2
Dawdon Crs SEA/MUR SR7 120 E2
Dawlish Cl SEA/MUR SR7 120 B2
Dawlish Gdns
LWF/SPW/WRK NE9 81 F2
Dawlish Pl WD/WHPE/BLK NE5 44 A7 2
Dawson Ter MLFD/PNYW SR4 84 E6
Daylesford Dr LGB/HTN NE7 47 F6
Daylesford Rd CRAM NE23 23 G5
Dayshield WD/WHPE/BLK NE5 54 D2
Deacon Cl
WD/WHPE/BLK NE5 53 K1 1
Deaconsfield Cl
SUNDSW SR3 109 K2 3
Deal Cl BLYTH NE24 25 G3
Dean Cl PLEE/EAS SR8 137 G5
Deanery St BDLGTN NE22 18 E5
Deanham Gdns
WD/WHPE/BLK NE5 55 G3
Dean Rd SSH NE33 61 F4 1
Deansfield Cl SUNDSW SR3 109 K2 4
Dean St CNUT NE1 5 L7
LWF/SPW/WRK NE9 69 F7
Deans' Wk DHAM DH1 125 G6
Dean Ter SSH NE33 61 F4
SWCK/CAS SR5 85 K4
Dean View Dr BLYTH NE24 20 D6
Dearham Gv CRAM NE23 23 G5
Debdon Gdns
BYK/HTN/WLK NE6 57 J2
Debdon Pl CRAM NE23 28 C2 3
Deckham Ter GATE NE8 11 J7
Deepbrook Rd
WD/WHPE/BLK NE5 55 G2 2
Deepdale WLSD/HOW NE28 48 B5
Deepdale Cl WICK/BNPF NE16 78 D1
Deepdale Crs
WD/WHPE/BLK NE5 55 H1
Deepdale Gdns LGB/KIL NE12 37 J6
Deepdale Rd TYNE/NSHE NE30 41 F7
Deepdale St HLH DH5 117 K7
Deepdene Gv
CLDN/WHIT/ROK SR6 74 D7
Deepdene Rd
CLDN/WHIT/ROK SR6 74 D7
Deerbolt Pl LGB/KIL NE12 47 J3 1
Deer Bush WD/WHPE/BLK NE5 54 D2
Deerness Hts
BDN/LAN/SAC DH7 133 G5
Dee Rd HEBB NE31 71 H1 2
Deer Park Wy BLAY NE21 66 C3
Dees Av WLSD/HOW NE28 48 D7
Dee St JRW NE32 60 A4 1
Defender Ct SWCK/CAS SR5 85 G5 1
Defoe Av HAR/WTLS NE34 73 F1
Deighton Wk
WD/WHPE/BLK NE5 54 D2 3
Delacour Rd BLAY NE21 66 A1
Delamere Ct SUNDSW SR3 110 A1 2
Delamere Crs CRAM NE23 23 G5
Delamere Rd GOS/KPK NE3 45 K5
Delaval Av NSHW NE29 50 C4
Delaval Ct BDLGTN NE22 19 J4
SSH NE33 61 H2
Delaval Crs BLYTH NE24 24 E3 3
Delavale Cl PLEE/EAS SR8 137 G5 1
Delaval Gdns
BW/LEM/TK/HW NE15 55 F7
Delaval Rd
BW/LEM/TK/HW NE15 55 F7
LGB/KIL NE12 47 K2
WBAY NE26 41 G5
Delaval St BLYTH NE24 24 D3
Delaval Ter BLYTH NE24 21 F6
GOS/KPK NE3 46 A6 1
Delight Bank STLY/ANP DH9 89 F7
Dellfield Dr MLFD/PNYW SR4 96 E2 1
The Dell HLS DH4 108 B4
Delta Bank Rd WICK/BNPF NE16 8 B2
Demesne Dr BDLGTN NE22 19 F6
Dempsey Rd DIN/WO NE13 36 B4 1
Denbeigh Pl LGB/KIL NE12 47 J3
Denbigh Av
CLDN/WHIT/ROK SR6 86 D1
WLSD/HOW NE28 49 J6
Denby Cl CRAM NE23 23 G5
Dene Av BW/LEM/TK/HW NE15 54 B5
DIN/WO NE13 36 A3
GOS/KPK NE3 46 E6
HLH DH5 108 E7
LGB/KIL NE12 37 G7 1
PLEE/EAS SR8 131 F4
ROWG NE39 77 F4
Denebank MONK NE25 40 C4
Dene Bank Av PLEE/EAS SR8 137 H4 1
Dene Bank Vw GOS/KPK NE3 45 J7 1
Dene Cl LGB/HTN NE7 57 G1
RYTON NE40 53 F6
Dene Ct BDN/LAN/SAC DH7 113 G7
CLS/BIR/GTL DH3 81 J7
WASHS NE38 82 E7
Dene Crs GOS/KPK NE3 46 E6
ROWG NE39 77 F4
RYTON NE40 53 F6
WBAY NE26 40 D3
WLSD/HOW NE28 59 F1
Dene Dr DHAM DH1 126 A4
Deneford LWF/SPW/WRK NE9 81 G4
Dene Gdns FELL NE10 13 L5
HLH DH5 117 J1
Dene Gv CRAM NE23 29 H6
GOS/KPK NE3 46 E6
Deneholm MONK NE25 40 C3
WLSD/HOW NE28 49 F7
Dene House Rd SEA/MUR SR7 111 J7
Dene La CLDN/WHIT/ROK SR6 86 D1 3
Dene Pk PONT/DH NE20 32 D6
SWCK/CAS SR5 85 G3
Dene Rd BLAY NE21 66 A1
ROWG NE39 77 F4
SEA/MUR SR7 120 C3
SWCK/CAS SR5 85 G4
TYNE/NSHE NE30 51 G2
Deneside BDN/LAN/SAC DH7 113 H4
BDN/LAN/SAC DH7 123 G1 1
CRAM NE23 29 H6
DUN/TMV NE11 67 K6
WD/WHPE/BLK NE5 44 D6
Deneside Av LWF/SPW/WRK NE9 80 E1
Dene St HLH DH5 117 K2
MLFD/PNYW SR4 85 K6
PLEE/EAS SR8 137 H3
SUNDSW SR3 98 A5
Dene Ter JRW NE32 59 J7
The Dene CLSW/PEL DH2 105 H7
HLS DH4 116 D5
MONK NE25 40 C4
Dene Vw BDLGTN NE22 19 J5
GOS/KPK NE3 46 E6
ROWG NE39 76 C2 1
Dene View Crs MLFD/PNYW SR4 85 F7
Dene Vw East BDLGTN NE22 19 J6
Dene Vw West BDLGTN NE22 19 H6
Dene Vls PLEE/EAS SR8 137 H4
Deneway ROWG NE39 77 J1
Dene Wy SEA/MUR SR7 111 J7
Denewell Av LGB/HTN NE7 47 G7
LWF/SPW/WRK NE9 69 F7
Denewood LGB/KIL NE12 38 A7
Denham Av
CLDN/WHIT/ROK SR6 86 D1
Denham Dr MONK NE25 30 A6
Denham Gv BLAY NE21 65 H4
Denhill Pk
BW/LEM/TK/HW NE15 55 H5
Denholm Av CRAM NE23 23 G5 2
Denmark St
BYK/HTN/WLK NE6 7 G4 1
GATE NE8 11 G5
Denshaw Cl CRAM NE23 23 G5
Dentdale HLS DH4 95 G7
Denton Av
BW/LEM/TK/HW NE15 54 B5
NSHW NE29 50 A4
Denton Ga
WD/WHPE/BLK NE5 44 E7 2
Denton Gv
WD/WHPE/BLK NE5 44 E7 3
Denton Rd
BW/LEM/TK/HW NE15 54 D6
Denton Vw BLAY NE21 65 K2
Dent St BLYTH NE24 25 H1
CLDN/WHIT/ROK SR6 86 D1
Denver Gdns BYK/HTN/WLK NE6 7 M6
Denway Gv WBAY NE26 30 E1
Denwick Cl CLSW/PEL DH2 105 G7
Denwick Ter TYNE/NSHE NE30 51 G3
Depot Rd BYK/HTN/WLK NE6 7 J2
Deptford Rd GATE NE8 6 D8
MLFD/PNYW SR4 14 A3
Deptford Ter MLFD/PNYW SR4 86 A5
Derby Crs HEBB NE31 59 F6
Derby Gdns WLSD/HOW NE28 48 C7 3
Derby Rd STLY/ANP DH9 102 C2
Derbyshire Dr DHAM DH1 126 A7
Derby St ASHBK/HED/RY SR2 14 C6
ELS/FEN NE4 4 F5
JRW NE32 60 A4
SSH NE33 3 H9
Dereham Cl WBAY NE26 31 G3
Dereham Ct
WD/WHPE/BLK NE5 45 F6 3
Dereham Rd WBAY NE26 31 G4
Dereham Wy NSHW NE29 49 K2
Derry Av CLDN/WHIT/ROK SR6 86 E1
Derwent Av DUN/TMV NE11 68 D7
HEBB NE31 71 G1 3
ROWG NE39 77 G4
Derwent Cl BDN/LAN/SAC DH7 113 G5
SEA/MUR SR7 111 J7
Derwent Crs WICK/BNPF NE16 66 E4
Derwentdale Gdns
LGB/HTN NE7 47 H7
Derwent Gdns WLSD/HOW NE28 49 J6
Derwenthaugh Rd BLAY NE21 66 E2
Derwent Rd PLEE/EAS SR8 137 F3
TYNE/NSHE NE30 41 F7
WBAY NE26 30 E2
Derwent St HLH DH5 118 A6
SUND SR1 14 D6
Derwent Vw BLAY NE21 65 K3
Derwent Wk WICK/BNPF NE16 66 D4
Derwentwater Rd GATE NE8 9 K7
Derwent Wy BLAY NE21 66 C3
LGB/KIL NE12 37 J6
Deuchar St JES NE2 57 F3
Devon Crs CLS/BIR/GTL DH3 81 H7
Devon Dr SUNDSW SR3 98 A6
Devon Gdns HAR/WTLS NE34 62 B4
Devonport HLS DH4 108 A4
Devon Rd HEBB NE31 71 H1
NSHW NE29 50 B2
Devonshire Dr LGB/KIL NE12 48 D1
SMOOR NE27 48 E1
Devonshire Gdns
WLSD/HOW NE28 48 B7
Devonshire Pl JES NE2 57 F2
Devonshire Rd DHAM DH1 125 K7
Devonshire St SSH NE33 61 F4
SWCK/CAS SR5 86 C4
Devonworth Pl BLYTH NE24 20 C7
Dewberry Cl BLYTH NE24 24 E3
Dewley CRAM NE23 28 C3
Dewley Pl
WD/WHPE/BLK NE5 44 C6 1
Dewley Rd WD/WHPE/BLK NE5 54 E2
Dewsgreen CRAM NE23 28 C2
Dexter Wy FELL NE10 12 B7
Deyncourt DHAM DH1 134 B4 1
PONT/DH NE20 33 F7
Deyncourt Cl PONT/DH NE20 43 F1
Diamond Ct GOS/KPK NE3 45 G5
Diamond St WLSD/HOW NE28 58 D1 3
Diana St ELS/FEN NE4 4 F6
Dickens Av HAR/WTLS NE34 73 F1
WICK/BNPF NE16 66 E4
Dickens St HLS DH4 108 B7
SWCK/CAS SR5 86 A4 3
Dickens Wynd DHAM DH1 134 B3
Didcot Av NSHW NE29 50 C6 2
Didcot Wy BOL NE36 72 D5
BOLCOL NE35 72 D5
Dillon St JRW NE32 59 J6
SEA/MUR SR7 120 E1
Dilston Av MONK NE25 41 F5
Dilston Cl PLEE/EAS SR8 136 D7
SMOOR NE27 39 H7
WASHS NE38 94 C2
Dilston Dr WD/WHPE/BLK NE5 44 C7
Dilston Gdns MLFD/PNYW SR4 97 K1 1
Dilston Rd DHAM DH1 124 E3 1
ELS/FEN NE4 4 C5
Dilston Ter JRW NE32 71 K1
Dimbula Gdns LGB/HTN NE7 57 K1
Dinsdale Av WLSD/HOW NE28 48 E5
Dinsdale Dr DHAM DH1 126 A5
Dinsdale Pl JES NE2 6 B3
Dinsdale Rd
CLDN/WHIT/ROK SR6 86 E3
JES NE2 6 B3
Dinsdale St ASHBK/HED/RY SR2 111 F1
Dinting Cl PLEE/EAS SR8 136 C5
Dipe La BOL NE36 72 E6
Dipton Gdns SUNDSW SR3 98 B4 3
Dipton Gv CRAM NE23 28 C2
Dipton Rd MONK NE25 40 B2
Dipwood Rd ROWG NE39 77 F4
Dipwood Wy ROWG NE39 77 F5
Disraeli St BLYTH NE24 21 F6
HLS DH4 107 K7
Dissington Pl
WD/WHPE/BLK NE5 55 G3
WICK/BNPF NE16 66 E7
Ditchburn Ter MLFD/PNYW SR4 85 K5
Dixon Pl DUN/TMV NE11 9 H7
Dixon Ri PLEE/EAS SR8 137 J4
Dixon Rd HLH DH5 117 G2
Dixon's Sq
CLDN/WHIT/ROK SR6 86 D4 2
Dixon St GATE NE8 10 B6
SSH NE33 61 G2 1
Dobson Cl ELS/FEN NE4 9 L1
Dobson Crs BYK/HTN/WLK NE6 7 H9
Dobson Ter SEA/MUR SR7 119 H5 1
Dock Rd NSHW NE29 2 C5
Dock Rd South NSHW NE29 2 D6
Dock St CLDN/WHIT/ROK SR6 15 G1
Dockwray Cl TYNE/NSHE NE30 2 F2
Dockwray Sq TYNE/NSHE NE30 2 F2
Doddfell Cl WASHN NE37 82 C7
Doddington Cl
BW/LEM/TK/HW NE15 53 K4
Doddington Dr CRAM NE23 28 B2
Dolphin St ELS/FEN NE4 55 H6
Dominies Cl ROWG NE39 77 H2
Dominion Rd
BDN/LAN/SAC DH7 133 G7
Donald Av RDHAMSE DH6 128 D1
Donald St GOS/KPK NE3 46 E5 5
Doncaster Rd JES NE2 6 B2
Doncrest Rd WASHN NE37 82 D4
Don Dixon Dr JRW NE32 71 K3 1
Don Gdns BOL NE36 72 D5
Donkin Rd WASHN NE37 82 B6
Donkin Ter TYNE/NSHE NE30 51 G3
Donnington Cl SWCK/CAS SR5 84 E4 1
Donnington Ct GOS/KPK NE3 47 F6
Donnini Pl DHAM DH1 17 J1
Donnison Gdns SUND SR1 15 H4 1
Donridge WASHN NE37 82 D4
Don Rd JRW NE32 60 B4
Don St DUN/TMV NE11 80 C1
Donvale Rd WASHN NE37 82 C4
Don Vw BOL NE36 72 D5
Dorcas Av
BW/LEM/TK/HW NE15 55 G6
Dorchester Cl
WD/WHPE/BLK NE5 43 K7 4
Dorchester Ct MONK NE25 29 K2
Dorchester Gdns
LWF/SPW/WRK NE9 81 F3
Doreen Av SEA/MUR SR7 120 A2
Doric Rd BDN/LAN/SAC DH7 132 E3
Dorking Av NSHW NE29 50 C6
Dorking Cl BLYTH NE24 25 G3
Dorking Rd
CLDN/WHIT/ROK SR6 86 D1
Dorlonco Vls
BDN/LAN/SAC DH7 133 H7
Dormand Dr PLEE/EAS SR8 136 D7
Dornoch Crs FELL NE10 70 A6 1
Dorrington Rd GOS/KPK NE3 45 J4
Dorset Av CLDN/WHIT/ROK SR6 86 E1
CLS/BIR/GTL DH3 93 J5
HAR/WTLS NE34 62 B4
HEBB NE31 59 H6
WLSD/HOW NE28 58 C1
Dorset Gv NSHW NE29 50 B1
Dorset La SUNDSW SR3 98 B7
Dorset Rd
BW/LEM/TK/HW NE15 54 D5
GATE NE8 6 C8
Dorset St HLH DH5 128 B1
Double Rw MONK NE25 29 J3
Douglas Cl HAR/WTLS NE34 61 G7 2
Douglas Ct STLY/ANP DH9 101 G4
Douglas Gdns DUN/TMV NE11 68 A5
Douglas Rd
CLDN/WHIT/ROK SR6 86 E1
Douglass St WLSD/HOW NE28 58 C1
Douglas St WLSD/HOW NE28 59 J2 4
Douglas Ter ELS/FEN NE4 4 F6
HLS DH4 95 K6
Douglas Vls DHAM DH1 17 G2
Doulting Cl LGB/KIL NE12 47 H4 3
Dove Av JRW NE32 72 A1
Dove Cl BDN/LAN/SAC DH7 133 F6 1
Dovecote Cl MONK NE25 40 A3 1
Dovecote Rd LGB/KIL NE12 48 A3
Dovedale Av BLYTH NE24 20 C7
Dovedale Gdns LGB/HTN NE7 47 G7
LWF/SPW/WRK NE9 81 G1
Dovedale Rd
CLDN/WHIT/ROK SR6 74 C7
Dover Cl BDLGTN NE22 18 D5
WD/WHPE/BLK NE5 44 A7
Dovercourt Rd
BYK/HTN/WLK NE6 58 C7
Dowling Av MONK NE25 40 D5
Downe Cl BLYTH NE24 25 G3 2
Downend Rd
WD/WHPE/BLK NE5 44 C7
Downfield WASHN NE37 83 F2 1
Downham WD/WHPE/BLK NE5 54 D2
Downhill La BOL NE36 84 C1 1
WASHN NE37 84 B1
Downs La HLH DH5 118 A3
Downs Pit La HLH DH5 118 C3
Downswood LGB/KIL NE12 38 B6 2
Dowsey Rd RDHAMSE DH6 126 C7
Dowson Sq SEA/MUR SR7 119 F5
Doxford Av HLH DH5 117 J2
Doxford Dr PLEE/EAS SR8 136 A4
Doxford Gdns
WD/WHPE/BLK NE5 55 H2 4
Doxford Park Wy SUNDSW SR3 109 J1
Doxford Pl CRAM NE23 28 C3 1
Doxford Ter HLH DH5 117 J2
Dragon La DHAM DH1 125 J7
Drake Cl SSH NE33 61 F3
The Dray PONT/DH NE20 32 D6
Drayton Rd
CLDN/WHIT/ROK SR6 86 D1
GOS/KPK NE3 45 J6
The Drive CLS/BIR/GTL DH3 93 K5
FELL NE10 12 E8
GOS/KPK NE3 46 C7
LGB/HTN NE7 47 H6
LWF/SPW/WRK NE9 69 F6
TYNE/NSHE NE30 51 H1
WASHN NE37 82 E4
WD/WHPE/BLK NE5 54 D3
WICK/BNPF NE16 67 G6
WLSD/HOW NE28 58 D1
Dronfield Cl CLSW/PEL DH2 105 F6
Drove Rd BW/LEM/TK/HW NE15 42 E7
Drummond Crs HAR/WTLS NE34 60 D6
Drummond Rd GOS/KPK NE3 45 K7
Drummond Ter
TYNE/NSHE NE30 51 F3
Drumoyne Cl SUNDSW SR3 109 F1
Drumoyne Gdns MONK NE25 40 B6
Drum Rd CLSW/PEL DH2 93 H7
Drumsheugh Pl
WD/WHPE/BLK NE5 55 F1
Druridge Av
CLDN/WHIT/ROK SR6 74 D7
Druridge Crs BLYTH NE24 24 D2
HAR/WTLS NE34 62 B3
Druridge Dr BLYTH NE24 24 D2
WD/WHPE/BLK NE5 55 H2

Drury La NSHW NE29 50 A3
SUND SR1 15 G4
Drybeck Ct CRAM NE23 23 K7
Drybeck Sq SUNDSW SR3 110 B1 5
Drybeck Wk CRAM NE23 23 K7 6
Dryborough St
MLFD/PNYW SR4 14 A3 1
Dryburgh WASHS NE38 94 E1
Dryburgh Cl NSHW NE29 50 C2
Dryburn Hl DHAM DH1 124 B5
Dryburn Rd DHAM DH1 124 B4
Dryden Cl HAR/WTLS NE34 73 F2
STLY/ANP DH9 102 E1
Dryden Rd LWF/SPW/WRK NE9 11 H8
Dryden St SWCK/CAS SR5 86 A3
Drysdale Ct DIN/WO NE13 36 A3
Drysdale Crs DIN/WO NE13 36 A3
Dubmire Cottages HLS DH4 107 H7
Dubmire Ct HLS DH4 107 J7
Duchess Crs JRW NE32 71 K1
Duchess Crs East JRW NE32 71 K1 2
Duchess Dr
BW/LEM/TK/HW NE15 54 E4
Duchess St WBAY NE26 40 E4
Duckpool La WICK/BNPF NE16 67 G5
Duddon Cl PLEE/EAS SR8 137 F4 3
Duddon Pl LWF/SPW/WRK NE9 81 H1
Dudley Av
CLDN/WHIT/ROK SR6 86 D1 4
Dudley Dr CRAM NE23 37 G1
Dudley Gdns SUNDSW SR3 109 G1
Dudley La CRAM NE23 28 B3
DIN/WO NE13 36 C1
Dugdale Rd GOS/KPK NE3 45 H5
Duke's Av HEBB NE31 59 F7
Dukes Dr GOS/KPK NE3 46 B1
Dukesfield CRAM NE23 28 C3 2
Dukes Meadow DIN/WO NE13 44 C2
Duke St FELL NE10 13 J5
MLFD/PNYW SR4 86 A7 4
SEA/MUR SR7 111 H7
WBAY NE26 40 E4
Duke St North
CLDN/WHIT/ROK SR6 86 D3
Dukesway DUN/TMV NE11 68 B7
Dulverston Cl
WD/WHPE/BLK NE5 44 A7 1
Dulverton Av SSH NE33 61 H4
Dumfries Crs JRW NE32 60 C7
Dunbar Cl WD/WHPE/BLK NE5 44 A7
Dunbar St MLFD/PNYW SR4 97 K1
Dunblane Crs
WD/WHPE/BLK NE5 54 D3
Dunblane Dr BLYTH NE24 25 G3
Dunblane Rd
CLDN/WHIT/ROK SR6 74 E7
Dunbreck Gv MLFD/PNYW SR4 98 A2
Duncan St BYK/HTN/WLK NE6 58 C5
GATE NE8 11 L6
MLFD/PNYW SR4 85 K6
Duncombe Crs STLY/ANP DH9 90 D6
Duncow La DHAM DH1 16 D5
Dun Cow St SUND SR1 14 D4 1
Dundas St CLDN/WHIT/ROK SR6 14 E1
Dundee Cl WD/WHPE/BLK NE5 44 A7
Dundrennan WASHS NE38 94 E3
Dunelm Dr BOL NE36 73 F5
HLS DH4 108 A7
Dunelm Rd HLH DH5 117 J4
Dunelm St SSH NE33 3 J9
Dunelm Wk PLEE/EAS SR8 136 E3 2
Dunford Gdns
WD/WHPE/BLK NE5 44 B6 1
Dunholm Cl HLH DH5 117 H1
Dunholme Cl DHAM DH1 124 C4
Dunholme Rd ELS/FEN NE4 4 A7
Dunira Cl JES NE2 57 F1 2
Dunkeld Cl BLYTH NE24 25 G3
Dunkirk Av HLH DH5 117 J1
Dunlin Cl RYTON NE40 53 G7 3
Dunlin Dr BLYTH NE24 25 G3
WASHS NE38 94 B3
Dunlop Cl LGB/HTN NE7 47 J6 3
Dunlop Crs HAR/WTLS NE34 62 A5
Dunmoor Cl GOS/KPK NE3 46 A6 2
Dunmore Av
CLDN/WHIT/ROK SR6 74 E7
Dunmorlie St BYK/HTN/WLK NE6 7 J5
Dunn Av SUNDSW SR3 98 A5
Dunning St SUND SR1 14 D3
Dunnlynn Cl SUNDSW SR3 109 J1 4
Dunnock Dr WASHS NE38 94 B4
WICK/BNPF NE16 78 E2
Dunn Rd PLEE/EAS SR8 136 E3
Dunn's Ter JES NE2 4 E1 1
Dunn St ELS/FEN NE4 9 L1
Dunnykirk Av GOS/KPK NE3 45 H5 4
Dunsdale Dr CRAM NE23 23 K7
Dunsdale Rd MONK NE25 30 B6
Dunsgreen PONT/DH NE20 33 G4
Dunsley Gdns DIN/WO NE13 35 F2
Dunsmuir Gv GATE NE8 10 D8
Dunstable Pl
WD/WHPE/BLK NE5 43 K7 5
Dunstanburgh BDLGTN NE22 18 D5
Dunstanburgh Cl BDLGTN NE22 18 D5
WASHS NE38 94 D2
Dunstanburgh Rd
BYK/HTN/WLK NE6 7 K7
Dunstan Cl CLSW/PEL DH2 105 G6
Dunston Bank DUN/TMV NE11 67 J5
Dunston Pl BLYTH NE24 20 D7
Dunston Rd DUN/TMV NE11 9 G5
Dunvegan CLS/BIR/GTL DH3 94 A4
Dunvegan Av CLSW/PEL DH2 105 H6
Durant Rd CNUT NE1 5 L5
Durban St BLYTH NE24 21 F5
Durham Av PLEE/EAS SR8 137 G2
WASHN NE37 82 D5
Durham Cl BDLGTN NE22 18 D5 2
Durham Dr BOLCOL NE35 71 K4
JRW NE32 71 K2
Durham Gdns
BDN/LAN/SAC DH7 113 G7
Durham Gv JRW NE32 71 J2
Durham La PLEE/EAS SR8 130 B6
Durham Pl CLS/BIR/GTL DH3 93 J5
GATE NE8 11 H6 1
Durham Rd ASHBK/HED/RY SR2 14 B6
BDN/LAN/SAC DH7 113 H6
CLS/BIR/GTL DH3 93 J1
CRAM NE23 23 J6
GATE NE8 11 G6
HLH DH5 108 D4
HLS DH4 108 C7
LWF/SPW/WRK NE9 81 F1
STLY/ANP DH9 101 J4
SUNDSW SR3 98 A3
Durham St ELS/FEN NE4 4 B8
HLS DH4 107 J7
SEA/MUR SR7 111 H7
WLSD/HOW NE28 58 E1
Durham St West
WLSD/HOW NE28 58 E1 5
Durham Ter SUNDSW SR3 98 A5
Durham Wy PLEE/EAS SR8 136 C7
Duxfield Rd LGB/HTN NE7 47 H7
Dwyer Crs ASHBK/HED/RY SR2 111 F1
Dyer Sq SWCK/CAS SR5 86 B3
Dykefield Av GOS/KPK NE3 45 J3
Dyke Heads La RYTON NE40 64 D2
Dykelands Rd
CLDN/WHIT/ROK SR6 86 D1
Dykelands Wy HAR/WTLS NE34 72 D1
Dykenook Cl WICK/BNPF NE16 78 E1
Dykes Wy FELL NE10 69 K7
Dymock Ct WD/WHPE/BLK NE5 45 F5

E

Eaglescliffe Dr LGB/HTN NE7 47 K7
Eaglesdene HLH DH5 117 K4 2
Eagle St DUN/TMV NE11 68 B6
Ealing Dr TYNE/NSHE NE30 51 G1
Eardulph Av CLS/BIR/GTL DH3 105 K4
Earlington Ct LGB/KIL NE12 48 A1 2
Earl's Dr BW/LEM/TK/HW NE15 54 E4
LWF/SPW/WRK NE9 81 F1
Earl's Gdns BLYTH NE24 20 E6 1
Earls Gn HLH DH5 117 G5
Earl St MLFD/PNYW SR4 14 A5
SEA/MUR SR7 111 G7
Earlsway DUN/TMV NE11 68 C5
Earlswood Av
LWF/SPW/WRK NE9 81 F1
Earlswood Gv BLYTH NE24 25 F4
Earnshaw Wy MONK NE25 40 B2
Earsdon Cl WD/WHPE/BLK NE5 54 E1
Earsdon Rd GOS/KPK NE3 45 J7
HLH DH5 108 D7 3
MONK NE25 40 B5
SMOOR NE27 39 G6
Earsdon Vw SMOOR NE27 39 H5
Easby Cl GOS/KPK NE3 46 D2
Easby Rd WASHS NE38 95 F2
Easdale Av GOS/KPK NE3 46 C1
Easedale WBAY NE26 31 F2
Easedale Gdns
LWF/SPW/WRK NE9 81 G1
Easington Av CRAM NE23 23 J5
LWF/SPW/WRK NE9 81 J2
Easington St PLEE/EAS SR8 130 E4 1
SWCK/CAS SR5 14 D2
Easington St North
SWCK/CAS SR5 14 D2
East Acre BLAY NE21 66 B2
East Acres DIN/WO NE13 35 F1
East Av HAR/WTLS NE34 62 A5
LGB/KIL NE12 47 K4
WASHS NE38 94 E5
East Back Pde
ASHBK/HED/RY SR2 15 K7
East Bailey LGB/KIL NE12 37 K5 7
LGB/KIL NE12 37 K6 2
East Boldon Rd
CLDN/WHIT/ROK SR6 73 K3 1
Eastbourne Av
BYK/HTN/WLK NE6 58 C4
GATE NE8 10 F7
Eastbourne Gdns
BYK/HTN/WLK NE6 58 C4
WBAY NE26 40 D3
Eastbourne Gv SSH NE33 3 K7 1
Eastcheap BYK/HTN/WLK NE6 57 J2 1
East Cleft Rd
ASHBK/HED/RY SR2 14 B6
East Clere BDN/LAN/SAC DH7 122 B3
Eastcliffe Av GOS/KPK NE3 46 A7
East Cl HAR/WTLS NE34 62 A5
Eastcombe Cl BOLCOL NE35 72 C2 5
Eastcote Ter BYK/HTN/WLK NE6 13 H1
East Crs BDLGTN NE22 19 K4
East Cross St SUND SR1 14 F3
Eastdene Rd SEA/MUR SR7 120 A1
Eastdene Wy PLEE/EAS SR8 137 G5
East Dr BLYTH NE24 24 E3 1
CLDN/WHIT/ROK SR6 73 J4
East End WBAY NE26 31 H4
Eastern Av BDN/LAN/SAC DH7 122 B3
DUN/TMV NE11 80 D1
Eastern Wy PONT/DH NE20 33 F6
WD/WHPE/BLK NE5 55 H1
Eastfield PLEE/EAS SR8 137 H5
Eastfield Av BYK/HTN/WLK NE6 58 C3
MONK NE25 40 B5
Eastfield Rd HAR/WTLS NE34 61 K3 1
LGB/KIL NE12 47 J4
East Flds CLDN/WHIT/ROK SR6 75 F4
Eastfield St MLFD/PNYW SR4 97 K1
Eastfield Ter LGB/KIL NE12 47 K4 2
East Forest Hall Rd
LGB/KIL NE12 48 A2 3
East Front JES NE2 5 L1
Eastgarth WD/WHPE/BLK NE5 44 E5
East Ga GATE NE8 11 G1
Eastgate STKFD/GP NE62 19 F1
East George Potts St
SSH NE33 61 H2 2
East Gra MONK NE25 30 C6
SWCK/CAS SR5 86 C2
East Grange Ct
PLEE/EAS SR8 130 C6 3
Eastgreen STKFD/GP NE62 19 F1
East Gv MLFD/PNYW SR4 97 F1
East Hill Rd GATE NE8 11 M5
Eastlands BLAY NE21 65 K3
LGB/HTN NE7 47 G7
East Lea BLAY NE21 66 A4
Eastlea Crs SEA/MUR SR7 120 B1
Eastlea Rd SEA/MUR SR7 120 A1
Eastleigh Cl BOLCOL NE35 72 C4
East Moffett St SSH NE33 61 H2 3
East Moor Rd MLFD/PNYW SR4 85 K6
East Park Gdns BLAY NE21 66 A3 2
East Park Rd
LWF/SPW/WRK NE9 69 F6
East Park Vw BLYTH NE24 21 H7
East Percy St TYNE/NSHE NE30 51 G4
East Riggs BDLGTN NE22 19 F6
East Side Av BDN/LAN/SAC DH7 123 F6
East Stevenson St SSH NE33 61 H2 4
East Stoneycroft
LGB/KIL NE12 38 A7 1
East St CLDN/WHIT/ROK SR6 75 F4
CLSW/PEL DH2 104 A2
GATE NE8 11 G1
ROWG NE39 76 B1
SSH NE33 3 G7
STLY/ANP DH9 91 F7
TYNE/NSHE NE30 51 J2
East Thorp WD/WHPE/BLK NE5 44 D5
East Vw CLDN/WHIT/ROK SR6 86 E2
HEBB NE31 59 F7
PLEE/EAS SR8 131 F3
SWCK/CAS SR5 85 G4 3
East View Ter
WICK/BNPF NE16 67 F4 1
East Vines SUND SR1 15 J3
Eastward Gn MONK NE25 40 B5
Eastway HAR/WTLS NE34 62 B6
Eastwood BDN/LAN/SAC DH7 113 H6
Eastwood Av BLYTH NE24 25 F4
Eastwood Cl CRAM NE23 37 J4 1
Eastwood Gdns FELL NE10 12 A5
GOS/KPK NE3 45 K6
LWF/SPW/WRK NE9 69 G6
Eastwood Pl CRAM NE23 23 J5 1
Eaton Pl ELS/FEN NE4 4 B6
Eavers Ct HAR/WTLS NE34 61 G6 7
Ebba Wk GOS/KPK NE3 46 D5
Ebchester Ct GOS/KPK NE3 45 G5
Ebchester St HAR/WTLS NE34 60 E6
Ebdon La CLDN/WHIT/ROK SR6 86 D1
Ebor St BYK/HTN/WLK NE6 57 J3
HAR/WTLS NE34 60 E7
Eccleston Cl SMOOR NE27 38 E5
Eccleston Rd SSH NE33 3 M9
Ecgfrid Ter JRW NE32 60 A6
Eddison Rd WASHS NE38 95 H2
Eddleston Av GOS/KPK NE3 46 A7
Eddrington Gv
WD/WHPE/BLK NE5 44 A7
Ede Av DUN/TMV NE11 9 G8
HAR/WTLS NE34 62 B5
Edenbridge Crs LGB/KIL NE12 47 H3
Eden Cl WD/WHPE/BLK NE5 54 A1
Edendale Av BLYTH NE24 20 D6
BYK/HTN/WLK NE6 58 C5
Edendale Ter GATE NE8 11 G8
PLEE/EAS SR8 137 G4 1
Edenfield STLY/ANP DH9 92 A7
Edenhill Rd PLEE/EAS SR8 137 F3
Eden House Rd
MLFD/PNYW SR4 14 A8
Eden La PLEE/EAS SR8 136 E2
Eden Pl TYNE/NSHE NE30 50 E1
Eden Rd DHAM DH1 124 D3
Eden St PLEE/EAS SR8 137 H3
WLSD/HOW NE28 58 D2 6
Eden St West CLS/BIR/GTL DH3 106 E7
SUND SR1 14 C4
Edgar St GOS/KPK NE3 47 F5
Edgecote WASHN NE37 83 H5
Edge Ct DHAM DH1 17 K3
Edgefield Av GOS/KPK NE3 45 K5
Edgefield Dr CRAM NE23 23 J5
Edge Hl PONT/DH NE20 42 D1
Edgehill Cl PONT/DH NE20 42 E1
Edge Mt LGB/KIL NE12 37 K5
Edgewood PONT/DH NE20 33 F7
Edgewood Av BDLGTN NE22 19 J5 2
Edgeworth Cl BOLCOL NE35 72 C2 6
Edgeworth Crs
CLDN/WHIT/ROK SR6 86 D3 2
Edgmond Ct
ASHBK/HED/RY SR2 98 E6
Edgware Rd GATE NE8 11 K7
Edhill Av HAR/WTLS NE34 60 D6
Edinburgh Rd JRW NE32 60 C7
Edington Gv TYNE/NSHE NE30 50 E1
Edington Rd TYNE/NSHE NE30 50 E1
Edison Gdns GATE NE8 10 E9
Edison St SEA/MUR SR7 119 H5
Edith Av BLAY NE21 66 A2
Edith St ASHBK/HED/RY SR2 15 H9
JRW NE32 59 J4
SEA/MUR SR7 121 F3
SWCK/CAS SR5 86 C3 2
TYNE/NSHE NE30 51 G2
Edlingham Cl GOS/KPK NE3 47 F6
Edlingham Ct HLH DH5 108 D7 4
Edlingham Rd DHAM DH1 124 D4
Edmondsley La
BDN/LAN/SAC DH7 113 G3
Edmund Pl
LWF/SPW/WRK NE9 69 F7 5
Edna Ter WD/WHPE/BLK NE5 44 E7
Edward Av PLEE/EAS SR8 137 G3
Edward Burdis St
SWCK/CAS SR5 86 B3 7
Edward Cain Ct
PLEE/EAS SR8 137 H3 1
Edward Pl ELS/FEN NE4 4 E6
Edward Rd BDLGTN NE22 19 K4 2
CLS/BIR/GTL DH3 93 H1
WLSD/HOW NE28 49 H7
Edwardson Rd
BDN/LAN/SAC DH7 133 J7
Edwards Rd WBAY NE26 41 G5
Edward St BLYTH NE24 21 F6
DHAM DH1 17 K2
GOS/KPK NE3 46 C5 1
HEBB NE31 58 E4 1
HLH DH5 117 K4
SEA/MUR SR7 120 E2 3
STLY/ANP DH9 103 G5
SUNDSW SR3 98 A7
Edward's Wk CNUT NE1 5 J4
Edward Ter BDN/LAN/SAC DH7 132 E2
Edwin Gv WLSD/HOW NE28 49 J7
Edwins Av LGB/KIL NE12 48 A2
Edwin's Av South LGB/KIL NE12 48 A2
Edwin St HLH DH5 108 C6
MLFD/PNYW SR4 85 J6
Egerton Rd HAR/WTLS NE34 61 G5
Egerton St ASHBK/HED/RY SR2 15 G7
BW/LEM/TK/HW NE15 55 G7
Eggleston Cl
CLS/BIR/GTL DH3 115 J1 1
DHAM DH1 125 F3
Eggleston Dr SUNDSW SR3 98 A4
Egham Rd WD/WHPE/BLK NE5 54 A1
Eglesfield Rd SSH NE33 61 G3
Eglinton St SWCK/CAS SR5 86 C4
Eglinton St North
SWCK/CAS SR5 86 C4
Egremont Dr
LWF/SPW/WRK NE9 69 H6 3
Egremont Gdns
LWF/SPW/WRK NE9 69 G6 4
Egremont Gv PLEE/EAS SR8 136 B7
Egremont Pl WBAY NE26 41 F5
Eider Cl BLYTH NE24 25 G4
Eighteenth Av BLYTH NE24 24 E2 2
Eighth Av BLYTH NE24 25 F2 2
BYK/HTN/WLK NE6 7 G1
CLSW/PEL DH2 105 H4
Eighth St PLEE/EAS SR8 137 H3
Eighton Ter LWF/SPW/WRK NE9 81 K2
Eishort Wy LGB/KIL NE12 47 H4
Eland Cl GOS/KPK NE3 45 H5
Eland Edge PONT/DH NE20 33 H3
Eland La PONT/DH NE20 33 H2
Elberfeld Ct JRW NE32 59 K5
Elder Cl BDN/LAN/SAC DH7 133 G1
Elder Gv HAR/WTLS NE34 61 K7
LWF/SPW/WRK NE9 69 F7 6
Elderwood Gdns
DUN/TMV NE11 68 B7
Eldon La CNUT NE1 5 K6
Eldon Pl BW/LEM/TK/HW NE15 54 B4
Eldon Rd BW/LEM/TK/HW NE15 54 B4
Eldon St GATE NE8 11 J3
MLFD/PNYW SR4 86 A7
SSH NE33 61 F2
WLSD/HOW NE28 59 J1
Eleanor St SSH NE33 3 K6
TYNE/NSHE NE30 41 G5
Elemore Cl
BDN/LAN/SAC DH7 122 A3 2
Elemore La HLH DH5 128 A1
RDHAMSE DH6 127 H3
Elemore St RDHAMSE DH6 126 E4
Elemore Vw RDHAMSE DH6 128 D2
Elenbel Av BDLGTN NE22 19 J5
Eleventh Av BLYTH NE24 25 G1 3
Eleventh St PLEE/EAS SR8 137 G3
RHTLP TS27 137 K6
Elford Cl MONK NE25 40 B4
Elfordleigh HLS DH4 108 A3 2
Elgar Av WD/WHPE/BLK NE5 54 A1 5
Elgar Cl STLY/ANP DH9 102 E2
Elgin Av SEA/MUR SR7 120 A1
WLSD/HOW NE28 49 H6
Elgin Cl NSHW NE29 50 A2 3
Elgin Gdns BYK/HTN/WLK NE6 58 B5
Elgin Gv STLY/ANP DH9 103 F1
Elgin Rd LWF/SPW/WRK NE9 11 L8
Elgin St JRW NE32 60 C7
Elgy Rd GOS/KPK NE3 46 B7
Elisabeth Av CLS/BIR/GTL DH3 81 H7
Elizabeth Ct LGB/KIL NE12 48 C2
Elizabeth Crs CRAM NE23 37 G1
Elizabeth Diamond Gdns
SSH NE33 61 F3 2
Elizabeth Dr LGB/KIL NE12 48 C2
Elizabeth Rd WLSD/HOW NE28 49 J7
Elizabeth St BYK/HTN/WLK NE6 6 D4
HLH DH5 108 C6
SEA/MUR SR7 120 D1 1
SWCK/CAS SR5 85 F4 3
SWCK/CAS SR5 86 C2 2
Ellam Av DHAM DH1 134 B2
Ell-dene Crs FELL NE10 12 E9
Ellersmere Gdns
TYNE/NSHE NE30 41 F7 1
Ellerton Wy CRAM NE23 23 J5 2
FELL NE10 12 A8
Ellesmere HLS DH4 107 F4
Ellesmere Av BYK/HTN/WLK NE6 7 M2
WD/WHPE/BLK NE5 54 E1
Ellesmere Ct
ASHBK/HED/RY SR2 98 E5
Ellesmere Dr SEA/MUR SR7 120 A1
Ellesmere Rd ELS/FEN NE4 55 J6
Ellington Cl
ASHBK/HED/RY SR2 111 F2 1
BW/LEM/TK/HW NE15 53 K4
Elliot Cl HLS DH4 95 K7
Elliot Rd FELL NE10 11 M5 1
Elliott Dr FELL NE10 12 D7
Elliott Gdns WLSD/HOW NE28 48 C6
Elliott Rd PLEE/EAS SR8 136 E3
Elliott St BLYTH NE24 24 D3
Elliott Ter ELS/FEN NE4 4 C6
Ellison Pl CNUT NE1 5 L5
JRW NE32 59 K3
LWF/SPW/WRK NE9 81 F1
Ellison Rd DUN/TMV NE11 9 G8
PLEE/EAS SR8 137 F3
Ellison St GATE NE8 11 G1
HEBB NE31 59 F5 2
JRW NE32 59 K4 4
Ellis Rd SWCK/CAS SR5 86 A2 1
Ellis Sq SWCK/CAS SR5 86 B2
Elm Av BDN/LAN/SAC DH7 133 G7
CLSW/PEL DH2 104 C1
DIN/WO NE13 35 F2
DUN/TMV NE11 9 H9
HAR/WTLS NE34 61 K7
WICK/BNPF NE16 8 A8
Elm Cl CRAM NE23 23 J5
Elm Ct WICK/BNPF NE16 67 F7
Elm Crs CLSW/PEL DH2 114 A5
Elm Croft Rd LGB/KIL NE12 48 A3
Elm Dr BDLGTN NE22 19 F7
CLDN/WHIT/ROK SR6 75 G3
Elmfield Av DHAM DH1 125 J6
Elmfield Cl SUNDSW SR3 109 F1
Elmfield Gdns WLSD/HOW NE28 48 B6
Elmfield Gv GOS/KPK NE3 46 B7
Elmfield Pk GOS/KPK NE3 46 B7
Elmfield Rd
BW/LEM/TK/HW NE15 53 G1 2
GOS/KPK NE3 46 B7
HEBB NE31 71 H1
Elmfield Ter HEBB NE31 59 H7
Elm Gv BDN/LAN/SAC DH7 133 G1
GOS/KPK NE3 45 K3
HAR/WTLS NE34 61 K7
LGB/KIL NE12 47 K1
WICK/BNPF NE16 77 H7
Elm Rd BLAY NE21 66 B2
NSHW NE29 49 K3
PONT/DH NE20 33 J4
Elmsford Gv LGB/KIL NE12 47 J4
Elmsleigh Gdns
CLDN/WHIT/ROK SR6 74 A1
The Elms HLH DH5 118 C7
Elm St BDN/LAN/SAC DH7 122 B3
CLS/BIR/GTL DH3 105 J4
DUN/TMV NE11 68 B6
JRW NE32 59 J4
STLY/ANP DH9 102 B3
WICK/BNPF NE16 79 F3
Elm St West WICK/BNPF NE16 79 F3
Elmtree Ct SEA/MUR SR7 120 D3
Elmtree Gdns MONK NE25 40 C6
Elmtree Gv GOS/KPK NE3 46 B6
Elm Trees BLYTH NE24 25 F1 2
Elmway CLSW/PEL DH2 105 G2
Elmwood Av DIN/WO NE13 36 B4
SWCK/CAS SR5 85 K2
Elmwood Crs
BYK/HTN/WLK NE6 58 B2 1
Elmwood Dr PONT/DH NE20 33 G2
Elmwood Gdns DUN/TMV NE11 68 B6
Elmwood Gv WBAY NE26 40 E3
Elmwood Rd MONK NE25 40 C5
Elmwood St ASHBK/HED/RY SR2 14 B7
HLS DH4 107 G6
Elrick Cl WD/WHPE/BLK NE5 54 A1 6
Elrington Gdns
WD/WHPE/BLK NE5 55 F3 2
Elsdon Av MONK NE25 30 A5
Elsdonburn Rd SUNDSW SR3 109 J2 3
Elsdon Cl BLYTH NE24 20 E7
PLEE/EAS SR8 136 D7
Elsdon Ct WICK/BNPF NE16 66 E7
Elsdon Dr LGB/KIL NE12 48 B2
Elsdon Gdns DUN/TMV NE11 9 J8
Elsdon Pl NSHW NE29 2 C4
Elsdon Rd DHAM DH1 124 E3
GOS/KPK NE3 46 C5
WICK/BNPF NE16 66 E6
Elsdon St NSHW NE29 2 C4
Elsdon Ter NSHW NE29 50 B6
Elsing Cl WD/WHPE/BLK NE5 45 F6
Elstob Pl BYK/HTN/WLK NE6 7 M9
SUNDSW SR3 98 A4
Elston Cl WD/WHPE/BLK NE5 54 A1 7
Elstree Ct DIN/WO NE13 45 F3 1
Elstree Gdns BLYTH NE24 25 F4 1
Elswick East Ter ELS/FEN NE4 4 F8
Elswick Rd ELS/FEN NE4 55 J7
Elswick Rw ELS/FEN NE4 4 E7
Elswick Wy HAR/WTLS NE34 60 E5
Elterwater Rd CLSW/PEL DH2 105 H6
Elton St East WLSD/HOW NE28 58 D2
Elton St West WLSD/HOW NE28 58 C2
Eltringham Cl
WLSD/HOW NE28 58 C1 2
Elvaston Rd RYTON NE40 52 E5
Elvet Br DHAM DH1 16 D4
Elvet Cl DIN/WO NE13 36 B3 2
Elvet Crs DHAM DH1 16 E5
Elvet Gn CLSW/PEL DH2 105 J5
HLH DH5 117 K7 1
Elvet Hill Rd DHAM DH1 16 C8
Elvet Waterside DHAM DH1 16 E4
Elvington St
CLDN/WHIT/ROK SR6 86 E2
Elwin Cl WBAY NE26 31 G3
Elwin Pl CLSW/PEL DH2 104 E1
Elwin Ter ASHBK/HED/RY SR2 14 C6
Elwyn Cl WBAY NE26 31 G3
Ely Cl LGB/KIL NE12 47 K6
Ely Rd DHAM DH1 124 E1 2
Elysium La GATE NE8 10 B6
Ely St GATE NE8 10 F5
Embankment Rd SEA/MUR SR7 111 H6
Embassy Gdns
BW/LEM/TK/HW NE15 55 F5
Emblehope WASHN NE37 82 C7
Emblehope Dr GOS/KPK NE3 46 A6
Embleton Av GOS/KPK NE3 46 A4 3
HAR/WTLS NE34 62 B3
WLSD/HOW NE28 49 G5
Embleton Cl DHAM DH1 124 E3 2
Embleton Crs NSHW NE29 50 A2
Embleton Dr BLYTH NE24 24 E2 3
Embleton Gdns
WD/WHPE/BLK NE5 55 H2 3
Embleton Rd FELL NE10 13 M3
NSHW NE29 50 A2
Embleton St SEA/MUR SR7 120 E3 1
Emden Rd GOS/KPK NE3 45 J4
Emily St BYK/HTN/WLK NE6 7 L5
GATE NE8 11 M5
Emily St East SEA/MUR SR7 120 E1 2
Emlyn Rd HAR/WTLS NE34 61 G5
Emmbrook Cl HLH DH5 117 G4 1
Emmerson Pl SMOOR NE27 39 G6
Empress Rd BYK/HTN/WLK NE6 58 D7
Empress St SWCK/CAS SR5 86 C4 3
Emsworth Rd SWCK/CAS SR5 86 A2
Enderby Rd MLFD/PNYW SR4 14 A3
Enfield Av WICK/BNPF NE16 67 F3

Enfield Gdns WICK/BNPF NE16 ... 67 F7
Enfield Rd LWF/SPW/WRK NE9 ... 11 C8
SEA/MUR SR7 ... 120 A1
Enfield St MLFD/PNYW SR4 ... 85 K6 2
Engine Inn Rd WLSD/HOW NE28 .. 49 H6
Engine La LWF/SPW/WRK NE9 ... 81 F1
Englemann Wy SUNDSW SR3 ... 109 J3
Enid Av CLDN/WHIT/ROK SR6 ... 86 D2
Enid St DIN/WO NE13 ... 36 A5 2
Ennerdale ASHBK/HED/RY SR2 ... 14 D9
CLS/BIR/GTL DH3 ... 93 K4
Ennerdale Cl DHAM DH1 ... 126 B5 2
SEA/MUR SR7 ... 120 A1
Ennerdale Crs BLAY NE21 ... 65 K4 3
HLS DH4 ... 95 J6 1
Ennerdale Gdns
LWF/SPW/WRK NE9 ... 69 G7
WLSD/HOW NE28 ... 49 J6 2
Ennerdale Rd BLYTH NE24 ... 20 B5
BYK/HTN/WLK NE6 ... 58 B5
TYNE/NSHE NE30 ... 40 E7
Ennerdale St HLH DH5 ... 117 H6
Enslin St BYK/HTN/WLK NE6 ... 13 G1
Epping Cl SEA/MUR SR7 ... 120 A2
Eppleton Cl BDN/LAN/SAC DH7 .. 122 A3
Eppleton Hall Cl SEA/MUR SR7 ... 110 E7
Eppleton Rw HLH DH5 ... 118 A4 1
Epsom Cl NSHW NE29 ... 2 A5
Epsom Ct GOS/KPK NE3 ... 45 G3
Epsom Wy BLYTH NE24 ... 25 F4
Epworth STLY/ANP DH9 ... 90 A6
Equitable St
WLSD/HOW NE28 ... 58 D2 2
Erick St CNUT NE1 ... 5 L6 1
Erith Ter MLFD/PNYW SR4 ... 85 K7
Ernest St ASHBK/HED/RY SR2 ... 15 H9
BOLCOL NE35 ... 72 E4
CLSW/PEL DH2 ... 92 E7
Ernest Ter STLY/ANP DH9 ... 90 D6 3
Ernwill Av SWCK/CAS SR5 ... 85 F4
Errington Cl PONT/DH NE20 ... 32 E7
Errington Dr STLY/ANP DH9 ... 90 A6
Errington Rd PONT/DH NE20 ... 32 E6
Errington Ter LGB/KIL NE12 ... 48 A1 3
Errol Pl CLS/BIR/GTL DH3 ... 93 K4
Erskine Rd SSH NE33 ... 3 J9
Erskine Wy SSH NE33 ... 3 K8
Escallond Dr SEA/MUR SR7 ... 120 A2
Esdale ASHBK/HED/RY SR2 ... 110 E1
Esher Gdns BLYTH NE24 ... 25 F4
Esh Hillside BDN/LAN/SAC DH7 .. 122 C3
Eshmere Crs
WD/WHPE/BLK NE5 ... 54 A1
Eshott Cl GOS/KPK NE3 ... 46 A4
WD/WHPE/BLK NE5 ... 54 E2
Eskdale CLS/BIR/GTL DH3 ... 94 A5
HLS DH4 ... 95 J6 2
Eskdale Av BLYTH NE24 ... 20 C6
WLSD/HOW NE28 ... 48 E6
Eskdale Cl SEA/MUR SR7 ... 120 A1
Eskdale Ct HAR/WTLS NE34 ... 61 G5
Eskdale Dr JRW NE32 ... 72 B1
Eskdale Gdns
LWF/SPW/WRK NE9 ... 81 G1
Eskdale Rd CLDN/WHIT/ROK SR6 .. 75 F6
Eskdale St HAR/WTLS NE34 ... 61 G6 3
HLH DH5 ... 117 J6
Eskdale Ter JES NE2 ... 5 L1
WBAY NE26 ... 41 G5
Eskdale Wk PLEE/EAS SR8 ... 137 F4 1
Esk St LWF/SPW/WRK NE9 ... 11 M9
Eslington Rd JES NE2 ... 5 M2 1
Eslington Ter JES NE2 ... 56 E3
Esmaralda Gdns CRAM NE23 ... 29 H7 1
Esplanade WBAY NE26 ... 41 F4
Espley Cl LGB/KIL NE12 ... 48 C2
Espley Ct GOS/KPK NE3 ... 45 J3 3
Essen Wy SUNDSW SR3 ... 98 B3
Essex Cl ELS/FEN NE4 ... 9 L1
Essex Crs SEA/MUR SR7 ... 120 A1
Essex Dr WASHN NE37 ... 83 F4 1
Essex Gdns HAR/WTLS NE34 ... 62 C4
WLSD/HOW NE28 ... 49 G7
Essex Gv SUNDSW SR3 ... 98 A6
Essex Pl PLEE/EAS SR8 ... 136 D2
Essington Wy PLEE/EAS SR8 ... 136 D2
Esst Vw HLH DH5 ... 118 C7
Esther Sq WASHS NE38 ... 95 G2
Esthwaite Av CLSW/PEL DH2 ... 105 H6
Eston Ct BLYTH NE24 ... 20 D6
WLSD/HOW NE28 ... 48 B5 2
Eston Gv SWCK/CAS SR5 ... 86 C2
Estuary Wy MLFD/PNYW SR4 ... 85 F6
Etal Av MONK NE25 ... 41 F5
NSHW NE29 ... 50 B6
Etal Crs JRW NE32 ... 60 B7
SMOOR NE27 ... 39 H6
Etal La WD/WHPE/BLK NE5 ... 44 E7
Etal Pl GOS/KPK NE3 ... 46 A3 2
Etal Rd BLYTH NE24 ... 24 D4 1
Etal Wy WD/WHPE/BLK NE5 ... 45 F6
Ethel Av ASHBK/HED/RY SR2 ... 111 G1
BLAY NE21 ... 66 A2 3
Ethel St CRAM NE23 ... 37 G3
ELS/FEN NE4 ... 55 H7
Ethel Ter HAR/WTLS NE34 ... 61 F6
SWCK/CAS SR5 ... 85 F4
Etherley Cl DHAM DH1 ... 124 E2
Etherley Rd BYK/HTN/WLK NE6 ... 7 J2
Etherstone Av LGB/HTN NE7 ... 57 J1
Eton Cl CRAM NE23 ... 23 J5 3
Eton Sq HEBB NE31 ... 59 H5
Ettrick Cl LGB/KIL NE12 ... 37 J5 1
Ettrick Gdns GATE NE8 ... 11 M7
MLFD/PNYW SR4 ... 97 J2
Ettrick Gv MLFD/PNYW SR4 ... 97 K2
SUNDSW SR3 ... 97 K3 1
Ettrick Rd JRW NE32 ... 59 J6
European Wy MLFD/PNYW SR4 ... 85 H5
Euryalus Ct SSH NE33 ... 61 K2
Eustace Av NSHW NE29 ... 2 A2
Evanlade FELL NE10 ... 70 D6
Eva St BW/LEM/TK/HW NE15 ... 54 A5
Evelyn St ASHBK/HED/RY SR2 ... 14 A8
Evenwood Gdns
LWF/SPW/WRK NE9 ... 69 H7
Everard St CRAM NE23 ... 23 H4
Everest Gv BOL NE36 ... 73 F5 3
Eversleigh Pl
BW/LEM/TK/HW NE15 ... 53 G1 3
Eversley Pl WLSD/HOW NE28 ... 49 H7 3
Everton Dr SEA/MUR SR7 ... 120 A1
Everton La SWCK/CAS SR5 ... 86 A2
Evesham MLFD/PNYW SR4 ... 84 E7
Evesham Av WBAY NE26 ... 40 D3
Evesham Cl BOLCOL NE35 ... 72 D3
Evesham Garth GOS/KPK NE3 ... 45 J7
Evesham Rd SEA/MUR SR7 ... 120 A1
Eve St PLEE/EAS SR8 ... 137 J4 2
Evistones Gdns
BYK/HTN/WLK NE6 ... 12 E1
Evistones Rd
LWF/SPW/WRK NE9 ... 69 F6 2
Ewart Crs HAR/WTLS NE34 ... 60 C7
Ewbank Av ELS/FEN NE4 ... 55 J4
Ewehurst Crs STLY/ANP DH9 ... 89 G5
Ewehurst Pde STLY/ANP DH9 ... 89 G5
Ewehurst Rd STLY/ANP DH9 ... 89 G5
WICK/BNPF NE16 ... 89 H4
Ewen Ct NSHW NE29 ... 49 K2
Ewesley WASHS NE38 ... 94 C6
Ewesley Cl WD/WHPE/BLK NE5 ... 54 E1
Ewesley Gdns DIN/WO NE13 ... 36 B3
Ewesley Rd MLFD/PNYW SR4 ... 97 K1
Ewing Rd MLFD/PNYW SR4 ... 14 A8 1
Exeby Cl GOS/KPK NE3 ... 46 D2
Exeter Cl CLS/BIR/GTL DH3 ... 115 H2
Exeter Rd WLSD/HOW NE28 ... 48 C5
Exeter St BYK/HTN/WLK NE6 ... 58 C7
GATE NE8 ... 10 F6
MLFD/PNYW SR4 ... 85 K6
Exmouth Cl SEA/MUR SR7 ... 120 B2 3
Exmouth Rd NSHW NE29 ... 50 A5
Exmouth Sq SWCK/CAS SR5 ... 86 A2
Extension Rd SUND SR1 ... 15 K5
Eyemouth La SWCK/CAS SR5 ... 86 A2
Eyemouth Rd NSHW NE29 ... 50 A5 2
Eyre St STLY/ANP DH9 ... 102 B2

F

Faber Rd SWCK/CAS SR5 ... 86 A2
Factory Rd BLAY NE21 ... 54 B7
Fairbairn Rd PLEE/EAS SR8 ... 136 E2
Fairburn Av HLH DH5 ... 117 H2
LGB/HTN NE7 ... 47 J6
Fairdale Av LGB/HTN NE7 ... 47 J6
Fairfalls Ter BDN/LAN/SAC DH7 .. 132 D2
Fairfield CLSW/PEL DH2 ... 92 D7
LGB/KIL NE12 ... 47 F4
STLY/ANP DH9 ... 101 H2
Fairfield Av BLYTH NE24 ... 25 F3
WICK/BNPF NE16 ... 66 E7
Fairfield Cl DUN/TMV NE11 ... 9 G6
Fairfield Dr
CLDN/WHIT/ROK SR6 ... 74 E2
MONK NE25 ... 40 A5
TYNE/NSHE NE30 ... 41 F7
Fairfield Gn MONK NE25 ... 40 A5
Fairfield Rd JES NE2 ... 56 D2
Fairfields RYTON NE40 ... 52 D7
Fair Gn MONK NE25 ... 40 A5
Fairgreen Cl SUNDSW SR3 ... 110 A2 1
Fairhaven LWF/SPW/WRK NE9 ... 82 B3
Fairhaven Av
BYK/HTN/WLK NE6 ... 58 C5
Fairhill Cl LGB/HTN NE7 ... 47 J6
Fairholme Av HAR/WTLS NE34 ... 61 K5
Fairholme Rd SUNDSW SR3 ... 98 C3 3
Fairholm Rd ELS/FEN NE4 ... 55 J6
Fairlands East
CLDN/WHIT/ROK SR6 ... 86 D3 3
Fairlands West SWCK/CAS SR5 ... 86 D3
Fairlawn Gdns MLFD/PNYW SR4 .. 97 J2
Fairles St SSH NE33 ... 3 J5
Fairmead Wy MLFD/PNYW SR4 ... 96 E1
Fairmile Dr SUNDSW SR3 ... 110 A2
Fairmont Wy LGB/HTN NE7 ... 47 J6 4
Fairney Cl PONT/DH NE20 ... 33 H3
Fairney Edge PONT/DH NE20 ... 33 H3
Fairspring WD/WHPE/BLK NE5 ... 54 E1
Fair Vw BDN/LAN/SAC DH7 ... 113 F7
Fairview Av HAR/WTLS NE34 ... 61 K4
Fairview Gn LGB/HTN NE7 ... 47 J6 5
Fairville Cl CRAM NE23 ... 23 H5
Fairville Crs LGB/HTN NE7 ... 47 J6
Fairway Cl GOS/KPK NE3 ... 46 B2
Fairways MONK NE25 ... 40 A4
SUNDSW SR3 ... 98 B7 2
Fairways Av LGB/HTN NE7 ... 47 J5 2
The Fairways BOL NE36 ... 72 E5 2
BOL NE36 ... 73 G5 2
STLY/ANP DH9 ... 102 B5
The Fairway BLAY NE21 ... 53 J7
GOS/KPK NE3 ... 46 B2
WASHN NE37 ... 83 F2
Falconar's Ct CNUT NE1 ... 5 J7
Falconar St JES NE2 ... 5 M5
Falcon Pl LGB/KIL NE12 ... 47 G3
Falcon Wy HAR/WTLS NE34 ... 61 F7
Faldonside
BYK/HTN/WLK NE6 ... 57 K1 3
Falkirk LGB/KIL NE12 ... 37 K5 3
Falkland Av GOS/KPK NE3 ... 45 K7
HEBB NE31 ... 59 G5
Falkland Rd MLFD/PNYW SR4 ... 85 J7
Falla Park Crs FELL NE10 ... 12 B8
Falla Park Rd FELL NE10 ... 12 B8
Falloden Av GOS/KPK NE3 ... 45 K2
Fallodon Gdns
WD/WHPE/BLK NE5 ... 55 H1 4
Fallodon Rd NSHW NE29 ... 50 B5
Fallowfeld FELL NE10 ... 70 C5
Fallowfield WASHS NE38 ... 95 G5
Fallowfield Av GOS/KPK NE3 ... 45 K4
Fallowfield Wy WASHS NE38 ... 95 F4
Fallow Park Av BLYTH NE24 ... 24 E1 3
Fallow Rd HAR/WTLS NE34 ... 62 D5
Fallsway DHAM DH1 ... 126 A4
Falmouth Cl SEA/MUR SR7 ... 120 B2 4
Falmouth Dr JRW NE32 ... 60 B6
Falmouth Rd BYK/HTN/WLK NE6 ... 6 E3
MLFD/PNYW SR4 ... 85 J6
NSHW NE29 ... 50 B1
Falmouth Sq MLFD/PNYW SR4 ... 85 J7
Falsgrave Pl WICK/BNPF NE16 ... 66 D7
Falstaff Rd NSHW NE29 ... 50 B4
Falstone FELL NE10 ... 70 B7
WASHS NE38 ... 95 G4
Falstone Av
BW/LEM/TK/HW NE15 ... 54 C3
HAR/WTLS NE34 ... 62 A5
Falstone Cl LGB/KIL NE12 ... 48 C2
Falstone Dr CLSW/PEL DH2 ... 105 F6
Falstone Sq GOS/KPK NE3 ... 46 A4 4
Falston Rd BLYTH NE24 ... 24 E2
Faraday Cl WASHS NE38 ... 95 K1
Faraday Gv GATE NE8 ... 10 D9
MLFD/PNYW SR4 ... 85 J7
Faraday Rd PLEE/EAS SR8 ... 137 F1
Faraday St SEA/MUR SR7 ... 119 H5 2
Faraday Ter RDHAMSE DH6 ... 128 D6
Fareham Gv BOLCOL NE35 ... 72 B4
Farlam Av TYNE/NSHE NE30 ... 50 E1
Farlam Rd
WD/WHPE/BLK NE5 ... 55 F3 3
Farleigh Ct NSHW NE29 ... 49 K2
Farm Cl WASHN NE37 ... 82 D4
WICK/BNPF NE16 ... 79 F3
Farm Ct BLAY NE21 ... 66 D2
Farmer Crs SEA/MUR SR7 ... 119 G5
Farm Hill Rd
CLDN/WHIT/ROK SR6 ... 74 A2
Farm Rd DHAM DH1 ... 134 E5
Farm St SWCK/CAS SR5 ... 86 B4
Farnborough Cl CRAM NE23 ... 23 H7
Farnborough Dr SUNDSW SR3 ... 98 B6
Farn Ct DIN/WO NE13 ... 45 H2
Farndale WLSD/HOW NE28 ... 48 B5
Farndale Av
CLDN/WHIT/ROK SR6 ... 75 F6
Farndale Cl BLAY NE21 ... 65 H4 1
DIN/WO NE13 ... 35 F2 2
Farndale Rd ELS/FEN NE4 ... 55 J6
Farne Av GOS/KPK NE3 ... 46 A2
HAR/WTLS NE34 ... 62 B4
Farne Rd LGB/KIL NE12 ... 48 A2
SMOOR NE27 ... 39 H6
Farne Sq MLFD/PNYW SR4 ... 85 H6
Farne Ter BYK/HTN/WLK NE6 ... 7 M5
Farnham Cl DHAM DH1 ... 124 D4
Farnham Gv BLYTH NE24 ... 25 F3
Farnham Rd DHAM DH1 ... 124 D3
HAR/WTLS NE34 ... 61 G5 2
Farnham St
BW/LEM/TK/HW NE15 ... 54 B5
Farnham Ter MLFD/PNYW SR4 ... 97 K1
Farnley Hey Rd DHAM DH1 ... 134 B1
Farnley Mt DHAM DH1 ... 134 B1 1
Farnley Rdg DHAM DH1 ... 134 B1
Farnley Rd BYK/HTN/WLK NE6 .. 57 J2 2
Farnon Rd GOS/KPK NE3 ... 46 A5
Farquhar St JES NE2 ... 57 F3
Farrier Cl WASHS NE38 ... 95 G4
Farriers Ct STKFD/GP NE62 ... 19 H1
Farringdon Rd TYNE/NSHE NE30 .. 40 E7
Farringdon Rw
MLFD/PNYW SR4 ... 14 B2
Farrington Av SUNDSW SR3 ... 97 G6
Farrow Dr CLDN/WHIT/ROK SR6 .. 74 E3
The Farthings WASHN NE37 ... 82 D3
Fatfield Pk WASHS NE38 ... 95 F5
Fatfield Rd WASHS NE38 ... 95 G2
Faversham Ct GOS/KPK NE3 ... 45 H3 1
Faversham Pl CRAM NE23 ... 23 H7
Fawcett St SUND SR1 ... 14 E4
Fawcett Ter
ASHBK/HED/RY SR2 ... 111 G1 1
Fawdon Cl GOS/KPK NE3 ... 45 J2
Fawdon La GOS/KPK NE3 ... 45 H3
Fawdon Park Rd
GOS/KPK NE3 ... 45 J3 4
Fawdon Pl NSHW NE29 ... 50 A4
Fawley Cl BOLCOL NE35 ... 72 C3 2
Fawn Rd MLFD/PNYW SR4 ... 85 G7
Feather Bed La
ASHBK/HED/RY SR2 ... 111 G1
Featherstone Gv BDLGTN NE22 ... 18 D4
JRW NE32 ... 71 J1
Featherstone Rd DHAM DH1 ... 124 E4
Featherstone St
CLDN/WHIT/ROK SR6 ... 87 F3
Federation Sq SEA/MUR SR7 ... 119 H6
Federation Wy DUN/TMV NE11 ... 8 E6
Feetham Av LGB/KIL NE12 ... 48 B2
Felixstowe Dr LGB/HTN NE7 ... 47 J7
Fell Bank CLS/BIR/GTL DH3 ... 93 K2
Fell Cl CLS/BIR/GTL DH3 ... 94 A3
WICK/BNPF NE16 ... 79 F3
Felldyke FELL NE10 ... 70 B7 1
Fellgate Av JRW NE32 ... 72 A3
Fellgate Gdns FELL NE10 ... 70 E4 1
Felling House Gdns FELL NE10 ... 12 C5
Felling Vw BYK/HTN/WLK NE6 ... 13 G2
Fellmere Av FELL NE10 ... 13 H7
Fell Rd CLSW/PEL DH2 ... 104 E4
LWF/SPW/WRK NE9 ... 82 B4
MLFD/PNYW SR4 ... 85 H6
Fellside HAR/WTLS NE34 ... 62 B6
PONT/DH NE20 ... 42 D1
Fellside Av WICK/BNPF NE16 ... 79 F2
Fellside Cl PONT/DH NE20 ... 42 D1
Fellside Ct WICK/BNPF NE16 ... 66 E5 3
Fellside Gdns DHAM DH1 ... 125 K5 2
Fellside Rd WICK/BNPF NE16 ... 66 D7
WICK/BNPF NE16 ... 78 A6
The Fell Side GOS/KPK NE3 ... 45 K6
Fells Rd DUN/TMV NE11 ... 68 D5
Fell Vw ROWG NE39 ... 76 C2
The Fell Wy
WD/WHPE/BLK NE5 ... 54 B2 3
Felsham Sq MLFD/PNYW SR4 ... 85 J7
Felstead Crs MLFD/PNYW SR4 ... 85 H6
Felstead Pl BLYTH NE24 ... 25 F3
Felstead Sq MLFD/PNYW SR4 ... 85 H7
Felton Av GOS/KPK NE3 ... 46 A4
HAR/WTLS NE34 ... 62 A5
MONK NE25 ... 41 F5
Felton Cl SMOOR NE27 ... 39 H6
Felton Crs GATE NE8 ... 68 E5
Felton Dr LGB/KIL NE12 ... 48 B1
Fencer Ct GOS/KPK NE3 ... 46 C2
Fence Rd CLS/BIR/GTL DH3 ... 107 G1
Fenham Cha ELS/FEN NE4 ... 55 H3
Fenham Hall Dr ELS/FEN NE4 ... 55 H3
Fenham Rd ELS/FEN NE4 ... 4 B4
Fenkle St CNUT NE1 ... 5 H7
Fennel Gv HAR/WTLS NE34 ... 73 J1
Fenside Rd ASHBK/HED/RY SR2 ... 99 F6
Fenton Cl CLSW/PEL DH2 ... 105 G6
Fenton Sq MLFD/PNYW SR4 ... 85 H7 1
Fenton Well La
CLS/BIR/GTL DH3 ... 115 F1
Fenwick Av BLYTH NE24 ... 25 F2 2
HAR/WTLS NE34 ... 60 E6
Fenwick Cl CLSW/PEL DH2 ... 105 F6
HLS DH4 ... 95 K6 1
Fenwick St HLS DH4 ... 95 K6
Ferens Cl DHAM DH1 ... 16 F1
Ferens Pk DHAM DH1 ... 16 F1
Ferguson Crs DIN/WO NE13 ... 36 A5
Ferguson's La
BW/LEM/TK/HW NE15 ... 54 E5
Ferguson St ASHBK/HED/RY SR2 .. 15 K6
Fern Av CLDN/WHIT/ROK SR6 ... 75 F2
CRAM NE23 ... 23 H5
GOS/KPK NE3 ... 45 K3
GOS/KPK NE3 ... 46 A3 3
JES NE2 ... 56 E2
NSHW NE29 ... 2 A1
SWCK/CAS SR5 ... 86 A3
Fern Crs SEA/MUR SR7 ... 120 D4
Ferndale DHAM DH1 ... 126 A6
Ferndale Av BOL NE36 ... 73 H5
GOS/KPK NE3 ... 46 D1
WLSD/HOW NE28 ... 58 E1
Ferndale Cl BLYTH NE24 ... 20 C6 2
Ferndale Gv BOL NE36 ... 73 H5
Ferndale La BOL NE36 ... 73 H5
Ferndale Rd HLS DH4 ... 95 J6
Ferndale Ter MLFD/PNYW SR4 ... 85 J5
Ferndene Crs MLFD/PNYW SR4 ... 85 K7
Ferndene Gv LGB/HTN NE7 ... 47 H7
Fern Dene Rd GATE NE8 ... 10 E8
Ferndown Ct RYTON NE40 ... 53 F7 1
Fern Dr CLDN/WHIT/ROK SR6 ... 73 K3
CRAM NE23 ... 37 G1
Fernhill Av WICK/BNPF NE16 ... 66 E5
Fernlea Cl WASHS NE38 ... 95 G4
Fernlea Gdns RYTON NE40 ... 52 C7 1
Fernley Vls CRAM NE23 ... 28 E2
Fern Rd BDN/LAN/SAC DH7 ... 113 J5
Fern St MLFD/PNYW SR4 ... 14 B3
Fernsway SUNDSW SR3 ... 98 B3 5
Fernville Av WICK/BNPF NE16 ... 79 F3
Fernville Rd GOS/KPK NE3 ... 46 B7
Fernville St MLFD/PNYW SR4 ... 14 A7 3
Fernwood Av GOS/KPK NE3 ... 46 D4
Fernwood Cl SUNDSW SR3 ... 110 A2 2
Fernwood Rd
BW/LEM/TK/HW NE15 ... 54 B5
JES NE2 ... 5 M1
Ferrand Dr HLS DH4 ... 108 B7
Ferriby Cl GOS/KPK NE3 ... 46 D2 2
Ferrisdale Wy GOS/KPK NE3 ... 45 K3
Ferryboat La SWCK/CAS SR5 ... 84 D5
Ferrydene Av GOS/KPK NE3 ... 45 K6
Ferry St JRW NE32 ... 59 K3
SSH NE33 ... 2 F7
Festival Park Dr DUN/TMV NE11 ... 9 M9
Festival Wy DUN/TMV NE11 ... 9 J6
Field Cl JES NE2 ... 6 B5
Field Fare Ct WICK/BNPF NE16 ... 90 A1
Fieldhouse La DHAM DH1 ... 124 B6
Field House Rd GATE NE8 ... 10 E9
Fielding Ct
WD/WHPE/BLK NE5 ... 44 E6 2
Fielding Pl LWF/SPW/WRK NE9 ... 11 M8
Field La FELL NE10 ... 13 H8
Fieldside CLDN/WHIT/ROK SR6 ... 74 E3
CLSW/PEL DH2 ... 92 E7
HLH DH5 ... 117 F5
Field Sq MLFD/PNYW SR4 ... 85 G7
Field St FELL NE10 ... 12 C6 1
GOS/KPK NE3 ... 46 E5
Field Ter JRW NE32 ... 59 K6
Fieldway BOLCOL NE35 ... 72 A4
JRW NE32 ... 72 B3 2
Fife Av JRW NE32 ... 72 C1
Fife St GATE NE8 ... 11 J6
SEA/MUR SR7 ... 119 J6
Fifteenth Av BLYTH NE24 ... 25 F1
Fifth Av BYK/HTN/WLK NE6 ... 7 G2
DUN/TMV NE11 ... 68 D7
Fifth St PLEE/EAS SR8 ... 137 H3
Filby Dr DHAM DH1 ... 126 A4
Filey Cl CRAM NE23 ... 23 H7
Filton Cl CRAM NE23 ... 23 H7
Finchale WASHS NE38 ... 94 E3
Finchale Av DHAM DH1 ... 125 G1
Finchale Cl ASHBK/HED/RY SR2 ... 15 H7
DUN/TMV NE11 ... 67 K6 1
HLS DH4 ... 108 B7
Finchale Gdns
BW/LEM/TK/HW NE15 ... 43 F7
Finchale Rd DHAM DH1 ... 124 E1
HEBB NE31 ... 71 G1
Finchale Ter JRW NE32 ... 60 B7
Finchale Vw DHAM DH1 ... 124 C2 2
HLS DH4 ... 116 B6
Finchdale Cl NSHW NE29 ... 2 B4
Finchley Crs BYK/HTN/WLK NE6 .. 58 C3
Findon Av BDN/LAN/SAC DH7 ... 113 G7
Findon Gv NSHW NE29 ... 50 C6
Findon Hl BDN/LAN/SAC DH7 ... 113 H6
Finsbury Av BYK/HTN/WLK NE6 ... 7 M5
Finsbury St SWCK/CAS SR5 ... 86 C4 4
Finsmere Av
WD/WHPE/BLK NE5 ... 55 F2 3
Finsmere Pl
WD/WHPE/BLK NE5 ... 55 F2 4
Finstock Ct LGB/HTN NE7 ... 47 F6
Fir Av BDN/LAN/SAC DH7 ... 133 G7
DHAM DH1 ... 17 L4
Firbank Av TYNE/NSHE NE30 ... 41 F7
Firbanks JRW NE32 ... 72 B3
Firfield Rd WD/WHPE/BLK NE5 ... 55 H1
Fir Gv HAR/WTLS NE34 ... 61 K6
Fir Pk BDN/LAN/SAC DH7 ... 123 G7
First Av BLYTH NE24 ... 25 F1
BYK/HTN/WLK NE6 ... 7 G2
CLSW/PEL DH2 ... 93 H6
DUN/TMV NE11 ... 68 C6
NSHW NE29 ... 49 K6
The Firs GOS/KPK NE3 ... 46 B6 2
Fir St JRW NE32 ... 59 J4
First St GATE NE8 ... 10 C6
PLEE/EAS SR8 ... 137 H3
Firth Sq MLFD/PNYW SR4 ... 85 H7
Firtree Av BYK/HTN/WLK NE6 ... 58 C2
LGB/KIL NE12 ... 47 K1
WASHS NE38 ... 94 E5
Fir Tree Cl DHAM DH1 ... 125 H5 1
Firtree Crs LGB/KIL NE12 ... 47 J1
Firtree Gdns MONK NE25 ... 40 D6
Firtree Rd WICK/BNPF NE16 ... 66 E6
Firtrees CLSW/PEL DH2 ... 105 H2
FELL NE10 ... 70 A7
Firtrees Av WLSD/HOW NE28 ... 49 K7
Firwood Crs ROWG NE39 ... 76 C2
Firwood Gdns DUN/TMV NE11 ... 68 B7
Fisher La CRAM NE23 ... 22 C7
DIN/WO NE13 ... 27 G5
Fisher Rd SMOOR NE27 ... 38 D3
Fisher St BYK/HTN/WLK NE6 ... 58 D4
WLSD/HOW NE28 ... 58 D4
Fisherwell Rd FELL NE10 ... 13 K4
Fitzpatrick Pl SSH NE33 ... 3 L9
Fitzsimmons Av
WLSD/HOW NE28 ... 48 D7
Flambard Rd DHAM DH1 ... 124 C4
Flass Av BDN/LAN/SAC DH7 ... 122 E7
Flassburn Rd DHAM DH1 ... 124 B6
Flasshall La BDN/LAN/SAC DH7 .. 122 A7
Flass St DHAM DH1 ... 16 A3
Flaunden Cl HAR/WTLS NE34 ... 62 B6 3
Flaxby Cl GOS/KPK NE3 ... 46 D2
Flax Sq MLFD/PNYW SR4 ... 85 G6 1
Fleet St SUND SR1 ... 15 K5
Fleming Gdns FELL NE10 ... 69 J5
Fleming Pl PLEE/EAS SR8 ... 136 E4 1
Fletcher Crs HLS DH4 ... 108 C1
Flexbury Gdns
BW/LEM/TK/HW NE15 ... 54 C4 2
FELL NE10 ... 12 B7
LWF/SPW/WRK NE9 ... 81 G3
Flint Hill Bank STLY/ANP DH9 ... 89 G5
Flodden LGB/KIL NE12 ... 37 K5
Flodden Cl CLSW/PEL DH2 ... 105 F6
Flodden Rd MLFD/PNYW SR4 ... 85 H7
Flodden St BYK/HTN/WLK NE6 ... 7 K6
Floral Dene MLFD/PNYW SR4 ... 84 E7
Florence Av
LWF/SPW/WRK NE9 ... 69 G6 5
Florence Crs SWCK/CAS SR5 ... 85 K3
Florence St BLAY NE21 ... 65 K3
Florida St MLFD/PNYW SR4 ... 85 K5
Flotterton Gdns
WD/WHPE/BLK NE5 ... 55 G4
Flour Mill Rd DUN/TMV NE11 ... 9 H4
The Fold MONK NE25 ... 40 C4
WICK/BNPF NE16 ... 77 J6
Folldon Av
CLDN/WHIT/ROK SR6 ... 86 D2 2
Follingsby Av FELL NE10 ... 71 G6
Follingsby Dr FELL NE10 ... 70 E5
Follingsby La FELL NE10 ... 71 G7
Follingsby Wy FELL NE10 ... 71 F6
Folly La RYTON NE40 ... 64 D2
Folly Ter DHAM DH1 ... 124 B2
The Folly BOL NE36 ... 72 E5
Fondlyset La STLY/ANP DH9 ... 89 F7
Fontaine Rd SUND SR1 ... 14 C3
Fontburn Ct SWCK/CAS SR5 ... 85 K1 1
Fontburn Pl LGB/HTN NE7 ... 47 G5
Fontburn Rd MONK NE25 ... 30 A5
Fontburn Ter TYNE/NSHE NE30 ... 51 F4
Fonteyn Pl CRAM NE23 ... 23 H5
STLY/ANP DH9 ... 103 F2
Fontwell Dr GATE NE8 ... 10 C9
Forbeck Rd MLFD/PNYW SR4 ... 85 H7
Forber Av HAR/WTLS NE34 ... 62 B5
Ford Av MLFD/PNYW SR4 ... 84 E7
NSHW NE29 ... 50 B6
Ford Crs JRW NE32 ... 71 K1
MLFD/PNYW SR4 ... 84 E7
SMOOR NE27 ... 39 G6
Ford Dr BLYTH NE24 ... 20 E7
Fordenbridge Crs
MLFD/PNYW SR4 ... 85 H7
Fordenbridge Rd
MLFD/PNYW SR4 ... 85 H7 2
Fordenbridge Sq
MLFD/PNYW SR4 ... 85 J7 1
Fordfield Rd MLFD/PNYW SR4 ... 85 G7
Ford Gv GOS/KPK NE3 ... 46 B3
Fordhall Dr MLFD/PNYW SR4 ... 85 J7 2
Fordham Rd DHAM DH1 ... 124 D4
MLFD/PNYW SR4 ... 85 H6
Fordham Sq MLFD/PNYW SR4 ... 85 J7
Fordland Pl MLFD/PNYW SR4 ... 85 K7
Ford Ov MLFD/PNYW SR4 ... 85 F6
Ford Rd DHAM DH1 ... 124 E2
Ford St BYK/HTN/WLK NE6 ... 6 D6
GATE NE8 ... 11 M5
Ford Ter WLSD/HOW NE28 ... 59 G1
Ford Vw CRAM NE23 ... 28 B7
Forest Av LGB/KIL NE12 ... 48 A2
Forest Dr WASHS NE38 ... 94 B6
Forest Hall Rd LGB/KIL NE12 ... 48 A1
Fore St JES NE2 ... 6 D1
Forest Rd BW/LEM/TK/HW NE15 ... 55 F7
MLFD/PNYW SR4 ... 85 H6
SSH NE33 ... 3 H8
Forest Vw BDN/LAN/SAC DH7 ... 132 E7
Forest Wy CRAM NE23 ... 29 G7
Forfar St SWCK/CAS SR5 ... 86 D3
Forge La CHPW NE17 ... 88 A1
CLS/BIR/GTL DH3 ... 106 D4
Forge Rd DUN/TMV NE11 ... 9 K8
Forres Ct STLY/ANP DH9 ... 103 F1
Forres Pl CRAM NE23 ... 23 H7
Forrest Rd WLSD/HOW NE28 ... 58 C2 2
Forster Av BDLGTN NE22 ... 18 E5
HAR/WTLS NE34 ... 61 J4 2
RDHAMSE DH6 ... 126 C7
Forster St BLYTH NE24 ... 21 H7
CLDN/WHIT/ROK SR6 ... 86 E4

Forsyth Rd JES NE2 56 D2
Forth Banks CNUT NE1 5 J9
Forth Cl PLEE/EAS SR8 136 E5
Forth Ct HAR/WTLS NE34 61 G6
Forth Pl CNUT NE1 5 H8
Forth St CNUT NE1 5 H9
Fortrose Av SUNDSW SR3 98 A3
Fort St SSH NE33 3 J4
Forum Ct BDLGTN NE22 19 F5
The Forum
BW/LEM/TK/HW NE15 54 D4
Forum Wy CRAM NE23 28 B2
Fossdyke FELL NE10 70 B7 2
Fossefeld FELL NE10 70 C5
Fosse Law
BW/LEM/TK/HW NE15 53 G2
Fosse Ter LWF/SPW/WRK NE9 69 H6 4
Fossway BYK/HTN/WLK NE6 7 K3
Foster St BYK/HTN/WLK NE6 58 D6
Foundry La BYK/HTN/WLK NE6 6 D5
Foundry Rd SEA/MUR SR7 121 F1
Fountain Cl BDLGTN NE22 19 F5 1
Fountain Gv HAR/WTLS NE34 61 K3
Fountain Head Bank
WBAY NE26 30 E2
Fountain La BLAY NE21 53 K7
Fountain Rw JES NE2 4 E2
Fountains Cl DUN/TMV NE11 68 A6 2
WASHS NE38 95 F2
Fountains Crs HEBB NE31 71 G1
HLS DH4 108 A5
Fouracres Rd WD/WHPE/BLK NE5 55 J1
Four Lane Ends HLH DH5 118 A6
Fourstones WD/WHPE/BLK NE5 54 E1
Fourstones Cl GOS/KPK NE3 45 H5
Fourstones Rd MLFD/PNYW SR4 85 J6
Fourth Av BLYTH NE24 25 F1 3
BYK/HTN/WLK NE6 7 G2
CLSW/PEL DH2 105 H4
DUN/TMV NE11 68 C7
Fourth St GATE NE8 10 C6
PLEE/EAS SR8 137 H3
Fowberry Crs ELS/FEN NE4 55 J4
Fowberry Rd
BW/LEM/TK/HW NE15 54 D7
Fowler Cl HLS DH4 108 A3 3
Fowler St SSH NE33 3 H7
Fox & Hounds La
BW/LEM/TK/HW NE15 55 G5
Fox & Hounds Rd
WD/WHPE/BLK NE5 55 G4
Fox Av HAR/WTLS NE34 60 D7
Foxcover La SUNDSW SR3 97 F7
Foxcover Rd MLFD/PNYW SR4 96 D4
Fox Covert La PONT/DH NE20 33 F3
Foxglove Ct HAR/WTLS NE34 60 E7
Foxhills Cl WASHS NE38 95 G4
Foxhills Covert
WICK/BNPF NE16 66 C7
Foxhunters Rd MONK NE25 40 D6
Foxlair Cl SUNDSW SR3 110 A3
Fox Lea Wk CRAM NE23 29 F7
Foxley WASHN NE37 83 G5
Foxley Cl LGB/KIL NE12 38 B5
Fox St ASHBK/HED/RY SR2 14 A8
SEA/MUR SR7 120 E2
Foxton Av GOS/KPK NE3 45 K3
TYNE/NSHE NE30 41 F6
Foxton Cl NSHW NE29 50 C7
Foxton Hall WASHN NE37 83 F2
Foxton Wy DHAM DH1 135 J5
FELL NE10 13 M3
Foyle St SUND SR1 14 F5
Framwelgate DHAM DH1 16 C2
Framwelgate Br DHAM DH1 16 C4
Framwelgate Peth DHAM DH1 124 C6
Framwelgate Waterside
DHAM DH1 16 D3
Frances St BLAY NE21 65 J2
Francis St CLDN/WHIT/ROK SR6 86 D3
Frankham St
WD/WHPE/BLK NE5 54 D1 3
Frankland Dr MONK NE25 40 C6
Frankland La DHAM DH1 16 D1
Frankland Rd DHAM DH1 124 C4
Franklin St MLFD/PNYW SR4 86 A6
SSH NE33 3 H7
Franklyn Av WBAY NE26 30 E1
Franklyn Rd PLEE/EAS SR8 136 C3
Frank Pl NSHW NE29 2 D1
Frank St DHAM DH1 17 M3
SWCK/CAS SR5 86 B3 6
WLSD/HOW NE28 58 D2
Fraser Cl SSH NE33 61 F3
Freda St SWCK/CAS SR5 85 K4
Frederick Gdns HLS DH4 95 J7 2
Frederick Rd SUND SR1 14 F4
Frederick St MLFD/PNYW SR4 84 E7 2
SEA/MUR SR7 120 E1
SSH NE33 61 G3
SUND SR1 14 F5 1
Frederick Ter RDHAMSE DH6 128 E3
Freeman Rd GOS/KPK NE3 47 F6
LGB/HTN NE7 47 F6
Freesia Gra WASHS NE38 95 G3 1
Freezemoor Rd HLS DH4 108 B1
Fremantle Rd HAR/WTLS NE34 62 B6
Frenchman's Wy
HAR/WTLS NE34 62 B4
French St BLYTH NE24 21 G6 5
Frensham WASHS NE38 95 J2 1
Frensham Wy
BDN/LAN/SAC DH7 133 H6 4
Frenton Cl
WD/WHPE/BLK NE5 54 A1 5
Friarage Av
CLDN/WHIT/ROK SR6 86 D2 5
Friar Rd MLFD/PNYW SR4 85 H7
Friars Dene Rd FELL NE10 12 A4
Friarsfield Cl SUNDSW SR3 109 J2
Friarside BDN/LAN/SAC DH7 123 G1
Friarside Crs ROWG NE39 77 F5
Friarside Gdns WICK/BNPF NE16 66 E6
Friarside Rd ELS/FEN NE4 55 J3
Friar Sq MLFD/PNYW SR4 85 H7
Friars' Rw DHAM DH1 125 G6
Friars St CNUT NE1 5 H7
Friars Wy WD/WHPE/BLK NE5 55 G3 1
Friar Wy JRW NE32 60 A4
Friary Gdns FELL NE10 12 A5
Frobisher Ct SUNDSW SR3 109 K2
Frobisher St HEBB NE31 59 H5
Frome Gdns LWF/SPW/WRK NE9 81 F3
Frome Pl CRAM NE23 23 H7
Frome Sq MLFD/PNYW SR4 85 G7 1
Front Rd MLFD/PNYW SR4 85 H7
Front St BDN/LAN/SAC DH7 113 G5
BDN/LAN/SAC DH7 123 F1
BDN/LAN/SAC DH7 133 K4
BLAY NE21 65 K3
BLYTH NE24 19 K7
BOL NE36 73 G5
BOLCOL NE35 72 C3
CLDN/WHIT/ROK SR6 74 A3
CLDN/WHIT/ROK SR6 74 E4
CLS/BIR/GTL DH3 105 J4
CLS/BIR/GTL DH3 115 H1
CLSW/PEL DH2 92 D7
CRAM NE23 28 C7
CRAM NE23 29 H7
DHAM DH1 17 M4
DHAM DH1 124 B3
DIN/WO NE13 27 G7
DIN/WO NE13 35 F2
HLH DH5 117 H7
HLS DH4 107 J7
HLS DH4 108 B4
LGB/HTN NE7 47 J5
LGB/KIL NE12 37 H4 2
MONK NE25 39 J4
MONK NE25 40 C5
NSHW NE29 50 C5
NSHW NE29 50 D2
RDHAMSE DH6 126 D3
RDHAMSE DH6 128 E6
RDHAMSE DH6 128 D1
STLY/ANP DH9 88 E7
STLY/ANP DH9 89 G5
STLY/ANP DH9 89 K4
STLY/ANP DH9 90 B2
STLY/ANP DH9 90 D7 3
STLY/ANP DH9 90 E7
STLY/ANP DH9 102 C1
STLY/ANP DH9 103 G4
TYNE/NSHE NE30 41 G6
TYNE/NSHE NE30 51 H3
WASHN NE37 83 G5 1
WICK/BNPF NE16 66 E5
WICK/BNPF NE16 77 G7
WICK/BNPF NE16 77 J7
WICK/BNPF NE16 89 J2
Front St East BDLGTN NE22 19 G6
Frosterley Cl CLS/BIR/GTL DH3 115 J1
DHAM DH1 124 E3 3
HLH DH5 118 C7 1
Frosterley Gdns SUNDSW SR3 98 B4 4
Frosterley Pl ELS/FEN NE4 4 D5
Froude Av HAR/WTLS NE34 73 F1
Fuchsia Pl
WD/WHPE/BLK NE5 55 H1 5
Fulbrook Rd GOS/KPK NE3 45 K5
Fulforth Cl
BDN/LAN/SAC DH7 123 F5 1
Fullerton Pl LWF/SPW/WRK NE9 11 J8
Fulmar Dr BLYTH NE24 25 G3
WASHS NE38 94 B3
Fulmar Wk CLDN/WHIT/ROK SR6 75 F5
Fulwell Av HAR/WTLS NE34 62 B4
Fulwell Gn
WD/WHPE/BLK NE5 55 F2 5
Fulwell Rd
CLDN/WHIT/ROK SR6 86 D4 3
PLEE/EAS SR8 137 G5
Furnace Bank BDLGTN NE22 19 K5
Furness Cl PLEE/EAS SR8 136 C4
Furrowfield FELL NE10 69 J6 1
Furzefield Rd GOS/KPK NE3 46 B6
Fylingdale Dr SUNDSW SR3 98 C7
Fyndoune Wy
BDN/LAN/SAC DH7 113 G7
Fynes Cl PLEE/EAS SR8 136 E2
Fynway BDN/LAN/SAC DH7 113 H6 1

G

The Gables DIN/WO NE13 45 F4
Gainers Ter WLSD/HOW NE28 58 E3
Gainford CLSW/PEL DH2 105 G4
Gainsborough Av
HAR/WTLS NE34 73 H1
WASHS NE38 95 G2
Gainsborough Cl MONK NE25 40 A2
Gainsborough Crs HLS DH4 107 H2
LWF/SPW/WRK NE9 11 M9
Gainsborough Pl CRAM NE23 28 C5
Gainsborough Rd
MLFD/PNYW SR4 97 G4
STLY/ANP DH9 102 D2
Gainsbro Gv ELS/FEN NE4 4 B5
Gairloch Dr CLSW/PEL DH2 93 F7
WASHS NE38 94 C3
Gairloch Rd MLFD/PNYW SR4 97 G3
Galashiels Gv HLS DH4 107 K2 3
Galashiels Rd MLFD/PNYW SR4 97 F3
Galashiels Sq
MLFD/PNYW SR4 97 G3 1
Gale St STLY/ANP DH9 102 B2
Galfrid Cl SEA/MUR SR7 120 A2 2
Gallalaw Ter GOS/KPK NE3 47 F5 5
Galley's Gill Rd SUND SR1 14 C4
Galloping Green Rd
LWF/SPW/WRK NE9 81 K3
Galloway Rd PLEE/EAS SR8 136 E3
Gallowgate CNUT NE1 5 H6
Galsworthy Rd HAR/WTLS NE34 72 E1
MLFD/PNYW SR4 97 G3
Galway Rd MLFD/PNYW SR4 97 F3 1
Gambia Rd MLFD/PNYW SR4 97 F4 1
Gambia Sq MLFD/PNYW SR4 97 F4 2
Ganton Av CRAM NE23 28 C4
Ganton Cl WASHN NE37 82 E3 2
Ganton Ct HAR/WTLS NE34 73 K1 2
Garasdale Cl BLYTH NE24 25 F3
Garden Av BDN/LAN/SAC DH7 122 A3
Garden Cl DIN/WO NE13 27 G7 1
Garden Cft LGB/KIL NE12 48 A2
Garden Dr HEBB NE31 59 F7 2
Garden House Est RYTON NE40 52 B7
Garden La SSH NE33 3 H7
Garden Pk WLSD/HOW NE28 49 H6 1
Garden Pl HLS DH4 95 K7
SUND SR1 14 D4 2
The Gardens CLSW/PEL DH2 105 H4
MONK NE25 40 D5
Garden St BLAY NE21 66 A1 2
HLS DH4 108 B4 1
Garden Ter MONK NE25 39 J4
RYTON NE40 52 B7
Gardiner Rd MLFD/PNYW SR4 96 E3
Gardiner Sq MLFD/PNYW SR4 97 F3 2
Gardner Pk NSHW NE29 2 B3
Gardner Pl NSHW NE29 2 D3 1
Garesfield Gdns ROWG NE39 77 G2 2
Garesfield La BLAY NE21 65 H5
Gareston Cl BLYTH NE24 20 D7
Garfield St MLFD/PNYW SR4 85 K6 3
Garforth Cl CRAM NE23 28 B4
Garleigh Cl LGB/KIL NE12 38 B6 3
Garner Cl WD/WHPE/BLK NE5 44 B7
Garnet St MLFD/PNYW SR4 85 K6
Garrick Cl NSHW NE29 50 A3
Garrick St SSH NE33 61 G3
Garrigill WASHS NE38 95 H5
Garron St SEA/MUR SR7 120 E2
Garsdale Av WASHN NE37 82 D5
Garsdale Rd WBAY NE26 31 H7
Garside Av CLS/BIR/GTL DH3 93 J1
Garside Gv PLEE/EAS SR8 136 C2
Garsin Cl LGB/HTN NE7 48 A7
Garth Cornfield PLEE/EAS SR8 137 G5
Garth Crs BLAY NE21 65 K3
HAR/WTLS NE34 62 A2
Garth Farm Rd BLAY NE21 65 K3
Garthfield Crs
WD/WHPE/BLK NE5 54 E1
Garth Heads CNUT NE1 6 A7
Garth Six LGB/KIL NE12 37 J6
Garth Sixteen LGB/KIL NE12 37 J5 3
The Garth GOS/KPK NE3 45 K6
WD/WHPE/BLK NE5 54 C2 4
Garth Thirteen LGB/KIL NE12 37 H5 3
Garth Thirty Three
LGB/KIL NE12 37 K6
Garth Thirty Two LGB/KIL NE12 38 A6
Garth Twelve LGB/KIL NE12 37 J5 5
Garth Twenty LGB/KIL NE12 38 A6
Garth Twenty Five
LGB/KIL NE12 38 B6 4
Garth Twenty Four
LGB/KIL NE12 38 B6 5
Garth Twenty Seven
LGB/KIL NE12 38 B6
Garth Twenty Two LGB/KIL NE12 38 A6
Gartland Rd MLFD/PNYW SR4 96 E3
Garvey Vls LWF/SPW/WRK NE9 69 J6
Garwood St SSH NE33 61 F3
Gas House La HLS DH4 108 B6
Gaskell Av HAR/WTLS NE34 73 F1
Gas La BLAY NE21 54 A7
Gas Works Rd SEA/MUR SR7 121 F2
Gatacre St BLYTH NE24 21 G6 6
Gateley Av BLYTH NE24 25 F3
Gatesgarth LWF/SPW/WRK NE9 69 G7
Gatesgarth Gv
CLDN/WHIT/ROK SR6 74 C7 4
Gateshead Hwy GATE NE8 11 H1
Gateshead Rd WICK/BNPF NE16 79 G2
Gatwick Rd MLFD/PNYW SR4 97 F3
Gayhurst Crs SUNDSW SR3 110 A1
Gayton Rd WASHN NE37 83 G4
Geddes Rd MLFD/PNYW SR4 97 F3
Gelt Crs HLH DH5 118 A6 1
General Graham St
MLFD/PNYW SR4 97 K1 2
General Havelock Rd
MLFD/PNYW SR4 85 J7
The General's Wd WASHS NE38 94 E6
Geneva Rd MLFD/PNYW SR4 97 F3 5
Genister Pl ELS/FEN NE4 55 H3 1
Geoffrey Av DHAM DH1 134 B2
Geoffrey St
CLDN/WHIT/ROK SR6 75 F3
Geoffrey Ter STLY/ANP DH9 102 B2
George Pit La CLS/BIR/GTL DH3 115 K2
George Rd BDLGTN NE22 19 K4 3
WLSD/HOW NE28 58 D3
George Scott St SSH NE33 3 K5
George Smith Gdns
FELL NE10 12 B4 1
Georges Rd ELS/FEN NE4 4 B8
George Stephenson Wy
NSHW NE29 2 B6
George St ASHBK/HED/RY SR2 111 G1
BLAY NE21 66 B1 1
BLYTH NE24 25 G1 4
CLS/BIR/GTL DH3 93 H2
CLS/BIR/GTL DH3 105 K5
DHAM DH1 134 B1
ELS/FEN NE4 5 G9
GOS/KPK NE3 46 A5 2
HLH DH5 117 K3
RDHAMSE DH6 128 E6
SEA/MUR SR7 119 H6
SEA/MUR SR7 120 D1
TYNE/NSHE NE30 2 F1
WD/WHPE/BLK NE5 53 H1
WICK/BNPF NE16 66 E5 4
WLSD/HOW NE28 59 K2
George St North
CLDN/WHIT/ROK SR6 14 F1
Georgian Ct LGB/KIL NE12 47 H1
MLFD/PNYW SR4 98 A2 3
Gerald St ELS/FEN NE4 55 H7
HAR/WTLS NE34 73 G1
Gerrard Cl CRAM NE23 28 C4
WBAY NE26 31 H7
Gerrard Rd MLFD/PNYW SR4 97 F3 3
WBAY NE26 31 H7
Gertrude St HLS DH4 108 B5 1
Ghyll Field Rd DHAM DH1 124 C4
Gibside CLSW/PEL DH2 105 G4
Gibside Cl STLY/ANP DH9 91 F7
Gibside Ct DUN/TMV NE11 67 K6 2
Gibside Gdns
BW/LEM/TK/HW NE15 55 F5
Gibside Vw BLAY NE21 65 K4
Gibside Wy WICK/BNPF NE16 67 F2
Gibson Ct BOLCOL NE35 72 D4 1
Gibson St CNUT NE1 6 B6
WLSD/HOW NE28 49 G6
Gifford Sq MLFD/PNYW SR4 97 G2
Gilbert Rd MLFD/PNYW SR4 97 F3
PLEE/EAS SR8 136 D3
Gilbert St SSH NE33 61 G3 3
Gilderdale HLS DH4 95 G6
Gilderdale Wy CRAM NE23 28 B5 1
CRAM NE23 28 C5 1
Gilesgate DHAM DH1 16 F3
Gilesgate Ct DHAM DH1 16 F3 1
Gilesgate Rd HLH DH5 118 A6
Gilhurst Gra SUND SR1 14 B5
Gillas La HLH DH5 117 K1
Gillas La East HLH DH5 117 J1
Gillas La West HLH DH5 117 H2
Gillies St BYK/HTN/WLK NE6 7 J5
Gillingham Rd MLFD/PNYW SR4 97 G3
Gill Rd SUND SR1 14 D3
Gill Side Gv CLDN/WHIT/ROK SR6 86 E3
Gill St ELS/FEN NE4 55 J6
Gilmore Cl WD/WHPE/BLK NE5 44 B7
Gilpin St HLS DH4 108 B7
Gilsland Av WLSD/HOW NE28 49 H7
Gilsland Gv CRAM NE23 23 H6 1
Gilsland St MLFD/PNYW SR4 86 A6 1
Gilwell Wy GOS/KPK NE3 46 B1
Gingler La RYTON NE40 64 C2
Girtin Rd HAR/WTLS NE34 73 H2
Girton Cl PLEE/EAS SR8 136 C5
Girvan Cl STLY/ANP DH9 103 F1
Gishford Wy
WD/WHPE/BLK NE5 55 F1
Givens St CLDN/WHIT/ROK SR6 86 E3
Gladeley Wy WICK/BNPF NE16 78 E3
The Glade JRW NE32 71 K3
WD/WHPE/BLK NE5 53 J1
Gladstonbury Pl LGB/KIL NE12 47 J4
Gladstone St BLYTH NE24 21 F6
BW/LEM/TK/HW NE15 54 A5 1
CLDN/WHIT/ROK SR6 86 D4
HEBB NE31 59 H5
HLS DH4 107 K7
STLY/ANP DH9 91 H7
STLY/ANP DH9 102 B2
WLSD/HOW NE28 59 K2 3
Gladstone Ter GATE NE8 11 G5
JES NE2 5 M3
Gladstone Ter West GATE NE8 10 F5
Gladwyn Rd MLFD/PNYW SR4 97 F4 3
Glaholm Rd ASHBK/HED/RY SR2 15 J6
Glaisdale Dr
CLDN/WHIT/ROK SR6 74 E6
Glaisdale Rd LGB/HTN NE7 47 G5 1
Glamis Av GOS/KPK NE3 36 C7
MLFD/PNYW SR4 97 G2
Glamis Ct HAR/WTLS NE34 73 K1
Glamis Crs ROWG NE39 77 J1
Glamis Vls CLS/BIR/GTL DH3 81 J7
Glanmore Rd
MLFD/PNYW SR4 97 F3 5
Glantlees WD/WHPE/BLK NE5 54 E1
Glanton Av MONK NE25 29 K5
Glanton Cl CLSW/PEL DH2 105 G5
Glanton Rd NSHW NE29 50 B3
Glanton Sq MLFD/PNYW SR4 97 G3 2
Glanton Wynd GOS/KPK NE3 46 B3
Glanville Cl DUN/TMV NE11 68 B5
Glanville Rd SUNDSW SR3 109 H2
Glasbury Av MLFD/PNYW SR4 97 G2 1
Glasgow Rd JRW NE32 72 C1
Glasshouse St BYK/HTN/WLK NE6 7 G9
Glastonbury WASHS NE38 95 F2 1
Glastonbury Gv JES NE2 57 F1
Gleaston Ct PLEE/EAS SR8 136 C7
Glebe Av LGB/KIL NE12 47 K3
WICK/BNPF NE16 67 F5
Glebe Cl WD/WHPE/BLK NE5 44 B7 1
Glebe Crs LGB/KIL NE12 47 K1
WASHS NE38 83 G7
Glebe Ms BDLGTN NE22 19 F5 2
Glebe Ri WICK/BNPF NE16 66 E5
Glebe Rd BDLGTN NE22 19 F5
LGB/KIL NE12 47 K1
Glebeside BDN/LAN/SAC DH7 123 G1
Glebe St ELS/FEN NE4 55 H5
Glebe Ter LGB/KIL NE12 47 K1
PLEE/EAS SR8 130 D5
Glebe Vls LGB/KIL NE12 47 J1
Glenallen Gdns
TYNE/NSHE NE30 51 G1
Glen Barr CLSW/PEL DH2 105 H3
Glenbrooke Ter
LWF/SPW/WRK NE9 81 F1
Glenburn Cl WASHS NE38 94 B3
Glencarron Cl WASHS NE38 94 C2
Glen Cl ROWG NE39 77 G2
Glencoe LGB/KIL NE12 37 K5
Glencoe Av CLSW/PEL DH2 105 H3
CRAM NE23 28 C5
Glencoe Rd MLFD/PNYW SR4 97 F4
Glencourse BOL NE36 73 J5
Glendale Av BLYTH NE24 20 A6
GOS/KPK NE3 46 A6
NSHW NE29 50 C4
WBAY NE26 40 E2
WICK/BNPF NE16 66 E6
WLSD/HOW NE28 48 D6 2
Glendale Cl BLAY NE21 65 H4
SUNDSW SR3 109 G1
WD/WHPE/BLK NE5 44 B6
Glendale Gdns
LWF/SPW/WRK NE9 69 H7
Glendale Gv NSHW NE29 2 A1
Glendale Rd SMOOR NE27 39 J6
Glendale Ter BYK/HTN/WLK NE6 7 G4
Glendford Pl BLYTH NE24 25 F3 2
Glendower Av NSHW NE29 50 B4 3
Glendyn Cl LGB/HTN NE7 57 G2
Gleneagle Cl
WD/WHPE/BLK NE5 44 B7 2
Gleneagles SSH NE33 61 J2 3
Gleneagles Cl LGB/HTN NE7 47 J5 3
Gleneagles Dr WASHN NE37 82 D3
Gleneagles Rd
LWF/SPW/WRK NE9 80 E2
MLFD/PNYW SR4 97 G3 3
Gleneagles Sq
MLFD/PNYW SR4 97 F4 4
Glenesk Gdns
ASHBK/HED/RY SR2 98 C4 2
Glenesk Rd ASHBK/HED/RY SR2 98 C3
Glenfield Av CRAM NE23 23 H6
Glenfield Rd LGB/KIL NE12 47 J3
Glengarvan Cl WASHS NE38 94 C3
Glenhurst Dr
WD/WHPE/BLK NE5 44 B7
WICK/BNPF NE16 78 D1
Glenhurst Gv HAR/WTLS NE34 61 K5
Glenhurst Rd PLEE/EAS SR8 130 E5
Glenleigh Dr MLFD/PNYW SR4 97 G3
Glen Luce Dr
ASHBK/HED/RY SR2 99 F4
Glenluce Dr CRAM NE23 28 B5
Glenmoor HEBB NE31 59 F4
Glenmore Av CLSW/PEL DH2 105 H3
Glenmuir Av CRAM NE23 28 B5 2
Glenorrin Cl WASHS NE38 94 C3
Glen Pth ASHBK/HED/RY SR2 98 D3
Glenridge Av BYK/HTN/WLK NE6 57 H2
Glenroy Gdns CLSW/PEL DH2 105 H3
Glenshiel Cl WASHS NE38 94 C3
Glen St HEBB NE31 59 F6
Glen Ter CLSW/PEL DH2 105 G3
The Glen ASHBK/HED/RY SR2 98 D3 1
Glenthorn Rd JES NE2 56 E1
Glenuce CLS/BIR/GTL DH3 94 A3
Gloria Av MONK NE25 30 A2
Glossop St ROWG NE39 76 B1
Gloucester Av
CLDN/WHIT/ROK SR6 86 E1
Gloucester Cl CLS/BIR/GTL DH3 115 H2
Gloucester Pl HAR/WTLS NE34 62 A6 2
PLEE/EAS SR8 136 C3
Gloucester Rd ELS/FEN NE4 4 D6
NSHW NE29 49 K3
Gloucestershire Dr DHAM DH1 125 K6
Gloucester Ter ELS/FEN NE4 4 D8
Gloucester Wy ELS/FEN NE4 4 E9
Glover Rd MLFD/PNYW SR4 97 F4
WASHN NE37 83 H5
Glynfellis FELL NE10 70 B7
Glynwood Cl CRAM NE23 23 H6 2
Glynwood Gdns
LWF/SPW/WRK NE9 69 G7
Goathland Av LGB/KIL NE12 47 J3
Goathland Cl SUNDSW SR3 98 C7
Goathland Dr SUNDSW SR3 98 B7
Godfrey Rd MLFD/PNYW SR4 96 E3
Goldcrest Rd WASHS NE38 94 B3
Goldlynn Dr SUNDSW SR3 109 H1
Goldsmith Rd MLFD/PNYW SR4 97 F4
Goldspink La JES NE2 6 B2
Golf Course Rd HLS DH4 107 H3
Gompertz Gdns SSH NE33 61 F3
Goodrich Cl HLS DH4 108 A2 2
Good St STLY/ANP DH9 90 C6
Goodwood LGB/KIL NE12 38 B6 6
Goodwood Av GATE NE8 10 B8
Goodwood Cl
WD/WHPE/BLK NE5 44 B7 3
Goodwood Rd
MLFD/PNYW SR4 96 E3 1
Goole Rd MLFD/PNYW SR4 97 G3
Gordon Av GOS/KPK NE3 46 C6 1
SWCK/CAS SR5 84 E5
Gordon Dr BOL NE36 73 H5
Gordon Rd HAR/WTLS NE34 61 G5
MLFD/PNYW SR4 96 E4
Gordon Sq BYK/HTN/WLK NE6 6 F6
WBAY NE26 41 G5
Gordon St GATE NE8 10 D4
SSH NE33 61 G3
Gordon Ter SWCK/CAS SR5 86 A3
Gorecock La STLY/ANP DH9 100 E6
Gorleston Wy SUNDSW SR3 109 K3
Gorse Av HAR/WTLS NE34 62 A6
Gorsedale Gv DHAM DH1 126 A6 1
Gorsedene Rd WBAY NE26 31 J7
Gorse Rd ASHBK/HED/RY SR2 14 E8
Gort Pl DHAM DH1 17 J1
Goschen St BLYTH NE24 21 F6 1
BLYTH NE24 21 G5 1
GATE NE8 10 D7
SWCK/CAS SR5 86 A3
Gosforth Av HAR/WTLS NE34 73 G1
Gosforth Park Wy LGB/KIL NE12 47 F3
Gosforth St JES NE2 6 A4
Gosforth Ter FELL NE10 13 H5
Gosport Wy BLYTH NE24 25 F3
Gossington WASHS NE38 95 J1
Goswick Av LGB/HTN NE7 57 H1
Goswick Dr GOS/KPK NE3 45 K2
Goundry Av
ASHBK/HED/RY SR2 111 G1
Gowanburn CRAM NE23 28 B5 3
WASHS NE38 95 G4
Gowan Ter JES NE2 57 F2
Gower Rd SWCK/CAS SR5 86 A3
Gower St BYK/HTN/WLK NE6 58 C7
Gower Wk FELL NE10 12 A7
Gowland Av ELS/FEN NE4 55 J4
Gracefield Cl
WD/WHPE/BLK NE5 44 B7 4
Grace Gdns WLSD/HOW NE28 48 C6
Grace St BYK/HTN/WLK NE6 7 H5
DUN/TMV NE11 9 G8
Grafton Rd WBAY NE26 41 G5
Grafton St MLFD/PNYW SR4 14 A3
Graham Av WICK/BNPF NE16 66 E4
Graham Ct
BDN/LAN/SAC DH7 113 H5 1
Graham Park Rd GOS/KPK NE3 46 C7
Grahamsley St GATE NE8 11 G3
Graham St SSH NE33 3 K9
The Graham Wy SEA/MUR SR7 120 B2
Grainger Park Rd ELS/FEN NE4 4 A8
Grainger St CNUT NE1 5 J7
Grampian Dr PLEE/EAS SR8 136 C5
Grampian Gv BOL NE36 73 F5 4

Grampian Pl LGB/KIL NE12 47 H1 2
The Granaries ROWG NE39 76 B1
Granby Cl SUNDSW SR3 98 B3
WICK/BNPF NE16 79 F2
Grand Pde TYNE/NSHE NE30 51 H2
Grandstand Rd JES NE2 55 K3
Grange Av BDLGTN NE22 19 K3
HLS DH4 107 J6
LGB/KIL NE12 48 A4
PLEE/EAS SR8 130 C6
SMOOR NE27 39 H5
Grange Cl BLYTH NE24 25 F3
MONK NE25 40 B5
PLEE/EAS SR8 136 D2
TYNE/NSHE NE30 41 F7 2
WLSD/HOW NE28 58 E1
Grange Crs FELL NE10 13 J9
RYTON NE40 52 E7
Grange Dr RYTON NE40 52 E7
Grange Est DUN/TMV NE11 80 C7
Grange Farm Dr
WICK/BNPF NE16 66 E7
Grange La WICK/BNPF NE16 66 E7
Grange Lonnen RYTON NE40 52 D6
Grangemere Cl
ASHBK/HED/RY SR2 99 F4
Grange Nook WICK/BNPF NE16 66 E7
Grange Pk MONK NE25 40 A6
Grange Park Av BDLGTN NE22 19 K3
SWCK/CAS SR5 86 C2
Grange Pl JRW NE32 59 K4
Grange Rd
BW/LEM/TK/HW NE15 53 G3
DHAM DH1 125 K5
ELS/FEN NE4 55 H5
FELL NE10 13 J9
GOS/KPK NE3 46 C3
JRW NE32 59 K4
PONT/DH NE20 33 G2
RYTON NE40 52 E6
STLY/ANP DH9 102 B1
SWCK/CAS SR5 84 E6
Grange Rd West JRW NE32 59 J4
Grange St CLSW/PEL DH2 104 E1
Grange St South
ASHBK/HED/RY SR2 99 F4
Grange Ter BOL NE36 73 H5 4
LWF/SPW/WRK NE9 11 K8
SWCK/CAS SR5 86 B3
The Grange BDLGTN NE22 18 A6
STLY/ANP DH9 90 A6
Grange Vw HLH DH5 117 G3
HLS DH4 108 B4
RYTON NE40 52 E7
SWCK/CAS SR5 86 C2
Grange Vls WLSD/HOW NE28 58 E1
Grantham Dr
LWF/SPW/WRK NE9 80 E1
Grantham Pl CRAM NE23 28 B4 1
Grantham Rd
CLDN/WHIT/ROK SR6 86 E3
JES NE2 6 A3
Grantham St BLYTH NE24 25 H1
Grants Crs SEA/MUR SR7 120 E1
Grant St JRW NE32 59 J4
PLEE/EAS SR8 137 H3 2
Granville Av LGB/KIL NE12 48 A1
WBAY NE26 31 G3
Granville Crs LGB/KIL NE12 48 A4
Granville Dr HLS DH4 108 A2
LGB/KIL NE12 48 A2
WD/WHPE/BLK NE5 44 B7
Granville Gdns JES NE2 57 G3 1
Granville Rd GOS/KPK NE3 46 C3
JES NE2 6 A1
PLEE/EAS SR8 137 G5
Granville St GATE NE8 11 G5
MLFD/PNYW SR4 14 A4
Grape La DHAM DH1 16 B4
Grasmere CLDN/WHIT/ROK SR6 74 A3
Grasmere Av BYK/HTN/WLK NE6 7 M6
FELL NE10 13 H7
HLH DH5 128 B1
JRW NE32 72 B1
Grasmere Ct LGB/KIL NE12 37 J6 2
Grasmere Crs BLAY NE21 65 K4 4
SWCK/CAS SR5 86 C2
WBAY NE26 40 D2
Grasmere Gdns
HAR/WTLS NE34 61 J5 2
Grasmere Pl GOS/KPK NE3 46 B3
Grasmere Rd CLSW/PEL DH2 105 H6
HEBB NE31 59 H6
PLEE/EAS SR8 137 F3
WICK/BNPF NE16 8 B9
WLSD/HOW NE28 58 C2
Grasmere St GATE NE8 10 E6
Grasmere St West GATE NE8 10 E6 1
Grasmere Ter RDHAMSE DH6 129 G2 1
SEA/MUR SR7 119 J6
Grasmoor Pl
BW/LEM/TK/HW NE15 53 K4 2
Grassdale DHAM DH1 126 A6
Grassholme Mdw SUNDSW SR3 98 B4
Grassholm Pl LGB/KIL NE12 47 G3
Grassington Dr CRAM NE23 28 B4
Grasslees WASHS NE38 94 B6
Grasswell Dr
WD/WHPE/BLK NE5 45 H7
Gravel Wks HLH DH5 108 C6
Gravesend Rd
MLFD/PNYW SR4 97 F4 5
Gravesend Sq
MLFD/PNYW SR4 97 G4 1
Gray Av DHAM DH1 124 B4
DIN/WO NE13 36 C2
RDHAMSE DH6 126 C7
SEA/MUR SR7 119 H5
Grayling Ct SUNDSW SR3 109 G2 1
Gray Rd ASHBK/HED/RY SR2 14 F9
ASHBK/HED/RY SR2 15 K7
Grays Ter BOLCOL NE35 72 C3 3
Graystones FELL NE10 70 D5
Gray St BLYTH NE24 21 G5
Graythwaite CLSW/PEL DH2 105 F4
Greathead St SSH NE33 61 F4 2
Great Lime Rd DIN/WO NE13 37 G4
LGB/KIL NE12 37 F6
Great North Forest Trail
HAR/WTLS NE34 62 D4
Great North Rd GOS/KPK NE3 46 C3
Grebe Cl BLYTH NE24 25 G2
Greely Rd WD/WHPE/BLK NE5 54 D1
Greenacres CLSW/PEL DH2 92 D7
Green Acres PONT/DH NE20 32 E7
Greenacres Cl RYTON NE40 64 C1 1
Green Av HLS DH4 108 B3 1
Greenbank BLAY NE21 66 A2
JRW NE32 59 K4
Greenbank Dr MLFD/PNYW SR4 96 E1
Greenbourne Gdns FELL NE10 69 J5 2
Green Cl TYNE/NSHE NE30 51 F1
Green Crs CRAM NE23 37 F1 2
Greencroft RDHAMSE DH6 129 G2
Greencroft Av
BYK/HTN/WLK NE6 58 C3
Greencroft Pkwy
STLY/ANP DH9 101 H6
Greendale Cl BLYTH NE24 20 C6 3
Greendale Gdns HLH DH5 117 J6
Greenfield Av
WD/WHPE/BLK NE5 54 E1
Greenfield Rd DIN/WO NE13 36 B7
GOS/KPK NE3 46 B1
Greenfinch Cl WASHS NE38 94 B3
Greenford DUN/TMV NE11 80 D7
Greenford La DUN/TMV NE11 80 E6
Greenford Rd
BYK/HTN/WLK NE6 13 J1
Greenhaugh LGB/KIL NE12 47 H1
Greenhead WASHS NE38 94 B2
Greenhills LGB/KIL NE12 37 K4
Greenhill Vw
WD/WHPE/BLK NE5 55 J1
Green Hill Wk HAR/WTLS NE34 62 C5
Greenholme Cl CRAM NE23 23 H5 2
Greenhow Cl
ASHBK/HED/RY SR2 111 F2 2
Greenlands STLY/ANP DH9 102 B3 1
Greenlands Ct MONK NE25 30 A4
Green La BOL NE36 73 H6
DHAM DH1 17 J2
DHAM DH1 17 G5
DIN/WO NE13 44 D2
FELL NE10 12 C4
FELL NE10 13 J6
HAR/WTLS NE34 61 F7
LGB/KIL NE12 38 A6 1
RDHAMSE DH6 127 K6
RDHAMSE DH6 128 C5
SEA/MUR SR7 118 D2
STLY/ANP DH9 102 C7
Greenlaw WD/WHPE/BLK NE5 54 C3
Greenlaw Rd CRAM NE23 28 B5
Green Lea BDN/LAN/SAC DH7 113 G7
Greenlea NSHW NE29 49 K1
Greenlea Cl MLFD/PNYW SR4 97 G3
ROWG NE39 76 C1
Greenlee Dr LGB/HTN NE7 47 K7
Greenock Rd
MLFD/PNYW SR4 97 F4 6
Green Pk WLSD/HOW NE28 48 A7
Greenrigg Gdns SUNDSW SR3 98 B3 6
Green's Bank STLY/ANP DH9 92 A7
Greenshields Rd
MLFD/PNYW SR4 97 F4
Greenside Av PLEE/EAS SR8 137 G3
WLSD/HOW NE28 49 H7
Greenside Crs
BW/LEM/TK/HW NE15 54 E4
Greenside Rd RYTON NE40 64 B1
Green's Pl SSH NE33 3 H4
Green St SEA/MUR SR7 120 E1
SUND SR1 14 E4
Green Ter SUND SR1 14 D5
The Green
BW/LEM/TK/HW NE15 53 H2
DHAM DH1 135 J6
GOS/KPK NE3 45 K7
HLH DH5 108 D6
MONK NE25 40 C3
PLEE/EAS SR8 136 B6
PONT/DH NE20 33 H1
SWCK/CAS SR5 86 A4
Green Va RYTON NE40 64 B2
Greenway ELS/FEN NE4 55 H3
WD/WHPE/BLK NE5 44 A6
The Greenway
MLFD/PNYW SR4 97 G2 2
Greenwell Cl BLAY NE21 65 J3 5
Greenwich Pl GATE NE8 6 D9
Greenwood LGB/KIL NE12 38 B6 7
Greenwood Av BDLGTN NE22 19 K3 1
BYK/HTN/WLK NE6 58 C2 3
HLS DH4 108 A7
Greenwood Gdns
DUN/TMV NE11 68 A7 3
FELL NE10 12 D4 1
Greenwood Rd
MLFD/PNYW SR4 97 F3
Greetlands Rd
ASHBK/HED/RY SR2 98 C3
Gregson St BDN/LAN/SAC DH7 113 H5
Gregson Ter SEA/MUR SR7 111 F6
Grenada Cl WBAY NE26 40 D1 1
Grenada Dr WBAY NE26 40 D1
Grenada Pl WBAY NE26 40 D1 2
Grenfell Sq MLFD/PNYW SR4 97 F4 7
Grenville Ct PONT/DH NE20 32 C5
Grenville Dr GOS/KPK NE3 46 B1
Grenville Wy WBAY NE26 40 C2
Gresford St SSH NE33 61 G5
Gresham Cl CRAM NE23 28 C4
Gresley Rd PLEE/EAS SR8 136 B4
Greta Gdns SSH NE33 61 H3
Greta Ter MLFD/PNYW SR4 98 A1
Gretna Dr HAR/WTLS NE34 72 D2 1
Gretna Rd
BW/LEM/TK/HW NE15 55 F4
Gretton Pl LGB/HTN NE7 47 G7 1
Grey Av CRAM NE23 28 B5
Greybourne Gdns
ASHBK/HED/RY SR2 98 C4 3
Greyfriars La LGB/KIL NE12 47 G4 3
Greystead Cl
WD/WHPE/BLK NE5 44 B7
Greystead Rd MONK NE25 39 K4
Greystoke Av
ASHBK/HED/RY SR2 98 C4
JES NE2 6 C2
WICK/BNPF NE16 67 F6
Greystoke Gdns
ASHBK/HED/RY SR2 98 C3 4
JES NE2 6 C1
LWF/SPW/WRK NE9 81 H3
WICK/BNPF NE16 67 F7
Greystoke Pk GOS/KPK NE3 46 C2
Greystoke Wk
WICK/BNPF NE16 67 F6 1
Grey St CNUT NE1 5 K6
DIN/WO NE13 36 A3 2
HLS DH4 108 B6
TYNE/NSHE NE30 51 F4
WLSD/HOW NE28 58 E1
Greywood Av ELS/FEN NE4 55 J4
Grieves' Rw CRAM NE23 37 G1
Grieve St BLYTH NE24 21 F5 1
Grimsby St BLYTH NE24 25 G1
Grindon Av MLFD/PNYW SR4 97 F1 3
Grindon Cl CRAM NE23 28 B5
MONK NE25 40 C7
Grindon Ct MLFD/PNYW SR4 97 G3
Grindon Gdns MLFD/PNYW SR4 97 G3
Grindon La MLFD/PNYW SR4 97 F7
SUNDSW SR3 97 J4 1
Grindon Pk MLFD/PNYW SR4 97 G3 4
Grindon Ter MLFD/PNYW SR4 98 A1
Grinstead Cl HAR/WTLS NE34 61 K4 1
Grinstead Wy DHAM DH1 126 A4
Grisedale Gdns
LWF/SPW/WRK NE9 81 G1
Grisedale Rd PLEE/EAS SR8 137 F4 5
Grizedale WASHN NE37 82 D7
Grizedale Ct
CLDN/WHIT/ROK SR6 74 C6
Grosvenor Av JES NE2 57 F2
WICK/BNPF NE16 67 F4
Grosvenor Cl CRAM NE23 28 B5 4
Grosvenor Ct
WD/WHPE/BLK NE5 44 B7 5
Grosvenor Crs HEBB NE31 71 H1
Grosvenor Dr
CLDN/WHIT/ROK SR6 73 J3
HAR/WTLS NE34 61 K3
MONK NE25 40 E5
Grosvenor Gdns
HAR/WTLS NE34 61 K5 2
JES NE2 57 G3 2
WLSD/HOW NE28 49 J7
Grosvenor Pl JES NE2 57 F2
NSHW NE29 50 E4
Grosvenor Rd HAR/WTLS NE34 61 J3
JES NE2 57 F2
Grosvenor St SWCK/CAS SR5 85 K3
Grosvenor Wy
WD/WHPE/BLK NE5 54 B1
Grotto Gdns HAR/WTLS NE34 62 D5
Grotto Rd HAR/WTLS NE34 62 D5
Grove Av GOS/KPK NE3 46 D6 1
Grove Rd BDN/LAN/SAC DH7 133 G7
BW/LEM/TK/HW NE15 53 J2
LWF/SPW/WRK NE9 69 G6
Grove St DHAM DH1 16 B6
Grove Ter BDN/LAN/SAC DH7 133 K4
The Grove ASHBK/HED/RY SR2 14 D9
ASHBK/HED/RY SR2 99 F7
DHAM DH1 124 B6
GOS/KPK NE3 46 D6
HLH DH5 117 H2
JES NE2 57 F1 3
JES NE2 57 F2 1
JRW NE32 71 K3
LGB/KIL NE12 47 K4
MONK NE25 40 D5
PLEE/EAS SR8 130 B5
PONT/DH NE20 33 F4
ROWG NE39 77 H4
SWCK/CAS SR5 85 F4 4
WD/WHPE/BLK NE5 54 B2
WICK/BNPF NE16 67 G6
Guardians Ct PONT/DH NE20 33 H2 2
Guelder Rd LGB/HTN NE7 47 J7
Guernsey Rd MLFD/PNYW SR4 97 F4
Guernsey Sq MLFD/PNYW SR4 97 F4
Guildford Pl BYK/HTN/WLK NE6 6 F3
Guildford St ASHBK/HED/RY SR2 15 H9
Guillemot Cl BLYTH NE24 25 G2 6
Guisborough Dr NSHW NE29 49 K2
Guisborough St
MLFD/PNYW SR4 97 K1
Gullane WASHN NE37 83 F2
Gullane Cl FELL NE10 70 E2
STLY/ANP DH9 103 F1
Gunnerston Gv GOS/KPK NE3 45 H5 5
Gunnerton Cl CRAM NE23 28 C4
Gunnerton Pl NSHW NE29 50 B4 4
Gunn St DUN/TMV NE11 9 G8
Gut Rd WLSD/HOW NE28 59 H1
Guyzance Av GOS/KPK NE3 46 A4

H

Hackworth Rd PLEE/EAS SR8 136 A1
Hackworth Wy NSHW NE29 2 B6
Haddington Rd MONK NE25 40 A2
Haddon Cl MONK NE25 39 K4
Haddon Gn MONK NE25 39 K4
Haddricksmill Rd GOS/KPK NE3 46 E6
Hadleigh Rd MLFD/PNYW SR4 97 H1
Hadrian Av CLS/BIR/GTL DH3 105 K2
Hadrian Ct PONT/DH NE20 42 D1
Hadrian Gdns BLAY NE21 66 B3
Hadrian Pl
BW/LEM/TK/HW NE15 53 F1
LWF/SPW/WRK NE9 69 H5 2
Hadrian Rd BLYTH NE24 24 E4
ELS/FEN NE4 55 J5
JRW NE32 60 B7
WLSD/HOW NE28 58 E2
Hadrians Ct DUN/TMV NE11 80 D1
Hadrian St MLFD/PNYW SR4 86 A6
Hadstone Pl
WD/WHPE/BLK NE5 55 G2 3
Haggerston Cl
WD/WHPE/BLK NE5 45 F6 4
Haggerston Ct
WD/WHPE/BLK NE5 45 F6 5
Haggerston Crs
WD/WHPE/BLK NE5 45 F6
Haggerston Dr
SWCK/CAS SR5 84 E5 1
Haggerston Ter JRW NE32 60 C7
Haggie Av WLSD/HOW NE28 49 F7 1
Haig Av MONK NE25 40 D5
Haig Crs BW/LEM/TK/HW NE15 54 E6
DHAM DH1 17 M5
Haig Rd BDLGTN NE22 19 H6
Hailsham Av LGB/KIL NE12 47 J3
Haininghead WASHS NE38 95 G4
Hainingwood Ter FELL NE10 13 L4 1
Haldane Ter JES NE2 56 E3
Hale Ri PLEE/EAS SR8 136 E4
Halewood Av GOS/KPK NE3 45 J6
Half Fields Rd BLAY NE21 65 K3
Half Moon La GATE NE8 5 M9 2
Halfway House La
ASHBK/HED/RY SR2 99 G3
Halidon Rd ASHBK/HED/RY SR2 98 D5
Halidon Sq
ASHBK/HED/RY SR2 98 D5 1
Halifax Rd DUN/TMV NE11 8 E5
Halkirk Wy CRAM NE23 23 G6
Hallam Rd PLEE/EAS SR8 136 E3 3
Hall Av BDN/LAN/SAC DH7 122 E7
Hall Cl HLS DH4 116 D6
SEA/MUR SR7 110 D7
Hall Dr LGB/KIL NE12 37 J4 2
Halleypike Cl LGB/HTN NE7 47 K7 2
Hall Farm DHAM DH1 135 G4 1
Hall Farm Rd SUNDSW SR3 109 K2
Hallfield Cl SUNDSW SR3 110 A2
Hallfield Dr PLEE/EAS SR8 130 B6
Hall Gdns BOL NE36 72 E5
FELL NE10 69 K5
Hallgarth La RDHAMSE DH6 126 E5
Hallgarth Rd BLAY NE21 65 K2
Hallgarth St DHAM DH1 16 F6
RDHAMSE DH6 126 C7
The Hallgarth DHAM DH1 16 F6
Hall Gn BLYTH NE24 20 D7
Halling Cl BYK/HTN/WLK NE6 58 C7 5
Hallington Dr MONK NE25 30 A5
Halliwell St HLS DH4 108 B6
Hall La DHAM DH1 135 G5
HLH DH5 117 H1
HLS DH4 116 D6
RDHAMSE DH6 128 E6
Hallow Dr BW/LEM/TK/HW NE15 53 F2
Hall Pk BLAY NE21 53 J7
Hall Rd HEBB NE31 59 G6
WASHN NE37 83 G5 2
Hallside Rd BLYTH NE24 24 D1
Hall Ter FELL NE10 13 M4
Hall Vw CLDN/WHIT/ROK SR6 75 F4
Hall Wks PLEE/EAS SR8 130 B6
Hallwood Cl BDLGTN NE22 18 A6
Halstead Sq MLFD/PNYW SR4 97 H1
Halterburn Cl GOS/KPK NE3 46 B6
Halton Rd DHAM DH1 124 E4 1
Hamar Cl NSHW NE29 50 A6
Hambard Wy WASHS NE38 95 F2
Hambledon Av
TYNE/NSHE NE30 40 E6
Hambledon Cl BOLCOL NE35 72 C4 1
Hambledon Gdns LGB/HTN NE7 47 G7
Hambledon Pl PLEE/EAS SR8 136 B5 1
Hambledon St BLYTH NE24 21 F6 2
Hambleton Dr SEA/MUR SR7 111 H7 2
Hambleton Rd WASHS NE38 94 D3
Hamilton Crs ELS/FEN NE4 4 E5
NSHW NE29 50 A2
Hamilton Dr WBAY NE26 40 D1
Hamilton St PLEE/EAS SR8 137 G3 2
Hamilton Ter
BDN/LAN/SAC DH7 113 G2
BOL NE36 72 E5 3
Hammer Square Bank
STLY/ANP DH9 91 K5
Hampden Rd
CLDN/WHIT/ROK SR6 86 E3
Hampden St SSH NE33 61 G3 4
Hampshire Ct ELS/FEN NE4 9 K2
Hampshire Pl WASHN NE37 83 F4 2
Hampshire Rd DHAM DH1 125 K6
Hampshire Wy
HAR/WTLS NE34 62 C4 1
Hampstead Cl BLYTH NE24 24 E4
Hampstead Rd ELS/FEN NE4 55 J6
MLFD/PNYW SR4 97 H2
Hampstead Sq
MLFD/PNYW SR4 97 G2 3
Hampton Cl CRAM NE23 28 E1 1
Hampton Ct CLS/BIR/GTL DH3 93 K7
Hampton Dr FELL NE10 12 A7
Hampton Rd TYNE/NSHE NE30 40 E7
Hamsterley Cl
CLS/BIR/GTL DH3 115 J1 2
Hamsterley Ct SUNDSW SR3 110 A1 3
Hamsterley Crs
BW/LEM/TK/HW NE15 53 K4 5
DHAM DH1 124 E3
LWF/SPW/WRK NE9 81 J2
Hamsterley Dr LGB/KIL NE12 37 J5
Hamsterley Gdns
STLY/ANP DH9 101 H3
Hanby Gdns SUNDSW SR3 98 A3 5
Hancock St CNUT NE1 5 K3
Handel St MLFD/PNYW SR4 86 A6 2
SSH NE33 3 K9
Handley St PLEE/EAS SR8 137 G3 3
Handy Dr DUN/TMV NE11 8 D4
Hangingstone La
STLY/ANP DH9 100 E5
Hangmans La HLH DH5 109 J4
Hanlon Ct JRW NE32 59 H4
Hannington St
BYK/HTN/WLK NE6 6 C5
Hanover Ct CRAM NE23 28 C7 1
Hanover Dr BLAY NE21 65 J3
Hanover Pl CRAM NE23 23 G5 3
MLFD/PNYW SR4 14 B1
Hanover St CNUT NE1 5 K9
Harbottle Av GOS/KPK NE3 46 A4
SMOOR NE27 39 H7
Harbottle Ct BYK/HTN/WLK NE6 7 H8
Harbottle Crs JRW NE32 71 K2
Harbour Dr SSH NE33 3 K3
The Harbour HLS DH4 107 K1 2
Harbour Vw
CLDN/WHIT/ROK SR6 87 F4
SSH NE33 3 H3
Harbour Wk SEA/MUR SR7 111 J7
Harcourt Rd
ASHBK/HED/RY SR2 98 D5 2
Harcourt St
LWF/SPW/WRK NE9 69 G7 2
Hardgate Rd
ASHBK/HED/RY SR2 98 E5 1
Hardie Av WICK/BNPF NE16 66 E4
Hardie Dr BOL NE36 72 E5
Hardwick Cl GATE NE8 11 K5 1
Hardwick Pl GOS/KPK NE3 46 A7 2
Hardwick Ri
CLDN/WHIT/ROK SR6 15 H1 1
Hardwick St PLEE/EAS SR8 137 H4
RHTLP TS27 137 K7
Hardyards Ct HAR/WTLS NE34 61 G6 9
Hardy Av HAR/WTLS NE34 73 F1
Hardy Gv WLSD/HOW NE28 48 C5
Hardy Sq SWCK/CAS SR5 86 A2
Hardy St SEA/MUR SR7 120 E1 8
Harebell Rd LWF/SPW/WRK NE9 81 J5
Harehills Av WD/WHPE/BLK NE5 45 H7
Harelaw Gdns STLY/ANP DH9 101 F1
Harelaw Gv
WD/WHPE/BLK NE5 54 B2 4
Hareside CRAM NE23 28 B3
Harewood Cl WICK/BNPF NE16 78 E1
Harewood Crs MONK NE25 39 K5 1
Harewood Dr BDLGTN NE22 19 J4
Harewood Gdns SUNDSW SR3 98 A3 4
Harewood Rd GOS/KPK NE3 46 C4
Hareydene WD/WHPE/BLK NE5 44 D5
Hargill Dr WASHS NE38 94 C5
Hargrave Ct BLYTH NE24 24 E1 4
Harland Wy WASHS NE38 95 F1
Harle Cl WD/WHPE/BLK NE5 54 C2 5
Harle Rd SMOOR NE27 39 F5
Harleston Wy FELL NE10 70 A6
Harle St WLSD/HOW NE28 58 D1 4
Harley Ter GOS/KPK NE3 46 D5
Harlow Av GOS/KPK NE3 45 K3
SMOOR NE27 39 F6
Harlow Green La
LWF/SPW/WRK NE9 81 G3
Harlow Pl LGB/HTN NE7 47 H7
Harlow St MLFD/PNYW SR4 14 A5
Harnham Av NSHW NE29 50 A5
Harnham Gdns
WD/WHPE/BLK NE5 55 G3
Harnham Gv CRAM NE23 28 B3
Harold St JRW NE32 60 A4
Harperley Dr SUNDSW SR3 98 B4
Harperley La STLY/ANP DH9 89 J5
Harperley Rd STLY/ANP DH9 101 H2
Harper St BLYTH NE24 21 F7
Harras Bank CLS/BIR/GTL DH3 93 J3
Harriet St BLAY NE21 66 A2
BYK/HTN/WLK NE6 7 J5
Harrington St
WLSD/HOW NE28 58 D1 5
Harriot Dr LGB/KIL NE12 37 G7
Harrison Cl PLEE/EAS SR8 137 F5
Harrison Gdns GATE NE8 68 D5 2
Harrison Garth
RDHAMSE DH6 126 C7 1
Harrison Pl JES NE2 5 M3
Harrison Rd WLSD/HOW NE28 49 J7
Harrogate St
ASHBK/HED/RY SR2 15 G7
Harrogate Ter SEA/MUR SR7 119 H5 3
Harrow Gdns DIN/WO NE13 36 C4
Harrow Sq MLFD/PNYW SR4 97 H1
Hartburn FELL NE10 70 C7
Hartburn Dr WD/WHPE/BLK NE5 44 B7
Hartburn Pl ELS/FEN NE4 4 A2
Hartburn Rd TYNE/NSHE NE30 50 D1
Hartburn Wk GOS/KPK NE3 45 H5
Hartford Bank CRAM NE23 22 C3
Hartford Br BDLGTN NE22 22 C3
Hartford Ct BDLGTN NE22 18 E6
Hartford Crs BDLGTN NE22 18 E6
Hartford Dr BDLGTN NE22 22 C2
Hartford Rd BDLGTN NE22 22 D1
GOS/KPK NE3 46 D3
HAR/WTLS NE34 60 E6
MLFD/PNYW SR4 97 H1
Hartforth Crs FELL NE10 13 M4
Harthope Av SWCK/CAS SR5 85 G2 1
Harthope Cl WASHS NE38 94 B6
Harthope Dr NSHW NE29 50 C7
Hartington Rd TYNE/NSHE NE30 50 E1
Hartington St
CLDN/WHIT/ROK SR6 86 E3
ELS/FEN NE4 4 C7
GATE NE8 11 G6
Hartington Ter SSH NE33 61 H3
Hartland Dr CLS/BIR/GTL DH3 93 K4
Hartlands BDLGTN NE22 18 E6
Hartleigh Pl BLYTH NE24 20 D7 2
Hartley Av WBAY NE26 40 C4
Hartleyburn Av HEBB NE31 71 F1
Hartley La MONK NE25 39 K3
Hartley St MONK NE25 29 K5
SUND SR1 15 J3
Hartley Ter BLYTH NE24 24 E3 5
Hartoft Cl HLS DH4 108 B4 2
Harton Gv HAR/WTLS NE34 61 J4
Harton House Rd
HAR/WTLS NE34 61 K4
Harton House Rd East
HAR/WTLS NE34 62 A4
Harton La HAR/WTLS NE34 61 G6
Harton Ri HAR/WTLS NE34 61 K4
Hartside BW/LEM/TK/HW NE15 54 A4
CLS/BIR/GTL DH3 93 K5
Hartside Crs BLAY NE21 65 H4

CRAM NE23 ... 23 G5 4
SMOOR NE27 ... 39 F5
Hartside Gdns HLH DH5 ... 118 B7
JES NE2 ... 57 F2 2
Hartside Pl GOS/KPK NE3 ... 46 C1 1
Hartside Vw
BDN/LAN/SAC DH7 ... 123 F5 2
DHAM DH1 ... 124 B2
Hart Sq MLFD/PNYW SR4 ... 97 H1
Hart Ter CLDN/WHIT/ROK SR6 ... 75 F6 1
Harvard Rd GOS/KPK NE3 ... 45 J5 3
Harvest Cl SUNDSW SR3 ... 109 K2 5
Harvey Cl PLEE/EAS SR8 ... 136 E3
WASHS NE38 ... 94 B1
Harvey Combe LGB/KIL NE12 ... 37 H6
Harvey Crs FELL NE10 ... 13 M8
Harwick Ct STLY/ANP DH9 ... 103 G1
Harwood Cl CRAM NE23 ... 28 B3
WASHS NE38 ... 94 C5 1
Harwood Dr LGB/KIL NE12 ... 38 B6
Hascombe Cl MONK NE25 ... 40 B3
Haslemere Dr SUNDSW SR3 ... 98 A3 3
Hassop Wy BDLGTN NE22 ... 19 F4
Hastings Av DHAM DH1 ... 134 B3
GOS/KPK NE3 ... 45 H3
LGB/KIL NE12 ... 47 K3 1
WBAY NE26 ... 30 E1 1
Hastings Ct BDLGTN NE22 ... 19 J4
Hastings Dr TYNE/NSHE NE30 ... 51 G2
Hastings Gdns MONK NE25 ... 30 A2
Hastings St ASHBK/HED/RY SR2 ... 98 E2
CRAM NE23 ... 28 D3
Hastings Ter ASHBK/HED/RY SR2 ... 99 F3
CRAM NE23 ... 23 K5
MONK NE25 ... 30 A1
Haswell Cl FELL NE10 ... 71 F5
Haswell Gdns TYNE/NSHE NE30 ... 50 E4
Hatfield Av HEBB NE31 ... 59 H5
Hatfield Cl DHAM DH1 ... 124 B3
Hatfield Dr CRAM NE23 ... 29 G6
Hatfield Gdns MONK NE25 ... 39 K5
SUNDSW SR3 ... 98 A3 6
Hathaway Gdns SUNDSW SR3 ... 98 A3 7
Hatherton Av TYNE/NSHE NE30 ... 41 F6
Hathery La BLYTH NE24 ... 23 K4
Haugh La RYTON NE40 ... 53 G5
Haughton Crs JRW NE32 ... 71 K2 2
WD/WHPE/BLK NE5 ... 54 C2
Haughton Ter BLYTH NE24 ... 21 G7
Hautmont Rd HEBB NE31 ... 59 H7
Hauxley LGB/KIL NE12 ... 37 K4 5
Hauxley Dr CLSW/PEL DH2 ... 105 F7
CRAM NE23 ... 23 G5
GOS/KPK NE3 ... 45 J3
Hauxley Gdns
WD/WHPE/BLK NE5 ... 55 H1 6
Havanna LGB/KIL NE12 ... 37 K4 4
Havannah Crs DIN/WO NE13 ... 35 F3 1
Havannah Rd WASHN NE37 ... 82 D6
Havant Gdns DIN/WO NE13 ... 36 B2
Havelock Cl GATE NE8 ... 10 E3
Havelock Crs BDLGTN NE22 ... 20 B3 1
Havelock Ms BDLGTN NE22 ... 20 B2
Havelock Rd SMOOR NE27 ... 39 F6
Havelock St SSH NE33 ... 61 G2 2
SUND SR1 ... 15 H3
Havelock Ter
ASHBK/HED/RY SR2 ... 14 B7
GATE NE8 ... 10 E4
JRW NE32 ... 59 K6
Haven Ct BLYTH NE24 ... 24 E1 5
DHAM DH1 ... 124 D1 2
The Haven HLS DH4 ... 107 K1 3
NSHW NE29 ... 2 C7
Havercroft FELL NE10 ... 70 D5
Haverley Dr SEA/MUR SR7 ... 110 E7
Haversham Pk SWCK/CAS SR5 ... 74 C7
Haversham Rd LGB/HTN NE7 ... 47 G5
Hawarden Crs MLFD/PNYW SR4 ... 98 A1
Hawes Av CLSW/PEL DH2 ... 105 J6
Hawes Ct CLDN/WHIT/ROK SR6 ... 74 C7
Hawes Rd PLEE/EAS SR8 ... 136 E3
Haweswater Cl
HAR/WTLS NE34 ... 61 H5 1
Hawick Ct STLY/ANP DH9 ... 103 F1
Hawick Crs BYK/HTN/WLK NE6 ... 6 F8
Hawkey's La NSHW NE29 ... 2 B1
Hawkhill Cl CLSW/PEL DH2 ... 105 G7
Hawkhurst WASHS NE38 ... 95 G4 1
Hawkins Ct SUNDSW SR3 ... 109 K1 2
Hawksbury WICK/BNPF NE16 ... 66 E5 3
Hawkshead Ct DIN/WO NE13 ... 45 H3 2
Hawkshead Pl
LWF/SPW/WRK NE9 ... 69 H7
Hawksley WD/WHPE/BLK NE5 ... 54 D1
Hawks Rd GATE NE8 ... 6 B9
Hawks St GATE NE8 ... 6 D9
Hawkwell Ri
BW/LEM/TK/HW NE15 ... 53 F2 3
Hawkser Cl SUNDSW SR3 ... 98 C7 2
Hawthorn Av DIN/WO NE13 ... 36 A4
SUNDSW SR3 ... 98 B6
Hawthorn Cl CLSW/PEL DH2 ... 114 A5
WICK/BNPF NE16 ... 79 F1
Hawthorn Cottages
RDHAMSE DH6 ... 129 G2
Hawthorn Crs DHAM DH1 ... 17 M1
Hawthorn Dr DUN/TMV NE11 ... 9 G8
JRW NE32 ... 72 B2
Hawthorne Av HAR/WTLS NE34 ... 61 K7
HEBB NE31 ... 59 H5
Hawthorne Cl
BDN/LAN/SAC DH7 ... 122 A3
SEA/MUR SR7 ... 119 J6
Hawthorne Rd BLYTH NE24 ... 21 H7 4
Hawthorne Ter
BDN/LAN/SAC DH7 ... 122 B2
Hawthorn Gdns GOS/KPK NE3 ... 45 K6
NSHW NE29 ... 50 D3 1
WBAY NE26 ... 40 D4
Hawthorn Pk
BDN/LAN/SAC DH7 ... 133 G6 2
Hawthorn Pl ELS/FEN NE4 ... 9 K1
LGB/KIL NE12 ... 37 J5 7
Hawthorn Rd BLAY NE21 ... 66 A2
DHAM DH1 ... 126 A4
GOS/KPK NE3 ... 46 C6
Hawthorn Rd West
GOS/KPK NE3 ... 46 C6
The Hawthorns BOL NE36 ... 73 H5
Hawthorn St JRW NE32 ... 59 J4 1
MLFD/PNYW SR4 ... 86 A7
PLEE/EAS SR8 ... 130 E4
Hawthorn Ter
CLDN/WHIT/ROK SR6 ... 74 E6 1
DHAM DH1 ... 16 A4
ELS/FEN NE4 ... 4 D8
WD/WHPE/BLK NE5 ... 53 J1
Hawthorn Vls CRAM NE23 ... 28 D2
Hawthorn Wy PONT/DH NE20 ... 33 F6
Haydock Dr FELL NE10 ... 70 D5
Haydon WASHS NE38 ... 95 G5
Haydon Pl WD/WHPE/BLK NE5 ... 54 E3
Haydon Sq MLFD/PNYW SR4 ... 97 H1
Hayes Wk DIN/WO NE13 ... 36 B3
Hayfield La WICK/BNPF NE16 ... 67 F6
Hayhole Rd NSHW NE29 ... 60 C1
Hayleazes Rd
BW/LEM/TK/HW NE15 ... 54 D4
The Hayricks STLY/ANP DH9 ... 90 B2
Hay St SWCK/CAS SR5 ... 14 D1
Hayton Av HAR/WTLS NE34 ... 62 A6
Hayton Cl CRAM NE23 ... 28 D1
Hayton Rd TYNE/NSHE NE30 ... 50 D1
Hazard La HLH DH5 ... 117 H5
Hazel Av BDN/LAN/SAC DH7 ... 133 F7
NSHW NE29 ... 50 D3
SUNDSW SR3 ... 98 B6 1
Hazeldene MONK NE25 ... 40 B4
Hazeldene Av GOS/KPK NE3 ... 45 G6
Hazeldene Ct TYNE/NSHE NE30 ... 51 G3
Hazeley Gv GOS/KPK NE3 ... 45 H5
Hazeley Wy GOS/KPK NE3 ... 45 H5 6
Hazel Gv CLSW/PEL DH2 ... 105 G2
Hazelgrove FELL NE10 ... 70 D5
Hazel Gv HAR/WTLS NE34 ... 61 K7
LGB/KIL NE12 ... 37 H7
Hazel Leigh CLS/BIR/GTL DH3 ... 115 H1
Hazelmere Av BDLGTN NE22 ... 18 E5
Hazelmere Crs CRAM NE23 ... 23 J7
Hazelmere Dene CRAM NE23 ... 29 F7 2
Hazelmoor HEBB NE31 ... 59 F4 5
Hazel Rd BLAY NE21 ... 66 B2
GATE NE8 ... 10 A7
Hazel St JRW NE32 ... 59 J4
Hazel Ter STLY/ANP DH9 ... 103 F4
Hazelwood LGB/KIL NE12 ... 38 B6 8
Hazelwood Av JES NE2 ... 56 E1
SWCK/CAS SR5 ... 85 K3
Hazelwood Cl LWF/SPW/WRK NE9 ... 81 K3
Hazelwood Ct
BDN/LAN/SAC DH7 ... 122 B3 1
Hazelwood Ter WLSD/HOW NE28 ... 59 J1
Hazledene Ter
MLFD/PNYW SR4 ... 85 K7 4
Hazlitt Av HAR/WTLS NE34 ... 73 F1
Hazlitt Pl CRAM NE23 ... 29 H7 2
Headlam St BYK/HTN/WLK NE6 ... 7 G5
Headlam Vw WLSD/HOW NE28 ... 59 J1
Healey Dr SUNDSW SR3 ... 98 B4
Heartsbourne Dr
HAR/WTLS NE34 ... 73 K1 3
Heath Cl DUN/TMV NE11 ... 9 M9
PLEE/EAS SR8 ... 137 F5
Heath Crs BW/LEM/TK/HW NE15 ... 54 E7
Heathdale Gdns LGB/HTN NE7 ... 47 H7
Heather Cl
CLDN/WHIT/ROK SR6 ... 74 A2 1
Heatherdale Crs DHAM DH1 ... 126 A6
Heather Dr HLH DH5 ... 117 K3
Heather Gv FELL NE10 ... 11 L3
Heather Lea STLY/ANP DH9 ... 89 G4 1
Heatherlea Gdns
SUNDSW SR3 ... 98 B3 7
Heather Pl ELS/FEN NE4 ... 55 J3
RYTON NE40 ... 52 C7
Heatherslaw Rd
WD/WHPE/BLK NE5 ... 55 G3
Heather Wy STLY/ANP DH9 ... 102 B1
Heatherwell Gn FELL NE10 ... 12 A9
Heathery La GOS/KPK NE3 ... 46 E3
Heathfield ASHBK/HED/RY SR2 ... 98 C4
Heathfield Crs
WD/WHPE/BLK NE5 ... 45 H7
Heathfield Gdns RYTON NE40 ... 64 C3
Heathfield Pl GOS/KPK NE3 ... 46 D1 3
Heathfield Rd
LWF/SPW/WRK NE9 ... 69 F6
Heath Gra HLH DH5 ... 108 C6
Heathmeads CLSW/PEL DH2 ... 104 C1
Heath Sq MLFD/PNYW SR4 ... 97 J1
Heathway JRW NE32 ... 72 A2
SEA/MUR SR7 ... 120 D3
Heathways DHAM DH1 ... 135 J5
Heathwell Gdns
WICK/BNPF NE16 ... 67 F4 2
Heathwell Rd
BW/LEM/TK/HW NE15 ... 54 D4
Heathwood Av
WICK/BNPF NE16 ... 66 E5 6
Heaton Gdns HAR/WTLS NE34 ... 73 G2
Heaton Gv BYK/HTN/WLK NE6 ... 6 E3
Heaton Hall Rd
BYK/HTN/WLK NE6 ... 6 E2
Heaton Park Rd
BYK/HTN/WLK NE6 ... 6 E3
Heaton Park Vw
BYK/HTN/WLK NE6 ... 6 E2
Heaton Pl BYK/HTN/WLK NE6 ... 6 F3
Heaton Rd BYK/HTN/WLK NE6 ... 6 F2
Heaton Ter BYK/HTN/WLK NE6 ... 6 D4
NSHW NE29 ... 50 C4
Heaviside Pl DHAM DH1 ... 17 J2
Heber St ELS/FEN NE4 ... 5 G6
Hebron Wy CRAM NE23 ... 28 B2
Hector St SMOOR NE27 ... 39 H5
Heddon Banks
BW/LEM/TK/HW NE15 ... 52 A2
Heddon Cl GOS/KPK NE3 ... 46 A4 5
Heddon Vw BLAY NE21 ... 65 K2
Heddon Wy HAR/WTLS NE34 ... 61 F5
Hedgefield Gv BLYTH NE24 ... 24 E4
Hedgefield Vw CRAM NE23 ... 28 B7
Hedgehope Rd
WD/WHPE/BLK NE5 ... 44 E6
Hedgelea RYTON NE40 ... 52 D6
Hedgelea Rd HLH DH5 ... 117 F5
Hedgeley Rd HEBB NE31 ... 59 G5
NSHW NE29 ... 50 B3 1
WD/WHPE/BLK NE5 ... 54 C3 2
Hedgeley Ter
BYK/HTN/WLK NE6 ... 58 B5 3
Hedley Ct BDN/LAN/SAC DH7 ... 123 F5
Hedley La WICK/BNPF NE16 ... 79 G7
Hedley Pl WLSD/HOW NE28 ... 58 D2 3
Hedley Rd MONK NE25 ... 30 B6
NSHW NE29 ... 2 B7
Hedley St GATE NE8 ... 10 C8
GOS/KPK NE3 ... 46 C5
SSH NE33 ... 3 H5
Hedley Ter
ASHBK/HED/RY SR2 ... 111 G1 2
GOS/KPK NE3 ... 46 C4
Hedworth Av HAR/WTLS NE34 ... 60 E7 2
Hedworth La BOLCOL NE35 ... 72 B3
JRW NE32 ... 72 B2
Hedworth Ter SUND SR1 ... 15 H5
Heighley St
BW/LEM/TK/HW NE15 ... 54 D6
Helen St BLAY NE21 ... 65 J2
CLDN/WHIT/ROK SR6 ... 86 E1
Helford Rd PLEE/EAS SR8 ... 136 D6
Helmdon WASHN NE37 ... 83 G5
Helmsdale Av FELL NE10 ... 12 C6 2
Helmsdale Rd MLFD/PNYW SR4 ... 97 H1
Helmsley Cl HLS DH4 ... 107 J1
Helmsley Ct SWCK/CAS SR5 ... 85 J2
Helmsley Dr WLSD/HOW NE28 ... 59 H1
Helmsley Rd DHAM DH1 ... 124 D2
JES NE2 ... 6 B3
Helston Ct
BW/LEM/TK/HW NE15 ... 53 K4 4
Helvellyn Av WASHS NE38 ... 94 C3
Helvellyn Rd
ASHBK/HED/RY SR2 ... 98 D4
Hemlington Cl
ASHBK/HED/RY SR2 ... 111 F1 2
Hemmel Cts
BDN/LAN/SAC DH7 ... 133 H5 1
Hemming St
ASHBK/HED/RY SR2 ... 99 F4 2
Hemsley Rd HAR/WTLS NE34 ... 61 K2
Henderson Av
WICK/BNPF NE16 ... 66 E4 3
Henderson Gdns FELL NE10 ... 13 L9
Henderson Rd HAR/WTLS NE34 ... 60 D6
MLFD/PNYW SR4 ... 97 K1
WLSD/HOW NE28 ... 48 D7 1
Hendersyde Cl
WD/WHPE/BLK NE5 ... 45 F7 1
Hendon Burn Av
ASHBK/HED/RY SR2 ... 15 H8
Hendon Burn Av West
ASHBK/HED/RY SR2 ... 15 H9 2
Hendon Cl NSHW NE29 ... 2 D6 1
Hendon Gdns JRW NE32 ... 72 B2
Hendon Rd LWF/SPW/WRK NE9 ... 11 L8
SUND SR1 ... 15 H4
Hendon Rd East SUND SR1 ... 15 K5
Hendon St SUND SR1 ... 15 J6
Hendon Valley Rd
ASHBK/HED/RY SR2 ... 15 G8
Henley Av CLSW/PEL DH2 ... 104 E4
Henley Cl CRAM NE23 ... 28 E1
Henley Gdns WLSD/HOW NE28 ... 49 K6
Henley Rd MLFD/PNYW SR4 ... 97 H1
TYNE/NSHE NE30 ... 51 F1
Henley Wy BOLCOL NE35 ... 72 C4
Henlow Rd
BW/LEM/TK/HW NE15 ... 54 A4 4
Henry Nelson St SSH NE33 ... 3 K5
Henry Sq JES NE2 ... 6 A5 1
Henry St GOS/KPK NE3 ... 46 C5
HLH DH5 ... 108 C6
NSHW NE29 ... 2 C4 1
SEA/MUR SR7 ... 111 K7 1
SSH NE33 ... 3 J4
Henry St East
ASHBK/HED/RY SR2 ... 15 J6
Hensby Ct
WD/WHPE/BLK NE5 ... 45 F6 6
Henshaw Gv MONK NE25 ... 30 C6
Henshaw Pl WD/WHPE/BLK NE5 ... 54 E4
Henshelwood Ter JES NE2 ... 56 E2 1
Henson Cl WASHS NE38 ... 95 F2
Hepburn Gdns FELL NE10 ... 12 A5
Hepburn Gv SWCK/CAS SR5 ... 84 D4 6
Hepple Ct BLYTH NE24 ... 24 E1 6
Hepple Wy GOS/KPK NE3 ... 46 A4 3
Hepscott Dr MONK NE25 ... 40 B3
Hepscott Ter HAR/WTLS NE34 ... 61 H4
Herbert St GATE NE8 ... 11 K5
Herbert Ter SEA/MUR SR7 ... 120 E1
Herd Cl BLAY NE21 ... 65 J3 6
Herd House La BLAY NE21 ... 65 H2
Herdinghill WASHN NE37 ... 82 B7
Herdlaw CRAM NE23 ... 28 B2
Hereford Ct
ASHBK/HED/RY SR2 ... 98 D5 3
DIN/WO NE13 ... 45 H2
Hereford Rd
ASHBK/HED/RY SR2 ... 98 D5
Herefordshire Dr DHAM DH1 ... 125 K6
Hereford Sq
ASHBK/HED/RY SR2 ... 98 D5 4
Hermiston MONK NE25 ... 40 C4
Heron Cl BLYTH NE24 ... 25 G4
WASHS NE38 ... 94 C4
Heron Dr SSH NE33 ... 3 G5
Heron Pl LGB/KIL NE12 ... 47 G3 2
Herrick St WD/WHPE/BLK NE5 ... 44 E7
Herring Gull Cl BLYTH NE24 ... 25 G4
Herrington Rd HLS DH4 ... 108 D1
SUNDSW SR3 ... 97 F7
Hersham Cl DIN/WO NE13 ... 45 H2 2
DIN/WO NE13 ... 45 G2 1
GOS/KPK NE3 ... 45 H3
Hertford LWF/SPW/WRK NE9 ... 81 F3
Hertford Av HAR/WTLS NE34 ... 62 B4
Hertford Cl MONK NE25 ... 40 A3
Hertford Crs HLH DH5 ... 117 J4
Hertford Gv CRAM NE23 ... 28 D1
Herton Cl PLEE/EAS SR8 ... 136 D3
Hesket Ct GOS/KPK NE3 ... 45 J3 5
Hesleyside Dr
WD/WHPE/BLK NE5 ... 55 F3
Hesleyside Rd MONK NE25 ... 39 K4
Hester Av MONK NE25 ... 30 A2
Hetton Rd HLH DH5 ... 117 H1
Hewitson Ter FELL NE10 ... 12 B9
Hewitt Av ASHBK/HED/RY SR2 ... 98 E6
Hewley Crs
BW/LEM/TK/HW NE15 ... 53 F2
Heworth Burn Crs FELL NE10 ... 12 F7
Heworth Gv WASHN NE37 ... 82 E5 1
Heworth Rd WASHN NE37 ... 83 F3
Heworth Wy FELL NE10 ... 13 J7
Hewson Pl
LWF/SPW/WRK NE9 ... 69 H6 5
Hexham WASHS NE38 ... 94 B2 1
Hexham Av BYK/HTN/WLK NE6 ... 58 B6
CRAM NE23 ... 28 E1
HEBB NE31 ... 71 G2
Hexham Cl NSHW NE29 ... 50 A3 2
Hexham Ct DUN/TMV NE11 ... 67 K6 3
Hexham Dr STLY/ANP DH9 ... 101 H2
Hexham Old Rd RYTON NE40 ... 52 E6
Hexham Rd
BW/LEM/TK/HW NE15 ... 53 F1
MLFD/PNYW SR4 ... 97 H1
WICK/BNPF NE16 ... 66 E3
Hextol Gdns
BW/LEM/TK/HW NE15 ... 54 D4 3
Heybrook Av NSHW NE29 ... 50 D2
Heyburn Gdns
BW/LEM/TK/HW NE15 ... 55 H6
Hibernian Rd JRW NE32 ... 59 K4 5
Hibernia Rd
BYK/HTN/WLK NE6 ... 58 C7 6
Hickling Ct WD/WHPE/BLK NE5 ... 45 F6
Hickstead Cl
WLSD/HOW NE28 ... 49 G3 2
Hickstead Gv CRAM NE23 ... 28 E1
Hiddleston Av LGB/HTN NE7 ... 47 H5
Higgins Ter SUNDSW SR3 ... 98 B7
Higham Pl CNUT NE1 ... 5 L5 1
High Back Cl JRW NE32 ... 59 J7
High Barnes Ter
MLFD/PNYW SR4 ... 98 A1 3
High Br CNUT NE1 ... 5 K7
Highbury FELL NE10 ... 12 E8
MONK NE25 ... 40 C4 1
Highbury Av
LWF/SPW/WRK NE9 ... 82 C3
Highbury Cl LWF/SPW/WRK NE9 ... 82 C3
High Carr Cl DHAM DH1 ... 124 C4
High Chare CLS/BIR/GTL DH3 ... 105 J4
Highcliffe Gdns GATE NE8 ... 11 K7
High Cft CLDN/WHIT/ROK SR6 ... 75 F3
WASHN NE37 ... 82 D4
High Croft Cl HEBB NE31 ... 59 F7 3
Highcroft Dr
CLDN/WHIT/ROK SR6 ... 74 E3 1
Highcross Rd TYNE/NSHE NE30 ... 40 E6
High Dene LGB/HTN NE7 ... 57 G2
Highfield BDN/LAN/SAC DH7 ... 113 H5
WICK/BNPF NE16 ... 79 F2
Highfield Cl
WD/WHPE/BLK NE5 ... 44 D7 3
Highfield Ct FELL NE10 ... 70 A5 3
Highfield Crs CLS/BIR/GTL DH3 ... 105 J2
Highfield Dr HAR/WTLS NE34 ... 61 K3
HLS DH4 ... 107 K7
Highfield Gra HLS DH4 ... 116 E1 1
Highfield Pl DIN/WO NE13 ... 36 A4 3
Highfield Ri CLS/BIR/GTL DH3 ... 105 J2
Highfield Rd GATE NE8 ... 11 K6
HAR/WTLS NE34 ... 61 K3
HLS DH4 ... 107 J1
ROWG NE39 ... 76 E4
WD/WHPE/BLK NE5 ... 54 D1
Highfield Ter
BYK/HTN/WLK NE6 ... 58 C7 7
High Flatworth NSHW NE29 ... 49 K5
Highgate Gdns JRW NE32 ... 72 B2 1
Highgate Rd MLFD/PNYW SR4 ... 97 H1
The High Ga GOS/KPK NE3 ... 45 J6
Highgreen Cha
WICK/BNPF NE16 ... 78 E1
High Gv RYTON NE40 ... 53 F7
Highgrove WD/WHPE/BLK NE5 ... 54 B1
High Hamsterley Rd
ROWG NE39 ... 88 C1
Highheath WASHN NE37 ... 82 C7 1
High Heworth La FELL NE10 ... 13 G8
High Horse Cl ROWG NE39 ... 77 J1
High Horse Close Wd
ROWG NE39 ... 77 J1
High House Gdns FELL NE10 ... 12 F6
Highland Rd
WD/WHPE/BLK NE5 ... 45 H7
High La HLS DH4 ... 108 D3
High Lane Rw HEBB NE31 ... 59 H3
High La FELL NE10 ... 13 H9
High Laws GOS/KPK NE3 ... 47 F6
High Level Br CNUT NE1 ... 5 L8
High Meadow HAR/WTLS NE34 ... 61 K3
High Mdw BDN/LAN/SAC DH7 ... 133 F5
High Mill Rd ROWG NE39 ... 88 C1
High Moor Pl
HAR/WTLS NE34 ... 61 G6 10
High Pasture WASHS NE38 ... 95 G5 1
High Rdg DIN/WO NE13 ... 36 B4 2
The High Rd HAR/WTLS NE34 ... 61 K5
High Rw BW/LEM/TK/HW NE15 ... 54 A5
High Sandgrove
CLDN/WHIT/ROK SR6 ... 74 A3
Highside Dr SUNDSW SR3 ... 98 A3
High Spen Ct ROWG NE39 ... 76 C1
Highstead Av CRAM NE23 ... 23 G6
High St BDN/LAN/SAC DH7 ... 133 K5
BLYTH NE24 ... 21 F7 1
BW/LEM/TK/HW NE15 ... 53 H4
DHAM DH1 ... 125 K5
DHAM DH1 ... 135 H4
FELL NE10 ... 12 C7
GATE NE8 ... 5 M9
GOS/KPK NE3 ... 46 C5
HLH DH5 ... 118 B7
JRW NE32 ... 60 A4
MLFD/PNYW SR4 ... 84 E7
RDHAMSE DH6 ... 126 E3
STLY/ANP DH9 ... 90 D7
High St East SUND SR1 ... 15 H3
WLSD/HOW NE28 ... 58 E2
High Street South Back
BDN/LAN/SAC DH7 ... 133 K5
High St West BYK/HTN/WLK NE6 ... 58 C2
SUND SR1 ... 14 E4
Hightree Cl SUNDSW SR3 ... 109 K2 6
SUNDSW SR3 ... 110 A2 3
High Vw PONT/DH NE20 ... 33 F7
WLSD/HOW NE28 ... 48 D7
High Vw North
WLSD/HOW NE28 ... 48 D6
Highwell La
WD/WHPE/BLK NE5 ... 54 C2 6
High West St GATE NE8 ... 10 F2
Highwood Rd
BW/LEM/TK/HW NE15 ... 54 D4
High Wood Vw DHAM DH1 ... 16 E7
Highworth Dr LGB/HTN NE7 ... 48 A7 2
LWF/SPW/WRK NE9 ... 82 B3
Hilda Av DHAM DH1 ... 17 M5
Hilda Cl DHAM DH1 ... 135 J1
Hilda Pk CLSW/PEL DH2 ... 105 H2
Hilda St CLDN/WHIT/ROK SR6 ... 86 D2 4
GATE NE8 ... 10 D6
Hilden Gdns LGB/HTN NE7 ... 57 J1
Hillary Av LGB/KIL NE12 ... 48 A2
Hillary Pl WD/WHPE/BLK NE5 ... 44 E7 3
Hill Av CRAM NE23 ... 29 H6
Hill Crs SEA/MUR SR7 ... 119 H5
SEA/MUR SR7 ... 121 F3
Hill Crest BDN/LAN/SAC DH7 ... 113 H6
WICK/BNPF NE16 ... 77 K7
Hillcrest DHAM DH1 ... 16 E2
DHAM DH1 ... 135 J5
HAR/WTLS NE34 ... 62 B7
JRW NE32 ... 72 A2
MONK NE25 ... 40 C4
SUNDSW SR3 ... 97 F7
Hillcrest Dr DUN/TMV NE11 ... 67 J5
Hill Crest Gdns JES NE2 ... 46 E6 5
Hillcroft LWF/SPW/WRK NE9 ... 69 G6
Hill Dyke LWF/SPW/WRK NE9 ... 81 J3
Hillfield MONK NE25 ... 40 B4
Hillfield Gdns SUNDSW SR3 ... 98 B3
Hillfield St GATE NE8 ... 10 E4
Hillgate GATE NE8 ... 5 M9
Hill Head Dr WD/WHPE/BLK NE5 ... 54 B2
Hillhead Gdns DUN/TMV NE11 ... 68 A6 3
Hillhead La WICK/BNPF NE16 ... 78 B4
Hillhead Pkwy
WD/WHPE/BLK NE5 ... 44 A7
Hill Head Rd WD/WHPE/BLK NE5 ... 54 B1
Hillheads Rd MONK NE25 ... 40 D6
Hillhead Wy WD/WHPE/BLK NE5 ... 44 C7
Hill House Rd
BW/LEM/TK/HW NE15 ... 52 D1
Hillingdon Gv MLFD/PNYW SR4 ... 96 E4
Hill La HLS DH4 ... 96 A5
Hill Mdw DHAM DH1 ... 135 H5
Hillmeads CLSW/PEL DH2 ... 114 A4
Hill Pk PONT/DH NE20 ... 33 F7
Hill Park Rd JRW NE32 ... 60 A6
Hill Ri RYTON NE40 ... 64 B1
WASHS NE38 ... 83 G7
Hillrise Crs SEA/MUR SR7 ... 110 D7
Hillsden Rd MONK NE25 ... 40 B2
Hillside BDN/LAN/SAC DH7 ... 113 G7
BLAY NE21 ... 65 K2
BOL NE36 ... 72 E5 4
CLS/BIR/GTL DH3 ... 93 K2
CLS/BIR/GTL DH3 ... 105 J3
DUN/TMV NE11 ... 67 J5
HAR/WTLS NE34 ... 62 B7
PONT/DH NE20 ... 42 E1
SUNDSW SR3 ... 98 C3
Hillside Av
BW/LEM/TK/HW NE15 ... 54 D4
Hillside Cl ROWG NE39 ... 77 G2 3
Hillside Crs
BW/LEM/TK/HW NE15 ... 54 E7
Hillside Dr CLDN/WHIT/ROK SR6 ... 74 E3
Hillside Gdns STLY/ANP DH9 ... 90 E6
SUNDSW SR3 ... 98 C3 5
Hillside Pl LWF/SPW/WRK NE9 ... 69 G6
Hillside Wy HLS DH4 ... 108 C6
Hillsleigh Rd
WD/WHPE/BLK NE5 ... 45 H7
Hill St JRW NE32 ... 59 J4
SEA/MUR SR7 ... 120 E2
SSH NE33 ... 2 E9
SUNDSW SR3 ... 98 A7
Hillsview Av GOS/KPK NE3 ... 45 K5 5
Hill Ter HLS DH4 ... 108 C1 1
Hillthorne Cl WASHS NE38 ... 95 H2 3
Hill Top BLAY NE21 ... 65 K3
CLS/BIR/GTL DH3 ... 93 K2
STLY/ANP DH9 ... 91 F7
Hill Top Av LWF/SPW/WRK NE9 ... 69 G7
Hill Top Gdns
LWF/SPW/WRK NE9 ... 69 G7
Hilltop Gdns SUNDSW SR3 ... 98 C7 3
Hilltop Rd BDN/LAN/SAC DH7 ... 123 F5
Hilltop Vw BDN/LAN/SAC DH7 ... 122 C3
Hillview SUNDSW SR3 ... 97 F7
Hillview Crs HLS DH4 ... 108 B4 3
Hill View Gdns SUNDSW SR3 ... 98 B3
Hillview Gv HLS DH4 ... 108 B4 4
Hill View Rd ASHBK/HED/RY SR2 ... 98 E4
Hillview Rd HLS DH4 ... 108 B4 5
Hill View Sq ASHBK/HED/RY SR2 ... 98 D4
Hilton Av WD/WHPE/BLK NE5 ... 55 F1
Hilton Cl CRAM NE23 ... 23 G5
Hilton Dr PLEE/EAS SR8 ... 136 E5
Hindley Cl RYTON NE40 ... 64 A1 1
Hindley Gdns ELS/FEN NE4 ... 55 H4
Hindmarch Dr BOL NE36 ... 72 E5
Hind St SUND SR1 ... 14 C5 1
Hinkley Cl SUNDSW SR3 ... 110 A1
Hipsburn Dr SUNDSW SR3 ... 98 A3
Hiram Dr BOL NE36 ... 73 H5
Histon Wy WD/WHPE/BLK NE5 ... 45 F7
Hither Gn JRW NE32 ... 72 B2 2
Hobart WBAY NE26 ... 40 D2
Hobart Av HAR/WTLS NE34 ... 60 D7

Hodgkin Park Crs
BW/LEM/TK/HW NE15 ... **55** G6
Hodgkin Park Rd
BW/LEM/TK/HW NE15 ... **55** G6
Hodgson's Rd *BLYTH* NE24 ... **21** F6
Hodkin Gdns
LWF/SPW/WRK NE9 ... **69** H6
Hogarth Dr *WASHS* NE38 ... **95** G3
Hogarth Rd *HAR/WTLS* NE34 ... **73** G2
Holbein Rd *HAR/WTLS* NE34 ... **73** G1
Holborn Pl
WD/WHPE/BLK NE5 ... **54** C2 7
Holborn Rd *MLFD/PNYW* SR4 ... **97** H2
Holborn Sq *MLFD/PNYW* SR4 ... **97** H2 2
Holburn Cl *RYTON* NE40 ... **53** F6 1
Holburn Ct
BDN/LAN/SAC DH7 ... **133** G1 1
RYTON NE40 ... **53** F6 2
Holburn Crs *RYTON* NE40 ... **53** G6
Holburn Gdns *RYTON* NE40 ... **53** G6
Holburn La *RYTON* NE40 ... **53** F6
Holburn Wk *RYTON* NE40 ... **53** G6
Holburn Wy *RYTON* NE40 ... **53** F6
Holden Pl *WD/WHPE/BLK* NE5 ... **55** H1 7
Holder House La
HAR/WTLS NE34 ... **73** J1
Holderness Rd
BYK/HTN/WLK NE6 ... **57** H2
WLSD/HOW NE28 ... **49** J7
Hole La *WICK/BNPF* NE16 ... **78** D1
Holeyn Rd
BW/LEM/TK/HW NE15 ... **52** E2 1
Holland Dr *JES* NE2 ... **4** E3
Holland Pk *WLSD/HOW* NE28 ... **48** A7
Holland Park Dr *JRW* NE32 ... **72** B2
Hollinghill Rd *MONK* NE25 ... **30** B6
Hollings Crs *WLSD/HOW* NE28 .. **48** D6 3
Hollingside La *DHAM* DH1 ... **16** D9
Hollington Av *LGB/KIL* NE12 ... **47** H4
Hollinhill *ROWG* NE39 ... **65** J7
Hollinhill La *ROWG* NE39 ... **77** H1
Hollinside Cl *WICK/BNPF* NE16 ... **66** E7
Hollinside Gdns
BW/LEM/TK/HW NE15 ... **55** F5
Hollinside Rd *MLFD/PNYW* SR4 ... **97** H2
WICK/BNPF NE16 ... **67** F2
Hollinside Sq *MLFD/PNYW* SR4 ... **97** G1
Hollinside Ter *ROWG* NE39 ... **77** F3 2
Hollowdene *HLH* DH5 ... **117** K5
Holly Av *BLAY* NE21 ... **66** A6
CLDN/WHIT/ROK SR6 ... **75** F4
DUN/TMV NE11 ... **9** H9
GOS/KPK NE3 ... **45** K4
HAR/WTLS NE34 ... **62** A6
HLH DH5 ... **108** C7
JES NE2 ... **56** E2
LGB/KIL NE12 ... **47** K1
MONK NE25 ... **39** K4
RYTON NE40 ... **52** E5 2
SUNDSW SR3 ... **98** B6
WBAY NE26 ... **40** E4
WLSD/HOW NE28 ... **58** E2
Holly Av West *JES* NE2 ... **56** E2 2
Hollybush Rd *FELL* NE10 ... **12** A8
Hollycarrside Rd
ASHBK/HED/RY SR2 ... **98** E6
Holly Crs *BDN/LAN/SAC* DH7 ... **113** H6
Hollydene *DUN/TMV* NE11 ... **80** D7
ROWG NE39 ... **77** H3
Holly Hvn *HLH* DH5 ... **117** G4
Holly Hl *FELL* NE10 ... **12** C7
Holly Hill Gdns *STLY/ANP* DH9 ... **102** D3
Holly Hill Gdns East
STLY/ANP DH9 ... **102** E3
Holly Hill Gdns West
STLY/ANP DH9 ... **102** D3
Hollymount Sq *BDLGTN* NE22 ... **19** G6
Holly Pk *BDN/LAN/SAC* DH7 ... **133** G6
BDN/LAN/SAC DH7 ... **133** F1
Holly Park Vw *FELL* NE10 ... **12** D7
Holly Rd *NSHW* NE29 ... **50** D3
The Hollys *CLS/BIR/GTL* DH3 ... **81** H6
Holly St *DHAM* DH1 ... **16** A4
JRW NE32 ... **59** J4
Hollywell Ct *BDN/LAN/SAC* DH7 .. **133** G1
Hollywell Gv *DIN/WO* NE13 ... **44** D2
Hollywell Rd *NSHW* NE29 ... **50** B4
Hollywood Av *GOS/KPK* NE3 ... **46** C4
SWCK/CAS SR5 ... **85** K3
Hollywood Crs *GOS/KPK* NE3 ... **46** D4
Hollywood Gdns
DUN/TMV NE11 ... **68** B7 2
Holme Av *BYK/HTN/WLK* NE6 ... **58** B2
WICK/BNPF NE16 ... **67** F5
Holme Gdns *SUNDSW* SR3 ... **98** B3
WLSD/HOW NE28 ... **59** J1 1
Holme Ri *WICK/BNPF* NE16 ... **67** F5
Holmesdale Rd
WD/WHPE/BLK NE5 ... **55** H2
Holmeside *SUND* SR1 ... **14** E5
Holmewood Dr *ROWG* NE39 ... **77** F5
Holmfield Av *HAR/WTLS* NE34 ... **61** J4
Holm Gn *MONK* NE25 ... **40** B5
Holmhill La *CLS/BIR/GTL* DH3 ... **114** D1
PLEE/EAS SR8 ... **130** E4
Holmland *BW/LEM/TK/HW* NE15 .. **55** G7
Holmlands *MONK* NE25 ... **40** C4 2
Holmlands Pk North
ASHBK/HED/RY SR2 ... **98** C2 3
Holmlands Pk South
ASHBK/HED/RY SR2 ... **98** C2 4
Holmside Av *DUN/TMV* NE11 ... **9** H8
Holmside Hall Rd
BDN/LAN/SAC DH7 ... **103** F7
Holmwood Av *MONK* NE25 ... **40** B5
Holmwood Gv *JES* NE2 ... **56** D1 1
Holyfields *SMOOR* NE27 ... **39** F7
Holylake Sq *MLFD/PNYW* SR4 ... **97** H1
Holyoake Gdns
CLS/BIR/GTL DH3 ... **93** J2 2
LWF/SPW/WRK NE9 ... **11** H8
Holyoake St *CLSW/PEL* DH2 ... **104** C1
Holystone Av *GOS/KPK* NE3 ... **46** B4
MONK NE25 ... **41** F5
Holystone Cl *BLYTH* NE24 ... **24** E2
HLS DH4 ... **107** K5 1
Holystone Crs *LGB/HTN* NE7 ... **47** G7
Holystone Dr *SMOOR* NE27 ... **38** E7
Holystone Gdns *NSHW* NE29 ... **50** B3
Holystone St *HEBB* NE31 ... **59** F5
Holywell Av *BYK/HTN/WLK* NE6 ... **12** F1
MONK NE25 ... **30** C6
WBAY NE26 ... **40** C3
Holywell Cl *ELS/FEN* NE4 ... **4** F4 1
MONK NE25 ... **30** C6
Holywell Dene Rd *MONK* NE25 ... **30** C7
Home Av *LWF/SPW/WRK* NE9 ... **81** F1
Home Pk *WLSD/HOW* NE28 ... **48** A7
Homestall Cl *HAR/WTLS* NE34 ... **61** H6 3
Honeycomb Cl *SUNDSW* SR3 ... **109** K2 7
Honeysuckle Av
HAR/WTLS NE34 ... **61** F7
Honeysuckle Cl *SUNDSW* SR3 ... **110** A2
Honister Av *JES* NE2 ... **46** E7
Honister Cl
BW/LEM/TK/HW NE15 ... **54** B4 3
Honister Dr *SWCK/CAS* SR5 ... **86** C2 3
Honister Pl
BW/LEM/TK/HW NE15 ... **54** B4
Honister Rd *TYNE/NSHE* NE30 ... **41** F7
Honister Wy *BLYTH* NE24 ... **24** E4
Honiton Cl *HLS* DH4 ... **108** A3 4
Honiton Ct
WD/WHPE/BLK NE5 ... **45** F4 1
Honiton Wy *NSHW* NE29 ... **49** K2
Hood Cl *SWCK/CAS* SR5 ... **86** C4 5
Hood St *CNUT* NE1 ... **5** K6
WICK/BNPF NE16 ... **66** E3 3
Hookergate La *ROWG* NE39 ... **76** C3
Hopedene *FELL* NE10 ... **70** C7
Hope Shield *WASHS* NE38 ... **94** B5
Hope St *HAR/WTLS* NE34 ... **61** F6 2
JRW NE32 ... **60** A4
SUND SR1 ... **14** C5
Hopgarth Gdns
CLS/BIR/GTL DH3 ... **105** K3
Hopkins Ct *MLFD/PNYW* SR4 ... **85** K6
Hopper Pl *GATE* NE8 ... **11** G2
Hopper Rd *FELL* NE10 ... **12** A9
Hopper St *GATE* NE8 ... **11** G2
NSHW NE29 ... **2** B2
WLSD/HOW NE28 ... **58** D1 6
Horatio St *CLDN/WHIT/ROK* SR6 .. **86** E4
Hornbeam Pl *ELS/FEN* NE4 ... **9** L1
Horncliffe Gdns *WICK/BNPF* NE16 .. **8** A7
Horncliffe Pl
BW/LEM/TK/HW NE15 ... **52** D1
Hornsea Cl *DIN/WO* NE13 ... **36** B4 3
Hornsey Ter *HLH* DH5 ... **118** A7 1
Horse Crofts *BLAY* NE21 ... **66** A1 3
Horsham Gdns *SUNDSW* SR3 ... **98** A3 8
Horsham Gv *NSHW* NE29 ... **50** C6
Horsley Av *RYTON* NE40 ... **64** A1
SMOOR NE27 ... **39** H7
Horsley Ct *GOS/KPK* NE3 ... **45** J4 1
Horsley Gdns *DUN/TMV* NE11 ... **9** J8
MONK NE25 ... **30** C6 2
Horsley Gv *SUNDSW* SR3 ... **98** A3
Horsley Hill Rd *SSH* NE33 ... **61** J2
Horsley Hill Sq
HAR/WTLS NE34 ... **62** B4 1
Horsley Rd *LGB/HTN* NE7 ... **57** H2
WASHS NE38 ... **83** J7
Horsley Ter
BYK/HTN/WLK NE6 ... **58** B6 1
Horsley V *HAR/WTLS* NE34 ... **61** K4
Horton Av *BDLGTN* NE22 ... **19** F6
HAR/WTLS NE34 ... **73** H1
SMOOR NE27 ... **39** H7
Horton Crs *DIN/WO* NE13 ... **35** F2 3
Hortondale Gv *BLYTH* NE24 ... **20** D7
Horton Dr *CRAM* NE23 ... **23** G6
Horton Pl *BLYTH* NE24 ... **24** D3 3
Horton Rd *BLYTH* NE24 ... **23** J1
Horwood Av
WD/WHPE/BLK NE5 ... **54** B1
Hospital Dr *HEBB* NE31 ... **59** F7 4
Hospital La
BW/LEM/TK/HW NE15 ... **53** K4
Hospital Rd *BDN/LAN/SAC* DH7 .. **122** A3
Hotch Pudding Pl
WD/WHPE/BLK NE5 ... **54** D3
Hotspur Av *BDLGTN* NE22 ... **19** F6
HAR/WTLS NE34 ... **61** J4 3
MONK NE25 ... **40** E5
Hotspur Rd *WLSD/HOW* NE28 ... **48** C5
Hotspur St *BYK/HTN/WLK* NE6 ... **6** C3
TYNE/NSHE NE30 ... **51** H2
Houghton Av *TYNE/NSHE* NE30 ... **41** F6
WD/WHPE/BLK NE5 ... **45** H7
Houghton Cut *HLH* DH5 ... **108** C6
Houghton Rd *HLH* DH5 ... **117** J2
HLS DH4 ... **108** B4
Houghton St *MLFD/PNYW* SR4 ... **86** A7
Houlskye Cl *SUNDSW* SR3 ... **98** C7 4
Houndelee Pl
WD/WHPE/BLK NE5 ... **55** G2 4
Hounslow Gdns *JRW* NE32 ... **72** B2 3
House Ter *WASHN* NE37 ... **83** F5
Houston Ct *ELS/FEN* NE4 ... **4** F8
Houston St *ELS/FEN* NE4 ... **4** F8
Houxty Rd *MONK* NE25 ... **39** K4
Hovingham Cl *PLEE/EAS* SR8 ... **137** F5
Hovingham Gdns
SUNDSW SR3 ... **98** A3 9
Howardian Cl *WASHS* NE38 ... **94** D3
Howard St *CNUT* NE1 ... **6** B6
FELL NE10 ... **69** J6
GATE NE8 ... **11** M6
JRW NE32 ... **60** A5
SWCK/CAS SR5 ... **86** D4 4
TYNE/NSHE NE30 ... **2** E2
Howarth St *MLFD/PNYW* SR4 ... **86** A7
Howat Av *WD/WHPE/BLK* NE5 .. **55** J2 1
Howdene Rd
BW/LEM/TK/HW NE15 ... **54** D5
Howdon La *WLSD/HOW* NE28 ... **49** J7
Howdon Rd *NSHW* NE29 ... **2** A6
WLSD/HOW NE28 ... **60** A1
Howe Sq *MLFD/PNYW* SR4 ... **97** G1
Howe St *GATE* NE8 ... **11** L6
HEBB NE31 ... **59** J5 2
Howick Av *GOS/KPK* NE3 ... **46** A3
Howletch La *PLEE/EAS* SR8 ... **136** D4
Howlett Hall Rd
BW/LEM/TK/HW NE15 ... **54** D5
Howley Av *SWCK/CAS* SR5 ... **85** G3 2
Hownam Cl *GOS/KPK* NE3 ... **46** A6 3
Hoy Crs *SEA/MUR* SR7 ... **111** F6
Hoylake Av *LGB/HTN* NE7 ... **47** J5
Hoyle Av *ELS/FEN* NE4 ... **55** J5
Hoyle Fold *SUNDSW* SR3 ... **110** A3
Hubert St *BOLCOL* NE35 ... **72** D4
Huddlestone Ri
CLDN/WHIT/ROK SR6 ... **15** H1 2
Huddleston Rd
BYK/HTN/WLK NE6 ... **7** J3
Hudson Av *BDLGTN* NE22 ... **19** H5
Hudson Rd *SUND* SR1 ... **15** G5
Hudson St *GATE* NE8 ... **10** F1 1
HAR/WTLS NE34 ... **61** F5
TYNE/NSHE NE30 ... **3** G1
Hudspeth Crs *DHAM* DH1 ... **124** B2
Hugh St *CLDN/WHIT/ROK* SR6 ... **86** E2
WASHS NE38 ... **95** H2 4
WLSD/HOW NE28 ... **58** D2
Hull St *ELS/FEN* NE4 ... **4** B8
Hulme Ct *PLEE/EAS* SR8 ... **136** D5 1
Hulne Av *TYNE/NSHE* NE30 ... **51** G3
Humber Gdns *GATE* NE8 ... **11** L6
Humber Hl *STLY/ANP* DH9 ... **102** E2
Humbert St *JRW* NE32 ... **59** K5 3
Humbleburn La
BDN/LAN/SAC DH7 ... **103** J6
Hume St *BYK/HTN/WLK* NE6 ... **6** D6
MLFD/PNYW SR4 ... **86** A6
Humford Gn *BLYTH* NE24 ... **20** B7
Humford Wy *BDLGTN* NE22 ... **19** G7
Humsford Gv *CRAM* NE23 ... **23** J7
Humshaugh Cl *LGB/KIL* NE12 ... **48** C2 1
Humshaugh Rd *NSHW* NE29 ... **50** A4 1
Hunstanton Ct
LWF/SPW/WRK NE9 ... **80** E2
Huntcliffe Av
CLDN/WHIT/ROK SR6 ... **74** E6
Huntcliffe Gdns
BYK/HTN/WLK NE6 ... **57** J2
Hunter Av *BDN/LAN/SAC* DH7 ... **122** E7
BLYTH NE24 ... **25** H1
Hunter Cl *BOL* NE36 ... **73** H6
Hunter Rd *PLEE/EAS* SR8 ... **136** B5
Hunters Cl *NSHW* NE29 ... **50** B7
Hunters Ct *WLSD/HOW* NE28 ... **58** E1 4
Hunters Hall Rd
MLFD/PNYW SR4 ... **14** A8 2
Hunters Ldg *WLSD/HOW* NE28 ... **58** D1
Hunter's Moor Cl *JES* NE2 ... **4** E1
Hunter's Pl *JES* NE2 ... **4** E1
Hunter's Rd *GOS/KPK* NE3 ... **47** F5
JES NE2 ... **4** D2
Hunter St *HLS* DH4 ... **107** J2
SSH NE33 ... **61** H2
Hunter Ter *ASHBK/HED/RY* SR2 ... **98** E3
Huntingdon Cl *DIN/WO* NE13 ... **45** G2
Huntingdon Gdns
SUNDSW SR3 ... **98** A3 10
Huntingdon Pl *TYNE/NSHE* NE30 .. **51** H3
Huntingdon Rd *PLEE/EAS* SR8 ... **136** D2
Huntingdonshire Dr
DHAM DH1 ... **126** A6 2
Huntington Dr *CRAM* NE23 ... **28** D1
Hunt Lea *WICK/BNPF* NE16 ... **66** C7 2
Huntley Av *SEA/MUR* SR7 ... **119** G5 1
Huntley Crs *BLAY* NE21 ... **65** J4
Huntley Sq *MLFD/PNYW* SR4 ... **97** H1 1
Huntly Rd *MONK* NE25 ... **40** A2
Hurst Ter *BYK/HTN/WLK* NE6 ... **7** M5
Hurstwood Rd *MLFD/PNYW* SR4 .. **98** A2
Hurworth Av *HAR/WTLS* NE34 ... **62** A5
Hurworth Pl *JRW* NE32 ... **59** K5
Hustledown Gdns
STLY/ANP DH9 ... **102** D3 1
Hustledown Rd *STLY/ANP* DH9 .. **102** C3
Hutton Cl *HLS* DH4 ... **108** A7
WASHS NE38 ... **94** B1
Hutton St *BOLCOL* NE35 ... **72** C3
MLFD/PNYW SR4 ... **14** A7
Hutton Ter *JES* NE2 ... **6** A2
LWF/SPW/WRK NE9 ... **81** F1
Huxley Crs *GATE* NE8 ... **10** D9
Hyacinth Ct *MLFD/PNYW* SR4 ... **14** A3 2
Hyde Pk *WLSD/HOW* NE28 ... **48** B7
Hydepark St *GATE* NE8 ... **10** D8
Hyde St *ASHBK/HED/RY* SR2 ... **99** F2
SSH NE33 ... **3** K9
Hyde Ter *GOS/KPK* NE3 ... **46** D5
Hylton Av *HAR/WTLS* NE34 ... **62** B5
Hylton Bank *MLFD/PNYW* SR4 ... **85** F7
Hylton Castle Rd *SWCK/CAS* SR5 .. **85** F4
Hylton Cl *BDLGTN* NE22 ... **18** D5
BDN/LAN/SAC DH7 ... **122** A3
Hylton Gra *SWCK/CAS* SR5 ... **84** D6
Hylton La *BOL* NE36 ... **72** E6
SWCK/CAS SR5 ... **84** E2
Hylton Park Rd *SWCK/CAS* SR5 ... **85** J4
Hylton Rd *DHAM* DH1 ... **124** D3
JRW NE32 ... **59** K7
MLFD/PNYW SR4 ... **14** A4
Hylton St *GATE* NE8 ... **11** L5
HLS DH4 ... **108** B5 2
MLFD/PNYW SR4 ... **86** A7
NSHW NE29 ... **2** C4
Hylton Wk *MLFD/PNYW* SR4 ... **96** E1 1
MLFD/PNYW SR4 ... **97** F1 2
Hymers Av *HAR/WTLS* NE34 ... **60** D7
Hyperion Av *HAR/WTLS* NE34 ... **60** E6

I

Ilchester St *SEA/MUR* SR7 ... **120** E2 4
Ilderton Pl
WD/WHPE/BLK NE5 ... **54** C3 3
Ilex St *DUN/TMV* NE11 ... **68** C6
Ilford Av *CRAM* NE23 ... **23** G6 4
Ilford Pl *GATE* NE8 ... **11** K8
Ilford Rd *JES* NE2 ... **46** D7
WLSD/HOW NE28 ... **49** H7
Ilfracombe Av *ELS/FEN* NE4 ... **55** J6
Ilminster Ct *GOS/KPK* NE3 ... **45** G4 2
Imeary Gv *SSH* NE33 ... **61** H2 3
Imeary St *SSH* NE33 ... **61** H2
Inchberry Cl *ELS/FEN* NE4 ... **55** J7
Inchbury Cl *ELS/FEN* NE4 ... **55** J7 1
Inchcliffe Crs
WD/WHPE/BLK NE5 ... **55** G1
Indigo St *DUN/TMV* NE11 ... **68** C6
Industrial Rd *WASHN* NE37 ... **83** G6
Industrial St *CLSW/PEL* DH2 ... **104** C1
Industry Rd *BYK/HTN/WLK* NE6 ... **57** K1
Ingham Gra *SSH* NE33 ... **61** J2 4
Ingham Gv *CRAM* NE23 ... **23** G6 5
Ingleby Ter *MLFD/PNYW* SR4 ... **98** A1 5
Ingleby Wy *BLYTH* NE24 ... **25** F4
Inglemere Pl
BW/LEM/TK/HW NE15 ... **54** E5 1
Ingleside *WICK/BNPF* NE16 ... **66** D6
Ingleside Rd *NSHW* NE29 ... **50** D3
Ingleton Dr
BW/LEM/TK/HW NE15 ... **52** D1
Ingleton Gdns *BLYTH* NE24 ... **24** E4
Inglewood Cl *BLYTH* NE24 ... **20** B7
Inglewood Pl *GOS/KPK* NE3 ... **46** C1 2
Ingoe Av *GOS/KPK* NE3 ... **45** K3 2
Ingoe Cl *BLYTH* NE24 ... **20** E7
Ingoe St *BW/LEM/TK/HW* NE15 ... **54** A5
WLSD/HOW NE28 ... **60** A1
Ingoldsby Ct *MLFD/PNYW* SR4 .. **97** J2 3
Ingram Av *GOS/KPK* NE3 ... **45** K2 3
Ingram Cl *CLSW/PEL* DH2 ... **105** G6
WLSD/HOW NE28 ... **49** H5 1
Ingram Dr *BLYTH* NE24 ... **20** D7
WD/WHPE/BLK NE5 ... **44** B6
Ingram Ter
BYK/HTN/WLK NE6 ... **58** C5 1
Inkerman Rd *WASHN* NE37 ... **83** F4
Inkerman St *SWCK/CAS* SR5 ... **86** A4
Inleborough Dr *RYTON* NE40 ... **53** F7
Innesmoor *HEBB* NE31 ... **59** F4
Inskip Ter *GATE* NE8 ... **11** H8
Institute Ter West
CLSW/PEL DH2 ... **93** F6
Inverness Rd *JRW* NE32 ... **72** C1
Inverness St
CLDN/WHIT/ROK SR6 ... **86** D3
Invincible Dr *ELS/FEN* NE4 ... **9** K2
Iolanthe Crs *BYK/HTN/WLK* NE6 ... **7** L2
Iolanthe Ter *SSH* NE33 ... **3** L9
Iona Pl *BYK/HTN/WLK* NE6 ... **58** C5 2
Iona Rd *FELL* NE10 ... **69** H5
JRW NE32 ... **72** C1
Irene Av *ASHBK/HED/RY* SR2 ... **99** F5
Iris Crs *CLSW/PEL* DH2 ... **93** F4
Iris Pl *ELS/FEN* NE4 ... **55** H4
Iris St *DUN/TMV* NE11 ... **68** C6
Iris Ter *RYTON* NE40 ... **64** B1
Iroko St *DUN/TMV* NE11 ... **68** C6
Ironside St *HLH* DH5 ... **108** C6
Irthing Av *BYK/HTN/WLK* NE6 ... **7** K8
Irton St *GOS/KPK* NE3 ... **46** C5
Irwin Av *WLSD/HOW* NE28 ... **48** D7
Isabella Rd *BLYTH* NE24 ... **24** E1
Isabella Wk
BW/LEM/TK/HW NE15 ... **53** F2 4
Isis Rd *PLEE/EAS* SR8 ... **136** D5
Ivanhoe *MONK* NE25 ... **40** C4
Ivanhoe Vw *LWF/SPW/WRK* NE9 .. **81** H3
Iveagh Cl *ELS/FEN* NE4 ... **55** H7
Iveson St *BDN/LAN/SAC* DH7 ... **113** G5
Iveston La *CON/LDGT* DH8 ... **100** B6
Iveston Ter *STLY/ANP* DH9 ... **90** D7
Ivor St *ASHBK/HED/RY* SR2 ... **99** G4
Ivy Av *RYTON* NE40 ... **52** E5 3
SEA/MUR SR7 ... **120** C1
Ivy Cl *ELS/FEN* NE4 ... **9** M1
Ivy La *LWF/SPW/WRK* NE9 ... **81** G2
Ivymount Rd *BYK/HTN/WLK* NE6 .. **57** H2
Ivy Rd *BYK/HTN/WLK* NE6 ... **58** B3
GOS/KPK NE3 ... **46** C6
LGB/KIL NE12 ... **48** A2
Ivy St *DUN/TMV* NE11 ... **68** C6
Ivyway *CLSW/PEL* DH2 ... **92** E7
Ixia St *DUN/TMV* NE11 ... **68** C6

J

Jackson Av *PONT/DH* NE20 ... **33** H2
Jackson St *BYK/HTN/WLK* NE6 .. **58** B5 4
GATE NE8 ... **11** G2
MLFD/PNYW SR4 ... **98** A1
TYNE/NSHE NE30 ... **51** F4
Jackson St West
TYNE/NSHE NE30 ... **51** F4
Jack's Ter *HAR/WTLS* NE34 ... **61** G6
Jacques St *MLFD/PNYW* SR4 ... **85** K6 4
Jacques Ter *CLSW/PEL* DH2 ... **105** H4
Jade Cl *BW/LEM/TK/HW* NE15 ... **54** A3
James Armitage St
SWCK/CAS SR5 ... **86** B3 9
James Mather St *SSH* NE33 ... **3** J6
James St *ELS/FEN* NE4 ... **4** A9
PLEE/EAS SR8 ... **130** E4
SEA/MUR SR7 ... **120** E2
SWCK/CAS SR5 ... **86** A3 4
WD/WHPE/BLK NE5 ... **54** D1 4
WICK/BNPF NE16 ... **66** E5 7
James Ter *HLH* DH5 ... **128** A1
HLS DH4 ... **107** J7
SUNDSW SR3 ... **98** B7
WLSD/HOW NE28 ... **58** D2 9
James Williams St *SUND* SR1 ... **15** H3
Jane Eyre Ter *GATE* NE8 ... **11** L5
Jane Ter *BYK/HTN/WLK* NE6 ... **58** C6
Janet St *BYK/HTN/WLK* NE6 ... **7** H8
Janus Cl *WD/WHPE/BLK* NE5 ... **44** A6 2
Jarrow Rd *HAR/WTLS* NE34 ... **60** E5
JRW NE32 ... **60** D5
Jarvis Rd *PLEE/EAS* SR8 ... **136** E2
Jasmin Av *WD/WHPE/BLK* NE5 ... **44** A6
Jasmine Cl *BYK/HTN/WLK* NE6 ... **58** A2
Jasmine Ct *MLFD/PNYW* SR4 ... **14** B4 2
Jasmine Crs *SEA/MUR* SR7 ... **120** D3
Jasper Av *RYTON* NE40 ... **64** D3
Jedburgh Cl *GATE* NE8 ... **11** H6 2
NSHW NE29 ... **50** C2
WD/WHPE/BLK NE5 ... **44** A6
Jedburgh Gdns
BW/LEM/TK/HW NE15 ... **55** F5
Jedburgh Rd *HLS* DH4 ... **107** K1 4
Jedmoor *HEBB* NE31 ... **59** F4
Jefferson Pl *ELS/FEN* NE4 ... **4** F5
Jellicoe Rd *BYK/HTN/WLK* NE6 ... **12** E1
Jenifer Gv *LGB/HTN* NE7 ... **47** G7
Jenison Av
BW/LEM/TK/HW NE15 ... **55** G6
Jennifer Av *SWCK/CAS* SR5 ... **85** F4 5
Jervis St *HEBB* NE31 ... **59** H5
Jesmond Dene Rd *JES* NE2 ... **56** D1
Jesmond Gdns *JES* NE2 ... **57** F2 3
Jesmond Pk East *LGB/HTN* NE7 ... **57** H1
Jesmond Pk West
LGB/HTN NE7 ... **57** H2 1
Jesmond Rd *JES* NE2 ... **5** K3
JES NE2 ... **57** G3 3
Jesmond Ter *WBAY* NE26 ... **40** E5
Jesmond V *BYK/HTN/WLK* NE6 ... **6** D2
Jesmond Vale La
BYK/HTN/WLK NE6 ... **6** E1
Jessel St *LWF/SPW/WRK* NE9 ... **81** F1
Joan Av *ASHBK/HED/RY* SR2 ... **99** F5
Joannah St *SWCK/CAS* SR5 ... **86** C2 4
Joan St *ELS/FEN* NE4 ... **55** H7
Jobling Av *BLAY* NE21 ... **65** J2
Joel Ter *FELL* NE10 ... **13** L3
John Av *RYTON* NE40 ... **64** D3
John Brown Ct *BDLGTN* NE22 ... **19** F5 3
John Candlish Rd
MLFD/PNYW SR4 ... **86** A6
John Clay St *SSH* NE33 ... **61** H2 6
John Dobson St *CNUT* NE1 ... **5** K4
John Reid Rd *HAR/WTLS* NE34 ... **60** D7
Johnson Cl *PLEE/EAS* SR8 ... **136** E2
Johnson St
BW/LEM/TK/HW NE15 ... **54** A5 2
DUN/TMV NE11 ... **9** H5
GATE NE8 ... **9** M5
SSH NE33 ... **61** G4
SUND SR1 ... **14** B4
Johnston Av *HEBB* NE31 ... **71** F1
John St *BDN/LAN/SAC* DH7 ... **113** H5
BLYTH NE24 ... **20** D6
DHAM DH1 ... **16** A4
FELL NE10 ... **13** H6
GATE NE8 ... **11** L5
GOS/KPK NE3 ... **46** A5
HLH DH5 ... **108** D7
HLH DH5 ... **117** K5
HLH DH5 ... **118** A5 1
HLS DH4 ... **107** J7
MLFD/PNYW SR4 ... **84** E6 2
MONK NE25 ... **39** J4
PLEE/EAS SR8 ... **131** F4
STLY/ANP DH9 ... **91** H7
STLY/ANP DH9 ... **102** B3
STLY/ANP DH9 ... **103** G5
SUND SR1 ... **14** F4 1
TYNE/NSHE NE30 ... **41** G5
WLSD/HOW NE28 ... **58** D1
John Taylor Ct *SWCK/CAS* SR5 ... **86** A2 2
John Williamson St *SSH* NE33 ... **61** F4
John Wilson Ct
PLEE/EAS SR8 ... **137** H3 3
Joicey Gdns *STLY/ANP* DH9 ... **90** D7 4
Joicey Rd *LWF/SPW/WRK* NE9 ... **69** F6
Joicey St *FELL* NE10 ... **13** J5 1
Jolliffe St *CLS/BIR/GTL* DH3 ... **105** K6
Jonadab Rd *FELL* NE10 ... **13** K3
Jonadab St *FELL* NE10 ... **13** J5
Jones St *CLS/BIR/GTL* DH3 ... **93** H2
Jonquil Cl *WD/WHPE/BLK* NE5 .. **44** A6 3
Joseph Cl *ELS/FEN* NE4 ... **55** J7
Joseph St *STLY/ANP* DH9 ... **102** C2 1
Jowett Sq *SWCK/CAS* SR5 ... **86** A3 5
Joyce Ter *SWCK/CAS* SR5 ... **85** F4 6
Jubilee Av *LWF/SPW/WRK* NE9 ... **81** J4
Jubilee Cl *BDN/LAN/SAC* DH7 ... **113** G1
Jubilee Crs *GOS/KPK* NE3 ... **46** A4
Jubilee Pl *DHAM* DH1 ... **135** H4 1
Jubilee Rd *BLYTH* NE24 ... **25** G1
CNUT NE1 ... **6** A6
GOS/KPK NE3 ... **46** A5
Jubilee Sq *HLH* DH5 ... **118** B7 1
Jubilee Ter *WICK/BNPF* NE16 ... **66** E3 4
Jude Pl *PLEE/EAS* SR8 ... **136** D2 1
PLEE/EAS SR8 ... **136** E2 1
Julian Av *BYK/HTN/WLK* NE6 ... **7** L2
SSH NE33 ... **3** J5
Julian Rd *FELL* NE10 ... **71** F4
Julian St *SSH* NE33 ... **3** J5
Juliet Av *NSHW* NE29 ... **50** B4 5
Julius Caesar St
SWCK/CAS SR5 ... **86** A3 6
June Av *BLAY* NE21 ... **66** A6
Juniper Cl *BLYTH* NE24 ... **24** E3
GOS/KPK NE3 ... **46** D1 4
Jupiter Ct *PLEE/EAS* SR8 ... **130** D5 2
Jutland Av *HEBB* NE31 ... **59** G5
Jutland Ter *STLY/ANP* DH9 ... **90** B6

K

Kalmia St *DUN/TMV* NE11 ... **68** C7
Kane Gdns *FELL* NE10 ... **69** J6
Katrine Cl *CLSW/PEL* DH2 ... **105** H5
Katrine Ct *SUNDSW* SR3 ... **110** A2 4
Kayll Rd *MLFD/PNYW* SR4 ... **85** K7
Kay St *STLY/ANP* DH9 ... **90** D7
Kearsley Cl *MONK* NE25 ... **30** A5 2
Kearton Av *WD/WHPE/BLK* NE5 .. **44** A7
Keats Av *BLYTH* NE24 ... **24** E2 4
BOLCOL NE35 ... **73** F4
SWCK/CAS SR5 ... **86** A3 7
Keats Cl *STLY/ANP* DH9 ... **102** E1
Keats Rd *BW/LEM/TK/HW* NE15 .. **53** J5
Keebledale Av
BYK/HTN/WLK NE6 ... **58** B4 1
Keelman's La *MLFD/PNYW* SR4 ... **85** F6
Keelman's Rd *MLFD/PNYW* SR4 ... **85** F6
Keir Hardie Av *FELL* NE10 ... **13** K8
STLY/ANP DH9 ... **102** D3
Keir Hardie St *HLS* DH4 ... **107** K7
Keir Hardie Wy *SWCK/CAS* SR5 ... **86** B4
Keith Cl *ELS/FEN* NE4 ... **55** J7
Keldane Gdns *ELS/FEN* NE4 ... **55** J6
Kelfield Gv *CRAM* NE23 ... **23** H5 3

Kellfield Av LWF/SPW/WRK NE9 69 G6
Kellfield Rd LWF/SPW/WRK NE9 69 G7
Kell Rd PLEE/EAS SR8 137 G4 2
Kells La LWF/SPW/WRK NE9 69 F7
Kellsway FELL NE10 70 B7 5
Kell's Wy ROWG NE39 77 G4
Kelly Rd HEBB NE31 71 G1
Kelsey Wy CRAM NE23 23 H5
Kelso Cl WD/WHPE/BLK NE5 44 A6 4
Kelso Dr NSHW NE29 50 C2
Kelso Gdns
BW/LEM/TK/HW NE15 55 F5
WLSD/HOW NE28 49 J6
Kelso Gv HLS DH4 107 J1 2
Kelson Wy
WD/WHPE/BLK NE5 44 A6 5
Kelso Pl GATE NE8 10 A8
Kelston Wy WD/WHPE/BLK NE5 55 G1
Kelvin Gv
CLDN/WHIT/ROK SR6 73 J3 2
CLDN/WHIT/ROK SR6 86 E3
GATE NE8 10 D8
HAR/WTLS NE34 61 K2
JES NE2 6 B2
NSHW NE29 50 E2
Kemble Cl CRAM NE23 23 H5 4
Kemp Rd PLEE/EAS SR8 136 D3
Kempton Gdns GATE NE8 10 B9
Kendal Av BLYTH NE24 25 F1 5
TYNE/NSHE NE30 41 F7
Kendal Cl PLEE/EAS SR8 136 B7
Kendal Crs LWF/SPW/WRK NE9 81 H1
Kendal Dr BOL NE36 73 G5
CRAM NE23 23 J7
Kendale Wk
WD/WHPE/BLK NE5 44 C7 4
Kendal Gdns WLSD/HOW NE28 49 J5
Kenilworth LGB/KIL NE12 37 K5
Kenilworth Rd ELS/FEN NE4 4 C8
MONK NE25 40 D5
Kenilworth Sq SWCK/CAS SR5 85 G1
Kenilworth Vw
LWF/SPW/WRK NE9 81 G3
Kenley Rd WD/WHPE/BLK NE5 54 E3
Kenmoor Wy
WD/WHPE/BLK NE5 44 A7
Kenmore Crs RYTON NE40 64 D2
Kennersdene TYNE/NSHE NE30 51 G2
Kennet Av JRW NE32 72 A1
Kennington Gv
BYK/HTN/WLK NE6 7 L6
Kenny Pl DHAM DH1 125 G6
Kensington Av GOS/KPK NE3 46 C3
Kensington Gdns
TYNE/NSHE NE30 51 F4 2
WLSD/HOW NE28 48 A7
Kensington Gv
TYNE/NSHE NE30 51 F3 1
Kensington Ter JES NE2 5 J2
Kent Av DUN/TMV NE11 9 J7 1
HEBB NE31 59 F6
WLSD/HOW NE28 59 H1
Kentchester Rd SWCK/CAS SR5 85 F1
Kent Gdns HLH DH5 117 J4
Kentmere Av BYK/HTN/WLK NE6 58 B5
CLDN/WHIT/ROK SR6 74 C7
Kentmere Cl CRAM NE23 29 H6
Kentmere Pl PLEE/EAS SR8 137 F4 6
Kenton Av GOS/KPK NE3 46 A7
Kenton Ct SSH NE33 61 H2
Kenton Crs GOS/KPK NE3 45 K6
Kenton Gv CLDN/WHIT/ROK SR6 86 D4
Kenton La GOS/KPK NE3 45 H6
WD/WHPE/BLK NE5 45 J6
Kenton Rd GOS/KPK NE3 46 A5
NSHW NE29 50 A3
Kent Pl HAR/WTLS NE34 61 K5
Kent St JRW NE32 59 J5
Kentucky Rd SWCK/CAS SR5 84 E1
Kenya Rd SWCK/CAS SR5 85 F1
Kepier Chare RYTON NE40 52 B7
Kepier Ct DHAM DH1 16 F2
Kepier Gdns MLFD/PNYW SR4 84 E7 3
Keppel St SSH NE33 3 H7
Kerry Cl BLYTH NE24 21 G6 7
Kerryhill Dr DHAM DH1 124 D1 3
Keston Dr CRAM NE23 23 H5
Kestrel Cl WASHS NE38 94 C4
Kestrel Ms WICK/BNPF NE16 66 E5 3
Kestrel Pl LGB/KIL NE12 47 H3
Kestrel St DUN/TMV NE11 68 C6
Kestrel Wy HAR/WTLS NE34 61 F7
NSHW NE29 2 B6
Keswick Av
CLDN/WHIT/ROK SR6 86 C1
Keswick Dr TYNE/NSHE NE30 41 F7
Keswick Gdns WLSD/HOW NE28 49 J7
Keswick Gv WD/WHPE/BLK NE5 54 E3
Keswick Rd PLEE/EAS SR8 137 F4
STLY/ANP DH9 102 B3
Keswick St GATE NE8 10 E6
Keswic Ter RDHAMSE DH6 128 D1
Kettering Pl CRAM NE23 23 J7 1
Kettlewell Ter TYNE/NSHE NE30 2 F1
Ketton Cl LGB/KIL NE12 47 H4 4
Kew Gdns WBAY NE26 40 D3
Keyes Gdns JES NE2 46 E7
Kibblesworth Bank
DUN/TMV NE11 80 B7
Kidderminster Dr
WD/WHPE/BLK NE5 44 A7 2
Kidderminster Rd
SWCK/CAS SR5 85 F2
Kidlandlee Gn
WD/WHPE/BLK NE5 44 E6 3
Kidlandlee Pl
WD/WHPE/BLK NE5 44 E6
Kielder Av CRAM NE23 27 J2
Kielder Cl BLYTH NE24 24 D2
LGB/KIL NE12 37 J5 3
WD/WHPE/BLK NE5 44 E6 4
Kielder Gdns JRW NE32 71 J1
Kielder Pl MONK NE25 39 K4
Kielder Rd
BW/LEM/TK/HW NE15 53 K4
MONK NE25 39 K4
Kielder Ter TYNE/NSHE NE30 51 F4 3
Kielder Wy GOS/KPK NE3 46 B3 2
Kier Hardie Av STLY/ANP DH9 102 D2
Kilburn Dr PLEE/EAS SR8 137 G1
Kilburne Cl LGB/HTN NE7 48 A7 3
Kilburn Gdns NSHW NE29 50 B7
Kildale HLS DH4 95 G6 3
Killin Cl WD/WHPE/BLK NE5 44 A6 6
Killingworth Av SMOOR NE27 38 C5
Killingworth Dr LGB/KIL NE12 37 H7
SUNDSW SR3 97 H2
Killingworth La LGB/KIL NE12 38 C6
Killingworth Pl CNUT NE1 5 J5
Killingworth Rd GOS/KPK NE3 47 F5
LGB/KIL NE12 48 A1
Killingworth Wy CRAM NE23 38 A4
LGB/KIL NE12 37 G5
Kiln Ri WICK/BNPF NE16 78 E1
Kilnshaw Pl GOS/KPK NE3 46 D1 3
Kimberley WASHS NE38 95 J1
Kimberley Av NSHW NE29 50 C4
Kimberley Gdns JES NE2 57 G3 4
Kimberley St BLYTH NE24 21 F6
MLFD/PNYW SR4 85 K7 5
Kingarth Av
CLDN/WHIT/ROK SR6 74 E7
Kingdom Pl NSHW NE29 2 C7
King Edward Pl GATE NE8 11 L5
King Edward Rd
BYK/HTN/WLK NE6 57 H2
MLFD/PNYW SR4 85 F7 2
RYTON NE40 53 G7
SEA/MUR SR7 120 E2
TYNE/NSHE NE30 51 G3
King Edward St GATE NE8 11 L6
Kingfisher Rd LGB/KIL NE12 47 G3
Kingfisher Wy BLYTH NE24 25 G3
WLSD/HOW NE28 49 J4
King George Av DUN/TMV NE11 9 G9
King George Rd GOS/KPK NE3 45 J4
HAR/WTLS NE34 61 J4
Kingham Ct LGB/HTN NE7 47 F6 2
King John's Ct PONT/DH NE20 32 C5
King John St BYK/HTN/WLK NE6 6 F1
King John Ter BYK/HTN/WLK NE6 6 F1
Kings Av CLDN/WHIT/ROK SR6 74 E7
HEBB NE31 59 H6
Kingsbridge LGB/KIL NE12 47 F3 1
Kings Cl GATE NE8 11 L5
Kingsdale Av BLYTH NE24 20 C7
Kingsdale Rd LGB/KIL NE12 47 F3
King's Dr WBAY NE26 40 E4
King's Gdns BLYTH NE24 20 E6
Kings Gv DHAM DH1 134 B3
Kingsland JES NE2 56 E3 2
King's La CLSW/PEL DH2 92 D7
Kingsley Av GOS/KPK NE3 46 D1
HAR/WTLS NE34 72 E1
MONK NE25 40 D5
Kingsley Cl SWCK/CAS SR5 86 A4 4
Kingsley Pl DUN/TMV NE11 9 H6 1
WICK/BNPF NE16 67 F4
WLSD/HOW NE28 49 H7 4
Kingsley Ter ELS/FEN NE4 4 C7
Kingsmere CLS/BIR/GTL DH3 93 J7
Kingsmere Gdns
BYK/HTN/WLK NE6 58 C7 3
Kings Pk STKFD/GP NE62 19 F1
King's Pl MLFD/PNYW SR4 86 A6
King's Rd BDLGTN NE22 19 K4
CNUT NE1 5 J4
LGB/KIL NE12 47 J1
WBAY NE26 40 D3
Kings Rd North
WLSD/HOW NE28 48 D6
Kings Rd South
WLSD/HOW NE28 48 D7
The King's Rd SWCK/CAS SR5 86 A3
King's Ter MLFD/PNYW SR4 85 K6
Kingston Av BDN/LAN/SAC DH7 123 F6
BYK/HTN/WLK NE6 7 K7
Kingston Cl WBAY NE26 40 D1
Kingston Dr WBAY NE26 40 D2
Kingston Park Av GOS/KPK NE3 45 G4
Kingston Park Rd DIN/WO NE13 45 H2
GOS/KPK NE3 45 K3
Kingston Rd GATE NE8 11 K7
Kingston Ter
CLDN/WHIT/ROK SR6 86 D3
King St BLYTH NE24 21 G6
CLDN/WHIT/ROK SR6 86 D1
CLS/BIR/GTL DH3 93 H2
CNUT NE1 5 M8
FELL NE10 13 K5
GATE NE8 10 B7
SSH NE33 3 G7
SUND SR1 14 E4
TYNE/NSHE NE30 51 F4
Kingsway BDN/LAN/SAC DH7 122 B3
BLYTH NE24 25 G1 5
ELS/FEN NE4 55 J3
HLH DH5 108 D7
PONT/DH NE20 33 G3
SSH NE33 61 K1
TYNE/NSHE NE30 51 G2
WICK/BNPF NE16 78 E2
Kingsway Av GOS/KPK NE3 46 C3
Kingsway North DUN/TMV NE11 68 C6
Kingsway Rd SWCK/CAS SR5 84 E1
Kingsway South
DUN/TMV NE11 80 D1
Kingswood Av JES NE2 46 D7 2
Kingswood Cl BOLCOL NE35 72 C3
Kingswood Dr PONT/DH NE20 32 E5
Kingswood Gv MLFD/PNYW SR4 96 D4
Kingswood Rd CRAM NE23 23 J7
King Ter STLY/ANP DH9 102 B2
Kinlett WASHS NE38 95 J1 2
Kinley Rd DHAM DH1 126 A4
Kinloch Ct CLSW/PEL DH2 105 H6
Kinloss Sq CRAM NE23 23 J7 2
Kinnaird Av
BW/LEM/TK/HW NE15 54 E5
Kinross Ct FELL NE10 13 M4
Kinross Dr GOS/KPK NE3 45 J5
STLY/ANP DH9 103 F1
Kinver Dr WD/WHPE/BLK NE5 44 A7
Kiphill Ct STLY/ANP DH9 90 E6
Kipling Av BOLCOL NE35 73 F4
HEBB NE31 59 H5
WICK/BNPF NE16 67 F4
Kipling Cl STLY/ANP DH9 102 E1
Kipling Ct WICK/BNPF NE16 67 F4 3
Kipling St SWCK/CAS SR5 86 A4 5
Kira Dr DHAM DH1 124 D1
Kirby Av DHAM DH1 124 B4
Kirby Cl HAR/WTLS NE34 60 D7
Kirkbride Pl CRAM NE23 23 J7 3
Kirkdale Gn ELS/FEN NE4 4 E8
Kirkdale St HLH DH5 117 J6
Kirkham Av GOS/KPK NE3 45 G3 1
Kirkham Rd DHAM DH1 124 E3
Kirkheaton Pl
WD/WHPE/BLK NE5 55 G3
Kirkland Hl PLEE/EAS SR8 136 E3
Kirklands CRAM NE23 37 J4
Kirkland Wk SMOOR NE27 39 G6
Kirklea Rd HLH DH5 108 D7
Kirkleatham Gdns
BYK/HTN/WLK NE6 57 K1 4
Kirkley Av HAR/WTLS NE34 62 A5
Kirkley Cl GOS/KPK NE3 46 B4
Kirkley Dr PONT/DH NE20 33 G2
Kirkley Rd SMOOR NE27 39 H7
Kirklinton Rd TYNE/NSHE NE30 40 E7
Kirknewton Cl HLH DH5 108 D7 3
Kirkside HLS DH4 108 C1
Kirkston Av
BW/LEM/TK/HW NE15 54 B4
Kirkstone CLS/BIR/GTL DH3 93 K4
Kirkstone Av JRW NE32 72 B1
PLEE/EAS SR8 137 F4
SWCK/CAS SR5 86 C2
TYNE/NSHE NE30 40 E7
Kirkstone Cl HLH DH5 108 D7
Kirkstone Dr DHAM DH1 125 K4
Kirkstone Gdns LGB/HTN NE7 47 G7 2
Kirkstone Rd FELL NE10 13 H6
Kirk Vw HLS DH4 108 B4 6
Kirkwall Cl SWCK/CAS SR5 84 E4
Kirkwood CRAM NE23 37 J4
Kirkwood Av MLFD/PNYW SR4 96 E4
Kirkwood Cl CRAM NE23 29 H6
Kirkwood Dr GOS/KPK NE3 45 K5 6
Kirkwood Gdns FELL NE10 13 L7
Kirton Av ELS/FEN NE4 55 J5
Kirton Wy CRAM NE23 23 J7
Kismet St SWCK/CAS SR5 86 A3
Kitchener Rd
CLDN/WHIT/ROK SR6 62 E7
Kitchener St
LWF/SPW/WRK NE9 11 J9
MLFD/PNYW SR4 97 K2
Kitchener Ter
ASHBK/HED/RY SR2 99 F4
JRW NE32 59 K6
TYNE/NSHE NE30 51 G3
Kitching Rd PLEE/EAS SR8 136 B1
Kittiwake Cl BLYTH NE24 25 G4
NSHW NE29 49 J3
Kittiwake Dr WASHS NE38 94 B3
Kittiwake St DUN/TMV NE11 68 C7
Kitty Brewster Rd BLYTH NE24 20 B6
Knaresborough Cl BDLGTN NE22 18 D4
Knaresborough Rd
SEA/MUR SR7 119 H5
Knaresdale CLS/BIR/GTL DH3 93 K5
Knarsdale Av NSHW NE29 50 B4
Knarsdale Pl
WD/WHPE/BLK NE5 54 C2 3
Kneller Cl STLY/ANP DH9 102 D1
Knightsbridge GOS/KPK NE3 46 C4
SUNDSW SR3 97 J6 2
Knightside Gdns
DUN/TMV NE11 67 K6 4
Knivestone Ct LGB/KIL NE12 38 A5
Knobbyends La BLAY NE21 65 H4
Knoll Ri DUN/TMV NE11 67 K5
Knollside Cl SUNDSW SR3 109 K2
Knott Pl BW/LEM/TK/HW NE15 54 E6
Knoulberry WASHN NE37 82 C7
Knoulberry Rd WASHN NE37 82 C7
Knowledge Hl BLAY NE21 65 K3
Knowle Pl LGB/KIL NE12 47 H5
Knowsley Ct
WD/WHPE/BLK NE5 45 F5 1
Knox Cl BDLGTN NE22 19 K4 4
Knox Rd BDLGTN NE22 19 H6
Knox Sq SWCK/CAS SR5 86 A2
Kristin Av JRW NE32 60 A7
Kyffin Vw HAR/WTLS NE34 62 B6
Kyle Cl ELS/FEN NE4 4 F9
Kyle Rd GATE NE8 10 B7
Kyloe Av MONK NE25 30 A6
Kyloe Cl GOS/KPK NE3 45 J3
Kyloe Pl WD/WHPE/BLK NE5 44 E7
Kyloe Vls WD/WHPE/BLK NE5 44 E7 5
Kyo Heugh Rd STLY/ANP DH9 101 J1
Kyo La STLY/ANP DH9 101 K2
Kyo Rd STLY/ANP DH9 101 H2

L

Laburnam Pk
BDN/LAN/SAC DH7 133 F7 1
Laburnam Rd
CLDN/WHIT/ROK SR6 86 D2 5
Laburnum Av BLYTH NE24 21 F6
BYK/HTN/WLK NE6 58 B3
DHAM DH1 16 A4
FELL NE10 13 J9
WLSD/HOW NE28 58 D1
Laburnum Ct LGB/KIL NE12 37 J5 5
Laburnum Crs DUN/TMV NE11 80 C7
SEA/MUR SR7 120 D4 1
Laburnum Gdns JRW NE32 59 J7
Laburnum Gv
CLDN/WHIT/ROK SR6 74 A3
HAR/WTLS NE34 61 K6
SWCK/CAS SR5 84 E5
WICK/BNPF NE16 66 E5 3
WICK/BNPF NE16 79 F2
Laburnum Rd BLAY NE21 66 A2
CLDN/WHIT/ROK SR6 86 D2 6
Lacebank SUNDSW SR3 109 J3
Ladock Cl ASHBK/HED/RY SR2 99 G6 1
Lady Anne Rd RDHAMSE DH6 126 C7
Ladybank WD/WHPE/BLK NE5 43 K7
Ladyhaugh Dr
WICK/BNPF NE16 78 E1 1
Ladykirk Rd ELS/FEN NE4 55 J6
Ladykirk Wy CRAM NE23 27 K2 1
Ladyrigg PONT/DH NE20 33 F5
Ladysmith Ct STLY/ANP DH9 102 E2
Lady's Piece La RDHAMSE DH6 126 D3
Lady's Wk SSH NE33 3 G5
Ladywell Rd BLAY NE21 66 A2
Ladywell Wy PONT/DH NE20 33 F2
Ladywood Pk HLS DH4 95 H6 2
Laet St NSHW NE29 2 E3
Laindon Av CLDN/WHIT/ROK SR6 86 D1
Laing Gv WLSD/HOW NE28 49 J7
Laith Rd GOS/KPK NE3 45 J5
Lake Ap BLAY NE21 66 D3 1
Lake Av HAR/WTLS NE34 62 C5
Lake Ct SUNDSW SR3 110 A1 3
Lakeland Dr PLEE/EAS SR8 137 F3
Lake Rd HLH DH5 108 C7
Lakeside BLAY NE21 66 D3
HAR/WTLS NE34 62 D5
Lake Vw HEBB NE31 59 F7
Lambden Cl NSHW NE29 50 C7
Lambert Rd WASHN NE37 82 B6
Lambeth Pl GATE NE8 11 K7 1
Lambley Av TYNE/NSHE NE30 41 F7
Lambley Cl WICK/BNPF NE16 78 E3
Lambley Crs HEBB NE31 71 F1
Lambourn Av LGB/KIL NE12 47 J3
NSHW NE29 50 B6
Lambourne Cl HLS DH4 107 G4
Lambourne Rd
ASHBK/HED/RY SR2 98 C3
Lamb St BYK/HTN/WLK NE6 58 C6 2
Lambton Av WICK/BNPF NE16 8 A8
Lambton Cl RYTON NE40 52 B7
Lambton Ct PLEE/EAS SR8 136 D7
SUNDSW SR3 97 G7 3
WASHS NE38 94 A6
Lambton Dr HLH DH5 117 K6
Lambton Rd HEBB NE31 59 H4 2
JES NE2 5 L1
Lambton St SUND SR1 14 F3
Lambton Ter JRW NE32 71 K1
Lampeter Cl
WD/WHPE/BLK NE5 45 F6 7
Lamport St HEBB NE31 58 E4 2
Lampton Ct BDLGTN NE22 19 J4 1
Lanark Cl NSHW NE29 50 A2
Lanark Dr JRW NE32 72 C1
Lancashire Dr DHAM DH1 126 A6
Lancaster Ct GOS/KPK NE3 45 H3 3
Lancaster Dr WLSD/HOW NE28 49 F3
Lancaster Rd DUN/TMV NE11 8 E6
Lancaster Ter CLS/BIR/GTL DH3 105 K5
Lancastrian Rd CRAM NE23 28 B3
Lancefield Av
BYK/HTN/WLK NE6 58 B7
Lanchester Av
LWF/SPW/WRK NE9 81 K2
Lanchester Cl FELL NE10 70 E6 1
Lanchester Gn BDLGTN NE22 19 F4 1
Lanchester Pk WASHS NE38 95 G4 2
Lanchester Rd
BDN/LAN/SAC DH7 101 J7
Lancing Ct GOS/KPK NE3 45 G3
Landseer Cl STLY/ANP DH9 102 D1
Landseer Gdns HAR/WTLS NE34 73 H2
LWF/SPW/WRK NE9 11 M9 1
Lane Cnr HAR/WTLS NE34 61 G6
Lanercost WASHS NE38 94 E1
Lanercost Av BLAY NE21 65 K2 1
Lanercost Dr
WD/WHPE/BLK NE5 55 F3
Lanercost Gdns
BW/LEM/TK/HW NE15 43 F7
FELL NE10 69 J6 2
Lanercost Rd NSHW NE29 50 C5
Langdale MONK NE25 40 C4
Langdale Cl LGB/KIL NE12 47 G4
Langdale Crs DHAM DH1 125 K4
Langdale Dr CRAM NE23 27 K2
Langdale Gdns
BYK/HTN/WLK NE6 58 C5 3
WLSD/HOW NE28 49 J6
Langdale Pl PLEE/EAS SR8 137 F4 7
Langdale Rd HLS DH4 95 J6
LWF/SPW/WRK NE9 69 G7
Langdale St HLH DH5 117 J6
Langdale Wy BOL NE36 73 G4
Langdon Cl NSHW NE29 50 D1 1
Langdon Rd WD/WHPE/BLK NE5 54 B1
Langford Dr BOLCOL NE35 72 C2
Langham Av NSHW NE29 50 A2
Langham Rd
BW/LEM/TK/HW NE15 54 D6 1
Langholm Rd BOL NE36 73 H4
GOS/KPK NE3 46 C3 1
Langhurst ASHBK/HED/RY SR2 98 E6
Langleeford Rd
WD/WHPE/BLK NE5 44 E7
Langley Av BLYTH NE24 20 D6
FELL NE10 70 D6
MONK NE25 40 B6
SMOOR NE27 39 J7
Langley Cl WASHS NE38 94 D2
Langley Crs BDN/LAN/SAC DH7 133 J5
Langley Rd BYK/HTN/WLK NE6 58 B5
DHAM DH1 124 D3
NSHW NE29 50 B4
SUNDSW SR3 98 B4
WD/WHPE/BLK NE5 54 D3
Langley St HLS DH4 108 B1
Langley Ter JRW NE32 71 K1
Langport Rd
ASHBK/HED/RY SR2 98 D3 2
Langton Cl MLFD/PNYW SR4 14 A5 1
Langton Ct PONT/DH NE20 32 D5
Langton Dr CRAM NE23 23 J5
Langton Lea DHAM DH1 135 K5 1
Langton Ter LGB/HTN NE7 57 H1 1
Lanivet Cl ASHBK/HED/RY SR2 99 F6
Lansbury Cl CLS/BIR/GTL DH3 81 H7
Lansbury Dr CLS/BIR/GTL DH3 81 H7
SEA/MUR SR7 119 H5 4
Lansbury Gdns FELL NE10 13 K8
Lansbury Rd WICK/BNPF NE16 67 G6
Lansbury Wy SWCK/CAS SR5 85 F4
Lansdowne ASHBK/HED/RY SR2 98 E7
Lansdowne Gdns JES NE2 6 D1
Lansdowne Rd LGB/KIL NE12 47 K2
Lansdowne St MLFD/PNYW SR4 14 A3
Lansdowne Ter NSHW NE29 2 B1
Lansdowne Ter West NSHW NE29 2 A1
Lanthwaite Rd
LWF/SPW/WRK NE9 69 G7
Lanton St HLS DH4 108 B1
Lapford Dr CRAM NE23 23 J6
Lapwing Cl BLYTH NE24 25 G3
WASHS NE38 94 B3
Lapwing Ct WICK/BNPF NE16 90 A1
L'arbre Crs WICK/BNPF NE16 66 D5
Larch Av CLDN/WHIT/ROK SR6 75 G3
HAR/WTLS NE34 62 A6
HLS DH4 108 B6
Larch Cl LWF/SPW/WRK NE9 81 K3
Larches Rd DHAM DH1 124 B6 1
The Larches WICK/BNPF NE16 77 K6 1
Larchlea PONT/DH NE20 32 E7
Larchlea South PONT/DH NE20 32 E7
Larch Rd BLAY NE21 66 B1
Larch Ter STLY/ANP DH9 89 J5
Larchwood WASHS NE38 94 D5
Larchwood Av
BYK/HTN/WLK NE6 58 A3
DIN/WO NE13 36 C4
GOS/KPK NE3 45 K3 3
Larchwood Gdns
DUN/TMV NE11 68 B7
Larchwood Gv
ASHBK/HED/RY SR2 98 C4 4
Larkfield Crs HLS DH4 107 J2 1
Larkfield Rd ASHBK/HED/RY SR2 98 C3
Lark Rise Cl LGB/HTN NE7 47 K7 3
Larkspur Cl STLY/ANP DH9 90 B6
Larkspur Rd WICK/BNPF NE16 66 E6
Larkspur Ter JES NE2 56 E2
Larne Crs LWF/SPW/WRK NE9 69 G7
Larriston Pl CRAM NE23 28 A2 1
Lartington Cl CLS/BIR/GTL DH3 115 J2
Lartington Gdns
GOS/KPK NE3 47 F5 4
Larwood Cl CLS/BIR/GTL DH3 106 A6
Larwood Ct STLY/ANP DH9 101 G4
Lascelles Av HAR/WTLS NE34 61 J6
Laski Gdns FELL NE10 13 L7
Latimer St TYNE/NSHE NE30 51 H2
Lauderdale Av WLSD/HOW NE28 48 D6
Launceston Cl DIN/WO NE13 45 H2
Launceston Dr SUNDSW SR3 97 G7
Laura St SUND SR1 14 F6
Laurel Av DHAM DH1 17 L3
GOS/KPK NE3 46 A4
LGB/KIL NE12 48 C1
SEA/MUR SR7 120 C1
Laurel Ct CLSW/PEL DH2 105 H2
Laurel Crs BYK/HTN/WLK NE6 58 B2
STLY/ANP DH9 92 B7
Laurel Gv ASHBK/HED/RY SR2 98 C4
Laurel Rd BLAY NE21 66 B2
Laurel St BW/LEM/TK/HW NE15 43 F7
WLSD/HOW NE28 58 E2
Laurel Wy RYTON NE40 64 C1
Laurelwood Gdns
DUN/TMV NE11 68 B7
Lauren Ct PLEE/EAS SR8 130 D5
Laurens Ct WASHN NE37 83 F5 1
Lavender Gdns
BDN/LAN/SAC DH7 113 J5
JES NE2 56 D2
Lavender Gv SWCK/CAS SR5 84 E4
Lavender La HAR/WTLS NE34 61 F6
Lavender Rd WICK/BNPF NE16 66 E6
Laverock Hall Rd BLYTH NE24 24 C4
Laverock Pl BLYTH NE24 24 D4 2
GOS/KPK NE3 45 H5 7
Lavington Rd HAR/WTLS NE34 61 J3
Lawe Rd SSH NE33 3 J4
Lawmill Wy
WD/WHPE/BLK NE5 55 F1 7
Lawn Dr BOL NE36 72 D6
The Lawns HLH DH5 118 B7
Lawnswood HLH DH5 117 J1
Lawrence Av BLAY NE21 66 A1
HAR/WTLS NE34 73 H1
Lawrence Ct BLAY NE21 66 A1 4
Lawrence St SUND SR1 15 H5
Lawson Av JRW NE32 60 A7
Lawson Crs
CLDN/WHIT/ROK SR6 86 D1
Lawson St NSHW NE29 2 D5
WLSD/HOW NE28 58 E2
Lawson Ter DHAM DH1 16 A4
ELS/FEN NE4 55 J7 2
HLH DH5 118 A7
Laws St CLDN/WHIT/ROK SR6 86 D1
Laxford Ct SUNDSW SR3 109 K2
Laybourn Gdns
HAR/WTLS NE34 60 E7 3
Layburn Gdns
BW/LEM/TK/HW NE15 54 C3 4
Layburn Pl PLEE/EAS SR8 136 C3
Layfield Rd GOS/KPK NE3 46 C1
Laygate SSH NE33 61 G3 3
Laygate Pl SSH NE33 61 G2
Laygate St SSH NE33 61 F2
Lea Av JRW NE32 72 A2
Leabank BW/LEM/TK/HW NE15 54 B3
Lead Rd RYTON NE40 64 C3
Leafield Crs HAR/WTLS NE34 62 A3
Lea Gn CLS/BIR/GTL DH3 94 A5
Leagreen Ct GOS/KPK NE3 46 A5 3
Leaholme Crs BLYTH NE24 24 E1
Lea La PLEE/EAS SR8 130 C3
Lealholm Rd LGB/HTN NE7 47 C5 2
Leam Gdns FELL NE10 70 E4
Leamington St MLFD/PNYW SR4 14 A6
Leam La FELL NE10 70 C7
JRW NE32 60 B7
JRW NE32 71 J3
LWF/SPW/WRK NE9 82 B1
Leamside FELL NE10 70 B6
JRW NE32 60 A7

Leander Av CLS/BIR/GTL DH3 93 K7
Leander Dr BOLCOL NE35 72 C4
Leaplish WASHS NE38 95 H4
Lea Riggs HLS DH4 116 D6 1
The Leas HLS DH4 108 B4
Leazes Ct DHAM DH1 16 E3
Leazes Crs CNUT NE1 5 H5
Leazes La CNUT NE1 5 J5
DHAM DH1 16 F3
Leazes Pde JES NE2 4 F4
Leazes Park Rd CNUT NE1 5 H5
Leazes Pkwy
BW/LEM/TK/HW NE15 52 E2
Leazes Pl DHAM DH1 16 E3
Leazes Ri PLEE/EAS SR8 137 G4
Leazes Rd DHAM DH1 16 E3
Leazes Ter CNUT NE1 5 H4
The Leazes HAR/WTLS NE34 61 K5
SUND SR1 14 B5
Leazes Vw ROWG NE39 77 F3
Lecondale FELL NE10 70 B7
Ledbury Rd ASHBK/HED/RY SR2 98 D3
Leechmere Rd
ASHBK/HED/RY SR2 98 C4
Leechmere Wy
ASHBK/HED/RY SR2 98 E6
Lee Cl WASHS NE38 95 K1
Leeds St CLDN/WHIT/ROK SR6 86 D3 4
Leeholme HLH DH5 117 J1
Leeholme Ct STLY/ANP DH9 101 J4 1
Leeming Gdns
LWF/SPW/WRK NE9 69 H6
Leesfield Dr BDN/LAN/SAC DH7 133 H7
Leesfield Gdns
BDN/LAN/SAC DH7 133 G7
Leesfield Rd
BDN/LAN/SAC DH7 133 H7 1
Lees St STLY/ANP DH9 90 D7
Lee St CLDN/WHIT/ROK SR6 86 D1
SWCK/CAS SR5 86 B4 3
Legg Av BDLGTN NE22 20 A3
Legges Dr DIN/WO NE13 26 C2
Legion Gv
BW/LEM/TK/HW NE15 54 D4 4
Legion Rd
BW/LEM/TK/HW NE15 54 D4 5
Leicester Cl WLSD/HOW NE28 48 C5
Leicestershire Dr DHAM DH1 126 A6 3
Leicester St BYK/HTN/WLK NE6 7 L6
Leighton Rd ASHBK/HED/RY SR2 98 D4
Leighton St BYK/HTN/WLK NE6 6 D5
SSH NE33 3 L9
Leith Ct HAR/WTLS NE34 61 G6
Leith Gdns STLY/ANP DH9 90 B5
Lemington Gdns
WD/WHPE/BLK NE5 55 G4
Lemington Rd
BW/LEM/TK/HW NE15 53 J4
Lemon St SSH NE33 61 F5
Lena Av MONK NE25 40 C5
Lenin Ter STLY/ANP DH9 102 E2
Leominster Rd
ASHBK/HED/RY SR2 98 D4
Leopold St JRW NE32 59 K5 1
Lesbury Av SMOOR NE27 39 G6
WLSD/HOW NE28 49 H7
Lesbury Cha GOS/KPK NE3 46 B4
Lesbury Cl CLSW/PEL DH2 105 F6
Lesbury Rd BYK/HTN/WLK NE6 57 H2
Lesbury St
BW/LEM/TK/HW NE15 54 B5
WLSD/HOW NE28 60 A2 2
Leslie Av HEBB NE31 59 G6
Leslie Cl RYTON NE40 53 G7
Leslie Crs GOS/KPK NE3 46 C7 1
Letch Av SEA/MUR SR7 130 B1
Leven Av CLSW/PEL DH2 105 H6
Levisham Cl SUNDSW SR3 98 C7 3
Lewis Crs ASHBK/HED/RY SR2 15 J8
Lewis Dr ELS/FEN NE4 4 A5
Lexington Ct
BDN/LAN/SAC DH7 133 F7
Leybourne Av LGB/KIL NE12 47 K1
Leyburn Cl CLSW/PEL DH2 92 D5
HLS DH4 108 A6
Leyburn Dr LGB/HTN NE7 47 G7
Leyburn Gv HLS DH4 108 A6
Leyburn Pl CLS/BIR/GTL DH3 81 H7
Leyfield Cl SUNDSW SR3 110 B2 2
Leyton Pl GATE NE8 11 K8
Liburn Cl BOL NE36 73 F4
Lichfield Av BYK/HTN/WLK NE6 7 M8
Lichfield Cl CLS/BIR/GTL DH3 115 H2 2
GOS/KPK NE3 45 H3
Lichfield Rd SWCK/CAS SR5 86 A2
Lidcombe Cl SUNDSW SR3 98 B7
Liddell St CLDN/WHIT/ROK SR6 14 F1
TYNE/NSHE NE30 2 F3
Liddell Ter GATE NE8 10 C6
Liddle Av RDHAMSE DH6 126 C7 2
Liddle Cl PLEE/EAS SR8 136 C2
Liddle Rd ELS/FEN NE4 4 D6
Lieven St DIN/WO NE13 36 A5 3
Liffey Rd HEBB NE31 71 H1
Lightbourne Rd
BYK/HTN/WLK NE6 58 C5
Lightwood Av
BW/LEM/TK/HW NE15 54 E7 1
Lilac Av BDN/LAN/SAC DH7 113 H5
BLYTH NE24 21 F6
CLDN/WHIT/ROK SR6 75 F1
DHAM DH1 124 C4
HAR/WTLS NE34 61 K6
LGB/KIL NE12 48 B2
SUNDSW SR3 98 B6
Lilac Cl WD/WHPE/BLK NE5 43 K6 5
Lilac Gdns LWF/SPW/WRK NE9 69 F6
WICK/BNPF NE16 66 E6
Lilac Gv CLSW/PEL DH2 105 G2
Lilac Pk BDN/LAN/SAC DH7 133 G1
Lilac Rd BYK/HTN/WLK NE6 58 C2
Lilac Sq HLS DH4 107 G4
Lilac St MLFD/PNYW SR4 84 E7
Lilburn Cl CLSW/PEL DH2 105 G7
Lilburn Gdns GOS/KPK NE3 47 F6
Lilburn Pl SWCK/CAS SR5 86 A4 6
Lilburn Rd SMOOR NE27 39 G7
Lilburn St NSHW NE29 2 A2
Lilian Av ASHBK/HED/RY SR2 98 E6
WLSD/HOW NE28 58 C2
Lilley Gv SWCK/CAS SR5 85 F4
Lily Av BDLGTN NE22 19 H6
JES NE2 56 E2
Lily Bank WLSD/HOW NE28 58 D1
Lily Crs CLDN/WHIT/ROK SR6 75 F1
JES NE2 56 E2
Lily Gdns STLY/ANP DH9 89 G6
Lily St MLFD/PNYW SR4 14 B3
Lily Ter WD/WHPE/BLK NE5 44 E7
Lilywhite Ter HLH DH5 118 A6
Lime Av HLS DH4 108 A7
Limecragg Av DHAM DH1 125 J6
Limecroft JRW NE32 72 A3
Lime Gv RYTON NE40 52 E6
Limekiln Rd WLSD/HOW NE28 59 F1
Lime Pk BDN/LAN/SAC DH7 133 G6
The Limes HLS DH4 95 K6
Limestone La PONT/DH NE20 32 B3
Lime St BLAY NE21 66 B3
CNUT NE1 6 C5
MLFD/PNYW SR4 14 A4
Limetrees Gdns
LWF/SPW/WRK NE9 69 F5
Limewood Gv DIN/WO NE13 36 B4
Linacre Cl DIN/WO NE13 45 F4
Linbridge Dr
WD/WHPE/BLK NE5 54 C2 9
Linburn WASHS NE38 94 C5
Lincoln Av SUNDSW SR3 98 A6
WLSD/HOW NE28 48 C7
Lincoln Gn GOS/KPK NE3 46 B1
Lincoln Rd CRAM NE23 23 J6 1
DHAM DH1 124 E2 1
HAR/WTLS NE34 62 B4
Lincolnshire Cl DHAM DH1 125 K6
Lincoln St GATE NE8 10 F6
MLFD/PNYW SR4 85 K6 5
Lindale Av WICK/BNPF NE16 66 E7
Lindale Rd ELS/FEN NE4 55 J3
Lindean Pl CRAM NE23 28 A2 2
Linden Av ELS/FEN NE4 55 H4
GOS/KPK NE3 46 C6 2
Linden Gdns
ASHBK/HED/RY SR2 98 C3 6
Linden Gv DUN/TMV NE11 9 J7
HLS DH4 108 B7 1
Linden Pk BDN/LAN/SAC DH7 133 G6 3
Linden Rd
ASHBK/HED/RY SR2 98 C3 7
BLAY NE21 66 B2
GOS/KPK NE3 46 C6
LGB/KIL NE12 47 K3
MONK NE25 29 J5
Linden Wy PONT/DH NE20 32 E7
Lindesfarne DHAM DH1 135 J5 1
Lindfield Av WD/WHPE/BLK NE5 55 F2
Lindisfarne PLEE/EAS SR8 136 D6
WASHS NE38 94 E2
Lindisfarne Av
CLS/BIR/GTL DH3 105 K4
Lindisfarne Cl HLS DH4 107 K6
JES NE2 47 F7
WD/WHPE/BLK NE5 54 D2 4
Lindisfarne Ct JRW NE32 60 D5
Lindisfarne Dr GATE NE8 11 H3
Lindisfarne Pl WLSD/HOW NE28 49 F7
Lindisfarne Recess JRW NE32 60 B7
Lindisfarne Rd DHAM DH1 124 E4
HEBB NE31 71 G1
JES NE2 57 F1
Lindisfarne Ter
TYNE/NSHE NE30 50 E3
Lindom Av CLS/BIR/GTL DH3 105 K4
Lindon Rd STLY/ANP DH9 102 C2
Lindrick Ct FELL NE10 70 E5
Lindsay Av BLYTH NE24 20 E6
Lindsay Cl ASHBK/HED/RY SR2 15 G7
Lindsay Rd
ASHBK/HED/RY SR2 15 H7 2
Lindsay St HLH DH5 118 A2
Lindsey Cl CRAM NE23 27 K2
Lindum Rd LWF/SPW/WRK NE9 11 H8
Lingdale DHAM DH1 126 A6
Lingdale Av
CLDN/WHIT/ROK SR6 74 E6
Lingey Gdns FELL NE10 70 E4
Lingey La FELL NE10 70 D5
Lingholme CLSW/PEL DH2 105 G3
Lingmell WASHN NE37 82 D7
Lingshaw FELL NE10 13 L9
Linhope Av GOS/KPK NE3 45 K3
Linhope Rd WD/WHPE/BLK NE5 54 D1
Link Av BDLGTN NE22 18 D5
Link Rd WD/WHPE/BLK NE5 55 J1 1
Links Av TYNE/NSHE NE30 41 G7
WBAY NE26 40 D2
Links Gn GOS/KPK NE3 46 D4
Links Rd BLYTH NE24 25 H4
TYNE/NSHE NE30 41 G7
WBAY NE26 25 K7
The Links DHAM DH1 126 A5 1
WBAY NE26 31 F2
Links Vw BLYTH NE24 24 E3
Linkway JRW NE32 72 B3
Linley Hl WICK/BNPF NE16 78 C1
Linnel Dr BW/LEM/TK/HW NE15 54 C4
Linnet Gv SWCK/CAS SR5 85 G4
Linskell ASHBK/HED/RY SR2 98 E6
Linskill Pl TYNE/NSHE NE30 51 F3
Linskill St TYNE/NSHE NE30 2 F2
Linskill Ter TYNE/NSHE NE30 51 F4
Lintfort CLS/BIR/GTL DH3 93 K7
Linthorpe Rd GOS/KPK NE3 46 C3
TYNE/NSHE NE30 51 F1
Linton Rd LWF/SPW/WRK NE9 81 F2
WBAY NE26 31 H7
Lintzford Gdns
BW/LEM/TK/HW NE15 54 C5 1
ROWG NE39 77 F5
Lintzford La ROWG NE39 76 D5
Lintzford Rd ROWG NE39 76 C7
Lintz Green La ROWG NE39 76 D6
Lintz La WICK/BNPF NE16 89 F2
Linum Pl ELS/FEN NE4 55 J3
Linwood Pl GOS/KPK NE3 46 C1 3
Lisa Av MLFD/PNYW SR4 96 E1
Lisburn Ter MLFD/PNYW SR4 86 A6
Lisle Gv WLSD/HOW NE28 49 J7
Lisle Rd HAR/WTLS NE34 61 K4
Lisle St WLSD/HOW NE28 58 D1
Lismore Av SSH NE33 61 H4 1
Lismore Pl
BW/LEM/TK/HW NE15 55 G5
Lister Av DUN/TMV NE11 9 G6
RYTON NE40 64 B4
Lister Cl HLH DH5 117 G2
Lister Rd PLEE/EAS SR8 136 B2
Litchfield La BLAY NE21 65 K3
Litchfield Rd DHAM DH1 124 E1
Little Bedford St NSHW NE29 2 E3
Littlebridge Ct DHAM DH1 124 B2 1
Littleburn Cl HLS DH4 108 A5 2
Littleburn La
BDN/LAN/SAC DH7 133 K5
Littleburn Rd
BDN/LAN/SAC DH7 133 K6
Littledene LWF/SPW/WRK NE9 69 F5
Little Eden PLEE/EAS SR8 136 E3
Littleton La RDHAMSE DH6 127 G7
Little Villiers St SUND SR1 14 F4 2
Little Wy BW/LEM/TK/HW NE15 55 F7
Littondale WLSD/HOW NE28 48 B6
Livingstone Rd SUND SR1 14 C4
Lizard La CLDN/WHIT/ROK SR6 74 E2
HAR/WTLS NE34 62 D5
Lloyd Av HLH DH5 117 F4
Lobban Av HEBB NE31 71 F1
Lobelia Av FELL NE10 11 M4
Lobelia Cl WD/WHPE/BLK NE5 44 A7 3
Lobley Gdns DUN/TMV NE11 68 A6
Lobley Hill Rd DUN/TMV NE11 68 A6
Lobleyhill Rd WICK/BNPF NE16 78 B5
Lochcraig Pl CRAM NE23 28 A2 3
Lochmaben Ter SWCK/CAS SR5 86 D3
Lockerbie Rd CRAM NE23 28 A2
Lockhaugh Rd ROWG NE39 77 H2
Locksley Cl NSHW NE29 49 K1
Locomotion Wy LGB/KIL NE12 37 H4
NSHW NE29 2 C6
Lodge Cl ROWG NE39 88 C1
Lodgeside Meadow
SUNDSW SR3 110 B2
The Lodges Rd
LWF/SPW/WRK NE9 80 E2
Lodore Gv JRW NE32 72 B1
Lodore Rd JES NE2 46 D7
Logan Rd BYK/HTN/WLK NE6 58 B2
Logan St HLH DH5 117 K5
Lola St DIN/WO NE13 35 K4 1
Lombard Dr CLS/BIR/GTL DH3 93 J7
Lombard St SUND SR1 15 H4
Lomond Ct SUNDSW SR3 110 A1 5
Lomond Pl CLSW/PEL DH2 105 H6
London Av WASHN NE37 82 D4
Londonderry Av DHAM DH1 17 M4
Londonderry St
SEA/MUR SR7 121 F3 1
SUNDSW SR3 98 A7
Londonderry Ter SUNDSW SR3 98 B7
Longacre HLS DH4 108 A7
WASHS NE38 95 G5 2
Long Acres DHAM DH1 17 J1
Long Bank CLS/BIR/GTL DH3 81 J6
LWF/SPW/WRK NE9 81 J5
Longborough Ct
LGB/HTN NE7 47 G6 2
Long Burn Dr CLSW/PEL DH2 105 F5
Long Close Rd ROWG NE39 88 B1
Long Dl CLSW/PEL DH2 105 F5
Longdean Cl HEBB NE31 58 E6 1
Longdean Pk CLS/BIR/GTL DH3 105 J1
Long Edge BDN/LAN/SAC DH7 112 C4
BDN/LAN/SAC DH7 112 A4
Longfield Rd
CLDN/WHIT/ROK SR6 86 D2
Longfield Ter BYK/HTN/WLK NE6 58 B7
Long Gair BLAY NE21 65 J4
Long Garth DHAM DH1 124 A5
Longhirst FELL NE10 70 C5
LGB/KIL NE12 37 K5
WD/WHPE/BLK NE5 54 D1
Longhirst Dr DIN/WO NE13 36 B4
Longlands Dr HLH DH5 117 H1
Longley St ELS/FEN NE4 4 D5
Long Meadow Cl RYTON NE40 64 B1 1
Longmeadows PONT/DH NE20 32 D6
SUNDSW SR3 109 G1
Longnewton St SEA/MUR SR7 120 E3
Longniddry WASHN NE37 82 E2
Longniddry Ct
LWF/SPW/WRK NE9 80 E2
Longridge Av LGB/HTN NE7 47 K7
WASHS NE38 94 C4
Longridge Dr WBAY NE26 40 C2
Long Ridge Rd RYTON NE40 64 E2
Longridge Sq
ASHBK/HED/RY SR2 98 D4 1
Longridge Wy CRAM NE23 28 A2
STKFD/GP NE62 19 G3
Longrigg FELL NE10 70 B5 2
Long Rigg WICK/BNPF NE16 66 E3 5
Longrigg Rd WICK/BNPF NE16 66 E3
Long Row SSH NE33 2 F6
Longsdale Av BLYTH NE24 20 A6
Longshank La CLS/BIR/GTL DH3 81 G7
Longston Av TYNE/NSHE NE30 41 F6
Longstone Ct LGB/KIL NE12 38 A5
Longstone Sq
WD/WHPE/BLK NE5 54 B2
Longwood Cl WICK/BNPF NE16 79 F2
Lonnen Av ELS/FEN NE4 55 H4
Lonnen Dr WICK/BNPF NE16 66 E4
The Lonnen HAR/WTLS NE34 62 B7
Lonsdale CLS/BIR/GTL DH3 94 A5
Lonsdale Av
CLDN/WHIT/ROK SR6 74 E6
Lonsdale Gdns WLSD/HOW NE28 49 J6
Lonsdale Rd
CLDN/WHIT/ROK SR6 86 E3
Lonsdale Ter JES NE2 56 E1
Loraine Ter
BW/LEM/TK/HW NE15 54 A5 3
Lord Byrons Wk SEA/MUR SR7 111 F6
Lordenshaw
WD/WHPE/BLK NE5 54 D1 5
Lord Nelson St HAR/WTLS NE34 61 F5
Lord St SEA/MUR SR7 120 E2
SSH NE33 61 J2
SUNDSW SR3 98 B7
Lorimers Cl PLEE/EAS SR8 136 C6
Lorne St HLH DH5 128 A1
Lorne Ter ASHBK/HED/RY SR2 14 D8
Lorrain Rd HAR/WTLS NE34 73 H2
Lorton Av TYNE/NSHE NE30 40 E7
Lorton Rd LWF/SPW/WRK NE9 81 G1
Losh Ter BYK/HTN/WLK NE6 58 B6
Lossiemouth Rd NSHW NE29 49 K5
Lothian Ct
WD/WHPE/BLK NE5 45 G7 5
Lotus Cl WD/WHPE/BLK NE5 43 K7
Lotus Pl ELS/FEN NE4 55 H4 2
Loudon St HAR/WTLS NE34 61 G6 11
Loughborough Av
ASHBK/HED/RY SR2 98 C3
Loughrigg Av CRAM NE23 27 K2
Louie Ter LWF/SPW/WRK NE9 69 G7
Louis Av CLDN/WHIT/ROK SR6 86 D2
Loup St BLAY NE21 66 A1 5
Lovaine Av MONK NE25 40 E5
Lovaine Pl NSHW NE29 2 C3
Lovaine Pl West NSHW NE29 2 B3 1
Lovaine Rw TYNE/NSHE NE30 51 H2
Lovaine St
BW/LEM/TK/HW NE15 53 G3
CLSW/PEL DH2 104 C1
Lovaine Ter NSHW NE29 2 C1
Love Av CRAM NE23 37 H2
Loveless Gdns FELL NE10 13 L9
Lowbiggin WD/WHPE/BLK NE5 45 G6
Low Chare CLS/BIR/GTL DH3 105 K4
Lowdham Av NSHW NE29 50 C6
Low Downs Rd HLH DH5 117 K2
Lower Dundas St
CLDN/WHIT/ROK SR6 14 F1 2
Lower Rudyerd St NSHW NE29 2 E3 1
Lowerson Av HLS DH4 107 J2
Lowery La STLY/ANP DH9 103 H5
Lowe's Barn Bank DHAM DH1 134 A3
Lowes Ct DHAM DH1 134 B2
Lowes Fall DHAM DH1 134 B2
Lowes Ri DHAM DH1 134 B3
Loweswater Av HLH DH5 128 B1
Loweswater Cl BLYTH NE24 20 B5
Loweswater Rd
WD/WHPE/BLK NE5 55 F2 6
Loweswood Cl LGB/HTN NE7 57 G2
Lowes Wynd DHAM DH1 134 B2
Lowfield Ter BYK/HTN/WLK NE6 58 B7
Low Flatts Rd CLSW/PEL DH2 105 H1
Low Friar St CNUT NE1 5 J7
Lowgate BW/LEM/TK/HW NE15 53 F2
Low Gosforth Ct
GOS/KPK NE3 46 D1 6
Low Gn DHAM DH1 135 G4
Low Haugh PONT/DH NE20 33 H2
Low Heworth La FELL NE10 13 G5
Low Heyworth La FELL NE10 13 G5
Lowhills Rd PLEE/EAS SR8 136 C2
Lowland Cl SUNDSW SR3 110 A2
Lowland Rd BDN/LAN/SAC DH7 133 G6
Low La HAR/WTLS NE34 61 G7
Low Meadow
CLDN/WHIT/ROK SR6 74 A3 1
Lownds Ter BYK/HTN/WLK NE6 7 M4
Low Quay BLYTH NE24 21 H7
Lowrey's La
LWF/SPW/WRK NE9 69 F7 2
Low Rd DHAM DH1 135 G4
Low Rw PLEE/EAS SR8 130 C5
Lowry Gdns HAR/WTLS NE34 73 H2
Lowry Rd CLDN/WHIT/ROK SR6 74 E7
Low Station Rd HLS DH4 116 B6
Low St SUND SR1 15 H3
Lowther Cl PLEE/EAS SR8 136 E3 3
Lowthian Crs BYK/HTN/WLK NE6 7 M6
Low West Av ROWG NE39 76 E4
Lucknow St SUND SR1 15 J3
Lucock St HAR/WTLS NE34 61 F6 3
Ludlow Av NSHW NE29 50 C2
Ludlow Ct GOS/KPK NE3 45 J3 3
Ludlow Dr MONK NE25 39 K5
Ludlow Rd ASHBK/HED/RY SR2 98 D4
Luffness Dr HAR/WTLS NE34 73 K1
Luke Crs SEA/MUR SR7 119 G5
Luke's La HEBB NE31 71 H2
Lulsgate SWCK/CAS SR5 84 E4
Lulworth Av JRW NE32 60 B6
Lulworth Ct SUNDSW SR3 97 G7 3
Lulworth Gdns
ASHBK/HED/RY SR2 98 C3 3
Lumley Av HAR/WTLS NE34 62 B5
WICK/BNPF NE16 67 F3
Lumley Cl WASHS NE38 94 D1
Lumley Ct BDLGTN NE22 19 J4 2
SUNDSW SR3 97 G7 5
Lumley Dr PLEE/EAS SR8 136 E7
Lumley Gdns GATE NE8 11 L6
Lumley New Rd
CLS/BIR/GTL DH3 106 B5
HLS DH4 107 F6
Lumley Rd DHAM DH1 124 D2
Lumley St HLS DH4 108 B5
MLFD/PNYW SR4 86 A7
Lumley Ter CLS/BIR/GTL DH3 105 K5
JRW NE32 71 K1
Lumsden Sq SEA/MUR SR7 119 G5 2
Lund Av DHAM DH1 124 B3
Lund's La CON/LDGT DH8 100 D7
Lunedale Av
CLDN/WHIT/ROK SR6 74 C7
Lunedale Dr
CLS/BIR/GTL DH3 115 J2 1
Lunesdale St HLH DH5 117 K6
Lupin Cl WD/WHPE/BLK NE5 44 A6 7
Luss Av JRW NE32 72 C1
Lutterworth Cl LGB/KIL NE12 47 H4 5
Lutterworth Dr LGB/KIL NE12 47 G4
Lutterworth Rd
ASHBK/HED/RY SR2 98 C3
LGB/KIL NE12 47 H5 3
Luxembourg Rd
MLFD/PNYW SR4 85 H6
Lydbury Cl CRAM NE23 23 J6 2
Lydcott WASHS NE38 95 K2
Lydford Ct HLS DH4 108 A4 2
WD/WHPE/BLK NE5 45 G4
Lydford Wy CLS/BIR/GTL DH3 93 K3
Lyncroft Rd NSHW NE29 50 C4
Lyndale CRAM NE23 23 J6
Lyndhurst Av CLS/BIR/GTL DH3 105 J1
JES NE2 56 D1
LWF/SPW/WRK NE9 81 F1
Lyndhurst Cl BLAY NE21 65 J4 5
Lyndhurst Crs
LWF/SPW/WRK NE9 81 G1
Lyndhurst Dr DHAM DH1 134 B1 2
LWF/SPW/WRK NE9 81 G1
Lyndhurst Gdns JES NE2 56 D1 2
Lyndhurst Gv
LWF/SPW/WRK NE9 81 G1
Lyndhurst Rd LGB/KIL NE12 47 K3
STLY/ANP DH9 102 B1 1
Lyndhurst St SSH NE33 3 K8
Lyndhurst Ter
MLFD/PNYW SR4 85 J5 1
Lyndon Cl BOL NE36 73 F5
Lyndon Dr BOL NE36 73 F5
Lyndon Gv BOL NE36 73 F5
Lyndon Wk BLYTH NE24 20 B6
Lyne Cl CLSW/PEL DH2 93 F6
Lyne's Dr BDN/LAN/SAC DH7 133 J5
Lynfield WBAY NE26 40 C1
Lynfield Ct
WD/WHPE/BLK NE5 45 F7 2
Lynfield Pl
WD/WHPE/BLK NE5 45 F7 3
Lynford Gdns
ASHBK/HED/RY SR2 98 C3 9
Lynholm Gv LGB/KIL NE12 47 K2 4
Lynmouth Pl LGB/HTN NE7 47 H7 1
Lynmouth Rd NSHW NE29 50 A5 3
Lynndale Av BLYTH NE24 20 C7
Lynnholme Gdns
LWF/SPW/WRK NE9 11 J8
Lynn Rd NSHW NE29 50 B3 2
WLSD/HOW NE28 58 C2
Lynn St BLYTH NE24 21 F7
Lynnwood Av ELS/FEN NE4 4 B6
Lynnwood Ter ELS/FEN NE4 4 B6
Lynthorpe ASHBK/HED/RY SR2 99 F6
Lyn-thorpe Gv
CLDN/WHIT/ROK SR6 86 E2 2
Lynton Av JRW NE32 60 C6
Lynton Ct HLS DH4 108 A4
Lynton Pl WD/WHPE/BLK NE5 45 F7
Lynton Wy WD/WHPE/BLK NE5 45 F7
Lynwood Av BLAY NE21 66 A1 6
MLFD/PNYW SR4 96 E4
Lynwood Cl PONT/DH NE20 32 E7
Lyons Av HLH DH5 118 A6
Lyons La HLH DH5 118 B7
Lyon St HEBB NE31 59 F5
Lyric Cl NSHW NE29 49 K2
Lysdon Av MONK NE25 30 A2
Lyster Cl SEA/MUR SR7 110 E6
Lytham Cl CRAM NE23 27 K2 2
WASHN NE37 82 E3 3
WLSD/HOW NE28 49 G3
Lytham Dr MONK NE25 40 B4
Lytham Gra HLS DH4 107 J3
Lytham Pl BYK/HTN/WLK NE6 7 L7
Lythe Wy LGB/KIL NE12 47 J4

M

Mabel St BLAY NE21 66 A1
Macadam St GATE NE8 10 C9
Maclynn Cl SUNDSW SR3 109 J1
Macmerry Cl SWCK/CAS SR5 84 D5 1
Macmillan Gdns FELL NE10 13 K7
Maddison St BLYTH NE24 21 G6
Maddox Rd LGB/KIL NE12 47 K4
Madeira Av WBAY NE26 40 D2
Madeira Cl WD/WHPE/BLK NE5 44 A6
Madeira Ter SSH NE33 61 H2
Madras St HAR/WTLS NE34 60 E7
Mafeking Pl NSHW NE29 49 K1
Mafeking St LWF/SPW/WRK NE9 11 J8
MLFD/PNYW SR4 85 K7
Magdalene Av DHAM DH1 125 K5
Magdalene Hts DHAM DH1 17 G2
Magdalene St DHAM DH1 17 H2
Magdelene Pl MLFD/PNYW SR4 85 K6
Magenta Crs
WD/WHPE/BLK NE5 44 A6
Maglona St SEA/MUR SR7 120 E3
Maiden La RYTON NE40 64 B2
Maiden Law HLS DH4 116 D1 1
Maiden St ELS/FEN NE4 9 M1 1
Maidstone Cl SUNDSW SR3 109 H1 1
Main Crs WLSD/HOW NE28 48 B6
Main Rd DIN/WO NE13 35 F2
DIN/WO NE13 45 F3
RYTON NE40 52 D6
Mainsforth Ter West
ASHBK/HED/RY SR2 15 H9
Mains Park Rd
CLS/BIR/GTL DH3 105 K5
Mainstone Cl CRAM NE23 28 B2 1
Main St PONT/DH NE20 33 G3
RYTON NE40 52 B7
Main St North CRAM NE23 38 A1
Makendon St HEBB NE31 59 G4
Malaburn Wy SWCK/CAS SR5 86 A4 7
Malaga Cl WD/WHPE/BLK NE5 43 K6
Malaya Dr BYK/HTN/WLK NE6 58 C6
Malcolm St BYK/HTN/WLK NE6 6 D4
SEA/MUR SR7 120 E2 3
Malden Cl CRAM NE23 28 A2
Maling Pk MLFD/PNYW SR4 85 F6 2
Malings Cl SUND SR1 15 J5
Maling St BYK/HTN/WLK NE6 6 D6 2
Mallard Cl WASHS NE38 94 B2
Mallard Wy BLYTH NE24 25 H4
WLSD/HOW NE28 49 J4
Mallowburn Crs GOS/KPK NE3 45 G6

Malmo Cl NSHW NE29 ... 49 K5
Malone Gdns CLS/BIR/GTL DH3 ... 81 K7
Maltby Cl WASHS NE38 ... 95 F2
Malton Cl BLYTH NE24 ... 20 D7 3
BW/LEM/TK/HW NE15 ... 54 C5 2
Malton Crs NSHW NE29 ... 50 C6
Malton Gdns WLSD/HOW NE28 ... 48 D7
Malvern Ct
BW/LEM/TK/HW NE15 ... 53 K4
Malvern Crs SEA/MUR SR7 ... 120 B1
Malvern Gdns
CLDN/WHIT/ROK SR6 ... 86 E2
DUN/TMV NE11 ... 68 A6 4
DUN/TMV NE11 ... 68 A5 2
Malvern Rd NSHW NE29 ... 50 C2
WBAY NE26 ... 31 G3
WLSD/HOW NE28 ... 49 H7
Malvern St ELS/FEN NE4 ... 4 C8
SSH NE33 ... 61 G4
Malvern Ter STLY/ANP DH9 ... 102 E2
Malvins Close Rd BLYTH NE24 ... 20 E7
Malvins Rd BLYTH NE24 ... 20 D6
Mandale Crs TYNE/NSHE NE30 ... 40 E6
Mandarin Cl WD/WHPE/BLK NE5 .. 43 K6
Mandela Cl STLY/ANP DH9 ... 102 B2
Mandela Wy DUN/TMV NE11 ... 8 C3
Mandeville WASHN NE37 ... 83 G5
Manet Gdns HAR/WTLS NE34 ... 61 H7
Mangrove Cl
WD/WHPE/BLK NE5 ... 43 K6
Manila St ASHBK/HED/RY SR2 ... 98 E2
Manisty Ter PLEE/EAS SR8 ... 130 D5
Mann Crs SEA/MUR SR7 ... 119 J4 1
Manningford Cl CRAM NE23 ... 28 B3 1
Manningford Dr SUNDSW SR3 ... 109 J2
Manor Av LGB/HTN NE7 ... 47 J5
Manor Chare CNUT NE1 ... 5 M7
Manor Cl GOS/KPK NE3 ... 46 D5 2
Manor Dr LGB/HTN NE7 ... 47 J5
STLY/ANP DH9 ... 101 H2
Manorfields LGB/KIL NE12 ... 47 K4
Manor Gdns FELL NE10 ... 13 M8
LGB/HTN NE7 ... 47 J5 4
Manor Gv BW/LEM/TK/HW NE15 .. 53 H4
HLS DH4 ... 96 D7
LGB/HTN NE7 ... 47 J5
Manor Hall Cl SEA/MUR SR7 ... 110 E7
Manor House Rd JES NE2 ... 57 F2
Manor Pl LGB/HTN NE7 ... 47 J5
Manor Rd LGB/HTN NE7 ... 47 J6
STLY/ANP DH9 ... 90 D7 5
TYNE/NSHE NE30 ... 51 H2
WASHN NE37 ... 83 F5
Manor Ter BLAY NE21 ... 66 A5
Manor Vw WASHN NE37 ... 83 F5
Manor Vw East WASHN NE37 ... 83 G5
Manor Wk LGB/HTN NE7 ... 47 J5 8
Manor Wy PLEE/EAS SR8 ... 137 F5
Manorway TYNE/NSHE NE30 ... 51 H2 4
Mansell Crs PLEE/EAS SR8 ... 137 F3
Mansell Pl GOS/KPK NE3 ... 45 J7
Mansfield Ct BOL NE36 ... 72 E5
Mansfield Crs
CLDN/WHIT/ROK SR6 ... 86 E2
Mansfield St ELS/FEN NE4 ... 4 E6
Manston Cl SUNDSW SR3 ... 109 H2
Manx Sq SWCK/CAS SR5 ... 86 B2
Maple Av DHAM DH1 ... 17 L3
DUN/TMV NE11 ... 9 J9
MONK NE25 ... 40 D6
SUNDSW SR3 ... 98 B6
Maplebeck Cl SUNDSW SR3 ... 109 H2 1
Maple Cl
BW/LEM/TK/HW NE15 ... 54 C5 3
Maple Ct BDN/LAN/SAC DH7 ... 132 E7
MONK NE25 ... 30 A2 1
Maple Crs BLYTH NE24 ... 20 B6
SEA/MUR SR7 ... 120 C4
Mapledene Rd GOS/KPK NE3 ... 45 K4
Maple Gv CLDN/WHIT/ROK SR6 ... 75 F3
FELL NE10 ... 12 E8
GATE NE8 ... 68 E5
HAR/WTLS NE34 ... 61 K6
Maple Pk BDN/LAN/SAC DH7 ... 133 G1
Maple Rd BLAY NE21 ... 66 A2
Maple Rw WICK/BNPF NE16 ... 67 F2
Maple St ELS/FEN NE4 ... 4 F9
JRW NE32 ... 59 J4
STLY/ANP DH9 ... 102 B3
Maple Ter ELS/FEN NE4 ... 4 E9
HLS DH4 ... 107 J2
Maplewood CLSW/PEL DH2 ... 105 H3
Maplewood Av SWCK/CAS SR5 ... 85 K2
Maplewood Ct
BDN/LAN/SAC DH7 ... 122 A3
Maplewood Dr
RDHAMSE DH6 ... 128 E6 2
Maplewood St HLS DH4 ... 107 G6
Mapperley Dr
BW/LEM/TK/HW NE15 ... 54 C4
Marblet Ct DUN/TMV NE11 ... 68 B5 1
Marbury Cl SUNDSW SR3 ... 109 H1 2
March Rd CRAM NE23 ... 37 H2 1
Marcia Av
CLDN/WHIT/ROK SR6 ... 86 D2 7
Marconi Wy WICK/BNPF NE16 ... 67 F3
Marcross Cl
WD/WHPE/BLK NE5 ... 53 K1 2
Marcross Dr SUNDSW SR3 ... 109 H2
Mardale WASHN NE37 ... 82 D6
Mardale Gdns
LWF/SPW/WRK NE9 ... 81 G2
Mardale Rd WD/WHPE/BLK NE5 .. 55 F2
Mardale St HLH DH5 ... 117 K6
Marden Av TYNE/NSHE NE30 ... 41 G6
Marden Ct WBAY NE26 ... 30 E1 2
Marden Crs WBAY NE26 ... 41 G5
Marden Rd South MONK NE25 ... 40 E5
Marden Ter TYNE/NSHE NE30 ... 41 G6
Mareburn Crs FELL NE10 ... 12 F7
Maree Cl SUNDSW SR3 ... 109 J2
Margaret Alice St
MLFD/PNYW SR4 ... 85 J6 1
Margaret Dr LGB/KIL NE12 ... 48 C2 2
Margaret Gv HAR/WTLS NE34 ... 60 E6 2
Margaret Rd WBAY NE26 ... 41 G5
Margaret St ASHBK/HED/RY SR2 .. 99 F4
SEA/MUR SR7 ... 120 E2
Margaret Ter ROWG NE39 ... 76 E4
Margery La DHAM DH1 ... 16 B5
Marguerite Ct
MLFD/PNYW SR4 ... 14 B4 3
Marian Ct GATE NE8 ... 10 C5
Marian Dr FELL NE10 ... 13 M3
Marian Wy HAR/WTLS NE34 ... 73 K1
PONT/DH NE20 ... 32 D7
Maria St ELS/FEN NE4 ... 55 J7
SEA/MUR SR7 ... 120 E1
SUNDSW SR3 ... 98 A7
Marie Curie Dr ELS/FEN NE4 ... 4 B8
Marigold Av FELL NE10 ... 11 M3
Marigold Ct MLFD/PNYW SR4 ... 14 A3
Marigold Crs HLS DH4 ... 107 G4
Marigold Wk HAR/WTLS NE34 ... 61 F6
Marina Av CLDN/WHIT/ROK SR6 ... 86 C1
Marina Ct
CLDN/WHIT/ROK SR6 ... 86 D2 8
Marina Dr MONK NE25 ... 39 K5
SSH NE33 ... 3 L7
Marina Gv
CLDN/WHIT/ROK SR6 ... 86 D2 9
Marina Ter
CLDN/WHIT/ROK SR6 ... 75 F3 2
Marina Veiw WLSD/HOW NE28 ... 59 H1
Marina Vw HEBB NE31 ... 59 F5
Marine Ap SSH NE33 ... 3 L8
Marine Av WBAY NE26 ... 40 E3 1
Marine Dr ASHBK/HED/RY SR2 ... 99 F6
HEBB NE31 ... 71 J1
JRW NE32 ... 71 J2
Marine Gdns WBAY NE26 ... 40 E4
Mariners' La TYNE/NSHE NE30 ... 51 G3
Marine Ter BLYTH NE24 ... 21 F7
Marine Wk CLDN/WHIT/ROK SR6 .. 87 F3
Marion St ASHBK/HED/RY SR2 ... 15 H9
Maritime Crs PLEE/EAS SR8 ... 131 G7
Maritime St SUND SR1 ... 14 E5 1
Marius Av BW/LEM/TK/HW NE15 .. 52 B1
Mariville East
ASHBK/HED/RY SR2 ... 111 G2
Mariville West
ASHBK/HED/RY SR2 ... 111 G2
Markby Cl SUNDSW SR3 ... 109 J2 4
Market La CNUT NE1 ... 5 K7
WICK/BNPF NE16 ... 66 E3
Market Pl HLH DH5 ... 108 D7
Market Sq JRW NE32 ... 59 K4 6
Market St CNUT NE1 ... 5 K6
CRAM NE23 ... 37 G1
HLH DH5 ... 118 A4
Market Wy DUN/TMV NE11 ... 68 D6
Markham Av
CLDN/WHIT/ROK SR6 ... 75 G4
Markham St
ASHBK/HED/RY SR2 ... 99 F4 3
Markington Dr
ASHBK/HED/RY SR2 ... 111 F1
Markle Gv HLH DH5 ... 117 G3
Mark Ri HLH DH5 ... 117 K3
Mark's La HLS DH4 ... 116 C4
Marlboro Av WICK/BNPF NE16 ... 67 F4
Marlborough Ap
GOS/KPK NE3 ... 46 C3 2
Marlborough Av GOS/KPK NE3 ... 45 J6
Marlborough Ct GOS/KPK NE3 ... 45 H3
HLH DH5 ... 117 H2 1
Marlborough Rd
MLFD/PNYW SR4 ... 96 D3
WASHN NE37 ... 83 G4
Marlborough St North
SSH NE33 ... 61 H3 4
Marlborough St South
SSH NE33 ... 61 H3
Marleen Av BYK/HTN/WLK NE6 ... 7 H1
Marleen Ct BYK/HTN/WLK NE6 ... 7 H1
Marley Crs SWCK/CAS SR5 ... 85 K2
Marlfield Ct
WD/WHPE/BLK NE5 ... 45 F7 4
Marlow Dr SUNDSW SR3 ... 109 H2
Marlowe Gdns GATE NE8 ... 11 H5
Marlowe Pl HLH DH5 ... 117 H1
Marlow Pl LGB/KIL NE12 ... 47 J4
Marlow St BLYTH NE24 ... 21 F7
Marmion Rd BYK/HTN/WLK NE6 .. 58 B3
Marmion Ter MONK NE25 ... 40 D4
Marne St HLS DH4 ... 107 K1
Marondale Av
BYK/HTN/WLK NE6 ... 58 B4
Marquis Av WD/WHPE/BLK NE5 ... 44 A5
Marr Rd HEBB NE31 ... 71 H2
Marsden Av
CLDN/WHIT/ROK SR6 ... 75 F2
Marsden Cl HLS DH4 ... 108 A7
Marsden Gv
LWF/SPW/WRK NE9 ... 81 K2 2
Marsden La HAR/WTLS NE34 ... 62 B4
WD/WHPE/BLK NE5 ... 44 E7
Marsden Rd
CLDN/WHIT/ROK SR6 ... 73 K4
HAR/WTLS NE34 ... 74 A3
Marshall St CLDN/WHIT/ROK SR6 .. 86 D1
Marshall Wallis Rd SSH NE33 ... 61 G3
Marsham Cl
BW/LEM/TK/HW NE15 ... 54 C4
CLDN/WHIT/ROK SR6 ... 74 A2
Marsham Rd
WD/WHPE/BLK NE5 ... 44 C7 5
Marsh Ct DUN/TMV NE11 ... 9 M9
Marske Ter BYK/HTN/WLK NE6 ... 7 M5
Marston LGB/KIL NE12 ... 37 K5 3
Martello Gdns LGB/HTN NE7 ... 57 K1
Martin Ct WASHS NE38 ... 94 B4
Martindale Av
CLDN/WHIT/ROK SR6 ... 74 C7
Martindale Pk HLH DH5 ... 117 H1
Martin Rd WLSD/HOW NE28 ... 59 H1
Marwell Dr WASHN NE37 ... 83 G3 1
Marwood Gv PLEE/EAS SR8 ... 136 D7
Mary Agnes St GOS/KPK NE3 ... 46 A5 4
Mary Av CLS/BIR/GTL DH3 ... 81 H7
Maryhill Cl ELS/FEN NE4 ... 55 J7 3
Mary's Pl BYK/HTN/WLK NE6 ... 58 D5
Mary St BLAY NE21 ... 65 J2
SEA/MUR SR7 ... 121 F1 2
SUND SR1 ... 14 D6 1
SUNDSW SR3 ... 98 A6
Mary Ter WD/WHPE/BLK NE5 ... 54 E1
Masefield Av
WICK/BNPF NE16 ... 67 F3 3
Masefield Cl STLY/ANP DH9 ... 91 F7
Masefield Dr HAR/WTLS NE34 ... 72 E2
Mason Rd WLSD/HOW NE28 ... 48 C6
Mason St BYK/HTN/WLK NE6 ... 7 G6
Mast La TYNE/NSHE NE30 ... 41 F6
Matamba Ter MLFD/PNYW SR4 ... 14 A5
Matanzas St ASHBK/HED/RY SR2 .. 98 E3
Matfen Av SMOOR NE27 ... 39 H6
Matfen Cl BLYTH NE24 ... 20 E7
BW/LEM/TK/HW NE15 ... 54 C5 4
Matfen Dr SUNDSW SR3 ... 109 H1 3
Matfen Gdns WLSD/HOW NE28 ... 49 H5
Matfen Pl ELS/FEN NE4 ... 4 A2
GOS/KPK NE3 ... 46 A4 7
Mather Rd ELS/FEN NE4 ... 4 E9
Matlock Gdns
WD/WHPE/BLK NE5 ... 44 D7 6
Matlock Rd JRW NE32 ... 60 A6 7
Matlock St SUND SR1 ... 14 E3
Matterdale Rd PLEE/EAS SR8 ... 137 G4
Matthew Bank JES NE2 ... 46 E7
Matthew Rd BLYTH NE24 ... 25 H2
Maudlin Pl
WD/WHPE/BLK NE5 ... 55 H2 6
Maudlin St HLH DH5 ... 118 A2
Mauds La SUND SR1 ... 15 H4
Maud St
BW/LEM/TK/HW NE15 ... 54 A5 4
CLDN/WHIT/ROK SR6 ... 86 E1
Maughan St BLYTH NE24 ... 21 H7
Maureen Ter SEA/MUR SR7 ... 120 D1
Maurice Rd WLSD/HOW NE28 ... 58 D3 2
Mautland St HLS DH4 ... 108 C6 1
Mavin St DHAM DH1 ... 16 F6
Maxton Cl SUNDSW SR3 ... 109 H2 2
Maxwell St GATE NE8 ... 10 D9
MLFD/PNYW SR4 ... 85 K6 5
SSH NE33 ... 3 H9
May Av BLAY NE21 ... 66 A5
RYTON NE40 ... 52 E5 4
Maydown Cl SWCK/CAS SR5 ... 84 D5 2
Mayfair Gdns GATE NE8 ... 11 K7
HAR/WTLS NE34 ... 61 J4
PONT/DH NE20 ... 33 H3
Mayfair Rd JES NE2 ... 56 D1 3
Mayfield WICK/BNPF NE16 ... 67 F7 4
Mayfield Av
BW/LEM/TK/HW NE15 ... 53 G2
CRAM NE23 ... 28 D2
Mayfield Ct
CLDN/WHIT/ROK SR6 ... 86 D2
Mayfield Dr
CLDN/WHIT/ROK SR6 ... 74 B4 1
Mayfield Gdns
BW/LEM/TK/HW NE15 ... 53 G2 2
JRW NE32 ... 59 J5
WLSD/HOW NE28 ... 48 B7 1
Mayfield Gv MLFD/PNYW SR4 ... 96 E4
Mayfield Pl DIN/WO NE13 ... 36 A4
Mayfield Rd GOS/KPK NE3 ... 46 B6
MLFD/PNYW SR4 ... 84 D7
Mayfield Ter
WD/WHPE/BLK NE5 ... 55 J2 2
May Gv CLDN/WHIT/ROK SR6 ... 75 F1
May Lea BDN/LAN/SAC DH7 ... 113 G7
Maynard's Rw DHAM DH1 ... 17 J3
Mayo Dr SUNDSW SR3 ... 109 J2 5
Mayoral Wy DUN/TMV NE11 ... 80 D3
Mayorswell Cl DHAM DH1 ... 16 F2
Mayorswell Fld DHAM DH1 ... 16 F2 1
Mayorswell St DHAM DH1 ... 16 F2 2
Maypole Cl SWCK/CAS SR5 ... 86 B4 4
May St BLAY NE21 ... 65 K3
CLS/BIR/GTL DH3 ... 93 J1
DHAM DH1 ... 16 A5
MLFD/PNYW SR4 ... 14 B4
SSH NE33 ... 61 H2 7
Mayswood Rd
CLDN/WHIT/ROK SR6 ... 86 D2
Maythorne Dr RDHAMSE DH6 ... 129 G3
Maywood Cl GOS/KPK NE3 ... 45 J6
Mcanany Av HAR/WTLS NE34 ... 61 H6
Mcclaren Wy HLS DH4 ... 96 D7
Mccracken Cl GOS/KPK NE3 ... 46 C2
Mccracken Dr DIN/WO NE13 ... 36 C2
Mcewan Gdns ELS/FEN NE4 ... 4 B7
Mcintyre Rd HEBB NE31 ... 59 H4 3
Mckendrick Vls
WD/WHPE/BLK NE5 ... 55 H2
Mcnally Pl DHAM DH1 ... 17 J2
Mcnamara Rd WLSD/HOW NE28 .. 49 G7
Meacham Wy WICK/BNPF NE16 ... 66 E7
Mead Av LGB/KIL NE12 ... 48 A2
Mead Crs LGB/KIL NE12 ... 48 A2
Meadowbank
BDN/LAN/SAC DH7 ... 122 A3 3
Meadowbrook Dr FELL NE10 ... 70 E5 3
Meadow Cl BLAY NE21 ... 65 H3
CRAM NE23 ... 29 G6 1
DUN/TMV NE11 ... 8 F6
HLH DH5 ... 117 J1
LGB/KIL NE12 ... 47 H4 6
RYTON NE40 ... 53 F6
Meadow Ct BDLGTN NE22 ... 18 E5
PONT/DH NE20 ... 33 G4
Meadowdale Crs BDLGTN NE22 ... 18 D5
WD/WHPE/BLK NE5 ... 45 H7
Meadow Dr CLSW/PEL DH2 ... 105 F5
DIN/WO NE13 ... 36 C1
SUNDSW SR3 ... 109 F2
Meadowfield MONK NE25 ... 40 B4
PONT/DH NE20 ... 33 G2
Meadowfield Av GOS/KPK NE3 ... 46 A4
Meadowfield Crs
RYTON NE40 ... 52 C7 2
Meadowfield Dr
CLDN/WHIT/ROK SR6 ... 74 A3
Meadowfield Gdns
BYK/HTN/WLK NE6 ... 58 C2 4
Meadowfield Rd
GOS/KPK NE3 ... 46 B6 3
Meadowfield Wy STLY/ANP DH9 .. 90 A6
Meadow Gdns SUNDSW SR3 ... 98 B3 9
Meadow Gra HLS DH4 ... 107 G5
Meadow Gv MLFD/PNYW SR4 ... 96 E1
Meadow La DUN/TMV NE11 ... 8 F5
RYTON NE40 ... 52 C7 3
Meadow Laws HAR/WTLS NE34 ... 62 A7
Meadow Ri WD/WHPE/BLK NE5 .. 45 F6
Meadow Rd
BW/LEM/TK/HW NE15 ... 54 B4
MONK NE25 ... 40 B5
WBAY NE26 ... 30 E2
WLSD/HOW NE28 ... 59 H2 1
Meadowside
ASHBK/HED/RY SR2 ... 98 B2
Meadows La HLS DH4 ... 116 E4
The Meadows GOS/KPK NE3 ... 45 K4
HLS DH4 ... 107 F4
HLS DH4 ... 116 D5
RYTON NE40 ... 53 F6
Meadow St HLH DH5 ... 117 F4
Meadow V ASHBK/HED/RY SR2 ... 14 D9
Meadowvale PONT/DH NE20 ... 32 C7
Meadow Vw MONK NE25 ... 30 A2
STLY/ANP DH9 ... 89 G5 1
SUNDSW SR3 ... 109 F2
Meadow Well Wy NSHW NE29 .. 50 C6 3
Mead Wk BYK/HTN/WLK NE6 ... 58 B5
Mead Wy LGB/KIL NE12 ... 48 B2
Meadway Dr LGB/KIL NE12 ... 48 B3
Means Dr CRAM NE23 ... 37 H4
Medburn Av TYNE/NSHE NE30 ... 41 G7
Medburn Rd
BW/LEM/TK/HW NE15 ... 53 K4
MONK NE25 ... 30 B6
Medham Cl FELL NE10 ... 70 A6 2
Medina Cl SUNDSW SR3 ... 109 J2 6
Medomsley Gdns
LWF/SPW/WRK NE9 ... 82 A1 1
Medomsly St MLFD/PNYW SR4 ... 86 A6
Medway JRW NE32 ... 72 A2
Medway Av HEBB NE31 ... 71 G1
Medway Cl PLEE/EAS SR8 ... 136 D6
Medway Crs GATE NE8 ... 11 L7
Medway Gdns
MLFD/PNYW SR4 ... 97 H2 3
TYNE/NSHE NE30 ... 50 E3 1
Medway Pl CRAM NE23 ... 23 J6
Megstone Av CRAM NE23 ... 28 B3
Megstone Ct LGB/KIL NE12 ... 38 A5
Melbeck Dr CLSW/PEL DH2 ... 92 E4
Melbourne Crs MONK NE25 ... 40 C6
Melbourne Gdns
HAR/WTLS NE34 ... 72 D1
Melbourne Pl MLFD/PNYW SR4 ... 97 J2
Melbourne St CNUT NE1 ... 5 M7
Melbury MONK NE25 ... 40 A3
Melbury Ct
CLDN/WHIT/ROK SR6 ... 86 D2 10
Melbury Rd LGB/HTN NE7 ... 57 G2
Melbury St SEA/MUR SR7 ... 120 E3
Meldon Av GOS/KPK NE3 ... 45 K3 4
HAR/WTLS NE34 ... 61 J5
Meldon Ct RYTON NE40 ... 64 A1 2
Meldon Gdns DUN/TMV NE11 ... 68 A7
Meldon Rd MLFD/PNYW SR4 ... 85 K6 7
Meldon St WLSD/HOW NE28 ... 60 A2
Meldon Ter BYK/HTN/WLK NE6 ... 6 F1
Meldon Wy BLAY NE21 ... 65 H4
DHAM DH1 ... 135 J5
STLY/ANP DH9 ... 101 K3
Melgarve Dr SUNDSW SR3 ... 109 J2
Melkington Ct
WD/WHPE/BLK NE5 ... 45 F7 5
Melkridge Pl CRAM NE23 ... 28 A3
Mellendean Cl
WD/WHPE/BLK NE5 ... 45 F7 6
Melling Rd CRAM NE23 ... 28 A2
Melmerby Cl GOS/KPK NE3 ... 46 D3
Melness Rd DIN/WO NE13 ... 36 A4
Melrose WASHS NE38 ... 95 F3
Melrose Av BDLGTN NE22 ... 19 K5
HEBB NE31 ... 71 G1
SEA/MUR SR7 ... 119 F6
SMOOR NE27 ... 38 E4
TYNE/NSHE NE30 ... 40 E7
Melrose Cl
BW/LEM/TK/HW NE15 ... 54 C5
GOS/KPK NE3 ... 36 B7 3
Melrose Ct BDLGTN NE22 ... 19 K4
Melrose Crs SEA/MUR SR7 ... 111 F7
Melrose Gdns
CLDN/WHIT/ROK SR6 ... 86 E2
WLSD/HOW NE28 ... 49 J6
Melrose Gv JRW NE32 ... 60 C7 1
Melsonby Cl SUNDSW SR3 ... 109 H1 4
Meltham Ct
WD/WHPE/BLK NE5 ... 53 K1 3
Meltham Dr SUNDSW SR3 ... 109 J2 7
Melton Av BYK/HTN/WLK NE6 ... 58 B6 2
Melton Crs WBAY NE26 ... 31 G4
Melton Dr MONK NE25 ... 30 A2
Melvaig Cl SUNDSW SR3 ... 109 J2
Melville Av BLYTH NE24 ... 25 F2
Melville Gdns MONK NE25 ... 40 A5
Melville Gv LGB/HTN NE7 ... 47 G7
Melville St CLS/BIR/GTL DH3 ... 105 J5
Melvin Pl WD/WHPE/BLK NE5 ... 55 F1
Melvyn Gdns
CLDN/WHIT/ROK SR6 ... 86 E2
Membury Cl SUNDSW SR3 ... 109 J2 8
Memorial Av PLEE/EAS SR8 ... 131 F4
Mendip Av CLSW/PEL DH2 ... 105 H5
Mendip Cl PLEE/EAS SR8 ... 136 C4
Mendip Dr WASHS NE38 ... 94 D3
Mendip Gdns DUN/TMV NE11 ... 68 B6 1
Mendip Ter STLY/ANP DH9 ... 102 E2
Mendip Wy LGB/KIL NE12 ... 47 F4 3
Menvill Pl SUND SR1 ... 15 H5
Mercantile Rd HLS DH4 ... 117 F1
Mercia Wy
BW/LEM/TK/HW NE15 ... 54 C6
Mere Dr DHAM DH1 ... 124 C2
Mere Knolls Rd
CLDN/WHIT/ROK SR6 ... 74 E7
Meresyde FELL NE10 ... 70 C5
Merevale Cl WASHN NE37 ... 83 G3
Meridan Wy LGB/HTN NE7 ... 47 K7
Merlay Dr DIN/WO NE13 ... 35 F3 2
Merle Ter MLFD/PNYW SR4 ... 85 K5 1
Merlin Cl SEA/MUR SR7 ... 111 J7
Merlin Crs WLSD/HOW NE28 ... 49 H7
Merlin Dr CLS/BIR/GTL DH3 ... 93 K7
Merlin Pl LGB/KIL NE12 ... 47 G3
Merlin Wy SMOOR NE27 ... 49 J1
Merrington Cl SUNDSW SR3 ... 109 H1 5
Merrion Cl SUNDSW SR3 ... 109 H1 6
Merryfield Gdns
CLDN/WHIT/ROK SR6 ... 86 E2 3
Mersey Pl GATE NE8 ... 11 M6
Mersey Rd GATE NE8 ... 11 M7
HEBB NE31 ... 71 G1
Merton Ct ELS/FEN NE4 ... 55 H7
Merton Rd BYK/HTN/WLK NE6 ... 13 H2
PONT/DH NE20 ... 33 G3 1
Merton Sq BLYTH NE24 ... 21 G6 8
Metcalfe Crs SEA/MUR SR7 ... 119 G5
Methven Wy CRAM NE23 ... 23 J5
The Mews BLAY NE21 ... 66 C2
HLS DH4 ... 116 D1 2
SUNDSW SR3 ... 97 F7
TYNE/NSHE NE30 ... 50 E4
Michaelgate BYK/HTN/WLK NE6 ... 7 G6
Mickle Cl WASHN NE37 ... 82 C7
Mickleton Cl
CLS/BIR/GTL DH3 ... 115 J1 3
Mickleton Gdns SUNDSW SR3 ... 98 B4 5
Middle Cl WASHS NE38 ... 94 D5
Middle Dr DIN/WO NE13 ... 44 D1
PONT/DH NE20 ... 32 D7
Middle Engine La SMOOR NE27 ... 49 J3
WLSD/HOW NE28 ... 49 H5
Middlefield CLSW/PEL DH2 ... 92 E7
Middlegarth
WD/WHPE/BLK NE5 ... 55 H1 8
Middle Ga WD/WHPE/BLK NE5 ... 54 B2
Middle Gn MONK NE25 ... 40 A5
Middleham Cl CLSW/PEL DH2 ... 92 E5
Middleham Ct SWCK/CAS SR5 ... 85 J2
Middleham Rd DHAM DH1 ... 124 E2
Middles Rd STLY/ANP DH9 ... 102 E4
Middle St BYK/HTN/WLK NE6 ... 58 B5
SUND SR1 ... 14 D4 3
TYNE/NSHE NE30 ... 51 H3
Middle St East
BYK/HTN/WLK NE6 ... 58 C5
Middleton Av ELS/FEN NE4 ... 55 J5
ROWG NE39 ... 77 H4 1
Middleton Cl SEA/MUR SR7 ... 110 E6
Middleton St BLYTH NE24 ... 21 G7
Middlewood Pk ELS/FEN NE4 ... 55 J3
Midfield Dr CLDN/WHIT/ROK SR6 .. 86 B3
Midgley Dr SUNDSW SR3 ... 109 J2
Midhill Cl BDN/LAN/SAC DH7 ... 133 G5
Midhurst Av HAR/WTLS NE34 ... 61 K3
Midhurst Cl SUNDSW SR3 ... 109 H1
Midhurst Rd LGB/KIL NE12 ... 47 K3
Midmoor Rd MLFD/PNYW SR4 ... 85 J6
Midsomer Cl SUNDSW SR3 ... 109 H2 1
Midway BYK/HTN/WLK NE6 ... 58 C5
Milbanke Cl CLSW/PEL DH2 ... 93 G5
Milburn Dr
BW/LEM/TK/HW NE15 ... 55 F5
Mildmay Rd JES NE2 ... 56 D1 4
Milecastle Ct
WD/WHPE/BLK NE5 ... 54 B1
Mile End Rd SSH NE33 ... 3 G4
Milfield Av SMOOR NE27 ... 39 H6
WLSD/HOW NE28 ... 48 E6
Milford Gdns GOS/KPK NE3 ... 46 B1
Milford Rd
BW/LEM/TK/HW NE15 ... 55 G6
Military Rd TYNE/NSHE NE30 ... 51 F4
Milk Market CNUT NE1 ... 6 A7
Millais Gdns HAR/WTLS NE34 ... 73 G2
Mill Bank SWCK/CAS SR5 ... 86 C1
Millbank Ct DHAM DH1 ... 16 A1 1
Millbank Pl BDLGTN NE22 ... 19 H6
Millbank Rd BDLGTN NE22 ... 19 H5
BYK/HTN/WLK NE6 ... 58 C7
Millbeck Gv HLH DH5 ... 117 G2 1
Millbrook NSHW NE29 ... 50 C5 1
Millbrook Rd CRAM NE23 ... 23 J6
Millburngate DHAM DH1 ... 16 C4
Millburn St MLFD/PNYW SR4 ... 14 A3
Mill Cl NSHW NE29 ... 50 C5 2
Mill Ct HLS DH4 ... 107 G5
Mill Crs HEBB NE31 ... 70 E2
Milldale SEA/MUR SR7 ... 111 F7
Milldale Av BLYTH NE24 ... 20 C7 3
Mill Dam SSH NE33 ... 2 F8
Milldene Av TYNE/NSHE NE30 ... 51 G2
Mill Dene Vw JRW NE32 ... 59 K6
Mill Dyke Cl MONK NE25 ... 40 A3
Millenium Wy SWCK/CAS SR5 ... 14 D1
Miller Gdns CLSW/PEL DH2 ... 104 D3
Miller's La WICK/BNPF NE16 ... 67 F3
Millers Rd BYK/HTN/WLK NE6 ... 7 H3
Miller St GATE NE8 ... 10 C7
Miller Ter SUNDSW SR3 ... 98 A6
Mill Farm Rd ROWG NE39 ... 76 C7
Millfield BDLGTN NE22 ... 19 G7
WBAY NE26 ... 31 G3
Millfield Av GOS/KPK NE3 ... 45 J7
Millfield Cl
BW/LEM/TK/HW NE15 ... 53 H3 2
CLSW/PEL DH2 ... 105 G6
Millfield Ct BDLGTN NE22 ... 19 G6
Millfield East BDLGTN NE22 ... 19 G6
Millfield Gdns BLYTH NE24 ... 21 F5 2
FELL NE10 ... 12 B8
TYNE/NSHE NE30 ... 51 G2
Millfield Gv TYNE/NSHE NE30 ... 51 G2
Millfield La
BW/LEM/TK/HW NE15 ... 53 H3
Millfield North BDLGTN NE22 ... 19 G6
Millfield Rd WICK/BNPF NE16 ... 67 F6
Millfield South BDLGTN NE22 ... 19 G7
Millfield West BDLGTN NE22 ... 19 G6
Millford FELL NE10 ... 70 C7
Mill Gv HAR/WTLS NE34 ... 62 B7
TYNE/NSHE NE30 ... 51 G2
Millgrove Vw GOS/KPK NE3 ... 45 K7 3
Mill Hl HLH DH5 ... 117 G2
PLEE/EAS SR8 ... 136 B2
Mill Hill Rd SUNDSW SR3 ... 109 K1
WD/WHPE/BLK NE5 ... 54 D3
Mill La BDN/LAN/SAC DH7 ... 133 F2
BLAY NE21 ... 65 K5
BW/LEM/TK/HW NE15 ... 42 B7

CLDN/WHIT/ROK SR6 .... 75 F1
CLSW/PEL DH2 .... 114 C4
CRAM NE23 .... 28 D7
DHAM DH1 .... 17 M2
DHAM DH1 .... 17 L9
ELS/FEN NE4 .... 4 C8
HEBB NE31 .... 71 F2
NSHW NE29 .... 2 E4
STLY/ANP DH9 .... 92 D4
Millne Ct BDLGTN NE22 .... 19 F5
Millom Ct PLEE/EAS SR8 .... 136 B7
Millom Pl LWF/SPW/WRK NE9 .... 69 H7
Mill Pit HLS DH4 .... 107 K1 5
Mill Ri GOS/KPK NE3 .... 46 E6
Mill Rd BDN/LAN/SAC DH7 .... 133 K5
GATE NE8 .... 6 B9
SEA/MUR SR7 .... 111 F7
Mills Gdns WLSD/HOW NE28 .... 48 D7
Mill St MLFD/PNYW SR4 .... 14 A5
Millthorp Cl
ASHBK/HED/RY SR2 .... 99 G5 2
Mill Vw BOL NE36 .... 72 E5
FELL NE10 .... 69 J5
Mill View Av
CLDN/WHIT/ROK SR6 .... 86 D2
Millview Dr TYNE/NSHE NE30 .... 51 G2
Millway LWF/SPW/WRK NE9 .... 11 K9
WBAY NE26 .... 31 G3
Milner Crs BLAY NE21 .... 65 J3 7
Milner St SSH NE33 .... 3 L9
Milne Wy GOS/KPK NE3 .... 45 K4 5
Milrig Cl SUNDSW SR3 .... 109 J2 5
Milsted Cl SUNDSW SR3 .... 109 H2 4
Milsted Ct
WD/WHPE/BLK NE5 .... 53 K1 4
Milton Av HEBB NE31 .... 59 G5
HLH DH5 .... 117 J1
Milton Cl JES NE2 .... 6 A3
SEA/MUR SR7 .... 120 C1
STLY/ANP DH9 .... 103 F1
Milton Gv NSHW NE29 .... 50 D4 2
Milton La PLEE/EAS SR8 .... 130 D5
Milton Pl JES NE2 .... 6 A3
LWF/SPW/WRK NE9 .... 82 A4
NSHW NE29 .... 50 D4 3
Milton Rd WICK/BNPF NE16 .... 67 F4
Milton St JRW NE32 .... 59 K3 1
MLFD/PNYW SR4 .... 86 A6
RYTON NE40 .... 64 A3
SSH NE33 .... 61 H2
Milton Ter NSHW NE29 .... 50 D4
Milvain Av ELS/FEN NE4 .... 55 J5
Milvain St GATE NE8 .... 11 H6 3
Milverton Ct GOS/KPK NE3 .... 45 G4
Mimosa Dr HEBB NE31 .... 71 G1
Mimosa Pl ELS/FEN NE4 .... 55 H3
Mindrum Ter BYK/HTN/WLK NE6 .. 58 B7
NSHW NE29 .... 50 B6
Mindrum Wy MONK NE25 .... 30 A5
Minehead Gdns SUNDSW SR3 .... 98 A6 3
Minerva Cl WD/WHPE/BLK NE5 .... 44 A6
Mingary Cl HLH DH5 .... 117 F4 1
Minorca Cl SUND SR1 .... 15 H5
Minorca Pl GOS/KPK NE3 .... 45 K7
Minskip Cl SUNDSW SR3 .... 109 H2 5
Minster Gv WD/WHPE/BLK NE5 .... 43 K7
Minster Pde JRW NE32 .... 60 A4 2
Minting Pl CRAM NE23 .... 28 A2
Minton Ct NSHW NE29 .... 2 B4
Minton La NSHW NE29 .... 2 B5
Minton Sq MLFD/PNYW SR4 .... 85 J6 2
Mirk La GATE NE8 .... 5 M9
Mirlaw Rd CRAM NE23 .... 28 A3 1
Mistletoe Rd JES NE2 .... 56 E2
Mistletoe St DHAM DH1 .... 16 A4
Mitcham Crs LGB/HTN NE7 .... 47 H7
Mitchell Av JES NE2 .... 56 E1
MONK NE25 .... 40 B5
Mitchell Cl PLEE/EAS SR8 .... 136 C2 2
Mitchell Gdns HAR/WTLS NE34 .... 61 K4
Mitchell St BYK/HTN/WLK NE6 .. 58 D6 1
DHAM DH1 .... 16 B3 2
STLY/ANP DH9 .... 102 B3
Mitford Av BLYTH NE24 .... 24 E1 7
MONK NE25 .... 29 K5
Mitford Cl DHAM DH1 .... 135 J5
WASHS NE38 .... 94 D2
Mitford Ct PLEE/EAS SR8 .... 136 E6 1
Mitford Dr RDHAMSE DH6 .... 126 D7
WD/WHPE/BLK NE5 .... 44 C7 6
Mitford Gdns DUN/TMV NE11 .... 68 A7
WLSD/HOW NE28 .... 49 H5
Mitford Pl GOS/KPK NE3 .... 46 A4 3
Mitford Rd HAR/WTLS NE34 .... 61 J5
Mitford St CLDN/WHIT/ROK SR6 .. 86 E1
WLSD/HOW NE28 .... 60 A1 1
Mitford Ter JRW NE32 .... 71 K2
Mitford Wy DIN/WO NE13 .... 35 F3
Mithras Gdns
BW/LEM/TK/HW NE15 .... 52 A1
Mitre Pl SSH NE33 .... 61 F3
Moat Gdns FELL NE10 .... 70 E4
Moffat Av JRW NE32 .... 60 C7
Moffat Cl NSHW NE29 .... 50 A2
Moine Gdns
CLDN/WHIT/ROK SR6 .... 86 E2
Molineux St BYK/HTN/WLK NE6 .... 6 E4
Mollyfair Cl RYTON NE40 .... 52 B7
Monarch Rd ELS/FEN NE4 .... 9 J2
Monarch Wy SUNDSW SR3 .... 109 G2
Mona St STLY/ANP DH9 .... 90 D7 6
Moncreiff Ter PLEE/EAS SR8 .... 130 D5
Monday Crs ELS/FEN NE4 .... 4 E4 1
Monday Pl ELS/FEN NE4 .... 4 E4
Money Slack DHAM DH1 .... 134 C5
Monkchester Rd
BYK/HTN/WLK NE6 .... 7 L8 1
Monk Ct PLEE/EAS SR8 .... 136 C7
Monkdale Av BLYTH NE24 .... 24 C1
Monkhouse Av
TYNE/NSHE NE30 .... 50 E1
Monkridge WBAY NE26 .... 40 C2
WD/WHPE/BLK NE5 .... 53 K1
Monkridge Gdns DUN/TMV NE11 .. 9 H9
Monks Av MONK NE25 .... 40 B6
Monks' Crs DHAM DH1 .... 125 G6
Monkseaton Dr MONK NE25 .... 40 A4
Monkseaton Rd MONK NE25 .... 39 K4
Monksfeld FELL NE10 .... 12 E9
Monksfield Cl SUNDSW SR3 .... 109 K2 8
Monkside Cl WASHS NE38 .... 94 C4
Monks Park Wy LGB/KIL NE12 .... 47 G4
Monks Rd MONK NE25 .... 40 A6
Monkstone Av
TYNE/NSHE NE30 .... 51 G2 1
Monkstone Cl
TYNE/NSHE NE30 .... 51 G2 2
Monkstone Crs
TYNE/NSHE NE30 .... 51 G2
Monk St CLDN/WHIT/ROK SR6 .. 86 D4 5
Monksway JRW NE32 .... 60 C5
Monks Wy TYNE/NSHE NE30 .... 51 G1
Monks Wd NSHW NE29 .... 50 C2
Monkswood Sq
SUNDSW SR3 .... 110 B1 4
Monkton FELL NE10 .... 70 B6
Monkton Av HAR/WTLS NE34 .... 60 D7
Monkton La HEBB NE31 .... 71 G2
JRW NE32 .... 59 H7
Monkton Rd JRW NE32 .... 59 K4 7
Monkton Ter JRW NE32 .... 59 K5
Monmouth Gdns
WLSD/HOW NE28 .... 49 J6
Monroe Pl
WD/WHPE/BLK NE5 .... 55 H1 9
Mons Av HEBB NE31 .... 59 G6
Montagu Av GOS/KPK NE3 .... 56 A1
Montagu Ct GOS/KPK NE3 .... 56 A1
Montague St
BW/LEM/TK/HW NE15 .... 54 B5
CLDN/WHIT/ROK SR6 .... 86 D2 11
Monterey SUNDSW SR3 .... 109 J2 10
WASHN NE37 .... 83 F4
Montfalcon Cl PLEE/EAS SR8 .. 136 D4 1
Montford Cl SUNDSW SR3 .... 109 H2 6
Montgomery Rd DHAM DH1 .... 17 J1
Montpellier Pl GOS/KPK NE3 .... 45 K7 4
Montpellier Ter
ASHBK/HED/RY SR2 .... 98 E2
Montrose Cl MONK NE25 .... 30 A2
Montrose Crs
LWF/SPW/WRK NE9 .... 11 M9
Montrose Dr FELL NE10 .... 70 E5
Montrose Gdns SUNDSW SR3 .... 98 A3
Monument Vw HLS DH4 .... 95 J6
Moor Cl NSHW NE29 .... 50 A2
Moor Ct CLDN/WHIT/ROK SR6 .... 74 E4
Moor Crs DHAM DH1 .... 17 M1
GOS/KPK NE3 .... 46 C7
Moorcroft Cl
BW/LEM/TK/HW NE15 .... 54 B4
Moorcroft Rd
BW/LEM/TK/HW NE15 .... 54 C4
Moordale Av BLYTH NE24 .... 24 C1 1
Moore Av HAR/WTLS NE34 .... 61 J5
Moore Crs South HLH DH5 .... 117 H1
Moor Edge BDN/LAN/SAC DH7 .... 133 G7
Moor Edge Rd SMOOR NE27 .... 39 G5
Moore St GATE NE8 .... 11 K5
STLY/ANP DH9 .... 102 C3 2
Moorfield JES NE2 .... 46 D7
Moorfield Gdns
CLDN/WHIT/ROK SR6 .... 74 A5 1
Moorfoot Av CLSW/PEL DH2 .... 105 J5
Moorfoot Gdns DUN/TMV NE11 .. 68 A5
Moorhead WD/WHPE/BLK NE5 .... 55 J2
Moorhill DUN/TMV NE11 .... 80 C7
Moorhouse Cl HAR/WTLS NE34 61 H6 4
Moorhouses Rd NSHW NE29 .... 50 A3 3
Moorland Av BDLGTN NE22 .... 20 A3
Moorland Ct BDLGTN NE22 .... 20 A3 2
Moorland Crs BDLGTN NE22 .... 20 A3 3
BYK/HTN/WLK NE6 .... 7 L3
Moorland Dr BDLGTN NE22 .... 20 A4
Moorlands JRW NE32 .... 72 B3
The Moorlands STLY/ANP DH9 .. 89 G5 2
Moorland Vls BDLGTN NE22 .... 20 A3
Moorland Wy CRAM NE23 .... 22 E6
Moor La BOL NE36 .... 73 J4
CLDN/WHIT/ROK SR6 .... 74 C4
HAR/WTLS NE34 .... 61 J5
PONT/DH NE20 .... 32 E5
WD/WHPE/BLK NE5 .... 45 H6
Moor La East HAR/WTLS NE34 .... 61 K5
Moormill La DUN/TMV NE11 .... 80 E7
Moor Park Ct NSHW NE29 .... 50 A3
Moor Park Rd NSHW NE29 .... 49 K3
Moor Pl GOS/KPK NE3 .... 46 C7
Moor Rd North GOS/KPK NE3 .... 46 D6
Moor Rd South JES NE2 .... 46 D7
Moorsburn Dr HLS DH4 .... 108 A6
Moors Cl HLS DH4 .... 107 K6
Moorsfield HLS DH4 .... 107 K7
Moorside WASHN NE37 .... 82 D6
Moorside North ELS/FEN NE4 .... 55 J2
Moorside Rd SUNDSW SR3 .... 109 H2
Moorside South ELS/FEN NE4 .... 4 A1
Moorsley Rd HLH DH5 .... 117 J6
Moor St SUND SR1 .... 15 H4
Moor Ter SUND SR1 .... 15 J5
Moorvale La
WD/WHPE/BLK NE5 .... 55 J1
Moor Vw
CLDN/WHIT/ROK SR6 .... 74 E4 1
LGB/KIL NE12 .... 37 J5
Moorview Crs
WD/WHPE/BLK NE5 .... 55 J1
Moorway WASHN NE37 .... 82 D7
Moorway Dr
BW/LEM/TK/HW NE15 .... 54 C4
Moralee Cl LGB/HTN NE7 .... 47 K7
Moran St
CLDN/WHIT/ROK SR6 .... 86 D1 5
Moray Cl CLS/BIR/GTL DH3 .... 93 K5
PLEE/EAS SR8 .... 136 D5
Moray St CLDN/WHIT/ROK SR6 .... 86 D3
Morcott Gdns NSHW NE29 .... 2 A5
Morden St CNUT NE1 .... 5 J5
Mordey Cl ASHBK/HED/RY SR2 .... 15 H7
Moreland Rd HAR/WTLS NE34 .... 73 H2
Moreland St
CLDN/WHIT/ROK SR6 .... 86 D3 5
Morgan St SWCK/CAS SR5 .... 86 B3
Morgans Wy BLAY NE21 .... 65 J2
Morland Av WASHS NE38 .... 95 G3
Morland Gdns
LWF/SPW/WRK NE9 .... 11 M9
Morley Av FELL NE10 .... 13 L4
Morley Hill Rd
WD/WHPE/BLK NE5 .... 54 D3 3
Morley Ter HLS DH4 .... 107 J7
Morningside
BDN/LAN/SAC DH7 .... 113 H4
WASHS NE38 .... 94 A6
Mornington Av GOS/KPK NE3 .... 45 K7
Morpeth Av DIN/WO NE13 .... 36 C2
HAR/WTLS NE34 .... 61 J4
JRW NE32 .... 71 K1 3
Morpeth Cl WASHS NE38 .... 94 C2
Morpeth Dr SUNDSW SR3 .... 109 H1
Morpeth St JES NE2 .... 4 F1
PLEE/EAS SR8 .... 137 G2
Morpeth Ter NSHW NE29 .... 50 B6
Morris Av HAR/WTLS NE34 .... 73 F1
Morris Crs BOLCOL NE35 .... 72 E4
Morris Gdns FELL NE10 .... 13 M8
Morrison St GATE NE8 .... 10 A4
Morris Rd WICK/BNPF NE16 .... 67 F4
Morris St CLS/BIR/GTL DH3 .... 93 H2
GATE NE8 .... 10 A7
Morston Dr
BW/LEM/TK/HW NE15 .... 54 C5
Mortimer Av NSHW NE29 .... 50 B4 6
WD/WHPE/BLK NE5 .... 44 E7
Mortimer Cha CRAM NE23 .... 23 H4 1
Mortimer Rd HAR/WTLS NE34 .... 61 J4
SSH NE33 .... 61 H3
Mortimer St MLFD/PNYW SR4 .... 85 K6
Morton Cl WASHS NE38 .... 95 F2 2
Morton Sq PLEE/EAS SR8 .... 136 D3
Morton St BYK/HTN/WLK NE6 .... 7 J5
SSH NE33 .... 3 J5
Morval Cl SUNDSW SR3 .... 109 H2
Morwick Cl CRAM NE23 .... 28 A3
Morwick Pl
WD/WHPE/BLK NE5 .... 55 H2 7
Morwick Rd NSHW NE29 .... 50 B2
Mosley St CNUT NE1 .... 5 K7
Moss Bank LWF/SPW/WRK NE9 .... 81 H2
Moss Cl BW/LEM/TK/HW NE15 .. 54 A3 4
Moss Crs RYTON NE40 .... 52 C7
Mossdale DHAM DH1 .... 126 A5
Moss Side LWF/SPW/WRK NE9 .... 81 H2
Mossway CLSW/PEL DH2 .... 92 D7
Moulton Pl WD/WHPE/BLK NE5 .... 55 G1
Mountbatten Av HEBB NE31 .... 59 G7
Mount Cl LGB/KIL NE12 .... 37 K5
MLFD/PNYW SR4 .... 85 F7
MONK NE25 .... 40 B6
Mountfield Gdns GOS/KPK NE3 .... 45 K6
Mountford Rd MONK NE25 .... 30 A1
Mount Gv MLFD/PNYW SR4 .... 98 A2
Mount La LWF/SPW/WRK NE9 .... 82 A5
Mount Pleasant BLAY NE21 .... 65 K3 3
CLS/BIR/GTL DH3 .... 93 J1
HLH DH5 .... 108 D7
STLY/ANP DH9 .... 89 G5 3
SWCK/CAS SR5 .... 86 A4 3
Mount Pleasant Ct
BW/LEM/TK/HW NE15 .... 53 F1 2
Mount Rd CLS/BIR/GTL DH3 .... 93 K1
LWF/SPW/WRK NE9 .... 82 A5
MLFD/PNYW SR4 .... 97 K2
Mountside Gdns DUN/TMV NE11 .. 67 K5
Mount Stewart St
SEA/MUR SR7 .... 120 E3
Mount Ter SSH NE33 .... 3 H8
The Mount
BW/LEM/TK/HW NE15 .... 52 E1
RYTON NE40 .... 52 E6
Mount Vw WICK/BNPF NE16 .... 67 F4
Mourne Gdns DUN/TMV NE11 .... 68 A6
Moutter Cl PLEE/EAS SR8 .... 137 F2
Mowbray Cl ASHBK/HED/RY SR2 .. 14 F8
Mowbray Rd
ASHBK/HED/RY SR2 .... 15 G8
LGB/KIL NE12 .... 47 K2
NSHW NE29 .... 50 B4
SSH NE33 .... 61 J2
Mowbray St BYK/HTN/WLK NE6 .... 6 C4
DHAM DH1 .... 16 A3
Mozart St SSH NE33 .... 3 K9
Muirfield MONK NE25 .... 40 B4
SSH NE33 .... 61 K2
Muirfield Dr FELL NE10 .... 69 K6
WASHN NE37 .... 82 E3
Muirfield Rd LGB/HTN NE7 .... 47 J5
Mulben Cl ELS/FEN NE4 .... 55 J7 4
Mulberry St FELL NE10 .... 12 B6
Mulcaster Gdns
WLSD/HOW NE28 .... 48 C7 4
Mulgrave Dr
CLDN/WHIT/ROK SR6 .... 15 H1
Mulgrave Ter GATE NE8 .... 10 F2
Mullen Dr RYTON NE40 .... 52 E7
Mullen Gdns WLSD/HOW NE28 .... 48 C6
Mullen Rd WLSD/HOW NE28 .... 48 C6
Mull Gv JRW NE32 .... 72 C1 2
Muncaster Ms PLEE/EAS SR8 .... 136 B7
Mundella Ter BYK/HTN/WLK NE6 .... 6 F2
Mundell St STLY/ANP DH9 .... 102 B3
Mundle Av BLAY NE21 .... 66 A6
Mundles La BOL NE36 .... 73 G5
Munslow Rd SUNDSW SR3 .... 97 G6 1
Muriel St STLY/ANP DH9 .... 102 C4
Murphy Gv
ASHBK/HED/RY SR2 .... 98 E7 1
Murray Av HLS DH4 .... 107 J6 2
Murrayfield CRAM NE23 .... 29 G6 2
Murrayfield Dr
BDN/LAN/SAC DH7 .... 133 F7
Murrayfield Rd
WD/WHPE/BLK NE5 .... 45 H7 3
Murrayfields SMOOR NE27 .... 49 F1
Murray Gdns DUN/TMV NE11 .... 9 J8
Murray Rd CLSW/PEL DH2 .... 105 H4
WLSD/HOW NE28 .... 49 H7
Murray St BLAY NE21 .... 66 A1
PLEE/EAS SR8 .... 137 H4
Murton La HLH DH5 .... 118 C7
NSHW NE29 .... 49 J1
Murton St SUND SR1 .... 15 G6
Muscott Gv
BW/LEM/TK/HW NE15 .... 54 E5 2
Musgrave Rd
LWF/SPW/WRK NE9 .... 69 F6
Musgrave Ter BYK/HTN/WLK NE6 .. 7 M4
Muswell Hl
BW/LEM/TK/HW NE15 .... 54 E6
Mutual St WLSD/HOW NE28 .... 58 D1
Mylord Crs LGB/KIL NE12 .... 37 H4
Myrella Crs ASHBK/HED/RY SR2 .... 98 C4
Myreside Pl LGB/KIL NE12 .... 47 H3 3
Myrtle Av CLDN/WHIT/ROK SR6 .... 75 F3
DUN/TMV NE11 .... 9 H9
Myrtle Crs LGB/KIL NE12 .... 47 K1
Myrtle Gv HAR/WTLS NE34 .... 61 K7 1
JES NE2 .... 56 E1
LWF/SPW/WRK NE9 .... 81 F1
SUNDSW SR3 .... 98 B7
WLSD/HOW NE28 .... 59 F2
Myrtle Rd BLAY NE21 .... 66 A3 3
Myrtles CLSW/PEL DH2 .... 105 H2

N

Nafferton Pl
WD/WHPE/BLK NE5 .... 55 G3
Nailsworth Cl BOLCOL NE35 .... 72 C2 7
Nairn Cl CLS/BIR/GTL DH3 .... 93 K4
WASHN NE37 .... 82 E3
Nairn Rd CRAM NE23 .... 28 C1
Nairn St JRW NE32 .... 72 C1
Naisbitt Av PLEE/EAS SR8 .... 137 F2
Nansen Cl
WD/WHPE/BLK NE5 .... 54 D1 6
Napier Rd SEA/MUR SR7 .... 111 G7
WICK/BNPF NE16 .... 66 E3 6
Napier St HAR/WTLS NE34 .... 61 F5
JES NE2 .... 6 A4
JRW NE32 .... 59 K4 3
Napier Wy BLAY NE21 .... 66 C2 1
Narvik Wy NSHW NE29 .... 49 K5
Nash Av HAR/WTLS NE34 .... 73 H1
Naters St WBAY NE26 .... 41 G5
Natley Av BOL NE36 .... 73 J5
Navenby Cl GOS/KPK NE3 .... 46 D2 3
Naworth Av TYNE/NSHE NE30 .... 50 E1
Naworth Ct PLEE/EAS SR8 .... 136 C7
Naworth Dr WD/WHPE/BLK NE5 .. 44 C7
Naworth Ter JRW NE32 .... 60 B7
Nawton Av SWCK/CAS SR5 .... 86 C3
Nayland Rd CRAM NE23 .... 28 B1
Naylor Av BLAY NE21 .... 66 A6
Naylor Pl WBAY NE26 .... 30 E1
Neale St CLDN/WHIT/ROK SR6 .... 86 D2
Nearlane Cl DIN/WO NE13 .... 36 C1 1
Neasdon Crs TYNE/NSHE NE30 .... 51 F1
Neasham Rd SEA/MUR SR7 .... 111 G6
Nedderton Cl
WD/WHPE/BLK NE5 .... 43 K6 6
Needham Pl CRAM NE23 .... 28 C1
Neill Dr WICK/BNPF NE16 .... 79 F3
Neilson Rd FELL NE10 .... 11 M3
Neil St HLH DH5 .... 118 B7
Nelson Av CRAM NE23 .... 22 E7
GOS/KPK NE3 .... 46 A5 5
SSH NE33 .... 3 L7
Nelson Cl PLEE/EAS SR8 .... 137 H3 4
Nelson Crs NSHW NE29 .... 50 B7 2
Nelson Dr CRAM NE23 .... 22 E7
Nelson Rd BYK/HTN/WLK NE6 .... 58 D7
CRAM NE23 .... 22 E6
MONK NE25 .... 39 K4
Nelson St ASHBK/HED/RY SR2 .. 99 F7 1
CLS/BIR/GTL DH3 .... 105 J5
CNUT NE1 .... 5 J6
DUN/TMV NE11 .... 9 G5
GATE NE8 .... 10 F1
HLH DH5 .... 117 K5 1
SEA/MUR SR7 .... 111 H7
SSH NE33 .... 3 G7 2
WASHS NE38 .... 95 G2
Nelson Ter NSHW NE29 .... 50 B7
Nelson Wy CRAM NE23 .... 22 D5
Nenthead Cl CLS/BIR/GTL DH3 .... 115 J1
Neptune Rd
BW/LEM/TK/HW NE15 .... 54 B5
WLSD/HOW NE28 .... 58 D3
Nesbit Rd PLEE/EAS SR8 .... 137 F5
Nesburn Rd MLFD/PNYW SR4 .... 98 A2
Nesham Pl HLH DH5 .... 108 C7
Ness Ct BLAY NE21 .... 65 J2
Nest Rd FELL NE10 .... 12 D3
Netherburn Rd SWCK/CAS SR5 .... 86 C3
Netherby Dr
WD/WHPE/BLK NE5 .... 55 G3
Netherdale BDLGTN NE22 .... 18 D5 3
Nether Farm Rd FELL NE10 .... 13 H6
Nether Riggs BDLGTN NE22 .... 19 F6 2
Netherton LGB/KIL NE12 .... 37 J4 3
Netherton Av NSHW NE29 .... 50 B3
Netherton Cl
BDN/LAN/SAC DH7 .... 122 A3
CLSW/PEL DH2 .... 105 F5
Netherton Gdns
DIN/WO NE13 .... 36 B3 3
Netherton Gv NSHW NE29 .... 50 B3 3
Netherton La BDLGTN NE22 .... 18 E5 4
Nettleham Rd SWCK/CAS SR5 .... 86 C3
Nettles La SUNDSW SR3 .... 110 B1
Neville Dene DHAM DH1 .... 134 A1
Neville Rd
BW/LEM/TK/HW NE15 .... 54 B4
MLFD/PNYW SR4 .... 85 K6
PLEE/EAS SR8 .... 136 D3
Neville's Cross Bank
DHAM DH1 .... 134 B2 1
Neville's Cross Rd HEBB NE31 .... 59 H6
Neville Sq DHAM DH1 .... 134 B3 2
Neville St CNUT NE1 .... 5 H8
DHAM DH1 .... 16 C4
Nevinson Av HAR/WTLS NE34 .... 73 H1
Nevis Cl WBAY NE26 .... 40 B1
Nevis Gv BOL NE36 .... 73 F5
New Acres BDN/LAN/SAC DH7 .... 123 F7
Newacres Rd STLY/ANP DH9 .... 102 C5
Newark Cl PLEE/EAS SR8 .... 136 D3
Newark Crs SEA/MUR SR7 .... 111 G7
Newark Dr CLDN/WHIT/ROK SR6 .. 75 F4
Newarth Cl
BW/LEM/TK/HW NE15 .... 54 B4
Newbiggin La
WD/WHPE/BLK NE5 .... 44 D7 7
Newbold Av SWCK/CAS SR5 .... 86 C3
Newbold St BYK/HTN/WLK NE6 .... 7 K6
Newbottle La HLS DH4 .... 116 C1
Newbottle St HLS DH4 .... 108 B5
Newbridge Av SWCK/CAS SR5 .... 86 C3 3
Newbridge Bank
CLS/BIR/GTL DH3 .... 106 A2
Newbridge Banks
CLSW/PEL DH2 .... 104 A3
New Bridge St CNUT NE1 .... 5 M5
New Bridge St West CNUT NE1 .... 5 L5 2
Newbrough Crs JES NE2 .... 56 E1 2
Newburgh Av MONK NE25 .... 29 K6
Newburn Av SWCK/CAS SR5 .... 86 C3
Newburn Bridge Rd BLAY NE21 .... 53 G5
Newburn Ct SSH NE33 .... 61 H2 3
Newburn Crs HLS DH4 .... 108 B6
Newburn Rd
BW/LEM/TK/HW NE15 .... 53 G2
STLY/ANP DH9 .... 90 E6
Newbury LGB/KIL NE12 .... 37 K5
Newbury Av GATE NE8 .... 10 C8
Newbury Cl
BW/LEM/TK/HW NE15 .... 54 B4
Newbury St SSH NE33 .... 61 H4 3
SWCK/CAS SR5 .... 86 C2
Newby La RDHAMSE DH6 .... 127 F4
Newby Pl LWF/SPW/WRK NE9 .... 81 H1
Newcastle Av PLEE/EAS SR8 .... 137 G2
Newcastle Bank
CLS/BIR/GTL DH3 .... 81 H6
Newcastle Rd BLYTH NE24 .... 24 E3
BOL NE36 .... 71 J5
CLS/BIR/GTL DH3 .... 81 J7 1
CLS/BIR/GTL DH3 .... 105 J2
DHAM DH1 .... 134 B2 2
HAR/WTLS NE34 .... 60 D6
SWCK/CAS SR5 .... 74 A7
Newcastle St NSHW NE29 .... 2 C2
New Dr SEA/MUR SR7 .... 111 H6
New Durham Rd
ASHBK/HED/RY SR2 .... 14 B7
New Elvet DHAM DH1 .... 16 E4
New Front STLY/ANP DH9 .... 101 H3
New Front St STLY/ANP DH9 .... 90 B5
New George St SSH NE33 .... 61 G3
New Grange Ter
CLSW/PEL DH2 .... 104 D3
New Green St SSH NE33 .... 61 G2 3
Newham Av DIN/WO NE13 .... 36 A5
Newhaven Av SWCK/CAS SR5 .... 86 C3
Newington Ct SWCK/CAS SR5 .... 86 C3
Newington Rd
BYK/HTN/WLK NE6 .... 6 C4
JES NE2 .... 6 B3
Newland Ct HAR/WTLS NE34 .. 61 G6 12
Newlands Av BLYTH NE24 .... 25 F2 3
GOS/KPK NE3 .... 46 C1
MONK NE25 .... 40 B6
SUNDSW SR3 .... 98 B3
Newlands Pl BLYTH NE24 .... 25 F2 4
Newlands Rd BLYTH NE24 .... 25 F2
DHAM DH1 .... 125 K5
JES NE2 .... 46 D7
Newlands Rd East
SEA/MUR SR7 .... 111 H7 3
Newlands Rd West
SEA/MUR SR7 .... 111 G6
Newlyn Crs NSHW NE29 .... 50 C5
Newlyn Dr CRAM NE23 .... 23 H7
JRW NE32 .... 60 B5
Newlyn Rd GOS/KPK NE3 .... 45 J5
Newman Ter GATE NE8 .... 11 J7
Newmarch St JRW NE32 .... 59 J4
New Mills ELS/FEN NE4 .... 4 E4
Newminster Cl HLS DH4 .... 107 K5
Newport Gv SUNDSW SR3 .... 98 A6 4
New Quay NSHW NE29 .... 2 E4 1
Newquay Gdns
LWF/SPW/WRK NE9 .... 81 F3
Newriggs WASHS NE38 .... 95 G4
New Rd BOLCOL NE35 .... 72 E4
DUN/TMV NE11 .... 68 B6
FELL NE10 .... 70 E7
STLY/ANP DH9 .... 91 K7
WICK/BNPF NE16 .... 77 J6
Newsham Cl
WD/WHPE/BLK NE5 .... 43 K6 7
Newsham Rd BLYTH NE24 .... 24 E2
Newstead Ct WASHS NE38 .... 94 E1 2
Newstead Rd HLS DH4 .... 108 A5
Newsteads Cl MONK NE25 .... 40 B4 1
Newsteads Dr MONK NE25 .... 40 A4
Newstead Sq SUNDSW SR3 .... 110 A1 6
New Strangford Rd
SEA/MUR SR7 .... 120 D1
New St DHAM DH1 .... 16 B3
MLFD/PNYW SR4 .... 84 E7 4
Newton Av TYNE/NSHE NE30 .... 41 F6
WLSD/HOW NE28 .... 49 H7
Newton Cl
BW/LEM/TK/HW NE15 .... 54 C4
Newton Dr DHAM DH1 .... 124 C4
Newton Gv HAR/WTLS NE34 .... 60 E6 3
Newton Pl LGB/HTN NE7 .... 57 H1
Newton Rd LGB/HTN NE7 .... 47 G7
Newton St BDN/LAN/SAC DH7 .... 123 F1
DUN/TMV NE11 .... 9 H5
GATE NE8 .... 10 C7
New York Rd NSHW NE29 .... 49 K1
SMOOR NE27 .... 39 G7
New York Wy SMOOR NE27 .... 49 J2
Nicholas Av
CLDN/WHIT/ROK SR6 .... 75 F4
Nicholas St HLH DH5 .... 118 A3
Nicholson Ter LGB/KIL NE12 .... 48 A1
Nichol St ELS/FEN NE4 .... 55 H6
Nickleby Chare DHAM DH1 .... 16 A9
Nidderdale Av HLH DH5 .... 117 J6
Nidderdale Cl BLYTH NE24 .... 20 C6
Nidsdale Av BYK/HTN/WLK NE6 .... 58 C4
Nightingale Cl MLFD/PNYW SR4 .. 96 E2

Nightingale Pl STLY/ANP DH9...... 103 F2
Nile Cl BW/LEM/TK/HW NE15 .... 54 A3
Nile St NSHW NE29 .... 2 D2
SSH NE33 .... 2 F9
SUND SR1 .... 15 G4
Nilverton Av
ASHBK/HED/RY SR2 .... 98 D3
Nimbus Ct SUNDSW SR3 .... 110 A1 7
Nine Lands HLS DH4...................... 108 A7
Ninth Av BLYTH NE24...................... 25 F1
BYK/HTN/WLK NE6 .... 7 G1
CLSW/PEL DH2.............................. 105 H4
Ninth St PLEE/EAS SR8 .... 137 H3 5
Nissan Wy WASHN NE37 .... 83 K6
Nixon St GATE NE8 .... 6 C9
Nixon Ter BLYTH NE24 .... 25 H1 2
Noble's Bank Rd
ASHBK/HED/RY SR2 .... 15 J7 2
Noble St ASHBK/HED/RY SR2 .... 15 J8
ELS/FEN NE4 .... 9 G1
FELL NE10 .... 12 D5 1
PLEE/EAS SR8.............................. 130 E4
Noble Ter ASHBK/HED/RY SR2 ... 15 J8 1
Noel Av BLAY NE21 .... 66 A6
Noel St STLY/ANP DH9 .... 90 E7
Noel Ter BLAY NE21 .... 66 B5
Noirmont Wy SUNDSW SR3 .... 109 J1
Nookside MLFD/PNYW SR4........... 97 H2
Nookside Ct MLFD/PNYW SR4 .. 97 G2 4
The Nook NSHW NE29 .... 2 A2
Nora St HAR/WTLS NE34 .... 61 G6
MLFD/PNYW SR4.......................... 97 K2
Norburn La BDN/LAN/SAC DH7 .. 112 E5
Norburn Pk BDN/LAN/SAC DH7 .. 113 F7
Norbury Gv BYK/HTN/WLK NE6 .... 7 K2
Nordale Wy BLYTH NE24 .... 20 C6
Norfolk Av CLS/BIR/GTL DH3 .... 93 J5
SUNDSW SR3 .... 97 K6
Norfolk Cl SEA/MUR SR7 .... 111 G6
Norfolk Dr WASHN NE37 .... 83 F3
Norfolk Gdns WLSD/HOW NE28 .... 49 G6
Norfolk Rd GATE NE8 .... 6 C9
HAR/WTLS NE34.............................. 62 C4
Norfolk St SUND SR1 .... 14 F4
TYNE/NSHE NE30............................ 2 E1
Norfolk Wk PLEE/EAS SR8 .... 136 D2 2
Norfolk Wy
BW/LEM/TK/HW NE15 .... 54 C5 5
Norham Av HAR/WTLS NE34.......... 62 A3
Norham Av North
HAR/WTLS NE34.............................. 62 A3
Norham Av South
HAR/WTLS NE34.............................. 62 A3
Norham Cl BLYTH NE24 .... 20 E7
DIN/WO NE13 .... 36 A4 5
Norham Dr PLEE/EAS SR8 .... 136 D7 2
WD/WHPE/BLK NE5 .... 44 C7 7
Norham Pl JES NE2 .... 56 E2 5
Norham Rd DHAM DH1 .... 124 D2
GOS/KPK NE3 .... 46 B4
MONK NE25 .... 40 D4
NSHW NE29 .... 50 A5 4
NSHW NE29 .... 50 A4 2
Norham Rd North NSHW NE29 .... 49 K5
Norham Ter JRW NE32.................. 59 K7
Norhurst WICK/BNPF NE16............ 66 C7
Norland Rd
BW/LEM/TK/HW NE15 .... 54 D6
Norley Av SWCK/CAS SR5 .... 86 C3
Norma Crs WBAY NE26 .... 41 H5
Norman Av SUNDSW SR3 .... 98 B7
Normanby Cl SEA/MUR SR7 .... 111 G6
Normandy Crs HLH DH5 .... 108 D7
Norman Rd ROWG NE39 .... 77 G4
Norman Ter WLSD/HOW NE28 ...... 59 K1
Normanton Ter ELS/FEN NE4.......... 4 D6
Normount Rd ELS/FEN NE4 .... 55 J6
Northampton Rd
PLEE/EAS SR8.............................. 136 D2
Northamptonshire Dr
DHAM DH1 .... 126 A6 4
North Ap CLSW/PEL DH2.............. 105 H3
North Av GOS/KPK NE3 .... 46 B6
HAR/WTLS NE34.............................. 61 J5
LGB/KIL NE12 .... 47 K4
PLEE/EAS SR8 .... 137 G3 4
WD/WHPE/BLK NE5 .... 54 D1
North Bailey DHAM DH1 .... 16 D5
Northbourne Rd HEBB NE31 .... 59 J5
Northbourne St ELS/FEN NE4 .... 4 A9
GATE NE8 .... 11 H7
North Brancepeth Cl
BDN/LAN/SAC DH7 .... 133 K4 1
North Bridge St
CLDN/WHIT/ROK SR6 .... 14 E1
SWCK/CAS SR5 .... 14 E2
North Burns CLS/BIR/GTL DH3 .... 105 J3
North Cl BYK/HTN/WLK NE6 .... 7 G3
HAR/WTLS NE34.............................. 61 K5
RYTON NE40.................................... 52 E6
Northcote WICK/BNPF NE16............ 66 E7
Northcote Av SUND SR1 .... 15 G6
WD/WHPE/BLK NE5 .... 54 A2
Northcote St ELS/FEN NE4.............. 4 D6
SSH NE33 .... 61 H3
North Crs PLEE/EAS SR8 .... 130 D6
WASHS NE38 .... 94 E5 1
North Cft LGB/KIL NE12.................. 48 A3
North Cross St GOS/KPK NE3 .... 46 C5
Northdene CLS/BIR/GTL DH3 .... 81 J7
Northdene Av SEA/MUR SR7 .... 111 K7
North Dr CLDN/WHIT/ROK SR6.......... 73 J3
CLS/BIR/GTL DH3 .... 93 K7
HEBB NE31 .... 58 E6
North Durham St SUND SR1 .... 15 H4
North End BDN/LAN/SAC DH7 .... 133 F5
DHAM DH1 .... 124 C6 1
Northern Wy SWCK/CAS SR5 .... 86 A3
North Farm BDLGTN NE22 .... 18 A5
North Farm Av MLFD/PNYW SR4.. 97 F4
North Farm Rd HEBB NE31............ 59 F6
Northfield BDLGTN NE22.................. 20 D2
Northfield Cl WICK/BNPF NE16 ...... 66 D7
Northfield Dr LGB/KIL NE12 .... 37 H7
MLFD/PNYW SR4 .... 97 F4 5
Northfield Gdns
HAR/WTLS NE34.............................. 61 K3
Northfield Rd GOS/KPK NE3.......... 46 B6
SSH NE33 .... 61 K2
Northgate LGB/KIL NE12.................. 37 K5
North Gra PONT/DH NE20.............. 33 G1
North Gv CLDN/WHIT/ROK SR6...... 86 E2
RYTON NE40.................................... 53 F6
North Guards
CLDN/WHIT/ROK SR6 .... 74 E4
North Hall Rd MLFD/PNYW SR4 .... 97 H2
North Hvn SEA/MUR SR7 .... 111 H7
North Hylton Rd SWCK/CAS SR5 .. 85 H3
North Jesmond Av JES NE2 .... 56 E1 5
North King St TYNE/NSHE NE30.... 51 F4
Northlands BLAY NE21 .... 65 K3 4
North La BOL NE36.......................... 73 G5
HLH DH5 .... 118 C3
Northlea
BW/LEM/TK/HW NE15 .... 54 C3 5
Northlea Rd SEA/MUR SR7 .... 111 G7
North Mason Ldg DIN/WO NE13 .. 34 E1
North Milburn St
MLFD/PNYW SR4 .... 14 A3 5
North Moor Ct SUNDSW SR3.......... 97 J5
North Moor La SUNDSW SR3 .... 97 J5
Northmoor Rd
BYK/HTN/WLK NE6 .... 7 M1
North Moor Rd SUNDSW SR3 .... 97 J5
Northolt Av CRAM NE23 .... 28 C1
North Pde WBAY NE26...................... 41 F4
North Railway St
SEA/MUR SR7 .... 120 E1 5
North Ravensworth St
MLFD/PNYW SR4 .... 14 A3 4
North Rdg BDLGTN NE22................ 18 D5
MONK NE25 .... 40 A4
North Rd BOL NE36 .... 73 G5
BOLCOL NE35 .... 72 C3
CLS/BIR/GTL DH3............................ 93 J7
DHAM DH1 .... 16 C3
HLH DH5 .... 117 H3
NSHW NE29 .... 50 D2
PONT/DH NE20 .... 33 G1
SEA/MUR SR7................................ 111 K6
STLY/ANP DH9 .... 89 G6
WLSD/HOW NE28............................ 58 D1
Northside Pl MONK NE25 .... 30 B6
North St BLAY NE21 .... 65 J2
CLDN/WHIT/ROK SR6 .... 74 A3
CNUT NE1 .... 5 K5
HLH DH5 .... 117 G3
HLS DH4 .... 108 B3
JRW NE32 .... 59 K4
SSH NE33 .... 3 G6
SUNDSW SR3 .... 98 A6
SWCK/CAS SR5 .... 86 C4 6
North Ter SEA/MUR SR7 .... 111 K7
SUNDSW SR3 .... 98 A6 5
WLSD/HOW NE28............................ 59 G1
Northumberland Av
BDLGTN NE22.................................. 18 E5
GOS/KPK NE3 .... 46 A6
LGB/KIL NE12 .... 47 K3
Northumberland Dock Rd
WLSD/HOW NE28............................ 60 A2
Northumberland Gdns
WD/WHPE/BLK NE5 .... 43 K7
Northumberland Pl
PLEE/EAS SR8 .... 136 C2 5
Northumberland Rd
BW/LEM/TK/HW NE15 .... 54 A5 5
CNUT NE1 .... 5 L4
RYTON NE40.................................... 52 E5
Northumberland Sq NSHW NE29 .. 2 D2
Northumberland St CNUT NE1 ...... 5 K5
PLEE/EAS SR8............................ 137 G2
WLSD/HOW NE28............................ 58 E1
Northumberland Ter
TYNE/NSHE NE30 .... 51 H3 1
Northumberland Vls
WLSD/HOW NE28............................ 59 G1
Northumberland Wy
WASHN NE37 .... 83 F3
WASHS NE38.................................... 95 G3
Northumbrian Rd CRAM NE23...... 23 J7
Northumbrian Wy LGB/KIL NE12.. 37 J7
NSHW NE29 .... 2 C6
Northumbria Pl STLY/ANP DH9 .... 90 E7
North Vw BYK/HTN/WLK NE6.......... 6 E4
CLDN/WHIT/ROK SR6 .... 86 D2
DIN/WO NE13.................................... 35 F2
HAR/WTLS NE34 .... 61 K3 2
HLH DH5 .... 118 C7
JRW NE32 .... 59 J5
LGB/KIL NE12 .... 47 K2 5
SWCK/CAS SR5 .... 85 G4
WBAY NE26...................................... 41 G5
WICK/BNPF NE16............................ 66 E5
WLSD/HOW NE28............................ 58 E1
North Walbottle Rd
WD/WHPE/BLK NE5 .... 53 J1
Northway
BW/LEM/TK/HW NE15 .... 43 F7
LWF/SPW/WRK NE9 .... 11 L9
Northwood Ct SWCK/CAS SR5 .. 86 C3 4
Northwood Rd SEA/MUR SR7 .... 111 H7
Norton Av SEA/MUR SR7.............. 111 G6
Norton Cl CLSW/PEL DH2 .... 105 F6
Norton Rd SWCK/CAS SR5.............. 86 A2
Norton Wy
BW/LEM/TK/HW NE15 .... 54 C5
Norway Av MLFD/PNYW SR4 .... 97 J2
Norwich Av DIN/WO NE13 .... 36 B4 4
Norwich Cl CLS/BIR/GTL DH3 ...... 115 H1
Norwich Rd DHAM DH1................ 124 E2
Norwood Av BYK/HTN/WLK NE6 .. 57 H2
GOS/KPK NE3 .... 36 C7
Norwood Rd
BW/LEM/TK/HW NE15 .... 54 B3
DUN/TMV NE11 .... 9 L9
Nottingham Pl PLEE/EAS SR8 .... 136 C2
Nottinghamshire Rd
DHAM DH1 .... 125 K6
Nuneaton Wy
WD/WHPE/BLK NE5 .... 43 K6
Nuns La CNUT NE1 .... 5 J7
GATE NE8 .... 11 G2
Nuns Moor Crs ELS/FEN NE4 .... 55 J4
Nuns Moor Rd ELS/FEN NE4.......... 55 J4
Nuns' Rw DHAM DH1 .... 125 G6
Nun St CNUT NE1 .... 5 J6
Nunwick Gdns NSHW NE29 ...... 50 A4 3
Nunwick Wy LGB/HTN NE7.............. 47 K7
Nursery Cl SUNDSW SR3 .... 98 A4
Nursery Gdns PLEE/EAS SR8........ 130 C6
Nursery La CLDN/WHIT/ROK SR6 .. 74 A3
Nursery Rd SUNDSW SR3 .... 98 A4
Nutley Pl BW/LEM/TK/HW NE15 .. 54 E6
Nye Dene SWCK/CAS SR5 .... 85 F4

O

Oakapple Cl BDLGTN NE22 .... 19 F5
Oak Av DHAM DH1 .... 17 L4
DIN/WO NE13 .... 35 G2
DUN/TMV NE11 .... 9 G9
HAR/WTLS NE34................................ 62 A6
Oak Crs CLDN/WHIT/ROK SR6 .... 75 G3
CLSW/PEL DH2 .... 114 B5
Oakdale BDLGTN NE22...................... 18 B6
Oakdale Cl
BW/LEM/TK/HW NE15 .... 54 B5
Oakenshaw
BW/LEM/TK/HW NE15 .... 54 B5
Oakerside Dr PLEE/EAS SR8 .... 136 D6
Oakes Pl ELS/FEN NE4 .... 4 F6
Oakeys Rd STLY/ANP DH9 .... 90 D5
Oakfield Av WICK/BNPF NE16.......... 67 F6
Oakfield Cl SUNDSW SR3 .... 109 G1
WICK/BNPF NE16............................ 67 F6
Oakfield Dr LGB/KIL NE12 .... 38 B6
WICK/BNPF NE16 .... 67 F6 2
Oakfield Gdns
BW/LEM/TK/HW NE15 .... 55 H6
WLSD/HOW NE28 .... 48 B7 2
Oakfield Gra DIN/WO NE13.............. 35 F2
Oakfield North RYTON NE40 ...... 52 D6 1
Oakfield Rd DUN/TMV NE11 .... 68 A6
GOS/KPK NE3 .... 46 B7
WICK/BNPF NE16.............................. 66 D7
Oakfields WICK/BNPF NE16 .... 77 K6
Oakfield Ter GOS/KPK NE3 .... 46 B6
Oakfield Wy CRAM NE23.................. 29 G7
Oakgreen Flats
BDN/LAN/SAC DH7 .... 133 G6
Oak Gv WLSD/HOW NE28 .... 59 F1
Oakham Av WICK/BNPF NE16.......... 66 D6
Oakham Dr DHAM DH1 .... 126 A4
Oakham Gdns NSHW NE29 .... 50 C6
Oakhurst Dr GOS/KPK NE3 .... 56 A1
Oakhurst Ter LGB/KIL NE12 ...... 47 K4 3
Oakland Rd JES NE2 .... 56 D1 5
MONK NE25 .... 40 B5
Oaklands GOS/KPK NE3.................... 46 C7
PONT/DH NE20 .... 33 F5
WICK/BNPF NE16................................ 8 A7
Oaklands Ct PONT/DH NE20............ 33 F5
Oaklands Crs SWCK/CAS SR5 .... 86 A3
Oaklands Ter
MLFD/PNYW SR4 .... 98 A1 6
Oak Lea BDN/LAN/SAC DH7............ 113 G7
Oaklea CLSW/PEL DH2 .... 105 G3
Oakleigh Gdns
CLDN/WHIT/ROK SR6 .... 74 A2 2
Oakley Cl CRAM NE23 .... 37 H1
Oakley Dr CRAM NE23 .... 28 D1
Oakmere Cl HLS DH4 .... 107 K1 6
Oakridge WICK/BNPF NE16.............. 66 D6
Oakridge Rd
BDN/LAN/SAC DH7 .... 123 F7
Oak Rd NSHW NE29.......................... 49 J3
PLEE/EAS SR8.................................. 130 E6
The Oaks RYTON NE40 .... 64 D3 1
Oak St BDN/LAN/SAC DH7 .... 122 B2 2
HLS DH4 .... 107 G6
JRW NE32 .... 59 J4
SUND SR1 .... 15 K5
Oak Ter CLSW/PEL DH2 .... 92 C7
SEA/MUR SR7.................................. 119 H5
STLY/ANP DH9 .... 103 F4
Oaktree Av WLSD/HOW NE28.......... 58 C2
Oaktree Gdns MONK NE25 .... 40 C6
Oakwellgate GATE NE8 .... 6 A9
Oakwood FELL NE10.......................... 70 A7
HEBB NE31 .... 58 E4
RDHAMSE DH6 .... 129 G3
Oakwood Av DIN/WO NE13 .... 36 C4
LWF/SPW/WRK NE9 .... 81 G2
Oakwood Gdns DUN/TMV NE11 .... 68 B7
Oakwood Pl
WD/WHPE/BLK NE5 .... 55 G2 5
Oakwood St ASHBK/HED/RY SR2.. 14 B7
Oates St MLFD/PNYW SR4.............. 86 A7
Oatlands Rd MLFD/PNYW SR4 ...... 97 J2
Oatlands Wy DHAM DH1 .... 124 D1
Oban Av WLSD/HOW NE28 .... 49 H6
Oban St FELL NE10 .... 12 A6
JRW NE32 .... 72 C1
Obelisk La DHAM DH1 .... 16 A2
Ocean Rd ASHBK/HED/RY SR2 .... 99 G4
SSH NE33 .... 3 H6
Ocean Vw ASHBK/HED/RY SR2........ 99 F7
WBAY NE26 .... 41 F4 1
Ochiltree Ct WBAY NE26 .... 31 G2
Octavia Cl BDLGTN NE22 .... 18 E4
Octavia Ct WLSD/HOW NE28 .... 49 G6
Octavian Wy DUN/TMV NE11 .... 80 C2
Offerton Cl MLFD/PNYW SR4 .... 84 D7
Offerton La MLFD/PNYW SR4.......... 84 D7
Offerton St MLFD/PNYW SR4 .... 86 A7
Office Pl HLH DH5.............................. 117 K5
Office St PLEE/EAS SR8 .... 131 G5
Ogden St MLFD/PNYW SR4.............. 86 A7
Ogle Av DIN/WO NE13 .... 36 A5 4
Ogle Dr BLYTH NE24.......................... 24 E1
Ogle Gv JRW NE32 .... 71 J1
O'hanlon Crs WLSD/HOW NE28 .... 48 C6
Oil Mill Rd BYK/HTN/WLK NE6.......... 58 D4
Okehampton Dr HLS DH4 .... 108 A3
Okehampton Sq
SWCK/CAS SR5 .... 86 A2 3
Old Coronation St SSH NE33 .... 3 G8
Old Course Rd
CLDN/WHIT/ROK SR6 .... 74 A4 1
Old Durham Rd GATE NE8.............. 11 H6
LWF/SPW/WRK NE9 .... 69 H7
Old Elvet DHAM DH1 .... 16 E4
Old Farm Ct WICK/BNPF NE16 ... 79 F3 1
Oldfield Rd BYK/HTN/WLK NE6 .... 13 H1
Old Fold Rd FELL NE10.................... 11 M4
Old Main St RYTON NE40.................. 64 A1
Old Mill La CLS/BIR/GTL DH3 .... 115 G2
Old Mill Rd ASHBK/HED/RY SR2 .... 15 K7
SWCK/CAS SR5 .... 86 A2
Old Station Ct PONT/DH NE20 ...... 32 E6
Oldstead Gdns MLFD/PNYW SR4 .. 97 J2
Old Well La BLAY NE21 .... 65 K3
Olive Gdns LWF/SPW/WRK NE9 .... 69 G6
Olive Pl ELS/FEN NE4 .... 55 H4
Oliver Pl DHAM DH1 .... 134 B3
Oliver St BW/LEM/TK/HW NE15 .... 55 F6
SEA/MUR SR7.................................. 111 H7
STLY/ANP DH9 .... 102 C3 3
Olive St CLSW/PEL DH2 .... 104 E6
SSH NE33 .... 61 F5
SUND SR1 .... 14 D6
Ollerton Dr
BW/LEM/TK/HW NE15 .... 52 D1
Ollerton Gdns FELL NE10.................. 69 J5
Olney Cl CRAM NE23 .... 28 E1
O'neil Dr PLEE/EAS SR8 .... 136 E5
Ongar Wy LGB/KIL NE12 .... 47 H3
Onslow Gdns
LWF/SPW/WRK NE9 .... 69 F7
Onslow St MLFD/PNYW SR4 ...... 85 J6 5
Orange Gv CRAM NE23 .... 28 C7
WICK/BNPF NE16................................ 8 A9
Orb Ct ELS/FEN NE4 .... 55 H4
Orchard Av ROWG NE39 .... 77 F4
Orchard Cl HAR/WTLS NE34 .... 61 F6
LGB/KIL NE12 .... 38 B7
ROWG NE39 .... 77 F5
STLY/ANP DH9 .... 104 A1
Orchard Ct RYTON NE40 .... 52 E6
RYTON NE40...................................... 64 B3
Orchard Dene ROWG NE39 .... 77 F4
Orchard Dr DHAM DH1 .... 17 G1
Orchard Gdns
CLDN/WHIT/ROK SR6 .... 74 E4
CLS/BIR/GTL DH3............................ 105 J6
LWF/SPW/WRK NE9 .... 81 G1
WLSD/HOW NE28.............................. 48 C7
Orchard-leigh
BW/LEM/TK/HW NE15 .... 54 B5
Orchard Pk CLS/BIR/GTL DH3.......... 93 J2
Orchard Pl JES NE2 .... 57 F2
Orchard Priory DHAM DH1 .... 16 B5 1
Orchard Rd ROWG NE39 .... 77 F4
WICK/BNPF NE16................................ 8 A9
The Orchards BLYTH NE24 .... 20 D6
Orchard St CLS/BIR/GTL DH3 .... 93 J2
CLSW/PEL DH2 .... 92 E7
CNUT NE1 .... 5 K8
MLFD/PNYW SR4 .... 85 K6
Orchard Ter CLS/BIR/GTL DH3 .... 105 J6
The Orchard
BW/LEM/TK/HW NE15 .... 54 B5 1
DHAM DH1 .... 124 C1
WICK/BNPF NE16 .... 67 G5 3
Orde Av WLSD/HOW NE28.............. 49 G7
Ordley Cl BW/LEM/TK/HW NE15 .. 54 C5
Ord St ELS/FEN NE4 .... 10 A1
Oriel Cl CLDN/WHIT/ROK SR6 .... 86 D4 6
Orkney Dr ASHBK/HED/RY SR2 ...... 98 D6
Orlando Rd NSHW NE29 .... 50 B4
Ormesby Rd
CLDN/WHIT/ROK SR6 .... 86 D2 12
Ormiscraig
BW/LEM/TK/HW NE15 .... 54 C5
Ormiston BW/LEM/TK/HW NE15 .. 54 C5
Ormonde Av
BW/LEM/TK/HW NE15 .... 54 E5
Ormonde St JRW NE32...................... 59 K4
MLFD/PNYW SR4 .... 97 K1
Ormskirk Cl
BW/LEM/TK/HW NE15 .... 54 B5
Ormskirk Gv CRAM NE23 .... 28 D1 1
Ormston St CRAM NE23 .... 23 H4
Orpen Av HAR/WTLS NE34 .... 73 G1
Orpington Av BYK/HTN/WLK NE6 .. 7 L3
Orpington Rd CRAM NE23 .... 28 D1
Orr Av SUNDSW SR3 .... 110 B1
Orton Cl ELS/FEN NE4 .... 55 J7 5
Orwell Cl HAR/WTLS NE34.............. 73 F2
PLEE/EAS SR8.................................. 136 C6
Orwell Gdns STLY/ANP DH9 .... 102 C3
Osbaldeston Gdns GOS/KPK NE3.. 46 B7
Osborne Av JES NE2.......................... 56 E3
SSH NE33 .... 61 H2
Osborne Cl BDLGTN NE22 .... 19 J4
Osborne Gdns NSHW NE29 .... 50 E3 2
WBAY NE26.. 40 D4
Osborne Rd JES NE2 .... 56 E3
SWCK/CAS SR5 .... 84 E6
Osborne St CLDN/WHIT/ROK SR6.. 86 D3
SSH NE33 .... 3 L9
Osborne Ter JES NE2 .... 5 M2
Oslo Cl NSHW NE29............................ 49 K6
Osman Cl ASHBK/HED/RY SR2 .... 15 G7
Osprey Dr BLYTH NE24 .... 25 G3
NSHW NE29 .... 49 J4
Osprey Wy HAR/WTLS NE34 .... 60 E7
Oswald Cl DHAM DH1...................... 17 M4
Oswald Ct DHAM DH1 .... 16 E6
Oswald Rd HLH DH5.......................... 117 K3
Oswald St MLFD/PNYW SR4 .... 86 A6 3
Oswald Ter ASHBK/HED/RY SR2.... 99 F4
GATE NE8 .... 10 D6
PLEE/EAS SR8 .... 130 E4 2
Oswald Ter South
SWCK/CAS SR5 .... 85 G4
Oswald Wk GOS/KPK NE3 .... 46 E5
Oswestry Pl CRAM NE23 .... 28 D1
Oswin Av LGB/KIL NE12.................... 48 A2
Oswin Ct LGB/KIL NE12 .... 48 A1
Oswin Ter NSHW NE29...................... 50 B5
Otley Cl CRAM NE23.......................... 28 E1
Otterburn Av MONK NE25................ 39 K5
Otterburn Cl LGB/KIL NE12 .... 48 B2
Otterburn Crs HLS DH4 .... 108 A6
Otterburn Gdns
DUN/TMV NE11 .... 68 A5 4
HAR/WTLS NE34.................................. 61 J5
LWF/SPW/WRK NE9 .... 80 E1
WICK/BNPF NE16................................ 67 F5
Otterburn Gv BLYTH NE24 .... 24 D1
Otterburn Rd NSHW NE29 .... 50 D3
Otterburn Ter JES NE2...................... 56 E2
Ottercap Cl
BW/LEM/TK/HW NE15 .... 54 B5
Otterington WASHS NE38 .... 95 J2
Ottershaw
BW/LEM/TK/HW NE15 .... 54 C5
Otto Ter ASHBK/HED/RY SR2 .... 14 B7
Ottovale Crs BLAY NE21 .... 65 J3
Ottringham Cl
BW/LEM/TK/HW NE15 .... 54 B5
Oulton Cl CRAM NE23 .... 28 E1
Ousby Ct DIN/WO NE13 .... 45 H3 4
Ouseburn Cl
ASHBK/HED/RY SR2 .... 99 F6 2
Ouseburn Rd BYK/HTN/WLK NE6.... 6 D2
CNUT NE1 .... 6 C5
Ouseburn Wy DUN/TMV NE11.......... 80 D7
Ouse St CNUT NE1 .... 6 D6
Ouslaw La DUN/TMV NE11 .... 80 B7
Ousterley Ter STLY/ANP DH9 .... 103 F5
Ouston Cl FELL NE10.......................... 70 E5
Ouston La CLSW/PEL DH2 .... 93 F7
Ouston St BW/LEM/TK/HW NE15.. 54 D6
Outram St HLH DH5 .... 108 C6
Oval Park Vw FELL NE10.................. 12 D9
FELL NE10 .... 69 K5 2
The Oval BDLGTN NE22 .... 19 J5
BLYTH NE24 .... 24 D4
BYK/HTN/WLK NE6 .... 7 K9
CLSW/PEL DH2 .... 93 F4
CLSW/PEL DH2 .... 114 C1
DIN/WO NE13.. 44 D2
HLS DH4 .... 108 A7
LGB/KIL NE12 .... 47 K4
Overdene
BW/LEM/TK/HW NE15 .... 54 D4 6
SEA/MUR SR7 .... 120 A3 1
Overfield Rd GOS/KPK NE3.............. 45 K5
Overton Cl
BW/LEM/TK/HW NE15 .... 54 B5
Overton Rd NSHW NE29 .... 50 C2 2
Ovingham Cl WASHS NE38 .... 95 H1
Ovingham Gdns
DIN/WO NE13 .... 36 B3 4
Ovington Gv
WD/WHPE/BLK NE5 .... 55 G3
Owen Brannigan Dr
CRAM NE23 .... 37 H1 4
Owen Dr BOL NE36.............................. 73 F4
Owengate DHAM DH1 .... 16 D4
Owen St HAR/WTLS NE34 .... 61 F6
Owlet Cl BLAY NE21 .... 65 J3 8
Oxbridge St ASHBK/HED/RY SR2 .. 99 F4
Oxclose Rd WASHS NE38.................... 95 G2
Oxford Av CRAM NE23........................ 28 D1
SSH NE33 .... 61 H3 5
WASHN NE37 .... 82 D5
WLSD/HOW NE28................................ 48 C7
Oxford Cl SUNDSW SR3 .... 97 K6
Oxford Crs HEBB NE31 .... 59 H5
Oxford Pl CLS/BIR/GTL DH3 .... 93 J5
Oxfordshire Dr DHAM DH1 ...... 125 K6 2
Oxford Sq MLFD/PNYW SR4 .... 85 J6
Oxford St BLYTH NE24 .... 21 H7 5
CNUT NE1 .... 5 L5
MLFD/PNYW SR4 .... 85 J6
SEA/MUR SR7.................................... 120 B1
SSH NE33 .... 61 H3
TYNE/NSHE NE30................................ 51 H3
WBAY NE26.. 41 F4
Oxnam Crs JES NE2 .... 4 E2
Oxted Cl CRAM NE23.......................... 28 E1
Oxted Pl BYK/HTN/WLK NE6.............. 12 F1
Oyston St SSH NE33.............................. 3 G8
Ozanan Cl CRAM NE23........................ 37 H2

P

Pacific Hall SEA/MUR SR7 .... 110 E7 1
Packham Rd MLFD/PNYW SR4...... 97 G1
Paddock Cl
CLDN/WHIT/ROK SR6 .... 73 J3 5
HLS DH4 .... 107 H2
Paddock Hl PONT/DH NE20 .... 33 H2
Paddock La SUNDSW SR3 .... 98 C7
The Paddock BLYTH NE24.................. 20 E7
BW/LEM/TK/HW NE15 .... 53 H2
CRAM NE23.. 28 E2
DIN/WO NE13.. 44 D2
FELL NE10.. 70 B6
HLS DH4 .... 96 D7
STLY/ANP DH9 .... 90 A6
Pader Cl DIN/WO NE13 .... 36 B4 5
Padgate Rd MLFD/PNYW SR4 .... 97 G1
Padstow Cl
ASHBK/HED/RY SR2 .... 99 F6 3
Padstow Rd NSHW NE29.................... 50 C6
Page Av HAR/WTLS NE34 .... 61 J4
Page St HEBB NE31 .... 59 H4 4
Paignton Av ELS/FEN NE4 .... 55 J6
MONK NE25 .... 40 B5
Paignton Sq SUNDSW SR3 .... 97 J4 2
Paisley Sq SUNDSW SR3 .... 97 J4 3
Palace Rd BDLGTN NE22 .... 19 K4
Palace St ELS/FEN NE4 .... 4 F8
Palermo St MLFD/PNYW SR4 .... 85 K5
Paley St SUND SR1 .... 14 C4 2
Palgrove Rd MLFD/PNYW SR4 .... 97 G1
Palgrove Sq MLFD/PNYW SR4 .... 97 G1
Pallinsburn Ct
WD/WHPE/BLK NE5 .... 45 F7 7
Pallion New Rd
MLFD/PNYW SR4.................................. 85 K5
Pallion Pk MLFD/PNYW SR4 .... 85 K5
Pallion Rd MLFD/PNYW SR4 .... 85 K7
Pallion Subway
MLFD/PNYW SR4 .... 85 K5 2
Palm Av ELS/FEN NE4 .... 55 H4
HAR/WTLS NE34.................................... 62 A6
Palmer Crs HEBB NE31 .... 59 H5
Palmer Rd PLEE/EAS SR8 .... 136 B5
STLY/ANP DH9 .... 89 G5
Palmers Garth DHAM DH1 .... 16 E5

Palmers Gn LGB/KIL NE12 48 B1
Palmer's Hill Rd
CLDN/WHIT/ROK SR6 14 F2
Palmerston Av
BYK/HTN/WLK NE6 7 M2
Palmerston Rd MLFD/PNYW SR4 97 F3
Palmer St JRW NE32 59 J4
STLY/ANP DH9 102 B2 1
Palm Lea BDN/LAN/SAC DH7 133 F6 2
Palmstead Rd MLFD/PNYW SR4 97 G1
Palmstead Sq MLFD/PNYW SR4 97 G1
Palm St BDN/LAN/SAC DH7 122 B2
Palm Ter STLY/ANP DH9 103 F4
Pancras Rd SUNDSW SR3 97 J4
Pandon CNUT NE1 5 M7
Pandon Bank CNUT NE1 5 M6
Pangbourne Cl
BW/LEM/TK/HW NE15 54 A3
Pankhurst Gdns FELL NE10 13 K8
Pankhurst Pl STLY/ANP DH9 103 F2 1
Pann La SUND SR1 14 E4
Panns Bank SUND SR1 14 F3
The Parade ASHBK/HED/RY SR2 15 K6
BYK/HTN/WLK NE6 58 C6
CLSW/PEL DH2 104 C1
Paradise Crs PLEE/EAS SR8 130 E5
Paradise La PLEE/EAS SR8 130 E5
Paradise Rw CRAM NE23 28 C2 4
Paradise St PLEE/EAS SR8 137 J4 3
Park Av BDLGTN NE22 20 A3
BLAY NE21 66 A2
CLDN/WHIT/ROK SR6 86 E2
DUN/TMV NE11 8 F9
GOS/KPK NE3 45 K3
HAR/WTLS NE34 61 K7
SMOOR NE27 39 H6
SUNDSW SR3 98 B7
TYNE/NSHE NE30 51 G3
WBAY NE26 40 E4
WLSD/HOW NE28 58 D1
Park Chare WASHS NE38 95 G1 1
Park Cl BDN/LAN/SAC DH7 122 C3
ELS/FEN NE4 4 D8 1
STLY/ANP DH9 101 J4
Park Crs SMOOR NE27 39 H6
TYNE/NSHE NE30 51 F4
Park Crs East TYNE/NSHE NE30 51 G3
Parkdale Ri WICK/BNPF NE16 66 D5
Park Dr BDN/LAN/SAC DH7 122 B3
BLYTH NE24 24 D3
GOS/KPK NE3 46 C1
LGB/KIL NE12 48 A2
WICK/BNPF NE16 8 A9
Parker Av GOS/KPK NE3 46 B7
Park Farm Vls BLYTH NE24 24 E5
Park Fld RYTON NE40 52 E6
Park Field Ter WBAY NE26 31 F2
Park Gdns WBAY NE26 40 E4
Park Ga CLDN/WHIT/ROK SR6 86 E2
Parkgate La BLAY NE21 65 K4
Park Gv SMOOR NE27 39 H6
WASHN NE37 83 F4
Parkham Cl CRAM NE23 23 H6 3
Parkhead STLY/ANP DH9 101 G5
Parkhead Gdns BLAY NE21 65 K4
Park Head Rd LGB/HTN NE7 57 G1
Parkhouse Av SWCK/CAS SR5 85 F5
Park House Cl
RDHAMSE DH6 126 C7 3
Park House Rd DHAM DH1 134 B3
Parkhurst Rd MLFD/PNYW SR4 97 F2
Parkland BLAY NE21 53 J7
LGB/KIL NE12 47 K4 4
Parkland Av BLAY NE21 65 K4
Parkland Ct SEA/MUR SR7 111 H7
Parklands PONT/DH NE20 32 D7
ROWG NE39 88 B1
Parklands Ct FELL NE10 70 E3
Parklands Wy FELL NE10 70 E3
Parkland Ter SEA/MUR SR7 111 H7
Park La BLAY NE21 65 K4
PLEE/EAS SR8 137 H3
SEA/MUR SR7 119 G5
SMOOR NE27 39 H6
SUND SR1 14 E6
Park Lea SUNDSW SR3 109 F1
Park Lea Rd
CLDN/WHIT/ROK SR6 86 E2
Parkmore Rd
MLFD/PNYW SR4 96 E3 2
Park Pde CLDN/WHIT/ROK SR6 86 E3
WBAY NE26 40 E4
Park Pl CLS/BIR/GTL DH3 105 K2
Park Ri BW/LEM/TK/HW NE15 54 A4
Park Rd ASHBK/HED/RY SR2 14 E7
BDLGTN NE22 19 G5
BW/LEM/TK/HW NE15 53 H3
ELS/FEN NE4 9 K1
GATE NE8 11 K2
HEBB NE31 59 G6
JRW NE32 59 J5 3
MONK NE25 29 K5
PLEE/EAS SR8 137 G2
ROWG NE39 77 F3 3
SMOOR NE27 39 H6
STLY/ANP DH9 102 B2
WBAY NE26 40 E3
WLSD/HOW NE28 58 D1
Park Road Central
CLS/BIR/GTL DH3 105 K4
Park Rd North
CLS/BIR/GTL DH3 105 J2
Park Rd South
CLS/BIR/GTL DH3 105 K5
Park Rw FELL NE10 12 C7
SWCK/CAS SR5 86 A4 9
Parkshiel HAR/WTLS NE34 61 K7
Parkside BDLGTN NE22 20 A3
BDN/LAN/SAC DH7 113 H5
BW/LEM/TK/HW NE15 53 G2
DUN/TMV NE11 9 H7
HEBB NE31 58 E7
STLY/ANP DH9 90 A5
TYNE/NSHE NE30 51 H1
WLSD/HOW NE28 49 F7 2
Parkside Av BLAY NE21 65 K3
LGB/HTN NE7 47 H5
Parkside Crs SEA/MUR SR7 120 D3
TYNE/NSHE NE30 51 H2
The Parks CLS/BIR/GTL DH3 106 A6
Parkstone Cl MLFD/PNYW SR4 96 E4
Park St SEA/MUR SR7 120 E2
Park St South SWCK/CAS SR5 85 G4 5
Park Ter BDLGTN NE22 19 J3
DUN/TMV NE11 9 G8
JES NE2 5 J2
PLEE/EAS SR8 137 H4
SWCK/CAS SR5 85 K3
TYNE/NSHE NE30 51 G4
WICK/BNPF NE16 66 E3
WLSD/HOW NE28 58 D1
Park Vw BLAY NE21 66 A6
BLYTH NE24 21 H7
BYK/HTN/WLK NE6 58 C6 3
CLSW/PEL DH2 114 A4
HLH DH5 117 K5
JRW NE32 59 K7
LGB/KIL NE12 47 K2 6
MONK NE25 30 A5
WBAY NE26 40 E4
WLSD/HOW NE28 58 D1
Parkway WASHS NE38 94 E1
WICK/BNPF NE16 66 C7
Park Wood Av
BDN/LAN/SAC DH7 123 F6
Parmeter St STLY/ANP DH9 102 C3 4
Parmontley St
BW/LEM/TK/HW NE15 54 D6 2
Parnell St HLS DH4 107 K7
Parry Dr CLDN/WHIT/ROK SR6 74 E3
Parson's Av BYK/HTN/WLK NE6 58 B6
Parsons Rd PLEE/EAS SR8 136 E1
WASHN NE37 82 D6
Partick Rd MLFD/PNYW SR4 97 F2
Partick Sq MLFD/PNYW SR4 97 G2 5
Partridge Cl WASHS NE38 94 B3
Passfield Wy PLEE/EAS SR8 136 B6
Pasteur Rd RDHAMSE DH6 128 E2 1
Paston Rd MONK NE25 30 A6
The Pastures BLYTH NE24 25 F3
Pathside JRW NE32 71 K2
Patience Av DIN/WO NE13 36 C1
Patina Cl
BW/LEM/TK/HW NE15 54 A3 5
Paton Rd SUNDSW SR3 97 K4
Paton Sq SUNDSW SR3 97 K4
Patrick Crs RDHAMSE DH6 128 D1
Patterdale Cl BOL NE36 73 G5 3
DHAM DH1 126 B5 3
Patterdale Gdns LGB/HTN NE7 47 H7
Patterdale Gv SWCK/CAS SR5 86 C1 3
Patterdale Rd BLYTH NE24 20 C6
Patterdale St HLH DH5 117 K6
Patterdale Ter GATE NE8 11 G8 1
Patterson St BLAY NE21 54 C7
Pattinson Gdns FELL NE10 12 A4
LWF/SPW/WRK NE9 11 L9
Pattinson Rd WASHS NE38 83 K7
Pauline Av
CLDN/WHIT/ROK SR6 86 D2 13
Pauline Gdns
BW/LEM/TK/HW NE15 54 E4
Pauls Gn HLH DH5 117 K2
Paulsway JRW NE32 60 C5
Pawston Rd ROWG NE39 64 C7
Paxford Cl LGB/HTN NE7 47 F5
Paxton Ter MLFD/PNYW SR4 86 A6 4
Peacock Ct DUN/TMV NE11 68 B5
Peacock St West
MLFD/PNYW SR4 85 K7
Pea Flatts La CLS/BIR/GTL DH3 115 K1
Peareth Gv CLDN/WHIT/ROK SR6 86 E2
Peareth Hall Rd
LWF/SPW/WRK NE9 82 B4
WASHN NE37 82 D3
Peareth Rd
CLDN/WHIT/ROK SR6 86 E1
Pear Lea BDN/LAN/SAC DH7 133 F6
Pearl Rd SUNDSW SR3 97 K4
Pearson Pl JRW NE32 60 A3 2
TYNE/NSHE NE30 2 F1
Pearson St SSH NE33 3 J4
STLY/ANP DH9 90 D6 4
Peartree Gdns
BYK/HTN/WLK NE6 58 B2
Peary Cl WD/WHPE/BLK NE5 54 D1
Pease Av BW/LEM/TK/HW NE15 55 G5
Peasemoor Rd MLFD/PNYW SR4 97 F1
Pease Rd PLEE/EAS SR8 136 A2
Pecket Cl BLYTH NE24 24 C2
Peebles Cl NSHW NE29 49 K2
Peebles Rd SUNDSW SR3 97 J4
Peel Av DHAM DH1 125 J6
Peel La CNUT NE1 5 H8
Peggy's Wicket STLY/ANP DH9 91 K6
Pegwood Rd
MLFD/PNYW SR4 97 G1 1
Pelaw Av CLSW/PEL DH2 105 H2
STLY/ANP DH9 90 E6
Pelaw Bank CLS/BIR/GTL DH3 105 J3
Pelaw Crs CLSW/PEL DH2 105 H2
Pelaw Grange Ct
CLS/BIR/GTL DH3 93 J6
Pelaw Leazes La DHAM DH1 16 F3
Pelaw Pl CLSW/PEL DH2 105 J2
Pelaw Rd CLSW/PEL DH2 105 H2
Pelaw Sq CLSW/PEL DH2 105 H2
MLFD/PNYW SR4 85 G6 2
Pelaw Wy FELL NE10 13 K7
Peldon Cl LGB/HTN NE7 47 F5
Pelham Ct GOS/KPK NE3 45 J3 7
Peltondale Av BLYTH NE24 24 C1
Pelton Fell Rd CLSW/PEL DH2 105 G3
Pelton La CLSW/PEL DH2 92 C7
Pelton Ms CLSW/PEL DH2 104 C1
Pelton Rd MLFD/PNYW SR4 97 G2 6
Pemberton Bank HLH DH5 118 A7
Pemberton Cl SWCK/CAS SR5 86 B4 5
Pemberton Gdns
SUNDSW SR3 98 B3 2
Pemberton St HLH DH5 117 K4 3
Pembroke Av BYK/HTN/WLK NE6 7 L2
CLS/BIR/GTL DH3 93 K5
SUNDSW SR3 110 A1
Pembroke Dr PONT/DH NE20 32 C4
Pembroke Gdns
WLSD/HOW NE28 49 J6
Pembroke Ter SSH NE33 61 G4 2
Pendeford WASHS NE38 95 J2
Pendle Cl WASHS NE38 94 D3
Pendleton Dr CRAM NE23 23 G6
Pendower Wy
BW/LEM/TK/HW NE15 55 G5
Penfold Cl LGB/HTN NE7 47 J6 6
Penhale Dr ASHBK/HED/RY SR2 99 F7
Penhill Cl CLSW/PEL DH2 92 E5
Penistone Rd MLFD/PNYW SR4 96 E2
Penman Sq MLFD/PNYW SR4 97 F2 1
Penman St NSHW NE29 2 C4
Pennant Sq MLFD/PNYW SR4 85 G7 2
Pennine Dr PLEE/EAS SR8 136 C4
Pennine Gdns DUN/TMV NE11 68 A5
STLY/ANP DH9 102 E2
Pennine Gv BOL NE36 73 F5
Pennine Wy LGB/KIL NE12 47 G4
Penn Sq MLFD/PNYW SR4 85 G7
Penn St ELS/FEN NE4 9 L2
Pennycross Rd MLFD/PNYW SR4 96 E2
Pennycross Sq
MLFD/PNYW SR4 96 E1 2
Pennyfine Cl NSHW NE29 50 E2 3
Pennyfine Rd WICK/BNPF NE16 79 G2
Pennygate Sq
MLFD/PNYW SR4 96 E1 3
Pennygreen Sq
MLFD/PNYW SR4 96 E1 4
Pennymore Sq
MLFD/PNYW SR4 96 E2 2
Pennywell Rd MLFD/PNYW SR4 97 G2
Penrith Av TYNE/NSHE NE30 40 E7
Penrith Gdns
LWF/SPW/WRK NE9 81 H1
Penrith Rd HEBB NE31 59 H7
SWCK/CAS SR5 86 C1
Penryn Av SEA/MUR SR7 119 J5
Penryn Wy BDN/LAN/SAC DH7 133 H6
Pensford Ct GOS/KPK NE3 45 G5 1
Penshaw Cl
BDN/LAN/SAC DH7 122 A3 4
Penshaw Gn
WD/WHPE/BLK NE5 45 H7
Penshaw La HLS DH4 95 K6
Penshaw Vw
BDN/LAN/SAC DH7 113 J6
FELL NE10 70 E4
HEBB NE31 59 F7 5
JRW NE32 59 K7 1
Penshaw Wy CLS/BIR/GTL DH3 94 A2
Pensher St FELL NE10 11 M5
MLFD/PNYW SR4 86 A7
Pensher St East FELL NE10 12 A5
Pentland Cl CRAM NE23 23 H6 4
NSHW NE29 50 D1 2
PLEE/EAS SR8 136 B5
WASHS NE38 94 D3
Pentland Gdns DUN/TMV NE11 9 J9
Pentland Gv LGB/KIL NE12 47 H1
Pentlands Ter STLY/ANP DH9 102 E2
Pentridge Cl CRAM NE23 28 D1
Penwood Rd MLFD/PNYW SR4 97 G1
Penyghent Wy WASHN NE37 82 C7
Penzance Bungs SEA/MUR SR7 119 J4
Penzance Rd MLFD/PNYW SR4 97 F2
Percival St MLFD/PNYW SR4 85 K6 3
Percy Av WBAY NE26 40 D4
Percy Ct NSHW NE29 50 B7
Percy Crs NSHW NE29 50 B7
Percy Gdns DUN/TMV NE11 68 A5
LGB/KIL NE12 47 K2 7
MONK NE25 40 E5
TYNE/NSHE NE30 51 J2
Percy La DHAM DH1 134 B1
Percy Pk TYNE/NSHE NE30 51 H2
Percy Park Rd TYNE/NSHE NE30 51 H2
Percy Rd WBAY NE26 41 F4
Percy Scott St HAR/WTLS NE34 71 G1
Percy Sq DHAM DH1 134 B3 3
Percy St BLYTH NE24 21 H6
BW/LEM/TK/HW NE15 54 A5 6
CNUT NE1 5 J5
CRAM NE23 28 D3
HLH DH5 118 A4
JRW NE32 60 A4
LGB/KIL NE12 48 B1
SSH NE33 3 J9
TYNE/NSHE NE30 51 H3 2
WLSD/HOW NE28 58 E1
Percy St South BLYTH NE24 21 H7 6
Percy Ter ASHBK/HED/RY SR2 98 E2
DHAM DH1 134 B1
MONK NE25 40 C4
Percy Ter South
ASHBK/HED/RY SR2 98 E3
Percy Wy BW/LEM/TK/HW NE15 53 J2
Peregrine Pl LGB/KIL NE12 47 G3
Perivale Rd MLFD/PNYW SR4 97 F2
Perrycrofts SUNDSW SR3 110 A3 3
Perry St GATE NE8 11 H8
Perth Av JRW NE32 72 B1
Perth Cl NSHW NE29 50 A2 4
WLSD/HOW NE28 49 H6 2
Perth Ct SUNDSW SR3 97 J5
Perth Gdns WLSD/HOW NE28 49 H6
Perth Rd SUNDSW SR3 97 J5
Perth Sq SUNDSW SR3 97 K4 1
Pesspool La RDHAMSE DH6 129 G5
Peterborough Rd DHAM DH1 125 F3
Peter's Bank STLY/ANP DH9 89 J7
Petersfield Rd MLFD/PNYW SR4 97 F2
Petersham Rd MLFD/PNYW SR4 85 G7
Petherton Ct GOS/KPK NE3 45 G4
Peth Gn HLH DH5 118 A7 2
Peth La RYTON NE40 53 F5
Petrel Cl SSH NE33 3 G6 1
Petrel Wy BLYTH NE24 25 H3
Petteril WASHS NE38 94 C5
Petwell Crs PLEE/EAS SR8 130 D5
Petwell La PLEE/EAS SR8 130 E4
Pevensey Cl NSHW NE29 50 D1 3
Philadelphia La HLS DH4 108 A2
Philiphaugh WLSD/HOW NE28 58 D3 3
Philip Pl ELS/FEN NE4 4 D4
Philipson St BYK/HTN/WLK NE6 58 B5
Philip Sq SUNDSW SR3 97 J4
Philip St ELS/FEN NE4 4 D4
Phillips Av WICK/BNPF NE16 66 E4 4
Phoenix Cha NSHW NE29 49 K2
Phoenix Rd MLFD/PNYW SR4 85 G7
WASHS NE38 82 A7
Phoenix Wy HLS DH4 117 F1
Piccadilly SUNDSW SR3 97 J6 3
Pickard Cl PLEE/EAS SR8 137 F3
Pickard St MLFD/PNYW SR4 86 A6 3
Pickering Rd MLFD/PNYW SR4 96 E3
Pickering Sq MLFD/PNYW SR4 97 F2
Pickhurst Rd MLFD/PNYW SR4 97 F3
Pickhurst Sq MLFD/PNYW SR4 97 F3 6
Picktree La CLS/BIR/GTL DH3 105 K3
WASHS NE38 94 A6
Picktree Ldg CLS/BIR/GTL DH3 93 K6
Pickwick Cl DHAM DH1 16 A9
Pier Pde SSH NE33 3 L5
Pier Rd TYNE/NSHE NE30 51 J3
Pier Vw CLDN/WHIT/ROK SR6 87 F3
Pikestone Cl WASHS NE38 94 C3
Pikesyde STLY/ANP DH9 88 D7
Pilgrim Cl SWCK/CAS SR5 86 C4
Pilgrim St CNUT NE1 5 M8 1
Pilgrims' Wy DHAM DH1 125 G6
Pilgrimsway JRW NE32 60 C5
LWF/SPW/WRK NE9 11 K9
Pilton Rd WD/WHPE/BLK NE5 44 D7
Pimlico DHAM DH1 16 C6
Pimlico Rd HLH DH5 118 A7
MLFD/PNYW SR4 97 F2
Pine Av DHAM DH1 17 L4
DIN/WO NE13 35 G2
GOS/KPK NE3 45 K3
HAR/WTLS NE34 62 A6
Pinedale Dr RDHAMSE DH6 128 E2
Pinegarth PONT/DH NE20 32 E7
Pine Lea BDN/LAN/SAC DH7 133 F6
Pine Pk BDN/LAN/SAC DH7 133 G1
Pine Rd BLAY NE21 66 A2 4
The Pines RYTON NE40 64 D3
Pine St BDN/LAN/SAC DH7 122 B2
CLS/BIR/GTL DH3 93 J1
CLSW/PEL DH2 104 A2
JRW NE32 59 J5
MLFD/PNYW SR4 85 K6 9
STLY/ANP DH9 102 B3
Pinesway SUNDSW SR3 98 B3
Pinetree Gdns MONK NE25 40 C6
Pinetree Wy WICK/BNPF NE16 67 F2
Pinewood HEBB NE31 58 E4 3
Pinewood Av CRAM NE23 23 H6 5
DIN/WO NE13 36 C4
GOS/KPK NE3 36 C4
WASHS NE38 94 E5
Pinewood Cl BYK/HTN/WLK NE6 58 A2
DIN/WO NE13 45 F4
Pinewood Gdns DUN/TMV NE11 68 A7
Pinewood Rd SWCK/CAS SR5 85 K3
Pinewood Sq SWCK/CAS SR5 85 K3 1
Pinewood St HLS DH4 107 G6
Pinewood Vls
HAR/WTLS NE34 62 A5 2
Pink La CNUT NE1 5 J8 1
Pinner Pl BYK/HTN/WLK NE6 7 L8
Pinner Rd MLFD/PNYW SR4 97 G1 2
Pipershaw WASHN NE37 82 B7
Pipe Track La ELS/FEN NE4 55 H7
Pipewellgate GATE NE8 10 D1
Pitcairn Rd MLFD/PNYW SR4 97 G1
Pithouse La HLS DH4 116 B5
Pit La BDN/LAN/SAC DH7 132 C5
DHAM DH1 124 D3
Pittington La DHAM DH1 126 B4
Pittington Rd HLH DH5 126 D1
Pitt St ELS/FEN NE4 4 F5
Plains Rd SUNDSW SR3 97 K4
Plaistow Sq MLFD/PNYW SR4 85 G7 3
Plaistow Wy CRAM NE23 23 H6 6
Planesway FELL NE10 70 A7 1
Planet Pl LGB/KIL NE12 37 J7
Planetree Av ELS/FEN NE4 55 H3
Plane Tree Ct SUNDSW SR3 109 J1 3
Plantation Av RDHAMSE DH6 127 G6
WICK/BNPF NE16 66 E4
Plantation Gv FELL NE10 13 M4
Plantation Rd MLFD/PNYW SR4 85 J6
Plantation Sq
MLFD/PNYW SR4 85 J6 4
Plantation St
WLSD/HOW NE28 58 D3 4
The Plantation
LWF/SPW/WRK NE9 69 G7
Plantation Vw STLY/ANP DH9 103 K1
Plantation Wk RDHAMSE DH6 128 E2
Plawsworth Gdns
LWF/SPW/WRK NE9 81 J2
Plawsworth Rd
BDN/LAN/SAC DH7 113 H5
Plenmeller Pl WICK/BNPF NE16 78 E2
Plessey Av BLYTH NE24 25 G1
Plessey Crs MONK NE25 41 F5
Plessey Gdns NSHW NE29 50 B5 3
Plessey Rd BLYTH NE24 21 H6 3
BLYTH NE24 24 D3
Plessey Ter LGB/HTN NE7 57 H1
Plough Rd SUNDSW SR3 109 K2
Plover Cl BLYTH NE24 25 G3
Plover Dr WICK/BNPF NE16 90 A1
Plunkett Rd STLY/ANP DH9 89 G5
Plunkett Ter CLSW/PEL DH2 104 D3
Plymouth Cl SEA/MUR SR7 120 A2 3
Plymouth Sq SUNDSW SR3 97 J4 4
Point Pleasant Ter
WLSD/HOW NE28 59 G1
Polden Cl PLEE/EAS SR8 136 B5
Polden Crs NSHW NE29 40 C7
Polebrook Rd
MLFD/PNYW SR4 85 G7 4
Pollard St SSH NE33 3 J6
Polmuir Rd SUNDSW SR3 97 J4
Polmuir Sq SUNDSW SR3 97 J4 5
Polperro Cl CLS/BIR/GTL DH3 93 K3
Polperro Cl ASHBK/HED/RY SR2 99 F7
Polton Sq MLFD/PNYW SR4 85 G7
Polwarth Crs GOS/KPK NE3 46 C2
Polwarth Dr GOS/KPK NE3 46 C1
Polwarth Rd GOS/KPK NE3 46 C1
Polworth Sq SUNDSW SR3 97 K4 2
Pontefract Rd
MLFD/PNYW SR4 97 F3 7
Ponteland Cl NSHW NE29 50 A3
WASHS NE38 94 B2
Ponteland Rd
BW/LEM/TK/HW NE15 43 F6
DIN/WO NE13 44 E3
ELS/FEN NE4 55 K2
PONT/DH NE20 33 J3
WD/WHPE/BLK NE5 45 F4
WD/WHPE/BLK NE5 55 J2
Ponthaugh ROWG NE39 77 H2
Pontop Pike La STLY/ANP DH9 100 E1
Pontop Sq MLFD/PNYW SR4 85 G7 5
Pontop St HLH DH5 117 F4
Pontopsyde STLY/ANP DH9 88 E7
Pontop Vw ROWG NE39 77 F3
Pont Vw PONT/DH NE20 33 H2
Poole Cl CRAM NE23 28 D1
Poole Rd MLFD/PNYW SR4 85 G7 6
Pooley Cl WD/WHPE/BLK NE5 55 F2
Pooley Rd WD/WHPE/BLK NE5 55 F2
Poplar Av BLYTH NE24 21 F5
BYK/HTN/WLK NE6 58 B2 2
DIN/WO NE13 35 G2
Poplar Crs CLS/BIR/GTL DH3 93 H1
DUN/TMV NE11 9 G9
GATE NE8 10 E4
Poplar Dr CLDN/WHIT/ROK SR6 75 F3
DHAM DH1 125 H6
Poplar Gv ASHBK/HED/RY SR2 98 E6
BDLGTN NE22 19 H5
HAR/WTLS NE34 61 K6
Poplar Lea BDN/LAN/SAC DH7 133 F6
Poplar Rd BLAY NE21 66 A3 4
DHAM DH1 126 A5 2
The Poplars GOS/KPK NE3 46 C7
HLH DH5 118 B7
SWCK/CAS SR5 85 K3 2
Poplar St CLS/BIR/GTL DH3 105 J4
STLY/ANP DH9 102 B3
Popplewell Gdns
LWF/SPW/WRK NE9 81 G1
Popplewell Ter NSHW NE29 50 E2 4
The Populars HLS DH4 95 K6
Porchester Dr CRAM NE23 28 D1
Porlock Ct CRAM NE23 23 G6
Porlock Rd JRW NE32 60 B6
Portadown Rd
MLFD/PNYW SR4 97 F3 8
Portberry St SSH NE33 61 F3
Portberry Wy SSH NE33 61 F2
Portchester Gv BOLCOL NE35 72 C4
Portchester Rd
MLFD/PNYW SR4 97 G1
Portchester Sq
MLFD/PNYW SR4 97 G2
Porter Ter SEA/MUR SR7 119 H5
Porthcawl Dr WASHN NE37 82 E3
Portland Av SEA/MUR SR7 120 B1
Portland Gdns CRAM NE23 28 D1
LWF/SPW/WRK NE9 81 F3
TYNE/NSHE NE30 50 E3
Portland Rd
BW/LEM/TK/HW NE15 53 G1
JES NE2 6 A3
SUNDSW SR3 97 K4
Portland Sq SUNDSW SR3 97 K3 2
Portland St BLYTH NE24 21 F5
ELS/FEN NE4 4 B8
FELL NE10 13 H6
Portland Ter JES NE2 5 M2
Portman Pl BYK/HTN/WLK NE6 12 E1
Portman Sq MLFD/PNYW SR4 97 G1
Portmeads Rd CLS/BIR/GTL DH3 93 K2
Portobello La
CLDN/WHIT/ROK SR6 86 D4
Portree Sq SUNDSW SR3 97 J5
Portrush Cl WASHN NE37 82 E3 4
Portrush Rd MLFD/PNYW SR4 85 G7
Portrush Wy LGB/HTN NE7 47 J5
Portslade Rd MLFD/PNYW SR4 97 F2
Portsmouth Rd
MLFD/PNYW SR4 97 F1
NSHW NE29 50 A5
Portsmouth Sq
MLFD/PNYW SR4 97 F2
Portugal Pl
WLSD/HOW NE28 58 D2 10
Post Office La NSHW NE29 50 E2 5
Post Office St BLYTH NE24 21 H6 8
Potterhouse La DHAM DH1 124 A1
Potter Pl STLY/ANP DH9 103 F2
Potters Bank DHAM DH1 16 A8
Potters Cl DHAM DH1 134 B3
Potter Sq SUNDSW SR3 97 J4
Potter St JRW NE32 59 J4
WLSD/HOW NE28 59 J2
Pottersway LWF/SPW/WRK NE9 69 G6
Pottery Bank
BYK/HTN/WLK NE6 13 H1
Pottery La CNUT NE1 10 B1
MLFD/PNYW SR4 84 E6 3
Pottery Rd SWCK/CAS SR5 86 A4
Pottery Yd HLS DH4 108 C7 2
Potts St BYK/HTN/WLK NE6 7 G4 2
Powburn Cl CLSW/PEL DH2 105 G6
Powburn Gdns ELS/FEN NE4 55 J3
Powis Rd SUNDSW SR3 97 K4
Powis Sq SUNDSW SR3 97 K4 3
Poynings Cl WD/WHPE/BLK NE5 45 G5
Praetorian Dr
WLSD/HOW NE28 58 D3 3
Prebends Fld DHAM DH1 125 G5
Prefect Pl
LWF/SPW/WRK NE9 69 G5 2
Premier Rd SUNDSW SR3 97 J4
Prendwick Av HEBB NE31 71 F1
Prendwick Cl CLSW/PEL DH2 105 G7
Prengarth Av
CLDN/WHIT/ROK SR6 86 D2
Prensgarth Wy
HAR/WTLS NE34 72 D1 2
Prescot Rd MLFD/PNYW SR4 85 G7
Press La SUND SR1 14 F4
Prestbury Av CRAM NE23 23 G6

Prestbury Rd MLFD/PNYW SR4 ... 96 E2
Prestdale Av BLYTH NE24 ... 20 C7
Presthope Rd MLFD/PNYW SR4 ... 96 E2
Preston Av TYNE/NSHE NE30 ... 50 E3
Preston North Rd NSHW NE29 ... 50 D1
Preston Pk NSHW NE29 ... 50 E3
Preston Rd ASHBK/HED/RY SR2 ... 15 J9
Preston Wd TYNE/NSHE NE30 ... 50 E1
Prestwick FELL NE10 ... 70 A7 2
Prestwick Av NSHW NE29 ... 50 A3
Prestwick Cl WASHN NE37 ... 82 E3 5
Prestwick Dr FELL NE10 ... 70 E5
Prestwick Gdns GOS/KPK NE3 ... 45 K6
Prestwick Rd MLFD/PNYW SR4 ... 85 G7
Pretoria Sq SUNDSW SR3 ... 97 J4 6
Pretoria St
BW/LEM/TK/HW NE15 ... 54 E7 2
Price St HEBB NE31 ... 58 E4 4
Priestfield Cl SUNDSW SR3 ... 109 K2
Priestley Ct HAR/WTLS NE34 ... 72 E1
Priestley Gdns FELL NE10 ... 13 L8
Priestly Crs MLFD/PNYW SR4 ... 14 A2
Priestman Ct
MLFD/PNYW SR4 ... 85 H7 3
Primate Rd SUNDSW SR3 ... 97 J4
Primrose Av HAR/WTLS NE34 ... 61 F6 4
Primrose Cl CRAM NE23 ... 37 G1
Primrose Crs
CLDN/WHIT/ROK SR6 ... 86 D2
HLS DH4 ... 107 G4
Primrose Gdns
WLSD/HOW NE28 ... 48 C6 2
Primrose Hl
LWF/SPW/WRK NE9 ... 69 G7 3
Primrose Prec
CLDN/WHIT/ROK SR6 ... 86 D2 14
Primrose St MLFD/PNYW SR4 ... 84 E7 5
Primrose Ter CLS/BIR/GTL DH3 ... 93 K2
JRW NE32 ... 60 A7
Prince Albert Ter JES NE2 ... 6 A5 2
Prince Consort La HEBB NE31 ... 59 F5
Prince Consort Rd GATE NE8 ... 10 F3
HEBB NE31 ... 58 E5
JRW NE32 ... 60 A5
Prince Consort Wy NSHW NE29 ... 2 C7
Prince Edward Gv
HAR/WTLS NE34 ... 62 C5
Prince Edward Rd
HAR/WTLS NE34 ... 61 K6
Prince Edward Rd East
HAR/WTLS NE34 ... 62 C5
Prince George Av
CLDN/WHIT/ROK SR6 ... 86 D1 6
Prince of Wales Cl
HAR/WTLS NE34 ... 61 J6 1
Prince Philip Cl
BW/LEM/TK/HW NE15 ... 55 G6
Prince Rd WLSD/HOW NE28 ... 48 D7
Princes Av CLDN/WHIT/ROK SR6 .. 74 E7
GOS/KPK NE3 ... 46 B4
Princes Cl GOS/KPK NE3 ... 46 B2
Prince's Gdns BLYTH NE24 ... 20 E6
CLDN/WHIT/ROK SR6 ... 74 E7 2
Prince's Meadow GOS/KPK NE3 .. 46 A5
Princes Pk DUN/TMV NE11 ... 68 B7
Princes Rd GOS/KPK NE3 ... 46 B1
Princess Dr GATE NE8 ... 9 K6
Princess Louise Rd BLYTH NE24 ... 21 F7
Princess Rd SEA/MUR SR7 ... 120 D1
Princess St ASHBK/HED/RY SR2 ... 14 D7
FELL NE10 ... 13 J6
WICK/BNPF NE16 ... 79 F3
Princes' St DHAM DH1 ... 16 A2
HLS DH4 ... 107 J2
TYNE/NSHE NE30 ... 51 F3
Prince St SUND SR1 ... 14 E4 2
Princesway DUN/TMV NE11 ... 68 C6
Princetown Ter SUNDSW SR3 ... 97 J4
Princeway TYNE/NSHE NE30 ... 51 F2
Pringle Cl BDN/LAN/SAC DH7 ... 132 D3
Pringle Gv BDN/LAN/SAC DH7 ... 132 E3
Pringle Pl BDN/LAN/SAC DH7 ... 132 E3
Prinn Pl WICK/BNPF NE16 ... 79 F3
Priors Cl DHAM DH1 ... 124 B7
Priors Gra RDHAMSE DH6 ... 126 E4
Prior's Ter TYNE/NSHE NE30 ... 51 H3
Priors Wy WLSD/HOW NE28 ... 59 G1
Priory Av MONK NE25 ... 40 D5
Priory Ct BDN/LAN/SAC DH7 ... 113 H6
Priory Gra BLYTH NE24 ... 20 E6
Priory Gv MLFD/PNYW SR4 ... 97 K1
Priory Pl DIN/WO NE13 ... 36 A4 6
Priory Rd DHAM DH1 ... 124 C4
JRW NE32 ... 60 A3 3
Priory Wy WD/WHPE/BLK NE5 ... 44 D6
Proctor Sq SUNDSW SR3 ... 97 K4 4
Proctor St BYK/HTN/WLK NE6 .. 58 C6 4
Promenade ASHBK/HED/RY SR2 .. 99 G3
SEA/MUR SR7 ... 111 K7
SSH NE33 ... 51 K7
WBAY NE26 ... 40 E3
Prospect Av MONK NE25 ... 29 K5
WLSD/HOW NE28 ... 48 D7
Prospect Av North
WLSD/HOW NE28 ... 48 D6
Prospect Crs HLH DH5 ... 128 B1
Prospect Gdns BOL NE36 ... 72 E5
Prospect Pl BDN/LAN/SAC DH7 .. 132 D2
ELS/FEN NE4 ... 4 D6
Prospect Rw SUND SR1 ... 15 J3
Prospect Ter
BDN/LAN/SAC DH7 ... 132 D2
TYNE/NSHE NE30 ... 51 G4
Prospect Vw HLS DH4 ... 116 C6
Providence Rw DHAM DH1 ... 16 E2
Provident St CLSW/PEL DH2 ... 104 C1
Provost Gdns ELS/FEN NE4 ... 55 H7 1
Prudhoe Gv JRW NE32 ... 71 J1
Prudhoe St MLFD/PNYW SR4 .. 85 K6 10
NSHW NE29 ... 2 D4
Prudhoe Ter
TYNE/NSHE NE30 ... 51 H2 5
Pudding Chare CNUT NE1 ... 5 K8
Purbeck Gdns CRAM NE23 ... 28 D1
Purbeck Rd LGB/KIL NE12 ... 47 H4
Purley WASHS NE38 ... 95 J2 2
Purley Cl WLSD/HOW NE28 ... 49 H6
Purley Gdns GOS/KPK NE3 ... 45 K6
Purley Rd SUNDSW SR3 ... 97 J4
Purley Sq SUNDSW SR3 ... 97 J4
Putney Sq MLFD/PNYW SR4 ... 97 F2
Pykerley Rd MONK NE25 ... 40 C4

Q

The Quadrant NSHW NE29 ... 50 C5
SUND SR1 ... 15 J3
Quality Rw BYK/HTN/WLK NE6 ... 6 D6
Quality Row Rd
WICK/BNPF NE16 ... 66 E3 7
Quantock Cl LGB/KIL NE12 ... 47 G4 2
NSHW NE29 ... 40 D7 1
Quantock Pl PLEE/EAS SR8 ... 136 B4
Quarry Crs BDN/LAN/SAC DH7 ... 123 F6
Quarryfield Rd GATE NE8 ... 6 B9
Quarryheads La DHAM DH1 ... 16 B6
Quarry House La DHAM DH1 ... 134 A1
HLH DH5 ... 117 G4
Quarry La HAR/WTLS NE34 ... 62 A6
HAR/WTLS NE34 ... 62 D5 1
Quarry Rd
BW/LEM/TK/HW NE15 ... 54 A5 7
HEBB NE31 ... 59 G6
STLY/ANP DH9 ... 90 D7
SUNDSW SR3 ... 98 B7 3
Quarry Rw FELL NE10 ... 12 C6
Quarry St SUNDSW SR3 ... 98 A7
Quay Rd BLYTH NE24 ... 21 H6 3
Quayside BLYTH NE24 ... 21 H6 5
CNUT NE1 ... 5 M8
The Quay HLH DH5 ... 117 K5
Quay Vw WLSD/HOW NE28 ... 59 H1
Queen Alexandra Rd
ASHBK/HED/RY SR2 ... 98 E4
NSHW NE29 ... 50 D3
SEA/MUR SR7 ... 120 E2
SUNDSW SR3 ... 98 B3
Queen Alexandra Rd West
NSHW NE29 ... 50 C3
Queen Elizabeth Av
LWF/SPW/WRK NE9 ... 69 H7
Queen Elizabeth Dr HLH DH5 ... 128 C1
Queen Elizabeth Ii Br CNUT NE1 .. 10 D1
Queens Av CLDN/WHIT/ROK SR6 .. 74 E7
Queensberry St
MLFD/PNYW SR4 ... 14 B4 4
Queensbridge LGB/KIL NE12 ... 47 F3 2
Queensbury Dr
WD/WHPE/BLK NE5 ... 53 K1
Queensbury Rd SEA/MUR SR7 ... 120 B1
Queen's Ct
BW/LEM/TK/HW NE15 ... 53 J2
GATE NE8 ... 10 A6
GOS/KPK NE3 ... 36 C7 1
Queen's Crs HEBB NE31 ... 59 F7
MLFD/PNYW SR4 ... 98 A1
WLSD/HOW NE28 ... 48 C7
Queen's Dr WBAY NE26 ... 40 E4
WICK/BNPF NE16 ... 67 F7
Queen's Gdns BLYTH NE24 ... 20 E6
Queens Gv DHAM DH1 ... 134 B3
Queensland Av HAR/WTLS NE34 .. 60 C7
Queens La CNUT NE1 ... 5 K8 2
Queensmere CLS/BIR/GTL DH3 ... 93 J7
Queen's Rd BDLGTN NE22 ... 19 K4
BW/LEM/TK/HW NE15 ... 53 J2
CRAM NE23 ... 28 C7
JES NE2 ... 57 F2
SWCK/CAS SR5 ... 86 B4 6
WBAY NE26 ... 31 G2
WBAY NE26 ... 40 D3
WD/WHPE/BLK NE5 ... 54 E1
Queen's Ter JES NE2 ... 57 F2
WLSD/HOW NE28 ... 58 D1
Queen St ASHBK/HED/RY SR2 ... 99 F6
CLSW/PEL DH2 ... 104 A2
CNUT NE1 ... 5 M8
GATE NE8 ... 10 A7
HLH DH5 ... 117 K3
SEA/MUR SR7 ... 120 D1
SSH NE33 ... 3 G7
SUND SR1 ... 14 D3 1
TYNE/NSHE NE30 ... 2 F1
Queen St East SUND SR1 ... 15 H4 2
Queensway ELS/FEN NE4 ... 55 H3
GOS/KPK NE3 ... 46 B1
HLH DH5 ... 108 D7 6
PONT/DH NE20 ... 33 F7
TYNE/NSHE NE30 ... 51 H2
Queensway North
DUN/TMV NE11 ... 10 A9
Queen Victoria Rd CNUT NE1 ... 5 J4
Queen Victoria St FELL NE10 ... 13 H6
Quentin Av GOS/KPK NE3 ... 45 H5
Quinn Cl PLEE/EAS SR8 ... 136 E5
Quilton Cl WD/WHPE/BLK NE5 ... 45 F6

R

Rabbit Banks Rd GATE NE8 ... 10 D2
Raby Av PLEE/EAS SR8 ... 131 F4
Raby Cl HLS DH4 ... 107 J6 3
Raby Dr SUNDSW SR3 ... 97 G7
Raby Gdns JRW NE32 ... 59 K7
Raby Rd DHAM DH1 ... 124 D2
WASHS NE38 ... 94 B1
Raby St BYK/HTN/WLK NE6 ... 7 G5
GATE NE8 ... 11 H7
MLFD/PNYW SR4 ... 14 A6
Raby Wy BYK/HTN/WLK NE6 ... 7 G6
Rachel Cl ASHBK/HED/RY SR2 ... 98 C7
Rackly Wy CLDN/WHIT/ROK SR6 .. 75 F4
Radcliffe Pl
WD/WHPE/BLK NE5 ... 55 H1 10
Radcliffe Rd SWCK/CAS SR5 ... 85 J3
Radcliffe St CLS/BIR/GTL DH3 ... 93 J3
Radlett Rd SWCK/CAS SR5 ... 85 H3
Radnor Gdns WLSD/HOW NE28 ... 49 J7
Radnor St CNUT NE1 ... 5 M4
Radstock Pl LGB/KIL NE12 ... 47 J3 2
Rae Av WLSD/HOW NE28 ... 48 D6
Raeburn Av WASHS NE38 ... 95 G3
Raeburn Gdns
LWF/SPW/WRK NE9 ... 11 M9
Raeburn Rd HAR/WTLS NE34 ... 73 H2
SWCK/CAS SR5 ... 85 G2 2
Raglan WASHS NE38 ... 94 C1
Raglan Av ASHBK/HED/RY SR2 ... 98 E3
Raglan Pl WICK/BNPF NE16 ... 77 K7
Railway Rw SUND SR1 ... 14 B5
Railway St DUN/TMV NE11 ... 9 G4
ELS/FEN NE4 ... 9 M2
HEBB NE31 ... 59 H4
HLH DH5 ... 117 K4 4
HLS DH4 ... 108 B5
JRW NE32 ... 59 J4
NSHW NE29 ... 2 D2 2
STLY/ANP DH9 ... 101 J4
STLY/ANP DH9 ... 103 G5
SUND SR1 ... 15 J5 1
Railway Ter ELS/FEN NE4 ... 9 L2
NSHW NE29 ... 2 D2
Raine Gv SUND SR1 ... 15 H6
Rainford Av ASHBK/HED/RY SR2 .. 98 E3
Rainhill Cl WASHN NE37 ... 83 G4
Rainhill Rd WASHN NE37 ... 83 G4
Rainton Cl FELL NE10 ... 70 E6 2
Rainton Gv HLH DH5 ... 117 H2 2
Rainton St HLS DH4 ... 95 K6
MLFD/PNYW SR4 ... 86 A7
SEA/MUR SR7 ... 120 E2
Rainton Vw HLS DH4 ... 116 C6
Rake La NSHW NE29 ... 50 A1
Raleigh Cl SSH NE33 ... 61 F3
Raleigh Rd SWCK/CAS SR5 ... 85 H3
Raleigh Sq SWCK/CAS SR5 ... 85 H3
Ralph Av ASHBK/HED/RY SR2 ... 98 E6
Ralph St HEBB NE31 ... 59 H4
Ramilies ASHBK/HED/RY SR2 ... 110 D1
Ramillies Rd SWCK/CAS SR5 ... 85 G2
The Ramparts
BW/LEM/TK/HW NE15 ... 54 C3
Ramsay St BLAY NE21 ... 65 K3 6
Ramsey Cl DHAM DH1 ... 17 M3
PLEE/EAS SR8 ... 136 E2
Ramsey St CLS/BIR/GTL DH3 ... 105 J5
Ramsgate Rd SWCK/CAS SR5 ... 85 J2
Ramside Vw DHAM DH1 ... 126 A4 3
Randolph St JRW NE32 ... 60 A4 3
Rangoon Rd SWCK/CAS SR5 ... 85 G2 3
Ranmere Rd
BW/LEM/TK/HW NE15 ... 54 E6
Ranmore Cl CRAM NE23 ... 28 C1
Rannoch Av CLSW/PEL DH2 ... 105 H6
Rannoch Cl FELL NE10 ... 70 E4
Rannoch Rd SWCK/CAS SR5 ... 85 G2
Ranson Crs HAR/WTLS NE34 ... 60 D6 1
Ranson St MLFD/PNYW SR4 ... 98 A2
Raphael Av HAR/WTLS NE34 ... 73 G1
Rathmore Gdns
TYNE/NSHE NE30 ... 50 E2
Ratho Ct FELL NE10 ... 70 A6
Ravenburn Gdns
BW/LEM/TK/HW NE15 ... 54 D5 1
Ravenna Rd SWCK/CAS SR5 ... 85 F2
Ravensbourne Av BOL NE36 ... 73 H4
Ravenscar Cl
WICK/BNPF NE16 ... 66 C7 3
Ravenscourt Rd SWCK/CAS SR5 ... 85 G3
Ravensdale Gv BLYTH NE24 ... 20 C7
Ravenshill Rd
WD/WHPE/BLK NE5 ... 54 B2
Ravenside Rd ELS/FEN NE4 ... 55 J3
Ravenstone WASHN NE37 ... 82 D6
Ravenswood Cl LGB/KIL NE12 ... 48 A2
Ravenswood Gdns
LWF/SPW/WRK NE9 ... 81 F2
Ravenswood Rd
BYK/HTN/WLK NE6 ... 57 J2
SWCK/CAS SR5 ... 85 G2
Ravenswood Sq SWCK/CAS SR5 ... 85 F2
Ravensworh St
MLFD/PNYW SR4 ... 14 A4
Ravensworth
ASHBK/HED/RY SR2 ... 110 D1
Ravensworth Av HLS DH4 ... 107 H6
LWF/SPW/WRK NE9 ... 81 J3
Ravensworth Cl
WLSD/HOW NE28 ... 59 H1
Ravensworth Ct
RDHAMSE DH6 ... 128 E2
Ravensworth Rd
CLS/BIR/GTL DH3 ... 93 H1
DUN/TMV NE11 ... 9 J6
Ravensworth St
WLSD/HOW NE28 ... 59 H1
Ravensworth Ter DHAM DH1 ... 16 F3
DUN/TMV NE11 ... 9 J7
JRW NE32 ... 71 K1 4
SSH NE33 ... 61 G4
Rawdon Rd SWCK/CAS SR5 ... 85 J2
Rawling Rd GATE NE8 ... 10 C7
Rawlston Wy
WD/WHPE/BLK NE5 ... 45 G7
Rawmarsh Rd SWCK/CAS SR5 ... 85 G2 4
Raydale SWCK/CAS SR5 ... 85 J2 1
Raydale Av WASHN NE37 ... 82 D5
Raylees Gdns DUN/TMV NE11 .. 68 A5 6
Rayleigh Dr DIN/WO NE13 ... 36 B2
Rayleigh Gv GATE NE8 ... 10 D9
Raynham Cl CRAM NE23 ... 28 A5
Readhead Av SSH NE33 ... 61 J2
Readhead Dr BYK/HTN/WLK NE6 .. 58 B7
Readhead Rd HAR/WTLS NE34 ... 61 J3
Reading Rd HAR/WTLS NE34 ... 61 H4
SWCK/CAS SR5 ... 85 G2
Reading Sq SWCK/CAS SR5 ... 85 G2
Rea Pl GOS/KPK NE3 ... 46 A5 6
Reasby Gdns RYTON NE40 ... 52 D6
Reavley Av BDLGTN NE22 ... 20 A3
Reay Crs BOLCOL NE35 ... 73 F4
Reay Gdns WD/WHPE/BLK NE5 ... 54 E1
Reay St FELL NE10 ... 13 L3
Rectory Bank BOL NE36 ... 72 E5 5
Rectory Ct WICK/BNPF NE16 ... 67 F5
Rectory Dr JES NE2 ... 46 E6
Rectory Gn BOL NE36 ... 72 D5 1
Rectory Gv GOS/KPK NE3 ... 46 D5
Rectory La BLAY NE21 ... 65 K3
WICK/BNPF NE16 ... 67 F6
Rectory Pl GATE NE8 ... 10 D5
Rectory Rd FELL NE10 ... 12 B9
GATE NE8 ... 10 D6
GOS/KPK NE3 ... 46 D6
HLH DH5 ... 117 K5 6
Rectory Rd East FELL NE10 ... 69 K5
Red Admiral Ct
DUN/TMV NE11 ... 68 B5 2
Red Barnes CNUT NE1 ... 6 B6
Red Berry Wy HAR/WTLS NE34 ... 61 F7
Redburn Cl HLS DH4 ... 108 A7 1
Redburn Rd WD/WHPE/BLK NE5 .. 44 D6
Redcar Rd BYK/HTN/WLK NE6 ... 57 K2
SWCK/CAS SR5 ... 85 J3
WLSD/HOW NE28 ... 49 J7
Redcar Sq SWCK/CAS SR5 ... 85 J3 1
Redcliffe Wy
WD/WHPE/BLK NE5 ... 45 F7
Redditch Sq SWCK/CAS SR5 ... 85 H2 1
Rede Av HEBB NE31 ... 59 G5 2
Redemarsh FELL NE10 ... 70 C6 2
Redesdale Av BLAY NE21 ... 65 H4
GOS/KPK NE3 ... 46 A5
Redesdale Cl LGB/KIL NE12 ... 47 J2 1
Redesdale Gdns DUN/TMV NE11 ... 9 H9
Redesdale Gv NSHW NE29 ... 50 A4
Redesdale Pl BLYTH NE24 ... 20 D7 4
Redesdale Rd CLSW/PEL DH2 ... 105 G6
NSHW NE29 ... 50 A4
SWCK/CAS SR5 ... 85 G2
Rede St DUN/TMV NE11 ... 68 C7
JRW NE32 ... 59 J6 1
Redewater Gdns
WICK/BNPF NE16 ... 66 E6 1
Redewater Rd ELS/FEN NE4 ... 55 J3
Red Firs BDN/LAN/SAC DH7 ... 133 G6
Redford Pl LGB/KIL NE12 ... 37 J4 4
Red Hall Dr LGB/HTN NE7 ... 47 K7
Redheugh Bridge Rd
ELS/FEN NE4 ... 10 A1
Redheugh Rd MONK NE25 ... 39 K4
Redhill CLDN/WHIT/ROK SR6 ... 74 E4
Redhill Dr WICK/BNPF NE16 ... 78 C1 1
Redhill Rd SWCK/CAS SR5 ... 85 H2
Redhills La DHAM DH1 ... 124 B7
Redhills Wy HLH DH5 ... 117 K6
Redhouse Cl
BDN/LAN/SAC DH7 ... 113 J6
Red House Dr MONK NE25 ... 40 A3
Red House Farm BDLGTN NE22 ... 18 C6
Red House Rd HEBB NE31 ... 59 H5
Redland Av GOS/KPK NE3 ... 45 H4
Red Lion La WASHN NE37 ... 82 E3
Redmires Cl CLSW/PEL DH2 ... 92 E5
Redmond Rd SWCK/CAS SR5 ... 85 J2
Redmond Sq SWCK/CAS SR5 ... 85 J2
Rednam Pl WD/WHPE/BLK NE5 ... 55 F1
Redruth Gdns
LWF/SPW/WRK NE9 ... 81 F3
Redruth Sq SWCK/CAS SR5 ... 85 H2 2
Redshank Cl WASHS NE38 ... 94 B4
Redshank Dr BLYTH NE24 ... 25 G3 3
Red Wk LGB/HTN NE7 ... 57 G1
Redwell Ct HAR/WTLS NE34 ... 62 C4 2
Redwell La HAR/WTLS NE34 ... 62 D4
Redwing Cl WASHS NE38 ... 94 B3
Redwood BDN/LAN/SAC DH7 ... 133 G6
Redwood Cl HLH DH5 ... 117 J5
LGB/KIL NE12 ... 37 J5 10
Reed Av LGB/KIL NE12 ... 37 J4
Reedham Ct
WD/WHPE/BLK NE5 ... 45 F6 8
Reedling Ct SWCK/CAS SR5 ... 85 G1 1
Reedside RYTON NE40 ... 53 F6
Reedsmouth Pl
WD/WHPE/BLK NE5 ... 55 F3
Reed St SSH NE33 ... 61 F3
TYNE/NSHE NE30 ... 51 F4
Reedswood Crs CRAM NE23 ... 28 E3
Reestones Pl GOS/KPK NE3 ... 45 H5
Reeth Rd SWCK/CAS SR5 ... 85 H3
Reeth Sq SWCK/CAS SR5 ... 85 H3
Reeth Wy BW/LEM/TK/HW NE15 .. 52 E2
Regal Rd MLFD/PNYW SR4 ... 86 A6
Regency Ct SEA/MUR SR7 ... 120 E1
Regency Dr SUNDSW SR3 ... 98 B6
WICK/BNPF NE16 ... 66 D6
Regency Gdns NSHW NE29 ... 50 C4
Regent Av GOS/KPK NE3 ... 46 B5
Regent Dr WICK/BNPF NE16 ... 78 D1
Regent Farm Rd GOS/KPK NE3 ... 46 A4
Regent Rd ASHBK/HED/RY SR2 .. 111 G2
GOS/KPK NE3 ... 46 C5
JRW NE32 ... 60 A5
WLSD/HOW NE28 ... 48 C7 5
Regents Ct WLSD/HOW NE28 ... 48 A6
Regents Dr TYNE/NSHE NE30 ... 51 G2
Regents Pk WLSD/HOW NE28 ... 48 A7
Regent St BLYTH NE24 ... 21 G6
HLH DH5 ... 117 K3
Regent Ter ASHBK/HED/RY SR2 ... 99 F4
GATE NE8 ... 10 F3
NSHW NE29 ... 50 C3
Reginald St BOLCOL NE35 ... 72 D4
GATE NE8 ... 11 M6
MLFD/PNYW SR4 ... 85 K6 11
Regina Sq SWCK/CAS SR5 ... 85 H2 3
Reid Av WLSD/HOW NE28 ... 48 D7
Reid Park Cl JES NE2 ... 57 F1 4
Reid Park Rd JES NE2 ... 57 F1
Reid's La CRAM NE23 ... 29 F7
Reigate Sq CRAM NE23 ... 28 C1
Rekendyke La SSH NE33 ... 61 F2
Relley Cl BDN/LAN/SAC DH7 ... 133 G1 2
Relly Pth DHAM DH1 ... 134 B2
Relton Av BYK/HTN/WLK NE6 ... 7 K8
Relton Cl HLS DH4 ... 116 D1
Relton Ter CLS/BIR/GTL DH3 ... 105 J5
MONK NE25 ... 40 C4
Rembrandt Av HAR/WTLS NE34 ... 73 G2
Remus Cl DIN/WO NE13 ... 36 B4 6
Rendel St DUN/TMV NE11 ... 9 G5
Rendle Rd BYK/HTN/WLK NE6 ... 58 D7
Renforth St DUN/TMV NE11 ... 9 H7
Renfrew Cl NSHW NE29 ... 50 A2
Renfrew Rd SWCK/CAS SR5 ... 85 H2
Rennie Rd SWCK/CAS SR5 ... 85 F2
Rennie Sq SWCK/CAS SR5 ... 85 F2 1
Rennington FELL NE10 ... 70 B7
Rennington Av
TYNE/NSHE NE30 ... 51 G1
Rennington Pl
WD/WHPE/BLK NE5 ... 55 H2 8
Renny's La DHAM DH1 ... 17 M2
Renny St DHAM DH1 ... 17 G2
Renoir Gdns HAR/WTLS NE34 ... 73 H2
Renwick Av GOS/KPK NE3 ... 45 J4
Renwick Rd BLYTH NE24 ... 21 F7
Renwick St BYK/HTN/WLK NE6 ... 7 K5
Resida Cl
BW/LEM/TK/HW NE15 ... 54 A3 6
Retford Rd SWCK/CAS SR5 ... 85 H2
Retford Sq SWCK/CAS SR5 ... 85 H2
The Retreat ASHBK/HED/RY SR2 .. 14 B6
Revell Ter WD/WHPE/BLK NE5 .. 55 J2 3
Revelstoke Rd SWCK/CAS SR5 ... 85 F2
Revesby St SSH NE33 ... 61 G5 3
Reynolds Av HAR/WTLS NE34 ... 73 H1
LGB/KIL NE12 ... 37 H7
WASHS NE38 ... 95 G2
Reynolds Cl STLY/ANP DH9 ... 102 D1
Reynolds Ct PLEE/EAS SR8 ... 137 J4 4
Rheims Ct MLFD/PNYW SR4 ... 85 H6
Rheydt Av WLSD/HOW NE28 ... 58 B1
Rhodesia Rd SWCK/CAS SR5 ... 85 H2
Rhodes St BYK/HTN/WLK NE6 ... 58 C6
Rhondda Rd SWCK/CAS SR5 ... 85 F2
Rhuddlan Ct
WD/WHPE/BLK NE5 ... 45 F6 9
Rhyl Sq SWCK/CAS SR5 ... 85 J2
Ribbledale Gdns
LGB/HTN NE7 ... 47 H7 2
Ribble Rd SWCK/CAS SR5 ... 85 G3 3
Ribblesdale HLS DH4 ... 95 K7
WLSD/HOW NE28 ... 48 B6 1
Ribblesdale Av BLYTH NE24 ... 20 C6 4
Richard Av MLFD/PNYW SR4 ... 98 A2
Richard Browell Rd
BW/LEM/TK/HW NE15 ... 53 F2
Richardson Av
HAR/WTLS NE34 ... 60 D7 1
Richardson Rd JES NE2 ... 4 F2
Richardson St WLSD/HOW NE28 .. 58 E1
Richardson Ter
ASHBK/HED/RY SR2 ... 111 G1
Richard St BLYTH NE24 ... 21 G7
HLH DH5 ... 117 K5
Richmond ASHBK/HED/RY SR2 ... 98 C7
Richmond Av FELL NE10 ... 70 E3
WASHS NE38 ... 83 F7
WICK/BNPF NE16 ... 67 F3
Richmond Cl BDLGTN NE22 ... 18 E4
Richmond Gdns
WLSD/HOW NE28 ... 49 G7
Richmond Gv NSHW NE29 ... 50 C5
Richmond Ms GOS/KPK NE3 ... 46 B7 1
Richmond Pk
WLSD/HOW NE28 ... 48 B7 3
Richmond Rd DHAM DH1 ... 124 E2
HAR/WTLS NE34 ... 61 G5
Richmond St SWCK/CAS SR5 ... 14 D2
Richmond Ter RDHAMSE DH6 ... 128 D6
WBAY NE26 ... 40 D2
Richmond Wy CRAM NE23 ... 28 B5 5
PONT/DH NE20 ... 32 C4
Rickaby St SUND SR1 ... 15 J2
Rickgarth FELL NE10 ... 70 B7
Rickleton Av CLS/BIR/GTL DH3 ... 105 K2
Rickleton Wy WASHS NE38 ... 94 B5
Riddell Av BW/LEM/TK/HW NE15 .. 55 G6
Riddings Rd SWCK/CAS SR5 ... 85 H2
Riddings Sq SWCK/CAS SR5 ... 85 H2 4
Ridgely Dr PONT/DH NE20 ... 33 J3
Ridge Ter BDLGTN NE22 ... 18 E5
The Ridge RYTON NE40 ... 52 E7
Ridgeway ASHBK/HED/RY SR2 ... 110 C1
ELS/FEN NE4 ... 55 J3
FELL NE10 ... 13 M9
Ridge Wy MONK NE25 ... 30 B7
Ridgeway Crs SUNDSW SR3 ... 98 B3
The Ridge Wy GOS/KPK NE3 ... 45 K6
The Ridgeway HAR/WTLS NE34 ... 73 K1
Ridgewood Crs GOS/KPK NE3 ... 47 F5
Ridgewood Gdns
GOS/KPK NE3 ... 46 E5 6
Ridgewood Vls GOS/KPK NE3 ... 46 E5 7
Riding Cl RYTON NE40 ... 64 A1 3
Riding Hill Rd STLY/ANP DH9 ... 101 H2
Riding La DUN/TMV NE11 ... 92 B2
Riding Lea BLAY NE21 ... 65 J3
The Ridings MONK NE25 ... 40 A3
The Riding GOS/KPK NE3 ... 45 J7
Ridley Av ASHBK/HED/RY SR2 ... 99 F7
BLYTH NE24 ... 21 H7
WLSD/HOW NE28 ... 49 J6
Ridley Cl GOS/KPK NE3 ... 45 K2 4
Ridley Gdns WICK/BNPF NE16 ... 66 E3 8
Ridley Gv HAR/WTLS NE34 ... 62 A4
Ridley Pl CNUT NE1 ... 5 K4
Ridley St BLYTH NE24 ... 21 H6 7
GATE NE8 ... 10 D7
STLY/ANP DH9 ... 90 D7
SWCK/CAS SR5 ... 86 B3 10
Ridley Ter ASHBK/HED/RY SR2 ... 15 J8
Ridsdale Av WD/WHPE/BLK NE5 .. 54 B2
Ridsdale Cl MONK NE25 ... 29 K5
WLSD/HOW NE28 ... 48 E6
Rievaulx WASHS NE38 ... 94 E3
Riga Sq SWCK/CAS SR5 ... 85 G2
The Riggs HLH DH5 ... 108 D7
Rignall WASHS NE38 ... 95 J1
Riley St JRW NE32 ... 59 J4
Ringmore Ct
ASHBK/HED/RY SR2 ... 98 C4 5
Ringway SWCK/CAS SR5 ... 84 E5
Ringwood Dr CRAM NE23 ... 28 C1 1
Ringwood Gn LGB/KIL NE12 ... 47 J3 3
Ringwood Rd SWCK/CAS SR5 ... 85 H2
Ringwood Sq SWCK/CAS SR5 ... 85 H2 5
Rink St BLYTH NE24 ... 21 H6
Ripley Av NSHW NE29 ... 50 C6
Ripley Cl BDLGTN NE22 ... 18 D4
Ripley Dr CRAM NE23 ... 28 A5
Ripley Ter BYK/HTN/WLK NE6 ... 7 M4
Ripon Cl CRAM NE23 ... 28 A5
Ripon Ct BDN/LAN/SAC DH7 ... 113 G5

Ripon Gdns JES NE2 57 G3
WLSD/HOW NE28 49 G7
Ripon Rd DHAM DH1 124 E1 3
Ripon St CLDN/WHIT/ROK SR6 86 E4
GATE NE8 10 F6
Ripon Ter SEA/MUR SR7 119 H5
The Rise BLAY NE21 53 J7
GOS/KPK NE3 45 J6
PONT/DH NE20 32 D7
WBAY NE26 31 G4
Rishton Sq SWCK/CAS SR5 85 G2 8
Ritson Av BDN/LAN/SAC DH7 123 F6
Ritson Cl NSHW NE29 50 C3
Ritson St CLDN/WHIT/ROK SR6 86 E1
STLY/ANP DH9 102 C1 1
Riverbank Rd SWCK/CAS SR5 85 H3
Riverdale SWCK/CAS SR5 85 F5
River Dr SSH NE33 3 G5
River La RYTON NE40 52 E5
Rivermead Wy WASHS NE38 95 G5 3
Riversdale Wy
BW/LEM/TK/HW NE15 53 K5
Riverside PONT/DH NE20 33 G3
Riverside Ct DUN/TMV NE11 9 J5
Riverside Pk MLFD/PNYW SR4 85 F6
Riverside Rd SWCK/CAS SR5 85 J3
Riverside Wy BLAY NE21 66 E1
ROWG NE39 77 F5
WICK/BNPF NE16 66 E1
River Vw BLAY NE21 65 K2
TYNE/NSHE NE30 51 G4
River View Cl BDLGTN NE22 19 K5
Roachburn Rd
WD/WHPE/BLK NE5 54 C1
Robertson Rd SWCK/CAS SR5 85 F2
Robertson Sq SWCK/CAS SR5 85 F3 2
Robert Sq SEA/MUR SR7 121 F2
Roberts St
BW/LEM/TK/HW NE15 54 E7
Roberts Ter JRW NE32 59 K6
Robert St MLFD/PNYW SR4 86 A6
SEA/MUR SR7 121 F2 1
SSH NE33 61 H2
SUNDSW SR3 98 B7
Robert Ter STLY/ANP DH9 90 D6 5
Robert Westall Wy NSHW NE29 2 C7
Robin Ct HLH DH5 117 F5
Robin Gv SWCK/CAS SR5 85 G4 8
Robin La HLH DH5 116 E6
Robinson Gdns
CLDN/WHIT/ROK SR6 75 F3 3
WLSD/HOW NE28 49 J7
Robinson St SSH NE33 3 J9 1
SSH NE33 61 H2 9
Robinson Ter
ASHBK/HED/RY SR2 15 K9
SUNDSW SR3 98 B7
Robsheugh Pl
WD/WHPE/BLK NE5 55 G3
Robson Av PLEE/EAS SR8 136 E3
Robson Pl ASHBK/HED/RY SR2 111 G1
Robson St BYK/HTN/WLK NE6 6 D4
LWF/SPW/WRK NE9 69 F7
Rochdale Rd SWCK/CAS SR5 85 H2
Rochdale St HLH DH5 117 K6
WLSD/HOW NE28 58 C2 3
Rochdale Wy SWCK/CAS SR5 85 H2 6
Roche Ct WASHS NE38 94 E2
Rochester Gdns DUN/TMV NE11 9 J8
Rochester Rd DHAM DH1 124 E2
Rochester St BYK/HTN/WLK NE6 58 C6
Rochford Gv CRAM NE23 28 A6
Rochford Rd SWCK/CAS SR5 85 G2 6
Rockcliffe SSH NE33 61 K2
Rockcliffe Gdns
BW/LEM/TK/HW NE15 54 D4 7
Rockcliffe St WBAY NE26 41 G4
Rockcliffe Wy
LWF/SPW/WRK NE9 81 J3
Rocket Wy LGB/KIL NE12 48 B2
Rock Gv LWF/SPW/WRK NE9 69 F7 8
Rockhope WASHS NE38 94 B6
Rockingham Rd SWCK/CAS SR5 85 G2
Rockingham Sq
SWCK/CAS SR5 85 G2 7
Rock Lodge Rd
CLDN/WHIT/ROK SR6 86 E2
Rockmore Rd BLAY NE21 66 A3
Rock Ter BDN/LAN/SAC DH7 132 E2
JES NE2 6 A4
Rockville
CLDN/WHIT/ROK SR6 86 E1 6
Rockwood Hill Est RYTON NE40 64 A4
Rockwood Hill Rd RYTON NE40 64 A4
Rodin Av HAR/WTLS NE34 73 H2
Rodney Cl
ASHBK/HED/RY SR2 110 C1 1
TYNE/NSHE NE30 51 H3
Rodney St BYK/HTN/WLK NE6 6 F6
Rodney Wy WBAY NE26 40 B2
Rodsley Av GATE NE8 10 F7
Roeburn Wy GOS/KPK NE3 45 K7
Roedean Rd SWCK/CAS SR5 85 J2
Roehedge FELL NE10 70 D6 4
Rogers Cl PLEE/EAS SR8 137 H4 2
Rogerson Ter
WD/WHPE/BLK NE5 44 C7
Roger St BYK/HTN/WLK NE6 6 E4
Rogues La ROWG NE39 64 C6
Rokeby Av
BW/LEM/TK/HW NE15 54 B5
Rokeby Dr GOS/KPK NE3 45 K6
Rokeby Sq DHAM DH1 134 B3 4
Rokeby St
BW/LEM/TK/HW NE15 54 B5
MLFD/PNYW SR4 14 A5
Rokeby Ter
BYK/HTN/WLK NE6 57 J2 3
Rokeby Vw LWF/SPW/WRK NE9 81 G4
Roker Av CLDN/WHIT/ROK SR6 14 F1
MONK NE25 40 C6
Roker Baths Rd
CLDN/WHIT/ROK SR6 86 E3
Rokerby Av WICK/BNPF NE16 67 G6
Roker Park Rd
CLDN/WHIT/ROK SR6 86 E3
Roker Park Ter
CLDN/WHIT/ROK SR6 87 F3
Roker Ter CLDN/WHIT/ROK SR6 87 F2
Roland Rd WLSD/HOW NE28 59 G1
Rollesby Ct
WD/WHPE/BLK NE5 45 F6 10
Rolling Mill Rd JRW NE32 59 J3
Romaldskirk Cl
MLFD/PNYW SR4 97 F1 3
Roman Av BYK/HTN/WLK NE6 7 L3
CLS/BIR/GTL DH3 105 K4
Roman Rd SSH NE33 3 J5
The Roman Wy
WD/WHPE/BLK NE5 54 B2
Romford Cl CRAM NE23 28 B5 6
Romford Pl LWF/SPW/WRK NE9 11 K9
Romford St MLFD/PNYW SR4 85 K7 6
Romilly St SSH NE33 3 J8
Romley Gv FELL NE10 71 F5 2
Romney Av
ASHBK/HED/RY SR2 98 E3 1
HAR/WTLS NE34 73 H1 1
WASHS NE38 95 G2
Romney Cl HLS DH4 108 A2
Romney Dr DHAM DH1 126 A4
Romney Gdns
LWF/SPW/WRK NE9 11 M9
Romsey Cl CRAM NE23 28 C1
Romsey Dr BOLCOL NE35 72 C3 4
Romsey Gv
BW/LEM/TK/HW NE15 54 A3
Ronald Dr
BW/LEM/TK/HW NE15 54 E5
Ronald Gdns HEBB NE31 59 F7
Ronaldsay Cl
ASHBK/HED/RY SR2 98 E6 1
Ronald Sq
CLDN/WHIT/ROK SR6 86 D2 15
Rookery Cl BLYTH NE24 20 D7
Rookery La WICK/BNPF NE16 78 C1 2
Rookswood Gdns ROWG NE39 77 G2
Rookwood Dr DIN/WO NE13 36 C1
Rookwood Rd
WD/WHPE/BLK NE5 54 E3
Roosevelt Rd DHAM DH1 117 K1
Ropery La CLS/BIR/GTL DH3 105 K5
CLS/BIR/GTL DH3 106 C5
HEBB NE31 59 F5 3
WLSD/HOW NE28 59 G1
Ropery Rd GATE NE8 9 L6
MLFD/PNYW SR4 86 A5
The Ropery BYK/HTN/WLK NE6 7 J9
Ropery Wk SEA/MUR SR7 121 F2 2
Rosalie Ter ASHBK/HED/RY SR2 15 H9
Rosalind Av BDLGTN NE22 19 G6
Rosamond Pl BLYTH NE24 21 H7 2
Rosa St SSH NE33 3 K9
Rose Av HLS DH4 107 H6
STLY/ANP DH9 102 B2
WICK/BNPF NE16 67 F5
Rosebank Cl
ASHBK/HED/RY SR2 98 E6 2
Rosebay Rd BDN/LAN/SAC DH7 133 K6
Roseberry Gra LGB/KIL NE12 48 C1 1
Roseberry St STLY/ANP DH9 91 H7
Roseberry Vls CLSW/PEL DH2 104 C2
Rosebery Av BLYTH NE24 21 F7 2
GATE NE8 11 J7
NSHW NE29 50 D2
SSH NE33 61 J2
Rosebery Crs JES NE2 6 B1
Rosebery Pl JES NE2 6 C1
Rosebery St SWCK/CAS SR5 86 D4 7
Roseby Rd PLEE/EAS SR8 137 G3
Rose Ct PLEE/EAS SR8 136 C7
Rose Crs BDN/LAN/SAC DH7 113 J5
CLDN/WHIT/ROK SR6 75 F2
Rosedale BDLGTN NE22 18 E5
WLSD/HOW NE28 48 B6
Rosedale Av
CLDN/WHIT/ROK SR6 74 E6
Rosedale Ct WD/WHPE/BLK NE5 54 B2
Rosedale Crs HLS DH4 108 A5 4
Rosedale Rd DHAM DH1 126 A5
RYTON NE40 64 B1
Rosedale St HLH DH5 117 H7
SUND SR1 14 B5
Rosedale Ter
CLDN/WHIT/ROK SR6 86 E1
JES NE2 6 A3
PLEE/EAS SR8 137 G3
TYNE/NSHE NE30 51 F3 2
Roseden Ct LGB/KIL NE12 47 J3 4
Rosedene Vls CRAM NE23 28 E2
Rose Gdns WLSD/HOW NE28 48 D6
Rosegill WASHN NE37 82 D7
Rosehill WLSD/HOW NE28 59 G1
Rosehill Rd WLSD/HOW NE28 59 H1
Rose Hill Wy WD/WHPE/BLK NE5 55 G2
Rose Lea BDN/LAN/SAC DH7 113 G7
Roselea Av ASHBK/HED/RY SR2 99 F7
Rosemary La PLEE/EAS SR8 130 C5
Rosemary Rd SWCK/CAS SR5 85 H2
Rosemary Ter BLYTH NE24 25 H1
Rosemount DHAM DH1 124 E1
MLFD/PNYW SR4 96 E1
WD/WHPE/BLK NE5 54 D1
Rosemount Cl WASHN NE37 82 E3 6
Rosemount Ct BOL NE36 73 F5 3
Rosemount Wy LGB/HTN NE7 47 J5 6
MONK NE25 40 A4
Rose St GATE NE8 10 A4
HEBB NE31 59 F6
MLFD/PNYW SR4 14 B4
Rose St West HLS DH4 95 K6
Rose Ter WD/WHPE/BLK NE5 55 J2
Roseville St MLFD/PNYW SR4 14 A8
Rosewell Pl WICK/BNPF NE16 78 E1
Rosewood LGB/KIL NE12 38 B6 6
Rosewood Av GOS/KPK NE3 46 D4
Rosewood Crs
BYK/HTN/WLK NE6 58 B2
WBAY NE26 31 G4
Rosewood Gdns GOS/KPK NE3 45 K6
LWF/SPW/WRK NE9 69 H6
Rosewood Sq
MLFD/PNYW SR4 96 E4 1
Rosewood Ter
WLSD/HOW NE28 59 J1 2
Roseworth Av GOS/KPK NE3 46 C6 3
Roseworth Crs GOS/KPK NE3 46 C7
Roslin Pk BDLGTN NE22 19 J5
Roslin Wy CRAM NE23 28 B5 7
Ross CLSW/PEL DH2 93 G4
Ross Av DUN/TMV NE11 9 G6
Rosse Cl WASHN NE37 82 D5
Rossendale Pl LGB/KIL NE12 47 F3 3
Ross Gv CRAM NE23 28 A1
Ross Lea HLS DH4 107 J3
Rosslyn Av ASHBK/HED/RY SR2 99 F7
GOS/KPK NE3 45 J5
Rosslyn St MLFD/PNYW SR4 86 A7
Ross St SWCK/CAS SR5 86 C4 7
Ross Wy GOS/KPK NE3 45 K2
WBAY NE26 40 C2
Rosyth Rd SWCK/CAS SR5 85 J2
Rosyth Sq SWCK/CAS SR5 85 J2
Rotary Wy BLYTH NE24 25 H3
NSHW NE29 50 C7
Rothay Pl WD/WHPE/BLK NE5 55 G1 2
Rothbury ASHBK/HED/RY SR2 110 D1
Rothbury Av BLYTH NE24 24 D1
FELL NE10 13 J5
GOS/KPK NE3 46 B4
JRW NE32 59 H7
PLEE/EAS SR8 137 G2
Rothbury Cl CLSW/PEL DH2 105 G6
LGB/KIL NE12 37 J5 11
Rothbury Gdns DUN/TMV NE11 68 A7
WLSD/HOW NE28 49 H7
Rothbury Rd DHAM DH1 124 D2
SWCK/CAS SR5 85 H2
Rothbury Ter BYK/HTN/WLK NE6 6 F1
NSHW NE29 50 A6
Rotherfield Cl CRAM NE23 28 C1
Rotherfield Gdns
LWF/SPW/WRK NE9 81 G3 1
Rotherfield Rd SWCK/CAS SR5 85 G2
Rotherfield Sq SWCK/CAS SR5 85 G2 8
Rotherham Cl HLH DH5 117 G2 2
Rotherham Rd SWCK/CAS SR5 85 G2
Rothley WASHS NE38 95 H4
Rothley Av WD/WHPE/BLK NE5 55 G4
Rothley Cl GOS/KPK NE3 46 D5 3
PONT/DH NE20 33 F2
Rothley Ct SWCK/CAS SR5 85 K1 2
Rothley Gdns TYNE/NSHE NE30 40 E7
Rothley Gv MONK NE25 29 K5 2
Rothley Wy WBAY NE26 40 C2
Rothsay CLSW/PEL DH2 93 F5
Rothwell Rd GOS/KPK NE3 46 C5
SWCK/CAS SR5 85 G2
Roundhill Av
WD/WHPE/BLK NE5 55 G1 3
The Roundway LGB/KIL NE12 47 H3 4
Rowan Av WASHS NE38 94 E5
Rowanberry Rd LGB/KIL NE12 47 H4
Rowan Cl BDLGTN NE22 19 F4
MLFD/PNYW SR4 97 F1
Rowan Ct BLYTH NE24 25 F1 3
Rowan Dr DHAM DH1 125 F1
GOS/KPK NE3 45 J4
HLH DH5 117 J4
PONT/DH NE20 33 G2
Rowan Lea BDN/LAN/SAC DH7 133 G6
Rowan Tree Av DHAM DH1 125 H5
Rowantree Rd
BYK/HTN/WLK NE6 58 C2
Rowanwood Gdns
DUN/TMV NE11 68 A7
Rowell Cl SUNDSW SR3 110 C1
Rowes Ms BYK/HTN/WLK NE6 7 H9
Rowlandson Crs FELL NE10 12 D8
Rowland Sq SEA/MUR SR7 119 G5
Rowley Cl BDN/LAN/SAC DH7 132 D3
Rowley Dr BDN/LAN/SAC DH7 133 G1
Rowley St BLYTH NE24 21 G7
Rowntree Wy NSHW NE29 2 C6
Rowsley Rd JRW NE32 60 A6 3
Roxburgh Cl BLAY NE21 65 J4
Roxburgh Pl BYK/HTN/WLK NE6 6 F2
Roxburgh St
CLDN/WHIT/ROK SR6 86 D3
Roxburgh Ter WBAY NE26 40 E4
Roxby Gdns NSHW NE29 50 C5
Royal Crs ELS/FEN NE4 55 J3
Royal Rd STLY/ANP DH9 90 C7
The Royalty ASHBK/HED/RY SR2 14 B6
Roydon Av
ASHBK/HED/RY SR2 98 E3 2
Royle St ASHBK/HED/RY SR2 99 F4
Royston Ter
BYK/HTN/WLK NE6 58 C7 9
Ruabon Cl CRAM NE23 28 B5
Rubens Av HAR/WTLS NE34 73 H1
Ruby St HLS DH4 108 B5
Rudby Cl GOS/KPK NE3 46 D2
Rudchester Pl
WD/WHPE/BLK NE5 55 G3
Rudyard Av
ASHBK/HED/RY SR2 98 E3 3
Rudyerd St NSHW NE29 2 D2
Rugby Gdns LWF/SPW/WRK NE9 81 K2
Ruislip Pl CRAM NE23 28 A5
Ruislip Rd MLFD/PNYW SR4 96 E1
Runcorn ASHBK/HED/RY SR2 98 C7
Runcorn Rd SWCK/CAS SR5 85 G2
Runhead Est RYTON NE40 53 F6
Runnymede
ASHBK/HED/RY SR2 98 D7 1
Runnymede Rd PONT/DH NE20 32 D5
SWCK/CAS SR5 85 H2
WICK/BNPF NE16 66 E6
Runnymede Wy GOS/KPK NE3 45 J6 2
SWCK/CAS SR5 85 H2
Runswick Av LGB/KIL NE12 47 F4
Runswick Cl SUNDSW SR3 98 C7
Rupert Sq SWCK/CAS SR5 85 J2
Rupert St CLDN/WHIT/ROK SR6 75 F3
Rushall Pl LGB/KIL NE12 47 H4
Rushey Gill
BDN/LAN/SAC DH7 133 F6 3
Rushford ASHBK/HED/RY SR2 98 D7
Rushie Av BW/LEM/TK/HW NE15 55 G6
Rushley Crs BLAY NE21 66 A1
Rushsyde Cl WICK/BNPF NE16 66 C7
Rushton Av
ASHBK/HED/RY SR2 98 E3 4
Rushyrig WASHN NE37 82 C7
Ruskin Av CLSW/PEL DH2 104 E4
DUN/TMV NE11 9 H6
HLH DH5 128 B1
LGB/KIL NE12 47 K1 1
Ruskin Cl STLY/ANP DH9 103 F1
Ruskin Crs HAR/WTLS NE34 73 F1
Ruskin Dr BOLCOL NE35 72 E4
LGB/HTN NE7 58 A1
Ruskin Rd CLS/BIR/GTL DH3 93 J2 3
LWF/SPW/WRK NE9 69 H5
WICK/BNPF NE16 66 E4
Russell Av HAR/WTLS NE34 62 A5
Russell Sq DIN/WO NE13 36 C1
Russell St JRW NE32 60 A4
NSHW NE29 2 D2
SSH NE33 3 H7
SUND SR1 15 G3
Russell Ter BDLGTN NE22 19 F6
JES NE2 6 A5 3
Ruswarp Dr SUNDSW SR3 110 B1
Rutherford Av SEA/MUR SR7 111 F7
Rutherford Rd SWCK/CAS SR5 85 F2
WASHN NE37 83 G4
Rutherford Sq SWCK/CAS SR5 85 F2
Rutherford St BLYTH NE24 25 G1 3
CNUT NE1 5 H7 2
WLSD/HOW NE28 49 K7
Rutherglen Rd SWCK/CAS SR5 85 J2
Rutland Av BYK/HTN/WLK NE6 58 C4
SUNDSW SR3 97 K7
Rutland Pl NSHW NE29 2 A1 1
NSHW NE29 50 C4 1
WASHN NE37 83 F3 2
Rutland Rd HEBB NE31 71 H1
WLSD/HOW NE28 58 C2
Rutland Sq CLS/BIR/GTL DH3 93 H1
Rutland St HAR/WTLS NE34 61 F5 2
MLFD/PNYW SR4 85 K6
Ryal Cl BLYTH NE24 20 D7
MONK NE25 30 A5
Ryal Ter BYK/HTN/WLK NE6 58 B6
Rydal FELL NE10 13 J7
Rydal Av HLH DH5 128 B1
STLY/ANP DH9 102 B3
TYNE/NSHE NE30 40 E7
Rydal Cl BDN/LAN/SAC DH7 113 G5
BOL NE36 73 G4
LGB/KIL NE12 38 B6
Rydal Crs BLAY NE21 65 K4
PLEE/EAS SR8 137 F4
Rydal Gdns HAR/WTLS NE34 61 J5
Rydal Mt PLEE/EAS SR8 130 E5
SWCK/CAS SR5 84 E5
SWCK/CAS SR5 86 C2
Rydal Rd BW/LEM/TK/HW NE15 54 B3
CLSW/PEL DH2 105 H6
GOS/KPK NE3 46 D5
Rydal St GATE NE8 10 E6
Ryde Pl CRAM NE23 28 C1
Rye Cl BW/LEM/TK/HW NE15 53 G2 3
Ryedale CLDN/WHIT/ROK SR6 75 F5
DHAM DH1 126 A6
WLSD/HOW NE28 48 B5
Rye Hl ELS/FEN NE4 4 E8
Ryehill Vw HLH DH5 117 F4
Ryelands Wy DHAM DH1 124 D1
Ryemount Rd
ASHBK/HED/RY SR2 98 D7
Rye View Rd
ASHBK/HED/RY SR2 99 F6
Ryhope Gdns
LWF/SPW/WRK NE9 81 K2
Ryhope Rd ASHBK/HED/RY SR2 14 F9
ASHBK/HED/RY SR2 99 F5
Ryhope St ASHBK/HED/RY SR2 98 E7
HLH DH5 108 D7
Rymers Cl PLEE/EAS SR8 130 B6
Ryton Ct SSH NE33 61 H2
Ryton Crs SEA/MUR SR7 120 B1
STLY/ANP DH9 90 D6 3
Ryton Hall Dr RYTON NE40 52 E5 3
Ryton Ter BYK/HTN/WLK NE6 58 B7

S

Sackville Rd BYK/HTN/WLK NE6 57 J2
SUNDSW SR3 97 J3
Sacriston Av SUNDSW SR3 97 K3 3
Sacriston La BDN/LAN/SAC DH7 123 F1
Saddleback WASHN NE37 82 D5
Saddler St DHAM DH1 16 D4
Saffron Pl BYK/HTN/WLK NE6 58 C6 3
Sage Cl BW/LEM/TK/HW NE15 54 A3 7
St Agnes' West House
RYTON NE40 52 A7
St Aidan's Av
ASHBK/HED/RY SR2 99 F5
DHAM DH1 124 B4
LGB/KIL NE12 48 E1
St Aidan's Cl NSHW NE29 50 B2 1
St Aidan's Crs DHAM DH1 124 B7
STLY/ANP DH9 101 H4
St Aidan's Rd SSH NE33 3 J5
WLSD/HOW NE28 58 C2 6
St Aidan's St GATE NE8 10 D6
St Aidan's Ter HLS DH4 108 C1
St Alban's Cl CLS/BIR/GTL DH3 115 J1
St Alban's Crs
BYK/HTN/WLK NE6 57 K1
St Alban's St
ASHBK/HED/RY SR2 98 E3
St Alban's Ter GATE NE8 10 F7
St Albans Vw SMOOR NE27 39 G7
St Aldwyn Rd SEA/MUR SR7 111 H7
St Aloysius Vw HEBB NE31 59 F5
St Andrews HLS DH4 107 K7
St Andrews Av WASHN NE37 82 D5
St Andrew's Dr
LWF/SPW/WRK NE9 80 E2
St Andrew's Rd STLY/ANP DH9 90 D5
St Andrew's St CNUT NE1 5 H6
HEBB NE31 58 E4 5
St Andrew's Ter
CLDN/WHIT/ROK SR6 86 E3 3
St Ann's Cl CNUT NE1 6 C6
St Ann's St CNUT NE1 6 B7
St Anselm Crs NSHW NE29 50 A3
St Anselm Rd NSHW NE29 50 A3
St Anthony's Rd
BYK/HTN/WLK NE6 7 M6
St Asaph Cl LGB/HTN NE7 47 K6
St Aubyn's Wy STLY/ANP DH9 91 F7 1
St Austell Cl
WD/WHPE/BLK NE5 45 G6 1
St Austell Gdns
LWF/SPW/WRK NE9 81 F3
St Barnabas HLS DH4 107 F4
St Barnabas Wy
ASHBK/HED/RY SR2 15 J8
St Bede's Cl DHAM DH1 134 B1
St Bede's Dr GATE NE8 11 H3
St Bedes Pl BLYTH NE24 24 D3
St Bedes Rd BLYTH NE24 24 D3 4
St Bedes Wy
BDN/LAN/SAC DH7 133 K5 1
St Brandon's Gv
BDN/LAN/SAC DH7 133 F6
St Buryan Crs
WD/WHPE/BLK NE5 45 G6
St Catherine's Ct SWCK/CAS SR5 85 H4
St Chad's Crs SUNDSW SR3 97 F7 1
St Chad's Rd SUNDSW SR3 97 F7
St Chad's Vls BOL NE36 73 H5 3
St Christopher's Rd
SUNDSW SR3 98 A4
Saint Ct SUNDSW SR3 110 A2
St Cuthbert Av
CLS/BIR/GTL DH3 105 K4
St Cuthberts Av DHAM DH1 124 B4
HAR/WTLS NE34 62 A3
St Cuthberts Ct BLYTH NE24 21 H7 3
St Cuthberts Dr
BDN/LAN/SAC DH7 113 G5
FELL NE10 13 G9
St Cuthberts Pk
WICK/BNPF NE16 78 E5
St Cuthbert's Pl GATE NE8 10 D5 1
St Cuthbert's Rd GATE NE8 10 D4
HLS DH4 108 B4 7
PLEE/EAS SR8 136 E5 1
WD/WHPE/BLK NE5 55 F4
WICK/BNPF NE16 78 E6
WLSD/HOW NE28 49 F7
St Cuthbert's Ter
MLFD/PNYW SR4 14 A3 5
St Cuthberts Wk
BDN/LAN/SAC DH7 133 K5
St Cuthberts Wy BLAY NE21 66 B1
St David's Wy WBAY NE26 40 D1
St Edmund's Dr FELL NE10 13 G9
St Edmund's Rd GATE NE8 11 H5
St Gabriel's Av
BYK/HTN/WLK NE6 57 H2
MLFD/PNYW SR4 85 K7
St George's Av SSH NE33 61 J3
St George's Cl JES NE2 56 E1
St Georges Crs MONK NE25 40 D5
NSHW NE29 2 A2
St George's Est WASHS NE38 94 E6 1
St George's Pl
BW/LEM/TK/HW NE15 54 C6 1
St George's Rd
BW/LEM/TK/HW NE15 54 C6 2
TYNE/NSHE NE30 41 F6
St George's Ter BOL NE36 73 H5
BW/LEM/TK/HW NE15 54 C6 3
CLDN/WHIT/ROK SR6 87 F3
JES NE2 56 E1
St George's Wy
ASHBK/HED/RY SR2 14 E7 1
St Giles Cl DHAM DH1 17 J3
St Godric's Cl DHAM DH1 124 D2
St Godric's Dr HLS DH4 116 D6
St Helen's Crs
LWF/SPW/WRK NE9 68 E7 3
St Heliers Wy STLY/ANP DH9 91 F7
St Hilda's Av
WLSD/HOW NE28 49 G7 2
St Hilda St SSH NE33 3 H8
St Hilds Ct DHAM DH1 17 M2
St Hild's La DHAM DH1 17 G3
St Ignatius Cl
ASHBK/HED/RY SR2 15 H7 3
St Ives Wy WD/WHPE/BLK NE5 45 G6
St James Ct GATE NE8 11 M6
St James' Crs
BW/LEM/TK/HW NE15 55 H7 2
St James' Rd
BW/LEM/TK/HW NE15 55 H6
GATE NE8 11 K4
St James Sq GATE NE8 11 K3
St James' St CNUT NE1 5 H5
GOS/KPK NE3 46 D5
St James' Ter NSHW NE29 50 B7
St Johns SUND SR1 15 J2 1
St John's Av HEBB NE31 59 F6
St John's Cl WBAY NE26 40 D1 3
St John's Crs BDLGTN NE22 19 K3
St John's Gn NSHW NE29 50 B7
St John's Pl BDLGTN NE22 19 K3
CLS/BIR/GTL DH3 93 J2
FELL NE10 12 C7
WBAY NE26 40 D1 3
St John's Rd BDLGTN NE22 19 K4
BDN/LAN/SAC DH7 133 K6
DHAM DH1 134 B1
ELS/FEN NE4 55 J7
St John's St NSHW NE29 50 B7
St John's Ter BOL NE36 73 J5
JRW NE32 59 K4 3
NSHW NE29 50 B7
St John St CNUT NE1 5 J7
St Johns V MLFD/PNYW SR4 96 E2 3
St John's Wk NSHW NE29 50 B7 3
St Joseph's Cl DHAM DH1 17 L2
St Joseph's Ct HEBB NE31 71 F1 2
St Joseph's Wy JRW NE32 71 K3
St Jude's Ter SSH NE33 61 G2
St Julien Gdns LGB/HTN NE7 47 K7
WLSD/HOW NE28 49 K7 2
St Lawrence Cl RDHAMSE DH6 127 F4
St Lawrence Rd BYK/HTN/WLK NE6 6 E7
RDHAMSE DH6 126 E4

St Lawrence Sq
BYK/HTN/WLK NE6 ... 6 E7
St Lucia Cl
ASHBK/HED/RY SR2 ... 15 G8 2
WBAY NE26 ... 40 C1
St Luke's Rd MLFD/PNYW SR4 .. 85 G6 3
St Luke's St NSHW NE29 ... 50 B7
St Luke's Ter MLFD/PNYW SR4 ... 85 K6
St Margaret's Av SWCK/CAS SR5 .. 84 E4
St Margaret's Ct DHAM DH1 ... 16 B4 1
St Margaret's Dr STLY/ANP DH9 ... 90 A3
St Margaret's Rd
BW/LEM/TK/HW NE15 ... 55 F7
St Margarets Av LGB/KIL NE12 .. 47 K4 3
St Mark's Rd MLFD/PNYW SR4 ... 14 A5
St Mark's Rd North
MLFD/PNYW SR4 ... 86 A6
St Mark's St BYK/HTN/WLK NE6 ... 7 G3
MLFD/PNYW SR4 ... 14 A5 2
St Mark's Ter MLFD/PNYW SR4 ... 14 A4
St Mark's Wy SSH NE33 ... 61 G2
St Martin's Cl WBAY NE26 ... 40 C2
St Mary Av HAR/WTLS NE34 ... 61 K5
WBAY NE26 ... 40 D2
St Marys Cl CLSW/PEL DH2 ... 105 H5
DHAM DH1 ... 135 G4
PLEE/EAS SR8 ... 130 B6 1
St Mary's Dr BLYTH NE24 ... 24 D2
HLS DH4 ... 116 D6 2
St Mary's Pl
BW/LEM/TK/HW NE15 ... 53 G1 1
CNUT NE1 ... 5 K4
St Mary's Rd DHAM DH1 ... 125 K5
St Mary's Ter BOL NE36 ... 73 H5
St Mary's Wy SUND SR1 ... 14 D4
St Mary's Wynd WBAY NE26 ... 31 H4
St Matthews Vw SUNDSW SR3 .. 98 A7 4
St Michaels HLS DH4 ... 107 K7
St Michael's Av MONK NE25 ... 30 B2
SSH NE33 ... 61 H2
St Michael's Av North SSH NE33 .. 61 H2
St Michael's Rd BYK/HTN/WLK NE6 .. 6 E6
St Michaels Wy SUND SR1 ... 14 C4
WICK/BNPF NE16 ... 8 B6
St Monica Gv DHAM DH1 ... 134 B1
St Nicholas Av GOS/KPK NE3 ... 46 C6 4
SUNDSW SR3 ... 98 B3
St Nicholas' Church Yd
CNUT NE1 ... 5 K7 1
St Nicholas Dr DHAM DH1 ... 124 A5
St Nicholas Rd BOL NE36 ... 72 E5 6
St Nicholas' St CNUT NE1 ... 5 K7
St Nicholas Ter PLEE/EAS SR8 .. 130 E5 1
St Omers Rd DUN/TMV NE11 ... 9 G4
St Oswald Av BYK/HTN/WLK NE6 ... 7 L3
St Oswald's Dr DHAM DH1 ... 134 B5
St Oswald's Gn BYK/HTN/WLK NE6 .. 7 L3
St Oswald's Rd HEBB NE31 ... 59 H4
WLSD/HOW NE28 ... 49 F6
St Oswin's Pl TYNE/NSHE NE30 ... 51 H3
St Oswin's St SSH NE33 ... 61 H4
St Pauls Dr HLS DH4 ... 95 G6
St Paul's Gdns MONK NE25 ... 40 E5
St Paul's Rd JRW NE32 ... 60 A4
St Peter's Av HAR/WTLS NE34 ... 61 J5
St Peter's Rd BYK/HTN/WLK NE6 ... 7 H8
WLSD/HOW NE28 ... 49 F6
St Peters' Wy
CLDN/WHIT/ROK SR6 ... 15 G2
St Peter's Whf BYK/HTN/WLK NE6 .. 7 H9
St Philips Cl ELS/FEN NE4 ... 4 E6
St Philips Wy ELS/FEN NE4 ... 4 E6 1
St Ronan's Dr WBAY NE26 ... 30 E1
St Ronan's Rd MONK NE25 ... 40 D5
St Ronan's Vw
LWF/SPW/WRK NE9 ... 81 G3
St Simon St HAR/WTLS NE34 ... 60 E7
St Stephen's Cl MONK NE25 ... 29 J5 1
St Stephen's Wy NSHW NE29 ... 60 B1
St Stevens Cl HLS DH4 ... 95 G6 3
St Thomas Cl PLEE/EAS SR8 ... 130 B6 2
St Thomas' Crs CNUT NE1 ... 5 J4
St Thomas' St CNUT NE1 ... 5 J4
LWF/SPW/WRK NE9 ... 69 G7 4
SUND SR1 ... 14 F4
St Vincent Ct GATE NE8 ... 11 K5
St Vincents Cl
BW/LEM/TK/HW NE15 ... 54 C3 3
St Vincent's Pl WBAY NE26 ... 40 D1 3
St Vincent St ASHBK/HED/RY SR2 .. 15 G7
GATE NE8 ... 11 K5
SSH NE33 ... 61 J2
St Vincent's Wy WBAY NE26 ... 40 D1 3
Salcombe Av JRW NE32 ... 60 B6
Salcombe Cl SEA/MUR SR7 ... 120 B2 5
Salcombe Gdns
LWF/SPW/WRK NE9 ... 81 F3
Salem Hl ASHBK/HED/RY SR2 ... 15 G8
Salem Rd ASHBK/HED/RY SR2 ... 15 G7
Salem St ASHBK/HED/RY SR2 ... 15 G7
JRW NE32 ... 60 A4
SSH NE33 ... 3 G6
Salem St South
ASHBK/HED/RY SR2 ... 15 G8
Salem Ter ASHBK/HED/RY SR2 .. 15 G7 1
Salisbury Av NSHW NE29 ... 50 D3
Salisbury Cl CLS/BIR/GTL DH3 ... 115 H2
CRAM NE23 ... 27 K2
Salisbury Gdns JES NE2 ... 57 G3
Salisbury Pl SSH NE33 ... 3 L7
Salisbury Rd DHAM DH1 ... 125 F2
Salisbury St ASHBK/HED/RY SR2 .. 14 F6
FELL NE10 ... 13 J6
SSH NE33 ... 3 K8
STLY/ANP DH9 ... 102 B2
Salkeld Gdns
LWF/SPW/WRK NE9 ... 11 J8
Salkeld Rd LWF/SPW/WRK NE9 ... 69 G6
Salmon St SSH NE33 ... 3 J5
Saltburn Gdns
WLSD/HOW NE28 ... 49 K7 3
Saltburn Rd SUNDSW SR3 ... 97 J3
Saltburn Sq SUNDSW SR3 ... 97 J3
Salterfen La ASHBK/HED/RY SR2 .. 99 G6
Salterfen Rd
ASHBK/HED/RY SR2 ... 99 G6
Salters Cl GOS/KPK NE3 ... 46 E4
Salter's La HLH DH5 ... 109 J5
HLH DH5 ... 118 D5
LGB/KIL NE12 ... 47 F4
RDHAMSE DH6 ... 128 D3
SEA/MUR SR7 ... 118 E2
Salters' Rd GOS/KPK NE3 ... 46 A6
Saltmeadows Rd GATE NE8 ... 6 D9
Saltwell Pl GATE NE8 ... 10 C7
Saltwell Rd GATE NE8 ... 10 C7
Saltwell Rd South
LWF/SPW/WRK NE9 ... 68 E6
Saltwell St GATE NE8 ... 10 D7
Saltwell Vw LWF/SPW/WRK NE9 .. 10 F9
Samson Cl LGB/KIL NE12 ... 37 H7
Sancroft Dr HLH DH5 ... 117 H1
Sandalwood HAR/WTLS NE34 ... 73 H1 2
Sandalwood Sq MLFD/PNYW SR4 .. 96 E4
Sanderling Cl RYTON NE40 ... 53 G7 3
Sanderson Rd JES NE2 ... 56 E1 3
Sanderson St ELS/FEN NE4 ... 9 H1
Sandfield Rd BDLGTN NE22 ... 20 D2
TYNE/NSHE NE30 ... 41 F6
Sandford Av CRAM NE23 ... 23 H6
Sandford Ms DIN/WO NE13 ... 35 K4
Sandgate CNUT NE1 ... 6 A7
STLY/ANP DH9 ... 101 K3
Sandgrove
CLDN/WHIT/ROK SR6 ... 74 A3 2
Sandholm Cl WLSD/HOW NE28 .. 49 H5 2
Sandhurst Av TYNE/NSHE NE30 ... 41 F7
Sandmere Pl
BW/LEM/TK/HW NE15 ... 54 E6 1
Sandmere Rd
ASHBK/HED/RY SR2 ... 98 E5 2
Sandoe Gdns
BW/LEM/TK/HW NE15 ... 55 F6
Sandon Cl SMOOR NE27 ... 38 E4
Sandown MONK NE25 ... 40 A4
Sandown Cl SMOOR NE27 ... 30 A7
Sandown Gdns GATE NE8 ... 10 B8
SUNDSW SR3 ... 97 K6 1
WLSD/HOW NE28 ... 49 H6
Sandpiper Cl BLYTH NE24 ... 25 G3
RYTON NE40 ... 53 F7 2
Sand Point Rd
CLDN/WHIT/ROK SR6 ... 86 E4
Sandray Cl CLS/BIR/GTL DH3 ... 93 K5
Sandringham Av LGB/KIL NE12 ... 47 J4
Sandringham Dr BLYTH NE24 ... 25 F4
MONK NE25 ... 39 K5
STLY/ANP DH9 ... 101 H2 1
WICK/BNPF NE16 ... 66 E5 10
Sandringham Gdns NSHW NE29 .. 50 E3
Sandringham Rd
CLDN/WHIT/ROK SR6 ... 86 D3
GOS/KPK NE3 ... 46 E6
WD/WHPE/BLK NE5 ... 54 C3 7
Sandringham Ter
CLDN/WHIT/ROK SR6 ... 86 E3
Sandringham Wy
PONT/DH NE20 ... 32 E5
Sandsay Cl ASHBK/HED/RY SR2 ... 98 D6
Sands Rd WICK/BNPF NE16 ... 66 E3
Sandstone Cl HAR/WTLS NE34 ... 72 D1
Sandwell Dr HLS DH4 ... 95 H6
Sandwich Rd NSHW NE29 ... 50 D1
Sandy Chare
CLDN/WHIT/ROK SR6 ... 74 E4
Sandy Crs BYK/HTN/WLK NE6 ... 7 M9
Sandyford CLSW/PEL DH2 ... 92 D7
Sandyford Rd CNUT NE1 ... 5 L4
JES NE2 ... 5 L3
Sandy La DIN/WO NE13 ... 35 H3
GOS/KPK NE3 ... 36 E5
LWF/SPW/WRK NE9 ... 81 K4
Sandypath La
WICK/BNPF NE16 ... 77 J6 1
Sans St South SUND SR1 ... 15 G5 1
Sargent Av HAR/WTLS NE34 ... 73 H2
Satley Gdns SUNDSW SR3 ... 98 B4
Saturn Cl PLEE/EAS SR8 ... 130 D5 3
Saturn St SEA/MUR SR7 ... 120 B1
Saunton Ct HLS DH4 ... 108 A4 3
Saville St SSH NE33 ... 3 J7
TYNE/NSHE NE30 ... 2 E2
Saville St West NSHW NE29 ... 2 D3
Savory Rd WLSD/HOW NE28 ... 49 H7
Sawmill La BDN/LAN/SAC DH7 ... 133 F6
Saxilby Dr GOS/KPK NE3 ... 46 D2
Saxon Cl CLDN/WHIT/ROK SR6 ... 73 J3 4
Saxon Crs SUNDSW SR3 ... 97 K3
Saxondale Rd GOS/KPK NE3 ... 45 J5
Saxon Dr TYNE/NSHE NE30 ... 51 G1
Saxon Wy JRW NE32 ... 60 A3
Saxton Gv LGB/HTN NE7 ... 47 G6
Scafell CLS/BIR/GTL DH3 ... 93 K4
Scafell Cl PLEE/EAS SR8 ... 137 F4
Scafell Dr WD/WHPE/BLK NE5 ... 45 H7
Scafell Gdns DUN/TMV NE11 ... 68 A6
Scalby Cl GOS/KPK NE3 ... 46 D2 4
Scarborough Ct
BYK/HTN/WLK NE6 ... 7 J5
Scarborough Rd
BYK/HTN/WLK NE6 ... 7 K5
SUNDSW SR3 ... 97 K6
Scardale Wy DHAM DH1 ... 126 B5
Sceptre Pl ELS/FEN NE4 ... 4 C7
Sceptre St ELS/FEN NE4 ... 4 C7
Schalksmuhle Rd BDLGTN NE22 .. 19 F5
Schimel St SWCK/CAS SR5 ... 86 B3 11
School Ap HAR/WTLS NE34 ... 62 A5
School Av DUN/TMV NE11 ... 9 G9
School Cl FELL NE10 ... 69 K6
Schoolhouse La
WICK/BNPF NE16 ... 78 C6
School La ROWG NE39 ... 76 C2
STLY/ANP DH9 ... 102 B2 2
WICK/BNPF NE16 ... 67 F5
School Loaning
HAR/WTLS NE34 ... 61 F6 5
School Rd BDLGTN NE22 ... 19 K3
HLH DH5 ... 117 F4
School St CLS/BIR/GTL DH3 ... 93 J2
HEBB NE31 ... 59 G4
PLEE/EAS SR8 ... 131 F5
SEA/MUR SR7 ... 120 E3 2
WICK/BNPF NE16 ... 66 E5
School Ter STLY/ANP DH9 ... 102 B2
School Vw HLH DH5 ... 128 C1
HLS DH4 ... 116 C7 1
Scorer's La CLS/BIR/GTL DH3 ... 106 D7
Scorer St NSHW NE29 ... 2 A2
Scotland Head BLAY NE21 ... 65 J5
Scotland St
ASHBK/HED/RY SR2 ... 111 G1
Scotswood Rd
BW/LEM/TK/HW NE15 ... 54 B6
CNUT NE1 ... 5 G9
ELS/FEN NE4 ... 8 E1
Scotswood Vw DUN/TMV NE11 ... 8 C4
WICK/BNPF NE16 ... 8 A3
Scott Av CRAM NE23 ... 23 F7
Scott Ct CLS/BIR/GTL DH3 ... 115 H1
Scott's Ter HLH DH5 ... 117 K4
Scott St CRAM NE23 ... 23 H4
STLY/ANP DH9 ... 102 C1
Scripton Gill BDN/LAN/SAC DH7 .. 133 F6
Scripton Gill Rd
BDN/LAN/SAC DH7 ... 132 E7
Scrogg Rd BYK/HTN/WLK NE6 ... 7 M3
Scruton Av SUNDSW SR3 ... 97 K4
Sea Banks TYNE/NSHE NE30 ... 51 J2
Seaburn Dr HLS DH4 ... 108 A7
Seaburn Gdns
CLDN/WHIT/ROK SR6 ... 86 E1
LWF/SPW/WRK NE9 ... 81 K2
Seaburn Gv WBAY NE26 ... 31 F2
Seaburn Hl
CLDN/WHIT/ROK SR6 ... 86 E1 7
Seaburn Ter
CLDN/WHIT/ROK SR6 ... 87 F1 1
Seaburn Vw MONK NE25 ... 30 A2
Seacombe Av TYNE/NSHE NE30 ... 41 F6
Seacrest Av TYNE/NSHE NE30 ... 41 F7
Seafield Rd BLYTH NE24 ... 25 G2 7
Seafields CLDN/WHIT/ROK SR6 ... 74 E7
Seafield Ter SSH NE33 ... 3 K6
Seafield Vw TYNE/NSHE NE30 ... 51 H2
Seaforth Rd SUNDSW SR3 ... 98 A3
Seaforth St BLYTH NE24 ... 21 G6 9
Seaham Cl HAR/WTLS NE34 ... 62 B5
Seaham Gdns
LWF/SPW/WRK NE9 ... 81 J3
Seaham Rd HLH DH5 ... 108 D7
Seaham St SEA/MUR SR7 ... 121 F3 2
SUNDSW SR3 ... 98 A7
Sea La CLDN/WHIT/ROK SR6 ... 86 E1
Sea Rd CLDN/WHIT/ROK SR6 ... 86 D1
SSH NE33 ... 3 L5
Seascale Pl LWF/SPW/WRK NE9 ... 81 H1
Seaside La PLEE/EAS SR8 ... 130 D5
Seaton Av BLYTH NE24 ... 24 E3
HLH DH5 ... 108 E7
Seaton Cl FELL NE10 ... 70 D6 5
Seaton Crs MONK NE25 ... 30 C6
MONK NE25 ... 40 C4
SEA/MUR SR7 ... 110 E6
Seaton Cft CRAM NE23 ... 37 J1 2
Seaton Gv SEA/MUR SR7 ... 110 D7
Seaton La SEA/MUR SR7 ... 110 E6
Seaton Pk SEA/MUR SR7 ... 111 F7
Seaton Pl BYK/HTN/WLK NE6 ... 12 F2
DIN/WO NE13 ... 36 A3
Seaton Rd SMOOR NE27 ... 39 J5
SUNDSW SR3 ... 97 H3
Seatonville Crs MONK NE25 ... 40 C6
Seatonville Rd MONK NE25 ... 40 C6
Sea Vw ASHBK/HED/RY SR2 ... 111 G1
PLEE/EAS SR8 ... 130 C6
Sea View Gdns
CLDN/WHIT/ROK SR6 ... 86 E2
PLEE/EAS SR8 ... 137 H2
Sea View Pk
CLDN/WHIT/ROK SR6 ... 74 D4
CRAM NE23 ... 28 E2
Sea View Rd ASHBK/HED/RY SR2 .. 98 E4
Sea View Rd West
ASHBK/HED/RY SR2 ... 98 E4
Sea View St ASHBK/HED/RY SR2 .. 99 F4
Sea View Wk SEA/MUR SR7 ... 119 K4
Sea Wy SSH NE33 ... 3 M7
Second Av BLYTH NE24 ... 25 F1 6
BYK/HTN/WLK NE6 ... 7 G1
CLSW/PEL DH2 ... 93 H6
CLSW/PEL DH2 ... 105 H5
DUN/TMV NE11 ... 68 C6
NSHW NE29 ... 49 K6
Second St GATE NE8 ... 10 C5
Sedgeletch Rd HLS DH4 ... 107 J6
Sedgemoor LGB/KIL NE12 ... 37 K5
Sedgemoor Av
BW/LEM/TK/HW NE15 ... 54 E7
Sedley Rd WLSD/HOW NE28 ... 58 D2
Sedling Rd WASHS NE38 ... 94 D4
Sefton Av BYK/HTN/WLK NE6 ... 57 H2
Sefton Ct CRAM NE23 ... 23 J6
Sefton Sq SUNDSW SR3 ... 97 J3
Selborne Gdns JES NE2 ... 6 C1
Selbourne Cl CRAM NE23 ... 27 K2 3
Selbourne St SSH NE33 ... 3 K8
Selby Cl CRAM NE23 ... 23 H6
Selby Gdns BYK/HTN/WLK NE6 ... 58 B3
WLSD/HOW NE28 ... 48 D7
Selby Sq SUNDSW SR3 ... 97 J3
Selkirk Crs CLS/BIR/GTL DH3 ... 81 J7
Selkirk Gv CRAM NE23 ... 23 J6
Selkirk Sq SUNDSW SR3 ... 97 H3 1
Selkirk St JRW NE32 ... 72 C1
Selkirk Wy NSHW NE29 ... 50 A2
Selsdon Av MLFD/PNYW SR4 ... 96 E4 2
Selsey Ct FELL NE10 ... 70 A6
Selwood Ct HAR/WTLS NE34 ... 61 K6 1
Selwyn Av MONK NE25 ... 40 B6
Serlby Cl WASHN NE37 ... 82 E4
Seton Av HAR/WTLS NE34 ... 60 D7
Setting Stones WASHS NE38 ... 94 C6
Sevenoaks Dr MLFD/PNYW SR4 ... 96 E3
Seventh Av BLYTH NE24 ... 25 F1
BYK/HTN/WLK NE6 ... 7 G2
CLSW/PEL DH2 ... 105 H4
Seventh St PLEE/EAS SR8 ... 137 H3
Severn Av HEBB NE31 ... 71 G1
Severn Cl PLEE/EAS SR8 ... 136 D6
Severn Dr JRW NE32 ... 72 A2
Severn Gdns GATE NE8 ... 11 L7
Severus Rd ELS/FEN NE4 ... 55 J4
Seymour Sq SUNDSW SR3 ... 97 J3 1
Seymour St DUN/TMV NE11 ... 9 J5
NSHW NE29 ... 2 C4
PLEE/EAS SR8 ... 137 J4
Seymour Ter HLH DH5 ... 118 A7
Shadforth Cl PLEE/EAS SR8 ... 136 B6
Shadon Wy CLS/BIR/GTL DH3 ... 94 A2
Shaftesbury Av
ASHBK/HED/RY SR2 ... 98 E7
HAR/WTLS NE34 ... 60 C6
JRW NE32 ... 60 B5
WBAY NE26 ... 40 D2
Shaftesbury Crs RHTLP TS27 ... 137 K6 1
SUNDSW SR3 ... 97 K3
TYNE/NSHE NE30 ... 40 E6
Shaftesbury Gv
BYK/HTN/WLK NE6 ... 6 E2
Shaftesbury Rd RHTLP TS27 ... 137 K5
Shaftoe Cl RYTON NE40 ... 64 B1
Shaftoe Rd SUNDSW SR3 ... 97 J4
Shaftoe Sq SUNDSW SR3 ... 97 H4 1
Shaftoe Wy DIN/WO NE13 ... 34 E2
Shafto St BW/LEM/TK/HW NE15 .. 54 E6
WLSD/HOW NE28 ... 49 G7
Shakespeare Av HEBB NE31 ... 59 G5
Shakespeare St HLH DH5 ... 117 H1
JRW NE32 ... 59 K3 2
SEA/MUR SR7 ... 120 E1 10
SSH NE33 ... 61 H2 10
SWCK/CAS SR5 ... 86 A2
WLSD/HOW NE28 ... 59 H1
Shakespeare Ter
ASHBK/HED/RY SR2 ... 14 C7
PLEE/EAS SR8 ... 130 D5
Shakespere Ter CLSW/PEL DH2 .. 104 E4
Shalcombe Cl SUNDSW SR3 ... 110 A1
Shallcross ASHBK/HED/RY SR2 ... 14 B9
Shalstone WASHN NE37 ... 83 H4 1
Shamrock Cl
BW/LEM/TK/HW NE15 ... 54 A3
Shandon Wy GOS/KPK NE3 ... 45 J5 4
Shanklin Pl CRAM NE23 ... 27 K2 4
Shannon Cl SWCK/CAS SR5 ... 84 E4 2
Shap Cl WASHS NE38 ... 95 F3
Shap La WD/WHPE/BLK NE5 ... 54 E2
Shap Rd TYNE/NSHE NE30 ... 40 E7
Sharnford Cl SMOOR NE27 ... 39 F4
Sharon Cl LGB/KIL NE12 ... 37 H7
Sharp Crs DHAM DH1 ... 17 M1
Sharpendon St HEBB NE31 ... 59 G4 1
Sharpley Dr SEA/MUR SR7 ... 110 E7
Shaw Av HAR/WTLS NE34 ... 61 F7
Shawdon Cl
WD/WHPE/BLK NE5 ... 45 F6 11
Shaw Gdns FELL NE10 ... 13 L8
Shaw St SEA/MUR SR7 ... 120 E1 11
Shaw Wood Cl DHAM DH1 ... 124 B6
Shearlegs Rd GATE NE8 ... 11 K2
Shearwater
CLDN/WHIT/ROK SR6 ... 75 F1
Shearwater Av LGB/KIL NE12 ... 47 G3
Shearwater Cl
WD/WHPE/BLK NE5 ... 45 F6 12
Shearwater Wy BLYTH NE24 ... 25 H3
Sheelin Av CLSW/PEL DH2 ... 105 J6
Sheen Cl HLS DH4 ... 116 D6 3
Sheen Ct WD/WHPE/BLK NE5 ... 45 F5
Sheepfolds North
SWCK/CAS SR5 ... 14 E2 1
Sheepfolds Rd SWCK/CAS SR5 ... 14 E2
Sheepfolds South
SWCK/CAS SR5 ... 14 E2 2
Sheep Hl WICK/BNPF NE16 ... 77 K7
Sheldon Gv CRAM NE23 ... 23 H6
GOS/KPK NE3 ... 55 K1
Sheldon Rd HAR/WTLS NE34 ... 61 K2
Sheldon St JRW NE32 ... 59 K4
Shelford Gdns
BW/LEM/TK/HW NE15 ... 54 C4 3
Shelley Av BOLCOL NE35 ... 72 E4
HAR/WTLS NE34 ... 62 B6
HLH DH5 ... 128 C1 1
LWF/SPW/WRK NE9 ... 82 A4
Shelley Ct CLSW/PEL DH2 ... 104 E4
Shelley Dr GATE NE8 ... 11 J4
Shelley Gdns CLSW/PEL DH2 ... 105 F4
Shelley Rd
BW/LEM/TK/HW NE15 ... 53 H4
Shelley St SEA/MUR SR7 ... 120 E1
Shepherd St MLFD/PNYW SR4 .. 86 A6 3
Shepherds Wy BOL NE36 ... 72 E5 7
Shepherd Wy WASHS NE38 ... 95 G4
Sheppard Ter SWCK/CAS SR5 ... 85 F4 7
Sheppey Ct SUNDSW SR3 ... 110 A1 3
Shepton Cottages
WICK/BNPF NE16 ... 79 G2
Sheraton FELL NE10 ... 70 C7
Sheraton St JES NE2 ... 4 F1
Sherborne Av NSHW NE29 ... 50 B2 2
Sherburn Gra North
JRW NE32 ... 59 J6 2
Sherburn Gra South
JRW NE32 ... 59 J7 1
Sherburn Gn ROWG NE39 ... 77 H2
Sherburn Gv HLS DH4 ... 108 A6
Sherburn Park Dr ROWG NE39 ... 77 H2
Sherburn Rd DHAM DH1 ... 17 M3 1
Sherburn Wy FELL NE10 ... 70 D6
Sherfield Dr LGB/HTN NE7 ... 57 K1
Sheridan Gn WASHS NE38 ... 94 C5
Sheridan Rd HAR/WTLS NE34 ... 72 E1
Sheridan St MLFD/PNYW SR4 ... 85 K6
Sheriffs Cl LWF/SPW/WRK NE9 ... 11 M8
Sheriff's Moor Av HLH DH5 ... 128 B1
Sheringham Av NSHW NE29 ... 50 B3
Sheringham Cl SUNDSW SR3 ... 110 A3 4
Sheringham Dr CRAM NE23 ... 27 K2
Sheringham Gdns
BW/LEM/TK/HW NE15 ... 52 D1
Sherringham Av GOS/KPK NE3 ... 45 J5
Sherwood Cl SMOOR NE27 ... 39 K7
WASHS NE38 ... 95 F1 1
Sherwood Ct SUNDSW SR3 ... 110 A1 9
Sherwood Pl GOS/KPK NE3 ... 36 C7
Sherwood Vw WLSD/HOW NE28 .. 48 C6
Shetland Ct SUNDSW SR3 ... 110 A1 10
Shibdon Bank BLAY NE21 ... 66 B2
Shibdon Crs BLAY NE21 ... 66 B2 1
Shibdon Park Vw BLAY NE21 ... 66 B2 2
Shibdon Rd BLAY NE21 ... 66 A1
Shibdon Wy BLAY NE21 ... 66 D2
Shield Av WICK/BNPF NE16 ... 67 F3 4
Shieldfield La JES NE2 ... 6 A5
Shield Rd CLDN/WHIT/ROK SR6 ... 74 C7
Shieldrow La STLY/ANP DH9 ... 101 J4
Shields Rd BDLGTN NE22 ... 22 B2
BYK/HTN/WLK NE6 ... 7 H3
CLDN/WHIT/ROK SR6 ... 74 B6
CLS/BIR/GTL DH3 ... 105 K2
FELL NE10 ... 13 G7
HAR/WTLS NE34 ... 73 K1
MONK NE25 ... 40 D7
Shields Rd West
BYK/HTN/WLK NE6 ... 6 D5
Shield St JES NE2 ... 6 A4
Shiel Gdns CRAM NE23 ... 27 K2
Shillaw Pl CRAM NE23 ... 37 H4 3
Shilmore Rd GOS/KPK NE3 ... 45 K5 7
Shilton Cl HAR/WTLS NE34 ... 62 B6 4
Shincliffe Av SWCK/CAS SR5 ... 85 G3 4
Shincliffe Gdns
LWF/SPW/WRK NE9 ... 81 J2
Shincliffe La DHAM DH1 ... 135 J3
Shinwell Ter SEA/MUR SR7 ... 119 G5
Shipcote La GATE NE8 ... 11 G7
Shipcote Ter GATE NE8 ... 11 H7
Shipley Av ELS/FEN NE4 ... 55 J5
Shipley Rd TYNE/NSHE NE30 ... 51 G3
Shipley St BW/LEM/TK/HW NE15 .. 54 A5
Shipton Cl BOLCOL NE35 ... 72 C3
Shire Cha DHAM DH1 ... 124 E1 4
Shirley Gdns SUNDSW SR3 ... 98 B3
Shirwood Av WICK/BNPF NE16 ... 66 E7
Shop Spouts BLAY NE21 ... 66 A1 7
Shoreham Sq SUNDSW SR3 ... 97 J3 2
Shorestone Av TYNE/NSHE NE30 .. 41 F6
Shore St CLDN/WHIT/ROK SR6 .. 86 D4 8
Short Gv SEA/MUR SR7 ... 119 F5
Shortridge St SSH NE33 ... 3 K6 1
Shortridge Ter JES NE2 ... 57 F2
Shot Factory La CNUT NE1 ... 10 B1
Shotley Av SWCK/CAS SR5 ... 86 B2
Shotley Gdns
LWF/SPW/WRK NE9 ... 11 J9
Shotton Av BLYTH NE24 ... 25 G1
Shotton Bank PLEE/EAS SR8 ... 136 A7
Shotton La CRAM NE23 ... 22 C5
MPTH NE61 ... 22 A7
PLEE/EAS SR8 ... 136 B6
RDHAMSE DH6 ... 136 A5
Shotton Rd PLEE/EAS SR8 ... 137 G3
Shotton Wy FELL NE10 ... 71 G6
Shrewsbury Cl LGB/KIL NE12 ... 47 K6
PLEE/EAS SR8 ... 136 C5
Shrewsbury Crs SUNDSW SR3 ... 97 K3
Shrewsbury Dr SMOOR NE27 ... 38 E4
Shrewsbury St DUN/TMV NE11 ... 9 G8
SEA/MUR SR7 ... 120 E3
Shrewsbury Ter SSH NE33 ... 61 G4 5
Shrigley Gdns GOS/KPK NE3 ... 45 K5
Shropshire Dr DHAM DH1 ... 125 K7
Shunner Cl WASHN NE37 ... 82 C7
Sibthorpe St NSHW NE29 ... 2 E3
Side CNUT NE1 ... 5 L8
Side Cliff Rd
CLDN/WHIT/ROK SR6 ... 86 D2
Sidegate DHAM DH1 ... 16 C2
Sidlaw Av CLSW/PEL DH2 ... 105 G5
NSHW NE29 ... 50 D1
Sidmouth Cl HLS DH4 ... 108 A3 5
SEA/MUR SR7 ... 120 A2
Sidmouth Rd
LWF/SPW/WRK NE9 ... 81 F2
NSHW NE29 ... 50 A4
Sidney Gv ELS/FEN NE4 ... 4 C5
GATE NE8 ... 10 C6
Sidney St BLYTH NE24 ... 21 F7
BOLCOL NE35 ... 72 D4
NSHW NE29 ... 2 D2
Sidney Ter STLY/ANP DH9 ... 90 B6
Silkey's La NSHW NE29 ... 2 A3
Silksworth Cl SUNDSW SR3 ... 97 K6 2
Silksworth Gdns
LWF/SPW/WRK NE9 ... 81 J3
Silksworth Hall Dr
SUNDSW SR3 ... 109 K1
Silksworth La
ASHBK/HED/RY SR2 ... 98 B2 2
SUNDSW SR3 ... 97 K6
Silksworth Rw SUND SR1 ... 14 C4 3
Silksworth Ter SUNDSW SR3 ... 98 A7 5
Silksworth Wy SUNDSW SR3 ... 109 H1
Silkwood Cl CRAM NE23 ... 23 H6
Silloth Av WD/WHPE/BLK NE5 ... 54 E3
Silloth Dr WASHN NE37 ... 82 E3
Silloth Pl TYNE/NSHE NE30 ... 41 F7
Silloth Rd SUNDSW SR3 ... 97 H4 2
Silver Cts BDN/LAN/SAC DH7 ... 133 G6
Silverdale SUNDSW SR3 ... 110 A3
Silverdale Av FELL NE10 ... 71 F5
Silverdale Dr BLAY NE21 ... 65 H3
Silverdale Rd CRAM NE23 ... 23 H6
Silverdale Ter GATE NE8 ... 11 G8
Silverdale Wy HAR/WTLS NE34 ... 72 D1
WICK/BNPF NE16 ... 78 D1
Silver Fox Wy SMOOR NE27 ... 49 H2
Silverhill Dr WD/WHPE/BLK NE5 .. 54 E4
The Silverlink North
SMOOR NE27 ... 49 G1
The Silverlink SMOOR NE27 ... 49 J3
Silver Lonnen
WD/WHPE/BLK NE5 ... 55 F3
Silvermere Dr RYTON NE40 ... 53 F7
Silverstone LGB/KIL NE12 ... 38 A6
Silverstone Rd WASHN NE37 ... 83 G5
Silver St DHAM DH1 ... 16 D3 1
SUND SR1 ... 15 J2
TYNE/NSHE NE30 ... 51 H3 5
Silverwood Gdns
DUN/TMV NE11 ... 68 B7
Simonburn Av ELS/FEN NE4 ... 55 J3
NSHW NE29 ... 50 A4
Simon Pl DIN/WO NE13 ... 36 A4 7
Simonside WBAY NE26 ... 31 G4
Simonside Av WLSD/HOW NE28 ... 49 H6
Simonside Rd BLAY NE21 ... 66 A3 5
SUNDSW SR3 ... 97 H3

Simonside Ter
BYK/HTN/WLK NE6 57 H3
Simonside Vw JRW NE32 60 A7
PONT/DH NE20 33 F2
Simonside Wy LGB/KIL NE12 38 B5
Simpson St BLYTH NE24 21 G6 10
MLFD/PNYW SR4 14 A2
NSHW NE29 50 C5
TYNE/NSHE NE30 41 G5 1
Simpson Ter JES NE2 6 A5
Sinclair Dr CLS/BIR/GTL DH3 93 K6
Sinclair Gdns MONK NE25 30 A5
Sinderby Cl GOS/KPK NE3 46 D2
Six-mile Br DIN/WO NE13 36 C1
Sixth Av BLYTH NE24 25 F1
BYK/HTN/WLK NE6 7 G2
Sixth St PLEE/EAS SR8 137 H3
Skaylock Dr WASHS NE38 94 C3
Skelder Av LGB/KIL NE12 47 H4
Skelton Ct GOS/KPK NE3 45 J2
Skerne Cl PLEE/EAS SR8 136 D6
Skiddaw Cl PLEE/EAS SR8 137 F4
Skiddaw Dr
CLDN/WHIT/ROK SR6 74 C7 5
Skiddaw Pl LWF/SPW/WRK NE9 81 H1
Skinnerburn Rd ELS/FEN NE4 10 A2
Skipton Cl BDLGTN NE22 18 D4
CRAM NE23 23 J6 3
Skirlaw Cl WASHS NE38 95 F2
Ski Vw SUNDSW SR3 97 K6
Skye Ct SUNDSW SR3 109 K1
Skye Gv JRW NE32 72 C2 3
Slaidburn Rd STLY/ANP DH9 90 D7 7
Slake Rd JRW NE32 60 B3
Slaley WASHS NE38 95 G5
Slaley Cl FELL NE10 70 E5
Slaley Ct BDLGTN NE22 19 G5
SUNDSW SR3 110 A1
Slatyford La WD/WHPE/BLK NE5 54 E3
Sledmere Cl PLEE/EAS SR8 136 E2 2
Sleekburn Av BDLGTN NE22 19 K3 2
Slingley Cl SEA/MUR SR7 110 E7 2
Slingsby Gdns LGB/HTN NE7 47 K7 2
Smailes La ROWG NE39 76 E3 1
Smailes St STLY/ANP DH9 102 C2
Smeaton Ct WLSD/HOW NE28 59 J2 5
Smeaton St WLSD/HOW NE28 59 J2 6
Smillie Cl PLEE/EAS SR8 136 E3
Smithburn Rd FELL NE10 12 E9
Smithfield DHAM DH1 124 C1
Smith Gv ASHBK/HED/RY SR2 110 E1
Smith St ASHBK/HED/RY SR2 111 F1
SSH NE33 61 F3
Smith Ter GATE NE8 9 M6
Smithyford LWF/SPW/WRK NE9 81 G4
Smithy La DUN/TMV NE11 80 E4
Smithy St SSH NE33 3 H7
Smyrna Pl SUND SR1 15 H5
Snipes Dene ROWG NE39 77 G2
Snowdon Gdns
DUN/TMV NE11 68 A6 5
Snowdon Gv BOL NE36 73 F5 6
Soane Gdns HAR/WTLS NE34 73 H1
Softley Pl BW/LEM/TK/HW NE15 54 D4
Solingen Est BLYTH NE24 25 H2
Solway Av TYNE/NSHE NE30 40 E7
Solway Rd HEBB NE31 59 G7
Solway Sq SUNDSW SR3 97 J3
Somersby Dr GOS/KPK NE3 45 J5
Somerset Gdns
WLSD/HOW NE28 48 C7 6
Somerset Gv NSHW NE29 50 B2 3
Somerset Pl ELS/FEN NE4 4 D7
Somerset Rd HEBB NE31 71 H1 3
SUNDSW SR3 97 H3
Somerset Sq SUNDSW SR3 97 H3 2
Somerset St SUNDSW SR3 98 A5 1
Somerton Ct GOS/KPK NE3 45 G4
Sophia St SEA/MUR SR7 120 E1
Sophy St SWCK/CAS SR5 86 B3 12
Sorley St MLFD/PNYW SR4 86 A7
Sorrel Gdns HAR/WTLS NE34 73 J1
Soulby Ct DIN/WO NE13 45 H2
Sourmilk Hill La
LWF/SPW/WRK NE9 69 G6
Souter Rd GOS/KPK NE3 46 A5 7
South Ap CLSW/PEL DH2 105 J5
South Av HAR/WTLS NE34 61 K6
South Bailey DHAM DH1 16 D6
South Bend GOS/KPK NE3 46 B1
South Bents Av
CLDN/WHIT/ROK SR6 74 E6
South Benwell Rd
BW/LEM/TK/HW NE15 55 G7
Southburn Cl HLS DH4 108 A7 2
South Burns CLS/BIR/GTL DH3 105 J3
South Cl HAR/WTLS NE34 61 K6
HLH DH5 128 C1
RYTON NE40 52 E7
Southcote WICK/BNPF NE16 66 E7
South Crs BOLCOL NE35 72 D4
SEA/MUR SR7 121 F1
WASHS NE38 94 D6
South Cft LGB/KIL NE12 48 A3
Southcroft WASHS NE38 95 F5
South Dene HAR/WTLS NE34 61 F6
South Dr CLDN/WHIT/ROK SR6 73 K3 2
DIN/WO NE13 26 D2
DIN/WO NE13 44 D2
HEBB NE31 58 E7
South Eldon St SSH NE33 61 F4
Southend Av BLYTH NE24 24 E1
Southend Rd
LWF/SPW/WRK NE9 69 H7
SUNDSW SR3 97 J4
Southern Rd BYK/HTN/WLK NE6 58 B7
Southern Wy RYTON NE40 52 E7 1
Southey St SSH NE33 61 H3 6
South Farm BDLGTN NE22 18 A6
Southfield CLSW/PEL DH2 92 E7
Southfield Gdns
WICK/BNPF NE16 67 G5
Southfield La CHPW NE17 88 B3
Southfield Rd HAR/WTLS NE34 61 K3
LGB/KIL NE12 47 J4
WICK/BNPF NE16 67 G6
Southfields CRAM NE23 37 G1 1
Southfield Ter
BYK/HTN/WLK NE6 58 C7 10
Southfield Wy DHAM DH1 124 B5
Southfork
BW/LEM/TK/HW NE15 54 A3
South Frederick St SSH NE33 61 F4 5
Southgate LGB/KIL NE12 37 K7
South Grange Pk SEA/MUR SR7 111 F5
South Gv RYTON NE40 53 F7
South Hetton Rd HLH DH5 128 C1
South Hill Rd GATE NE8 10 B6
Southhill Rd HAR/WTLS NE34 62 A5
Southlands JRW NE32 72 B3
LGB/HTN NE7 57 G1
TYNE/NSHE NE30 51 F2
South La BOL NE36 73 G5
South Lea BDN/LAN/SAC DH7 123 G1
South Market St HLH DH5 118 A4
Southmayne Rd
MLFD/PNYW SR4 97 H2 4
Southmead Av
WD/WHPE/BLK NE5 55 F2
South Mdw STLY/ANP DH9 89 F6
South Moor Rd STLY/ANP DH9 102 C3
South Nelson Rd CRAM NE23 22 E7
South Newsham Rd BLYTH NE24 24 E4
South Pde FELL NE10 13 L4
WBAY NE26 41 F4
South Preston Gv NSHW NE29 2 B2
South Railway St
SEA/MUR SR7 120 E1
South Rdg GOS/KPK NE3 46 B2
South Riggs BDLGTN NE22 19 F6
South Rd DHAM DH1 134 D4
South Rw GATE NE8 6 D9
South Shore Rd GATE NE8 6 B8
South Side PLEE/EAS SR8 130 C6
South St CLSW/PEL DH2 105 H3
CNUT NE1 5 J9
DHAM DH1 16 C5
GATE NE8 11 H6
GOS/KPK NE3 46 A5 8
HLH DH5 117 F4 2
HLS DH4 108 B4
ROWG NE39 76 B1
SMOOR NE27 39 H5
SUND SR1 14 E4
South Ter DHAM DH1 124 B4
PLEE/EAS SR8 137 G3
SEA/MUR SR7 121 F1 3
SWCK/CAS SR5 86 B4 7
WLSD/HOW NE28 59 G1
South Vw BDN/LAN/SAC DH7 133 H7
BLYTH NE24 24 E3
CLDN/WHIT/ROK SR6 86 D2
CLS/BIR/GTL DH3 93 K2
HLH DH5 128 C2
JRW NE32 59 J5
SEA/MUR SR7 120 A3
STLY/ANP DH9 89 K4
WASHS NE38 95 G5
WD/WHPE/BLK NE5 54 C3
South View Rd MLFD/PNYW SR4 96 E1
South View Ter HLS DH4 107 K7
WICK/BNPF NE16 67 F4
South Vw West
BYK/HTN/WLK NE6 6 D4
Southward WBAY NE26 31 G3
Southward Cl WBAY NE26 31 G3 1
Southward Wy MONK NE25 30 B7
Southway
BW/LEM/TK/HW NE15 54 C4
LWF/SPW/WRK NE9 69 H6
PLEE/EAS SR8 136 D5
Southwick Rd SWCK/CAS SR5 14 E1 1
SWCK/CAS SR5 86 D4 9
Southwold Gdns
SUNDSW SR3 97 K6 3
Southwold Pl CRAM NE23 27 K2 5
South Woodbine St SSH NE33 3 K7
Southwood Gdns GOS/KPK NE3 45 K6
Sovereign Pl ELS/FEN NE4 4 C8
Spalding Cl LGB/HTN NE7 47 J6 7
Sparkwell Cl HLS DH4 108 B3 2
Spartylea WASHS NE38 95 H5 1
Spa Well Cl BLAY NE21 65 K4
Spa Well Dr SWCK/CAS SR5 85 G3
Spelter Works Rd
ASHBK/HED/RY SR2 99 F3
Spen Burn ROWG NE39 76 C1
Spencer Cl STLY/ANP DH9 103 F1
Spencer Ct BLYTH NE24 20 D5
Spencer Gv WICK/BNPF NE16 67 F4 4
Spencer Rd BLYTH NE24 20 D5
Spencers Bank
WICK/BNPF NE16 66 E3 9
Spencer St BYK/HTN/WLK NE6 7 H1
NSHW NE29 2 D3 2
Spence Ter NSHW NE29 2 B2
Spenfield Rd
WD/WHPE/BLK NE5 45 H7 4
Spen La ROWG NE39 76 C1
RYTON NE40 64 B5
Spen Rd ROWG NE39 76 B1
Spenser St JRW NE32 59 K3 8
Spen St STLY/ANP DH9 102 C2
Spinneyside Gdns
DUN/TMV NE11 67 K5
The Spinney CRAM NE23 37 J1
PLEE/EAS SR8 130 B5
WASHS NE38 95 F4
Spire Hollin PLEE/EAS SR8 136 D4
Spire Rd WASHN NE37 83 H6
Spires La BYK/HTN/WLK NE6 7 H5
Spital Ter GOS/KPK NE3 46 C5
Split Crow Rd GATE NE8 11 J7
Spohr Ter SSH NE33 61 H2
Spoor St DUN/TMV NE11 9 H6
Spout La WASHN NE37 83 F6
WASHS NE38 83 F7
Springbank Rd JES NE2 6 C2
SUNDSW SR3 97 H3
Springbank Sq SUNDSW SR3 97 H3 3
Springfield NSHW NE29 2 C1 2
Springfield Av
LWF/SPW/WRK NE9 81 J4
Springfield Crs SEA/MUR SR7 120 D2
Springfield Gdns
CLS/BIR/GTL DH3 105 J2
WLSD/HOW NE28 48 B7
Springfield Gv MONK NE25 40 C6
Springfield Pk DHAM DH1 124 B6
Springfield Pl
LWF/SPW/WRK NE9 69 G6
Springfield Rd BLAY NE21 65 K2
HLS DH4 108 B4 8
WD/WHPE/BLK NE5 55 G2 6
Spring Garden Cl SUND SR1 15 H4 3
Springhill Gdns
BW/LEM/TK/HW NE15 55 H5
Spring Pk BDLGTN NE22 19 G6
Springside BDN/LAN/SAC DH7 113 H5
The Springs CLS/BIR/GTL DH3 93 K3
Spring St ELS/FEN NE4 4 F5 1
Springsyde Cl
WICK/BNPF NE16 66 C7 4
Spring Ter NSHW NE29 2 C1
Springwell Av
BDN/LAN/SAC DH7 122 B3
BYK/HTN/WLK NE6 7 L8
DHAM DH1 124 B6
JRW NE32 60 A5
LWF/SPW/WRK NE9 81 J3 1
Springwell Cl
BDN/LAN/SAC DH7 122 B3 2
Springwell Rd DHAM DH1 124 B6
JRW NE32 59 K6
LWF/SPW/WRK NE9 81 K2
MLFD/PNYW SR4 97 H3
Springwood HEBB NE31 58 E4
Squires Gdns FELL NE10 69 K5
Stack Garth BDN/LAN/SAC DH7 133 H5
Stadium Wy SWCK/CAS SR5 14 D1
Stafford Gv
ASHBK/HED/RY SR2 110 E1 1
SWCK/CAS SR5 86 B3
Stafford Pl PLEE/EAS SR8 136 C3
Staffordshire Dr DHAM DH1 126 A6
Staffords La
CLDN/WHIT/ROK SR6 75 F4 2
Stafford St SUND SR1 15 J2
Stagshaw LGB/KIL NE12 37 J4 5
Staindrop FELL NE10 70 C7
Staindrop Rd DHAM DH1 124 E3
Staines Rd BYK/HTN/WLK NE6 7 K8 2
Stainmore Dr CLS/BIR/GTL DH3 115 J2
Stainton Dr FELL NE10 12 D7
Stainton Gv
CLDN/WHIT/ROK SR6 74 C7
Stainton St East SSH NE33 61 H2 11
Stainton Wy PLEE/EAS SR8 136 D4
Staithes Av LGB/KIL NE12 47 J4
Staithes Rd WASHS NE38 95 J3
Staithes St BYK/HTN/WLK NE6 58 D5
Staith La BLAY NE21 53 J7
Staiths Rd DUN/TMV NE11 9 J5
Stalks Rd DIN/WO NE13 36 B3
Stamford Av MONK NE25 30 B6
SUNDSW SR3 97 K3
Stamfordham Av NSHW NE29 50 B5
Stamfordham Cl
WLSD/HOW NE28 58 C1 3
Stamfordham Ms
WD/WHPE/BLK NE5 55 H2 9
Stamfordham Rd
PONT/DH NE20 42 B2
WD/WHPE/BLK NE5 43 H4
Stampley Cl BLAY NE21 65 J4 6
Stamps La SUND SR1 15 J3
Standfield Gdns FELL NE10 70 E4 2
Standish St STLY/ANP DH9 102 B2
Stanelaw Wy STLY/ANP DH9 90 D5
Staneway FELL NE10 82 A1
Stanfield Ct LGB/HTN NE7 48 A7 4
Stanhope WASHS NE38 94 B1
Stanhope Cl
BDN/LAN/SAC DH7 133 H6 5
DHAM DH1 124 E2
HLS DH4 117 G1
Stanhope Pde SSH NE33 61 H3 7
Stanhope Rd
CLDN/WHIT/ROK SR6 86 E1
HAR/WTLS NE34 61 F5
JRW NE32 60 B6
SSH NE33 61 H4
Stanhope St ELS/FEN NE4 4 D5
SSH NE33 3 H6
Stanley Gdns
LWF/SPW/WRK NE9 81 J3
Stanley Gv BDLGTN NE22 19 H5
LGB/HTN NE7 47 G7
Stanley St BLYTH NE24 21 H6 3
ELS/FEN NE4 4 A9 1
HAR/WTLS NE34 61 F6
JRW NE32 60 A4
NSHW NE29 2 D3
SEA/MUR SR7 111 H7
SWCK/CAS SR5 85 F4 8
WLSD/HOW NE28 49 H7
Stanley St West NSHW NE29 2 C3
Stanmore Rd
BYK/HTN/WLK NE6 57 J2
Stannerford Rd RYTON NE40 52 A6
Stannington Av
BYK/HTN/WLK NE6 6 E2
Stannington Gdns
ASHBK/HED/RY SR2 98 C4 6
Stannington Gv
ASHBK/HED/RY SR2 98 C4
Stannington Pl
BYK/HTN/WLK NE6 6 F2
PONT/DH NE20 33 G1
Stannington Rd NSHW NE29 50 A5
Stannington St BLYTH NE24 21 H7
Stansfield St
CLDN/WHIT/ROK SR6 86 E4
Stanstead Cl SWCK/CAS SR5 84 E5 2
Stanton Av BLYTH NE24 24 D2
HAR/WTLS NE34 61 J4
Stanton Cl FELL NE10 71 F5
Stanton Rd SMOOR NE27 39 G7
TYNE/NSHE NE30 50 D1
Stanton St ELS/FEN NE4 4 D5
Stanway Dr LGB/HTN NE7 47 G7
Stanwick St TYNE/NSHE NE30 51 H2 6
Stapeley Vw GOS/KPK NE3 45 H5
Staple Rd JRW NE32 59 K3
Stapylton Dr
ASHBK/HED/RY SR2 98 B2
Starbeck Av JES NE2 6 A2
Starbeck Ms JES NE2 6 A2 1
Stardale Av BLYTH NE24 24 C1
Stargate La RYTON NE40 53 G7
Starlight Crs MONK NE25 29 K5 3
Startforth Cl
CLS/BIR/GTL DH3 115 J1 4
Station Ap BOL NE36 73 J5
DHAM DH1 16 B3
LGB/KIL NE12 47 K4 6
SSH NE33 3 H6 1
Station Av BDN/LAN/SAC DH7 133 H6
HLH DH5 117 K5
Station Bank DHAM DH1 16 C3 1
RYTON NE40 52 E5
Station Crs SEA/MUR SR7 111 H7
Station Est East SEA/MUR SR7 119 F5
Station Est North
SEA/MUR SR7 119 F5
Station Est South
SEA/MUR SR7 119 F5
Station Field Rd STLY/ANP DH9 90 D5
Station La CLS/BIR/GTL DH3 93 H2
CLSW/PEL DH2 104 D1
DHAM DH1 17 G2
Station Rd ASHBK/HED/RY SR2 111 G1
BDLGTN NE22 19 J4
BDN/LAN/SAC DH7 132 E1
BDN/LAN/SAC DH7 133 H6
BOLCOL NE35 72 C2
BW/LEM/TK/HW NE15 52 B1
BW/LEM/TK/HW NE15 53 H4
CLS/BIR/GTL DH3 105 J4
CLSW/PEL DH2 105 J4
CRAM NE23 28 C1 2
CRAM NE23 29 G7
CRAM NE23 37 F1
DIN/WO NE13 45 F4
FELL NE10 13 L3
GOS/KPK NE3 46 E5
HEBB NE31 59 F5
HLH DH5 117 K5
HLS DH4 95 H6
HLS DH4 107 J1 3
HLS DH4 108 B6
HLS DH4 116 C7
LGB/KIL NE12 37 H6
LGB/KIL NE12 47 K4
LWF/SPW/WRK NE9 68 E7
NSHW NE29 50 B6
PLEE/EAS SR8 131 G5
RDHAMSE DH6 126 D2
ROWG NE39 77 H4
SEA/MUR SR7 111 F7
SEA/MUR SR7 119 F5
SMOOR NE27 39 F6
SSH NE33 3 G8
STLY/ANP DH9 90 D7
STLY/ANP DH9 91 J6
STLY/ANP DH9 101 H4
SWCK/CAS SR5 86 C1
TYNE/NSHE NE30 41 G6
WASHS NE38 95 G1
WASHS NE38 95 G5
WBAY NE26 41 F5
WLSD/HOW NE28 48 B5
WLSD/HOW NE28 58 C1
WLSD/HOW NE28 58 E2
WLSD/HOW NE28 59 J2
Station Rd North LGB/KIL NE12 47 K2 8
Station St BLYTH NE24 21 G6
RDHAMSE DH6 128 E6
SUND SR1 14 E4
Station Ter TYNE/NSHE NE30 51 H3
Station Vw HLH DH5 117 K5
Staveley Rd
CLDN/WHIT/ROK SR6 74 C7
PLEE/EAS SR8 137 F4
Stavordale St SEA/MUR SR7 120 E2 6
Stavordale St West
SEA/MUR SR7 120 E3 5
Stavordale Ter
LWF/SPW/WRK NE9 11 K9
Staward Av MONK NE25 30 A6
Staward Ter
BYK/HTN/WLK NE6 58 B7 2
Staynebrigg FELL NE10 70 C6 3
Stead La BDLGTN NE22 19 H5
Stead St WLSD/HOW NE28 49 J7
Stedham Cl WASHN NE37 83 G3
Steep Hl SUNDSW SR3 97 F6
Stella Bank BLAY NE21 53 H6
Stella Hall BLAY NE21 53 J7
Stella La BLAY NE21 53 H7
Stella Rd BLAY NE21 53 J7
Stephenson Cl HLH DH5 118 A4 2
Stephenson Rd
BYK/HTN/WLK NE6 57 H2
PLEE/EAS SR8 136 D1
WASHN NE37 83 G3
Stephenson St GATE NE8 10 C8
SEA/MUR SR7 119 H5 6
TYNE/NSHE NE30 2 E1
TYNE/NSHE NE30 51 H3 4
WLSD/HOW NE28 59 K2
Stephenson Ter FELL NE10 12 C9
Stephenson Wy BLAY NE21 65 K4
STKFD/GP NE62 19 G2
Stephens Rd SEA/MUR SR7 119 G5
Stephen St BLYTH NE24 21 G6
BYK/HTN/WLK NE6 6 D5
Stepney Bank CNUT NE1 6 C5
Stepney La CNUT NE1 6 A6
Stepney Rd JES NE2 6 B4
Sterling St MLFD/PNYW SR4 86 A7
Steward Crs HAR/WTLS NE34 62 A4
Stewart Av ASHBK/HED/RY SR2 110 E1
Stewart Dr BOL NE36 73 F5 7
Stewart St MLFD/PNYW SR4 86 A7
PLEE/EAS SR8 130 E5
SEA/MUR SR7 121 F2
SUNDSW SR3 98 A7
Stileford FELL NE10 13 K9
Stirling Av JRW NE32 60 C7
ROWG NE39 77 G4
Stirling Cl WASHS NE38 95 H2
Stirling Dr BDLGTN NE22 19 J4
NSHW NE29 50 A2
Stirling La ROWG NE39 77 G4
Stobart St
BDN/LAN/SAC DH7 113 G1 1
SWCK/CAS SR5 14 D1
Stockholm Cl NSHW NE29 49 K5
Stockley Av SWCK/CAS SR5 85 G3 5
Stockley Ct BDN/LAN/SAC DH7 133 H1
Stocksfield Av
WD/WHPE/BLK NE5 55 G4
Stockton Rd
ASHBK/HED/RY SR2 14 D7
ASHBK/HED/RY SR2 111 F2
DHAM DH1 16 E7
NSHW NE29 2 A6
PLEE/EAS SR8 130 B7
SEA/MUR SR7 111 F5
SEA/MUR SR7 130 B1
SUND SR1 14 D6 2
Stockton St SEA/MUR SR7 111 H7
Stockwell Gn BYK/HTN/WLK NE6 58 B3
Stoddart St HAR/WTLS NE34 61 G5 4
JES NE2 6 B4
Stoker Av HAR/WTLS NE34 60 D7
Stoker Ter ROWG NE39 76 C2 2
Stokesley Gv LGB/HTN NE7 47 G7
Stone Cellar Rd WASHN NE37 82 D3
Stonechat Pl LGB/KIL NE12 47 G3
Stonecroft Gdns LGB/HTN NE7 47 K7
Stonefold Cl
WD/WHPE/BLK NE5 45 F7 8
Stonehaugh Wy PONT/DH NE20 32 D7
Stoneleigh Av LGB/KIL NE12 47 G3
Stoneleigh Cl HLS DH4 108 A6 1
Stone Rw CLSW/PEL DH2 104 A2
Stonesdale HLS DH4 95 G6
Stone St FELL NE10 69 J6
Stoneygate La FELL NE10 12 E6
Stoneyhurst Av
BW/LEM/TK/HW NE15 55 F6 3
Stoneyhurst Rd GOS/KPK NE3 46 E6
Stoney La LWF/SPW/WRK NE9 82 B4
SWCK/CAS SR5 86 A4 10
Stoneylea Cl RYTON NE40 64 A1 3
Stoneylea Rd
WD/WHPE/BLK NE5 54 D3
Stonyheap La CON/LDGT DH8 100 D5
Stony La STLY/ANP DH9 92 A6
Store St
BW/LEM/TK/HW NE15 54 A5 8
Storey La BLAY NE21 53 J7 1
Stormont St NSHW NE29 2 B3
Stotfold Cl SEA/MUR SR7 110 E7
Stothard St JRW NE32 60 A4
Stotts Rd BYK/HTN/WLK NE6 58 C3
Stowell St CNUT NE1 5 H7
The Stow LGB/KIL NE12 47 G5
Straker St JRW NE32 60 B5
Straker Ter HAR/WTLS NE34 61 F6
The Strand SUNDSW SR3 97 J6 4
Strangford Rd SEA/MUR SR7 120 C1
Strangways St SEA/MUR SR7 120 E2 7
Stranton Ter
CLDN/WHIT/ROK SR6 86 D3
Stratfield St MLFD/PNYW SR4 85 J6 5
Stratford Av
ASHBK/HED/RY SR2 98 E3
Stratford Cl CRAM NE23 27 K1
LGB/KIL NE12 38 A6
Stratford Gdns
LWF/SPW/WRK NE9 69 F6 3
Stratford Gv West
BYK/HTN/WLK NE6 6 C3
Stratford Rd BYK/HTN/WLK NE6 6 D3
Strathearn Wy GOS/KPK NE3 45 K3
Strathmore Av ROWG NE39 77 G4 1
Strathmore Cl STLY/ANP DH9 91 F7
Strathmore Crs ELS/FEN NE4 55 J6
Strathmore Rd GOS/KPK NE3 46 C3
LWF/SPW/WRK NE9 11 M9
ROWG NE39 77 F4
SUNDSW SR3 97 J4
Strathmore Sq SUNDSW SR3 97 J4 7
Stratton Cl ASHBK/HED/RY SR2 99 G6
Stratus Ct SUNDSW SR3 110 A1
Strawberry Gdns
WLSD/HOW NE28 48 C6
Strawberry La CNUT NE1 5 H5
DHAM DH1 135 H6
Strawberry Pl CNUT NE1 5 H6
Street Gate Pk WICK/BNPF NE16 79 G2
Stretton Cl HLS DH4 116 D1 3
Stretton Wy SMOOR NE27 38 E4
Stridingedge WASHN NE37 82 C7
Strothers Rd ROWG NE39 64 B7
Stuart Ct GOS/KPK NE3 45 F4
Stuart Gdns
BW/LEM/TK/HW NE15 52 E1
Stubbs Av WICK/BNPF NE16 66 E4 5
Studdon Wk GOS/KPK NE3 45 H5
Studley Gdns
LWF/SPW/WRK NE9 69 F7 9
MONK NE25 40 E5
Studley Ter ELS/FEN NE4 4 A3
Studley Vls LGB/KIL NE12 48 A3 1
Sturdee Gdns JES NE2 46 E7
Styford Gdns
BW/LEM/TK/HW NE15 54 C4 4
Success Rd HLS DH4 107 K2
Sudbury Wy CRAM NE23 27 K1
Suddick St SWCK/CAS SR5 86 B4 8
Suez St TYNE/NSHE NE30 2 E1
Suffolk Gdns HAR/WTLS NE34 62 C4
WLSD/HOW NE28 49 G6
Suffolk Pl CLS/BIR/GTL DH3 93 K5
GATE NE8 6 C9
Suffolk Rd HEBB NE31 71 H1
Suffolk St ASHBK/HED/RY SR2 15 H8
JRW NE32 59 K5
Suffolk Wk PLEE/EAS SR8 136 D2 3
Suffolk Wy DHAM DH1 124 E1 5
Sugley Dr BW/LEM/TK/HW NE15 54 B5
Sugley St BW/LEM/TK/HW NE15 54 B5
Sulgrave Rd WASHN NE37 83 H4
Sullivan Wk HEBB NE31 59 G6

Summerfield STLY/ANP DH9 104 A1
Summerfield Rd
LWF/SPW/WRK NE9 11 H9
Summerhill BLAY NE21 65 K1
JRW NE32 72 B3
SUNDSW SR3 97 F7
Summerhill Av GOS/KPK NE3 46 D1
Summerhill Gv ELS/FEN NE4 4 F7
Summerhill Rd HAR/WTLS NE34 61 K4
Summerhill St ELS/FEN NE4 4 F8
Summerhill Ter CNUT NE1 5 G8
Summerhouse Farm
HLH DH5 117 G3 1
Summerson St HLH DH5 118 A4
Summerson Wy BDLGTN NE22 19 K4
Summer St FELL NE10 12 C6
Summerville DHAM DH1 16 B5
Sunbury Av JES NE2 56 E1
Sunderland Av PLEE/EAS SR8 137 G2
Sunderland Hwy WASHS NE38 82 B7
Sunderland Rd BOL NE36 73 J5
CLDN/WHIT/ROK SR6 74 B4
DHAM DH1 17 K2
FELL NE10 13 G7
FELL NE10 71 F4 1
GATE NE8 11 H3
HAR/WTLS NE34 61 J4
HLS DH4 108 C4
PLEE/EAS SR8 130 C5
SEA/MUR SR7 130 C3
SSH NE33 61 H3
SWCK/CAS SR5 86 A3
Sunderland St CNUT NE1 5 H8
HLH DH5 108 C6
HLS DH4 108 C7 3
Sundew Rd LWF/SPW/WRK NE9 69 J7
Sundridge Dr FELL NE10 70 E5
Sunholme Dr WLSD/HOW NE28 48 C5
Sunlea Av TYNE/NSHE NE30 41 G7
Sunnidale WICK/BNPF NE16 66 C7
Sunnilaws HAR/WTLS NE34 62 A7
Sunningdale SSH NE33 61 J2 5
Sunningdale Av
BYK/HTN/WLK NE6 58 C5 4
WLSD/HOW NE28 58 E1 5
Sunningdale Cl FELL NE10 69 K5
Sunningdale Dr WASHN NE37 82 E3 7
Sunningdale Rd SUNDSW SR3 97 H3
Sunnirise HAR/WTLS NE34 62 A7
Sunniside MLFD/PNYW SR4 84 E7
NSHW NE29 50 B5
Sunniside Ct WICK/BNPF NE16 79 F3
Sunniside Dr HAR/WTLS NE34 62 A7
Sunniside Gdns
BW/LEM/TK/HW NE15 55 F5 4
Sunniside La
CLDN/WHIT/ROK SR6 74 B2
Sunniside Rd WICK/BNPF NE16 67 F7
Sunniside Ter
CLDN/WHIT/ROK SR6 74 A2
Sunnybank Av
BW/LEM/TK/HW NE15 55 H6
Sunny Blunts PLEE/EAS SR8 136 D6
Sunny Brae RYTON NE40 64 B4 1
Sunnybrow SUNDSW SR3 97 K6
Sunnycrest Av
BYK/HTN/WLK NE6 58 B5
Sunny Ter STLY/ANP DH9 90 C7
Sunnyway WD/WHPE/BLK NE5 55 G1
Surrey Av SUNDSW SR3 110 A1
Surrey Pl ELS/FEN NE4 4 D7
Surrey Rd HEBB NE31 71 H1
NSHW NE29 50 B4 7
Surrey St JRW NE32 59 J5
Surtees Dr DHAM DH1 124 B7
Surtees Rd PLEE/EAS SR8 137 F4
Sussex Gdns WLSD/HOW NE28 49 G6
Sussex Pl WASHN NE37 83 F4 3
Sussex St BLYTH NE24 21 H6 3
JRW NE32 59 J5 4
Sutherland Av ELS/FEN NE4 55 J4
Sutherland Ct
HAR/WTLS NE34 73 H2 1
Sutherland Gra HLS DH4 108 B1 1
Sutherland St
CLDN/WHIT/ROK SR6 86 D3
SEA/MUR SR7 111 H7
Sutton Cl HLS DH4 107 J1
Sutton Ct WLSD/HOW NE28 48 B5
Sutton St BYK/HTN/WLK NE6 7 M1
DHAM DH1 16 B3
Sutton Wy HAR/WTLS NE34 62 B6
Swainby Cl GOS/KPK NE3 46 D2
Swaledale CLDN/WHIT/ROK SR6 75 F5
WLSD/HOW NE28 48 B5 3
Swaledale Av BLYTH NE24 20 C7
Swaledale Cl HLH DH5 117 H7
Swaledale Crs HLS DH4 95 J6
Swaledale Gdns LGB/HTN NE7 47 H7
MLFD/PNYW SR4 97 K1 3
The Swallows WLSD/HOW NE28 49 G3
Swallow Tail Ct
HAR/WTLS NE34 61 F7 1
Swallow Tail Dr DUN/TMV NE11 9 M9
Swalwell Bank WICK/BNPF NE16 66 E3
Swan Av WLSD/HOW NE28 49 F7 3
Swan Dr GATE NE8 9 K6
Swan Rd BYK/HTN/WLK NE6 58 D7
PLEE/EAS SR8 136 A5
WASHS NE38 95 H3
Swan St GATE NE8 11 G1 1
STLY/ANP DH9 101 G2
SWCK/CAS SR5 86 C4
Swanton Cl WD/WHPE/BLK NE5 45 F6
Swards Rd FELL NE10 70 A5
Swarland Av LGB/HTN NE7 47 H5
Swarland Rd MONK NE25 30 A6
Swarth Cl WASHN NE37 82 C7
Sweetbriar Wy BLYTH NE24 24 E3
Sweethope Av BLYTH NE24 21 F6 3
Swiftden Dr MLFD/PNYW SR4 96 E2
Swinbourne Gdns WBAY NE26 40 D3
Swinbourne Ter JRW NE32 71 K1
Swinburne Pl GATE NE8 10 F1 2
Swinburne St GATE NE8 10 F1
JRW NE32 60 C5
Swinburn Rd MONK NE25 30 A6
Swindale Dr LGB/KIL NE12 37 J6
Swindon Rd SUNDSW SR3 97 H3
Swindon Sq SUNDSW SR3 97 J3 3
Swindon St HEBB NE31 59 F5
Swindon Ter
BYK/HTN/WLK NE6 57 H2 2
Swing Br CNUT NE1 5 L8
Swinhoe Gdns DIN/WO NE13 36 B2
Swinhope WASHS NE38 94 C6
Swinley Gdns
BW/LEM/TK/HW NE15 54 D5
Swinside Dr DHAM DH1 125 K5
The Swirle CNUT NE1 6 B7 1
Sycamore Av BLYTH NE24 21 F5
DIN/WO NE13 35 G2
HAR/WTLS NE34 61 K7
MONK NE25 40 D5
PONT/DH NE20 33 F5
Sycamore Cl JES NE2 57 F1 5
Sycamore Dr SWCK/CAS SR5 86 B2
Sycamore Gv FELL NE10 12 E8
LWF/SPW/WRK NE9 82 B4
Sycamore Rd BLAY NE21 66 A2
CLDN/WHIT/ROK SR6 75 F3
CLSW/PEL DH2 114 A5
The Sycamores
ASHBK/HED/RY SR2 98 E3
WICK/BNPF NE16 90 A1
Sycamore St
BW/LEM/TK/HW NE15 43 F7
WLSD/HOW NE28 58 E2 2
Sydenham Ter MLFD/PNYW SR4 98 A1
SSH NE33 3 K7
Sydney Gdns HAR/WTLS NE34 72 D1
Sydney Gv WLSD/HOW NE28 48 C5
Sydney St HLS DH4 107 G5
STLY/ANP DH9 92 A7
Syke Rd WICK/BNPF NE16 77 H7
Sylvia Ter STLY/ANP DH9 90 D6
Symington Gdns
SUNDSW SR3 97 K6 4
Syon St TYNE/NSHE NE30 51 H2
Syron WICK/BNPF NE16 66 D6
Syston Cl HLS DH4 116 D1

T

Taberna Cl
BW/LEM/TK/HW NE15 52 A1
Tadcaster Rd SUNDSW SR3 97 G5
Tadema Rd SSH NE33 61 K1
Talbot Cl WASHS NE38 95 F2
Talbot Gn WD/WHPE/BLK NE5 54 D3
Talbot Pl SEA/MUR SR7 120 E1
Talbot Rd CLDN/WHIT/ROK SR6 86 E2
HAR/WTLS NE34 61 G5
Talgarth WASHS NE38 95 K1
Talley Ct WASHS NE38 94 E1
Tamar Cl NSHW NE29 50 A2
PLEE/EAS SR8 136 D5
Tamar St HLH DH5 128 B1
Tamerton Dr CLS/BIR/GTL DH3 93 K4
Tamerton St MLFD/PNYW SR4 85 K7 2
Tamworth Rd ELS/FEN NE4 4 C5
Tamworth Sq SUNDSW SR3 97 G5 1
Tanfield Gdns HAR/WTLS NE34 62 B5
Tanfield Pl LWF/SPW/WRK NE9 81 J3
Tanfield Rd
BW/LEM/TK/HW NE15 54 E5
LWF/SPW/WRK NE9 81 J3
SUNDSW SR3 97 H5
Tanfield St MLFD/PNYW SR4 85 J6 6
Tangmere Cl CRAM NE23 28 D1
Tankerville Pl JES NE2 56 E2 4
Tankerville Ter JES NE2 56 E3
Tanmeads CLSW/PEL DH2 114 A4
Tanners' Bank TYNE/NSHE NE30 51 G4
Tantobie Rd
BW/LEM/TK/HW NE15 54 E5
Tarlton Crs FELL NE10 12 B8
Tarn Cl PLEE/EAS SR8 137 F4 3
Tarn Dr ASHBK/HED/RY SR2 99 F6
Tarragon Wy HAR/WTLS NE34 73 H1
Tarrington Cl
WLSD/HOW NE28 49 H5 3
Tarset Rd MONK NE25 39 K4
Tarset St CNUT NE1 6 C6
Tasmania Rd HAR/WTLS NE34 72 D1
Tasman Rd SUNDSW SR3 97 G6
Tate St BLYTH NE24 21 H6 9
Tatham St SUND SR1 15 G5
Tatham Street Back SUND SR1 15 G5
Tattershall ASHBK/HED/RY SR2 98 B2
Taunton Av JRW NE32 60 C6
NSHW NE29 50 B2 4
Taunton Cl WLSD/HOW NE28 49 H5
Taunton Pl CRAM NE23 23 H7
Taunton Rd SUNDSW SR3 97 H5
Tavistock Ct HLS DH4 108 A4 4
Tavistock Pl JRW NE32 60 B6
SUND SR1 14 F5
Tavistock Rd JES NE2 56 E1
Tavistock Sq SUNDSW SR3 98 A6
Taylor Av BDN/LAN/SAC DH7 123 G6
DIN/WO NE13 36 C3
ROWG NE39 77 H4
Taylor Gdns WBAY NE26 31 G2
Taylor St BLYTH NE24 20 C6
SSH NE33 61 F4
STLY/ANP DH9 101 G2
Taynton Gv CRAM NE23 29 G6 3
Tay Rd SUNDSW SR3 97 G4
Tay St HLH DH5 128 B1
Teal Av BLYTH NE24 25 H3
Teal Cl WASHS NE38 94 B3
Team St GATE NE8 9 L5
Teasdale St
ASHBK/HED/RY SR2 15 J8 2
Tebay Dr WD/WHPE/BLK NE5 54 D3
Teddington Cl DIN/WO NE13 45 F3
Teddington Sq SUNDSW SR3 97 G4 2
Tedham Rd
BW/LEM/TK/HW NE15 54 A4
Tees Cl PLEE/EAS SR8 136 D6
Tees Ct HAR/WTLS NE34 61 G5
Tees Crs STLY/ANP DH9 102 D2
Teesdale Av HLS DH4 95 J6
Teesdale Gdns LGB/HTN NE7 47 H7
Teesdale Gv LGB/KIL NE12 47 K2 3
Teesdale Pl BLYTH NE24 20 B6
Tees Rd HEBB NE31 71 G1
Tees St HLH DH5 128 C1 3
PLEE/EAS SR8 137 H3
SEA/MUR SR7 111 K7
Teign Cl PLEE/EAS SR8 136 D5
Teindland Cl ELS/FEN NE4 55 J7
Tel-el-kebir Rd
ASHBK/HED/RY SR2 98 E2
Telford Cl DHAM DH1 135 J6
SMOOR NE27 38 E4
Telford Ct WLSD/HOW NE28 60 A1
Telford Rd SUNDSW SR3 97 H4
Telford St GATE NE8 10 D9
WLSD/HOW NE28 60 A1
Temperance Ter
BDN/LAN/SAC DH7 122 E7
Tempest Rd SEA/MUR SR7 120 E1
Tempest St BLAY NE21 53 J7 2
SUNDSW SR3 98 A7 6
Temple Gn GATE NE8 10 B7
HAR/WTLS NE34 61 J6
Temple Park Rd HAR/WTLS NE34 61 H5
Temple St CNUT NE1 5 H8
FELL NE10 12 D5
SSH NE33 61 F4
Temple St West SSH NE33 61 F3 3
Temple Town SSH NE33 61 F3
Tenbury Crs LGB/KIL NE12 47 J3
NSHW NE29 50 C1
Tenby Rd SUNDSW SR3 97 G6 2
Tenby Sq CRAM NE23 23 J7 4
Ten Flds HLH DH5 117 J5
Tennant St HAR/WTLS NE34 60 E7
Tennyson Av BOLCOL NE35 73 F4
HEBB NE31 59 H5 1
Tennyson Crs
WICK/BNPF NE16 66 E4 6
Tennyson Rd CLSW/PEL DH2 104 E4
PLEE/EAS SR8 130 E5 2
Tennyson St SWCK/CAS SR5 86 A3 8
Tennyson Ter NSHW NE29 2 E4 2
Tenter Ter DHAM DH1 16 C3
Tenth Av BLYTH NE24 25 F2
BYK/HTN/WLK NE6 7 G1
DUN/TMV NE11 80 D3
Tenth Av West DUN/TMV NE11 80 C3
Tenth St PLEE/EAS SR8 137 H3
Tern Cl BLYTH NE24 25 H3
Terrace Pl CNUT NE1 5 H5
Terrier Cl BDLGTN NE22 19 J5
Territorial La DHAM DH1 16 E4
Tetford Pl LGB/KIL NE12 47 J3
Teviot WASHS NE38 94 C5
Teviotdale Gdns LGB/HTN NE7 47 H7
Teviot St GATE NE8 11 K7
HLH DH5 128 B1 1
Teviot Wy JRW NE32 59 J6 3
Tewkesbury LGB/KIL NE12 37 K5 10
Tewkesbury Rd
BW/LEM/TK/HW NE15 54 A4
Thackeray Rd SUNDSW SR3 97 H4
Thames Av JRW NE32 72 A1
Thames Crs HLS DH4 107 J7
STLY/ANP DH9 102 D3
Thames Gdns
WLSD/HOW NE28 58 D2 11
Thames Rd HEBB NE31 59 H7
PLEE/EAS SR8 136 D5
SUNDSW SR3 97 G6 3
Thames St GATE NE8 11 K7
HLH DH5 128 B1
Thanet Rd SUNDSW SR3 97 H5
Tharsis Rd HEBB NE31 59 F6
Thatcher Cl WICK/BNPF NE16 66 E7
Thelma St MLFD/PNYW SR4 14 A6
Theme Rd SUNDSW SR3 97 G6
Theresa St BLAY NE21 66 A1
The Sands DHAM DH1 16 E1
Third Av BLYTH NE24 25 F1
BYK/HTN/WLK NE6 7 G2
CLSW/PEL DH2 93 H7
DUN/TMV NE11 68 C7
NSHW NE29 49 K5
Third St PLEE/EAS SR8 137 H3
Thirkeld Pl HLS DH4 95 K7 3
Thirlington Cl
WD/WHPE/BLK NE5 45 F7
Thirlmere CLDN/WHIT/ROK SR6 74 A3
CLS/BIR/GTL DH3 94 A4
FELL NE10 13 J7
Thirlmere Av CLSW/PEL DH2 105 H6
HLH DH5 128 B1
TYNE/NSHE NE30 40 E7
Thirlmere Cl LGB/KIL NE12 38 B6
Thirlmere Ct HEBB NE31 59 H7 3
Thirlmere Crs BLAY NE21 65 K4 3
HLS DH4 107 K1
Thirlmere Rd PLEE/EAS SR8 137 F3
Thirlmere Wy BLYTH NE24 20 C5
WD/WHPE/BLK NE5 55 F2
Thirlmoor WASHN NE37 82 C7
Thirlwell Gv JRW NE32 71 J1
Thirlwell Rd GATE NE8 6 C9
Thirsk Rd SUNDSW SR3 97 H4 3
Thirston Dr CRAM NE23 28 D2
Thirston Pl NSHW NE29 50 B3 4
Thirston Wy GOS/KPK NE3 45 H5 8
Thistle Av RYTON NE40 52 C7
Thistlecroft HLH DH5 117 H1
Thistledon Av WICK/BNPF NE16 66 D7
Thistle Rd BDN/LAN/SAC DH7 134 A6
SUNDSW SR3 97 G5
Thistley Cl BYK/HTN/WLK NE6 58 A3 1
Thomas Hawksley Pk
SUNDSW SR3 98 A3
Thomas St ASHBK/HED/RY SR2 111 F1
LWF/SPW/WRK NE9 81 K4
PLEE/EAS SR8 131 F4
SSH NE33 3 H7
STLY/ANP DH9 103 H4
WICK/BNPF NE16 66 E5 11
Thomas St North
CLDN/WHIT/ROK SR6 14 E1
Thomas St South
ASHBK/HED/RY SR2 111 F1
SWCK/CAS SR5 86 A4
Thompson Av LGB/KIL NE12 37 J5 12
Thompson Crs SWCK/CAS SR5 85 F4 9
Thompson Gdns
WLSD/HOW NE28 58 D1 7
Thompson Pl FELL NE10 12 C7
Thompson Rd SWCK/CAS SR5 86 C3
Thompson St BLYTH NE24 21 G6 11
BLYTH NE24 21 F6 4
BLYTH NE24 21 G5 2
HAR/WTLS NE34 61 F6 6
PLEE/EAS SR8 137 H2
Thorburn St
CLDN/WHIT/ROK SR6 86 D1 7
Thornbank Cl SUNDSW SR3 110 A3 5
Thornbridge WASHS NE38 95 J1
Thornbury Av CRAM NE23 29 G6
Thornbury Cl BOLCOL NE35 72 C3 5
DIN/WO NE13 45 F4
Thornbury Dr MONK NE25 40 A3
Thornbury St MLFD/PNYW SR4 86 A6
Thorncliffe Pl NSHW NE29 2 A2 1
NSHW NE29 50 C5 3
Thorn Cl DIN/WO NE13 36 A4 3
Thorndale Pl BLYTH NE24 20 C6 5
Thorndale Rd
BW/LEM/TK/HW NE15 54 D6
DHAM DH1 126 A6
SUNDSW SR3 97 G5
Thorne Av FELL NE10 13 M8
Thorne Brake FELL NE10 70 C5 1
Thorne Rd SUNDSW SR3 97 G5 2
Thornes Cl PLEE/EAS SR8 137 G5 2
Thorne Sq SUNDSW SR3 97 G5
Thorne Ter BYK/HTN/WLK NE6 7 M3
Thorneyburn Cl HLS DH4 108 A5 4
Thorneyburn Wy BLYTH NE24 20 E7 2
Thorney Close Rd SUNDSW SR3 97 H5
Thorneyford Pl
PONT/DH NE20 33 G2 1
Thorneyholme Ter
STLY/ANP DH9 102 C1
Thornfield Gv
ASHBK/HED/RY SR2 98 E4 1
Thornfield Pl ROWG NE39 77 G2 4
Thornfield Rd GOS/KPK NE3 46 B6 4
Thorngill WASHN NE37 82 D7
Thornhaugh Av
WICK/BNPF NE16 66 D6 1
Thornhill Cl MONK NE25 30 A6
Thornhill Gdns
ASHBK/HED/RY SR2 14 C9
Thornhill Pk ASHBK/HED/RY SR2 14 C8
PONT/DH NE20 33 G2 2
Thornhill Rd LGB/KIL NE12 47 K4
PONT/DH NE20 33 G2
Thornhill St HLS DH4 108 B7
Thornhill Ter
ASHBK/HED/RY SR2 14 C7
Thornholme Av HAR/WTLS NE34 62 B5
Thornholme Rd
ASHBK/HED/RY SR2 14 B9
Thornhope Cl WASHS NE38 83 H7 1
Thornlea Gdns
LWF/SPW/WRK NE9 69 F6
Thornleigh Gdns
CLDN/WHIT/ROK SR6 74 A2
Thornleigh Rd JES NE2 56 E2 5
Thornley Av CRAM NE23 28 D2
FELL NE10 70 D6 6
Thornley Cl BDN/LAN/SAC DH7 133 G1
WICK/BNPF NE16 78 E1
Thornley La BLAY NE21 65 J6
ROWG NE39 77 J1
Thornley Rd WD/WHPE/BLK NE5 54 C2
Thornley Vw ROWG NE39 77 H3
Thornton Cl HLS DH4 95 J7
Thornton Ct WASHS NE38 94 E1
Thornton Crs BLAY NE21 66 A1
Thornton La CLSW/PEL DH2 92 D7
Thornton St CNUT NE1 5 H8
Thorntree Av DIN/WO NE13 27 G7
Thorn Tree Dr BDLGTN NE22 19 F4
Thorntree Dr
BW/LEM/TK/HW NE15 54 E4
MONK NE25 39 K5
Thorntree Ter STLY/ANP DH9 91 F7
Thorntree Wy BLYTH NE24 20 B7
Thornwood Gdns
DUN/TMV NE11 68 B7
Thorp Cl BLYTH NE24 24 D2 1
Thorpe Cl ELS/FEN NE4 4 D5
Thorpe Dr RYTON NE40 53 F6
Thorpeness Rd SUNDSW SR3 97 G5 3
Thorpe Rd PLEE/EAS SR8 130 C6 4
Thorpe St PLEE/EAS SR8 131 F4
PLEE/EAS SR8 137 H3 6
Threap Gdns WLSD/HOW NE28 49 G6
Three Rivers Ct BOL NE36 72 E5 3
Threlkeld Gv
CLDN/WHIT/ROK SR6 74 C7 3
Thrift St NSHW NE29 2 C4 2
Thristley Gdns
ASHBK/HED/RY SR2 98 C3
Throckley Wy HAR/WTLS NE34 61 F5
Thropton Av BLYTH NE24 24 E2 3
LGB/HTN NE7 47 H5
Thropton Cl DHAM DH1 135 J5 2
FELL NE10 70 E5
Thropton Ct BLYTH NE24 24 E1 3
Thropton Crs GOS/KPK NE3 46 B4
Thropton Pl NSHW NE29 50 B3
Thropton Ter LGB/HTN NE7 57 H1
Thrush Gv SWCK/CAS SR5 85 G4 7
Thursby Av TYNE/NSHE NE30 41 F7
Thurso Cl SUNDSW SR3 97 F5 1
Tiberius Cl WLSD/HOW NE28 58 D2
Tilbeck Sq SUNDSW SR3 110 A1 11
Tilbury Cl HLS DH4 108 A2
Tilbury Gdns SUNDSW SR3 97 G6 4
Tilbury Gv MONK NE25 40 E6
Tilbury Rd SUNDSW SR3 97 G6
Tileshed La BOL NE36 73 G3
Till Av BLAY NE21 65 K2
Tilley Rd WASHS NE38 94 B1
Tillmouth Av MONK NE25 30 A6
Tillmouth Gdns ELS/FEN NE4 55 G5
Tillmouth Park Rd
BW/LEM/TK/HW NE15 53 F2
Till St BYK/HTN/WLK NE6 7 H8 1
Tilson Wy GOS/KPK NE3 45 K4 6
Timber Beach Rd SWCK/CAS SR5 85 H4
Timber Rd PLEE/EAS SR8 137 H1
Timlin Gdns WLSD/HOW NE28 49 K7
Tindal Cl ELS/FEN NE4 4 E6
Tindale Av CRAM NE23 28 D2
Tindale Dr WICK/BNPF NE16 66 E6
Tindal St ELS/FEN NE4 4 F7
Tintagel Cl CRAM NE23 23 H7
SUNDSW SR3 97 F5 2
Tintagel Dr SEA/MUR SR7 111 J7
Tintern WASHS NE38 94 E3
Tintern Cl HLS DH4 108 A5
Tintern Crs BYK/HTN/WLK NE6 6 F2
NSHW NE29 50 B2
Tintern St MLFD/PNYW SR4 14 A5 3
Tiree Cl BDN/LAN/SAC DH7 133 H5
Tiree Ct SUNDSW SR3 110 A1 12
Tirril Pl WD/WHPE/BLK NE5 54 E2
Titan Rd BYK/HTN/WLK NE6 58 C5
Titchfield Rd WASHS NE38 94 E2
Titian Av HAR/WTLS NE34 73 G2
Titlington Gv HEBB NE31 71 F1
Tiverton Av ELS/FEN NE4 55 J6
NSHW NE29 50 A2
Tiverton Cl WLSD/HOW NE28 49 H5
Tiverton Gdns
LWF/SPW/WRK NE9 81 F2
Tiverton Pl CRAM NE23 23 H7
Tiverton Sq SUNDSW SR3 97 G5
Toberty Gdns FELL NE10 13 L8
Toft Crs SEA/MUR SR7 119 H5
Togstone Pl
WD/WHPE/BLK NE5 55 G2 7
Toll Bar Rd ASHBK/HED/RY SR2 98 D5
Toll Bridge Rd BLAY NE21 66 D1
Tollerton Dr SWCK/CAS SR5 84 D4
Tollgate Flds HLS DH4 116 C7 2
Tollgate Rd ROWG NE39 88 B1
Toll House Rd DHAM DH1 124 A7
Tolls Cl MONK NE25 40 A4
Toll Sq TYNE/NSHE NE30 3 G1
Tomlea Av BDLGTN NE22 19 K5
Tonbridge Av NSHW NE29 50 C5
Toner Av HEBB NE31 71 F1
Topaz St SEA/MUR SR7 120 B1
Topcliff CLDN/WHIT/ROK SR6 15 H1
Torcross Wy CRAM NE23 23 H7
Toronto Rd SUNDSW SR3 97 H4
Toronto Sq SUNDSW SR3 97 H4
Torquay Gdns
LWF/SPW/WRK NE9 81 F2
Torquay Rd SUNDSW SR3 97 H4
Torrens Rd SUNDSW SR3 97 H4
Torrington Cl HLS DH4 108 A3 6
Torver Cl DIN/WO NE13 36 A4
Torver Crs CLDN/WHIT/ROK SR6 74 C7
Torver Pl LWF/SPW/WRK NE9 81 H1
Torver Wy TYNE/NSHE NE30 40 D7
Tosson Pl NSHW NE29 50 B5 3
Tosson Ter BYK/HTN/WLK NE6 57 J2 3
Totnes Dr CRAM NE23 23 H7
Toward Rd ASHBK/HED/RY SR2 15 G9
SUND SR1 14 F5
Toward St BYK/HTN/WLK NE6 6 E4 1
Tower Bank BDN/LAN/SAC DH7 101 G7
Tower Gdns RYTON NE40 52 E6
Tower Pl ASHBK/HED/RY SR2 15 H8 3
Tower Rd BDN/LAN/SAC DH7 101 J7
STLY/ANP DH9 101 G5
WASHN NE37 83 G6
Towers Av JES NE2 46 E7
Towers Cl BDLGTN NE22 19 G6
Towers Pl HAR/WTLS NE34 60 C6
Tower St ASHBK/HED/RY SR2 15 J8
CNUT NE1 5 M7
PLEE/EAS SR8 131 G4
Tower St West
ASHBK/HED/RY SR2 15 H9
The Towne Ga
BW/LEM/TK/HW NE15 52 A1
Townend Ct HAR/WTLS NE34 61 G6
Townfield Gdns
BW/LEM/TK/HW NE15 53 H3
Townley Flds ROWG NE39 77 H3
Townley Rd ROWG NE39 77 F3 4
Townsend Rd SUNDSW SR3 97 G6
Townsville Av MONK NE25 40 B6
Towton LGB/KIL NE12 37 K5 11
Toynbee WASHS NE38 95 J1
Tracey Av BOL NE36 73 F4
Trafalgar Rd WASHN NE37 83 H4 2
Trafalgar St CNUT NE1 5 M6 1
Trafford LWF/SPW/WRK NE9 81 G3
Trafford Rd SWCK/CAS SR5 86 A4
Trafford Wk
WD/WHPE/BLK NE5 44 C7 3
Trajan Av SSH NE33 3 J4
Tranwell Cl GOS/KPK NE3 45 K2 3
Tranwell Dr MONK NE25 30 B6
Treby St MLFD/PNYW SR4 86 A6
Tredegar Cl
WD/WHPE/BLK NE5 45 F6 13
Treecone Cl SUNDSW SR3 110 A2
Treen Crs SEA/MUR SR7 119 J5 1
Trefoil Rd STLY/ANP DH9 90 B6
Tregoney Av SEA/MUR SR7 119 J5
Treherne Rd JES NE2 46 D7 3
Trent Av HEBB NE31 71 G1
Trent Dr JRW NE32 72 A2
Trent Gdns GATE NE8 11 M7
Trentham Av LGB/HTN NE7 47 H5
Trenton Av WASHS NE38 83 F7 1
Trent Rd SUNDSW SR3 97 G5
Trent St HLH DH5 128 B1
Trevarren Dr
ASHBK/HED/RY SR2 99 F6
Trevelyan Av BDLGTN NE22 19 H5
BLYTH NE24 24 E1
Trevelyan Cl SUNDSW SR3 97 F5 3
Trevelyan Dr
WD/WHPE/BLK NE5 44 E7
Trevethick St GATE NE8 10 C8
Trevone Pl CRAM NE23 29 H6
Trevone Sq SEA/MUR SR7 119 J5

Trevor Gv *CLDN/WHIT/ROK* SR6 74 A4
Trevor Ter *TYNE/NSHE* NE30 50 E3
Trewhitt Rd
BYK/HTN/WLK NE6 57 J3 5
Tribune Pl *LWF/SPW/WRK* NE9 69 H6
Trident Rd *SUNDSW* SR3 98 A7
Trimdon St *MLFD/PNYW* SR4 14 B3
Trimdon St West
MLFD/PNYW SR4 14 A3
Trinity Ctyd *BYK/HTN/WLK* NE6 7 J9 1
Trinity Gv *CRAM* NE23 29 H6
Trinity Pk *HLS* DH4 107 K2
Trinity Pl *NSHW* NE29 2 D4 1
Trinity St *NSHW* NE29 2 D4
SWCK/CAS SR5 85 K3
Trinity Wk *SSH* NE33 61 F2
Trojan Av *BYK/HTN/WLK* NE6 7 L2
Tromso Cl *NSHW* NE29 49 K5
Trool Ct *SUNDSW* SR3 110 A2
Troon Cl *WASHN* NE37 82 E3 8
Trotter Gv *BDLGTN* NE22 19 J5 3
Trotter Ter *ASHBK/HED/RY* SR2 111 F1
Troutbeck Av
BYK/HTN/WLK NE6 58 B6 3
Troutbeck Rd
CLDN/WHIT/ROK SR6 74 C7 7
Troutbeck Wy *HAR/WTLS* NE34 72 D1
PLEE/EAS SR8 137 F3 4
Troutdale Pl *LGB/KIL* NE12 47 F4 4
Trout's La *DHAM* DH1 123 J2
Trowbridge Wy *GOS/KPK* NE3 45 K5
Truro Av *SEA/MUR* SR7 119 J4
Truro Gv *NSHW* NE29 50 B2
Truro Rd *SUNDSW* SR3 97 H5 1
Tuart St *CLS/BIR/GTL* DH3 105 J4
Tudor Av *NSHW* NE29 50 C4
Tudor Ct *PONT/DH* NE20 32 E5
Tudor Dr *STLY/ANP* DH9 90 B3 1
Tudor Gra *PLEE/EAS* SR8 130 B6
Tudor Gv *SUNDSW* SR3 97 K3
Tudor Rd *CLS/BIR/GTL* DH3 105 K2
SSH NE33 2 F9
Tudor Wy *GOS/KPK* NE3 45 G4
WD/WHPE/BLK NE5 45 F5
Tudor Wynd *BYK/HTN/WLK* NE6 57 K2
Tulip St *GATE* NE8 12 A6
Tumulus Av *BYK/HTN/WLK* NE6 58 C3
Tunbridge Rd *SUNDSW* SR3 97 H4
Tundry Wy *BLAY* NE21 54 D7
Tuneside *FELL* NE10 13 L9
Tunis Rd *SUNDSW* SR3 97 J4 8
Tunstall Av *BYK/HTN/WLK* NE6 7 J4
HAR/WTLS NE34 62 B5
Tunstall Bank *SUNDSW* SR3 98 C7
Tunstall Hill Cl
ASHBK/HED/RY SR2 98 C4 7
Tunstall Pk *ASHBK/HED/RY* SR2 98 C2
Tunstall Rd *ASHBK/HED/RY* SR2 14 D6
SUNDSW SR3 98 B5
Tunstall Ter *ASHBK/HED/RY* SR2 14 D6
Tunstall Ter West
ASHBK/HED/RY SR2 14 C6
Tunstall V *ASHBK/HED/RY* SR2 14 D9
Tunstall Vw *SUNDSW* SR3 98 B6
Tunstall Village Gn *SUNDSW* SR3 98 B7
Tunstall Village Rd *SUNDSW* SR3 98 B7
Tunstall Vls *SUNDSW* SR3 98 B7 4
Turbinia Gdns *LGB/HTN* NE7 57 J1
Turnberry *CLSW/PEL* DH2 93 F4
MONK NE25 40 A4
SSH NE33 61 J2 6
Turnberry Cl *WASHN* NE37 82 E3 9
Turnberry Wy *GOS/KPK* NE3 46 E4 1
Turnbull St *SUND* SR1 15 J2
Turner Av *HAR/WTLS* NE34 73 H1
Turner Cl *RYTON* NE40 53 F7
Turner Crs *GOS/KPK* NE3 46 A5 9
Turner St *SMOOR* NE27 49 G1
Turnham Rd *SUNDSW* SR3 97 G5
Turnstone Dr *WASHS* NE38 94 B3
Turret Rd *BW/LEM/TK/HW* NE15 54 D4
Tuscan Cl *BDN/LAN/SAC* DH7 132 D3
Tuscan Rd *SUNDSW* SR3 97 G5
Tweed Cl *ASHBK/HED/RY* SR2 99 F6
CLSW/PEL DH2 93 F6
PLEE/EAS SR8 136 D5
Tweed Gv *BW/LEM/TK/HW* NE15 54 A4
Tweed St *ELS/FEN* NE4 4 B7
HEBB NE31 59 F5
HLH DH5 128 B1 2
JRW NE32 59 J6
WASHS NE38 95 G2
Tweed Ter *STLY/ANP* DH9 102 D2
Tweedy St *BLYTH* NE24 20 C6 6
Tweedy Ter
BYK/HTN/WLK NE6 58 B6 4
Twelfth Av *BLYTH* NE24 25 F1
CLSW/PEL DH2 105 H3
Twelfth St *PLEE/EAS* SR8 137 G3
Twentieth Av *BLYTH* NE24 25 F2 5
Twentyfifth Av *BLYTH* NE24 25 F2 6
Twentysecond Av
BLYTH NE24 24 E2 6
Twentysixth Av *BLYTH* NE24 24 E2
Twentythird Av *BLYTH* NE24 24 E2
Twickenham Ct *CRAM* NE23 29 G6
Twickenham Rd *SUNDSW* SR3 97 G4
Twizell La *STLY/ANP* DH9 103 J2
Twizell Pl *PONT/DH* NE20 33 G2
Twizell St *BLYTH* NE24 25 H1 3
Twyford Cl *CRAM* NE23 23 H7
Tyldesley Sq *SUNDSW* SR3 97 G5 4
Tyne Ap *JRW* NE32 59 J3
Tynebank *BLAY* NE21 65 K2
Tyne Br *CNUT* NE1 5 M8
Tynedale Av *WBAY* NE26 40 D3
WLSD/HOW NE28 48 D6
Tynedale Crs *HLS* DH4 95 K7
Tynedale Dr *BLYTH* NE24 20 C7
Tynedale Rd *HAR/WTLS* NE34 61 J3
Tynedale St *HLH* DH5 117 H7
Tynedale Ter *LGB/KIL* NE12 47 K4 7
Tyne Gdns *WASHN* NE37 83 F4
Tyne Main Rd *FELL* NE10 12 A2
Tynemouth Gv
BYK/HTN/WLK NE6 7 G3
JRW NE32 71 J2
TYNE/NSHE NE30 51 G4
WLSD/HOW NE28 49 K7 4
Tynemouth Sq *SUNDSW* SR3 97 H5 2
Tynemouth Ter
TYNE/NSHE NE30 51 H3 5
Tyne Rd *STLY/ANP* DH9 102 C2
Tyne Rd East *GATE* NE8 10 B3
STLY/ANP DH9 102 C2
Tyneside Rd *ELS/FEN* NE4 9 M1
Tyne St *BLAY* NE21 54 A7
CNUT NE1 6 C7
FELL NE10 12 F3
HLH DH5 128 B1
JRW NE32 59 K3
SEA/MUR SR7 120 E1 12
TYNE/NSHE NE30 2 F2
Tyne Ter *HAR/WTLS* NE34 61 F6
Tynevale Av *BLAY* NE21 65 K3
Tyne Vw *BW/LEM/TK/HW* NE15 54 A5
HEBB NE31 58 E5
Tyne View Av *WICK/BNPF* NE16 8 A7
Tyne View Pl *GATE* NE8 9 M5
Tyne View Ter *WLSD/HOW* NE28 59 K2
Tyne-Wear Trail *DUN/TMV* NE11 8 D4
WICK/BNPF NE16 67 H7
Tyzack St *BDN/LAN/SAC* DH7 113 F1

U

Ugly La *CLSW/PEL* DH2 114 A4
Uldale Ct *GOS/KPK* NE3 45 J3 8
Ullerdale Cl *DHAM* DH1 126 B5
Ullswater Av *HLH* DH5 128 B1
JRW NE32 72 B1
Ullswater Cl *BLYTH* NE24 20 A6
Ullswater Crs *BLAY* NE21 65 K4 6
Ullswater Dr *LGB/KIL* NE12 38 B6
Ullswater Gdns *HAR/WTLS* NE34 61 H4
Ullswater Gv *SWCK/CAS* SR5 86 C1 4
Ullswater Rd *CLSW/PEL* DH2 105 H6
Ullswater Wy
WD/WHPE/BLK NE5 55 F2
Ulverstone Ter
BYK/HTN/WLK NE6 7 M3
Ulverston Gdns
LWF/SPW/WRK NE9 81 H2
Underhill Rd
CLDN/WHIT/ROK SR6 73 K4
Underwood Gv *CRAM* NE23 23 G6
Union Aly *SSH* NE33 3 G7
Union Hall Rd
BW/LEM/TK/HW NE15 54 A3
Union La *CLSW/PEL* DH2 114 C1
SUND SR1 15 H3 2
Union Quay *TYNE/NSHE* NE30 3 G2
Union Rd *BYK/HTN/WLK* NE6 7 H4
TYNE/NSHE NE30 3 H1
Union St *BLYTH* NE24 21 G6
HLH DH5 117 K4
JES NE2 6 B5
JRW NE32 59 K3
MLFD/PNYW SR4 84 E7 6
NSHW NE29 2 E3
SEA/MUR SR7 120 E2 8
SSH NE33 61 F5 3
SUND SR1 14 E4
WLSD/HOW NE28 58 D3
Unity Ter *STLY/ANP* DH9 89 K4
STLY/ANP DH9 89 G7
Uplands *MONK* NE25 40 B4
The Uplands *CLS/BIR/GTL* DH3 93 K1
GOS/KPK NE3 45 K6
Uplands Wy *LWF/SPW/WRK* NE9 82 B4
Upper Camden St
TYNE/NSHE NE30 2 D1
Upper Elsdon St *NSHW* NE29 2 C4 3
Upper Norfolk St
TYNE/NSHE NE30 2 E1 2
Upper Pearson St
TYNE/NSHE NE30 2 E1
Upper Queen St
TYNE/NSHE NE30 2 F1 2
Upton St *GATE* NE8 10 A6 1
Urswick Ct *WD/WHPE/BLK* NE5 45 F5
Urwin St *HLH* DH5 118 A5
Ushaw Rd *HEBB* NE31 59 H5
Usher Av *RDHAMSE* DH6 126 C7
Usher St *SWCK/CAS* SR5 86 B4 9
Usk Av *JRW* NE32 72 A1
Usworth Station Rd
WASHN NE37 83 G5 3

V

Valebrooke Av
ASHBK/HED/RY SR2 14 C9
Valebrooke Gdns
ASHBK/HED/RY SR2 14 D8
Valehead *MONK* NE25 40 B4
Valentia Av *BYK/HTN/WLK* NE6 7 L2
Valeria Cl *WLSD/HOW* NE28 49 F4
Valerian Av
BW/LEM/TK/HW NE15 52 B1
Valeside *BW/LEM/TK/HW* NE15 52 E1
Vale St *HLH* DH5 128 A1
MLFD/PNYW SR4 14 A7 4
Vale St East *MLFD/PNYW* SR4 14 A7 5
Vale Wk *JES* NE2 6 D2
Valley Crs *BLAY* NE21 65 J2
Valley Dr *DUN/TMV* NE11 9 G9
LWF/SPW/WRK NE9 11 J9
WICK/BNPF NE16 66 E4
Valley Forge *WASHS* NE38 83 F7
Valley Gdns *LWF/SPW/WRK* NE9 11 J9
MONK NE25 40 B4
WLSD/HOW NE28 49 F7
Valley La *HAR/WTLS* NE34 62 C5
Valley Rd *CLSW/PEL* DH2 104 E3
MONK NE25 30 C6
Valley Vw *BDN/LAN/SAC* DH7 113 G6
BDN/LAN/SAC DH7 133 G1
BW/LEM/TK/HW NE15 54 A4
CLS/BIR/GTL DH3 81 H6
JES NE2 57 F2
JRW NE32 59 K7
ROWG NE39 77 F3
WASHS NE38 95 G5
WICK/BNPF NE16 77 H6
Vallum Rd
BW/LEM/TK/HW NE15 53 G1
BYK/HTN/WLK NE6 7 M4
Vallum Wy *ELS/FEN* NE4 4 E6
Vanborough Ct *MONK* NE25 30 A6 1
Vancouver Dr *LGB/HTN* NE7 57 K1
Vane St *PLEE/EAS* SR8 131 F5
SUNDSW SR3 98 A7 7
Vane Ter *ASHBK/HED/RY* SR2 15 K7
SEA/MUR SR7 111 K7 2
Van Mildert Cl *PLEE/EAS* SR8 136 C6 1
Vardy Ter *HLS* DH4 96 C7
Vauxhall Rd *BYK/HTN/WLK* NE6 58 C3
Vedra St *SWCK/CAS* SR5 86 B4 10
Velville Ct *WD/WHPE/BLK* NE5 45 F4
Ventnor Av *ELS/FEN* NE4 4 A7
Ventnor Crs *LWF/SPW/WRK* NE9 68 E6
Ventnor Gdns
LWF/SPW/WRK NE9 68 E6
WBAY NE26 40 E3
Vera St *RYTON* NE40 64 B4
Verdun Av *HEBB* NE31 59 G5
Vermont *WASHN* NE37 83 F5
Verne Rd *NSHW* NE29 50 B5
Vernon Cl *SSH* NE33 61 F3
Vernon Dr *MONK* NE25 40 C5
Vernon St *WASHN* NE37 83 F5
Veryan Gdns *SUNDSW* SR3 98 B3
Vespasian Av *SSH* NE33 3 J5
Viador *CLS/BIR/GTL* DH3 105 J3
Viaduct St *WLSD/HOW* NE28 59 G1
Vicarage Cl *CLSW/PEL* DH2 92 E7 1
SUNDSW SR3 97 K7
Vicarage Flats
BDN/LAN/SAC DH7 133 G6 4
Vicarage La *MLFD/PNYW* SR4 84 E7 2
Vicarage Rd *SUNDSW* SR3 98 A7
Vicarage St *NSHW* NE29 2 C3 2
Vicarsholme Cl *SUNDSW* SR3 109 J2
Vicars' La *LGB/HTN* NE7 47 G5
Vicars Wy *LGB/KIL* NE12 47 F4
Viceroy St *SEA/MUR* SR7 120 E1
Victoria Av *ASHBK/HED/RY* SR2 99 F3
BDN/LAN/SAC DH7 133 H6
FELL NE10 12 A8
LGB/KIL NE12 47 K3
MLFD/PNYW SR4 85 F7
WLSD/HOW NE28 58 D1 8
Victoria Av West
ASHBK/HED/RY SR2 98 E4
Victoria Crs *NSHW* NE29 2 B4
Victoria Ms *BLYTH* NE24 25 F1
Victoria Rd *GATE* NE8 10 A7
SSH NE33 61 G2
WASHN NE37 83 F5
Victoria Rd East *HEBB* NE31 59 H5
Victoria Rd West *FELL* NE10 70 E2
HEBB NE31 70 E2
Victoria Sq *JES* NE2 5 L2
Victoria St *DUN/TMV* NE11 9 J6
ELS/FEN NE4 4 F8
HLH DH5 117 K4 5
NSHW NE29 2 D5
RYTON NE40 52 B7 2
SEA/MUR SR7 120 D1
Victoria Ter *JRW* NE32 59 J5
WBAY NE26 41 F4
Victor St *CLS/BIR/GTL* DH3 105 J4
Victory St *MLFD/PNYW* SR4 85 J6
Victory St East *HLH* DH5 118 A4 3
Victory St West *HLH* DH5 118 A4 4
Victory Wy *SUNDSW* SR3 109 G2
Viewforth Dr *SWCK/CAS* SR5 86 C2
Viewforth Rd
ASHBK/HED/RY SR2 111 F2
Viewforth Ter *SWCK/CAS* SR5 86 B2
View La *STLY/ANP* DH9 90 D7
View Pk *MONK* NE25 30 A5
Vigo La *CLS/BIR/GTL* DH3 93 K5
WASHS NE38 94 B6
Village Centre *WASHS* NE38 95 F2 5
Village Ct *WBAY* NE26 40 D4
Village East *RYTON* NE40 52 E5
Village Farm
BW/LEM/TK/HW NE15 53 J2 1
Village La *WASHS* NE38 83 F7
Village Rd *CRAM* NE23 28 D2
The Village *ASHBK/HED/RY* SR2 111 G1
Villa Pl *GATE* NE8 10 E5
Villa Vw *LWF/SPW/WRK* NE9 69 G6 6
Villette Brook St
ASHBK/HED/RY SR2 15 G9 1
Villette Pth *ASHBK/HED/RY* SR2 15 H9
Villette Rd *ASHBK/HED/RY* SR2 98 E2
Villiers St *SUND* SR1 15 G4
Villiers St South *SUND* SR1 15 G5
Vimy Av *HEBB* NE31 59 G5
Vincent St *PLEE/EAS* SR8 131 F5 1
SEA/MUR SR7 120 E2 9
Vine La *CNUT* NE1 5 K4
Vine Pl *HLS* DH4 108 C7
SUND SR1 14 D6
Vine St *SSH* NE33 61 G5
WLSD/HOW NE28 58 E2
Viola Crs *BDN/LAN/SAC* DH7 113 H6
CLSW/PEL DH2 93 F4
Viola St *WASHN* NE37 83 F5
Violet Cl *ELS/FEN* NE4 55 H7 3
Violet St *HLS* DH4 108 B7
MLFD/PNYW SR4 14 B4
MLFD/PNYW SR4 84 E7
Viscount Rd *SUNDSW* SR3 98 A7 8
Vivian Crs *CLSW/PEL* DH2 105 J5
Vivian Sq
CLDN/WHIT/ROK SR6 86 D2 16
Voltage Ter *HLS* DH4 108 B3 3
Vulcan Pl *BDLGTN* NE22 19 G6

W

Waddington St *DHAM* DH1 16 A3
Wadsley Sq *ASHBK/HED/RY* SR2 98 E3
Wagon Wy *WLSD/HOW* NE28 59 F1
Wagonway Rd *HEBB* NE31 59 F4
Wagtail La *STLY/ANP* DH9 102 E6
Wagtail Ter *STLY/ANP* DH9 103 G5
Wakefield Av *HAR/WTLS* NE34 62 B6
Wakenshaw Rd *DHAM* DH1 17 J1
Walbottle Rd
BW/LEM/TK/HW NE15 53 H2
Walden Cl *CLSW/PEL* DH2 92 D5
Waldo St *NSHW* NE29 2 E3
Waldridge La *CLSW/PEL* DH2 105 G5
Waldridge Rd *CLSW/PEL* DH2 105 H5
Waldron Sq *ASHBK/HED/RY* SR2 98 E3
Walkerburn *CRAM* NE23 28 C5
Walkergate *DHAM* DH1 16 D3
Walker Pl *TYNE/NSHE* NE30 3 G1 1
Walker Rd *BYK/HTN/WLK* NE6 7 L9
Wallace Gdns
LWF/SPW/WRK NE9 82 A1
Wallace St *DUN/TMV* NE11 9 J6 1
HLS DH4 108 B7
JES NE2 4 F2
SWCK/CAS SR5 86 C4
Wallingford Av
ASHBK/HED/RY SR2 98 E4
Wallington Av *DIN/WO* NE13 36 A3
TYNE/NSHE NE30 50 E1
Wallington Cl *BDLGTN* NE22 19 J4
Wallington Ct *MONK* NE25 30 A5 3
Wallington Dr
BW/LEM/TK/HW NE15 54 C3
Wallis St *HLS* DH4 95 K6 2
SSH NE33 3 G7 5
Wallnook La *BDN/LAN/SAC* DH7 122 C2
Wallridge Dr *MONK* NE25 30 B7
Wallsend Rd *NSHW* NE29 50 B6
WLSD/HOW NE28 50 A7
Wall St *GOS/KPK* NE3 46 A5
Wall Ter *BYK/HTN/WLK* NE6 7 L3
Walnut Gdns *GATE* NE8 10 A8
Walnut Pl *GOS/KPK* NE3 45 K7
Walpole Cl *SEA/MUR* SR7 120 A2
Walpole Ct *MLFD/PNYW* SR4 85 K7 8
Walpole St *BYK/HTN/WLK* NE6 7 L1
Walsham Cl *BLYTH* NE24 24 D2
Walsh Av *HEBB* NE31 59 G4
Walsingham *WASHS* NE38 94 E3
Walter St *JRW* NE32 59 K3
Walter Ter *ELS/FEN* NE4 4 D3
HLH DH5 118 A7
Walter Thomas St
SWCK/CAS SR5 85 K3 3
Waltham *WASHS* NE38 95 F2
Waltham Cl *WLSD/HOW* NE28 48 B7 4
Waltham Pl
WD/WHPE/BLK NE5 55 F1 8
Walton Av *BLYTH* NE24 20 E6
NSHW NE29 50 D3
SEA/MUR SR7 120 A2
Walton Cl *STLY/ANP* DH9 102 E2
Walton La *SUND* SR1 15 H3
Walton Pk *NSHW* NE29 50 D2
Walton Rd *WASHS* NE38 95 K1
WD/WHPE/BLK NE5 54 E2
Waltons Ter *BDN/LAN/SAC* DH7 132 E2
Walwick Av *NSHW* NE29 50 B4
Walwick Rd *MONK* NE25 39 K4
Walworth Av *HAR/WTLS* NE34 62 C5
Walworth Gv *JRW* NE32 71 K1
Wandsworth Rd
BYK/HTN/WLK NE6 6 E3
Wanebeck *WASHS* NE38 94 C5
Wanlass Ter *DHAM* DH1 16 E2
Wanley St *BLYTH* NE24 21 G6
Wanlock Cl *CRAM* NE23 28 C5
Wanny Rd *BDLGTN* NE22 19 H5 1
Wansbeck Av *BLYTH* NE24 25 G1
STLY/ANP DH9 102 D2
TYNE/NSHE NE30 41 G6
Wansbeck Cl *CLSW/PEL* DH2 93 F6
WICK/BNPF NE16 78 E2
Wansbeck Gv *MONK* NE25 30 A2 2
Wansbeck Rd *CRAM* NE23 37 F1
JRW NE32 59 J6
Wansbeck Rd North
GOS/KPK NE3 46 A3 4
Wansbeck Rd South
GOS/KPK NE3 46 A4 5
Wansfell Av *WD/WHPE/BLK* NE5 45 H7
Wansford Av
WD/WHPE/BLK NE5 55 F2
Wantage Av *NSHW* NE29 50 B6
Wantage Rd *DHAM* DH1 126 A4
Wantage St *SSH* NE33 61 H4
Wapping St *SSH* NE33 3 G4
Warbeck Cl *WD/WHPE/BLK* NE5 45 F4
Warburton Crs
LWF/SPW/WRK NE9 11 K8
Warcop Ct *GOS/KPK* NE3 45 J3
Warden Law La *SUNDSW* SR3 109 J1
Wardill Gdns
LWF/SPW/WRK NE9 69 H5
Wardle Av *SSH* NE33 61 J2
Wardle Dr *CRAM* NE23 37 H1
Wardle Gdns *FELL* NE10 12 F9
Wardle St *GOS/KPK* NE3 46 E5 8
STLY/ANP DH9 102 C4
Wardley Ct *FELL* NE10 71 F4
Wardley Dr *FELL* NE10 71 F4
Wardley La *FELL* NE10 70 E3
Warenford Cl *CRAM* NE23 28 D4 3
Warenford Pl
WD/WHPE/BLK NE5 55 G4 3
Warenmill Cl
BW/LEM/TK/HW NE15 53 K4
Warennes St *MLFD/PNYW* SR4 85 J6 7
Warenton Pl *NSHW* NE29 49 K1
Waring Av *WBAY* NE26 30 E1
Waring Ter *SEA/MUR* SR7 120 A2
Wark Av *NSHW* NE29 50 A4
SMOOR NE27 39 H5
Wark Crs *JRW* NE32 71 K2
Warkdale Av *BLYTH* NE24 24 C1 2
Warkworth Av *BLYTH* NE24 25 G2
HAR/WTLS NE34 62 B4
WLSD/HOW NE28 48 E6
Warkworth Cl *WASHS* NE38 94 D2
Warkworth Crs *GOS/KPK* NE3 46 B4
SEA/MUR SR7 119 K1
Warkworth Dr *CLSW/PEL* DH2 105 G7
DIN/WO NE13 36 C2
Warkworth Rd *DHAM* DH1 124 D2
Warkworth St
BW/LEM/TK/HW NE15 54 A5
Warkworth Ter *JRW* NE32 71 K1
TYNE/NSHE NE30 51 H2 7
Warnham Av
ASHBK/HED/RY SR2 98 E4
Warnhead Rd *BDLGTN* NE22 19 H5
Warren Av *BYK/HTN/WLK* NE6 58 C3
Warren Cl *HLS* DH4 108 A3 7
Warrenmor *FELL* NE10 13 K9
Warren St *PLEE/EAS* SR8 137 H4
Warrington Rd *ELS/FEN* NE4 4 D8
GOS/KPK NE3 45 J4
Warton Ter
BYK/HTN/WLK NE6 57 J3 8
Warwick Av *WICK/BNPF* NE16 66 E7
Warwick Cl *CRAM* NE23 29 F7 3
WICK/BNPF NE16 66 E7 1
Warwick Ct *DHAM* DH1 134 B3 5
GOS/KPK NE3 45 H3
Warwick Dr *HLH* DH5 117 H2
SUNDSW SR3 97 G7
WASHN NE37 83 F3
WICK/BNPF NE16 67 F7
Warwick Gv *BDLGTN* NE22 18 D5
Warwick Hall Wk *LGB/HTN* NE7 57 K1
Warwick Pl *PLEE/EAS* SR8 136 C2
Warwick Rd *HAR/WTLS* NE34 61 H4
HEBB NE31 71 H1 4
WD/WHPE/BLK NE5 54 C3 8
WLSD/HOW NE28 58 D2
Warwickshire Dr *DHAM* DH1 126 A7 1
Warwick St *BLYTH* NE24 24 D3
GATE NE8 11 G3
JES NE2 6 B3
SWCK/CAS SR5 86 D4
Warwick Ter *SUNDSW* SR3 98 A6
Wasdale Cl *CRAM* NE23 28 C5
PLEE/EAS SR8 137 F4
Wasdale Ct
CLDN/WHIT/ROK SR6 74 C7 8
Wasdale Rd *WD/WHPE/BLK* NE5 55 F3
Washington Hwy *WASHN* NE37 82 C5
WASHS NE38 94 E4
Washington Rd *SWCK/CAS* SR5 84 D2
Washington St
MLFD/PNYW SR4 85 K7 9
Washingwell La
WICK/BNPF NE16 67 H5
Washingwell Pk
WICK/BNPF NE16 67 G6
Waskdale Crs *BLAY* NE21 65 K4 7
Waskerley Cl *WICK/BNPF* NE16 78 E2
Waskerley Rd *WASHS* NE38 95 H1
Watch House Cl *NSHW* NE29 2 C7
Watcombe Cl *WASHN* NE37 83 H3 1
Waterbeach Pl
WD/WHPE/BLK NE5 54 E1
Waterbeck Cl *CRAM* NE23 28 C5
Waterbury Rd *GOS/KPK* NE3 46 B1
Waterfield Rd *BDLGTN* NE22 20 D2
Waterford Cl *HLH* DH5 117 G4 2
WBAY NE26 31 G2 2
Waterford Pk *DIN/WO* NE13 35 K3
Waterloo Pl *NSHW* NE29 50 E4
SUND SR1 14 E5
Waterloo Rd *BLYTH* NE24 21 G7
MONK NE25 39 J4
WASHN NE37 83 G4
Waterloo Sq *SSH* NE33 3 H7 1
Waterloo St *BLAY* NE21 65 J3 9
CNUT NE1 5 H8
Waterlow Cl *SWCK/CAS* SR5 85 K1 3
Watermill *RYTON* NE40 53 F6
Watermill La *FELL* NE10 12 E8
Water Rw *BW/LEM/TK/HW* NE15 53 G4
Waterside Dr *DUN/TMV* NE11 8 E4
Waterson Crs
BDN/LAN/SAC DH7 113 G7
Water St *BDN/LAN/SAC* DH7 113 H5
ELS/FEN NE4 9 L2
Waterville Rd *NSHW* NE29 50 B6
Waterworks Rd *SUND* SR1 14 B5
Watford Cl *SWCK/CAS* SR5 85 K1 4
Watkin Crs *SEA/MUR* SR7 119 H5
Watling Av *SEA/MUR* SR7 120 A2
Watling Pl
LWF/SPW/WRK NE9 69 H6 6
Watling St *HAR/WTLS* NE34 61 F6 7
Watson Av *HAR/WTLS* NE34 62 B6
Watson Cl *SEA/MUR* SR7 120 A2
Watson Gdns
WLSD/HOW NE28 49 J7 1
Watson Pl *HAR/WTLS* NE34 62 B6 5
Watson St *JRW* NE32 60 A3
STLY/ANP DH9 90 D6
WICK/BNPF NE16 77 K7 2
Watt's Rd *WBAY* NE26 40 E3
Watts St *SEA/MUR* SR7 119 H5 6
Watt St *GATE* NE8 10 D9
Wavendon Crs *MLFD/PNYW* SR4 97 H2
Waveney Gdns *STLY/ANP* DH9 102 C3
Waveney Rd *PLEE/EAS* SR8 136 C6
Waverdale Av
BYK/HTN/WLK NE6 58 C4
Waverdale Wy *SSH* NE33 61 F5
Waverley Av *BDLGTN* NE22 19 J4 3
MONK NE25 40 D5
Waverley Cl *BLAY* NE21 65 H4 2
Waverley Crs
BW/LEM/TK/HW NE15 54 B4
Waverley Dr *BDLGTN* NE22 19 J4
Waverley Rd *ELS/FEN* NE4 4 E9
LWF/SPW/WRK NE9 81 G3
Waverley Ter *MLFD/PNYW* SR4 85 J6
Waverton Cl *CRAM* NE23 28 C5
Wawn St *SSH* NE33 61 H3 8
Wayfarer Rd *SWCK/CAS* SR5 86 A4
Wayland Sq *ASHBK/HED/RY* SR2 98 E5
Wayman St *SWCK/CAS* SR5 86 C4
Wayside *ASHBK/HED/RY* SR2 14 A9
BW/LEM/TK/HW NE15 55 F6
Wealcroft *FELL* NE10 70 B7 4
Wear Ct *HAR/WTLS* NE34 61 G6
Weardale Av *BLYTH* NE24 20 B6

BYK/HTN/WLK NE6 58 C4
CLDN/WHIT/ROK SR6 74 E5
LGB/KIL NE12 47 K2
WASHN NE37 82 E5
WLSD/HOW NE28 48 D6 4
Weardale Crs HLS DH4 95 K7
Weardale St HLH DH5 117 H7
Wearfield SWCK/CAS SR5 85 J4
Wear Ldg CLS/BIR/GTL DH3 93 J7
Wearmouth Av
SWCK/CAS SR5 86 D3 6
Wearmouth Br SUND SR1 14 E3
Wearmouth Dr SWCK/CAS SR5 86 C3
Wearmouth St
SWCK/CAS SR5 86 D4 10
Wear Rd HEBB NE31 59 G7
STLY/ANP DH9 102 D2
Wearside Dr DHAM DH1 16 E1
Wear St HLH DH5 117 K5
HLS DH4 116 D1
JRW NE32 59 K4 10
MLFD/PNYW SR4 84 E6
SEA/MUR SR7 120 E1 13
SUND SR1 15 J5
SWCK/CAS SR5 86 A4
Wear Vw DHAM DH1 16 F2
Weathercock La
LWF/SPW/WRK NE9 69 F7 10
Weatherside BLAY NE21 65 K3 6
Webb Av SEA/MUR SR7 119 H4
SEA/MUR SR7 119 K1
Webb Gdns FELL NE10 13 K8
Webb Sq PLEE/EAS SR8 137 F1
Wedgewood Cottages
BW/LEM/TK/HW NE15 54 B5 2
Wedgwood Rd SEA/MUR SR7 119 K2
Wedmore Rd
WD/WHPE/BLK NE5 54 B1
Weetman St SSH NE33 61 F2 2
Weetslade Crs CRAM NE23 37 G2
Weetslade Rd CRAM NE23 37 G2
Weetwood Rd CRAM NE23 28 D4 4
Weidner Rd
BW/LEM/TK/HW NE15 55 H6
Welbeck Rd BYK/HTN/WLK NE6 7 H6
Weldon Av
ASHBK/HED/RY SR2 98 E4 2
Weldon Crs LGB/HTN NE7 57 H1
Weldon Pl NSHW NE29 50 B2
Weldon Rd CRAM NE23 29 F3 1
LGB/KIL NE12 47 H4
Weldon Ter CLS/BIR/GTL DH3 105 K5
Weldon Wy GOS/KPK NE3 46 B4
Welfare Cl PLEE/EAS SR8 131 F5
Welfare Crs RHTLP TS27 137 K7
Welfare Rd HLH DH5 117 K4
Welford Av GOS/KPK NE3 46 A5
Welland Cl PLEE/EAS SR8 136 D6
Welland La CLDN/WHIT/ROK SR6 74 E3
Wellands Cl
CLDN/WHIT/ROK SR6 74 E3
Wellands Ct
CLDN/WHIT/ROK SR6 74 E3
Well Bank Rd WASHN NE37 82 D5
Wellburn Rd WASHN NE37 82 D4
Well Close Wk
WICK/BNPF NE16 66 E6 2
Wellesley St JRW NE32 59 K6
Wellesley Ter ELS/FEN NE4 4 C6
Wellfield Cl
BW/LEM/TK/HW NE15 52 E2
Wellfield Ct RYTON NE40 64 A2
Wellfield La
WD/WHPE/BLK NE5 55 F1 9
Wellfield Rd ELS/FEN NE4 55 H6
ROWG NE39 76 E3
SEA/MUR SR7 119 G5
Wellington Av MONK NE25 39 J4 2
Wellington Dr SSH NE33 3 G5
Wellington La MLFD/PNYW SR4 14 A2
Wellington Rd DUN/TMV NE11 8 D6
Wellington St BLYTH NE24 21 H7 8
ELS/FEN NE4 5 G5
FELL NE10 12 B7
HEBB NE31 59 F6
Well La SMOOR NE27 39 K7
Well Ridge Cl MONK NE25 40 A3
Well Ridge Pk MONK NE25 40 A2
Wells Cl LGB/KIL NE12 47 K6 1
Wells Crs SEA/MUR SR7 120 A1
Wells Gdns LWF/SPW/WRK NE9 81 F3
Wells Gv HAR/WTLS NE34 62 A4
Well St MLFD/PNYW SR4 85 K6
Welsh Ter STLY/ANP DH9 101 J4
Welwyn Av BDLGTN NE22 19 K2
Welwyn Cl SWCK/CAS SR5 84 E5
WLSD/HOW NE28 48 B6
Wembley Av MONK NE25 40 C5
Wembley Rd SWCK/CAS SR5 85 K2
Wendover Cl SWCK/CAS SR5 85 J1
Wendover Wy SWCK/CAS SR5 85 J1
Wenham Sq
ASHBK/HED/RY SR2 98 B2 4
Wenlock WASHS NE38 94 E2
Wenlock Dr NSHW NE29 50 C2
Wenlock Rd HAR/WTLS NE34 60 E6
Wensley Cl CLSW/PEL DH2 92 E5
Wensleydale
WLSD/HOW NE28 48 B5 4
Wensleydale Av HLS DH4 95 J7
WASHN NE37 82 E5 2
Wens Leydale Dr
LGB/KIL NE12 47 K2 10
Wensleydale Ter BLYTH NE24 21 F5
Wentworth SSH NE33 61 J2
Wentworth Cl FELL NE10 69 K5 4
Wentworth Ct PONT/DH NE20 32 E5
Wentworth Dr WASHN NE37 82 E3
Wentworth Gdns MONK NE25 40 A4
Wentworth Pl ELS/FEN NE4 4 D8
Wentworth Ter
MLFD/PNYW SR4 14 A4
Werhale Gn FELL NE10 12 D8
Wesley Dr LGB/KIL NE12 48 D1
Wesley Gv RYTON NE40 64 A1
Wesley Mt RYTON NE40 64 A1
Wesley St
LWF/SPW/WRK NE9 69 F7 11
Wesley Wy
BW/LEM/TK/HW NE15 53 F1
LGB/KIL NE12 48 D1
SEA/MUR SR7 120 A1
Wessex Cl SWCK/CAS SR5 85 K1
Wessington Wy SWCK/CAS SR5 84 D6
SWCK/CAS SR5 85 J4
SWCK/CAS SR5 86 A4 11
Westacre Gdns
WD/WHPE/BLK NE5 55 G4 4
West Acres DIN/WO NE13 35 F1 1
Westacres Av WICK/BNPF NE16 79 F1
Westacres Crs
BW/LEM/TK/HW NE15 55 G5 3
West Av CLDN/WHIT/ROK SR6 74 E3
GOS/KPK NE3 46 C6
HAR/WTLS NE34 61 J5
LGB/KIL NE12 47 K4
NSHW NE29 50 B5
PLEE/EAS SR8 131 F4
ROWG NE39 77 F4 2
SEA/MUR SR7 119 H5 7
WASHS NE38 94 D5
WD/WHPE/BLK NE5 54 D1
West Bailey LGB/KIL NE12 37 K5 12
LGB/KIL NE12 37 K6 3
Westbourne Av
BYK/HTN/WLK NE6 58 B3
GATE NE8 10 E7
GOS/KPK NE3 46 C3
Westbourne Dr HLS DH4 107 J1
Westbourne Rd SUND SR1 14 B5
Westburn Gdns
WLSD/HOW NE28 48 B6 2
Westburn Ms RYTON NE40 64 A1 5
Westburn Ter
CLDN/WHIT/ROK SR6 86 E3
Westbury Av BYK/HTN/WLK NE6 58 B3
Westbury Rd NSHW NE29 50 D2 1
Westcliff Cl PLEE/EAS SR8 130 B6 3
Westcliffe Rd
CLDN/WHIT/ROK SR6 87 F1 2
Westcliffe Wy HAR/WTLS NE34 62 C1
West Clifton LGB/KIL NE12 37 J5 13
West Copperas
BW/LEM/TK/HW NE15 54 C4 5
Westcott Av SSH NE33 61 J2
Westcott Dr DHAM DH1 124 B4
Westcott Rd HAR/WTLS NE34 61 G6
PLEE/EAS SR8 136 E3
West Crs FELL NE10 70 E4
Westcroft Rd LGB/KIL NE12 48 A2
West Dene Dr TYNE/NSHE NE30 50 E2
West Denton Cl
BW/LEM/TK/HW NE15 54 B3
West Denton Rd
BW/LEM/TK/HW NE15 54 B3
West Denton Wy
WD/WHPE/BLK NE5 54 B1
WD/WHPE/BLK NE5 54 E1
West Dr BLYTH NE24 24 E3 6
CLDN/WHIT/ROK SR6 73 J3
CLSW/PEL DH2 105 F5
West End Front St
BDLGTN NE22 19 F6 3
Westerdale HLS DH4 95 G6
WLSD/HOW NE28 48 B6
Westerdale Pl
BYK/HTN/WLK NE6 58 D5
Westerham Cl SWCK/CAS SR5 85 K1
Westerhope Gdns
WD/WHPE/BLK NE5 55 H2 10
Westerhope Rd WASHS NE38 95 H1
Westerkirk CRAM NE23 28 C4
Western Ap SSH NE33 61 G2
Western Av MONK NE25 29 K5
WD/WHPE/BLK NE5 54 B2
Western Dr ELS/FEN NE4 4 A6 1
Western Hwy WASHS NE38 94 C4
Western Hl ASHBK/HED/RY SR2 14 A6
Westernmoor WASHN NE37 82 B7
Western Rd JRW NE32 59 J4
WLSD/HOW NE28 59 H1
Western Ter BOL NE36 72 E5
CRAM NE23 37 F1
Western Wy BLAY NE21 66 C2
BW/LEM/TK/HW NE15 42 C2
PONT/DH NE20 32 C5
RYTON NE40 52 E7
WBAY NE26 40 D1
West Farm Av LGB/KIL NE12 47 F4 5
West Farm Ct CRAM NE23 28 C1 3
West Farm Rd BYK/HTN/WLK NE6 7 M3
CLDN/WHIT/ROK SR6 74 B4
WLSD/HOW NE28 49 G7
West Farm Wynd LGB/KIL NE12 47 F5
Westfield GOS/KPK NE3 56 B1
Westfield Av DIN/WO NE13 36 A3
GOS/KPK NE3 46 C7
MONK NE25 40 B5
RYTON NE40 64 B1
Westfield Ct MLFD/PNYW SR4 97 J2 4
WLSD/HOW NE28 58 D3
Westfield Crs RYTON NE40 64 B1
Westfield Dr GOS/KPK NE3 46 B7
Westfield Gv GOS/KPK NE3 46 B7
MLFD/PNYW SR4 97 J2
Westfield La RYTON NE40 52 D5
Westfield Pk WLSD/HOW NE28 58 C1
Westfield Rd
BW/LEM/TK/HW NE15 55 G6
GATE NE8 10 E7
Westfield Ter GATE NE8 10 F7
Westgarth WD/WHPE/BLK NE5 44 C6
Westgate Av SUNDSW SR3 98 A6
Westgate Cl MONK NE25 40 A3
Westgate Gv SUNDSW SR3 98 A6
Westgate Hill Ter CNUT NE1 5 G8
Westgate Rd CNUT NE1 5 G7
ELS/FEN NE4 55 J5
West George Potts St
SSH NE33 61 H2 12
West Gra SWCK/CAS SR5 86 C2
Westgreen STKFD/GP NE62 18 E1
West Gv MLFD/PNYW SR4 97 F1
Westheath Av
ASHBK/HED/RY SR2 98 E5
West High Horse Cl ROWG NE39 77 H1
West Hl MLFD/PNYW SR4 97 J2
Westhills STLY/ANP DH9 89 J4 1
Westhills Cl BDN/LAN/SAC DH7 113 G3
West Holborn SSH NE33 61 F2
Westholme Gdns
BW/LEM/TK/HW NE15 55 H5
Westhope Cl HAR/WTLS NE34 62 A4
Westhope Rd HAR/WTLS NE34 62 A4
West Jesmond Av JES NE2 56 E1 5
Westlands
BW/LEM/TK/HW NE15 54 A2
JRW NE32 72 B3
LGB/HTN NE7 47 G7
TYNE/NSHE NE30 51 F1
WBAY NE26 30 E2
West La BLAY NE21 65 J4
CLS/BIR/GTL DH3 105 J5
LGB/KIL NE12 47 K1
RDHAMSE DH6 129 J3
SEA/MUR SR7 130 A2
WICK/BNPF NE16 78 A4
West Lawn ASHBK/HED/RY SR2 14 D9
West Lawson St NSHW NE29 2 C5
West Lea BLAY NE21 66 A4
Westleigh Ct
MLFD/PNYW SR4 85 K7 10
Westleigh Rd HLS DH4 108 A3
Westley Av WBAY NE26 31 H7
Westley Cl WBAY NE26 31 H7
Westloch Rd CRAM NE23 28 C5
Westmacott St
BW/LEM/TK/HW NE15 53 G3 1
West Mdw
WD/WHPE/BLK NE5 44 B6 2
West Meadows Dr
CLDN/WHIT/ROK SR6 74 A4
West Meadows Rd
CLDN/WHIT/ROK SR6 74 A4
Westminster Av NSHW NE29 49 K2
Westminster Crs HEBB NE31 71 G2
Westminster Dr
DUN/TMV NE11 67 K6 5
Westminster St GATE NE8 10 E8
Westminster Wy LGB/HTN NE7 47 J6
West Moffett St SSH NE33 61 H2 13
West Moor Dr
CLDN/WHIT/ROK SR6 74 A5
Westmoor Dr LGB/KIL NE12 47 H1
Westmoor Rd MLFD/PNYW SR4 85 H6
Westmoreland St
WLSD/HOW NE28 58 E1
Westmorland Av BDLGTN NE22 18 E5
WASHN NE37 83 F3
WLSD/HOW NE28 59 K2 4
Westmorland Gdns
LWF/SPW/WRK NE9 69 F7 12
Westmorland La CNUT NE1 5 H8
Westmorland Rd CNUT NE1 5 G8
ELS/FEN NE4 4 B9
HAR/WTLS NE34 62 C4
NSHW NE29 49 K3
Westmorland Wk ELS/FEN NE4 9 H1
Westmorland Wy CRAM NE23 28 A2
West Mt MLFD/PNYW SR4 97 J1
Westoe Av SSH NE33 61 J2
Westoe Dr SSH NE33 61 J2
Westoe Rd SSH NE33 3 J9
Westoe Village SSH NE33 61 J3
Weston Av WICK/BNPF NE16 66 D7
Weston Vw PLEE/EAS SR8 136 D3
West Ousterley Rd
STLY/ANP DH9 102 E5
Westover Gdns
LWF/SPW/WRK NE9 69 F5
West Pde ELS/FEN NE4 4 E8
HEBB NE31 59 F7
West Pk SUNDSW SR3 109 F1
West Park Gdns BLAY NE21 66 A3
West Park Rd
CLDN/WHIT/ROK SR6 74 A3
LWF/SPW/WRK NE9 68 E5
SSH NE33 61 G3
West Park Vw CRAM NE23 37 F1
West Pastures BOL NE36 72 A7
West Percy Rd NSHW NE29 2 A3
West Percy St NSHW NE29 2 C2
Westport Cl SWCK/CAS SR5 85 K1 5
West Quay Rd SWCK/CAS SR5 85 K4
West Riggs BDLGTN NE22 19 F6
The West Rig GOS/KPK NE3 45 J6
West Rd BDLGTN NE22 19 K4
PONT/DH NE20 33 F3
STLY/ANP DH9 89 J5
STLY/ANP DH9 101 H4
West Salisbury St BLYTH NE24 21 F6
West Stainton St SSH NE33 61 H2 14
West Stevenson St
SSH NE33 61 H2 15
West Stoneycroft
LGB/KIL NE12 38 A7 2
West St CLS/BIR/GTL DH3 93 J2
CLSW/PEL DH2 104 A2
GATE NE8 10 F1
HEBB NE31 59 G4
ROWG NE39 76 B1
SEA/MUR SR7 120 E1
SMOOR NE27 49 F1
STLY/ANP DH9 90 B6
SUND SR1 14 D4
SUNDSW SR3 98 A6 6
WICK/BNPF NE16 66 E5
WLSD/HOW NE28 58 C1
West Sunniside SUND SR1 14 F4
Westsyde PONT/DH NE20 32 C6
West Ter DHAM DH1 16 A2
WBAY NE26 31 G2
West Thorp WD/WHPE/BLK NE5 44 D5
West Vallum
BW/LEM/TK/HW NE15 54 D4 8
West Vw BDLGTN NE22 19 J3
BDN/LAN/SAC DH7 133 H7
BLAY NE21 66 A1
BW/LEM/TK/HW NE15 54 A5
CLDN/WHIT/ROK SR6 86 D2
DHAM DH1 17 H2
DUN/TMV NE11 80 D7
ELS/FEN NE4 4 A9
HLS DH4 107 K3
LGB/KIL NE12 47 K2 11
SWCK/CAS SR5 85 F4 10
West Walls CNUT NE1 5 H7
West Walpole St SSH NE33 61 F2
Westward Ct
WD/WHPE/BLK NE5 44 C7 9
Westward Pl WASHS NE38 94 D5
West Wy DUN/TMV NE11 9 J8
SSH NE33 61 G4
Westway BLAY NE21 65 K2 2
BW/LEM/TK/HW NE15 43 F7
PLEE/EAS SR8 136 D5 2
West Wear St SUND SR1 14 E3
Westwell Ct LGB/HTN NE7 47 F6 8
West Wellington St
NSHW NE29 2 D2 8
Westwood Av
BYK/HTN/WLK NE6 57 J2 6
Westwood Cl WICK/BNPF NE16 77 K6
Westwood Gdns GOS/KPK NE3 45 J6
Westwood Rd GOS/KPK NE3 46 C1
Westwood St
MLFD/PNYW SR4 85 K7 11
Westwood Vw RYTON NE40 64 A1
West Wynd LGB/KIL NE12 37 K6
Wetheral Gdns
LWF/SPW/WRK NE9 81 G2
Wetheral Ter
BYK/HTN/WLK NE6 58 B7 3
Wetherburn Av SEA/MUR SR7 119 G5
Wetherby Gv GATE NE8 10 C9
Wetherby Rd
ASHBK/HED/RY SR2 99 G5
Wettondale Av BLYTH NE24 20 C7
Weybourne Sq
ASHBK/HED/RY SR2 98 E4 3
Weyhill Av NSHW NE29 50 B6
Weymouth Dr SEA/MUR SR7 120 B2
Weymouth Gdns
LWF/SPW/WRK NE9 81 F3
Whaggs La WICK/BNPF NE16 67 F6
Whalton Av GOS/KPK NE3 46 A4
Whalton Cl FELL NE10 70 E5
Whalton Ct HAR/WTLS NE34 61 J5 3
Wharfdale Pl BYK/HTN/WLK NE6 58 C5
Wharfedale HLS DH4 95 J6 3
WLSD/HOW NE28 48 B5
Wharfedale Av WASHN NE37 82 D5
Wharfedale Dr SSH NE33 61 G4 4
Wharfedale Gdns BLYTH NE24 20 C6
Wharmlands Rd
BW/LEM/TK/HW NE15 54 D4
Wharncliffe St SUND SR1 14 B5
Wharrier St BYK/HTN/WLK NE6 58 B7
Wharton St BLYTH NE24 24 D3
SSH NE33 3 K9
Wheatall Dr
CLDN/WHIT/ROK SR6 75 F2
Wheatfield Gv LGB/KIL NE12 47 H3
Wheatfield Rd
WD/WHPE/BLK NE5 44 D7
Wheatley Gdns BOL NE36 72 E5
Wheatley Green La
BDN/LAN/SAC DH7 103 H7
Wheatleywell La
CLS/BIR/GTL DH3 114 D3
Whernside Pl CRAM NE23 28 C5 2
Whernside Wk RYTON NE40 53 F7 3
Whickham Cl HLS DH4 108 A7
Whickham Hwy DUN/TMV NE11 67 J5
WICK/BNPF NE16 8 C9
Whickham Ldg
WICK/BNPF NE16 67 G5
Whickham Pk WICK/BNPF NE16 8 A9
Whickham Rd HEBB NE31 59 F6
Whickham St
CLDN/WHIT/ROK SR6 15 G1
PLEE/EAS SR8 130 E5 3
Whickham St East
CLDN/WHIT/ROK SR6 86 E4
Whickham Vw
BW/LEM/TK/HW NE15 54 E5
LWF/SPW/WRK NE9 69 G7
Whickhope WASHS NE38 95 G4
Whinbank PONT/DH NE20 33 F7
Whinbrooke FELL NE10 70 C6
Whinbush Pl
BW/LEM/TK/HW NE15 54 E6
Whinfell Cl CRAM NE23 28 D5
Whinfell Rd PONT/DH NE20 33 F6
Whinfield Ter ROWG NE39 77 F3
Whinfield Wy ROWG NE39 76 E4
Whinlatter Gdns
LWF/SPW/WRK NE9 81 G1
Whinmoor Pl
WD/WHPE/BLK NE5 55 J2
Whinney Cl BLAY NE21 65 J4 7
Whinneyfield Rd
BYK/HTN/WLK NE6 58 B4
Whinney Hl DHAM DH1 16 F7
Whinshaw FELL NE10 70 B5
Whistler Gdns HAR/WTLS NE34 73 H1
Whitbay Crs LGB/KIL NE12 47 J4
Whitbeck Rd
WD/WHPE/BLK NE5 54 E3
Whitbourne Cl WASHN NE37 83 G3 2
Whitburn Bents Rd
CLDN/WHIT/ROK SR6 75 F5 1
Whitburn Cl
BDN/LAN/SAC DH7 122 A3 5
Whitburn Gdns
LWF/SPW/WRK NE9 81 K2
Whitburn Pl CRAM NE23 28 C5
Whitburn Rd
CLDN/WHIT/ROK SR6 73 K4
CLDN/WHIT/ROK SR6 87 F1
Whitburn Rd East
CLDN/WHIT/ROK SR6 74 B3
Whitburn St
CLDN/WHIT/ROK SR6 14 F1
Whitburn Ter BOL NE36 73 H5
CLDN/WHIT/ROK SR6 86 D1 8
Whitby Av CLDN/WHIT/ROK SR6 75 F6
Whitby Dr WASHS NE38 95 F3
Whitby Gdns WLSD/HOW NE28 49 G6
Whitby St TYNE/NSHE NE30 51 F4
Whitchurch Cl BOLCOL NE35 72 C3 6
SWCK/CAS SR5 85 K1 6
Whitchurch Rd SWCK/CAS SR5 85 K1
Whitebark SUNDSW SR3 109 J3 1
Whitebridge Cl GOS/KPK NE3 46 C2
Whitebridge Ct GOS/KPK NE3 46 C3 3
Whitebridge Pk GOS/KPK NE3 46 D3
White Cedars
BDN/LAN/SAC DH7 133 F7
Whitecliff Cl NSHW NE29 50 D2
Whitecroft Rd LGB/KIL NE12 37 G7
Whitefield Crs HLS DH4 95 J7
Whitefield Gdns RYTON NE40 64 B4 2
Whitefield Gv FELL NE10 12 C7
Whitefield Ter
BYK/HTN/WLK NE6 57 K2
Whiteford Pl CRAM NE23 29 H6
Whitefriars Wy LGB/KIL NE12 47 G5
White Gates Dr HLH DH5 118 A6 2
Whitegates Rd RDHAMSE DH6 126 C6
Whitehall Rd
BW/LEM/TK/HW NE15 53 H1
GATE NE8 10 F6 1
Whitehall St SSH NE33 61 G5
Whitehead St SSH NE33 61 F4 4
Whitehill FELL NE10 70 B7
Whitehill Crs CLSW/PEL DH2 104 E3
Whitehill Dr FELL NE10 69 K6
Whitehill Hall Gdns
CLSW/PEL DH2 105 G3
Whitehill Rd CRAM NE23 23 G6 6
White Hill Rd HLH DH5 128 B1
Whitehorn Crs
WD/WHPE/BLK NE5 55 H1
White Horse Vw
HAR/WTLS NE34 62 C5 1
Whitehouse Crs
LWF/SPW/WRK NE9 82 A1
Whitehouse La
BDN/LAN/SAC DH7 122 E7
NSHW NE29 50 B2
White House Pl
ASHBK/HED/RY SR2 15 J6 1
White House Rd
ASHBK/HED/RY SR2 15 H7 4
Whitehouse Rd
BW/LEM/TK/HW NE15 55 F7
White House Wy FELL NE10 70 A7
Whitehouse Wy PLEE/EAS SR8 136 A4
RDHAMSE DH6 136 A6
Whitelaw Pl CRAM NE23 28 D4 5
White Lea Cl PLEE/EAS SR8 137 G5
Whiteleas Wy HAR/WTLS NE34 61 G7
Whitelees Ct GOS/KPK NE3 45 J3 9
White Le Head Gdns
STLY/ANP DH9 89 J4 2
Whiteley Cl RYTON NE40 64 C3
Whiteley Rd BLAY NE21 54 C7
Whitemere Cl
ASHBK/HED/RY SR2 98 E4
White Mere Gdns FELL NE10 70 E4
Whiteoak Av DHAM DH1 125 J6
White Oaks FELL NE10 70 A7
White Rocks Gv
CLDN/WHIT/ROK SR6 75 F1
Whites Gdns HEBB NE31 58 E5
Whitesmocks DHAM DH1 124 B5
Whitesmocks Av DHAM DH1 124 A6
White St BYK/HTN/WLK NE6 58 D6
Whitewell La RYTON NE40 52 E6
Whitewell Rd BLAY NE21 66 A2
Whitfield Dr LGB/KIL NE12 47 J4
Whitfield Rd
BW/LEM/TK/HW NE15 54 D6
LGB/KIL NE12 47 K2 12
MONK NE25 30 A5
Whitgrave Rd
WD/WHPE/BLK NE5 45 H7
Whithorn Ct BLYTH NE24 20 E7 5
Whitley Rd LGB/KIL NE12 48 A4
MONK NE25 39 J4
WBAY NE26 41 F5
Whitmore Rd BLAY NE21 66 A1
Whittingham Rd
TYNE/NSHE NE30 41 G7
WD/WHPE/BLK NE5 44 D6 2
Whittington Gv
WD/WHPE/BLK NE5 55 G4
Whittleburn FELL NE10 70 B7
Whitton Av BLYTH NE24 24 D2
Whitton Gdns NSHW NE29 50 B3 5
Whitton Pl LGB/HTN NE7 47 G6
MONK NE25 30 A5
Whittonstall WASHS NE38 95 H5
Whitton Wy GOS/KPK NE3 46 B4
Whitwell Acres DHAM DH1 135 J6
Whitworth Cl
BYK/HTN/WLK NE6 58 C6 8
GATE NE8 68 D5 6
Whitworth Rd PLEE/EAS SR8 136 A4
WASHN NE37 82 B6
Whorlton Pl
WD/WHPE/BLK NE5 44 C7 10
Whyndyke FELL NE10 70 A7
Whytrigg Cl MONK NE25 29 J4
Widdrington Av
HAR/WTLS NE34 62 B3
Widdrington Gdns
DIN/WO NE13 36 C3 2
Widdrington Rd BLAY NE21 66 A2
Widnes Pl LGB/KIL NE12 47 J3
Wigeon Cl WASHS NE38 94 B4
Wigmore Av BYK/HTN/WLK NE6 7 L9
Wilber Ct MLFD/PNYW SR4 85 K7 12
Wilberforce St JRW NE32 60 A4
WLSD/HOW NE28 58 D3 6
Wilber St MLFD/PNYW SR4 85 K7 13
Wilbury Pl
WD/WHPE/BLK NE5 55 G1 4
Wilden Ct SUNDSW SR3 98 B4 6
Wilden Rd WASHS NE38 95 H3
Wildshaw Cl CRAM NE23 28 D5
Wilfred St BOLCOL NE35 72 D5
BYK/HTN/WLK NE6 6 D5
CLS/BIR/GTL DH3 105 J5
MLFD/PNYW SR4 85 J6 8
Wilfrid St CLS/BIR/GTL DH3 93 J3
Wilkes Cl WD/WHPE/BLK NE5 54 D1 7
Wilkinson Av HEBB NE31 71 F1 3
Wilkinson Rd PLEE/EAS SR8 137 F1

Wilkwood Cl CRAM NE23 .... 28 D4 5
Willerby Dr GOS/KPK NE3 .... 46 D2
Willerby Gv PLEE/EAS SR8 .... 136 D3 2
William Armstrong Dr
ELS/FEN NE4 .... 8 F2
William Cl LGB/KIL NE12 .... 48 C2 5
William Morris Av ROWG NE39 ..... 76 D3
William Pl DHAM DH1 .... 17 J3
Williams Cl STLY/ANP DH9 .... 102 E2
Williamson Ter
CLDN/WHIT/ROK SR6 .... 14 F1 5
Williams Rd SEA/MUR SR7 .... 119 H5
William St BLYTH NE24 .... 21 G7
FELL NE10 .... 12 D6
GOS/KPK NE3 .... 46 E5
HEBB NE31 .... 59 F4
SUND SR1 .... 14 F3
WICK/BNPF NE16 .... 66 E5 12
William St West HEBB NE31 .... 59 F5
NSHW NE29 .... 2 C3 2
Willington Ter WLSD/HOW NE28 .. 49 G7
Willis St HLH DH5 .... 117 K3 5
Willmore St MLFD/PNYW SR4 .... 86 A7
Willoughby Dr WBAY NE26 .... 40 C2
Willoughby Rd NSHW NE29 .... 50 B4
Willow Av BLYTH NE24 .... 21 F5
DUN/TMV NE11 .... 9 G8
ELS/FEN NE4 .... 55 H3
Willowbank Gdns JES NE2 .... 46 E6 5
Willow Bank Rd
ASHBK/HED/RY SR2 .... 98 C3 10
Willow Cl BDN/LAN/SAC DH7 .... 133 G6
Willow Ct RYTON NE40 .... 53 F5
Willow Crs BLYTH NE24 .... 24 E3
HLH DH5 .... 118 C7
Willowdene LGB/KIL NE12 .... 48 A1 5
Willowfield Av GOS/KPK NE3 .... 45 K4
Willow Gdns LGB/KIL NE12 .... 37 J5 14
Willow Gra JRW NE32 .... 59 J4 2
Willow Gv HAR/WTLS NE34 .... 61 K6
PLEE/EAS SR8 .... 137 J5
WLSD/HOW NE28 .... 59 F1
Willow Pl PONT/DH NE20 .... 33 G5
Willow Rd BLAY NE21 .... 66 B2
HLS DH4 .... 108 A7
Willows Cl DIN/WO NE13 .... 36 A4 9
The Willows
BW/LEM/TK/HW NE15 .... 53 F2
WASHS NE38 .... 95 H2
Willowtree Av DHAM DH1 .... 125 H5
Willow Tree Av DHAM DH1 .... 135 G4
Willow Wy PONT/DH NE20 .... 33 G7
Wilmington Cl
WD/WHPE/BLK NE5 .... 45 F4
Wilson Av BDLGTN NE22 .... 20 D2
CLS/BIR/GTL DH3 .... 93 J1
Wilson Dr BOL NE36 .... 73 F4 1
Wilson Gdns GOS/KPK NE3 .... 46 B7
Wilson Pl PLEE/EAS SR8 .... 136 E2
Wilson's La LWF/SPW/WRK NE9 .... 69 F7
Wilson St DUN/TMV NE11 .... 9 H8
MLFD/PNYW SR4 .... 86 A6
SSH NE33 .... 61 G2
WLSD/HOW NE28 .... 58 D1
Wilson St North SWCK/CAS SR5 .... 14 D2
Wilson Ter LGB/KIL NE12 .... 47 K2 13
SUNDSW SR3 .... 98 A6
Wilsway BW/LEM/TK/HW NE15 .... 52 E1
Wilton Av BYK/HTN/WLK NE6 .... 7 L8
Wilton Cl CRAM NE23 .... 28 D5
MONK NE25 .... 39 K4
Wilton Dr MONK NE25 .... 39 K5
Wilton Gdns North
BOLCOL NE35 .... 72 C2 9
Wilton Gdns South
BOLCOL NE35 .... 72 C3
Wiltshire Cl DHAM DH1 .... 125 K6 3
SWCK/CAS SR5 .... 85 J1 1
Wiltshire Dr WLSD/HOW NE28 .... 48 B5
Wiltshire Gdns WLSD/HOW NE28 .. 48 B7
Wiltshire Pl WASHN NE37 .... 83 F3
Wiltshire Rd SWCK/CAS SR5 .... 85 K1 1
Wimbledon Cl SWCK/CAS SR5 .... 85 K2 1
Wimborne Cl BOLCOL NE35 .... 72 C4 2
Wimbourne Av
MLFD/PNYW SR4 .... 97 J2 5
Wimbourne Gn
WD/WHPE/BLK NE5 .... 44 D7 5
Wimpole Cl WASHN NE37 .... 83 G3 5
Wimslow Cl WLSD/HOW NE28 .... 48 B7
Winalot Av ASHBK/HED/RY SR2 .... 98 E4
Wincanton Pl NSHW NE29 .... 50 C6 4
Winchcombe Pl LGB/HTN NE7 .. 47 G7 5
Winchester Av BLYTH NE24 .... 21 G7
Winchester Cl CLS/BIR/GTL DH3 .. 115 H1
Winchester Ct JRW NE32 .... 71 K3
MLFD/PNYW SR4 .... 85 K7 14
Winchester Dr PLEE/EAS SR8 .. 136 A5 1
Winchester Rd DHAM DH1 .... 125 F2
Winchester St SSH NE33 .... 3 J7
Winchester Ter ELS/FEN NE4 .... 4 F7
Winchester Wk DIN/WO NE13 .... 36 B4
Winchester Wy BDLGTN NE22 .... 19 F4
Wincomblee Rd
BYK/HTN/WLK NE6 .... 13 K1
Windburgh Dr CRAM NE23 .... 28 C5
Windermere
CLDN/WHIT/ROK SR6 .... 74 A3 5
Windermere Av CLSW/PEL DH2 .. 105 J6
FELL NE10 .... 13 H7
HLH DH5 .... 128 B1
Windermere Cl CRAM NE23 .... 28 C5
Windermere Crs BLAY NE21 .... 65 K4 8
HAR/WTLS NE34 .... 61 J5
HEBB NE31 .... 59 H6
HLS DH4 .... 107 K1
JRW NE32 .... 72 B1
Windermere Gdns
WICK/BNPF NE16 .... 8 B9
Windermere Rd RDHAMSE DH6 .. 129 G1
SEA/MUR SR7 .... 119 K1
WD/WHPE/BLK NE5 .... 55 F3 4
Windermere St
ASHBK/HED/RY SR2 .... 99 F4
GATE NE8 .... 10 E6
Windermere St West GATE NE8 .... 10 E6
Windermere Ter NSHW NE29 .... 2 B1
Windhill Rd BYK/HTN/WLK NE6 .... 13 H1
The Winding DIN/WO NE13 .... 35 F2 4
Windlass Ct HAR/WTLS NE34 .... 61 G6 13
Windlass La WASHN NE37 .... 82 E6
Windmill Ct JES NE2 .... 5 G1 1
Windmill Gv BLYTH NE24 .... 20 C6
Windmill Hl SSH NE33 .... 61 F2 5
Windmill Sq SWCK/CAS SR5 .... 86 C1 5
Windmill Wy HEBB NE31 .... 59 G3
Winds La SEA/MUR SR7 .... 119 G6
Winds Lonnen Est
SEA/MUR SR7 .... 119 F5
Windsor Av GATE NE8 .... 10 E7
Windsor Cl WICK/BNPF NE16 .... 78 D1
Windsor Cottages
WLSD/HOW NE28 .... 49 J6 5
Windsor Ct BDLGTN NE22 .... 19 F6
CRAM NE23 .... 23 G6
GOS/KPK NE3 .... 45 J3
Windsor Crs HEBB NE31 .... 59 H5
HLH DH5 .... 108 D7
WBAY NE26 .... 41 G5
WD/WHPE/BLK NE5 .... 44 E7
Windsor Dr CLDN/WHIT/ROK SR6 .. 73 J3
HLH DH5 .... 117 H2
RDHAMSE DH6 .... 128 E1
STLY/ANP DH9 .... 101 H2
SUNDSW SR3 .... 98 A7
WLSD/HOW NE28 .... 49 J7
Windsor Gdns BDLGTN NE22 .... 19 F6
FELL NE10 .... 12 A8 1
HAR/WTLS NE34 .... 61 J4
NSHW NE29 .... 50 E3
WBAY NE26 .... 40 D3
Windsor Pk WLSD/HOW NE28 .... 48 B7
Windsor Pl PONT/DH NE20 .... 32 D5
SMOOR NE27 .... 48 E1
Windsor Rd CLS/BIR/GTL DH3 .... 81 H7
LWF/SPW/WRK NE9 .... 82 A4
MONK NE25 .... 40 C4
SEA/MUR SR7 .... 120 A1
Windsor St WLSD/HOW NE28 .... 58 D1
Windsor Ter GOS/KPK NE3 .... 46 E6
JES NE2 .... 5 K2
PLEE/EAS SR8 .... 137 J4
RDHAMSE DH6 .... 128 D6
SEA/MUR SR7 .... 119 J5 2
SEA/MUR SR7 .... 119 J6 5
WBAY NE26 .... 41 G5
Windsor Wy GOS/KPK NE3 .... 45 G3
Windt St DIN/WO NE13 .... 36 A4 10
Windy Nook Rd
LWF/SPW/WRK NE9 .... 69 H6
Windy Ridge Vls FELL NE10 .... 69 J5 4
Wingate Cl
BW/LEM/TK/HW NE15 .... 54 C5
HLS DH4 .... 108 B7
Wingate Gdns
LWF/SPW/WRK NE9 .... 81 K1
Wingrove ROWG NE39 .... 77 F4 5
Wingrove Av
CLDN/WHIT/ROK SR6 .... 86 E1
ELS/FEN NE4 .... 4 A4
Wingrove Gdns ELS/FEN NE4 .... 4 A4
Wingrove Rd ELS/FEN NE4 .... 55 J2
Winifred St CLDN/WHIT/ROK SR6 .. 86 E2
Winifred Ter SUND SR1 .... 15 G6 1
Winshields CRAM NE23 .... 28 D4
Winship Cl HAR/WTLS NE34 .... 73 G2
Winship St BLYTH NE24 .... 24 E2
Winskell Rd HAR/WTLS NE34 .... 60 D7
Winslade Cl SUNDSW SR3 .... 98 B6 2
Winslow Cl BOLCOL NE35 .... 72 D2
BYK/HTN/WLK NE6 .... 58 C5 5
SWCK/CAS SR5 .... 85 K1
Winslow Crs SEA/MUR SR7 .... 120 A1
Winslow Gdns
LWF/SPW/WRK NE9 .... 68 E7 4
Winslow Pl BYK/HTN/WLK NE6 .... 58 C5
Winsten WASHS NE38 .... 94 C5
Winston Crs MLFD/PNYW SR4 .... 97 J2 5
Winston Gn HLS DH4 .... 95 H6
Winton Cl CRAM NE23 .... 29 H6
Winton Wy GOS/KPK NE3 .... 45 K5 5
Wishaw Cl CRAM NE23 .... 28 D4
Wishaw Ri
BW/LEM/TK/HW NE15 .... 54 C4
Witham Rd HEBB NE31 .... 71 H1
Witherington Cl LGB/HTN NE7 .. 48 A7 5
Withernsea Gv
ASHBK/HED/RY SR2 .... 98 D7
Witney Cl SWCK/CAS SR5 .... 85 J1
Witney Wy BOL NE36 .... 72 C5
Witton Av BDN/LAN/SAC DH7 .... 113 H5
HAR/WTLS NE34 .... 62 A5
Witton Ct GOS/KPK NE3 .... 45 J4
SUNDSW SR3 .... 98 B4
Witton Gdns JRW NE32 .... 71 K1
Witton Garth PLEE/EAS SR8 .... 136 D7
Witton Gv DHAM DH1 .... 124 A5
HLS DH4 .... 117 F1
Witton Rd BDN/LAN/SAC DH7 .... 113 G6
HEBB NE31 .... 59 H3
SMOOR NE27 .... 39 H6
Witty Av HEBB NE31 .... 59 H6
Woburn WASHS NE38 .... 95 F2
Woburn Cl CRAM NE23 .... 23 G6
WLSD/HOW NE28 .... 48 B7 5
Woburn Dr BDLGTN NE22 .... 19 J4
SUNDSW SR3 .... 110 A1
Woburn Wy WD/WHPE/BLK NE5 .. 54 E1
Wolmer Rd BLYTH NE24 .... 25 H2
Wolseley Cl GATE NE8 .... 10 A5
Wolseley Gdns JES NE2 .... 6 C1
Wolseley Ter
MLFD/PNYW SR4 .... 98 A1 2
Wolsey Ct HAR/WTLS NE34 .... 61 G5
Wolsey Rd SEA/MUR SR7 .... 119 K2
Wolsingham Ct CRAM NE23 .... 28 A1
Wolsingham Dr DHAM DH1 .... 124 E3
Wolsingham Rd GOS/KPK NE3 .... 46 B6
Wolsingham St ELS/FEN NE4 .... 9 H1
Wolsley Rd BLYTH NE24 .... 21 G6
Wolveleigh Ter GOS/KPK NE3 .... 46 D5
Woodbine Av WLSD/HOW NE28 .... 58 D1
Woodbine Cl ELS/FEN NE4 .... 4 A8
Woodbine Rd DHAM DH1 .... 124 B2
GOS/KPK NE3 .... 46 C6
Woodbine St GATE NE8 .... 10 E5 1
SSH NE33 .... 3 J5
SUND SR1 .... 15 J5
Woodbine Ter BLYTH NE24 .... 25 H1
FELL NE10 .... 11 M7
MLFD/PNYW SR4 .... 85 K5
Woodbrook Av
WD/WHPE/BLK NE5 .... 54 E3
Woodburn FELL NE10 .... 70 A7
STLY/ANP DH9 .... 90 A6
Woodburn Av ELS/FEN NE4 .... 55 J2
Woodburn Cl BLAY NE21 .... 65 J4 5
Woodburn Dr HLS DH4 .... 108 A6
WBAY NE26 .... 40 C2
Woodburn Gdns DUN/TMV NE11 .. 68 A6
Woodburn Sq WBAY NE26 .... 40 B2
Woodburn St
BW/LEM/TK/HW NE15 .... 54 A4 5
Woodchurch Cl LGB/KIL NE12 .... 47 K6
Woodcroft Cl CRAM NE23 .... 28 B7
Woodend PONT/DH NE20 .... 32 E7
Woodend Wy GOS/KPK NE3 .... 45 G2
Woodfield PLEE/EAS SR8 .... 136 D4 2
Wood Flds PONT/DH NE20 .... 33 H3
Woodford LWF/SPW/WRK NE9 .... 81 F4
Woodford Cl SWCK/CAS SR5 .... 85 K1 5
Woodgate Gdns FELL NE10 .... 13 M5
Woodgate La FELL NE10 .... 13 M4
Wood Gv BW/LEM/TK/HW NE15 .. 54 D4
Woodhall Spa HLS DH4 .... 107 J3
Woodhead Rd BYK/HTN/WLK NE6 .. 7 M1
Woodhill Rd CRAM NE23 .... 28 D4 2
Woodhorn Gdns DIN/WO NE13 .... 36 B3
Woodhouses La
WICK/BNPF NE16 .... 78 C1 5
Woodhurst Gv
MLFD/PNYW SR4 .... 96 E4 5
Woodland Cl
BDN/LAN/SAC DH7 .... 123 F6
Woodland Crs
BW/LEM/TK/HW NE15 .... 55 F7
Woodland Dr MLFD/PNYW SR4 .... 97 J2
Woodland Gra HLS DH4 .... 107 H6
Woodland Ri SUNDSW SR3 .... 109 J1
Woodlands
BW/LEM/TK/HW NE15 .... 52 E1
GOS/KPK NE3 .... 46 C7
NSHW NE29 .... 50 E2
PONT/DH NE20 .... 33 F6
WASHS NE38 .... 94 A6
Woodlands Cl MONK NE25 .... 39 J4
ROWG NE39 .... 76 C2 5
Woodlands Dr
CLDN/WHIT/ROK SR6 .... 74 A4
Woodlands Gra LGB/KIL NE12 .... 48 A1
Woodlands Park Dr BLAY NE21 .... 66 B2
Woodlands Rd
BW/LEM/TK/HW NE15 .... 54 B4 4
CLDN/WHIT/ROK SR6 .... 73 K4
ROWG NE39 .... 77 F3
Woodlands Ter FELL NE10 .... 12 B8 1
Woodlands Vw
CLDN/WHIT/ROK SR6 .... 74 A4
Wood La BDLGTN NE22 .... 19 H5
Wood Lea HLH DH5 .... 117 K1
Woodlea LGB/KIL NE12 .... 47 K1
Woodlea Cl HLH DH5 .... 117 K4
Woodlea Ct NSHW NE29 .... 50 C7 1
Woodlea Gdns GOS/KPK NE3 .... 46 E3
Woodlea Sq NSHW NE29 .... 50 C7
Woodleigh Rd MONK NE25 .... 40 C5
Woodleigh Vw
WD/WHPE/BLK NE5 .... 45 J7 2
Woodman St WLSD/HOW NE28 .... 49 K7
Woodmans Wy
WICK/BNPF NE16 .... 78 C1
Woodnansey Cl PLEE/EAS SR8 .... 136 C3
Woodpack Av WICK/BNPF NE16 .. 66 D6
Woodside ASHBK/HED/RY SR2 .... 14 D8
BDLGTN NE22 .... 19 J5
BLYTH NE24 .... 25 H1 4
PONT/DH NE20 .... 32 E7
Woodside Av
BDN/LAN/SAC DH7 .... 123 F6
BW/LEM/TK/HW NE15 .... 53 G1
MONK NE25 .... 30 A6
Woodside Bank CON/LDGT DH8 .. 100 B7
Woodside Cl RYTON NE40 .... 52 D6
Woodside Crs LGB/KIL NE12 .... 48 A2
Woodside Gdns DUN/TMV NE11 .. 67 K5
STLY/ANP DH9 .... 103 F4
Woodside La HLS DH4 .... 116 B7
RYTON NE40 .... 52 D7
Woodside Rd RYTON NE40 .... 52 D6
Woodside Ter SUNDSW SR3 .... 109 G1
Woodside Wk ROWG NE39 .... 76 E4
Woodside Wy RYTON NE40 .... 52 D6 2
SSH NE33 .... 61 F4
Woods Ter GATE NE8 .... 11 H6
SEA/MUR SR7 .... 119 J5
Woodstock Rd
BW/LEM/TK/HW NE15 .... 54 E6
LWF/SPW/WRK NE9 .... 81 G3
Wood St CLSW/PEL DH2 .... 92 E7
DUN/TMV NE11 .... 9 H8
MLFD/PNYW SR4 .... 86 A6 2
Wood Ter FELL NE10 .... 13 L4
JRW NE32 .... 59 J7
SSH NE33 .... 61 H3
Woodthorne Rd JES NE2 .... 46 E7 1
Woodvale PONT/DH NE20 .... 32 E7
Woodvale Dr HEBB NE31 .... 58 E7
Woodvale Gdns
LWF/SPW/WRK NE9 .... 69 J6 5
Woodvale Rd BLAY NE21 .... 66 B3
LGB/KIL NE12 .... 37 J5
Wood Vw BDN/LAN/SAC DH7 .... 122 B2
Woodville Ct MLFD/PNYW SR4 .. 97 J2 2
Woodville Crs
MLFD/PNYW SR4 .... 97 J2 5
Woodville Rd
BW/LEM/TK/HW NE15 .... 54 B3
Wooler Av NSHW NE29 .... 50 B6
Wooler Crs GATE NE8 .... 10 B7
Wooler Sq ASHBK/HED/RY SR2 .... 98 E3
DIN/WO NE13 .... 36 C2 2
Woolerton Dr
BW/LEM/TK/HW NE15 .... 54 C4
LWF/SPW/WRK NE9 .... 69 H6 2
Wooler Wk JRW NE32 .... 59 J7
Wooley Dr BDN/LAN/SAC DH7 .... 133 H1
Wooley St WLSD/HOW NE28 .... 58 D2
Woolmer Ct LGB/HTN NE7 .... 48 A7 5
Woolsington Ct
MLFD/PNYW SR4 .... 85 K7 15
Woolsington Gdns
DIN/WO NE13 .... 44 D2
Woolsington Pk South
DIN/WO NE13 .... 44 D2
Woolsington Rd NSHW NE29 .... 50 A3
Woolwich Cl SWCK/CAS SR5 .... 85 K1
Woolwich Rd SWCK/CAS SR5 .... 85 K1
Wooperton Gdns
WD/WHPE/BLK NE5 .... 55 G4
Worcester Cl CLS/BIR/GTL DH3 .. 115 H1
Worcester Rd DHAM DH1 .... 124 E2
Worcester St
ASHBK/HED/RY SR2 .... 14 D7 1
Worcester Ter
ASHBK/HED/RY SR2 .... 14 D7 2
Worcester Wy DIN/WO NE13 .... 36 B4
Wordsworth Av BLYTH NE24 .... 24 E2
CLSW/PEL DH2 .... 104 E5
HEBB NE31 .... 59 G5
HLH DH5 .... 128 C1 4
SEA/MUR SR7 .... 119 K1
WICK/BNPF NE16 .... 67 F4
Wordsworth Rd PLEE/EAS SR8 .. 130 D5
Wordsworth St GATE NE8 .... 11 J5
Worley Cl ELS/FEN NE4 .... 4 D6
Worley St ELS/FEN NE4 .... 4 D6
Worm Hill Ter WASHS NE38 .... 95 G5
Worsdell St BLYTH NE24 .... 21 G5 5
Worsley Cl WLSD/HOW NE28 .... 48 B7
Worswick St CNUT NE1 .... 5 L6
Worthing Cl WLSD/HOW NE28 .. 48 B7 6
Wouldhave Ct SSH NE33 .... 3 K6
Wraysbury Ct GOS/KPK NE3 .... 45 H3 5
Wreigh St HEBB NE31 .... 59 F5
Wreken Gdns FELL NE10 .... 70 E4
Wrekenton Rw
LWF/SPW/WRK NE9 .... 81 J3
Wren Cl WASHS NE38 .... 94 C3
Wren Gv SWCK/CAS SR5 .... 85 G4 5
Wretham Pl JES NE2 .... 6 A4
Wright Dr CRAM NE23 .... 37 G2
Wrightson St CRAM NE23 .... 23 H4
Wright St BLYTH NE24 .... 21 F6
Wright Ter HLS DH4 .... 107 J2
Wroxham Ct
ASHBK/HED/RY SR2 .... 98 E4
WD/WHPE/BLK NE5 .... 45 F6 14
Wroxton WASHS NE38 .... 94 E3
Wuppertal Ct JRW NE32 .... 59 K5
Wychcroft Wy
WD/WHPE/BLK NE5 .... 55 G1 5
Wych Elm Crs LGB/HTN NE7 .... 47 J7
Wycliffe Av GOS/KPK NE3 .... 45 K7
Wycliffe Rd MLFD/PNYW SR4 .... 97 K2
SEA/MUR SR7 .... 119 K1
Wye Av JRW NE32 .... 72 A1
Wye Rd HEBB NE31 .... 71 G1
Wylam Av MONK NE25 .... 30 C6
Wylam Cl HAR/WTLS NE34 .... 61 J6 2
WASHN NE37 .... 83 G4 1
Wylam Gdns WLSD/HOW NE28 .... 49 H6
Wylam Gv SUND SR1 .... 15 H6
Wylam Rd NSHW NE29 .... 2 A7
STLY/ANP DH9 .... 90 E7
Wylam St JRW NE32 .... 59 K4
STLY/ANP DH9 .... 103 G5
Wylam Ter STLY/ANP DH9 .... 90 D6 2
Wylam Vw BLAY NE21 .... 65 K2
Wynbury Rd
LWF/SPW/WRK NE9 .... 69 G7 5
Wyncote Ct LGB/HTN NE7 .... 57 H1 2
The Wynde HAR/WTLS NE34 .... 61 G6
PONT/DH NE20 .... 33 F5
Wyndfall Wy GOS/KPK NE3 .... 46 A7
Wyndham Av GOS/KPK NE3 .... 45 K7
Wyndham Wy NSHW NE29 .... 49 K2
The Wynding BDLGTN NE22 .... 18 E4
CRAM NE23 .... 28 B7
Wyndley Cl WICK/BNPF NE16 .... 66 D7
Wyndley Pl GOS/KPK NE3 .... 45 K7
Wyndsail Pl GOS/KPK NE3 .... 46 A7 5
The Wynd
BW/LEM/TK/HW NE15 .... 53 F2 5
CLSW/PEL DH2 .... 104 E1
GOS/KPK NE3 .... 46 A6
TYNE/NSHE NE30 .... 50 E2
Wyndtop Pl GOS/KPK NE3 .... 46 A7 4
Wyndways Dr STLY/ANP DH9 .... 89 G5
Wynn Gdns FELL NE10 .... 13 H5
Wynyard CLSW/PEL DH2 .... 105 G4
Wynyard Dr BDLGTN NE22 .... 19 J3
Wynyard Gdns
LWF/SPW/WRK NE9 .... 81 J3
Wynyard Sq ASHBK/HED/RY SR2 .. 98 E3
Wynyard St DUN/TMV NE11 .... 9 G8
HLS DH4 .... 107 J7
SEA/MUR SR7 .... 120 E3
SUNDSW SR3 .... 98 A7
Wyvern Sq ASHBK/HED/RY SR2 .... 98 E4

Y

Yardley Cl SUNDSW SR3 .... 110 A2
Yardley Gv CRAM NE23 .... 23 G7 1
Yarmouth Cl SEA/MUR SR7 .... 120 B2 5
Yarmouth Dr CRAM NE23 .... 23 G7
Yatesbury Av
WD/WHPE/BLK NE5 .... 55 F1
Yelverton Ct CRAM NE23 .... 23 G7
Yelverton Crs
BYK/HTN/WLK NE6 .... 13 G2
Yeoman St NSHW NE29 .... 2 E4
Yeovil Cl CRAM NE23 .... 23 G7 2
Yetholm Av CLSW/PEL DH2 .... 105 H5
Yetholm Pl
WD/WHPE/BLK NE5 .... 44 E6 5
Yetholm Rd GATE NE8 .... 9 M5
Yetlington Dr GOS/KPK NE3 .... 46 A6
Yewbank Av DHAM DH1 .... 125 J6
Yewburn Wy LGB/KIL NE12 .... 47 H4
Yewcroft Av
BW/LEM/TK/HW NE15 .... 54 D5
Yewdale Gdns
LWF/SPW/WRK NE9 .... 81 G1 1
Yewtree Av SWCK/CAS SR5 .... 85 K3
Yew Tree Dr BDLGTN NE22 .... 19 F4
Yewtree Gdns
BYK/HTN/WLK NE6 .... 58 C2
Yewtrees FELL NE10 .... 70 A7 5
Yewvale Rd WD/WHPE/BLK NE5 .. 55 H2
Yoden Av PLEE/EAS SR8 .... 137 G2
Yoden Crs PLEE/EAS SR8 .... 137 G2
Yoden Rd PLEE/EAS SR8 .... 136 E3
Yoden Wy PLEE/EAS SR8 .... 137 G4
York Av JRW NE32 .... 71 K1 5
York Cl CRAM NE23 .... 23 G7
York Crs DHAM DH1 .... 124 E1
HLH DH5 .... 117 J4
Yorkdale Pl
BYK/HTN/WLK NE6 .... 58 C5 5
York Dr WLSD/HOW NE28 .... 58 C2
York Rd CLS/BIR/GTL DH3 .... 93 J5
PLEE/EAS SR8 .... 136 D2
WBAY NE26 .... 41 F4
Yorkshire Dr DHAM DH1 .... 126 A6
York St ELS/FEN NE4 .... 4 E7
FELL NE10 .... 13 J6
HLH DH5 .... 117 H7
JRW NE32 .... 59 J5
SUND SR1 .... 14 E4
York Ter CLS/BIR/GTL DH3 .... 105 K5
York Wy HAR/WTLS NE34 .... 62 A5
Yorkwood HEBB NE31 .... 58 E4
Young Rd LGB/KIL NE12 .... 48 B1
Young St DHAM DH1 .... 17 K2

Z

Zetland Dr MONK NE25 .... 40 D7
Zetland St CLDN/WHIT/ROK SR6 .. 86 E4
Zion St SUND SR1 .... 15 H4 5
Zion Ter SWCK/CAS SR5 .... 86 C2

Index - featured places

Abbey Sports Centre
DHAM DH1 .... 124 D1
Acre Rigg Junior & Infant School
PLEE/EAS SR8 .... 136 C2
Adamsez West Industrial Estate
BLAY NE21 .... 54 D7
Adelaide Row Medical Centre
SEA/MUR SR7 .... 120 E1
Airport Church
WD/WHPE/BLK NE5 .... 55 G1
Akhurst Preparatory School
JES NE2 .... 57 F1
Albert Elliott County Junior Mixed School
HAR/WTLS NE34 .... 73 G2
Albert Road Surgery
JRW NE32 .... 59 K5
Alexandra Business Park
MLFD/PNYW SR4 .... 85 J5
Algernon Industrial Estate
SMOOR NE27 .... 49 H1
All Saints Junior Mixed School
HAR/WTLS NE34 .... 61 F7
Amberley First School
LGB/KIL NE12 .... 38 A5
AMF Bowling
ELS/FEN NE4 .... 4 B6
AMF Bowling
WASHS NE38 .... 94 E1
Amphitheatre
SSH NE33 .... 3 M6
Annfield Plain County Junior Mixed School
STLY/ANP DH9 .... 101 J4
Annfield Plain Cricket Club
STLY/ANP DH9 .... 101 G4
Annfield Plain Infants School
STLY/ANP DH9 .... 101 H4
Appletree Gardens First School
MONK NE25 .... 40 C5
Arbeia Roman Fort & Museum
SSH NE33 .... 3 H4

Archbishop Runcie C of E School *GOS/KPK* NE3 46 D4
Archibald First School *GOS/KPK* NE3 46 B5
Arena Business Park *HLS* DH4 117 G2
Argyle House School *ASHBK/HED/RY* SR2 14 C8
The Art Gallery *SUND* SR1 14 E5
Arthurs Hill Clinic *ELS/FEN* NE4 4 F5
Arthur Street Surgery *BDN/LAN/SAC* DH7 122 E7
Ascham House School *GOS/KPK* NE3 46 C6
Ashburne Medical Centre *ASHBK/HED/RY* SR2 15 G9
Ashleigh School *TYNE/NSHE* NE30 2 F1
Ashley Road County JMI School *HAR/WTLS* NE34 61 G5
Astley Community High School *MONK* NE25 29 K5
Atkinson House School *CRAM* NE23 29 G6
Atkinson Road Primary School *BW/LEM/TK/HW* NE15 55 G7
The Avenues Medical Practice *GOS/KPK* NE3 46 C7
Aykley Heads Business Centre *DHAM* DH1 124 C5
Ayton Primary School *WASHS* NE38 94 B3
Backworth County First School *SMOOR* NE27 38 E4
Bailey Green First School *LGB/KIL* NE12 37 J5
Balliol Business Park *LGB/KIL* NE12 47 G2
Balliol First School *LGB/KIL* NE12 47 H4
Barley Mow Primary School *CLS/BIR/GTL* DH3 93 K4
Barmston Medical Centre *WASHS* NE38 83 H7
Barmston Village Primary School *WASHS* NE38 95 H1
Barnes Junior School *MLFD/PNYW* SR4 97 K2
Barnwell Primary School *HLS* DH4 95 K6
Battle Hill First School *WLSD/HOW* NE28 49 F5
Bbc North & Radio Newcastle *JES* NE2 4 D2
Beaconhill County First School *CRAM* NE23 27 K2
Beamish County School *STLY/ANP* DH9 91 H7
Beamish Park Golf Club *STLY/ANP* DH9 91 G4
Beaumont Park Surgery *MONK* NE25 40 B3
Bebside County Middle School *BLYTH* NE24 20 B6
Bebside Social Club House *BLYTH* NE24 19 K7
Bede Infant School *FELL* NE10 11 M4
Bedewell School *HEBB* NE31 59 G7
Bedlington Community High School *BDLGTN* NE22 19 K4
Bedlington Station County First School *BDLGTN* NE22 19 K3
Bedlington Stead County First School *BDLGTN* NE22 19 J5
Belford House Sports Club *ASHBK/HED/RY* SR2 98 D3
Bellway Industrial Estate *LGB/KIL* NE12 48 B3
Belmont C of E (Controlled) Junior School *DHAM* DH1 125 K6
Belmont Comprehensive School *DHAM* DH1 125 K6
Belmont County Infant School *DHAM* DH1 125 K6
Belmont Grange Clinic *DHAM* DH1 125 K5
Belvedere Retail Park *GOS/KPK* NE3 45 G4
Benedict Biscop C of E School *SUNDSW* SR3 109 H2
Benfield Comprehensive School *BYK/HTN/WLK* NE6 58 A2
Bensham District Clinic *GATE* NE8 10 D7
Bensham Family Practice *GATE* NE8 10 C6
Bensham Synagogue *GATE* NE8 10 D6
Benton Park Primary School *LGB/HTN* NE7 47 H6
Benwell Hill Cricket Club *BW/LEM/TK/HW* NE15 55 F4
Bernard Gilpin Primary School *HLH* DH5 108 C7
Bessie Surtees House *CNUT* NE1 5 L8
Bewicke Health Centre *WLSD/HOW* NE28 59 J1
Bewick Road Medical Centre *GATE* NE8 11 G5
Bexhill Primary School *SWCK/CAS* SR5 84 D2
Biddick Hall County Infant School *HAR/WTLS* NE34 72 E1
Biddick Hall County Junior School *HAR/WTLS* NE34 61 F7
Biddick School *WASHS* NE38 95 G3
Bill Quay Cricket Club *FELL* NE10 13 M4
Birtley East Primary School *CLS/BIR/GTL* DH3 81 J7
Birtley Lane Surgery *CLS/BIR/GTL* DH3 93 J2
Birtley Medical Group Practice *CLS/BIR/GTL* DH3 93 J3
Birtley St Josephs RC School *CLS/BIR/GTL* DH3 93 J2
Birtley Swimming Baths *CLS/BIR/GTL* DH3 93 J3
Blackfell Primary School *WASHN* NE37 82 C7
Blackfriars Craft Centre *CNUT* NE1 5 H6
Black Gate *CNUT* NE1 5 K8
Blackhall Primary School *RHTLP* TS27 137 K7
Blakelaw Health Centre *WD/WHPE/BLK* NE5 55 G1
Blakelaw School *WD/WHPE/BLK* NE5 55 G1
Blaydon Business Centre *BLAY* NE21 66 C1
Blaydon Business Park *BLAY* NE21 54 D7
Blaydon Cricket Club *BLAY* NE21 66 A2
Blaydon Haugh Industrial Estate *BLAY* NE21 66 C1
Blaydon Industrial Park *BLAY* NE21 66 B1
Blaydon Rugby Football Club *WICK/BNPF* NE16 66 D3
Blaydon Swimming Pool *BLAY* NE21 66 C2
Blaydon West Primary School *BLAY* NE21 66 A1
Bloemfontein County Junior Mixed School *STLY/ANP* DH9 102 E4
Blyth Delaval County Middle School *BLYTH* NE24 25 F2
Blyth New Delaval County First School *BLYTH* NE24 24 D3
Blyth Newsham County First School *BLYTH* NE24 24 E2
Blyth Plessey Road County First School *BLYTH* NE24 21 H7
Blyth Spartans AFC *BLYTH* NE24 25 G1
Blyth Sports Centre *BLYTH* NE24 21 F7
Blyth Tynedale County High School *BLYTH* NE24 20 C7
Blyth Tynedale County Middle School *BLYTH* NE24 20 C7
Blyth Valley Borough Council *BLYTH* NE24 20 D5
Blyth Valley Borough Council *BLYTH* NE24 21 F7
Blyth Valley Borough Council *MONK* NE25 29 K5
Boker Lane Health Centre *BOLCOL* NE35 73 F4
Bolam Business Park *CRAM* NE23 22 D7
Boldon Comprehensive School *BOLCOL* NE35 72 E4
Boldon Lane Health Centre *HAR/WTLS* NE34 61 G7
Bow School *DHAM* DH1 16 D7
Brandling Primary School *FELL* NE10 12 C6
Brandon & Byshottles Parish Council *BDN/LAN/SAC* DH7 133 J5
Brandon Cricket Club *BDN/LAN/SAC* DH7 133 J5
Brandon Modern School *BDN/LAN/SAC* DH7 133 G6
Brandon United Football Club *BDN/LAN/SAC* DH7 133 H5
Brewery *ELS/FEN* NE4 5 G6
Brewery *SUND* SR1 14 D3
Bridges Shopping Centre *SUND* SR1 14 D5
Brighton Avenue Primary School *GATE* NE8 10 D6
Brinkburn School *HAR/WTLS* NE34 61 H6
Broadway East First School *GOS/KPK* NE3 46 D3
Broadway Junior School *MLFD/PNYW* SR4 97 H2
Broadwood Junior & Infant School *BW/LEM/TK/HW* NE15 54 D4
Brockwell Clinic *CRAM* NE23 23 H7
Brockwell County Middle School *CRAM* NE23 23 H7
Broomside Lane Surgery *DHAM* DH1 125 K5
Browney County Primary School *BDN/LAN/SAC* DH7 133 J7
Browns Gallery *JES* NE2 56 E1
Brunswick Beech Special School *DIN/WO* NE13 36 A3
Buddle Industrial Estate *WLSD/HOW* NE28 58 D3
Buddle Industrial Estate *WLSD/HOW* NE28 58 E3
Bugatti Industrial Park *NSHW* NE29 50 A5
Bullion Lane Primary School *CLSW/PEL* DH2 105 H5
Burnmoor Cricket Club *HLS* DH4 107 G3
Burnopfield Primary School *WICK/BNPF* NE16 77 H7
Burnside County First School *CRAM* NE23 23 J6
Burnside High School *WLSD/HOW* NE28 59 F1
Burnside JMI School *STLY/ANP* DH9 103 F2
Burnside Primary School *HLS* DH4 108 B6
Burradon First School *CRAM* NE23 37 J4
Byermoor RC Aided Junior & Infant School *WICK/BNPF* NE16 78 B6
Byker Primary School *BYK/HTN/WLK* NE6 6 F6
Caedman Primary School *GATE* NE8 10 F6
Cambois County First School *BLYTH* NE24 20 E2
Camden Square Secondary School *SEA/MUR* SR7 120 D1
Carr Hill Infant & Junior School *LWF/SPW/WRK* NE9 11 L9
Cartmel Business Centre *FELL* NE10 13 J6
Carville First School *WLSD/HOW* NE28 58 D3
Castle *DHAM* DH1 16 D4
Castle Dene Special School *GOS/KPK* NE3 47 F6
Castle Keep *CNUT* NE1 5 L8
Castle Leazes Halls *JES* NE2 4 F3
Castle View School *SWCK/CAS* SR5 84 E4
Catchgate Primary School *STLY/ANP* DH9 101 G3
Cedars Special School *LWF/SPW/WRK* NE9 81 G2
Central First School *WLSD/HOW* NE28 59 F1
Central High School *GOS/KPK* NE3 46 C6
Central Newcastle High School *JES* NE2 5 L1
Central Surgery *SUND* SR1 14 F5
Cestria Health Centre *CLSW/PEL* DH2 105 F5
Cestria Primary School *CLS/BIR/GTL* DH3 105 K4
Chapel House Middle School *WD/WHPE/BLK* NE5 53 K1
Chapel Park Shopping Centre *WD/WHPE/BLK* NE5 44 B6
Chase School *WICK/BNPF* NE16 67 F5
Chastleton Surgery *DHAM* DH1 124 C3
Chester Le Street Leisure Centre *CLS/BIR/GTL* DH3 105 K4
Chester Le Street C of E Junior School *CLSW/PEL* DH2 105 H3
Chester Le Street Cricket Club *CLS/BIR/GTL* DH3 105 K5
Chester Le Street District Council *CLS/BIR/GTL* DH3 105 J3
Chester Le Street District Council *CLSW/PEL* DH2 105 G4
Chester Le Street Health Centre *CLS/BIR/GTL* DH3 105 K3
Chester Road Surgery *MLFD/PNYW* SR4 86 A7
Cheveley Park Medical Centre *DHAM* DH1 126 A6
Cheveley Park Primary School *DHAM* DH1 126 A5
Cheviot County Junior Mixed School *HAR/WTLS* NE34 62 A3
Cheviot First School *WD/WHPE/BLK* NE5 44 E6
Chevyside Middle School *WD/WHPE/BLK* NE5 44 E6
Childrens Hospital *SUNDSW* SR3 98 A2
Chillingham Industrial Estate *BYK/HTN/WLK* NE6 7 H2
Chillingham Road Primary School *BYK/HTN/WLK* NE6 7 G1
Choppington County First School *STKFD/GP* NE62 18 E1
The Chorister School *DHAM* DH1 16 C6
Christ Church C of E Primary School *JES* NE2 5 M5
Church of England Primary School *WLSD/HOW* NE28 59 G1
Church View Medical Centre *SUNDSW* SR3 98 A7
Cinema *SUND* SR1 14 E6
City Council *DHAM* DH1 16 F2
City Hall *CNUT* NE1 5 L4
City of Sunderland College *ASHBK/HED/RY* SR2 98 E4
City of Sunderland College *HLS* DH4 107 K2
City of Sunderland College *SUND* SR1 14 E4
City of Sunderland College *SWCK/CAS* SR5 85 H3
City of Sunderland College *SWCK/CAS* SR5 86 C3
City Pool *CNUT* NE1 5 K4
Civic Centre *CLS/BIR/GTL* DH3 105 K3
Civic Centre *CNUT* NE1 5 K4
Civic Centre *GATE* NE8 10 F3
Civic Centre *SUND* SR1 14 E6
Civic Hall *WLSD/HOW* NE28 58 D1
Civil Service Sports Club *LGB/KIL* NE12 48 A5
Claremont Footcare Surgery *WBAY* NE26 40 C2
Claypath Medical Practice *DHAM* DH1 16 F3
Clayton Street Indoor Mini Market *CNUT* NE1 5 J7
Cleadon Village C of E Infant School *CLDN/WHIT/ROK* SR6 74 B3
Cleadon Village County JM School *CLDN/WHIT/ROK* SR6 73 K3
Club House *DHAM* DH1 134 C4
Club House *HLH* DH5 109 F7
Collierley County Primary School *STLY/ANP* DH9 88 E6
Collingwood Primary School *NSHW* NE29 50 B5
Community College *SEA/MUR* SR7 111 J7
Coquet Park First School *WBAY* NE26 40 E3
Corrymella Scott Gallery *JES* NE2 56 D3
Cotsford Junior School *PLEE/EAS* SR8 137 J3
County Durham Health Authority *PLEE/EAS* SR8 136 E4
County Hall Durham County Council *DHAM* DH1 124 C5
County Hospital *DHAM* DH1 16 B3
County Junior & Infant School *BDN/LAN/SAC* DH7 123 G6
County Junior & Infant School *RDHAMSE* DH6 128 D6
County Junior Middle & Infant School *STLY/ANP* DH9 103 K1
Cowgate Leisure Centre *WD/WHPE/BLK* NE5 45 H7
Cowgate Primary School *ELS/FEN* NE4 55 J2
Cragside County First School *CRAM* NE23 28 C4
Cragside Primary School *LGB/HTN* NE7 47 G7
Craigievar School *CLDN/WHIT/ROK* SR6 86 E2
Cramlington Football Club *CRAM* NE23 28 E2
Crawcrook Medical Centre *RYTON* NE40 52 B7
Crawcrook RC Junior & Infant School *RYTON* NE40 52 A7
Crook Hall *DHAM* DH1 16 D1
Crookhill Junior School *RYTON* NE40 53 G6
Crown Court *CNUT* NE1 5 L8
Crowtree Leisure Centre *SUND* SR1 14 D5
Cruddas Park Health Centre *ELS/FEN* NE4 4 D9
Cruddas Park Surgery *ELS/FEN* NE4 4 E9
Cullercoats Primary School *TYNE/NSHE* NE30 41 G6
Custom House *CNUT* NE1 5 M8
Dame Allans Boys School *ELS/FEN* NE4 55 J4
Dame Dorothy Street School *CLDN/WHIT/ROK* SR6 15 G1
Davenport School *HLH* DH5 117 H2
Deerness Park Medical Centre *ASHBK/HED/RY* SR2 15 H7
Deerness Sports Centre *BDN/LAN/SAC* DH7 133 F1
Deerness Valley Comprehensive School *BDN/LAN/SAC* DH7 123 F6
Delaval Primary School *BW/LEM/TK/HW* NE15 55 F6
Denbigh Community First School *WLSD/HOW* NE28 49 J7
Dene House County Mixed Modern School *PLEE/EAS* SR8 137 H4
Deneside Junior & Infant School *SEA/MUR* SR7 120 B2
Deneside Medical Centre *SEA/MUR* SR7 120 C1
Denton Park Middle School *WD/WHPE/BLK* NE5 54 D1
Denton Road Primary School *BW/LEM/TK/HW* NE15 54 D6
Derwenthaugh Industrial Estate *BLAY* NE21 66 D1
Derwent Infant School *GATE* NE8 10 A6
Derwentside College *BDN/LAN/SAC* DH7 122 A2
Derwentside District Council *STLY/ANP* DH9 101 J5
Derwentside District Council *STLY/ANP* DH9 102 D1
Diamond Hall Junior & Infant School *MLFD/PNYW* SR4 85 K6
Dinnington Village First School *DIN/WO* NE13 35 G2
Dipton Surgery *STLY/ANP* DH9 88 E6
DLI Museum & Arts Centre *DHAM* DH1 124 D6
Donwell Primary School *WASHN* NE37 82 E4
Downhill Primary School *SWCK/CAS* SR5 85 F1
Dragonville Industrial Park *DHAM* DH1 125 J7
Dr Chandys Surgery *PLEE/EAS* SR8 137 H3
Dr Dhuny's Surgery *STLY/ANP* DH9 103 F4
The Drive Primary School *FELL* NE10 12 F7
Dr Krishnans Surgery *GATE* NE8 10 C7
Dr Rannus Surgery *DUN/TMV* NE11 9 J7
Dr Reg Carrs Surgery *BLYTH* NE24 21 H7
Dryburn Hospital *DHAM* DH1 124 B5
DSS *SUND* SR1 14 C4
Dubmire County Junior & Infant School *HLS* DH4 107 J7
Dudley Surgery *CRAM* NE23 37 H1
Dunelm Medical Practice *BDN/LAN/SAC* DH7 123 G6
Dunelm Medical Practice *DHAM* DH1 17 K2
Dunholme School *DHAM* DH1 124 C4
Dunston Federation Football Club *DUN/TMV* NE11 8 F5
Dunston Health Centre *DUN/TMV* NE11 8 F8
Dunston Hill Hospital *DUN/TMV* NE11 8 D9
Dunston Hill Junior & Infant School *DUN/TMV* NE11 8 F8
Dunston Industrial Estate *DUN/TMV* NE11 8 E5
Dunston Riverside Primary School *DUN/TMV* NE11 9 H5
Dunston Swimming Pool *DUN/TMV* NE11 8 F9
Durham Baths *DHAM* DH1 16 F4
Durham Blue Coat C of E (Aided) Junior School *DHAM* DH1 124 D3
Durham Business Centre *BDN/LAN/SAC* DH7 133 K5
Durham Cathedral *DHAM* DH1 16 D5
Durham City Amateur Football Club *DHAM* DH1 125 J5
Durham City Cricket Club *DHAM* DH1 17 H5
Durham City Rugby Club *DHAM* DH1 17 H5
Durham County Constabulary *PLEE/EAS* SR8 136 E4
Durham County Council *CLS/BIR/GTL* DH3 115 J1
Durham County Council *DHAM* DH1 124 D2
Durham County Council *DHAM* DH1 124 C4
Durham County Council *DHAM* DH1 125 K7
Durham County Council *PLEE/EAS* SR8 136 D1
Durham County Council *PLEE/EAS* SR8 137 G2
Durham County Council *SEA/MUR* SR7 119 H5
Durham County Council *STLY/ANP* DH9 102 C1
Durham County Cricket Club *CLS/BIR/GTL* DH3 106 A5
Durham County NHS Trust *DHAM* DH1 123 K2
Durham Crown Court *DHAM* DH1 16 E5
Durham Gilesgate Comprehensive School *DHAM* DH1 125 H6
Durham High School *DHAM* DH1 134 C5

Durham Johnston Comprehensive School *DHAM* DH1 17 G6
Durham Johnston Comprehensive School *DHAM* DH1 124 B7
Durham Markets Co *DHAM* DH1 16 D3
Durham Newton Hall County Infant School *DHAM* DH1 124 D3
Durham St Hilds C of E (Aided) Primary School *DHAM* DH1 17 M2
Durham School *DHAM* DH1 16 B6
Durham Sixth Form Centre *DHAM* DH1 16 D2
Earls House Hospital *DHAM* DH1 123 K3
Easington C of E School *PLEE/EAS* SR8 130 B6
Easington Colliery Primary School *PLEE/EAS* SR8 130 D5
Easington Comprehensive School *PLEE/EAS* SR8 130 B6
Easington District Council *PLEE/EAS* SR8 130 C5
Easington District Council *PLEE/EAS* SR8 136 A1
Easington District Council *PLEE/EAS* SR8 136 E1
Easington District Council *SEA/MUR* SR7 119 J5
Easington District Council *SEA/MUR* SR7 120 D3
Easington District Council *SEA/MUR* SR7 120 B1
Easington District Leisure Centre *SEA/MUR* SR7 120 C1
Easington Lane Primary School *HLH* DH5 128 C1
East Boldon Junior School *BOL* NE36 73 G5
Eastcliffe Grammar School *GOS/KPK* NE3 46 D6
East Durham Community College *PLEE/EAS* SR8 136 E4
East Herrington Primary School *SUNDSW* SR3 97 G7
Eastlea First School *CRAM* NE23 23 J7
East Rainton JMI School *HLH* DH5 117 F4
Eden Hall Infant School *PLEE/EAS* SR8 137 F3
Edmondsley JMI School *BDN/LAN/SAC* DH7 113 G1
Eldon Square Shopping Centre *CNUT* NE1 5 K5
Elemore Leisure Centre *HLH* DH5 118 B7
Ellison C of E JMI School *JRW* NE32 59 K5
Elswick Way Industrial Estate *HAR/WTLS* NE34 60 E5
Emmanuel College *DUN/TMV* NE11 67 K7
Emmaville Primary School *RYTON* NE40 52 B7
Empire Theatre *SUND* SR1 14 C4
English Martyrs RC Primary School *SWCK/CAS* SR5 85 J3
Epinay Special School *JRW* NE32 60 A5
Eppleton Cricket Club *HLH* DH5 117 K2
The Evergreen Gallery *CNUT* NE1 5 J8
Eye Clinic *CNUT* NE1 5 K4
Farne First School *WD/WHPE/BLK* NE5 44 E7
Farnham Medical Centre *HAR/WTLS* NE34 61 G5
Farringdon School *SUNDSW* SR3 97 H7
Farrington Infant School *SUNDSW* SR3 97 H6
Farrington Junior School *SUNDSW* SR3 97 H6
Fatfield Junior & Infant School *WASHS* NE38 95 F4
Felldyke Primary & Infant School *LWF/SPW/WRK* NE9 81 K2
Fellgate Jmi School *JRW* NE32 71 K3
Felling Business Centre *FELL* NE10 12 C3
Fellrose Surgery *CLSW/PEL* DH2 104 E3
Fellside County Primary School *WICK/BNPF* NE16 66 E6
Fell Tower Medical Centre Whereis Building *LWF/SPW/WRK* NE9 81 F1
Felstead School *MLFD/PNYW* SR4 85 H7
Fence Houses Surgery *HLS* DH4 107 G5
Finchale County Infant School *DHAM* DH1 125 F2
Finchale Priory *DHAM* DH1 115 J5
Fire Station *CNUT* NE1 5 L6
Fire Station *SUND* SR1 14 B5
First School *MONK* NE25 29 J4
Fordley Clinic *CRAM* NE23 37 G1
Formica Social & Sports Club *NSHW* NE29 49 K3
Framwellgate Moor Comprehensive School *DHAM* DH1 124 C3
Framwellgate Moor Junior & Infant School *DHAM* DH1 124 C3
Freeman Hospital *LGB/HTN* NE7 47 G6
Front Street Industrial Estate *RDHAMSE* DH6 128 E2
Front Street Junior & Infant School *WICK/BNPF* NE16 66 E5
Front Street Surgery *BLAY* NE21 65 K3
Fulling Mill *DHAM* DH1 16 C5
Fulwell Grange Christian School *SWCK/CAS* SR5 86 C2
Fulwell Junior School *CLDN/WHIT/ROK* SR6 86 E1
Fulwell Medical Centre *CLDN/WHIT/ROK* SR6 86 D1
Fyndoune Community College *BDN/LAN/SAC* DH7 113 H6
The Gables Medical Group *BDLGTN* NE22 19 K4
Galactic Zoo *CNUT* NE1 5 H8
Gallery of Fine Art *CNUT* NE1 5 J5
The Gallery *CLSW/PEL* DH2 114 C1
The Gambling Man Gallery *TYNE/NSHE* NE30 2 F4
Garden Park Surgery *WLSD/HOW* NE28 49 J6
The Garrick Gallery *STLY/ANP* DH9 102 C1
Gateshead Area Health Authority *BLAY* NE21 66 D2
Gateshead Area Health Authority *DUN/TMV* NE11 68 A6
Gateshead Area Health Authority *GATE* NE8 10 A5
Gateshead Area Health Authority *GATE* NE8 10 F4
Gateshead Area Health Authority *LWF/SPW/WRK* NE9 69 H6
Gateshead Area Health Authority *WICK/BNPF* NE16 67 F5
Gateshead College *LWF/SPW/WRK* NE9 11 G9
Gateshead Complimentary Health Centre *GATE* NE8 10 E6
Gateshead Fell Cricket Club *LWF/SPW/WRK* NE9 69 G6
Gateshead Health Care *FELL* NE10 70 D6
Gateshead Health NHS Trust *LWF/SPW/WRK* NE9 11 J9
Gateshead Hospitals NHS Trust *GATE* NE8 68 D5
Gateshead International Stadium *FELL* NE10 12 A2
Gateshead Jewish Boys School *GATE* NE8 10 F5
Gateshead Jewish Primary School *GATE* NE8 10 F6
Gateshead Leisure Centre *GATE* NE8 11 G7
Gateshead Little Theatre *GATE* NE8 10 F8
Gateshead Magistrates Court *GATE* NE8 11 G4
Gateshead Metropolitan Borough Council *BLAY* NE21 66 B1
Gateshead Metropolitan Borough Council *CLS/BIR/GTL* DH3 93 J1
Gateshead Metropolitan Borough Council *DUN/TMV* NE11 80 D2
Gateshead Metropolitan Borough Council *FELL* NE10 12 C8
Gateshead Metropolitan Borough Council *GATE* NE8 10 E4
Gateshead Metropolitan Borough Council *GATE* NE8 11 L2
Gateshead Metropolitan Borough Council *GATE* NE8 11 G2
Gateshead Metropolitan Borough Council *LWF/SPW/WRK* NE9 69 H5
Gateshead Metropolitan Borough Council *LWF/SPW/WRK* NE9 69 F7
Gateshead Metropolitan Borough Council *LWF/SPW/WRK* NE9 81 G2
Gateshead Metropolitan Borough Council *ROWG* NE39 76 E3
Gateshead Metropolitan Borough Council *WICK/BNPF* NE16 67 F5
Gateshead & South Tyneside Health Authority *SSH* NE33 61 H2
Gateshead Talmudical College *GATE* NE8 10 D6
George Stephenson High School *LGB/KIL* NE12 37 K7
Gibside School *WICK/BNPF* NE16 66 E7
Gilesgate County Junior School *DHAM* DH1 17 L1
Gilesgate County Junior School *DHAM* DH1 125 H6
Glebe School *WBAY* NE26 40 C1
Glebe Village Primary School *WASHS* NE38 95 F1
Glen Dene School *PLEE/EAS* SR8 130 B5
The Globe Gallery *TYNE/NSHE* NE30 2 E2
Glover Industrial Estate *WASHN* NE37 83 H6
Glynwood Primary School *LWF/SPW/WRK* NE9 69 G7
Goathland Primary School *LGB/KIL* NE12 47 J4
Gosforth Central Middle School *GOS/KPK* NE3 46 C4
Gosforth Cricket Club *GOS/KPK* NE3 46 C6
Gosforth High School *GOS/KPK* NE3 46 C4
Gosforth Industrial Estate *GOS/KPK* NE3 46 D4
Gosforth Memorial Health Centre *GOS/KPK* NE3 46 D5
Gosforth West Middle School *GOS/KPK* NE3 46 B5
Grainger Market *CNUT* NE1 5 J6
Grange First School *GOS/KPK* NE3 46 B4
Grange Park Primary School *SWCK/CAS* SR5 86 C3
Grange Terrace Surgery *ASHBK/HED/RY* SR2 14 D7
Grangetown Family Dental Health Centre *ASHBK/HED/RY* SR2 98 E4
Grangetown Junior & Infant School *ASHBK/HED/RY* SR2 99 F3
Grangewood Surgery *HLS* DH4 107 J1
Greencroft Comprehensive School *STLY/ANP* DH9 101 G3
Greencroft Comprehensive School *STLY/ANP* DH9 101 K3
Greenesfield Business Centre *GATE* NE8 10 E1
Greenfields Special School *HEBB* NE31 59 H4
Greenland County Jmi School *STLY/ANP* DH9 102 B3
Greenside Cricket Club *RYTON* NE40 64 C3
Greenside JMI School *RYTON* NE40 64 B3
Grey College *DHAM* DH1 16 D9
Grindon Infants School *MLFD/PNYW* SR4 97 F3
Hadrian JMI School *SSH* NE33 3 H4
Hadrian Park First School *WLSD/HOW* NE28 49 G3
Hadrian Park Middle School *WLSD/HOW* NE28 49 G3
Hadrian School *BW/LEM/TK/HW* NE15 55 G5
Halls of Residence *MLFD/PNYW* SR4 14 A6
Hancock Museum *JES* NE2 5 K3
Harlow Green Infant School *LWF/SPW/WRK* NE9 81 G3
Harraton Primary School *WASHS* NE38 94 D5
Hartlepool Community Care NHS Trust *PLEE/EAS* SR8 136 E4
Harton School *HAR/WTLS* NE34 62 A5
Hatfield College *DHAM* DH1 16 D5
Havelock Primary School *MLFD/PNYW* SR4 85 H7
Hawthorn House Medical Centre *BYK/HTN/WLK* NE6 7 G4
Hawthorn Primary School *ELS/FEN* NE4 4 D8
Hawthorns Hospital *PLEE/EAS* SR8 137 F5
Hazlewood Community Primary School *DIN/WO* NE13 36 B4
Headway Theatre *BLYTH* NE24 21 H6
Heaton Manor Lower School *LGB/HTN* NE7 57 G1
Heaton Manor Upper School *LGB/HTN* NE7 47 J6
Hebrew Synagogue *WBAY* NE26 40 E4
Heddon on the Wall C of E Controlled First School *BW/LEM/TK/HW* NE15 52 A1
Hedworthfield Comprehensive School *JRW* NE32 71 K3
Heritage Centre *DHAM* DH1 16 E5
Herrington Medical Centre *HLS* DH4 108 A1
Hetton Health Centre *HLH* DH5 117 K4
Hetton Lyons School *HLH* DH5 117 K6
Hetton Primary School *HLH* DH5 117 J5
Hetton Secondary School *HLH* DH5 117 J5
Hetton UDC Swimming Baths *HLH* DH5 117 J5
Heworth Grange Comprehensive School *FELL* NE10 13 H8
High Farm Middle School *WLSD/HOW* NE28 48 D5
High Fell Special School *LWF/SPW/WRK* NE9 11 K9
Highfield County Infant School *HAR/WTLS* NE34 62 A2
Highfield Hospital *CLS/BIR/GTL* DH3 105 J2
Highfield Junior & Infant School *ROWG* NE39 76 D3
High Spen Industrial Estate *ROWG* NE39 64 B7
High Spen Industrial Estate *ROWG* NE39 77 H2
Hillcrest Day Special School *CRAM* NE23 28 C2
Hillsview Surgery *GOS/KPK* NE3 45 J4
Hill Top School *LWF/SPW/WRK* NE9 82 A1
Hillview Clinic *ASHBK/HED/RY* SR2 98 D4
Hill View Infant School *ASHBK/HED/RY* SR2 98 D4
Hill View Junior School *ASHBK/HED/RY* SR2 98 D4
Hilton Primary School *WD/WHPE/BLK* NE5 55 F1
Hindu Temple *ELS/FEN* NE4 55 H5
HM Prison *DHAM* DH1 16 F5
HMS Calliope Cadet Training Centre *GATE* NE8 6 A8
The Hobart Gallery *GOS/KPK* NE3 46 C6
Hollyhurst Medical Centre *BLAY* NE21 65 K3
Holly Park Primary School *WASHS* NE38 94 B3
Holmside & South Moor Hospital *STLY/ANP* DH9 102 E3
Holy Cross RC Primary School *WLSD/HOW* NE28 49 H6
Holystone First School *SMOOR* NE27 38 E7
Holywell County First School *MONK* NE25 30 C6
Hookergate Comprehensive School *ROWG* NE39 76 D2
Horden Cotsford County Infant School *PLEE/EAS* SR8 137 J4
Horden & Easington RC Primary School *PLEE/EAS* SR8 137 G1
Horton Grange First School *BLYTH* NE24 20 B6
Hotspur Primary School *BYK/HTN/WLK* NE6 6 D4
Houghall College *DHAM* DH1 17 H8
Houghton Colliery Welfare Cricket Club *HLS* DH4 108 A6
Houghton Health Centre *HLH* DH5 108 C7
Houghton Kepier School *HLS* DH4 108 B7
Howden Green Industrial Estate *WLSD/HOW* NE28 59 K1
Howletch Lane Junior & Infant School *PLEE/EAS* SR8 136 C4
Hudson Road Primary School *SUND* SR1 15 G6
Hylton Castle *SWCK/CAS* SR5 85 F3
Hylton Castle Health Centre *SWCK/CAS* SR5 85 F3
Hylton Castle Junior School *SWCK/CAS* SR5 84 D3
Imex Business Centre *DHAM* DH1 124 C1
Industrial Estate *BDN/LAN/SAC* DH7 113 H5
Ivy Road Primary School *LGB/KIL* NE12 48 A2
Jewish Boarding School *GATE* NE8 10 F5
Jewish High School *GATE* NE8 11 G5
Jewish Infant School *GATE* NE8 11 G5
John Spence Community High School *TYNE/NSHE* NE30 50 E2
Joseph Swan School *LWF/SPW/WRK* NE9 80 E2
Jubilee Infant School *SEA/MUR* SR7 119 J5
Kelvin Grove Primary School *GATE* NE8 10 E8
Kenton Comprehensive School *GOS/KPK* NE3 45 H6
Kenton Lodge Residential School *ELS/FEN* NE4 56 B1
Kepier Clinic *DHAM* DH1 17 L1
Kibblesworth Primary School *DUN/TMV* NE11 80 D7
Killingworth Middle School *LGB/KIL* NE12 37 K7
King Edward Junior & Infant School *TYNE/NSHE* NE30 51 F3
Kingfisher Industrial Estate *SEA/MUR* SR7 111 G7
King George Comprehensive School *HAR/WTLS* NE34 73 K1
Kingsmeadow Comprehensive School *DUN/TMV* NE11 8 E7
Kings School *TYNE/NSHE* NE30 51 H3
Kingston Park Primary School *GOS/KPK* NE3 45 G4
Kingsway First School *BLYTH* NE24 25 G1
Knoplaw First School *WD/WHPE/BLK* NE5 54 A1
Laing Art Gallery *CNUT* NE1 5 L5
Lancaster University *CNUT* NE1 5 K8
Langley Moor Primary School *BDN/LAN/SAC* DH7 133 K4
Langley Park Primary School *BDN/LAN/SAC* DH7 122 B3
Larkspur Primary School *LWF/SPW/WRK* NE9 81 J1
La Sagesse Convent High School *JES* NE2 46 E7
Laurel Avenue County Junior & Infant School *DHAM* DH1 17 K4
Law Courts *CNUT* NE1 5 M7
Laygate Lane County Infant School *SSH* NE33 61 G2
Laygate School *SSH* NE33 61 G2
Leadgate Industrial Estate *CON/LDGT* DH8 100 A5
Leafield House School *CLS/BIR/GTL* DH3 93 K3
Lemington Clinic *BW/LEM/TK/HW* NE15 54 B5
Lemington First School *BW/LEM/TK/HW* NE15 54 B5
Lemington Middle School *BW/LEM/TK/HW* NE15 54 B3
Linden School *LGB/KIL* NE12 47 K2
Lindisfarne County Primary School *GATE* NE8 11 H3
Lingey House Primary School *FELL* NE10 70 D5
Linhope First School *WD/WHPE/BLK* NE5 54 D1
Little Theatre *CLDN/WHIT/ROK* SR6 74 A3
Live Theatre *CNUT* NE1 5 M8
Lobley Hill Junior & Infant School *DUN/TMV* NE11 68 A7
Longbenton Community College *LGB/KIL* NE12 47 J3
Longrigg Medical Centre *FELL* NE10 70 C5
Lord Chancellors Department *CNUT* NE1 5 J8
Lord Chancellors Department *GATE* NE8 10 F2
Lord Lawson of Beamish Secondary School *CLS/BIR/GTL* DH3 93 K3
Louisa Surgery *STLY/ANP* DH9 102 C1
Low Fell Clinic *LWF/SPW/WRK* NE9 81 G1
Low Fell Junior & Infant School *LWF/SPW/WRK* NE9 69 F7
Lumley County Infant School *CLS/BIR/GTL* DH3 106 C7
Lumley Junior Middle & Infant School *CLS/BIR/GTL* DH3 115 J1
Lynnwood Business Centre *ELS/FEN* NE4 4 B7
Malvins Close County First School *BLYTH* NE24 20 E6
Maplewood School *SWCK/CAS* SR5 85 J2
Marden Bridge Middle School *MONK* NE25 40 E5
Marden High School *TYNE/NSHE* NE30 51 F1
Marine Avenue Medical Centre *WBAY* NE26 40 D4
Marine Park Jmi School *SSH* NE33 3 K7
Market Place Industrial Estate *HLH* DH5 108 D6
Marlborough Clinic *SEA/MUR* SR7 120 D1
Marley Hill Primary School *WICK/BNPF* NE16 78 E5
Mary Trevelyan Primary School *ELS/FEN* NE4 9 H1
Masonic Temple *ASHBK/HED/RY* SR2 14 E7
Mayfield Medical Centre *JRW* NE32 59 J5
Meadowfield Clinic *BDN/LAN/SAC* DH7 133 J6
Meadowfield Sports Centre *BDN/LAN/SAC* DH7 133 J6

Meadow Well Primary School *NSHW* NE29 50 B6
Megabowl *LGB/KIL* NE12 48 C3
Metrocentre East Business Park *DUN/TMV* NE11 8 D4
Metropolitan Borough of North Tyneside Council *TYNE/NSHE* NE30 2 E1
Millburngate Shopping Precinct *DHAM* DH1 16 C3
Monkhouse Primary School *TYNE/NSHE* NE30 51 F1
Monkseaton Clinic *MONK* NE25 40 C5
Monkseaton High School *MONK* NE25 40 C7
Monkseaton Medical Centre *MONK* NE25 40 B5
Monkseaton Middle School *MONK* NE25 40 C5
Monkton County Infant School *HAR/WTLS* NE34 60 E7
Monkton County Junior Mixed School *HAR/WTLS* NE34 60 D7
Monkton Hall Hospital *HEBB* NE31 59 H7
Monkwearmouth Health Centre *SWCK/CAS* SR5 14 E1
Monkwearmouth Hospital *SWCK/CAS* SR5 86 C3
Monkwearmouth Railway Station Museum *SWCK/CAS* SR5 14 E2
Montagu Junior & Infant School *WD/WHPE/BLK* NE5 45 J7
Moor Edge First School *LGB/KIL* NE12 37 H6
Moorside Community Primary School *ELS/FEN* NE4 4 D4
Mortimer Comprehensive School *HAR/WTLS* NE34 61 H4
Mosque *BYK/HTN/WLK* NE6 57 H3
Mosque *MLFD/PNYW* SR4 14 A6
Mosque *SSH* NE33 61 F2
Mountbatten Medical Centre *HEBB* NE31 59 F6
Mountfield Primary School *GOS/KPK* NE3 45 J5
Murton Primary School *SEA/MUR* SR7 119 J5
Museum & Art Gallery *SSH* NE33 3 H6
Museum of Science and Industry *ELS/FEN* NE4 4 F8
Music School *DHAM* DH1 16 D5
National Glasscentre *CLDN/WHIT/ROK* SR6 15 H2
The Natural Therapy Clinic *TYNE/NSHE* NE30 2 D1
Nature Reserve *LGB/KIL* NE12 48 E3
Nelson Health Centre *NSHW* NE29 2 C2
Nettlesworth Primary School *CLSW/PEL* DH2 114 A4
Nevilles Cross Primary School *DHAM* DH1 134 A1
Newbottle Primary School *HLS* DH4 108 A4
New Brancepeth Primary School *BDN/LAN/SAC* DH7 132 E3
Newburn Hall Motor Museum *BW/LEM/TK/HW* NE15 53 H3
Newburn Industrial Estate *BW/LEM/TK/HW* NE15 53 J5
Newburn Leisure Centre *BW/LEM/TK/HW* NE15 53 G3
Newburn Manor First School *BW/LEM/TK/HW* NE15 53 H3
Newcastle Antiques & Independent Museum *CNUT* NE1 5 J7
Newcastle Area Health Authority *BW/LEM/TK/HW* NE15 55 F6
Newcastle Area Health Authority *ELS/FEN* NE4 4 C8
Newcastle Area Health Authority *JES* NE2 5 H2
Newcastle Arena *ELS/FEN* NE4 10 A1
Newcastle City Council *BW/LEM/TK/HW* NE15 53 H3
Newcastle City Council *BW/LEM/TK/HW* NE15 53 F2
Newcastle City Council *BW/LEM/TK/HW* NE15 55 F7
Newcastle City Council *BYK/HTN/WLK* NE6 7 G8
Newcastle City Council *BYK/HTN/WLK* NE6 13 G1
Newcastle City Council *CNUT* NE1 5 J5
Newcastle City Council *ELS/FEN* NE4 4 B8
Newcastle City Council *ELS/FEN* NE4 55 H6
Newcastle City Council *GOS/KPK* NE3 45 K7
Newcastle City Council *JES* NE2 5 K3
Newcastle City Council *JES* NE2 6 C5
Newcastle City Council *JES* NE2 46 E7
Newcastle City Council *WD/WHPE/BLK* NE5 44 D7
Newcastle City Council *WD/WHPE/BLK* NE5 55 H2
Newcastle City Council *WD/WHPE/BLK* NE5 55 F2
Newcastle Clinic *JES* NE2 46 E7
Newcastle College *ELS/FEN* NE4 4 F9
Newcastle College Concert Hall *ELS/FEN* NE4 4 F9
Newcastle Falcons Rugby Football Club *DIN/WO* NE13 45 F3
Newcastle General Hospital *ELS/FEN* NE4 4 A6
Newcastle Nuffield Hospital *JES* NE2 56 E3
Newcastle Playhouse & Gulbenkian Studio Theatre *JES* NE2 5 J3
Newcastle Preparatory School *JES* NE2 5 L1
Newcastle Reform Synagogue *GOS/KPK* NE3 46 A6
The New City Medical Centre *SUND* SR1 15 G5
New College Durham *DHAM* DH1 16 A8
New College Durham *DHAM* DH1 124 B4
New College Durham *DHAM* DH1 134 B2
Newgate Shopping Mall *CNUT* NE1 5 J7
Newker Junior & Infant School *CLSW/PEL* DH2 105 H5
New Seaham Primary School *SEA/MUR* SR7 111 F6
Newsham Surgery *BLYTH* NE24 24 E3
NHS Clinic *SEA/MUR* SR7 119 J5
Norfolk Clinic *SUND* SR1 14 F4
Norham Community High School *NSHW* NE29 50 B5
North Biddick Club House *WASHS* NE38 95 F6
North Blunts Primary School *PLEE/EAS* SR8 136 E4
Northburn County First School *CRAM* NE23 23 H6
North Durham NHS Trust *CLS/BIR/GTL* DH3 105 J5
North East Aircraft Museum *SWCK/CAS* SR5 84 B3
Northern Land & Leisure Centre *DHAM* DH1 124 C5
Northern Rugby Club *GOS/KPK* NE3 46 C2
North Fawdon Primary School *GOS/KPK* NE3 45 K3
North Heaton Sports Club *BYK/HTN/WLK* NE6 57 J3
North Sands Business Centre *CLDN/WHIT/ROK* SR6 15 H1
North Shields Rugby Club *NSHW* NE29 50 D2
North Tyne Industrial Estate *LGB/KIL* NE12 48 C2
North Tyneside Area Health Authority *LGB/KIL* NE12 37 K6
North Tyneside Area Health Authority *NSHW* NE29 2 C1
North Tyneside Area Health Authority *WLSD/HOW* NE28 48 E7
North Tyneside Area Health Authority *WLSD/HOW* NE28 49 G3
North Tyneside Borough Council *NSHW* NE29 2 D3
North Tyneside College *WLSD/HOW* NE28 49 G5
North Tyneside Council *LGB/KIL* NE12 37 H6
North Tyneside Council *LGB/KIL* NE12 47 G4
North Tyneside Council *LGB/KIL* NE12 47 K2
North Tyneside Council *NSHW* NE29 2 D2
North Tyneside Council *NSHW* NE29 2 D3
North Tyneside Council *TYNE/NSHE* NE30 2 F1
North Tyneside Council *WLSD/HOW* NE28 59 K2
North Tyneside Council *WLSD/HOW* NE28 59 F2
North Tyneside Council Offices *WBAY* NE26 41 F4
North Tyneside Metropolitan Borough Council *NSHW* NE29 2 A5
Northumberland Area Health Authority *BLYTH* NE24 20 D7
Northumberland County Council *BLYTH* NE24 20 B6
Northumberland County Council *BLYTH* NE24 21 H7
Northumberland County Council *BLYTH* NE24 24 E2
Northumberland County Council *CRAM* NE23 27 K1
Northumberland County Council *CRAM* NE23 28 B2
Northumberland County Council *GOS/KPK* NE3 46 D1
Northumberland County Cricket Club *JES* NE2 57 F3
Northumberland Mental Health NHS Trust *CRAM* NE23 28 C1
Northumbria Sports Centre *WASHN* NE37 83 G2
Novacastrians Rugby Football Club *LGB/HTN* NE7 47 H6
Oakfield College *ELS/FEN* NE4 55 H5
Oakfield Junior School *LWF/SPW/WRK* NE9 81 F2
Oakleigh Gardens School *CLDN/WHIT/ROK* SR6 74 B2
Observatory *DHAM* DH1 16 B7
The Old Forge Surgery *MLFD/PNYW* SR4 85 K6
The Open University *GOS/KPK* NE3 46 C4
The Osborne Clinic *JES* NE2 57 F2
Our Lady of Peace RC School *HLS* DH4 95 J7
Our Lady & St Annes Primary School *ELS/FEN* NE4 4 F8
Ouston County Infant School *CLSW/PEL* DH2 93 F5
Ouston Junior School *CLSW/PEL* DH2 92 E5
Oxclose Community School *WASHS* NE38 94 C2
Pallion Health Centre *MLFD/PNYW* SR4 85 K7
Pallion Primary School *MLFD/PNYW* SR4 85 J5
Palmer Community Hospital *JRW* NE32 59 K4
Parkside Infant School *SEA/MUR* SR7 120 C3
Parkside Middle School *CRAM* NE23 28 C1
Parkside School *WLSD/HOW* NE28 48 C5
The Parks Sports Centre *NSHW* NE29 2 B5
Park View Community School *CLS/BIR/GTL* DH3 105 K4
Park View Comprehensive School *CLS/BIR/GTL* DH3 93 J7
Parkway Medical Centre *WD/WHPE/BLK* NE5 54 A1
Parkway School *WD/WHPE/BLK* NE5 54 B1
Pelaw County Infant School *CLSW/PEL* DH2 105 H2
Pelton County Junior & Infant School *CLSW/PEL* DH2 93 F7
Pelton Fell Surgery Building *CLSW/PEL* DH2 104 E3
Pelton Health Clinic *CLSW/PEL* DH2 93 F7
Pendower Clinic *BW/LEM/TK/HW* NE15 55 F6
Pennywell Comprehensive School *MLFD/PNYW* SR4 97 F1
Percy Main Cricket Club *NSHW* NE29 50 B7
Percy Main Primary School *NSHW* NE29 60 B1
Percy St Johns Primary School *NSHW* NE29 50 C7
Peterlee College *PLEE/EAS* SR8 136 D3
Peterlee Leisure Centre *PLEE/EAS* SR8 136 E5
Peterlee Town Council *PLEE/EAS* SR8 136 C6
Philadelphia Cricket Club *HLS* DH4 108 A2
Phoenix Theatre *BLYTH* NE24 21 H7
Plawsworth Road County Infant School *BDN/LAN/SAC* DH7 113 H5
Plessey Road County Junior School *BLYTH* NE24 21 H7
Police Headquarters and Magistrates Court *SUND* SR1 14 D4
Ponteland County First School *PONT/DH* NE20 33 H2
Ponteland County High School *PONT/DH* NE20 33 G4
Ponteland County Middle School *PONT/DH* NE20 33 H4
Ponteland Darras Hall County First School *PONT/DH* NE20 32 E6
Ponteland Health Centre *PONT/DH* NE20 33 G2
Ponteland Leisure Centre *PONT/DH* NE20 33 H3
Ponteland Parish Council *PONT/DH* NE20 33 G3
Portland School *SUNDSW* SR3 98 A4
Portobello County Junior Infant School *CLS/BIR/GTL* DH3 93 K4
Primrose Hill Hospital *JRW* NE32 60 A7
Princess Louise First School *BLYTH* NE24 21 F7
Princess Road Junior School *SEA/MUR* SR7 120 D1
Priory Primary School *TYNE/NSHE* NE30 51 H2
Priory Theatre *TYNE/NSHE* NE30 51 H2
Queen Elizabeth Hospital *LWF/SPW/WRK* NE9 69 J6
Queen Elizabeth Hospital *LWF/SPW/WRK* NE9 69 H7
Raby Cross Medical Centre *BYK/HTN/WLK* NE6 6 F4
Ramside Hall (Hotel) *DHAM* DH1 126 B3
Ravenswood Infant & Primary School *BYK/HTN/WLK* NE6 57 J2
Ravensworth Surgery *SSH* NE33 61 J2
Ravensworth Terrace Primary School *CLS/BIR/GTL* DH3 93 J2
RC JMI School *BDN/LAN/SAC* DH7 113 G4
Recreation Centre *CNUT* NE1 5 K6
Redesdale First School *WLSD/HOW* NE28 48 B6
Red House Junior Mixed School *SWCK/CAS* SR5 85 H3
Red Rose Primary School *CLS/BIR/GTL* DH3 105 K6
Redwell Hills Clinic *CON/LDGT* DH8 100 A3
Regent Farm First School *GOS/KPK* NE3 46 A4
Regional National Blood Transfusion Centre *JES* NE2 4 E3
Register Office *DHAM* DH1 16 F4
Richard Avenue Primary School *MLFD/PNYW* SR4 98 A2
Richard Coates Church of England Middle School *PONT/DH* NE20 33 G2
Richardson Dees First School *WLSD/HOW* NE28 59 F1
Rickleton Primary School *WASHS* NE38 94 B6
Riverview House Business Centre *SUND* SR1 14 F3
Roman Road Primary School *FELL* NE10 70 C7
Ronald Moore Gallery *TYNE/NSHE* NE30 51 F3
Ropery Walk Primary School *SEA/MUR* SR7 121 F1
Roseberry Primary School *CLSW/PEL* DH2 104 C2
Rowlands Gill Infant School *ROWG* NE39 77 H2
Rowlands Gill Junior School *ROWG* NE39 77 H2
Rowletch Burn Industrial Estate *CLS/BIR/GTL* DH3 93 H2
Royal College of Nursing *CNUT* NE1 5 K7
Royal Grammar School *JES* NE2 5 L2
Royalty Theatre *ASHBK/HED/RY* SR2 14 B6
Royal Victoria Infirmary *JES* NE2 5 H3
Rye Hill Sports Centre *ELS/FEN* NE4 4 F8
Ryhope General Hospital *ASHBK/HED/RY* SR2 111 F2
Ryhope Health Centre *ASHBK/HED/RY* SR2 98 E7
Ryhope Junior & Infant School *ASHBK/HED/RY* SR2 98 E7
Ryhope Village C of E Primary School *ASHBK/HED/RY* SR2 111 F1
Ryton Comprehensive School *RYTON* NE40 52 C6
Ryton Industrial Estate *BLAY* NE21 53 J6
Ryton Junior & Infant School *RYTON* NE40 52 C6
Ryton Rugby Club *RYTON* NE40 52 C7
Sacred Heart Primary School *ELS/FEN* NE4 55 H4
Sacriston Cricket Club *BDN/LAN/SAC* DH7 113 G5
Sacriston Junior School *BDN/LAN/SAC* DH7 113 H6
Sacriston Swimming Baths *BDN/LAN/SAC* DH7 113 G5
St Aidans College *DHAM* DH1 16 B9
St Aidans RC Comprehensive School *ASHBK/HED/RY* SR2 98 C2
St Albans Medical Group *FELL* NE10 12 C8
St Aloysius RC Infants School *HEBB* NE31 59 G4
St Aloysius RC Junior School *HEBB* NE31 59 G4
St Andrews RC Aided First School *BLYTH* NE24 20 E7
St Annes Mixed High School *SSH* NE33 61 J3
St Annes RC Primary School *MLFD/PNYW* SR4 97 F1
St Anthonys Health Centre *BYK/HTN/WLK* NE6 58 B7
St Anthonys RC School *ASHBK/HED/RY* SR2 14 C7
St Augustines RC Infant School *FELL* NE10 70 B6
St Bede Medical Centre *CLDN/WHIT/ROK* SR6 14 F1
St Bedes First School *BDLGTN* NE22 18 E5
St Bedes RC Comprehensive School *PLEE/EAS* SR8 136 D4
St Bedes RC Infants School *JRW* NE32 60 A4
St Bedes RC JMI School *JRW* NE32 60 A4
St Bedes RC Primary School *BW/LEM/TK/HW* NE15 54 D4
St Bedes RC Primary School *SSH* NE33 3 H9
St Bedes RC Primary School *WASHN* NE37 83 F4
St Benet Biscops RC High School *BDLGTN* NE22 18 E6
St Benets Primary RC School *CLSW/PEL* DH2 93 F5
St Benets RC Primary School *CLDN/WHIT/ROK* SR6 86 D3
St Bernadettes RC First School *WLSD/HOW* NE28 48 D5
St Catherines RC Primary School *JES* NE2 6 B1
St Chads College *DHAM* DH1 16 D5
St Charles RC Primary School *GOS/KPK* NE3 46 B4
St Columbas RC First School *WLSD/HOW* NE28 58 C1
St Cuthberts C of E Junior School *GATE* NE8 10 A6
St Cuthberts High School *BW/LEM/TK/HW* NE15 55 F5
St Cuthberts RC Lower School *BW/LEM/TK/HW* NE15 55 F5
St Cuthberts RC Primary School *BW/LEM/TK/HW* NE15 53 H1
St Cuthberts RC Primary School *CLS/BIR/GTL* DH3 105 K5
St Cuthberts RC Primary School *GOS/KPK* NE3 45 H6
St Cuthberts RC Primary School *NSHW* NE29 2 C3
St Cuthberts RC School *SEA/MUR* SR7 110 E7
St Edmunds RC Comprehensive School *LWF/SPW/WRK* NE9 81 K1
St Georges RC Primary School *BW/LEM/TK/HW* NE15 54 B6
St Godrics RC Junior & Infant School *DHAM* DH1 124 D3
St Hilda Industrial Estate *SSH* NE33 3 G8
St Hildas RC School *SWCK/CAS* SR5 86 A3
St Hild & St. Bede College *DHAM* DH1 17 H3
St James Park (Newcastle United FC) *CNUT* NE1 5 H5
St John Bosco RC Primary School *SWCK/CAS* SR5 84 E1
St John Boste RC Primary School *WASHS* NE38 94 C1
St John Vianney School *WD/WHPE/BLK* NE5 54 B2
St Joseph RC Junior Primary School *BW/LEM/TK/HW* NE15 55 G7
St Josephs Infant School *CLS/BIR/GTL* DH3 93 H1
St Josephs RC School *BDN/LAN/SAC* DH7 123 F7
St Josephs RC School *DHAM* DH1 17 L3
St Josephs RC School *MLFD/PNYW* SR4 85 K6
St Josephs RC School *SEA/MUR* SR7 119 H6
St Josephs School *NSHW* NE29 50 C6
St Josephs School *ROWG* NE39 76 D3
St Josephs School *WASHS* NE38 83 F7
St Lawrence RC Primary School *BYK/HTN/WLK* NE6 7 H5
St Leonards Junior & Infants School *SUNDSW* SR3 98 B6
St Leonards RC Comprehensive School *DHAM* DH1 16 A1
St Margarets C of E Infants School *DHAM* DH1 16 A6
St Margarets C of E Infants School *DHAM* DH1 134 B2
St Margarets C of E Primary School *DHAM* DH1 16 A5
St Marks RC Primary School *WD/WHPE/BLK* NE5 44 D6
St Mary Magdalene R C Primary School *SEA/MUR* SR7 111 J7
St Marys College *ELS/FEN* NE4 55 H4
St Marys Junior & Infant School *STLY/ANP* DH9 102 D3
St Marys RC Comprehensive School *LGB/HTN* NE7 47 G5
St Marys RC Primary School *ASHBK/HED/RY* SR2 98 B2
St Marys RC Primary School *JRW* NE32 72 B1
St Marys RC Primary School *TYNE/NSHE* NE30 40 E7
St Marys RC Primary School *WICK/BNPF* NE16 8 A9
St Mary's Roman Catholic Cathedral *CNUT* NE1 5 H8
St Michaels Industrial Estate *BYK/HTN/WLK* NE6 6 E6

St Michaels RC Primary School *ELS/FEN* NE4 9 J1
St Nicholas Cathedral *CNUT* NE1 5 L8
St Oswalds C E Junior Mixed & Infant School *HEBB* NE31 59 H4
St Oswalds Clinic *FELL* NE10 12 C8
St Oswalds C of E Infants School *DHAM* DH1 16 D6
St Oswalds RC Infant & Junior School *LWF/SPW/WRK* NE9 81 J2
St Patricks RC School *ASHBK/HED/RY* SR2 111 F1
St Patricks RC School *BDN/LAN/SAC* DH7 133 K5
St Pauls C of E Primary School *ELS/FEN* NE4 4 F8
St Pauls RC First School *CRAM* NE23 28 C3
St Peter RC Junior & Infant School *LWF/SPW/WRK* NE9 69 G6
St Peters JMI School *JRW* NE32 60 A3
St Peters RC Middle School *CRAM* NE23 28 C4
St Robert of Newminster RC Comprehensive School *WASHS* NE38 95 F4
St Stephens RC Primary School *LGB/KIL* NE12 47 H3
St Teresas RC Primary School *BYK/HTN/WLK* NE6 6 E1
St Thomas More RC (Aided) Comprehensive School *BLAY* NE21 65 K1
St Thomas Mores RC School *DHAM* DH1 126 A6
St Thomas Street Business Centre *CNUT* NE1 5 J5
St Vincents RC Primary School *BYK/HTN/WLK* NE6 7 L9
St Wilfreds RC Junior & Infant School *FELL* NE10 11 M3
St Wilfrids Middle School *BLYTH* NE24 21 F7
St Wilfrids RC Comprehensive School *HAR/WTLS* NE34 61 H5
Sam Smiths Sports Ground *BYK/HTN/WLK* NE6 58 A2
Sanderson Hospital *GOS/KPK* NE3 46 B6
Saville Clinic *CNUT* NE1 5 K5
Seaburn Dene Primary School *CLDN/WHIT/ROK* SR6 74 D7
Seaham College *SEA/MUR* SR7 120 E1
Seaham Comprehensive School *SEA/MUR* SR7 111 F6
Seaham Town Council *SEA/MUR* SR7 120 E1
Seaton Delaval Whytrig County Middle School *MONK* NE25 29 J4
Seaton Sluice Middle School *WBAY* NE26 30 E1
Segedunum Business Centre *WLSD/HOW* NE28 58 E2
Seghill County First School *CRAM* NE23 29 G7
Shanklea First School *CRAM* NE23 28 C1
Shieldfield Health Centre *JES* NE2 6 A4
Shield Row Junior & Infants School *STLY/ANP* DH9 90 E6
Shincliffe C of E Junior & Infant School *DHAM* DH1 135 J5
Shiney Row Primary School *HLS* DH4 107 K1
Shipley Art Gallery *GATE* NE8 11 G7
Shiremoor First School *SMOOR* NE27 39 G6
Shiremoor Middle School *SMOOR* NE27 39 H5
Shopping Centre *GOS/KPK* NE3 45 K4
Shopping Centre *WD/WHPE/BLK* NE5 54 A1
The Shopping Centre *STLY/ANP* DH9 102 D2
Shotton Hall Comprehensive School *PLEE/EAS* SR8 136 C6
Shotton Hall Junior School *PLEE/EAS* SR8 136 C6
The Side Gallery *CNUT* NE1 5 L8
Sidegate Gallery *WICK/BNPF* NE16 79 F2
Sikh Temple *ELS/FEN* NE4 4 E6
Silksworth Health Centre *SUNDSW* SR3 98 A7
Silverlink Business Park *WLSD/HOW* NE28 49 J4
Simonside First School *WD/WHPE/BLK* NE5 44 D5
Simonside Industrial Estate *HAR/WTLS* NE34 60 C6
Sir GB Hunter Memorial Hospital *WLSD/HOW* NE28 58 E1
Smiths Surgery *BOLCOL* NE35 72 C4
South Benwell Primary School *ELS/FEN* NE4 55 J7
South Gosforth First School *JES* NE2 46 E6
South Hetton Health Centre *RDHAMSE* DH6 128 E2
South Hetton Primary School *RDHAMSE* DH6 128 E2
South Hylton Primary School *MLFD/PNYW* SR4 84 E7
Southlands Middle School *CRAM* NE23 28 C5
Southlands School *TYNE/NSHE* NE30 50 E2
Southmoor School *ASHBK/HED/RY* SR2 98 E3
Southridge First School *MONK* NE25 40 B3
South Shields FC *JRW* NE32 60 C5
South Stanley Comprehensive School *STLY/ANP* DH9 102 C2
South Stanley County Junior Mixed School *STLY/ANP* DH9 102 C2
South Street County Primary School *GATE* NE8 11 H6
South Tyneside Area Health Authority *HAR/WTLS* NE34 62 A4
South Tyneside Borough Council *HEBB* NE31 59 F6
South Tyneside College *HEBB* NE31 71 F2
South Tyneside College *SSH* NE33 61 J3
South Tyneside Health Care Trust *HAR/WTLS* NE34 61 H6
South Tyneside Health Care Trust *HEBB* NE31 59 G6
South Tyneside Health Care Trust *SSH* NE33 3 K6
South Tyneside Magistrates Court *SSH* NE33 3 G9
South Tyneside Metropolitan Borough Council *HAR/WTLS* NE34 62 B4
South Tyneside Metropolitan Borough Council *SSH* NE33 3 K8
South Tyneside Metropolitan Borough Council *SSH* NE33 3 J7
South Wellfield First School *MONK* NE25 39 K5
Southwick Health Centre *SWCK/CAS* SR5 86 A4
Springfield Clinic *GATE* NE8 11 H8
Springfield Comprehensive School *JRW* NE32 59 K6
Spring Gardens Primary School *NSHW* NE29 2 B2
Spring Terrace Health Centre *NSHW* NE29 2 C1
Springwell Health Centre *SUNDSW* SR3 97 J3
Springwell House Surgery *SUNDSW* SR3 97 J4
Springwell Village Primary School *LWF/SPW/WRK* NE9 82 B4
Stanhope County Infants School *SSH* NE33 61 G4
Stanhope County Junior Mixed School *SSH* NE33 61 F5
Stanhope Parade Health Centre *SSH* NE33 61 G3
Stanley Health Centre *STLY/ANP* DH9 102 C1
Stanley RC Junior Mixed & Infants School *STLY/ANP* DH9 90 D7
Star Clinic *DHAM* DH1 16 D3
Stephenson Railway Museum *SMOOR* NE27 49 J3
Stephenson Street *TYNE/NSHE* NE30 2 E2
Stonelaw County Middle School *CRAM* NE23 28 B4
Studio Gallery *TYNE/NSHE* NE30 51 H3
Sunderland AFC Club Shop *SUND* SR1 14 E4
Sunderland Area Health Authority *ASHBK/HED/RY* SR2 14 D9
Sunderland Bowling Centre *SWCK/CAS* SR5 86 C4
Sunderland City Council *HLS* DH4 108 B7
Sunderland City Council *SUND* SR1 14 F5
Sunderland Counselling Services *MLFD/PNYW* SR4 97 G1
Sunderland County Court *SUND* SR1 14 F5
Sunderland Cricket & Rugby Football Club House *ASHBK/HED/RY* SR2 98 C2
Sunderland District General Hospital *MLFD/PNYW* SR4 85 K7
Sunderland Eye Infirmary *ASHBK/HED/RY* SR2 98 D3
Sunderland Football Club *SWCK/CAS* SR5 14 D1
Sunderland High School *ASHBK/HED/RY* SR2 14 E9
Sunderland Museum & Art Gallery *SUND* SR1 14 F6
Sunderland Retail Park *CLDN/WHIT/ROK* SR6 86 D4
Sunderland Royal Hospital *MLFD/PNYW* SR4 85 K7
Sunderland Royal Infirmary *ASHBK/HED/RY* SR2 14 B7
Sunderland Talmudical College *GATE* NE8 11 G7
Sunderland University *SUND* SR1 14 F4
Swalwell Cricket Club *WICK/BNPF* NE16 66 D3
Talbot House Special School *BW/LEM/TK/HW* NE15 53 G1
Tanfield Lea County Junior Mixed & Infant School *STLY/ANP* DH9 90 B6
Tanfield Lea County Junior Mixed & Infantschool *STLY/ANP* DH9 90 A5
Tanfield View Surgery *STLY/ANP* DH9 102 C1
Tax Office *SUND* SR1 14 D4
Team Valley Business Centre *DUN/TMV* NE11 68 D6
Team Valley Trading Estate Post Office *DUN/TMV* NE11 80 E3
Tedco Business Centre *HEBB* NE31 59 H3
Tedco Business Park *JRW* NE32 59 J3
Theatre Royal *CNUT* NE1 5 K6
Thockley First School *BW/LEM/TK/HW* NE15 52 E1
Thomas Bewick Special School *WD/WHPE/BLK* NE5 54 A1
Thomas Hepburn Community School *FELL* NE10 70 A5
Thornhill Comprehensive School *ASHBK/HED/RY* SR2 14 C9
Throckley Industrial Estate *BW/LEM/TK/HW* NE15 43 F7
Throckley Middle School *BW/LEM/TK/HW* NE15 52 E1
Throckley Surgery *BW/LEM/TK/HW* NE15 53 F1
The Toco Gallery *JES* NE2 56 E1
Toner Avenue County Infant School *HEBB* NE31 71 F1
Townend Primary School *SWCK/CAS* SR5 84 D1
Town Hall & Civic Offices *SSH* NE33 3 J8
Trevelyan College *DHAM* DH1 16 C9
Trinity Maritime Museum *CNUT* NE1 5 M7
Trinity Medical Centre *SSH* NE33 61 G2
Trinity School *BLAY* NE21 66 C3
Trouts Lane School *DHAM* DH1 123 K2
Tynemouth Business Centre *TYNE/NSHE* NE30 51 F4
Tynemouth College *NSHW* NE29 50 D4
Tynemouth Cricket Club *TYNE/NSHE* NE30 51 F2
Tyne Point Industrial Estate *JRW* NE32 60 C5
Tyne Tees TV Studios *CNUT* NE1 6 B7
Tyne Theatre and Opera House *CNUT* NE1 5 G7
Tyneview Primary School *BYK/HTN/WLK* NE6 58 C6
Tyne View Primary School *GATE* NE8 10 B4
Tyne & Wear County Council *SSH* NE33 3 H7
Univeristy Halls of Residence *SUND* SR1 15 G3
University College *DHAM* DH1 16 C4
University for Industry *SUND* SR1 14 E4
University Library *DHAM* DH1 16 C4
University of Durham *DHAM* DH1 16 E5
University of Durham *DHAM* DH1 16 E7
University of Durham *DHAM* DH1 16 E9
University of Durham *DHAM* DH1 16 D5
University of Durham *DHAM* DH1 16 E4
University of Durham *DHAM* DH1 16 F4
University of Durham *DHAM* DH1 16 A9
University of Durham *DHAM* DH1 16 B9
University of Durham *DHAM* DH1 16 C8
University of Durham *DHAM* DH1 16 C9
University of Durham *DHAM* DH1 16 D6
University of Durham *DHAM* DH1 17 G5
University of Durham *DHAM* DH1 17 H5
University of Durham *DHAM* DH1 17 H8
University of Durham *DHAM* DH1 125 J4
University of Newcastle Upon Tyne *CNUT* NE1 5 J3
University of Newcastle Upon Tyne *JES* NE2 5 H2
University of Newcastle Upon Tyne *JES* NE2 5 G4
University of Newcastle Upon Tyne *JES* NE2 5 L1
University of Newcastle Upon Tyne *LGB/HTN* NE7 47 J7
University of Northumbria at Newcastle *CNUT* NE1 5 L3
University of Northumbria at Newcastle *LGB/HTN* NE7 47 J6
University of Sunderland *ASHBK/HED/RY* SR2 14 E7
University of Sunderland *ASHBK/HED/RY* SR2 14 F8
University of Sunderland *ASHBK/HED/RY* SR2 98 D2
University of Sunderland *CLDN/WHIT/ROK* SR6 15 G2
University of Sunderland *CLDN/WHIT/ROK* SR6 86 E4
University of Sunderland *MLFD/PNYW* SR4 85 J5
University of Sunderland *SUND* SR1 14 C5
University of Sunderland *SWCK/CAS* SR5 85 F5
University of Sunderland *WASHN* NE37 82 C6
University of Sunderland (Library) *SUND* SR1 14 C6
University Technology Park *ASHBK/HED/RY* SR2 14 C6
Ushaw College *BDN/LAN/SAC* DH7 122 C5
Ushaw Moor Cricket Club *BDN/LAN/SAC* DH7 132 E1
Ushaw Moor Infant School *BDN/LAN/SAC* DH7 122 E7
Ushaw Moor Junior School *BDN/LAN/SAC* DH7 123 F7
Usworth Colliery Junior School *WASHN* NE37 83 G4
Usworth Grange Primary School *WASHN* NE37 83 H4
Usworth Secondary School *WASHN* NE37 83 F3
Valley Road Infant School *ASHBK/HED/RY* SR2 15 J9
Valley Road Junior School *ASHBK/HED/RY* SR2 15 J9
Valley View County Infant School *JRW* NE32 59 K7
Valley View County Infant School *JRW* NE32 71 K2
Van Mildert College *DHAM* DH1 134 C4
Victoria Industrial Estate *FELL* NE10 70 E1
Victoria Medical Centre *HEBB* NE31 59 F5
Victoria Road Health Centre *WASHN* NE37 83 F5
Viking Gallery *JRW* NE32 59 K4
Village Gallery *WICK/BNPF* NE16 67 F5
Wagonway Industrial Estate *HEBB* NE31 59 G3
Walker Comprehensive School *BYK/HTN/WLK* NE6 58 B5
Walkerdene Special School *BYK/HTN/WLK* NE6 58 B5
Walkergate Hospital *BYK/HTN/WLK* NE6 58 A3
Walkergate Infant School *BYK/HTN/WLK* NE6 7 M1
Wallsend Business Centre *WLSD/HOW* NE28 58 E2
Wallsend Sports Centre *WLSD/HOW* NE28 58 B1
Wansbeck District Council *BDLGTN* NE22 19 F6
Wardley Primary School *FELL* NE10 13 L7
War Memorial *SUND* SR1 14 F6
Washington Albany Infants School *WASHN* NE37 82 D6
Washington Football Club *WASHN* NE37 83 F6
Washington F Pit Museum *WASHN* NE37 82 E6
Washington Hospital *WASHS* NE38 94 A6
Washington Secondary School *WASHN* NE37 83 F6
Washington Village Primary School *WASHS* NE38 83 G7
Washingwell Primary School *WICK/BNPF* NE16 67 G6
Waterloo Medical Group *BLYTH* NE24 21 F6
Waterville Primary School *NSHW* NE29 2 B4
Waverley First School *BW/LEM/TK/HW* NE15 54 C5
Waygood Gallery & Studios *CNUT* NE1 5 K7
Wearside College *SUNDSW* SR3 97 K3
Welbeck Primary School *BYK/HTN/WLK* NE6 7 K6
Wellbank Special School *WASHN* NE37 82 D4
West Boldon Junior Mixed School *BOL* NE36 72 E4
Westbourne Surgery *HLS* DH4 107 J1
West Denton First School *WD/WHPE/BLK* NE5 54 B2
West Denton High School *WD/WHPE/BLK* NE5 54 C1
Westerhope Clinic *WD/WHPE/BLK* NE5 44 D7
Westerhope First School *WD/WHPE/BLK* NE5 44 C7
Westerhope Small Business Park *WD/WHPE/BLK* NE5 44 C6
Western First School *WLSD/HOW* NE28 58 C1
Western Infant School *NSHW* NE29 2 B4
Western Middle School *WLSD/HOW* NE28 58 C2
Westfield School *GOS/KPK* NE3 46 B7
West Gate Community College *ELS/FEN* NE4 55 H5
Westgate Hill Primary School *ELS/FEN* NE4 4 C6
West Jesmond Junior School *JES* NE2 56 E2
West Lane Junior & Infant School *BLAY* NE21 65 J4
Westlea Junior School *SEA/MUR* SR7 110 E7
West Moor First School *LGB/KIL* NE12 47 J1
Westmoor Middle School *LGB/KIL* NE12 47 H1
Westmorland Business Centre *ELS/FEN* NE4 5 G8
Westoe Gallery *SSH* NE33 3 J9
Westovian Theatre Society *SSH* NE33 3 L5
West Rainton Primary School *HLS* DH4 116 C6
West Walker School *BYK/HTN/WLK* NE6 58 C7
Whickham Comprehensive School *WICK/BNPF* NE16 66 E6
Whickham Parochial C of E Junior & Infant School *WICK/BNPF* NE16 66 D7
Whinfield Industrial Estate *ROWG* NE39 76 E4
Whitburn Comprehensive School *CLDN/WHIT/ROK* SR6 75 G4
Whitburn Cricket Club *CLDN/WHIT/ROK* SR6 75 F4
Whitburn Junior Mixed School *CLDN/WHIT/ROK* SR6 74 E4
Whitburn Surgery *CLDN/WHIT/ROK* SR6 74 E4
Whitehouse Industrial Estate *BW/LEM/TK/HW* NE15 55 G7
Whitehouse Primary School *NSHW* NE29 50 A3
Whitehouse Primary School *NSHW* NE29 50 C2
Whitley Bay Cricket Club *MONK* NE25 40 E6
Whitley Bay Football Club *MONK* NE25 40 E6
Whitley Bay High School *MONK* NE25 40 C3
Whitley Bay Ice Rink *MONK* NE25 40 D6
Whitley Bay Rockcliff RFC *MONK* NE25 40 E6
Whitley Lodge First School *WBAY* NE26 40 C1
Whitley Memorial School *BDLGTN* NE22 19 G6
Willington High School *WLSD/HOW* NE28 49 H5
Windmill Hills County Primary School *GATE* NE8 10 E4
Windy Nook Primary School *FELL* NE10 69 K6
Wingrove Primary School *ELS/FEN* NE4 55 J5
Winlaton Park Junior School *BLAY* NE21 66 A4
Winlaton Vulcans Rugby Club *BLAY* NE21 66 A3
Witherwack Primary School *SWCK/CAS* SR5 85 K1
Witton Gilbert County School *BDN/LAN/SAC* DH7 123 F1
Woodlands Park Health Centre *DIN/WO* NE13 36 B4
Woodlea County Primary School *HLS* DH4 107 G6
Wrekenton Health Centre *LWF/SPW/WRK* NE9 81 K2
Yates Jewish School for Girls *GATE* NE8 10 F6
The Yemeni School *SSH* NE33 61 F2
Yoden Primary School *PLEE/EAS* SR8 137 J4

Page 14
A5
1 Langton Cl
2 St Mark's St
3 Tintern St
A7
1 Beachcross Rd
2 Beachville St
3 Fernville St
4 Vale St
5 Vale St East
B4
1 Dahlia Ct
2 Jasmine Ct
3 Marguerite Ct
4 Queensberry St

Page 21
H6
1 Ballast Hl
2 Beaconsfield St
3 Plessey Rd
4 Post Office St
5 Quay Rd
6 Quayside
7 Ridley St
8 Sussex St
9 Tate St

Page 23
G7
1 Yardley Gv
2 Yeovil Cl

Page 28
D3
1 Barrasford Rd
2 Brownrigg Dr
3 Carlcroft Pl
4 Coldbeck Ct
5 Cranshaw Pl
D4
1 Cobden Rd
2 Coomside
3 Warenford Cl
4 Weetwood Rd
5 Whitelaw Pl
6 Wilkwood Cl
7 Woodhill Rd

Page 29
G6
1 Meadow Cl
2 Murrayfield
3 Taynton Gv

Page 35
F3
1 Havannah Crs
2 Merlay Dr

Page 36
A4
1 Arundel Cl
2 Austral Pl
3 Charles St
4 Highfield Pl
5 Norham Cl
6 Priory Pl
7 Simon Pl
8 Thorn Cl
9 Willows Cl
10 Windt St

Page 37
J5
1 Alder Wy
2 Beech Wy
3 Cowans Av
4 Ettrick Cl
5 Garth Sixteen
6 Garth Twelve
7 Hawthorn Pl
8 Kielder Cl
9 Laburnum Ct
10 Redwood Cl
11 Rothbury Cl
12 Thompson Av
13 West Clifton
14 Willow Gdns
K5
1 Agincourt
2 Alresford
3 Bannockburn
4 Blenheim
5 Cannock
6 Culloden Wk
7 East Bailey
8 Falkirk
9 Marston
10 Tewkesbury
11 Towton
12 West Bailey

Page 41
F7
1 Ellersmere Gdns
2 Grange Cl

Page 45
F6
1 Brecon Cl
2 Caernarvon Cl
3 Dereham Ct
4 Haggerston Cl
5 Haggerston Ct
6 Hensby Ct
7 Lampeter Cl
8 Reedham Ct
9 Rhuddlan Ct
10 Rollesby Ct
11 Shawdon Cl
12 Shearwater Cl
13 Tredegar Cl
14 Wroxham Ct
G2
1 Hersham Cl
H7
1 Beaufort Cl
2 Bowfell Cl
3 Murrayfield Rd
4 Spenfield Rd
K2
1 Ancroft Wy
2 Boulmer Cl
3 Ingram Av
4 Ridley Cl
5 Tranwell Cl
K3
1 Cornhill Av
2 Ingoe Av
3 Larchwood Av
4 Meldon Av
K4
1 Bellfield Av
2 Bodmin Wy
3 Brandon Rd
4 Brunton Gv
5 Milne Wy
6 Tilson Wy
K5
1 Ambridge Wy
2 Carrfield Rd
3 Colgrove Wy
4 Crantock Rd
5 Hillsview Av
6 Kirkwood Dr
7 Shilmore Rd
8 Winton Wy
K7
1 Aylyth Pl
2 Braebridge Pl
3 Millgrove Vw
4 Montpellier Pl

Page 46
A4
1 Ain Wk
2 Beadnell Wy
3 Embleton Av
4 Falstone Sq
5 Heddon Cl
6 Hepple Wy
7 Matfen Pl
8 Mitford Pl
9 Wansbeck Rd South
A5
1 Agnes Maria St
2 George St
3 Leagreen Ct
4 Mary Agnes St
5 Nelson Av
6 Rea Pl
7 Souter Rd
8 South St
9 Turner Crs
E5
1 Bowes St
2 Bowsden Ct
3 Christon Cl
4 Commercial Rd
5 Donald St
6 Ridgewood Gdns
7 Ridgewood Vls
8 Wardle St
E6
1 Alnmouth Dr
2 Balmoral Av
3 Craghall Dene
4 Craghall Dene Av
5 Hill Crest Gdns
6 Willowbank Gdns
E7
1 Woodthorne Rd

Page 47
F3
1 Kingsbridge
2 Queensbridge
3 Rossendale Pl
J6
1 Birkdale Cl
2 Carnoustie Cl
3 Dunlop Cl
4 Fairmont Wy
5 Fairview Gn
6 Penfold Cl
7 Spalding Cl
K2
1 Albany Av
2 Avondale Av
3 Cambridge Av
4 Lynholm Gv
5 North Vw
6 Park Vw
7 Percy Gdns
8 Station Rd North
9 Teesdale Gv
10 Wens Leydale Dr
11 West Vw
12 Whitfield Rd
13 Wilson Ter
K3
1 Hastings Av
K4
1 Belvedere Gdns
2 Eastfield Ter
3 Oakhurst Ter
4 Parkland
5 St Margargets Av
6 Station Ap
7 Tynedale Ter
K6
1 Wells Cl
K7
1 Candelford Cl
2 Halleypike Cl
3 Lark Rise Cl

Page 48
D6
1 Birkdale Cl
2 Glendale Av
3 Hollings Crs
4 Weardale Av
E5
1 Barnwood Cl
2 Basildon Gdns
3 Baywood Gv
4 Beamish Cl
5 Beaufort Gdns
6 Beckford Cl
7 Bedale Cl
8 Belford Cl
9 Belper Cl
10 Belsay Cl
11 Berry Cl
12 Briar Cl

Page 49
F5
1 Banbury Gdns
2 Barmouth Cl
3 Barnstaple Cl
4 Barton Cl
5 Bewley Gdns
6 Boreham Cl
7 Bridlington
8 Bromley Gdns
9 Buxton Cl
F7
1 Haggie Av
2 Parkside
3 Swan Av

Page 50
D6
1 Morcott Gdns
D7
1 Hackworth Wy
2 Stockton Rd
E2
1 Argyle Pl
2 Bulman's La
3 Pennyfine Cl
4 Popplewell Ter
5 Post Office La
E3
1 Medway Gdns
2 Osborne Gdns
E4
1 Albion Ter
2 Ashfield Gv
3 Ayre's Ter
4 Church Wy
5 Cleveland Crs
6 Cleveland Ter
7 Frank Pl
8 Lovaine Ter
9 Northumberland Sq
10 Springfield
11 Spring Ter
12 Upper Camden St
13 West Percy Rd
E5
1 Beaumont St
2 Bedford St
3 Brannen St
4 Gardner Pl
5 Lovaine Av
6 Newcastle St
7 Nile St
8 Railway Ter
9 Rudyerd St
10 Saville St West
11 South Preston Gv
12 Spencer St
13 Stanley St
14 West Percy St
15 West Wellington St
16 William St
E6
1 Coronation St
2 Elsdon Pl
3 Elsdon St
4 Hylton St
5 Penman Pl
6 Penman St
7 Thrift St
8 Trinity Pl
9 Upper Elsdon St
10 West Lawson St
E7
1 Atkinson Gdns
2 Hendon Cl
3 Kingdom Pl
4 Watch House Cl

Page 51
F5
1 Bedford St
2 Camden St
3 Dockwray Cl
4 Lower Rudyerd St
5 Sibthorpe St
H7
1 Brodrick St
2 Catherine St
3 Eastbourne Gv
4 Saville St
5 Shortridge St
6 Sydenham Ter
7 Winchester St
8 Woodbine St

Page 54
A1
1 Ainsdale Gdns
2 Alderney Gdns
3 Anglesey Gdns
4 Arncliffe Gdns
5 Elgar Av
6 Elrick Cl
7 Elston Cl
8 Frenton Cl
A7
1 Cochran St
C2
1 Allerwash
2 Beltingham
3 Burnstones
4 The Garth
5 Harle Cl
6 Highwell La
7 Holborn Pl
8 Knarsdale Pl
9 Linbridge Dr
C3
1 The Close
2 Hedgeley Rd
3 Ilderton Pl
4 Layburn Gdns
5 Northlea
6 St Vincents Cl
7 Sandringham Rd
8 Warwick Rd
D1
1 Barents Cl
2 Bruce Cl
3 Frankham St
4 James St
5 Lordenshaw
6 Nansen Cl
7 Wilkes Cl
D4
1 Castlenook Pl
2 Copperas La
3 Hextol Gdns
4 Legion Gv
5 Legion Rd
6 Overdene
7 Rockcliffe Gdns
8 West Vallum
E3
1 Ashleigh Crs
E5
1 Inglemere Pl
2 Muscott Gv
E6
1 Sandmere Pl
E7
1 Lightwood Av
2 Pretoria St

Page 55
F1
1 Abercrombie Pl
2 Amersham Pl
3 Blakelaw Rd
4 Bonington Wy
5 Chandra Pl
6 Curzon Pl
7 Lawmill Wy
8 Waltham Pl
9 Wellfield La
F3
1 Allonby Wy
2 Elrington Gdns
3 Fairdale Av
4 Windermere Rd
H1
1 Brieryside
2 Coldingham Gdns
3 Crossbrook Rd
4 Fallodon Gdns
5 Fuchsia Pl
6 Hauxley Gdns
7 Holden Pl
8 Middlegarth
9 Monroe Pl
10 Radcliffe Pl
H3
1 Genister Pl
J7
1 Inchbury Cl
2 Lawson Ter
3 Maryhill Cl
4 Mulben Cl
5 Orton Cl
K4
1 Baldwin Av
K5
1 Agricola Rd
2 Crossley Ter
3 Fenham Rd
K6
1 Eaton Pl
2 Lynnwood Av
3 Mcewan Gdns
K7
1 Ashtree Cl
2 Centenary Ct
3 Chesterfield Rd
4 Croftsway
5 Marie Curie Dr
6 Portland St

Page 56
B5
1 Avison Pl
2 Avolon Pl
3 Bassington Cl
4 Frosterley Pl
5 Hamilton Crs
6 Holywell Cl
7 Jefferson Pl
8 Monday Crs
9 Monday Pl
10 Spring Garden La
B6
1 Buckingham St
2 Colliery La
3 Cookson Cl
4 Cottenham Chare
5 Cottenham St
6 Cross Villa Place No 4
7 Cross Villa Place No 5
8 Douglas Ter
9 Edward Pl
10 Elswick St
11 High Swinburne Pl
12 Lancaster St
13 Mansfield Pl
14 Quarry Bank
15 Ravensworth Ter
16 St Philips Cl
17 St Philips Wy
18 Tindal Cl
19 Tindal St
20 Worley Cl
21 Worley St
B7
1 Belgrave Pde
2 Cambridge St
3 Cross Pde
4 Hawthorn Pl
5 Houston Ct
6 Kirkdale Gn
7 Mather Rd
8 Palace St
9 Victoria St
10 Waverley Rd
C7
1 Back George St
2 Blandford Sq
3 Churchill St
4 Forth Pl
5 Lord St
6 Neville St
7 Peel St
8 Sunderland St
9 Westmorland Rd
D6
1 Cloth Market
2 Grey St
3 St Nicholas' Church Yd
4 Shakespeare St
D7
1 Clavering Pl
2 Orchard St
3 Queens La
4 South St
5 Stephenson's La
E3
2 Kingsland
E4
1 Archbold Ter
2 Eslington Rd
3 Gladstone Pl
4 Gladstone Ter
5 Harrison Pl
6 Osborne Ter
7 Sandyford Rd
8 Windsor Pl
E5
1 Oxford St
E6
1 Broad Chare
2 Carliol Pl
3 Carliol Sq
4 Carliol St
5 Cowgate
6 Croft St
7 Cross Carliol St
8 Manor Chare
9 Minden St
10 New Bridge St West
11 Pandon Bank
12 Pilgrim St
13 Trafalgar St
E7
1 Akenside Hl
2 Bridge St
3 Cannon St
4 Castle Garth
5 Dog Bank
6 Hills St
7 King St
8 Lombard St
9 Mirk La
10 Pilgrim St
11 Pipewellgate
12 Quayside
13 Queen St
14 William Iv Yd

Page 57
F4
1 Back Coldspink La
2 Portland Ms
3 Starbeck Av
4 Starbeck Ms
F5
1 Beadnell Pl
2 Bermondsey St
3 Coppice Wy
4 Field Cl
5 Gosforth St
6 Henry Sq
7 Ingham Pl
8 Prince Albert Ter
9 Rock Ter
10 Russell Ter
11 Wesley St
G5
1 Back Stephen St
2 Byker Buildings
3 Claypath St
4 Coquet St
5 Foundry La
6 Hannington Pl
7 Leighton St
8 Ouseburn Rd
9 Shields Rd West
10 Wilfred St
H5
1 Albion Rw
2 Back Heaton Park Rd
3 Brinkburn St
4 Dalton St
5 Edwin St
6 Flora St
7 Grafton St
8 Matthew St
9 Molineux St
10 Toward St
J4
1 Denmark St
2 Depot Rd
3 Fifth Av
4 Fourth Av
J5
1 Algernon Rd
2 Denmark St
3 Glendale Ter
4 Headlam St
5 Jane St
6 Michaelgate
7 Robinson St
8 Warkworth St
J6
1 Janet St
2 Mason St
3 Priory Pl
J7
1 Fenning Pl
2 Merchants Whf
3 The Moorings
4 Rowes Ms
5 St Peter's Whf
K1
1 Allerton Gdns
2 Benton Hall Wk
3 Faldonside
4 Kirkleatham Gdns
K2
1 Danby Gdns
K5
1 Blount St
2 Canterbury St
3 Cresswell St
4 Harriet St
5 Scarborough Ct
6 Tunstall Av
K6
1 Bywell St
2 Cresswell St
3 Dunstanburgh Cl
K7
1 Callaly Wy
2 Chatsworth Gdns
3 St Peter's Quayside East
4 Trinity Ctyd

Page 58
D1
1 Albert Av
2 Clifton Av
3 Diamond St
4 Harle St
5 Harrington St
6 Hopper St
7 Thompson Gdns
8 Victoria Av
D2
1 Atkinson St
2 Benton Wy
3 Border Rd
4 Chadwick St
5 Curzon Rd West
6 Eden St
7 Equitable St
8 Hedley Pl
9 James Ter
10 Portugal Pl
11 Thames Gdns
D6
1 Mitchell St
E1
1 Alexandra St
2 Croft Av
3 Durham St West
4 Hunters Ct
5 Sunningdale Av
E2
1 Chestnut St
2 Sycamore St
E4
1 Edward St
2 Lamport St
3 Pinewood
4 Raine St
5 St Andrew's St
E6
1 Longdean Cl

Page 59
K4
1 Albert Rd
2 Burns St
3 Clayton St
4 Ellison St
5 Hibernian Rd
6 Market Sq
7 Monkton Rd
8 Napier St
9 St John's Ter
10 Wear St
K5
1 Arthur St
2 Bede Burn Rd
3 Humbert St
4 Leopold St
K7
1 Penshaw Vw

Page 61
F3
1 Barnes' Rd
2 Elizabeth Diamond Gdns
3 Temple St West
G6
1 Afton Ct
2 Awnless Ct
3 Bensham Ct
4 Browntop Pl
5 Claypool Ct
6 Coxfoot Ct
7 Eavers Ct
8 Eskdale St
9 Hardyards Ct
10 High Moor Pl
11 Loudon St
12 Newland Ct
13 Windlass Ct
H1
1 Beethoven St
2 Berkely St
3 Bolingbroke St
4 Burleigh St
5 Dunelm St
6 Elizabeth St
7 Graham St
8 Handel St
9 Lyndhurst St
10 Percy St
11 Salisbury St
12 Selbourne St
H2
1 Chichester Rd
2 East George Potts St
3 East Moffett St
4 East Stevenson St
5 Imeary Gv
6 John Clay St
7 May St
8 Newburn Ct
9 Robinson St
10 Shakespeare St
11 Stainton St East
12 West George Potts St
13 West Moffett St
14 West Stainton St
15 West Stevenson St
H3
1 Alansway Gdns
2 Albany St East
3 Albany St West
4 Marlborough St North
5 Oxford Av
6 Southey St
7 Stanhope Pde
8 Wawn St
J1
1 Aldwych St
2 Fitzpatrick Pl
J2
1 August Pl
2 Catherine Cookson Ct
3 Gleneagles
4 Ingham Gra
5 Sunningdale
6 Turnberry
J3
1 College Dr
J4
1 Armstrong Av
2 Forster Av
3 Hotspur Av
J5
1 Buttermere Gdns
2 Grasmere Gdns
3 Whalton Ct
J6
1 Prince Of Wales Cl
2 Wylam Cl
K3
1 Eastfield Rd
2 North Vw
K4
1 Grinstead Cl
K5
1 Central Gdns
2 Grosvenor Gdns
K6
1 Selwood Ct
K7
1 Myrtle Gv

Page 65
J3
1 Birchgate Cl
2 Brockwell Cl
3 The Close
4 Daryl Cl
5 Greenwell Cl
6 Herd Cl
7 Milner Crs
8 Owlet Cl
9 Waterloo St
K4
1 Buttermere Crs
2 Coniston Crs
3 Ennerdale Crs
4 Grasmere Crs
5 Thirlmere Crs
6 Ullswater Crs
7 Waskdale Crs
8 Windermere Crs

Page 66
E4
1 Brinkburn Av
2 Burns Crs
3 Henderson Av
4 Phillips Av
5 Stubbs Av
6 Tennyson Crs
E5
1 Axwell Vw
2 Castle Cl
3 Fellside Ct
4 George St
5 Hawksbury
6 Heathwood Av
7 James St
8 Kestrel Ms
9 Laburnum Gv
10 Sandringham Dr
11 Thomas St
12 William St

Page 68
A3
1 Athol Gn
2 Castlegate Gdns
3 Ravensworth Ct
4 Riverside Ct
5 Seymour Ct
6 Swan Dr
7 Wallace St
B1
1 Back Mitford St
2 Blackthorn Pl
3 Charlotte Cl
4 Clasper St
5 Dobson Cl
6 Hornbeam Pl
7 Maiden St
8 Mulberry Pl
9 Tyneside Rd
10 Whitebeam Pl
D4
1 Audouins Rw
2 Chepstow Gdns
3 Coschen St
4 Miller St
5 Newton St
6 Ridley St
7 Stephenson St
D5
1 Cartmel Gv
2 Harrison Gdns
3 Wetherby Gv
4 Whitworth Cl
E3
1 Claremont St
2 Ely St
3 Grasmere St
4 Grasmere St West
5 Lincoln St
6 Sedgewick Pl
7 Villa Pl
E4
1 Westfield Ter
E5
1 Bartram Gdns
E7
1 Alum Well Rd
2 Brackendene Dr
3 St Helen's Crs
4 Winslow Gdns

Page 69
F3
1 Abbey Ct
2 Camborne Pl
3 Camilla St
4 Cross St
5 Durham Pl
6 Jedburgh Cl
7 Marlowe Gdns
8 Milvain Cl
9 Milvain St
10 Richmond Ct
11 St Alban's Ter
12 St Edmund's Rd
13 Shipley Ct
14 South St
15 Sutherland St
16 Whitby Cl
F7
1 Albert Dr
2 Alum Well Rd
3 Belle Vue Gv
4 Clement St
5 Edmund Pl
6 Elder Gv
7 Lowrey's La
8 Rock Gv
9 Studley Gdns
10 Weathercock La
11 Wesley St
12 Westmorland Gdns
G4
1 Chiswick Gdns
2 Conway Sq
3 Grange Ter
4 Highcliffe Gdns
5 Kitchener St
6 Lambeth Pl
7 Lynnholme Gdns
8 Mafeking St
9 Mayfair Gdns
10 Methuen St
11 Newman Ter
12 Rosebery Av
13 Teviot St
14 Warburton Crs
H4
1 Bayswater Rd
2 Ettrick Gdns
3 Fielding Pl
4 Landseer Gdns
5 Leyton Pl
6 Trent Gdns
H6
1 Centurion Wy
2 Church La
3 Egremont Dr
4 Fosse Ter
5 Hewson Pl
6 Watling Pl
7 Woolerton Dr
J4
1 Brearley Wy
2 Ellerbeck Cl
3 Flexbury Gdns
4 Millfield Gdns
5 Tarlton Crs
6 Warkworth Gdns
7 Windsor Gdns
8 Woodlands Ter
J5
1 Blackburn Gn
2 Greenbourne Gdns
3 Heatherwell Gn
4 Windy Ridge Vls
J6
1 Furrowfield
2 Lancercost Gdns
3 Woodvale Gdns
K2
1 Felling House Gdns
2 George Smith Gdns
3 Greenwood Gdns
K3
1 Brandling La
2 Brandling Pl
3 Field St
4 Helmsdale Av
5 Noble St
6 Providence Pl
7 Quarry Rw
K4
1 Croudace Rw
2 Davidson St
3 Elliott Dr
4 Holly Park Vw
5 Park Rw
6 Stainton Dr
7 Thompson Pl
8 Werhale Gn
K5
1 Belgrave Ter
2 Oval Park Vw
3 Picherwell
4 Wentworth Cl
K6
1 College Cl
K7
1 Campion Gdns

Page 70
D2
1 Bamburgh Dr
2 Brack Ter
3 Braemar Ct
4 Christon Wy
5 Elgin Ct
6 Hainingwood Ter
7 Hall Ter
8 Wood Ter
D5
1 Ashridge Ct
D6
1 Alderwyk
2 Beaufront Cl
3 Cropthorne
4 Roehedge
5 Seaton Cl
6 Thornley Av
E4
1 Fellgate Gdns
2 Standfield Gdns
E5
1 Berkhamstead Ct
2 Bradbury Cl
3 Meadowbrook Dr
E6
1 Lanchester Cl
2 Rainton Cl

Page 72
E5
1 Avondale Gdns
2 The Fairways
3 Hamilton Ter
4 Hillside
5 Rectory Bank
6 St Nicholas Rd
7 Shepherds Wy
8 Three Rivers Ct

Page 73
G1
1 Brodie Cl
2 Cameron Cl

Page 77
F5
1 Bowes Lyon Cl

Page 82
E3
1 Blackheath Cl
2 Canton Cl
3 Lytham Cl
4 Portrush Cl
5 Prestwick Cl
6 Rosemount Cl
7 Sunningdale Dr
8 Troon Cl
9 Turnberry Cl

Page 83
F4
1 Essex Dr
2 Hampshire Pl
3 Sussex Pl

Page 84
E7
1 Cambria Gn
2 Frederick St
3 Kepier Gdns
4 New St
5 Primrose St
6 Union St
7 Vicarage La

Page 85
F2
1 Rennie Sq
F3
1 Coleridge Rd
2 Robertson Sq
F4
1 Alder St
2 Ashwood Gv
3 Elizabeth St
4 The Grove
5 Jennifer Av
6 Joyce Ter
7 Sheppard Ter
8 Stanley St
9 Thompson Crs
10 West Vw
F6
1 Claxheugh Rd
2 Maling Pk
F7
1 Coronation Ter
2 King Edward Rd
G1
1 Reedling Ct
G2
1 Harthope Av
2 Raeburn Rd
3 Rangoon Rd
4 Rawmarsh Rd
5 Rishton Sq
6 Rochford Rd
7 Rockingham Sq
8 Rotherfield Sq
G3
1 Bowburn Av
2 Howley Av
3 Ribble Rd
4 Shincliffe Av
5 Stockley Av
G4
1 Barron St South
2 Castle St South
3 Colima Av
4 East Vw
5 Park St South
6 Robin Gv
7 Thrush Gv
8 Wren Gv
G5
1 Defender Ct
G6
1 Flax Sq
2 Pelaw Sq
3 St Luke's Rd
G7
1 Frome Sq
2 Pennant Sq
3 Plaistow Sq
4 Polebrook Rd
5 Pontop Sq
6 Poole Rd
H2
1 Redditch Sq
2 Redruth Sq
3 Regina Sq
4 Riddings Sq
5 Ringwood Sq
6 Rochdale Wy
H7
1 Fenton Sq
2 Fordenbridge Rd
3 Priestman Ct
J1
1 Wiltshire Cl
J2
1 Raydale
J3
1 Redcar Sq
J5
1 Lyndhurst Ter
J6
1 Margaret Alice St
2 Minton Sq
3 Onslow St
4 Plantation Sq
5 Stratfield St
6 Tanfield St
7 Warennes St
8 Wilfred St
J7
1 Fordenbridge Sq
2 Fordhall Dr
K1
1 Fontburn Ct
2 Rothley Ct
3 Waterlow Cl
4 Watford Cl
5 Westport Cl
6 Whitchurch Cl
7 Wiltshire Rd
8 Woodford Cl
K2
1 Wimbledon Cl
K3
1 Pinewood Sq
2 The Poplars
3 Walter Thomas St
K4
1 Clockwell St
K5
1 Merle Ter
2 Pallion Subway
K6
1 Amethyst St
2 Enfield St
3 Garfield St
4 Jacques St
5 Lincoln St
6 Maxwell St
7 Meldon Rd
8 Percival St
9 Pine St
10 Prudhoe St
11 Reginald St
K7
1 Arlington St
2 Bell St
3 Brookland Rd
4 Hazledene Ter
5 Kimberley St
6 Romford St
7 Tamerton St
8 Walpole Ct
9 Washington St
10 Westleigh Ct
11 Westwood St
12 Wilber Ct
13 Wilber St
14 Winchester Ct
15 Woolsington Ct

Page 86
A2
1 Ellis Rd
2 John Taylor Ct
3 Okehampton Sq
A3
1 Cato St
2 Churchill Av
3 Clarence St
4 James St
5 Jowett Sq
6 Julius Caesar St
7 Keats Av
8 Tennyson St
A4
1 Camden St
2 Church Bank
3 Dickens St
4 Kingsley Cl
5 Kipling St
6 Ulburn Pl
7 Malaburn Wy
8 Mount Pleasant
9 Park Rw
10 Stoney La
11 Wessington Wy
A6
1 Gilsland St
2 Handel St
3 Oswald St
4 Paxton Ter
5 Pickard St
6 Shepherd St
7 Wood St
A7
1 Brunton Ter
2 Catharine St West
3 Chester St West
4 Duke St
B2
1 Burnhope Dr
2 Clarendon Sq
B3
1 Amy St
2 Church St
3 Coldstream Av
4 Collingwood St
5 Columba St
6 Cornhill Rd
7 Edward Burdis St
8 Frank St
9 James Armitage St
10 Ridley St
11 Schimel St
12 Sophy St
B4
1 Attwood Gv
2 Close St
3 Lee St
4 Maypole Cl
5 Pemberton Cl
6 Queen's Rd
7 South Ter
8 Suddick St
9 Usher St
10 Vedra St
B5
1 Priestly Crs
B6
1 Alliance Pl
2 Alliance St
3 Cirencester St
4 Dryborough St
5 Hyacinth Ct
6 Hylton Rd
7 Jasmine Ct
8 Lansdowne St
9 Marguerite Ct
10 Marigold Ct
11 Millburn St
12 North Ravensworth St
13 Queensberry St
14 St Cuthbert's Ter
B7
1 Chepstow St
2 Chester St East
3 Chester Ter North
4 East Cleft Rd
5 Gilhurst Gra
6 Harlow St
7 Langton Ct
8 The Leazes
9 The Retreat
10 The Royalty
11 St Mark's St
12 St Mark's Ter
13 Tintern St
14 Waterworks Rd
15 Western Hl
C1
1 Cairns Rd
2 Cairns Sq
3 Patterdale Gv
4 Ullswater Gv
5 Windmill Sq
C2
1 Bywell Av
2 Elizabeth St
3 Honister Dr
4 Joannah St
C3
1 Boundary St
2 Edith St
3 Newbridge Av
4 Northwood Ct
C4
1 Chilton St
2 Crozier St
3 Empress St
4 Finsbury St
5 Hood Cl
6 North St
7 Ross St
C5
1 Easington St North
2 Stadium Wy
C6
1 Dun Cow St
2 Dunning St
3 Eden St West
4 Galley's Gill Rd
5 Garden Pl
6 Middle St
7 Paley St
8 Queen St
C7
1 Clanny St
2 Crowtree Rd
3 Crowtree Ter
4 Elwin Ter
5 Green Ter
6 Hope St
7 Mary St
8 St Michaels Wy
9 Silksworth Rw
10 Stockton Rd
11 Tunstall Rd
12 Tunstall Ter West
D1
1 Atkinson Rd
2 Bower St
3 Dene La
4 Dudley Av
5 Moran St
6 Prince George Av
7 Thorburn St
8 Whitburn Ter
D2
1 Alexander Ter
2 Folldon Av
3 Friarage Av
4 Hilda St
5 Laburnam Rd
6 Laburnum Rd
7 Marcia Av
8 Marina Ct
9 Marina Gv
10 Melbury Ct
11 Montague St
12 Ormesby Rd
13 Pauline Av
14 Primrose Prec
15 Ronald Sq
16 Vivian Sq
D3
1 Burscough Crs
2 Edgeworth Crs
3 Fairlands East
4 Leeds St
5 Moreland St
6 Wearmouth Av
D4
1 Abbs St
2 Dixon's Sq
3 Fulwell Rd
4 Howard St
5 Monk St
6 Oriel Cl
7 Rosebery St
8 Shore St
9 Southwick Rd
10 Wearmouth St
D5
1 Barclay St
2 Causeway
3 Dundas St
4 George St North
5 Liddell St
6 Lower Dundas St
7 North Bridge St
8 Sheepfolds North
9 Sheepfolds Rd
10 Southwick Rd
11 Whitburn St
12 Williamson Ter
D6
1 Back Bridge St
2 Bedford St
3 Bridge Crs
4 Bridge St
5 Charman St
6 Cumberland St
7 Fawcett St
8 Frederick Rd
9 Green St
10 John St
11 Lambton St
12 Pann La
13 Press La
14 Prince St
15 Queen St
16 Sheepfolds South
17 Station St
18 Union St
19 West Sunniside
20 York St
D7
1 Athenaeum St
2 Cowan Ter
3 Fawcett St
4 Frederick St
5 King St
6 Maritime St
7 Park La
8 Tavistock Pl
9 Waterloo Pl
E1
1 Calderbourne Av
2 Cambourne Av
3 Chapman St
4 Cliftonbourne Av
5 Cressbourne Av
6 Rockville
7 Seaburn Hl
E2
1 Claremont Av
2 Lyn-thorpe Gv
3 Merryfield Gdns
E3
1 Association Rd
2 Clockstand Cl
3 St Andrew's Ter
E4
1 Brandling St South
2 Cooper St
E5
1 Huddlestone Ri
E6
1 Cross Pl
2 Donnison Gdns
3 Russell St
4 Spring Garden Cl
5 Zion St
E7
1 Besford Gv
2 Bishop Morton Gv
3 Churchill St
4 Menvill Pl
5 Winifred Ter

Page 89
G6
1 Bradley Lodge Dr

Page 95
F3
1 Beauly

Page 97
F1
1 Grindon Av
2 Hylton Wk
3 Romaldskirk Cl
F2
1 Penman Sq
F3
1 Galway Rd
2 Gardiner Sq
3 Geneva Rd
4 Gerrard Rd
5 Clanmore Rd
6 Pickhurst Sq
7 Pontefract Rd
8 Portadown Rd
F4
1 Gambia Rd
2 Gambia Sq
3 Gladwyn Rd
4 Gleneagles Sq
5 Gravesend Rd
6 Greenock Rd
7 Grenfell Sq
8 Northfield Dr
F5
1 Thurso Cl
2 Tintagel Cl
3 Trevelyan Cl
F7
1 St Chad's Crs
G1
1 Pegwood Rd
2 Pinner Rd
G2
1 Glasbury Av
2 The Greenway
3 Hampstead Sq
4 Nookside Ct
5 Partick Sq
6 Pelton Rd
G3
1 Galashiels Sq
2 Glanton Sq
3 Gleneagles Rd
4 Grindon Pk
G4
1 Gravesend Sq
2 Teddington Sq
G5
1 Tamworth Sq
2 Thorne Rd
3 Thorpeness Rd
4 Tyldesley Sq
G6
1 Munslow Rd
2 Tenby Rd
3 Thames Rd
4 Tilbury Gdns
G7
1 Algiers Rd
2 Berkeley Cl
3 Lambton Ct
4 Lulworth Ct
5 Lumley Ct
H1
1 Huntley Sq
H2
1 Broadmayne Gdns
2 Holborn Sq
3 Medway Gdns
4 Southmayne Rd
H3
1 Selkirk Sq
2 Somerset Sq
3 Springbank Sq
H4
1 Shaftoe Sq
2 Silloth Rd
3 Thirsk Rd
H5
1 Truro Rd
2 Tynemouth Sq
H6
1 Alloa Rd
2 Archer Sq
H7
1 Aldershot Rd
2 Aldershot Sq
3 Aldwych Rd
4 Allendale Rd
5 Anglesey Sq
6 Anthony Rd
7 Appleby Sq
8 Ashford Rd
9 Ashwell Rd
10 Aston Sq
11 Conway Gdns
J2
1 Arncliffe Av
2 Corry Ct
3 Ingoldsby Ct
4 Westfield Ct
5 Wimbourne Av
6 Winston Crs
7 Woodbine Ct
8 Woodville Crs
J3
1 Seymour Sq
2 Shoreham Sq
3 Swindon Sq
J4
1 Grindon La
2 Paignton Sq
3 Paisley Sq
4 Plymouth Sq
5 Polmuir Sq
6 Pretoria Sq
7 Strathmore Sq
8 Tunis Rd
J6
1 Buckingham
2 Knightsbridge
3 Piccadilly
4 The Strand
K1
1 Dilston Gdns
2 General Graham St
3 Swaledale Gdns
K3
1 Ettrick Gv
2 Portland Sq
3 Sacriston Av
K4
1 Perth Sq
2 Polworth Sq
3 Powis Sq
4 Proctor Sq
K6
1 Sandown Gdns
2 Silksworth Cl
3 Southwold Gdns
4 Symington Gdns
K7
1 Cavalier Wy

Page 98
A1
1 Burnaby St
2 Co-operative Ter
3 Cranford Ter
4 High Barnes Ter
5 Ingleby Ter
6 Oaklands Ter
7 Wolseley Ter
A2
1 Chatsworth Crs
2 Chatsworth St South
3 Georgian Ct
A3
1 Albyn Gdns
2 Alpine Wy
3 Hanby Gdns
4 Harewood Gdns
5 Haslemere Dr
6 Hatfield Gdns
7 Hathaway Gdns
8 Horsham Gdns
9 Hovingham Gdns
10 Huntingdon Gdns
A5
1 Somerset St
A6
1 Bedford Pl
2 Cypress Sq
3 Minehead Gdns
4 Newport Gv
5 North Ter
6 West St
A7
1 Athol Gv
2 Britannia Rd
3 Comet Sq
4 St Matthews Vw
5 Silksworth Ter
6 Tempest St
7 Vane St
8 Viscount Rd
B1
1 Beachcross Rd
2 Beachville St
3 Beresford Pk
4 Burnville Rd South
5 Elmwood St
6 Ewing Rd
7 Fernville St
8 Havelock Ter
9 Hunters Hall Rd
10 Oakwood St
11 Roseville St
12 Vale St
13 Western Hl
B2
1 Birchfield Rd
2 Silksworth La
3 Wayside
4 Wenham Sq
B3
1 Bamburgh Gdns
2 Bowbank Cl
3 Braemar Gdns
4 Brentwood Gdns
5 Fernsway
6 Greenrigg Gdns
7 Heatherlea Gdns
8 Meadow Gdns
9 Pemberton Gdns
B4
1 Brignall Ri
2 Butsfield Gdns
3 Dipton Gdns
4 Frosterley Gdns
5 Mickleton Gdns
6 Wilden Ct
B6
1 Hazel Av
2 Winslade Cl

B7

1 Ainthorpe Cl
2 Fairways
3 Quarry Rd
4 Tunstall Vls

C1

1 Argyle Sq
2 Argyle St
3 Azalea Ter North
4 Valebrooke Gdns
5 Worcester St
6 Worcester Ter

C2

1 Avenue Ter
2 Brookside Gdns
3 Holmlands Pk North
4 Holmlands Pk South

C3

1 Ashbrooke Cross
2 Ashbrooke Range
3 Fairholme Rd
4 Greystoke Gdns
5 Hillside Gdns
6 Linden Gdns
7 Linden Rd
8 Lulworth Gdns
9 Lynford Gdns
10 Willow Bank Rd

C4

1 Brackenwood Gv
2 Glenesk Gdns
3 Greybourne Gdns
4 Larchwood Gv
5 Ringmore Ct
6 Stannington Gdns
7 Tunstall Hill Cl

C6

1 Camberley Cl

C7

1 Boulby Cl
2 Hawsker Cl
3 Hilltop Gdns
4 Houlskye Cl
5 Levisham Cl

D1

1 Ashmore St
2 Burdon Rd
3 St George's Wy

D2

1 Ashburne Ct
2 Corby Ga
3 Corby Hall Dr

D3

1 The Glen
2 Langport Rd

D4

1 Longridge Sq

D5

1 Halidon Sq
2 Harcourt Rd
3 Hereford Ct
4 Hereford Sq

D7

1 Runnymede

E1

1 Lindsay Cl
2 Osman Cl
3 St Ignatius Cl

E2

1 Beaumont St
2 Capulet Ter
3 Edith St
4 Villette Brook St

E3

1 Romney Av
2 Roydon Av
3 Rudyard Av
4 Rushton Av

E4

1 Thornfield Gv
2 Weldon Av
3 Weybourne Sq

E5

1 Hardgate Rd
2 Sandmere Rd

E6

1 Ronaldsay Cl
2 Rosebank Cl

E7

1 Murphy Gv

Page 99

F5

1 Acomb Ct

Page 108

B4

1 Garden St
2 Hartoft Cl
3 Hillview Crs
4 Hillview Gv
5 Hillview Rd
6 Kirk Vw
7 St Cuthbert's Rd
8 Springfield Rd

Page 109

H1

1 Maidstone Cl
2 Marbury Cl
3 Matfen Dr
4 Melsonby Cl
5 Merrington Cl
6 Merrion Cl

Page 110

A1

1 Arran Ct
2 Delamere Ct
3 Hamsterley Ct
4 Lake Ct
5 Lomond Ct
6 Newstead Sq
7 Nimbus Ct
8 Sheppey Ct
9 Sherwood Ct
10 Shetland Ct
11 Tilbeck Sq
12 Tiree Ct

Page 115

J2

1 Lunedale Dr

Page 117

G1

1 Brandon Cl

Page 119

J4

1 Mann Crs

Page 120

E2

1 Beaumont St
2 Benevente St
3 Edward St
4 Ilchester St
5 Malcolm St
6 Stavordale St
7 Strangways St
8 Union St
9 Vincent St

Page 123

G6

1 Byland Ct

Page 137

F4

1 Burdon Pl
2 Coniston Cl
3 Duddon Cl
4 Eskdale Wk
5 Grisedale Rd
6 Kentmere Pl
7 Langdale Pl
8 Tarn Cl